THE MIND
OF AMERICA
1820 · 1860

RUSH WELTER

THE
MIND OF
AMERICA
1820·1860

COLUMBIA UNIVERSITY PRESS
NEW YORK AND LONDON

1975

LIBRARY OF CONGRESS CATALOGING IN PUBLICATION DATA

Welter, Rush.

The mind of America, 1820–1860.

Bibliography: p.

1. United States—Intellectual life. 2. Public
opinion—United States. I. Title.

E165.W46   917.3'03'5   74-14976

ISBN 0-231-02963-2

❧ FOR JONATHAN ❦

PREFACE

More than any other generation, the adult Americans who flourished between 1820 and 1850 gave the United States its distinctive character and direction. When we today seek to understand American social patterns, to explain the significance of American democracy, or to comprehend the failures of American institutions, we are likely to trace them to the epoch that has been variously identified with the rise of the common man, the presidency of Andrew Jackson, or the triumph of egalitarian beliefs. By the same token, we continue to behold in Alexis de Tocqueville, who visited the United States in 1831 and 1832, the preeminent foreign commentator on American institutions and American practices, whom we read as well as revere because he seems to have caught the Americans in the very process of defining themselves. Even during recent years, when we have been busy reassessing our past and groping our way into an unprecedented future, we have done so primarily by reacting against standards and practices that derive almost without change from that earlier epoch. As often as not, our reactions against the past have also reflected assumptions and expectations that date from the same period. In almost every respect, the Middle Period of American history has provided us with the social imperatives we still honor as well as the errors we now contend against.

My study of antebellum thought began within the framework of this general hypothesis, which my subsequent explorations of American thought have tended largely to confirm. This book was not undertaken to test the hypothesis, however, nor was it conceived as an essay in modern "relevance." It is, instead, a study of national attitudes that is focused so far as possible on the social opinions and beliefs of one generation of the American people. Partly as a result of my training in "American Studies," partly for other reasons, I have sought to establish not the formal and theoretically sophisticated "philosophy" with which educated men sought to comprehend the national experience, but the inarticulate premises and unresolved dilemmas of men and women who did not write formal treatises or major works of literature. It seemed to me when I began, and it seems to me now, that their often inchoate ideas were far more important than the deeply considered statements of the well-educated elite in setting the terms in which the American people conducted their lives. Acting on this premise, I set out to overcome the rationalist bias that afflicts most studies of intellectual history by reading as widely as I could in the published statements of relatively ordinary men and women to discover how the Americans of their generation conceived their society and its problems.

My effort was less familiar when I began than when I concluded it. In recent years, motivated in part by a revisionist wish to pursue the history of the common man in preference to the history of elite members of society, a good many historians, often of a radical persuasion, have interested themselves in establishing the "ideology" of the inarticulate masses. In doing so they have acted on many premises I share, but in their zeal for a democratic history they have also tended to repudiate the idea that the printed remains of men who achieved sufficient recognition in their own lifetimes to find publication for their views can be used to define the attitudes of the lower ranks of American society. These scholars' doubts are well taken, but—theories about ideology or popular culture notwithstanding—they do not point to any truly satisfactory method for establishing how and what a generation probably thought. Hence I have persevered in studying a host of ephemeral documents in the hope of identifying the intellectual preoccupations of the age by reading between the lines of its published materials, treating the relatively sophisticated statements of educated men as indices to popular thought only when it seemed to me that less elegant statements by a wider variety of men pointed in the same direction. I have discussed most of my theoretical presuppositions in the *Journal of American History*, and I present a brief account of my approach to the available documents in the bibliographical note to this volume.*

I should, however, add one *caveat*. Although I have attempted to deal with every major social theme that appears in the literature I have studied, it will be readily apparent that I have taken some widespread convictions of that era for granted (e.g., the inferiority of women and the abstract belief in justice as equity) as well as ignored some that other

* See "The History of Ideas in America: An Essay in Redefinition," *Journal of American History* 51 (1965), 599–614, and page 521 in this book.

investigators might find significant (e.g., attitudes toward children and marriage). Above all, I have made little effort to deal with the religious beliefs and moral convictions that played a large role in shaping the thought and behavior of the generation. My neglect of such matters hardly indicates a lack of concern for them; rather, I believe that they require a much more comprehensive study than could be attempted here. Given suitable opportunity, I hope to write a second volume dealing with religious attitudes and moral sentiments, if I can discover how to approach them systematically. When we have grasped these attitudes and sentiments in the same fashion and by substantially the same means as I have employed here, taking note of theological developments but examining the writings of the ministry only as the first step in a more general inquiry, I think we shall have begun to understand the mind of the Middle Period.

RUSH WELTER

North Pownal, Vermont
28 September 1973

ACKNOWLEDGMENTS

As the size and character of this volume will undoubtedly suggest to most readers, it owes its very existence to the labors of many persons whose names I neither cite nor otherwise identify. First among them are my friends and colleagues who read large sections of the manuscript while it was in preparation and whose counsel often sustained me as well as guided me during that taxing period; I particularly wish to acknowledge the assistance I have received from George A. Billias of Clark University and from R. Arnold Ricks, Anne V. Schlabach, and Wallace P. Scott of Bennington College. In addition, the manuscript has benefited greatly from the critical advice provided me through Columbia University Press; especially that of an anonymous scholarly reader who read an early version of the work and persuaded me to rewrite it; of Robert J. Tilley, long an editor and for several years an assistant director of the Press, who kept me at it through thick and thin; and of Maria Caliandro, who has edited these complex essays with taste, discretion, and modesty. Finally, I have been much aided in my reading of the proofs by my long-time colleague Lionel Nowak and by my friends Ruth Levin and Virginia Sandy, who have worked overtime to help bring my many quotations to the standard of their originals. I hope that all of these invisible assistants feel that the result vindicates their efforts, although I am far from wishing to implicate them in my lapses.

This study is equally indebted, though in a different way, to a host of libraries, large and small, which have provided me with the raw materials on which it is based. My dependence upon them is reflected in my bibliography, which often indicates which library supplied a given primary source, but the conventional symbols I employ for the purpose cannot express my sense of the investment of time, money, and personal energy that I have been able to lay claim to as one of their clients. I have depended most heavily, and in approximately equal measure, on the New York Public Library (chiefly the Astor, Lenox, & Tilden Foundations), the American Antiquarian Society, and the New York State Library. Each has a magnificent collection and each its own indispensable strengths; all three are notable for the courtesy and efficiency with which they have responded to my sometimes voracious demands. In addition, I have made considerable use of the libraries of Harvard University and that of the New-York Historical Society, while the personnel of the State Library of Indiana have gone out of their way to provide me with copies of the materials it holds.

Beyond this, I have been aided by some twenty-four other institutions, which have supplied me with anything from the microcopy of a single rare pamphlet or broadside to copies of a dozen or more rare imprints; they include (in alphabetical order) the Alabama Department of Archives and History, the University of Alabama, the Boston Public Library, the Chicago Historical Society, the library of Columbia University, the Congregational Library (Boston), the Library of Congress, the Henry E. Huntington Library, the Illinois State Historical Society, the Indiana Historical Society, the libraries of Indiana University, the Kansas State Historical Society, the Mississippi Department of Archives and History, the State Historical Society of Missouri, the Newberry Library, the New Orleans Public Library, the library of New York University, the Presbyterian Historical Society (Philadelphia), the St. Louis Mercantile Library Association, the St. Louis Public Library, the library of the University of South Carolina, the Tennessee State Library, the library of the University of Texas, and the Union College Library.

Drawing on these specialized libraries for fugitive materials, I have also made truly burdensome use of more general libraries closer to home. Although it is small and oriented largely to teaching, the library of Bennington College has played a major role in the preparation of this book, accommodating me with many reference services as well as numerous interlibrary loans, not to say basic books in my fields of interest. So, too, the library of Williams College has most generously allowed me repeated access to its collections of nineteenth-century publications (some of them quite rare) as well as modern materials.

I owe still other debts to Bennington College. Although it has absorbed too much of my time over the years, it has also given me the opportunity to work out the details of this study without compelling me to publish it prematurely or in fragments. Furthermore, my seminars at Bennington (and occasionally elsewhere) have proved to be one of the main props to this enterprise; if my students were not always experts in the field, they nevertheless demanded the best that was within me, as I did of them, and they have often expanded my perceptions or deepened my judgments of the patterns of American thought. Not least important, Bennington College has made available small grants in aid of research from sums donated to it in memory of William C. Fels and by Charles and Elizabeth Dollard and the Ford Foundation. This financial assistance was the more welcome in the absence of even token support from the foundations and other agencies to which a historian most often applies for aid to his scholarly projects.

Finally, my study has depended for many years on the largely silent acquiescence of my wife Thelma and my son Jonathan in its distracting labors. Though they cannot be said to have taken any direct part in its formulation, they have watched it from afar with tolerance and undaunted sympathy. In the world of scholarship as elsewhere, they also serve who only stand and wait.

R. W.

CONTENTS

PART FIVE
· CONSEQUENCES ·

THE MIND
OF AMERICA
1820 · 1860

HISTORY

❧ I ❧

MACROHISTORY:
THE LONG VIEW

The American Revolution is the greatest political event in history," the *Albany Argus* proclaimed in the fall of 1828 "—every thing that belongs to it is consecrated." [1] The occasion that elicited this extravagant claim was the presidential contest between John Quincy Adams and Andrew Jackson, and the *Argus* went on to solicit votes for Jackson as the last surviving "Revolutionary Patriot" who might be elected to the nation's highest office. While it voiced a partisan plea in a campaign that was already distinguished for its partisanship, it voiced something else as well, the fundamental historical convictions of a young people who were conscious of their place in time and for whom the long span of history bore special meanings. Not the accuracy of their historical vision, but its assumptions and implications, will concern us here, for the Americans' sense of their place in the history of mankind went far toward establishing the terms in which they were to conduct themselves as a nation.

THE AMERICAN IDEA OF PROGRESS

The *Argus*'s pronouncement could make sense only on the supposition that the American Revolution represented a political achievement long delayed but ultimately triumphant. By 1828, indeed, virtually all Americans subscribed to a belief that the history of the world was a progressive phenomenon, one marked by a long series of steps or turning points that had brought the human race ever closer to realizing the ultimate ideals of humanity. In this respect they were virtually indistinguishable from contemporary European liberals, who had made the idea of progress one of the chief doctrines of their age. Their common doctrine represented a fairly sharp break with historic European concepts: with the cyclical

NOTE: There are two kinds of notes to this book, both of which are found at the back. Letters refer to substantive notes and comments on the literature of the field, which appear in the Appendices, beginning on p. 395. Citations in support of the text appear in the Notes, which begin on p. 443.

view of history, characteristic of classical antiquity, which took for granted that human experience only repeats itself; and with the theocentric view of history, expressed by medieval writers, which deprecated the events of this world in favor of the divine drama of redemption. By the middle of the eighteenth century, influenced by a wide variety of phenomena such as the Renaissance, the Age of Discovery, and the actual material accomplishments of their own time, European thinkers had fused the secular traditions of classical historiography with the teleological traditions of religious historiography to produce a historical vision of the world in process of achieving the *summum bonum*.[a]

Nevertheless, the particulars of the Americans' belief served both to make their idea of history distinctive and to inculcate lessons that few European writers taught. Far from portraying a nation that was simply one stage in advance of Europe, they held that the American people had already achieved historic European hopes and implied that the United States had already fulfilled the progressive dreams of mankind. "Until the successful termination of our Revolution and the establishment of our Government," the Reverend Leander Ker told the Athenaean Society of the University of Missouri in 1845, "Liberty was an exile and a fugitive in the earth; without a local habitation, character or name; yea not so much as a place to rest her head in safety. But that era, in her history; the most eventful and important in the political annals of the world, has changed her position from the defensive to the offensive." By the same token, John K. Porter took the occasion of a Washington's Birthday address in 1850 to assure the young men of Albany (New York) that the American Revolution had succeeded where other struggles for liberty had failed. "Governments had existed," he said, "which the world called free, but their history had been uniform. The garb of patriotism was assumed by the demagogue as a convenient cloak to be put on or off as might suit his purposes, his interests or his caprice. The multitude tore down the throne by day, and it rose again by night. . . . Such had been the history of most of the struggles between the spirit of arbitrary power and the spirit of popular liberty, before the American revolution." [2]

Men of a more innovative temperament than Ker and Porter, who were conventional in sentiment and conservative in politics, also depicted

American accomplishments in extraordinarily complacent terms.* In 1830 Robert Walker, a professedly radical workingman speaking at a dinner held to celebrate the July Revolution in France, hailed the American Revolution as "one of the greatest and most glorious events which the annals of the world can boast of," and went on to explain that "its consummation marks a new and important era in the history of man." William S. Balch expressed much the same faith in an address to the free suffrage convention of Rhode Island. "Altho numerous attempts had been made, in all sincerity, to obtain political liberty for man," he declared, "it was not till the 4th day of July, 1776, that the great truth that 'all men are created equal' was fairly developed and erected into a chief corner stone on which to found a great and growing nation. And it was not till then that the world was prepared for the practical adoption of this fundamental principle." [3]

Claiming this happy situation, the Americans of the Middle Period tended to see themselves as heirs of all the ages, who had at one and the same time put ancient ideals into practice and transcended the very best that had first given impetus to those ideals. Three very different Fourth of July orations exemplify this conviction.[c] Although the Reverend William Sparrow of Alexandria (Virginia) recognized that the American colonists had begun by adopting European principles of government, he also held in 1852 that they had adopted the best available principles and then gone on to leave the Old World behind. Similarly, in 1835 James S. Allan told the students of Centre College in Kentucky that "this country did not merely stop even with the best lights in the old world; it took a step a century beyond," while Robert Rantoul Jr., the Democratic reformer from Massachusetts, admonished an audience at Gloucester in 1833, "The independence of the United States of America is not only a marked epoch in the course of time, but it is indeed the end from which the new order of things is to be reckoned. It is the dividing point in the history of mankind; it is the moment of the political regeneration of the world." [4] American history—the history of American liberty—represented a departure from the achievements of European liberty as well as a fruition of all that was best in the Old World.

* I discuss my working definitions of "conservative" and "democrat" in appendix b to this chapter.

Frequently, especially in New England, Americans saw the divine hand directly at work to secure this result. "Long ere our Revolution began," the Reverend Josiah Bent Jr. declared in an oration at Braintree (Massachusetts) on the fiftieth anniversary of the Declaration of Independence, "we trace his hand in relation to our present glory. It was He that saved this New world, so long unknown to the overloaded Old world, to be the theatre of new scenery to our race. And when the Old had testified long enough what man could do, and brought to the full its bitter fruits; He opens the uncorrupted New, and, having given birth to the Revival of learning and the Reformation of the church, selects a precious few, *here* to plant the principles that are to renovate the earth." [5] But it was not only New Englanders and clergymen who attributed American achievements to a providential design; a secular commentator like William Kent (son of the Chancellor, and himself a well-known lawyer) also celebrated special advantages that time had bestowed on the American experiment. "During the night of the middle ages," he told the Phi Beta Kappa Society of Union College in 1841, "the Western continent lay dark, unattainable and unknown. . . . The appropriation of America was reserved for the sixteenth century, when learning and liberty had become established in Europe, and the modern arts and sciences had commenced their brilliant and unceasing progress." [6] By now, a providential past was a common heritage of all Americans.

Providential or not, the chief characteristic of American innovations was that they surpassed all that had gone before. For some writers—especially, perhaps, westerners and Democrats—American achievements were so unprecedented as to support the belief they were entirely unrelated to the past. "With the Past we have literally nothing to do, save to dream of it," B. Gratz Brown told his constituents in Missouri in 1850. "Its lessons are lost and its tongue is silent. We are ourselves at the head and front of all political experience. Precedents have lost their virtue and all their authority is gone." But the more common and also the more significant view held that although many American innovations were traceable to the futile efforts of European heroes, their successful institution in the United States meant that the American people were uniquely free to achieve goals that other nations had not been able to reach. "Much as we are supposed to have borrowed from England—much as our institutions are reputed to resemble hers," Philip Lindsley argued in Nashville

(Tennessee) in 1832 "—it is notorious that Englishmen seem absolutely incapable of comprehending the genius and practical operations of our government. When they speak of the *people*, they mean the populace—the rabble—the mob—and without an aristocracy, in some form, to control their anarchical and tumultuary tendencies, they cannot conceive of any stable security for life or property or law or religion. Now we have no *populace* in the European sense of the term—we never had a populace. . . . We have but one *order*—and all the people belong to it." [7]

In expressing such views, Lindsley took direct issue with commentators like Porter, who devoted part of his address at Albany to an extended encomium upon English legal precedents. But though conservative commentators could always be found to invoke specific European precedents against specific contemporary innovations, they more characteristically visualized a future freed from the encumbrances of the past. "Whatsoever European experience has developed, favorable to the freedom and happiness of man; whatsoever European genius has invented for his improvement or gratification; whatsoever of refinement or polish the culture of European society presents for his adoption or enjoyment," Daniel Webster told the House of Representatives in 1826 "—all this is offered to man in America, with the additional advantages of the full power of erecting forms of Government on free and simple principles, without overturning institutions suited to times long passed, but too strongly supported either by interests or prejudices, to be shaken without convulsions." In short, Americans of almost every political persuasion testified to a belief that the United States had somehow appropriated the progress of liberty to itself. In their eyes, the history of the world had culminated in a nation that was uniquely free and uniquely progressive. [8]

THE IMPLICATIONS OF AMERICAN PROGRESS

The existence of a common belief in the special qualities of American life was itself significant in a nation that had as yet to prove itself in the world; its corollaries and ramifications were even more so. At first glance, the American idea of progress had ambiguous implications. On the one hand, it pointed toward a continuous national process of experimentation and innovation like that envisaged by William Ellery Channing in his famous *Remarks on a National Literature* (1830). Speaking both to and for a number of literary figures, Channing wrote that "we cannot admit the thought that this country is to be only a repetition of the old world. We delight to believe that God in the fulness of time, has brought a new continent to light, in order that the human mind should move here with a new freedom, should frame new social institutions, should explore new paths, and reap new harvests." On the other hand, many of Channing's contemporaries apparently took the common vision of a progressive country to mean that in having already fulfilled the main principles of liberty the American people had acquired an exemption from further epochal change; they held, in effect, that the large-scale historic process (which I shall call "macrohistory") had stopped when the American democracy was born. "In the old world," Benjamin F. Hallett declared at Oxford (Massachusetts) in 1841, "the struggle of the oppressed millions is to reform and change government. Under our institutions, the struggle only need be to make the administration of the government conform to the Constitution." [9]

Contemporary European attitudes indicate the importance that attached to the way in which Americans resolved this ambiguity. In Europe, the idea of progress connoted epoch-making achievements in the future as well as in the past, foretold a series of fundamental changes that would bring mankind ever closer to the perfection of liberty, government, and other human institutions. Often, indeed, the European idea had truly radical overtones, anticipating the overthrow of established governments or even (as in the Communist Manifesto) the overturn of the whole social order. It is of course understandable that, during a period of monarchical rule and counter-revolutionary triumphs, the European friends of democratic institutions should have looked to radical change in the future as an indispensable element of progress. It is also understandable that some of them should have believed that the United States had already achieved goals that only radical change could secure in Europe.[10] Nevertheless, the Americans' version of their own history cast a peculiar light on their future. In the United States, their statements often suggested, the future would be an occasion only for the elaboration and extension of institutions the Americans had already introduced.[d]

The attraction such a point of view might hold for conservative writers is obvious, and they often invoked it.[e] But liberals also held that the future would and should consist of an extension from the present, and—given their successes in American politics—their conviction spoke volumes about typical American beliefs. Certainly Hallett was a liberal Democrat in 1841, and other spokesmen for the liberal wing of his party shared his static conception of time. One of them was Henry D. Gilpin of Pennsylvania, who assured loyal Democrats of its Third Congressional District in 1834 that, thanks to popular vigilance, "We shall meet together, as we now do, on many a future anniversary of our independence, to rejoice in the unmoved grandeur of our political institutions." Other Democrats invoked the same perspective on the hustings: in the fall of 1836 the party's state convention of New York urged upon the electorate the need "from time to time to resurvey the political ground which we have occupied; to look up ancient monuments, and see whether we are within the pale of our original faith." Four years later the anonymous polemicist who drafted *The Crisis Met* hailed the triumph of the democratic idea through the "stern courage of our Revolutionary sires" and observed that "their blood and sufferings and sweat cemented the foundation stones on which we may hope shall safely repose for centuries to come the temple of freedom." [11] Such remarks clearly indicated that further progress in America must take the form of incidental improvement rather than substantial change in the political system adopted in 1789.[f]

Democrats typically embraced a restricted vision of the changes the future might bring; other men pressed against the limits the democrats took for granted. Besides Channing and the Transcendentalists, these philosophical progressives included such lesser men as Daniel D. Barnard, the conservative Whig congressman who told the literary societies of Amherst College in 1839, "the plain [*sic*] of man's pathway onward in his future career, will be by an angle of elevation equal at least to that of the course he has trodden hitherto, and by which he has been brought up already from a state of extreme degradation to one of comparative excellence and dignity." In much the same vein, Horace Mann pointed out in his Twelfth Report as Secretary of the Board of Education of Massachusetts (1848) that "from history and from consciousness, we find ourselves capable of ever-onward improvement; and therefore it seems to be a denial of first principles—it seems no better than impiety—to suppose that we shall ever become such finished scholars, that the works of

the All-wise will have no new problem for our solution, and will, therefore, be able to teach us no longer." Indeed, in 1845 Horace Bushnell
looked forward to a day when not the United States but other nations,
probably those in the southern hemisphere, would be in the vanguard of
human progress. Conservatives were not lacking to challenge the complacency that seemed to attach to the Americans' vision of history.[12]

Some liberal Democrats also placed the continuous improvement of
human institutions in the balance against American achievements to
date. In an essay on "Radicalism," the *Democratic Review* observed in
1838 that "The visions of the last age, have become the realities of this,
and opinions which are now deemed absurd and impracticable, may to-
morrow be adopted with success. . . . There are all around us refreshing
indications of progress and improvement, and who will limit the march
of improvement?" More pointedly, Churchill C. Cambreleng of New
York told the House of Representatives in 1835 that "the spirit of our age
cannot be mistaken—reform or revolution must ultimately be the fate of
every enlightened country," while in 1846 his fellow Democrat Walt
Whitman urged readers of the *Brooklyn Daily Eagle*, "Let us not think
because we are ahead of the tyrannical system of the Old World, that *we*
of the New have no advance to make. . . . In less than twenty years
from this time, we venture to predict, with every assurance of safety, the
nation will find, boldly promulgated in its midst, and supported by numerous and powerful advocates, notions of law, government and social
custom, as different from the present day as Leggett's and Jefferson's to
those of past ages." [13]

Nevertheless, much of this dissent from American complacency was
more apparent than real. For example, neither Barnard nor Mann suggested that the continuous process of improvement he pointed to connoted any fundamental alteration of American society, and even Bushnell visualized the future more or less in terms of innovations the United
States already took pride in.[14] Meanwhile the political innovators also
cast doubt on the urgency of their own demands for change. In 1839 the
editor of the *Democratic Review* explained that "the last order of civilization, which is the democratic, received its first permanent existence in
this country," and in general his essays insisted on purifying but not on
surpassing established political institutions. So, too, did Cambreleng—
his radicalism was focused on separating bank from state—and Whitman

elaborated his plea for innovation with a telling juxtaposition of heroes: Jefferson and William Leggett were not chronologically contemporaries, but they were apparently contemporary in being spokesmen for a truth that had been enunciated in Jefferson's day.[15] Somehow most of the proponents of further progress, of future departures from the present comparable to the present's departures from the past, managed to find their hopes embodied in the achievements America already boasted.

Their predilection was clearly demonstrated in the state constitutional conventions that met during the 1830s and 1840s, in which reform-minded delegates repeatedly invoked the progress of their age to override constitutional provisions that were hardly fifty years old. In North Carolina, for example, Kenneth Rayner sought to do away with the religious test for office on the grounds that "the spirit of liberty and reform is making its way in every corner of the globe, and sooner or later, will consign to one common ruin, all those despotic institutions, which are the time-worn relics of a feudal age." Similarly, during Iowa's first convention, Richard Quinton acknowledged the force of arguments in favor of an appointive judiciary, only to conclude that "this was said to be an age of progress, and he believed he should support the proposition to elect the Judges." For that matter, delegates frequently repudiated past precedents in the name of progress. In 1845, Solomon W. Downs pressed the convention of Louisiana to limit the residence requirement for voters to twelve months on the grounds that "we might, with as much reason insist that science should make no progress, as to attempt to arrest the progress of political government. By a parity of argument, it would be as logical to assume that the old machinery originally employed to propel steamboats was better adapted to that purpose than the new machinery, which has been perfected by experience, and that the first steamboats on the Mississippi . . . were superior to the floating palaces that now adorn our port." [16]

Such pronouncements notwithstanding, few if any delegates visualized themselves as drafting a second Declaration of Independence or launching a new experiment in popular government. Seeking to abolish the grand jury system in the Michigan convention of 1850, C. E. Beardsley invoked the American Revolution not as a precedent to be imitated but as an achievement-in-being that was threatened by arguments drawn from pre-Revolutionary antiquity. "If it was an ancient system," he held, "that was no reason why it should be retained. If institutions were venerable and useful for the reason of their antiquity, there was no object in the American revolution. . . . The arguments of the gentleman would lead back to the old system of government, and destroy our republican institutions." Similarly, John D. Pierce pressed for a clause that would revoke existing charters in thirty years' time on the grounds that peaceful constitutional change was the American alternative to revolutionary means of removing unbearable evils. Both arguments suggested that innovators claimed the privilege of further change primarily on the basis that the United States had already achieved the political system in which it was feasible.[17]

More generally, constitutional reformers claimed no more radical right for their generation than the right to amend the constitutions an earlier generation had drafted. Even in Rhode Island, where an intransigent legislature refused to provide for extension of the suffrage, agitators for political reform often declined to invoke radical change or appeal to unfamiliar rights; instead they argued that "the doctrines of liberty and equality, first promulgated in modern times by the immortal founders of our State, and re-asserted by the illustrious author of the declaration of independence, lie at the foundation of all that is just and free in our political institutions; and . . . the vindication of these doctrines, when impaired, and the development of them in all their force and effect, are duties of the most sacred and imperative obligations, and enjoined upon us by the venerable fathers." [18]

What was good for this generation was also good for the next; this was the anomalous conclusion toward which appeals to the right of each generation to govern itself ultimately led. Typically, convention delegates who demurred at the efforts of their colleagues to impose tightly constructed frames of government on their successors argued only that continued progress required leaving subsequent generations a necessary discretion. Isaac T. Preston told the Louisiana convention in 1845, "We have it in our power to do speedy justice in our own day and generation. . . . Let us struggle for right and justice and equality now, with the certainty that its attainment and enjoyment in our day, will be the best guarantee that our children, growing up in our principles, will maintain the same rights and equality, when they ascend the stage of action, and we descend to our original clay." Solomon Downs used the same argument in behalf of easing the amending process: "We are constantly improving in the science of government, as in all else, and we ought not to tie either our own hands or the hands of those who are to come after us." [19] Politically motivated though these Democrats' appeals may have been, they were hardly addressed to a revolutionary future; rather, they took for granted that familiar constitutional structures would work more perfectly if they retained a necessary degree of flexibility, and such change as they visualized was only that, not historic but incidental.

Even the proponents of "Young America" typically betrayed a more familiar allegiance than their occasional radical pronouncements indicated. For every George H. Evans who argued that "In this country we already possess most or all of those means of progress, for which the reformers of the old world are now chiefly contending: YOUNG AMERICA, then, must embody something more *ultimate* than they," there were ten members of Congress committed to nothing more innovative than a vigorous foreign policy. We shall deal more fully with their enthusiasms in chapter III; here it is important to note that when such spokesmen repudiated the precedents of the founding fathers they did so primarily on the grounds that time-honored policies no longer met the needs or reflected the capacities of a growing nation. Some of these Congressmen espoused "intervention" in European affairs while others advocated territorial expansion of the United States; almost all implied that the spread of liberal institutions on the existing American model was the key to their demand for change. (That is, they visualized a horizontal reduplication of institutions they already knew, not a restless search for new principles of government.) Even at their most aggressively radical, American democrats were little likely to visualize a future truly different from the past they had inherited from 1776. [20]

CONSERVATIVE DEMURRERS AND DOUBTS

Democrats won most national elections and they acquitted themselves very well in most of the states, but they were by no means universally successful. Hence it is appropriate to ask how far, whatever their party, the opponents of democratic innovations in politics or economics or foreign policy challenged liberal Americans' consensus on the progressive nature and implications of their history.

A small group of irreconcilable conservatives clearly took issue with even the most gradual of democratic reforms, and among them Chancellor Kent of New York was probably most inclined to visualize the present juncture of affairs in terms of a radical choice between established liberties and drastic innovations. "Universal suffrage once granted," he told the state's constitutional convention in 1821, "is granted forever, and never can be recalled. There is no retrograde step in the rear of democracy. However mischievous the precedent may be in its consequences, or however fatal in its effects, universal suffrage never can be recalled or checked, but by the strength of the bayonet. We stand, therefore, this moment, on the brink of fate, on the very edge of the precipice. If we let go our present hold on the senate, we commit our proudest hopes and our most precious interests to the waves." [21]

Kent's remarks have become famous since he spoke, but largely because they were so extreme as to seem irrelevant even in his own time. The more common conservative position was exemplified in the second Michigan convention by defenders of the grand jury system. There, Joseph R. Williams appealed not only to the federal Bill of Rights and the constitutions of the older states but also to Anglo-Saxon precedent: "It is one of those institutions which the Anglo Saxons every where cherish with pride, with affection, with undying tenacity. It has followed the Anglo Saxon race as a shadow. It is one of the mile stones that mark their progress in constitutional law and constitutional liberty. As a citizen of Michigan, I would not reject one of the noble characteristics of the race of which it is our pride and boast to be a part." Kent might well have agreed, but the thrust of his argument was different. In his view, any step toward democracy was by definition both radical and hazardous, and the easy-going progress most democrats visualized was impossible. For the Michigan conservative, on the other hand, the danger lay in the possibility that in their pursuit of an otherwise desirable progress his contemporaries might abandon the historic achievements of their race. [22]

Similarly, conservatives who objected to contemporary innovations did so with obvious confidence in the innovations that had already been established. Certainly this was the basis on which many Whig spokesmen sought to discredit the Democratic party: "It is the party," the Whig State Convention of Indiana argued in 1844, "which claims *progression*, for its great principle, because, for the sake of popularity, it unites contempt for the experience of the past, with a reckless opposition to all that is present; and which calls itself Democratic, and yet violates every principle and desecrates every institution, which Jefferson and Madison and Monroe developed, cherished, and sustained; because forsooth Democracy is *progressive.*" So, too, John Pendleton Kennedy burlesqued the opposition in *Quodlibet* (1840) in such a fashion as to indicate that he was more than content with the achievements that had already distinguished American history. The novel has Middleton Flam, a leading Democrat, defend the architectural character of his residence, a fraudulent manor house, on the grounds that "there is no reproach in the fact that we neither build, legislate, think nor determine for the next generation. We attend to *ourselves*—that is genuine New Light democracy. We oppose Vested Rights, we oppose Chartered Privileges, we oppose Pledges to bind future legislatures, we oppose Tariffs, Internal Improvements, Colleges and Universities, on the broad democratic ground, that we have nothing to do with Posterity. Posterity will be as free as we are. Let it take care of itself. I glory, sir, in saying New Light democracy riots in Gimcrack and Gingerbread." [23]

The *American Review* demonstrated, in turn, the ambiguities of the position Whig partisans tried to maintain in order to differentiate themselves from the Democrats. On the one hand, in its introductory statement of 1844 (the Whig counterpart to John L. O'Sullivan's introduction to the *Democratic Review* in 1837), the Whig monthly denounced its antagonists for unsettling the country's institutions by their attacks on an appointive judiciary, on corporations, and on the ideal of government by law. "There is scarcely any dangerously radical opinion," it held, "any specious, delusive theory, on social, political, or moral points, which does not, in some part of the country, find its peculiar aliment and growth among the elements of that party." On the other hand, the same editorial sought to claim a devotion to "progress" for the Whigs, as distinguished from the Democrats' love for mere change, and subsequent articles and reviews reinforced that complex position. [24]

In July 1845, it is true, an anonymous author in the *American Review* developed a lugubrious refutation of American ideas of progress, quarreling with the notion that the United States had progressed beyond earlier nations, that it was protected from their errors, and that its people were capable of maintaining liberty. But a year later, in an essay on "Civilization: American and European" that began by pointing up deficiencies in the American national character, the *Review* ended by hailing American advantages and praising American prospects. Significantly, those advantages included "a heroic age in our early settlement and happy revolution," and they terminated in the observation that "above all, in erecting our fabric of society, we have no antiquated edifices to remodel, no crumbling walls to prop up, no rubbish to remove; but an abundance of new and sound materials all around us." The upshot was a remarkably optimistic view of the nation's future prospects: "It has germinated, has waxed with a rapid and vigorous growth, and put forth magnificent buds of promise; and, though it has by no means reached the grandeur and maturity of the parent tree, though it is exposed to many casualties and enemies, yet it is the hope of the world; it contains the best, if not the only, promise of social regeneration for the race." By 1850, in fact, the journal had come to the point of criticizing Guizot (whom it had quoted with approbation in 1846) for his obstinate defense of the status quo in France, and of suggesting that changes in established ways of viewing society and politics were necessary even in the United States. By now its chief admonition was not that progress was hazardous, but that it must be guided by the voice of enlightened reason.[25]

Other instances in which men of a conservative temperament expressed doubts about the nation's infatuation with progress led to much the same results. One of the chief forums for such cautionary exercises was the gatherings of college literary societies at which young men were nerved to contend with the vagaries of a society that no longer deferred to educated men. Speaking before the Phi Beta Kappa Society of Dartmouth College in 1846, the Chief Justice of New Hampshire stressed the ways in which the contemporary age had not progressed beyond earlier times, if indeed it had not lost ground because of its passion for wealth and distinction. Nevertheless, he concluded that with improved education, better ethical training in the home, and the influence of higher learning, the world's progress in ethical matters might still match its evident progress in material and mechanical affairs. In the same year Joel T. Headley observed to the literary societies of the University of Vermont that the only certain instance of progress in modern history was the inexorable extension of the democratic principle, which he thought might well bring ruin in its train if the masses acted unwisely. The inference the New York editor drew was, however, remarkably open-ended: "With virtue and intelligence to guide it, this encroaching revolutionary movement may work the world's regeneration; without it, it will finish in a circle, and man at last will flee to despotism to escape anarchy." [26]

In invoking the metaphor of a circle and in visualizing a time when men might willingly substitute despotism for anarchy, Headley appealed to a time-honored conception of history as a cyclical process, placing a classical image of the world in the balance against the modern "progressive" image. This too was a staple of academic analysis, one that reached unusually erudite expression in Alexander H. Everett's "Discourse on the Progress and Limits of Social Improvement" before the literary societies of Amherst College in 1833. There Everett denied the perfectibility of man, insisted on "the common course of progress, maturity, decline and fall," and denied even that successive nations or races could be said to carry mankind permanently forward. Yet in his final observations he also dwelt on circumstances that promised to raise the United States above the level of any previous civilization, and in speeches he delivered both before and after his academic exercise he testified to an even greater enthusiasm for the unique historic role of his country.[27]

Everett's example indicates that the cyclical theory of history that many orators adopted neither denied American achievements nor supported exclusively conservative perspectives on the future. The fact was clearly demonstrated by Levi Slamm, a self-professed "radical" in the Democratic party of New York City, who wrote in 1844, "The day now is, when the people of the United States boast of enjoying a greater degree of liberty and happiness than any other nation. But, if there is truth in the remark, that every form of Government that the ingenuity of man can devise, contains within its elements the seeds of dissolution, the day *may* come when the freedom of our Republic will exist only in the history of bygone days. Let us beware then, and by every honest effort, attempt to proscrastinate that awful day, and thus preserve and perpetuate the blessings of liberty and independence to the remotest ages of posterity." [28] For a wide range of Americans, the metaphor of cyclical history was hortatory rather than descriptive, a challenge to their initiative rather than a prediction of inevitable events.[g]

In other words, most conservatives neither denied the desirability of progress nor invoked a cyclical pattern of history to discount America's claims to an extraordinary place in the annals of mankind; their only stipulation was that Americans must not confuse aberration with excellence. Their position was neatly summarized by the Whig delegation in the New York legislature when it announced in 1844 that "The whig party is devoted to progress, but it does not destroy. It seeks to establish perfect equality of political rights; but it levels upwards, not downwards, by education and benignant legislation, not by subverting established laws or institutions. It is the party of law, of order, of enterprise, of improvement, of beneficence, of hope, and of humanity. Through the action of this great and generous party, every attainable national good may be ultimately secured; and through its action we can best promote the more comprehensive interests of freedom and of humanity throughout the world." In the light of such a statement it is difficult to say wherein Whigs differed from Democrats except in claiming to represent the American idea of progress better than they.[29]

SECULAR PROGRESS AND DIVINE OBLIGATION

Liberals and conservatives, Democrats and Whigs, adhered to remarkably similar perspectives on the implications the history of the world held for the United States. At the same time there were genuine dissidents who systematically challenged the complacent inferences Americans typically drew from their history, but the most significant fact about them is that their intensely felt criticisms of American belief testified to the widespread authority those inferences had.

One such group of dissidents accepted the commonplace version of macrohistory only to turn it against itself. Henry David Thoreau put their argument very precisely in "Resistance to Civil Government" (1849). "The progress from an absolute to a limited monarchy, from a limited monarchy to a democracy, is a progress toward a true respect for the individual . . . ," he declared. "Is a democracy, such as we know it, the last improvement possible in government?" Posing such a question, he challenged his contemporaries to abandon beliefs that most of them accepted without reflection, but there is no evidence that he converted them to his way of viewing the world. Meanwhile his friend Ralph Waldo Emerson would seem to have played the anomalous role of confirming his compatriots' complacency by the manner in which he challenged them to transcend their present experience. "Here stars, here woods, here hills, here animals, here men abound," he declared in his lecture on the Young American, "and the vast tendencies concur of a new order. If only the men are employed in conspiring with the designs of the Spirit who led us hither and is leading us still, we shall quickly enough advance out of all hearing of others' censures, out of all regrets of our own, into a new and more excellent social state than history has recorded." [30]

A different sort of challenge came from the *Harbinger*, which was devoted to radical social reform. "The high idea of our Fathers, which was Hope in the Future," George Ripley declared in 1845 in a squib published just before the Fourth of July, "has become a petrifaction. We are so tickled with the praises of the present that we leave unfinished the work which they began." Perhaps the most notable expression of this sort of dissent appeared, however, in Parke Godwin's *Democracy, Constructive and Pacific* (1844). There Godwin excoriated his contemporaries for their complacent belief in material progress and their callous disregard for the torments their economy and their polity imposed on the laboring classes, but the whole point of his book was to advance the cause of associational socialism by condemning the evils of the existing state of society.[31] In other words, he dissented simultaneously from the facts of American history and from the Americans' sense of their history, and he could only identify—not alter—their vision.[h]

Meanwhile many members of the Protestant clergy demanded of Americans that they live up to the requirements of the millennium. In one sense this fact meant that the clergy described an obligation far more radical than any of the demands that the most radical secular historiography might make. In another sense, it meant that they confirmed American patriots in their extraordinary sense of well-being.[32]

Much of the history of American millennialism belongs exclusively to religious history, which this volume does not seek to trace, but in this instance religious tradition blended so directly with secular thought as to require some attention. According to the traditional idea of the millennium, which flourished during the Reformation, secular history consists of a series of stages in which mankind has moved ever closer to the point in time at which God will transform the earth into a replica of His kingdom. According to this traditional view, however, the transformation will come about as a result of His impatience with the kingdoms of this world, and in addition it will depend, as salvation also depends, upon an extraordinary exercise of His will. From this view arose the classic European form of millennial enthusiasm, a belief that the evils of the present day betokened the imminent arrival of the time at which God would impose His judgment on the world and call His saints to their final reward.

The disciples of William Miller, who foretold the end of the world in 1843, demonstrate that premillennialism (as it is now called) could find sympathizers in the United States. But the typical American commitment to the millenarian faith was, instead, postmillennial: the belief that humanity might progress so far toward perfection while still inhabiting the secular world as to persuade the Divinity that they were prepared for the Second Coming, which would then occur in recognition of human felicity rather than in retribution for human sins.[i] Seen in this perspective, the millennium appeared to be, not an extraordinary goal beyond the power of men to secure, nor a stunning antithesis to the history they had already experienced, but a destiny available to them through their history. The Reverend John Fowler voiced one version of this postmillennial hope in addressing the Young Men's Association of Utica (New York) in 1843. There, the former pastor of the city's First Presbyterian Church traced the influence of American example and the effect of American agency on the history of society, only to conclude that the millennium would arrive by natural means in a country that was already distinguished for its pious origins, its political genius, its religious observances, its geographical advantages, and its free press.[33]

Fowler was obviously an enthusiast, but other clergymen who refused to be drawn into his extreme position none the less continued to insist in the name of the millennium that their communicants, and more generally the nation as a whole, live up to obligations that their religious hopes placed upon them. The very magnitude of those hopes often led the clergy to make extraordinary demands of their contemporaries: that they eradicate sin, blot out natural corruption, purge the nation of all of its evils. In the last analysis, however, their sense that it was possible for Americans to triumph over secular evils as no other people ever had can only have reinforced the Americans' sense that they were peculiarly situated in history and peculiarly able to realize human hopes.[34] To a remarkable degree, the men who should have been most inclined to question the American people's good estate represented the country they knew as the Kingdom of God in process of achievement.[j]

On the other hand, clergymen and laymen who expressed a recurrent anxiety that the American people might not prove worthy of their heritage, but who did not explicitly invoke the millennium, also tended to portray the long reach of history in unusually reassuring terms; they joined in an attack on American complacency which inevitably implied that complacency would be warranted if the Americans were true to their history. Doing so, they also helped to obliterate the lines of distinction between secular and religious ideas of progress. It is difficult if not impossible to say now how far the Americans' sense of history derived from secular sources, how far from their religious background; the best answer would seem to be that by the 1830s the two traditions were inextricably fused. Secular and religious at the same time, the Americans' extraordinary historiography taught them that they would lead the world to its regeneration if their devotion did not falter.[k]

The Reverend Benjamin F. Tefft, professor of classics at Indiana Asbury University, expressed a theological version of this synthesis in 1845. "This is his [sic] chosen land," he explained, speaking particularly of the Mississippi Valley, which westerners and eastern missionaries alike were wont to consider the key to the nation's destiny. "For this he has been for ages watching and preparing. The past he has made our servant. All climes and countries have been working for us. The elements of a glorious order of civilization are now ready. If the great enterprise fail here; if in this valley man is not raised to his highest destiny; the toil and struggle of six thousand years are lost, and lost forever!" The Reverend M. Augustus Jewett celebrated the Fourth of July in Terre Haute (Indiana) in much the same vein in 1840: "This immortal declaration is due to circumstances which, in the history of a world, can never occur again. We have seen the spirits who called it into being, sifted by events from the intellect of the world: we have seen a new world opened to receive and nourish them: we have increased beyond all previous calculation: we are surrounded by comforts; we are removed from the yet enduring evils of the old world; and if, from any cause, we forget the ages of struggle, the streams of blood, the heaven directed events, which brought us to this condition of happiness, and criminally sacrifice the principles of this declaration, they can never be restored." [35]

Lay commentators expressed similar anxieties in almost identical terms. Pressing his contemporaries to join in a crusade against the evils of avarice, demagogism, a vicious press, and excessive zeal for office, Charles D. Drake (son of Dr. Daniel Drake) admonished the Franklin Society of St. Louis in 1837 that the nation must choose between liberty and despotism. If we fail to purge ourselves, he declared,

the expiring cries of Liberty shall be heard in accents of agony, bewailing the fate of her last and loveliest abode. . . .

But, on the other hand, how fills the heart with joy and gratitude at the picture of a nation, mindful of its duties, and faithful in their discharge! . . . In such a nation, freedom is perpetual, and the happiness which smiles over the whole land, attests her universal presence. . . . *Then*, will the glory of the American nation have reached the zenith of its splendor,—defying alike domestic feud and foreign aggression;—and with the impress of unending existence upon her brow, the genius of America, like the star in the east, will lead earth's people to the shrine of freedom, that with America, they may worship and be free.

Nor was the sentiment Drake expressed mere western hyperbole. Fifteen years later, addressing the literary societies of the University of Georgia, William H. Stiles underlined the cosmic importance that attached to the preservation of American liberties: "There are no more continents to be discovered, no new *Atlantis* to realize the visions of Plato's Critias, no fresh races to perform what we may neglect, or restore what we may ruin. In the great battle of human rights, we are *the world's last reserve*. When an army's last reserve has been brought into action, every soldier knows the battle must now be won or lost; he must now triumph, or he and his cause must perish together. In the progress of the world, the last reserve has been advanced to the conflict, the death-struggle has come, and the whole cause of Intelligence, of Liberty, and of Christianity, for the whole earth and for all time, must triumph with us, or with us they must perish for ever." [36] American moralists challenged their countrymen to rise to the level on which history had already placed them.

THE IDEA OF AN AMERICAN EXPERIMENT

Secular and religious, conservative and liberal, the ideas Americans held of their history came to a focus in their belief that they were engaged in a profound national "experiment." Modern writers brought up in secular and scientific categories of thought often exaggerate the open-ended and tentative aspects of the commitment the Americans expressed, and so miss the precise meanings they attached to the term.

So far as its dictionary meaning is concerned, the noun "experiment" bore the primary definition of "a trial; an act or operation to discover some unknown truth, principle, or effect." But it also retained an older connotation of making a known principle manifest, in the sense in which a high-school teacher today performs an experiment in chemistry for the instruction of his pupils.[37] In this latter sense, the American "experiment" was as important for demonstrating established truths as it was for discovering unknown laws or measuring the comparative validity of competing hypotheses, and Americans characteristically invoked it with this connotation in mind.

Their confidence that they were demonstrating established truths apparently derived specifically from the sense of national achievement they had gained from the successful conclusion of the War of 1812, and more generally from their continued success in exploiting the continent. It represented a distinct shift in attitudes since the 1790s; when the founding fathers had declared that they were launching a perilous political experiment, they had also taken for granted that only time would tell whether the institutions they had devised would serve their intended purposes. (Significantly, in illustrating the primary scientific meaning of the word in 1828, Noah Webster quoted John Adams to the effect that "a political experiment cannot be made in a laboratory, nor determined in a few hours.") By contrast, Americans of the Middle Period commonly took it for granted their national experience had already demonstrated the validity of their national principles. Even a critic of the idea that the United States was engaged in a national experiment confirmed the common faith by the manner in which he refuted it. "I cannot believe that our government is to be a perpetual 'experiment,' " George Camp wrote in Democracy (1841), "that its practicability can never be demonstrated."[38]

On the other hand, commentators who insisted that the national experiment was still in process did so in terms of a fear that mankind might not be capable of living up to American institutions—not a fear that those institutions might need to be altered to suit the character of mankind. Father Sparrow expressed this idea very clearly in his admonitory sermon at Alexandria. The nation's calling, he declared, was "to try the experiment for the sister nations of the earth, whether fallen man is capable of self-government in any great degree. The experiment has often been tried before, but never with perfect and permanent success: generally, it has been a total failure." [39] Even when it raised the most anxious doubts about the outcome of the American experience, this perspective was like other American perspectives in portraying the United States as the home of perfected human institutions. Successful or not, the outcome of the American experiment would be a judgment on human virtue, not on the institutions the fathers had adopted.[1]

Secular spokesmen adopted this same ambivalent perspective in their charges to their contemporaries. In 1832 Henry Clay admonished the National Republican Convention of Young Men that "it belongs to you, and the young men of your age, to decide whether [the] great blessings of Liberty and Union shall be defended and preserved. The responsibility which attaches to you is immense. It is not our own country alone that will be affected by the result of the great experiment of self-government which will be shortly committed exclusively to your hands. The eyes of all civilized nations are intensely gazing upon us; and it may be truly asserted that the fate of Liberty throughout the World, mainly depends upon the maintenance of American Liberty." Three years later, William J. Duane invoked a more pessimistic version of the same theme in a letter to the Great Whig Festival in Baltimore: "The practicability of institutions such as ours has been a problem for more than two thousand years. The experiment has been often made in vain, and we have been for about half a century engaged in making it ourselves. In his day, Mr. Jefferson said it was successful. Have we the same confidence still?" [40]

For their part, liberals and Democrats were probably more inclined than conservatives and Whigs to proclaim that the national experiment was already a success, but their claim expressed only a greater degree of confidence in the virtue of the American people, not a challenge to the common national sense of what was at stake. "The great experiment has been gloriously successful," Benjamin F. Butler declared in 1841. "The United States, in every stage of their career; in peace and in war; in the arts of social life; in political science; in knowledge and morals and religion; have vindicated the wisdom, the safety, the beneficence of Representative Government, founded on the broadest basis of Democratic Liberty." Moreover, Andrew Jackson took the occasion of his Farewell

Address (which was a sort of secular Democratic sermon) to express much the same warnings that his Whig antagonists had voiced: "You have the highest of human trusts committed to your care. Providence has showered on this favored land blessings without number, and has chosen you as the guardians of freedom, to preserve it for the benefit of the human race. May He who holds in His hands the destinies of nations make you worthy of the favors He has bestowed and enable you, with pure hearts and pure hands and sleepless vigilance, to guard and defend to the end of time the great charge He has committed to your keeping." [41]

As Jackson's exhortation indicates, the logical corollary of experimentation as the Americans understood it was much the same as the logical corollary of the millennium as they understood it: to be true to the institutions with which history had favored them. The exhortation to be true to yourselves runs all through the public literature of the Middle Period and its context makes clear that the self to be honored was the virtuous American whom speakers of every description postulated as the perfect citizen. Conservatives and Whigs understandably expressed doubts whether their contemporaries could adhere to the necessary standards of virtue, whereas liberals and Democrats often took it for granted that they had already done so, but partisans of every description joined in proclaiming a common faith and deriving national obligations from that faith. [42] In its religious version their faith was a reformed Protestantism, in its secular version a purified republicanism; in both it represented the achievements of the future in terms of remaining true to the achievements of the past. Seen in these terms, the differences between anxious conservatives and cock-sure democrats were as insignificant as the differences among the leading Protestant sects, which disappeared before their common nondenominational commitment to bringing the Lord's work to fruition in their own time.

❧ II ❧

MICROHISTORY:
THE VIEW SINCE 1776

For most Americans, history in the large sense stopped with the American Revolution, but history in a more restricted sense (which I shall refer to as "microhistory") did not. Rather, it continued as the setting in which Americans strove to keep faith with their special destiny. Macrohistory logically culminated in a microhistory of human effort no less significant because it took place in a new environment and according to new rules.

This proposition is especially important because of modern historical analyses that point to a concept or quality of "timelessness" in the Americans' views of their history. According to this interpretation, which frequently embodies a judgment on American values as well as an analysis of American thought, the American people saw themselves as outside of time and freed from its burdens. The judgment is more appropriate than the description is accurate. By contrast with Europeans, perhaps, and by contrast with many modern writers, the Americans of the Middle Period lacked a sense of time. In their own terms, however, they saw themselves as living at the end of one kind of time—Greenwich Mean Time, one is tempted to call it—and immersed in another. Time came to a focus in their national experience, and microhistory recorded their struggle to live up to their responsibilities in the New World.[1]

HISTORY ON THE HUSTINGS

The American sense of obligation is exemplified in the development during the Middle Period of an almost obsessive concern with the historic patterns of American politics. During the 1830s and 1840s, political partisans of every hue appealed to the history of American political parties to influence contemporary political choices by relating them to the choices made by the generation of 1776, or that of 1800.

Partisan microhistory of this sort obviously coincided with the larger perspective in which Americans saw themselves as a nation. The events of the heroic age that had preceded them were important to Americans of the Middle Period because they had established the terms in which it was intended that Americans should conduct themselves from that point forward. Hence appeals made to the electorate could logically state the issues of any given election as a mere *reprise* of issues already settled at an earlier day. On this view, the object of any political campaign was to revive public virtue by invoking the precedent of the founding fathers.[2]

Nevertheless, partisan appeals to recent history also typically involved an exaggerated sense of the efforts that were still necessary to secure American liberties. If macrohistory taught Americans to be complacent, microhistory pressed them to locate themselves in an unending struggle between the forces of good and of evil for mastery in the American republic. This attitude was particularly characteristic of Democratic partisans. On the one hand, Democrats maintained that they alone kept faith with the founding fathers. On the other hand, they argued that the faith of the fathers had itself been weakened by antidemocratic prejudices the Whigs still shared. Hence they lent to the details of American history since 1776 a tension that history up to 1776 had seemingly lacked. "The political history of the country," New York State's delegates to the national Democratic convention of 1832 told their constituents, "is, in a word, the history of a struggle, more or less remitted as the power of the opposition has increased or declined, to maintain in their purity the original principles on which the government is founded."[3] The purported object of Democratic politics was not simply to remain faithful to historic precedents, but to combat evils that had threatened American liberty since the days of the fathers.[a]

Democratic accounts of the writing of the Constitution exemplified both elements of this rather ambiguous rendering of national history. According to John A. Dix, for example, the precursors of the Federalist party had sought to draft an "aristocratic" constitution independent of the popular will. "If the constitution had been framed upon such principles," he told the Democrats assembled at Herkimer (New York) in 1840, "we should have been removed but a single step from the colonial vassalage which was thrown off by the war of the revolution. We should merely have exchanged foreign masters for irresponsible rulers of our own. Happily, the great body of the people were democratic then, as they are now: and through the firmness and perseverance of their representatives in the convention, a constitution, conforming in its general provisions to the true standard of democracy, was secured to us." [4]

The same ambiguous doctrine explained why the Constitution that democrats had rescued in 1787 nevertheless required their most strenuous partisan efforts in 1800 and continued to require them at every succeeding election. "Two great political parties have struggled for the mastery in our country ever since the formation of the federal constitution," the Democratic convention of Indiana declared in 1836. "The true republican or democratic party, have ever contended for a strict construction of the constitution, and have uniformly resisted the exercise of powers by Congress, not clearly delegated by that instrument. . . . The federalists, on the contrary, under the pretext of consulting the 'general welfare' and the vague and indefinable doctrine of 'expediency' and claiming a free construction of the constitution, have exercised powers in derogation of its letter and spirit, and in 'violation of many of the rights of the states.' " [5]

The upshot of Democratic microhistory understood as an ambiguous but obviously tendentious history of the early republic was an unambiguous but equally tendentious portrait of contemporary Whigs as "Federalists." The charge was made on every conceivable occasion. It led to laborious efforts to "prove" that the Whig party was composed of former Federalists and that its candidates had served Federalist masters. It also led to repeated forays into the writings of John Adams and the early writings of John Quincy Adams to demonstrate their intractable "aristocratic" bias. Above all, it led to a long series of attacks on the Alien and Sedition Acts and on the Hartford Convention. In Democratic eyes, these events were not merely instances of evil ways into which the country had fallen and from which it had recovered, but evidence of a continuing conspiracy against national liberty in which Whig "aristocrats" and imperfect republicans were still engaged. So far as they could, Democrats deprecated Whig claims to office by tracing Whig policies to their roots in a discredited Federalism. [6]

Even the fact that they gradually came to accept a two-party system as a legitimate form of political competition did not diminish the Democrats' enthusiasm for relegating the Whigs to an unacceptable past. While party leaders may have waxed philosophical about the existence of alternative parties in a republic supposedly committed to virtue, as Richard

Hofstadter argues they did, they also often visualized those parties in a kind of dialectical relationship, the opposition representing a force for good primarily by keeping one's own party alert and faithful to its professions. In addition, party managers were far less philosophical than the intellectuals Hofstadter chiefly describes, and in his *Inquiry into the Origin and Course of Political Parties in the United States* even Martin Van Buren—one of the first politicians to pay homage to the two-party system—represented his own party in heroic terms as the heir of the true American tradition.[7]

Democratic historiography of this sort was far from authentic, but it spoke to an authentic American need: members of the generation that elevated Andrew Jackson to the Presidency felt compelled to locate themselves in the mainstream of American liberalism. Hence they presented the Whigs with an almost insoluble problem. On any objective view of history the Whigs had reason to claim that it was they rather than the Democrats who were most consistently faithful to the founding fathers, and occasionally a bold politician or a discriminating party historian was willing to accept the historic ties that linked him to the Federalists.[8] More characteristically, however, they attempted to counteract the effects of Democratic microhistory by substituting their own competing version.

Sometimes their effort took the form of rebutting Democratic allegations that the Whigs were only Federalists in disguise by insisting that the disintegration of the country's original parties had redistributed political partisans among contemporary political organizations.[9] More often it led to rewriting national political history in order to represent the Whigs rather than the Democrats as true heirs of the tradition of popular liberty that Democrats had made the center of their cause. Far from seeking to maintain a distinctive version of history to compete with the Democratic version, Whigs typically accepted the Democratic version and then sought to populate it with their own candidates.

Their efforts led them in various directions. One was a truly fascinating if largely unpersuasive effort to counteract the invidious terminology the Democrats had succeeded in imposing on American political discourse. During the campaign of 1840, Joseph R. Underwood, a prominent Whig from Kentucky, professed to be unable to understand the political terms that divided his contemporaries. "Sir," he declared in the

House of Representatives, "there is something in the fascination of
names too deep for my philosophy. . . . The religious world runs after
its peculiar sectarian name; and the manner in which politicians use the
terms Federalists, Republicans, Democrats, Aristocrats, States rights,
&c. &c., without sense or meaning, is enough to make one think, that
words are no longer used as the signs of ideas, but because they possess
some magic power to influence the conduct of men." (Apparently the
term "Whig" gave him no such difficulties.) In the same campaign the
Whigs of Tennessee betrayed a nice sensitivity to the tactics Underwood
described when they defended William Henry Harrison on the grounds
he had been appointed to office by "four Republican Presidents" (among
whom they named George Washington) and "two called Federal Presidents," while in 1844 Calvin Colton devoted a whole *Junius Tract* to
proving both that all Americans were Democrats and that the Democrats
were not as democratic as the Whigs.[10]

Other Whigs sought as far as they could to claim the democratic-
republican tradition for themselves. When Charles Miner addressed a
"Democratic Whig Festival" at Wilkes-Barre (Pennsylvania) in 1840 he
freely acknowledged that he had been a Federalist, but he also insisted
that as a Federalist he had always been "a true Democratic Republican in
the best sense of those words." (The platform on which he appeared also
testified to his eagerness to deprive his Federalism of its distinctive historic significance.) Similarly, Judge Jacob Burnet of Ohio, like Miner a
former Federalist, told the Whig National Convention of 1839 (which
presented itself to the world as the "Democratic Whig National Convention") that Harrison "has always been a Democratic Republican of the
school of Washington, Jefferson and Madison." In 1844, moreover, Calvin
Colton made much of the fact that as a "young champion of democracy"
Henry Clay had signally helped Thomas Jefferson to win the election of
1800 and repudiate the Alien and Sedition Acts.[11]

The most striking effort of historical redefinition the Whigs engaged
in, however, was their attempt to identify the Democrats as latter-day
Federalists. Miner managed the trick in spite of his principles by arguing
that ultra-Democrats had joined with their natural allies the ultra-
Federalists (those who had never accepted democracy) to form the modern Democratic party. Calvin Colton, ever faithful to Whig Doctrine,
was to make the same charge in 1844, while in 1838 the Whigs of Penn-

sylvania, posing as "Democratic Young Men for Ritner" in that state's gubernatorial campaign, charged the Democratic party both with glaring inconsistencies in policy and with a consistent disloyalty to Democratic precepts. "Claiming descent from the Democracy of 1798," the 'Young Men' declared, "they have extended the prerogatives of the President, to fearful limits,—transcending the most extravagant notions of the original Federalists." Ten years later an anonymous Whig tract charged Lewis Cass with having delivered a Federalist Fourth of July oration in 1803 or 1804, and a similar charge was to be leveled against James Buchanan in 1856.[12]

Beset by Democratic victories, in short, the Whigs sought to vindicate their aspirations to power by invoking the same traditions and claiming the same sanctions as the Democrats. Accepting the Democratic version of American history as a continuous struggle for liberty against "aristocratic" and antidemocratic forces, they found it easy in 1840, although they were usually hostile to "revolutions" and critical even of "experiments" in national policy, to proclaim that they were fighting a second American Revolution intended to retrieve the hopes of the first. *"This contest has had no parallel since the period of the Revolution,"* Henry Clay declared at Taylorsville (Virginia) during the presidential campaign. *"In both instances there is a similarity of object. That was to achieve, this is to preserve the liberties of the country."* Indeed, the very name of their party, adopted during the 1830s, deliberately invoked memories of the earlier revolution. According to the view that self-proclaimed "Whigs" presented to the electorate, the great battle for human liberty that had been fought in 1776 remained the battle each generation must fight in order to be free. For a brief moment, the party of American conservatives succeeded in identifying itself with the most vigorous traditions of the democracy.[13]

AMERICA AND THE PROBLEMS OF EUROPE

The great battle for liberty also committed the Americans (or so they held) to struggle against dangers that emanated from Europe. If macrohistory taught them they had left Europe behind, microhistory taught them that Europe still existed as a potential hazard to the American experiment.

For many Democrats, of course, the threat of "Federalism" was identical with the threat of British institutions. According to the standard partisan view, Federalist sympathizers had consistently sought to impose British principles on vulnerable American democrats. British loyalties had underlain their efforts to establish an aristocratic constitution; British loyalties had led Alexander Hamilton and other Federalist leaders to adopt the controversial measures of Washington's administration; British loyalties had generated the Hartford Convention; and British loyalties continued to influence Whig policy.[b] On this view British precedent for any controversial policy was enough to condemn it. "The English Doctrine is that a 'Public Debt is a public blessing' and the Federal Doctrine in the United States, from the period of the 'funding system' of Hamilton, has been in accordance with it," Democrats told the people of Tennessee in 1840, one year after James K. Polk, their candidate for governor, had belabored the "American System" of Henry Clay on the same grounds.[14]

There were sound polemical reasons why Democrats should keep the specter of British policy before the American electorate. Not only had the United States twice gone to war with Britain; not only had Federalists and Whigs often betrayed an explicit sympathy with British social patterns and policies; but there was also a long-standing American tradition, fed by Scots-Irish Presbyterianism as well as other dissident faiths, of hostility to Britain on religious and ethnic grounds. If Democrats could maintain the fiction that the Whigs were more British than American, half their political battles were already won. However, the mere fact of this appeal to national prejudice should not blind us to its larger significance: the fear of British influence that partisans voiced was also historical. History in the large sense had carried Americans beyond the practices of Great Britain, and history since 1776 came to a focus in the struggle to throw off legacies that previous history had left. "The Fourth of July, 1776, was the date of our political separation from Great Britain," Robert Rantoul Jr. declared at Scituate (Massachusetts) in 1836. "The separation left the Colonies, Independent States. But political Independence was only a single step towards freedom from foreign influence. Much remained to be done—alas! much yet remains to be done—before these United States can be pronounced to be completely and in the broadest sense independent of Great Britain." [15]

Under these circumstances, Democrats came to identify national ob-

ligations with departures from British practice even when they expressed
no sense that British influences directly impinged on the United States.
Sometimes their argument took the form simply of drawing contrasts between British and American policy to the implicit advantage of the latter.[16] At other times, however, they appealed to their compatriots not to
suffer the United States to imitate Britain. During debate in the New
York constitutional convention of 1846, Robert H. Morris declared that
he supported restrictions on legislative incorporations because "he did
not wish to see women and children carrying baskets for the emolument
of those who did not labor, or children from an early age trudging off to
factories to toil from early day to night-fall for the good of others. This
in Great Britain did exist; and the system might in some measure be
traced to the law of primogeniture.—He proceeded to shew that what
primogeniture did on the other side of the Atlantic, corporations would
do here." One object of American history was not simply to throw off
British loyalties, but to throw off the evils that British loyalties entailed.[17]

Ultimately, moreover, Great Britain was only the most available
among many targets for Democratic demands for national autonomy.
Morris had begun by saying that his object "was to prevent the establishment of the same kind of society here which had been described as existing in other countries," and other commentators took all of Europe as the
point from which America should depart. "The moment we admit the
principle, that no change in government can take place without permis-
sion of the existing authorities," Thomas W. Dorr told the constituent
assembly of Rhode Island in 1842, "we revert to the worn-out theory of
the monarchies of Europe; and whether we are the subjects of the Czar
of Russia, or of the monarch of Great Britain, or of a landed oligarchy,
the difference to us is only in degree, and we have lost the reality,
though we may retain the forms of a Democratic Republic." The same
broad target was also useful on the hustings. In 1843 the Democrats of
Tennessee charged that Whig social theory led to measures that would
culminate "in changing our simple republican system of government into
one, similar in all essential respects, to the odious European systems,"
while the *Western Review* declared editorially in 1846, "The aim of the
whigs, is, to build up a state of society closely resembling that which
prevails in Europe." [18]

Democrats sought to associate Whiggery with the Old World in order to discredit it; Whigs sought to denigrate Democratic policies by associating them with the same phenomenon. Hence they often argued that Democratic policies represented a capitulation to British interests if not an actual betrayal of American loyalty. In 1831, National Republicans in Maine charged that the Administration's tariff measures were pro-British, while as late as 1850 the *American Whig Review* complained (after the fashion of John L. O'Sullivan in the *Democratic Review*) that Great Britain "has succeeded, through her literary and political influence on this continent, in breaking down our system of independent industry, to the incalculable advantage of her own home industry, both agricultural and mechanical." Meanwhile, broadening the attack, Daniel Webster had asked a campaign audience in Saratoga (New York) in 1840, "Where in Europe, where in any part of the world out of our country, shall we find labor thus rewarded, and the general condition of the people so good? Nowhere! Away, then, with the injustice and the folly of reducing the cost of productions with us to what is called the common standard of the world. Away, then, away at once and forever, with the miserable policy which would bring the condition of a laborer in the United States to that of a laborer in Russia or Sweden, in France or Germany, in Italy or Corsica." [19] Whigs as well as Democrats viewed the whole of the European experience as a foil for the American experiment.[c]

As a result, Whigs often spoke as if the United States were and should be the antithesis of Europe. The proposition was labored by Whig apologists who represented American social practices as if they were intended primarily to be a corrective to European evils. It was a truism of Whig apologetics that the American factory system was admirable because it was unlike the factory system of the Old World, and the same mode of argument could be invoked in behalf of other American practices. In 1833, for example, Edward Everett used it to support an appeal for private contributions to western colleges. Calvin Colton drew upon the same contrast in its most egregious and probably its most persuasive form when he wrote in 1844 that "the great battle of the world is between freedom and despotism; and we take upon us to say, that, more than in anything or all things else, the *form* under which that contest is now carried on, is between European capital and labor on one side, and American capital and labor on the other. On this pivot, in our regard, turns the destiny of nations. SUSTAIN the position of American capital and labor, . . . and freedom will prevail all the world over." [20]

But Democrats had long since equated national independence with national uniqueness, and Democrats also argued that the United States was epitomized by its contrasts with Europe. Speaking at Union College, Benjamin F. Butler took pride in the fact that the United States had not been compelled to suffer the bloody revolutions that European nations had undergone since 1776 during the course of their efforts to achieve long-overdue reforms. In his eyes, Europeans' aspirations to American conditions of liberty and democracy did little to commend their practices to American eyes, but only vindicated the American experiment. More typically, Democrats simply ignored contemporary European achievements to underline the disparities that existed between their nation and all others. "Go the world over, from sea to sea, and from Indus to the Poles," D. V. Bradford proclaimed at a Democratic rally in Cincinnati in 1840, "and you find the liberty of speech, and of the Press, muffled and gagged—you find *'the rich and the well born,'* the *tenantry and the serf—the noble and the menial—the bond and the free, in all lands* BUT THIS. No where else, is man allowed to walk upright and assume the dignity of his nature." [21]

Even American reformers who denied that the United States was the antithesis of Europe commonly did so in order to secure the adoption of policies that would make it so; in dissent, they testified both to a popular bias in favor of the antithesis, which they sought to invoke in behalf of their cause, and to their own sense that the antithesis was still within reach as an object of national effort. In 1833 William Gouge brought his case against the contemporary banking system to a focus by declaring that "the difference between England and the United States, is simply this: in the former country, exclusive privileges are conferred on individuals who are called *Lords;* in the latter, exclusive privileges are conferred on corporations which are called *Banks.* The effect on the people of both countries is the same. In both the many live and labor for the benefit of the few." Fifteen years later, in his Twelfth Report, Horace Mann differentiated "the European theory [that] men are divided into classes" from "the Massachusetts theory [that] all are to have an equal chance for earning, and equal security in the enjoyment of what they earn," only to ask, "But is it not true that Massachusetts, in some respects, instead of adhering more and more closely to her own theory, is becoming emulous of the baneful examples of Europe?" Both versions of the comparison between Europe and America were challenges to Americans to make sure that they were true to themselves.[22]

The tactic Gouge and Mann employed also demonstrated that the Americans' sense of their differences from Europe was more than a merely complacent inference drawn from advantages the United States already possessed. Much has been made of the Americans' sense of "uniqueness" and "exemption," which these two statements certainly exemplify. But the terms connote a static position in history, whereas the Americans of the Middle Period characteristically looked upon the position they had attained as a point of departure for still more extraordinary achievements. Looking at themselves in the context of macrohistory, indeed, they anticipated no striking departures from the innovations they had already launched; they had already arrived at their destination via the American Revolution. Looking at themselves in the context of microhistory, on the other hand—and quite apart from the belief in the millennium that many of them shared—they anticipated a continuous process of national growth and development on the lines already laid down. Under these circumstances the proposition that America was the antithesis of Europe was prelude to a proposition that Americans would be able to fulfill the promise of their national experiment so long as they continued to avoid European evils.[d]

To put matters another way, the Americans' sense of their national identity ultimately depended, not on the degree to which they had escaped from the human condition, nor on the extent to which they succeeded in transcending the practices of Europe, but on the opportunities for full manhood that American institutions peculiarly afforded them. In 1847, in an address devoted to celebrating the advantages of the United States, Abram P. Maury declared that the American experiment had prospered because "no disturbing causes, no time-honored and inveterate abuses, no social frame-work, radically defective in its fundamental principles, existed in the midst of this new community, to fetter the free growth of its youthful limbs. . . . Far removed from extraneous influences; too distant from other orbs for their powers of attraction to give complexity or perturbation to its motions, this lone western star rose gradually above the horizon and advanced steadily towards the zenith of the political system."[23]

Maury was a Whig, and perhaps it is significant that he celebrated accomplishments recorded in the past rather than progress to be achieved in the future. Certainly Calvin Colton sought to capitalize on achievements already reached when he wrote in 1844, "Providence has assigned us a rich, productive, and glorious heritage, and established among us and over us a new, regenerate, and admirable system of Government. It has been abused, indeed; but it is good. All we want is good and faithful men at the head of it." But he also went on to say, "The wealth of the country is inexhaustible, and the enterprise of the people is unsubdued, notwithstanding all our late misfortunes. Give them a good Government, and they can not help going ahead, and outstripping every nation on the globe." In the same fashion, other Whig spokesmen portrayed exaggerated material prospects for the nation as a corollary of keeping faith with its origins.[24]

Materialistic and secular though it was, this Whiggish stance found parallels in the writings of eminent moralists. "The great distinction of our country," Channing wrote in 1830, "is, that we enjoy some peculiar advantages for understanding our own nature. . . . In Europe, political and artificial distinctions have, more or less, triumphed over and obscured our common nature. In Europe, we meet kings, nobles, priests, peasants. How much rarer is it to meet *men;* by which we mean, human beings conscious of their own nature, and conscious of the utter worthlessness of all outward distinctions, compared with what is treasured up in their own souls." Similarly, Catharine Beecher looked forward with confidence to the ultimate success of her crusade to effect nationwide moral and social reform by training women as teachers. "In the aristocratic countries of Europe," she wrote in *The Evils Suffered by American Women and American Children* (1841), "the wrongs of the neglected and oppressed are so inwrought in the framework of society, that it is an almost hopeless task to attempt to rectify them. All that can be done is to try to *alleviate, at least a little.* But to us opens a fairer prospect. Every one of the evils here portrayed, it is in the power of American women fully to remedy and remove. Nothing is wanting but a knowledge of the evils, and a well-devised plan for uniting the energies of our countrywomen in the effort, and the thing will be speedily and gloriously achieved." [25]

In other words, critics of American social patterns as well as defenders of the status quo argued that Americans were peculiarly free, not to say peculiarly obligated, to fulfill the possibilities of American liberty. So did Democratic reformers who appealed to Americans to abandon colonial precedents and strike out for a fuller freedom. "Let us keep up with the spirit of the age," John Norvell declared in Michigan's first constitutional convention, "and not revert back to the times of our country's infancy, when, just emerging from their colonial vassalage, our ancestors inherited the contracted notions of Europe upon most subjects, except the great leading and general principles of human liberty. Let us show to the world by our institutions and our practical adherence, in all respects, to the liberality which they breathe throughout, that thus directed and governed,

> 'Our country was designed
> To be the sacred refuge of mankind.' "

On the one hand, they appealed to their compatriots to repudiate a past that still lingered in their institutions. On the other, they sought to exorcise that past in order to realize the full potential of those institutions.[26]

Democrats and conservatives could seldom agree on specific measures toward this end, but they did agree on the obligation history had laid upon them. In the long range of time, Europe was unmistakably the source of evils that the United States should renounce, not only in 1776 but also in the present and future. To this extent it may have been what psychologists call a negative reference group; but if it defined the American identity by negation, it also pointed to a positive American obligation. Not being Europeans, Americans had inherited in place of a debt to the past a continuing obligation to be true to their own highest ideals.

AMERICANISM AS A NATIONAL CREED

The obligation Americans felt found its ultimate expression in "Americanism," a loyalty apparently determined by geography and governed by the status quo. Daniel Boorstin has argued that national loyalty so understood created a blanket opposition to deviations from familiar American practice, while Louis Hartz has pointed out that "un-American" became a prominent category in American political discourse not matched by similar categories in other countries. (One does not hear of a Committee on Un-British Activities.) As is so often the case, however, these very telling observations miss part of the pattern of American belief, and the critical stance they suggest may cause us to deprecate rather than to understand a belief that was persuasive to many Americans. By any legitimate rules of historical inquiry, that belief must be understood in its own terms before it can be evaluated in ours.[27]

This general proposition holds true even for the brand of Americanism espoused by the nativist movement of the 1830s and 1840s and the American Party of the 1850s. But we are not concerned with Native Americanism here; our object is not to deal with what seems to have been an aberration from commonplace American belief, but to elicit the meanings of a much more widely held commitment. The problem to be considered is what ordinary Americans meant when they gratuitously invoked the adjective "American" and made use of the neologism "Americanism" to identify their scheme of values.

There is no doubt that Americans of both parties often invoked the national label in a cheaply partisan way to demean their political opponents by associating them with hostility to national institutions.[28] In the same way, the practice of employing it in other dubious or at least meaningless contexts continued to grow. In 1832 Philip Lindsley took pains to assert that George Washington had been "*American* in all his feelings, sentiments and policy"; in 1847 the *Boston Post* hailed Democratic victories in New England as indications of a "sound Americanism at the north that has not been appealed to in vain"; in 1851 Stephen A. Douglas insisted that "we should have an *American* policy in our foreign relations"; and subsequently the *New Orleans Bulletin* held that the outcome of the election of 1852 demonstrated a popular demand for "*American* statesmen, *American* diplomatists, *American* policies, *American* standards of thought and action." On any sort of occasion, it seemed, Americans were likely to appeal to an italicized national identity.[29]

So much for the crude display of Americanism as a creed: it existed; it was questionable on philosophical and historical grounds; and it flourished in spite of that fact. Nevertheless, it also betokened popular attitudes that are not immediately apparent. Its larger import is evident in the checkered career of the "American System," which was the major Whig contribution to American political discourse.

When Henry Clay first used the term American System in 1824 to characterize his elaborate proposals for a home market supplied by domestic manufacturers and enhanced by a national transportation network, he probably intended it to invoke unthinking national loyalties as well as the vision of a continental economic system. Although he explicitly disclaimed any wish to draw an invidious distinction between an "American" and a "foreign" economic policy, he also made clear that he hoped to raise the United States to the point at which it would be truly free of Great Britain, and (in view of the vision of national power and national greatness he invoked on this and other occasions) it is difficult to believe that he meant to use the term only descriptively when he introduced it. Indeed, he had already invoked its counterpart in 1820 to depict a *pan*-American system of trade intended to squeeze British merchants and merchandise out of the liberated Spanish colonies. The fact that he narrowed his application of the term to the United States in 1824 suggests that when he used it the second time he fully intended to give it a nationalistic meaning.[30]

Certainly proponents of the American System other than Clay identified it with a narrow national patriotism. In 1828 the National Republicans of Indiana urged John Quincy Adams' candidacy for president on the grounds that he stood for the American System and with it American independence from England, while in 1844 Calvin Colton (Clay's biographer and partisan as well as a veteran Whig polemicist) argued repeatedly that free trade would subject American well-being to foreign hostility and caprice. For that matter, Andrew Jackson had invoked the same argument in his well-known letter on the tariff before he became the Democratic standard-bearer. "In short, sir," he wrote in 1824, "we have been too long subject to the policy of the British merchants. It is time we should become a little more *Americanized*, and instead of feeding the paupers and laborers of Europe, feed our own." [31]

But Jackson's closing words suggested what classic Whig appeals also demonstrated, that the American System properly understood embraced significant positive values far more important than the negative and invidious attitudes the term probably appealed to. In the eyes of its sponsors, it was a scheme for lifting the whole national economy to an unprecedented level of prosperity by arranging for the mutually advantageous disposition of natural resources, industrial effort, and population. To be sure, its proponents were not loathe to emphasize the military advantages that national economic development would bring, but those advantages were decidedly defensive—their object was to secure American liberties at home, not impose American institutions abroad—

and in any event the implicit premise of their arguments was that a nation raised to such an economic level need have no fear of foreign incursions. In a very real sense the American System domesticated the vision of human felicity proclaimed by Adam Smith in *The Wealth of Nations* and took as its aim the fulfilling of Smith's hopes in one country.[32]

In other words, if Whig politicians often embraced Americanism narrowly understood and invidiously proclaimed, they also embraced under the same rubric a broader and more generous vision of human hopes. By the same token, Democrats who belabored "foreign" economic policies and advocated "American" principles in their stead also invoked something more than national prejudice when they appealed to the nationalistic catchword. One of the principal charges Andrew Jackson leveled against the Second Bank of the United States was that its securities might pass into the hands of foreign investors, whose control of the currency in case of war would be "more formidable and dangerous than the naval and military power of the enemy." It followed that "if we must have a bank with private stockholders, every consideration of sound policy and every impulse of American feeling admonishes that it should be *purely American*." But unless his words are to be taken out of context, it is significant that they appeared in a veto message that invoked a broad range of social values against the Bank. "Americanism" presumably stood for this range of values when Jackson employed it. Seen in this light, it expressed a national commitment to the fullest possible realization of the promise of American life.[33]

Much the same point may be made of American attitudes toward territorial expansion, which often originated in hostility to European influences (real or imaginary) and took form in an unmistakable chauvinism, yet also found expression in a grandiose vision of American liberty overspreading the (accessible) world. We shall examine typical manifestations of the idea of Manifest Destiny in chapter III; here they are important only to reinforce the proposition that even in its least prepossessing forms the Americans' commitment to Americanism often involved broad liberal hopes that they associated with their country because history taught that their country uniquely provided for them. Chauvinistic and self-centered as it often seemed, especially in foreign eyes, Americanism as the Americans viewed it addressed itself to the needs of the world as well as the prejudices of the nation that clung to it.[34]

Certainly this was the case when John Norvell invoked it in behalf of alien suffrage during Michigan's first constitutional convention. "To be an American citizen," he declared, "was justly our pride and our boast. But what was it that rendered it a source of satisfaction and exultation? Was it the soil on which we tread[?] Was it the natural atmosphere which we breathe? No, sir, it was the free and tolerant principles embodied in our institutions, that riveted our attachment to the name of American citizen, and extorted the admiration of the world." Norvell's appeal may well have been rhetorical—the product of a wish to secure the vote for men who were likely to be Democrats—but it also testified to his sense that American loyalty was a loyalty to principle rather than to place or precedent. So did James Brent's argument in a similar cause in the Louisiana convention of 1845: "I yield to no one in attachment and devotion to my native land; but I love it not merely because it is my native land—not because my eyes first happened to open to the light of day upon its soil, but I love it for the same reason that William Tell loved the glaciers and ice-ribbed mountains of Switzerland—because it is the abode of freedom. . . . I love her because here it is we have established a government of freedom and equality—here it is we have asserted and vindicated the rights of man, and here we have established an asylum where the exile can lie down in peace, and where all are left free and undisturbed in the pursuit and enjoyment of happiness." [35]

Conservatives and Whigs, who were often apprehensive about immigration and opposed to alien suffrage, articulated the same faith. Ruth Miller Elson points out that typical American textbooks, written for the most part by conservative New Englanders, sought above all to inculcate a national loyalty, but that they also increasingly tended to represent that loyalty as the natural attitude for men to take toward a nation characterized by the institutions the United States boasted. In this fashion, in 1844 a pamphlet entitled *Fifty Reasons why Hon. Henry Clay should be Elected President of the United States*, ostensibly written by "an adopted Irish citizen" but betraying the rhetorical style of a native Whig conservative, listed as one of its primary reasons the fact that "Henry Clay is an American." Given the constitutional provision that only a native-born citizen is eligible for the presidency, this was at best a superfluous argument, but the author went on to spell out his meaning in terms very similar to Brent's: it is not that Clay inhabits the land, consumes its produce, and enjoys its benefits, but "because, WHERE LIBERTY DWELLS

THERE IS HIS COUNTRY.—Every great measure in this country's glorious epoch, bears the impress of his gigantic intellect and devoted patriotism." [36]

Similarly, in assessing William Leggett's *Political Writings*, the *New-York Review* praised the Locofoco journalist for his insistent Americanism and invited others to imitate him. "Our political systems have little affinity with any that have ever yet existed," it said; "but nevertheless our literature, our education, with all its prejudices, and our social habits, continue to be immeasurably influenced, if not governed, by the old systems which were long ago rejected. There is an invincible opposition between the systems of the old world and the new, and all those ideas which had their origin in different principles of government are inapplicable to this new state of things." Even a Whig who rebuked American efforts to alleviate the condition of Hungary by giving aid to Louis Kossuth conveyed a sense that Americanism narrowly conceived took its justification from an idealism vindicated by history. "I love progress of the right sort," Representative Presley Ewing of Kentucky declared in 1852 "—that progress which has been for fifty years an American idea. There was in that idea of an 'ocean-bound Republic' at least something patriotic, something which stirred the heart and appealed to the pride of every lover of his country. I love natural, American progress, the development of true principles, in all their consequences, the advance to true happiness and true greatness. But let us not turn back and attempt, what I fear is a hopeless task, to regenerate the old, worn-out, *effete* institutions of Europe." [37]

While Americanism might well be employed to support reactionary policies, in short—policies hostile either to traditional American liberties or to European hopes of sharing them—it also called to mind the highest aspirations of the liberal American tradition. Its role was most tellingly exemplified in the fact that American critics of nativism frequently argued, in effect if not in so many words, that it was un-American. "This doctrine of Native Americanism smacks strongly of the flavor of Pekin and Hong-Kong," James F. Brent told the Louisiana constitutional convention. "It is much better adapted to the meridian of that empire, which is governed by the 'cousin to the sun and the brother to the moon,' than it is to the meridian of the free and enlightened States of the American confederacy." [38] If their statements in behalf of the aliens' rights sometimes had an oddly chauvinistic sound, it was because they took it for granted that no true American would abandon the principles of liberty with which history had favored his country.

By the same token, Americanism epitomized the accommodation Americans had reached between their overriding confidence in the nation's position in history (the pattern of macrohistory) and their recurrent anxieties lest it be subverted (the pattern of microhistory). Had history seemed progressive in the European sense, pointing to further secular achievements that would one day relegate the United States to the past, loyalty to the nation would have conflicted with loyalty to progress. Inasmuch as the Americans stood at the climax of history, however, the only burden that it placed upon them for the future was that they be true to the progress they already knew. Yet far from seeming an easy task, this was a most demanding obligation, for it reminded them that they were vulnerable to every sort of danger, not only foreign invasion and the casualties of other nations, but failure to live up to their own high hopes. Americanism expressed both their confidence and their anxieties.

As a creed it was probably regrettable, but instead of condemning it out of hand we should recognize the values it embraced. It was a plausible and philosophically acceptable substitute for national loyalty based simply on place; if place came to take precedence over the history of liberty, it was none the less true that the history of liberty had given place its significance. Similarly, if it reinforced the American people's belief in their superiority, it also tempered the belief by suggesting that while they were uniquely free they must also be vigilant to maintain their freedom. (Their creed would have been no more plausible and far less attractive had they read history as the genesis of a people who could not suffer evil.) Finally, it served to reinforce their dedication to the ideals of their fathers even while it used those ideals polemically to discredit other ideals that could not be found in their national history. The difficulty with Americanism was not that it was always hostile to liberal ideals, but that in subsuming them it might in the long run take precedence over them.

⚜ III ⚜

THE MISSION OF
AMERICA

Americans typically believed that the lessons of their nation's history might be summed up in "Americanism" and they adopted a correspondingly idiosyncratic vision of their country's place in the further history of the world. On the one hand, they generally accepted the proposition that it was destined and in some sense obligated to help other peoples overcome the burdens of their history and triumph over evils the American people had left behind them. On the other hand, they feared that if they involved themselves in the struggle against those evils they would jeopardize the freedoms they enjoyed and deprive their national experiment of its only possible basis of success. The upshot of these conflicting perspectives was the American doctrine of mission, which was no less significant because it sought to reconcile essentially irreconcilable positions. If Americanism connoted loyalty to the United States in order to further the cause of liberty at home, the mission of America came down to much the same thing with respect to liberty in the rest of the world.

To recognize this fact is to find a way around a dilemma in which classic interpretations of the American sense of mission have left us. Reading American expressions of foreign obligation uncritically, historians have implied that nineteenth-century speakers who invoked images of a world mission for the United States intended thereby to express the kind of foreign-policy commitment that Woodrow Wilson was to voice so eloquently in 1917 and 1918. In doing so, they have left out of account the long span of time (both before and after the First World War) during which the Americans simply ignored their alleged commitment to the world in order to concentrate on exploiting their own continent. Reacting in turn against this oversight, historians like David Noble (not to mention literary critics who have occupied themselves with images of Paradise, Nature, and Adamic man in American thought) have insisted that the Americans sought to escape history entirely by remaining aloof from the world beyond the oceans. There is much to be said for this proposition, but it is incompatible with the traditional view, and it points to a degree of indifference to the world that it is difficult to substantiate in the sources.[1]

It also fails to account for the ambiguities of American foreign policy, which has included strenuous efforts at territorial expansion and at least one extraordinary attempt to make the world safe for democracy, as well as long periods of theoretical if not practical isolation. Taken seriously, these ambiguities, like our own conflicting interpretations of the American idea of mission, admonish us that we have yet to grapple successfully with the intellectual dynamics of American foreign policy. They also suggest that we can do so, so far as the Middle Period is concerned, only by recognizing that American perspectives on foreign affairs were corollaries of Americanism broadly understood.[a]

THE IDEA OF AMERICAN EXAMPLE

Americans' attitudes toward their mission in the world centered on the idea of example, and example was important to them because it answered to their contradictory needs. On the one hand, it bespoke a national obligation in the world; on the other, it served to protect the republic against untoward consequences arising from that obligation.

Sometimes Americans visualized their obligation as a simple *quid pro quo* for the blessings God had brought them. "While dwelling with pleasing satisfaction upon the superior excellence of our political institutions," John Quincy Adams declared in his first annual message, "let us not be unmindful that liberty is power; that the nation blessed with the largest portion of liberty must in proportion to its numbers be the most powerful nation upon earth, and that the tenure of power by man is, in the moral purposes of his Creator, upon condition that it shall be exercised to ends of beneficence, to improve the condition of himself and his fellow-men." Nor was this sentiment peculiar to New Englanders; in 1830, at any rate, William Wirt incorporated it into an address to the citizens of Baltimore on the late revolution in France. "We stand under a fearful responsibility to our Creator and our fellow creatures," he declared. "It has been his divine pleasure that we should be sent forth as the harbingers of free government on the earth, and in this attitude we are now before the world. The eyes of the world are upon us; and our example will probably be decisive of the cause of human liberty." [2]

Taken simply as a religious duty, that is, benevolence admonished every American to repay the kindnesses Providence had bestowed on him. But both the president and Wirt also implied that the American people's duty was historic as well as religious; the advantages they experienced were not only gifts of God that called for good deeds commensurate with their magnificence, but products of a history that laid special obligations on Americans.[b] Other commentators enforced this proposition on appropriate occasions. "Nature has isolated us for great ends," William W. Greenough told the inhabitants of Boston on the Fourth of July, 1849. "Beyond the reach of external influences, to solve the problem of free institutions—to invent and to apply the only safe formula of civil, political, and religious liberty, yet exhibited for the examination and approval of the world." Similarly, Edward Everett rebuked his countrymen in 1823 for being preoccupied with petty domestic questions when Greece was fighting for liberty against the Turks. "We hope better things of our country," he wrote in the *North American Review*. "In the great Lancastrian school of the nations, liberty is the lesson, which we are appointed to teach. . . . It is taught in our settlement, taught in our revolution, taught in our government; and the nations of the world are resolved to learn." Both arguments suggested strongly that the history of the world would terminate successfully only if Americans lived up to their obligations to see that it did.[3]

Spokesmen for less constricted faiths than those of Greenough and Everett, who were Unitarians in theology and Whiggish in politics, clearly testified to the same sense of obligation. When they spoke of the responsibility Americans bore for the success of their national experiment, for example, both Benjamin Tefft, a Methodist, and M. Augustus Jewett, a Congregationalist, held that the outcome of the experiment would determine the fate of the rest of the world.[4] Meanwhile partisan Democrats of an essentially secular cast of mind had made the same point. In 1838, the *Democratic Review* praised a Fourth of July oration by Edwin Forrest, the noted Shakespearean actor, on the grounds that no one could read it "without feeling and believing that he is an American, true to his national vocation, and who fully appreciates the peculiar mission of his country. . . . The fervor of his language attests the strength of his patriotism—patriotism deeply imbued with the philanthropy which contemplates his country as designed, by her example, to shed the light of her moral truth, by gradual progression, into the remotest corners of the earth, for man's emancipation." Fourteen years earlier, Representative Silas Wood of New York had invoked much the same prospect during debate over Congressional resolutions expressing sympathy with the Greeks. "Much has been said, during this debate, about the spirit of the age," he declared. "The present age is distinguished from the last by liberality of sentiment in religion and politics. The American Revolution, Bible societies, and Christian missions, aided by the extension of commerce, have produced this change. It does not need the aid of physical means—such aid would obstruct its influence. This moral influence is all powerful, but does not irritate—does not excite alarm—does not provoke opposition. . . . Let it, then, operate as it has done, and we may expect it will continue to produce more and more important results, till the governments of the world are reformed." [5]

In short, it is clear that even when allowance is made for the temptations of rhetorical excess, Americans of different creeds and various political allegiances frequently visualized their country as playing a major role in the further history of the world. But it was also important that they defined that role primarily in terms of "example," of the proposition that the mere presence of the United States on the world stage, abetted perhaps by measures we have yet to discuss, would serve to fulfill the nation's historic obligations. The idea of example was a limitation on American efforts as well as a stimulus to them.

Its limiting effect is apparent in the fact that Representative Wood invoked the idea *against* involving the United States in the affairs of Greece: on his view, to be an exemplary nation was to contribute all that was required to further the consummation Americans devoutly hoped for in history. Other critics of a vigorous foreign policy adopted much the same position. "We can not witness the struggle between the oppressed and his oppressor anywhere without the deepest sympathy for the former and the most anxious desire for his triumph," Millard Fillmore declared in his annual message to Congress at the time of the Kossuth agitation, only to argue that "our policy is wisely to govern ourselves, and thereby to set such an example of national justice, prosperity, and true glory as shall teach to all nations the blessings of self-government and the unparalleled enterprise and success of a free people." Henry Clay expressed this idea directly to Kossuth, while conservative Democrats other than Wood had long since invoked the same doctrine with similar purposes in mind.[6]

These were admittedly conservative appeals intended to circumvent contemporary enthusiasms for abandoning the traditional American policy of isolation. Hence they may seem to have been either unrepresentative or disingenuous if not both, calculated efforts to bend accepted doctrine to narrowly restrictive purposes. But even if we disregard the fact that such appeals were apparently broadly persuasive—in spite of all the agitation, few Americans actually involved themselves significantly in the affairs of Europe—we cannot ignore the fact that liberal democrats also invoked the idea of example to define American obligations. Democrats as well as Whigs were remarkably circumspect when they came to consider the Americans' mission.

We shall discuss specific issues of policy that serve to test this general proposition in the next section of this chapter; here it is important to recognize the characteristic logic of liberal belief in an American example. Liberal democrats and Democrats were much more likely than conservatives and Whigs to voice sympathy with European revolutions and to suggest that Americans bore some responsibility for guiding them and aiding them. Yet they were equally likely to sum up that responsibility as one of congratulation and instruction rather than any more energetic obligation. Robert Walker expressed their peculiar vision in quasi-philosophical terms in 1830 when he told the workingmen's dinner held to celebrate the July Revolution in France, "The lesson which the heroes of your revolution practically taught the haughty aristocracy of Britain, stood, in the political wilderness, as a pillar of fire to light the way of the oppressed of every clime to the hallowed temple of liberty. Your fathers' noble daring stood as a bright beacon to degraded man, and successfully established the maxim, 'That a nation to be free need but will it.' " So understood, freedom of the will meant that the ends the United States hoped for would be achieved by the voluntary efforts of oppressed peoples who had learned of the American example. It did not preclude strife in Europe, but it did relieve the United States of any need to think of spilling its own blood.[7]

Other enthusiasts for democracy spoke with much the same accents. In 1844 Levi Slamm recognized that American voters had to make a difficult choice between providing for the happiness of their own compatriots and "enfranchising" the "oppressed millions of Europe." Because he was a typical free-trade zealot he was inclined to put domestic happiness first, but he also dispensed with the necessity of choosing by observing that "there is no method by which the citizens of the United States can benefit the oppressed of mankind so effectually, as that of exhibiting to them a free, prosperous and happy Government, based upon the theory that man is capable of self-government, thereby proving to the people of the Governments of the world, that if they wish to be happy they must follow our example." The *Western Review* expressed an even more telling version of aggressively democratic hopes when it pointed out in 1846 that the Americans were not and had not been "propagandists" of the French Revolutionary persuasion: "We have never declared, through Congress, as the French did through their National Convention, that we are ready to give aid and assistance to all who are struggling for freedom. . . . There is no necessity for our issuing any such declaration, because we are doing the same thing in another way—we are sending democracy throughout the world, 'conquering and to conquer,' without making any parade about the matter." [8]

Statements such as these, made by enthusiasts on the left wing of the Democratic party, argue strongly that even when Americans disagreed about specific issues of foreign policy they agreed very largely on its major premise. On both the conservative and the radical view of foreign affairs, the object of American policy was to maintain the force of American example in the belief that example would serve the historic ends of mankind. Differences might well exist over particular choices of policy, but they would be differences over the technique, not the substance, of the national obligation. Furthermore, a good many Americans apparently felt that obligation; the enthusiasm they expressed for the Greeks and Kossuth implies that their policy was intended to be, not one of isolation for its own sake or for their own sakes, but of isolation with greater ends in view. The object of American foreign policy was, quite literally, the object of example.

Implausible as it may seem in our eyes, the idea gains authority as an expression of American missionary zeal when we recognize how closely it fitted American concepts of history. On the level of macrohistory, the idea that the United States would and should serve as an example to mankind corresponded with the basic perspective in which Americans saw their European past. They assumed that their country had progressed beyond the Old World; they assumed that no additional radical changes lay in store for themselves; and they could easily infer that the objective of contemporary Europeans, like the object of future history, was to reach the level the United States had already reached. Hence the very existence of the United States, confirming man's potential for self-government, would serve a profound historic purpose. In 1842 the Reverend Edgar Buckingham, son of the editor of the *Boston Courier*, gave a particularly effusive expression to this idea during the course of a Fourth of July oration at Trenton (New York). "The cause of our country is the cause of the world," he announced. "It is for the interest of the people of all nations to secure our peace and prosperity. All nations have reason to be our friends; all people to rejoice with us:—would that we could say that kings and nobles so saw and loved the interests of their people, that they would cherish the peace and hail the prosperity of America! Happy nation! the world prospers in your prosperity! Happy people! you can be patriots, and wish all men well." [9]

At the same time, on the level of microhistory Americans were so deeply conscious of their differences from Europe, and of the evils that European practices betokened, that they leaned over backwards to throw off European institutions and disavow European precedents. So, too, would they disavow involvements in Europe that might cause them to revert to practices they believed they had found means to leave behind—military conscription was one example, heavy taxation for war and defense another—the more so as they feared that imitating Europe in any one aspect of its life was likely to involve them in imitating it in others. If the outcome of their sense of microhistory was "Americanism," its corollary in foreign affairs was "example," which left Americans free to act their own part in the security of their own continent. According to Charles Brooks, a cosmopolitan Unitarian minister and New York University professor who had studied in Europe for four years, "Our country must make its own character; and if it would draw others within the sphere of its attraction, it must, free of all foreign disturbing influence, majestically decree its own orbit in time and space." [10]

But Americanism had constructive implications for the United States, and example had comparable implications for the world. Both looked toward maintaining the United States inviolate as the necessary first step in fulfilling historic hopes for human liberty. Hence Americans frequently portrayed their primary obligation abroad in terms of keeping faith with their national experiment. Representative William Cabell Rives of Virginia gave classic expression to this juxtaposition of ideas during Congressional debate over the Panama Mission: "We do, indeed, owe a solemn responsibility to all mankind, in this and future ages, for the fate of the experiment of free Government, which has been committed to our hands. The success of this experiment does, in my opinion, mainly depend upon our keeping clear of entangling connexions with other People, who may be less blessed with an aptitude and capacity for freedom than ourselves, and whose interests and passions might involve us in enterprises foreign to our sober and peaceful pursuits. Sir, if *other* nations are destined to lose *their liberties*, let *us* acquit ourselves of the high trust which Providence has devolved upon us, and endeavor to preserve *our own*; that *one* beacon-light, *at least*, may be left to cheer the darkness of the political world, and to guide those nations who may have lost their liberties, through the sea of revolution, upon which they must embark to recover them." [11]

In other words, although Americans were often isolationists in fact, their isolationism involved much the same sense of obligation in foreign policy that their complacency did in domestic: they were obligated by history, and not merely by their natural national preferences, to be true to themselves. The ultimate outcome of their reflections on their place in the world was the extraordinary proposition that the highest objective they could adopt was to keep the faith of their fathers, not alone because they were content with the position to which history had brought them, but because they sought to influence it elsewhere. "If we are true to the vocation whereunto we are called," Abram P. Maury declared in 1847,

if we shall vindicate the capacity of man for self-government, and the consequent superiority of our institutions over those of other countries, . . . we will become a beacon and a land-mark on the cliffs of time, to the nations of the earth—by whose light they may be guided in the reconstruction of their own defective forms of polity. But if we should become corrupt and unprincipled; if passion should dominate over reason; faction be paramount to patriotism; liberty degenerate into licentiousness; . . . no horoscope will be needed to forecast our destinies? Ours and not ours only, but—bound up indissolubly with them—the fortunes of free institutions all the world over, will suffer disastrous shipwreck; and, borne on time's unebbing tide, will finally be lost in that great ocean of the past, where, already, in numbers numberless,

　　　"The graves of buried empires heave like passing waves." [12]

To be true to themselves was the highest kind of idealism: it embodied the obligations macrohistory had laid upon the Americans, guarded them against the evils microhistory could bring, and fulfilled a missionary obligation to mankind.

According to many spokesmen of the Middle Period, in short, the isolation Americans practiced was a highly principled policy, and although they could not know it then, the premise on which it was based would help lead a later generation to war in 1917 when it was convinced that American example was ineffective in the face of German militarism and suspicious that German militarism would not confine itself to the Old World. Meanwhile Americans clung to isolation both because it would serve historic human purposes without jeopardizing American freedoms and because it would serve those purposes better by not jeopardizing those freedoms. In the eyes of that earlier generation, the fact of its splendid example was America's greatest contribution to the further history of the world. [c]

THE IDEA OF INTERVENTION IN EUROPE

In general, Americans of the Middle Period adhered to a foreign policy of example rather than mission, or (to speak more precisely) to example as the embodiment and vehicle of mission. Enthusiasts sometimes challenged the policy of national isolation to which it led, however, and to this extent they took issue with the consequences if not the categories of American belief. Hence it is incumbent on us to examine the thought of major proponents of intervention in European affairs in order to determine how far they may be said to have departed from the established maxims of American foreign policy. We may best do so by considering the Americans' response to the European revolutions of 1848, the reception they accorded Louis Kossuth during his visit to the United States in 1851–52, and Senate debate on the resolution of 1852 proclaiming a foreign policy of nonintervention in European struggles. [d]

Most Democrats probably welcomed the revolutions of 1848, whereas many Whigs looked askance at them, but it is significant that partisans of both persuasions tested European events by the same criterion. Whigs doubted whether the Europeans would be able to imitate the example of the American Revolution while Democrats insisted that they would; the difference between them lay in their competing perspectives on European capabilities rather than in their sense of what those capabilities should be. Nor was this underlying bond of agreement insignificant in shaping American responses to events as they transpired. Although Democrats initially expressed an optimism that few Whigs could muster, they were easily discouraged by news of developments that did not accord with their hopes. Confronted with the failure of the Frankfurt Assembly or with the radical social experiments of the French revolutionaries, they were quick to decide that the men who had participated in them were not capable of securing free institutions. They also shifted their attention and their enthusiasm from one country to another as the tides of revolution ebbed and flowed. In effect, they declared that they would be faithful to their European mission only so long as Europeans remained faithful to the American example.[13]

Their view was understandable, given the typical American vision of macrohistory as a process leading other nations along a path the United States had already marked out, but it also meant that men whose sympathies were readily enlisted in the cause of European liberty measured that cause by oddly parochial standards. A similar kind of parochialism characterized their commitment to recognition of the revolutionary regimes. There is no doubt that the interventionists' behavior severely taxed the normal forms of diplomatic intercourse, and historians trained to the niceties of diplomatic history have helped unintentionally to lend credibility to the view that the rambunctious democrats of the 1840s threatened to revolutionize American foreign policy. Nevertheless, even if we grant the zeal of those democrats, it seems at least highly likely that recognition meant far less to them than it did to professional diplomats or conservative politicians. It is clear that few enthusiasts expected it to bring war or any other untoward event in its train. It also seems clear that even when they were not just talking for domestic political effect—and much interventionist oratory seems to have had this character—assertive American democrats simply did not credit the seriousness with which tradition-bound Europeans might respond to offenses against the conventions of diplomatic intercourse; or if they did, they repudiated it, like Stephen A. Douglas in 1851, on the grounds that European precedents should not control American practices.[14] Whatever consequences American recognition of revolutionary regimes might have brought in fact, we have reason to think that its proponents did not recognize them and cannot therefore be said to have intended them. Seen in this light, diplomatic recognition was a gratifying project but not a very assertive extension of the traditional American practice of diplomacy by example.[e]

In addition, the recognition that advocates contended for ultimately involved an abdication rather than an acceptance of American responsibility for the course of European events. William H. Seward, the leading Whig spokesman for an energetic foreign policy, made this fact clear during debate on proposals to welcome Kossuth to Washington, when he defended "alliances" with revolutionary nations, by which he meant at most the formalities of diplomatic recognition. "Is it wise to deny ourselves the benefits of alliances with States kindred in political interests and constitutions?" he asked in the Senate. "Far otherwise; true wisdom dictates that we lend to European nations, struggling for civil liberty, all possible moral aid to sustain them until they can mature and perfect their strength for that great conflict, through which they are doomed to pass. The nations that we thus lawfully aid to raise up, will constitute a lasting and impregnable bulwark for ourselves." On this view, recognition would still leave Europe to pass through predestined historic struggles without any expectation that American blood might be spent to accelerate the process, diminish the agony, or safeguard the result.[15]

To put matters another way, typical interventionist attitudes closely resembled the attitudes Americans now take toward spectator sports, which they view as occasions for cheering on sympathetic figures but would not dream of engaging in themselves. The analogy is made more persuasive by the fact that during his tour of the Middle West Kossuth apparently elicited great local enthusiasm, including donations of arms and money and promises of armed intervention in Europe, all of which came to very little a few months later when he left the United States without funds, without arms, and without assistance. Experts on the subject refer to a Kossuth "fad," but the sporting metaphor seems equally appropriate. For the moment, the Americans participated vicariously in the European struggle.[16] Meanwhile conservative critics of these diplomatic innovations probably intensified the satisfaction and reinforced the seriousness with which the interventionists viewed their own hortatory gestures; the very energy with which the critics pointed out the danger of ignoring diplomatic proprieties must have served to obscure the extent to which the liberals shared their premises.

Even enthusiasts who clearly repudiated the policies of example and insisted upon giving vigorous support to European revolutionaries did so in an oddly ambiguous fashion.[f] When Lewis Cass proposed in 1850 that the United States consider breaking diplomatic relations with Austria, he made clear that he sought only a "moral interposition" in European affairs although he freely acknowledged that Austria would persevere in the atrocities he abhorred until she was actually defeated by the Hungarians. Like Seward, he implied that the United States had no obligation to help Hungary avoid her fate if avoiding it meant calling on the United States for further assistance. Similarly, Senator Henry S. Foote of Mississippi supported Cass's resolution partly on the grounds that the United States had no good reason to man diplomatic posts abroad when they might involve it in foreign mischiefs, yet held that the country would fulfill its duty to the world by the mere act of withdrawing recognition. Only Representative Alexander Buel of Michigan seems to have recognized the consequences to which American enthusiasm for European liberty might conceivably lead, and he drew back from them even as he accepted them. Although he insisted that Americans must be "propagandists" for freedom, and argued that their own revolutionary past admonished them to extend sympathy to revolutionaries elsewhere, he also declared that he "would by no means involve this Government in a mere crusade against other nations in the name of civilization, but yet the world will justly hold us responsible for the use or neglect of those means which Providence has placed in our hands for the benefit of mankind." The means he referred to came down to the recognition of Hungarian independence.[17]

The national reception of Kossuth added little to these precedents. When Senator Foote sponsored a joint resolution in Congress calling for a congressional delegation to receive the Hungarian leader in the capital and to tender him the respect and sympathy of the American people, he adverted to the "great struggle going on at this moment in all parts of the civilized world between the principles of freedom and the principles of slavery," but his enthusiasm for that struggle terminated in the proposition that the United States could "stand by the cause of freedom" simply by welcoming the refugee. For his part, Lewis Cass insisted that the nation had a right to welcome Kossuth whether or not other nations approved, asserted its right to defend its interests in the world by war if necessary, and declared that he would not tie American hands by premature declarations of neutrality. But he also weakened the force of his argument by proclaiming, "It is not physical force that every true lover of his country would desire to employ on this occasion. It is moral force; that powerful lever in the affairs of the world, which sooner or later will do its work. Like truth, it is mighty and will prevail." Similarly, Stephen A. Douglas portrayed a world confrontation between republicanism and despotism and refused to abjure any measure that might prove to be necessary to further the cause of liberty, only to subordinate the taxing questions of how to implement these principles to the propriety of welcoming Kossuth.[18]

Less prominent figures challenged these happy evasions without really threatening to undo them. Condemning the very idea of neutrality as irrelevant to a nation now in the full flower of manhood, portraying the world as engaged in a struggle over principles that could not be compromised, Senator Isaac P. Walker of Wisconsin insisted that the United States must denounce Russian intervention in the Austro-Hungarian conflict. He also accepted the ultimate practical responsibility his measure might entail: "This declaration I would make good, too, when occasion should demand, by the blood and treasure of the land." But he added that "with such a declaration, the occasion would never arise: we would have no occasion to shed the one or to expend the other." His assurance on this point suggested not only that he embraced great hopes for the effect of American exhortations but also that he felt free to contemplate the possibility of more strenuous exertions precisely because his sense of history declared they would be unnecessary.[19]

Even at their most belligerent, other Congressional enthusiasts clearly limited the practical effect of their appeals to arms. In January, Representative Charles Sweetser of Ohio invoked "all the force we can command" against despotic incursions on free nations, but he also suggested that the only object his constituents demanded was a "fair fight" between

European adversaries, a demand that left the United States in a position of leaving liberty to fend for itself on the Continent. Speaking on the same occasion, Representative Richard Yates of Illinois insisted that Americans had a right to express their democratic sympathies even if it meant war with Austria and Russia, but he also made clear that the war he envisaged would be a war of national defense conducted exclusively on American soil, from which the United States could "bid defiance to the despotisms of the world." "Bright glories have covered our arms in three wars already," he added in a telling burst of patriotic fervor; "but in this last and final struggle between freedom and despotism, our good old flag would be borne aloft in triumph, the glorious ensign of liberty to the world." Men who appeared to be aggressive world reformers were firm only in their resolve to fight for their nation's right to be a symbolic force—not a conclusive influence—in European affairs, save as they took their nation's existence to be itself a force of major proportions.[20]

Expressions of sympathy for Hungary and Kossuth outside of Congress revealed the same ambiguities. The speeches that prominent figures made at the Congressional banquet for Kossuth in January 1852 are notorious primarily because Daniel Webster, now Secretary of State, grossly offended against the diplomatic proprieties in expressing sympathy for Hungarian aspirations, just as he had offended against propriety in his famous letter to Chevalier Hülsemann, the Austrian *chargé* to the United States. But impropriety here was much like impropriety on other occasions, a characteristic aberration of American politics rather than evidence of a clear national commitment to do anything about foreign problems, and none of the major speakers at the banquet significantly challenged American commitment to a policy of gesture masquerading as a policy of force.[21]

Webster evaded the critical issues of policy by declaring, "Freedom, human liberty, and human rights are gaining the ascendent upon earth; and the part we have to act in all this great drama is to show ourselves in favor of those rights, to uphold that ascendency, and to carry it on until we shall see it culminate in the highest heavens over our heads." For his part, Stephen A. Douglas sounded much more energetic, aggressively asserting the nation's right to recognize Hungary, and propounding the hypothesis that the United States might one day intervene still more forcefully in European affairs, but treating sympathy as a sufficient

weapon in the present case although it was clear that Kossuth was a refugee who was unlikely to be able to free his country even if he returned to
it. Two Congressional spokesmen for the armed services, Representative
Frederick P. Stanton for the Navy and Senator James Shields for the
Army, took the view that their respective services were willing and able
to fight if necessary, but the practical import of the proceedings as a
whole was summed up in a toast proposed by William A. Graham, Secretary of the Navy: *"The moral influence of American example and sympathy
upon the political destiny of our race:* It has already accomplished much for
the nations of Europe, and will continue to guide, to cheer, and establish
them in the principles of freedom." [22]

The proceedings at the banquet that the Jackson Democratic Association of Washington tendered Kossuth on the following night were less
restrained but no more significant than those at the Congressional affair.
Except for Francis P. Blair, who devoted a large part of his opening
address to detailing the aid France had granted the thirteen colonies during the American Revolution, the speakers generally ignored foreign
issues to discuss domestic politics. (We should remember this fact; in
pursuing expressions of liberal enthusiasm in foreign policy we may
forget that we are pursuing concerns that apparently attracted the attention of only a minority of American citizens.) When they did address
themselves to Kossuth and the Hungarian question, on the other hand,
they seemingly looked with favor on his doctrine of "intervention for
nonintervention," which called for American involvement in European
affairs to maintain the "fair fight" that Sweetser and Senator Robert F.
Stockton also advocated.[23]

Nevertheless, Douglas used the occasion primarily to belabor the incumbent Whig administration for adopting a policy of neutrality that cut
off arms and assistance to Hungary while permitting them to Austria.
He did not press an alternative Democratic policy, except (perhaps) for
laissez-faire, and even Cass went no further than proclaiming—not proposing to enforce—the right of "every country in the world" to "establish
and to change its own institutions at its own pleasure." Belligerently as
he criticized the Czar of Russia for infringing on this right, Cass concluded his remarks on foreign policy simply by hailing the Democratic
party for making the United States a great power—"a power that will
have a controlling influence over the destinies of the world"—which ob-

viously left matters much as they already stood. General Joseph Lane
was the only speaker who proposed a specific policy rather than a vague
effusion of sentiment, and his policy was to extend the Monroe Doctrine
to liberated peoples as soon as they had gained their liberty. From one
point of view, he would have committed the nation to an extraordinary
foreign responsibility; but it was also important that he apparently
looked to American example to secure objectives that the United States
might then, and only then, foster.[24]

Agitation over the Hungarian question reached its final stage when
Senator John H. Clarke of Rhode Island introduced a resolution calling
upon the United States to extend *de facto* recognition to all foreign powers on the grounds that it should recognize their right to govern themselves. This consciously conservative proposal set the stage for renewed
debate on the policy of intervention in foreign affairs, in which liberal
Democrats once again joined as partisans of European liberty.

Not surprisingly, they rehearsed familiar arguments and practiced familiar evasions. In the major Democratic speech on the question, Cass
reiterated that the United States had a right to interest itself in European
affairs, held that the legitimate pursuit of the American mission could
and might one day necessitate war—and insisted that no such contingency was now at stake. "Propagandism is no part of our creed," he
declared, "unless it be that propagandism which works its own way by
the force of example, thus inviting the oppressed nations of the earth to
do as we have done, and to be as free and happy as we are." Hence, although he went on to insist that "we cannot be indifferent to the condition of the human race, however widely scattered," he acquiesced in
what he apparently took to be the fact that American exertions as he
defined them would *not* serve European liberty in his time. "Can any one
doubt," he asked, "that the evidences of sympathy which are borne to
Europe from this great Republic will cheer the hearts, even when they
do not aid the purposes, of the downtrodden masses, to raise themselves,
if not to power, at least to protection?" It followed that he should ultimately defend his policy of intervention-by-expostulation on the grounds
that it was perfectly safe. As he explained in some detail, European nations' protests at their neighbors' actions had *not* led to war even when
they were ignored. And this was the context in which he developed his

most enthusiastic argument that American opinion would influence events abroad.[25]

In short, the Progressive Democratic commitment to American involvement in Europe, intended to accelerate the course of history by promoting the cause of liberty, all but terminated in the proposition that the United States could do little more than express pious hopes for the future liberation of mankind—unless, perchance, European nations chose to react so aggressively to these expressions as to force the country to defend its territorial integrity and thereby vindicate its role in world history. But before we conclude that a foreign policy conducted on these premises was bound to be ineffectual, we must also note that the enthusiasts for European liberty held out one very plausible reason for believing that American example alone might yet be sufficient to shape the history of the world. Cass expressed it most explicitly when he observed, during the same speech on nonintervention,

We have at length reached the condition of one of the great Powers of the earth, and yet we are but in the infancy of our career. The man yet lives, who was living, when a primitive forest extended from the Allagheny to the Rocky Mountains, trodden only by the Indian, and by the animals. . . . Then a narrow strip upon the sea-coast, thirteen remote and dependent colonies, and less than three millions of people, constituted what is now this vast Republic, stretching across the continent and extending almost from the Northern Tropic to the Arctic Circle. And the man is now living, who will live to see one hundred and fifty millions of people, free, prosperous, and intelligent, swaying the destinies of this country, and exerting a mighty influence upon those of the world.

Like the promise of American loyalty, the promise of American example bore the hopes of a greater destiny for all mankind. As the interventionists clearly demonstrated, the Americans were not simply isolationists, but isolationists with a historic purpose they hoped to serve better by virtue of their isolation.[26]

AMERICA AS ASYLUM

In moments of high enthusiasm, liberal Democrats and their Whig counterparts spoke vaguely but no less strenuously of intervening in European affairs to secure the triumph of righteousness.[g] More typically, they adopted still another version of foreign policy intended to achieve historic American ends without jeopardizing historic American institutions. This was the policy of "asylum"—offering the material, political, and spiritual benefits of American civilization to any inhabitants of the Old World who chose to seek them out.

This too was predominantly a Democratic policy. Democrats' allegiance to the policy of unrestricted admission of European immigrants was much strengthened by the political advantages their party stood to gain by admitting substantial numbers of foreign voters, while the Whigs' characteristic antipathy toward political innovation and unreliable voters was often reinforced by their recognition of the same fact. By the same token, the country as a whole tolerated and even welcomed immigrants primarily because it saw them digging its canals, building its railroads, and developing its resources; in all probability the concept that the United States offered an asylum to the oppressed of other climes was often only a rationalization for national economic interests. But it was something more than a rationalization; the long history of American hospitality to a truly extraordinary influx of increasingly alien peoples is a fact of American foreign policy at least as significant as the fact that it terminated so abruptly and so invidiously in 1922. (It is no mere coincidence that Woodrow Wilson, a good nineteenth-century Democrat, vetoed legislation intended to curtail immigration as well as preached intervention in Europe, only to see both immigration and his European crusade repudiated after the First World War.) Whatever role direct material interests may have played in shaping American policies toward immigrants, American perspectives on history would also seem to have been important in shaping the ways Americans treated newcomers.[h]

Certainly a number of historical assumptions ran through their discussions of the subject. One was the historical judgment, which was really just a corollary of the Americans' sense of their own place in time, that immigrants came to the United States because they recognized and chose to take advantage of the same opportunities native Americans perceived. On this view, advantages to the nation and advantages to the immigrants simply ran together, as the *Democratic Review* demonstrated in 1837 when it observed in passing, "The greater the number of the oppressed of other countries who come to seek shelter under the shadow of the broad wings of our eagle, bringing with them strong hands and honest hearts, and a voluntary desire to enjoy the benefits of the free institutions denied

to them in the land of their birth, the better!" *The Crisis Met*, also published in New York, made the same telling juxtaposition of ideas in
1840. "The Old World has had its youth-time and its manhood," its author declared. "Evident marks of age are creeping over it. Myriads of its
population are crossing the deep, allured by our rich and cheap lands,
and by our free and equalizing institutions. From the log cabin of the
remote West, from forest and prairie, from city and country, we hear the
voice of the foreign emigrant blended in delightful harmony with that of
those whose birthright is American. This is right. The New World is a
patrimony to the oppressed of all nations, and the spirit of Democracy is
to make the Alien welcome." [27]

Both statements also exemplified the high idealism that was felt, or at
least could be appealed to, against conservative spokesmen who sought to
curtail the rights of immigrants. "Heaven has bounded our Republic
with two mighty oceans," Representative Albert G. Brown of Mississippi declared in 1852, "thus placing a barrier deep and wide between us
and the despots of the old world. I would not impiously defy the protection of Providence by crossing this barrier to attack despotism in its
stronghold; but upon every breeze that sweeps the Atlantic I would send
a message to the oppressed millions of Europe, bidding them come—
come to an asylum on these shores, prepared by the Almighty, and
defended by his chosen people." Grandiloquent as they may have been,
Brown's words conveyed a certain magnanimity as well as a striking
identification between immigration and the national mission.[1] In the Michigan constitutional convention of 1835, John Norvell invoked much
the same historic idealism to justify giving aliens the vote:

The member says, that the cause of popular institutions is, in a measure, committed to our hands. This is true as to the institutions of our own state, and, to a
certain degree, of the United States. But what is that cause, which is to be
promoted by aristocratic prejudice? Are popular institutions to be promoted by
refusing to admit those to the enjoyment of liberty, who have migrated hither
from their love of liberty? Is this the way to promote the cause of popular institutions? What is it that gives to foreigners so high an idea of our country? It is
because they admire the general spirit of our institutions, and their influence
upon mankind; because they breathe a spirit of tolerance, and enable the foreigner to participate in all the blessings of liberty; because they look upon this
country, as peculiarly designed to be the refuge of the oppressed of every nation.
This, sir, is the highest encomium, which can be passed upon our institutions.

Here American mission, immigrants' choices, and republican safety all came together in support of the idea of an American asylum.[28]

At the same time, the idea of asylum could well stand for a version of the American mission that precluded the United States from doing anything about foreign oppression save offering refuge to its victims. Lewis Cass recognized as much when he protested in 1851 that asylum was not a sufficient boon to offer Kossuth, and the *Cincinnati Weekly Gazette* underlined the limiting effect asylum might have when it urged that the proper American mission to Kossuth and all other Europeans who aspired in vain to liberty was to make the United States "truly an independent land—a land of freedom—a land independent of aid, or sustenance of any character, from any other land—a land of equality." "This soil should be preserved, forever," it added, "as the refuge of the downtrodden and struggling sons of freedom, of every other nation, till, from Atlantic to Pacific, our soil is all occupied, and no more room remains. This is *our* destiny—this our future." [29]

Soon afterward William H. Seward demonstrated that even American statesmen who spoke up in favor of intervention abroad might nevertheless conclude by urging asylum in its stead. Rebuking politicians who sought to give the idea of example a narrow application, he declared during Senate debate on the Clarke Resolution, "I have heard frequently, here and elsewhere, that we can promote the cause of freedom and humanity only by our example, and it is most true. But what should that example be but that of performing not one national duty only, but all national duties. Not those due to ourselves only, but those which are due to other nations and to all mankind." Here, indeed, was a challenge to settled American policy, but it culminated in no more than a plea to the Senate to offer Kossuth asylum, as if asylum would somehow serve all of Kossuth's purposes. It was a not ignoble plea, but it suggested that American enthusiasm for liberty came to a focus in enjoying American advantages.[30]

Americans' attitudes toward foreign needs were limited in still another way, likewise a corollary of their sense of history. In all but a handful of cases, the choice they visualized for immigrants was a choice between oppression in the Old World and free institutions in the New, not a conscious search for a new environment in which to practice innovations they desired. As Cecil Eby points out in a perceptive analysis of the idea of asylum between 1775 and 1860, the term initially implied a continent that was to be a lodging-place for European liberty, but it rapidly acquired the somewhat different connotation of a refuge for Europeans. The first view was compatible with further experimentation and innovation precluded by European oppression; the second, with finding and maintaining a congenial home.[31]

During debate on the war with Mexico, Senator John A. Dix underlined the national self-confidence that accompanied this shift of meaning. "Our country has long been a refuge for those who desire a larger liberty than they enjoy under their own rulers. It is an outlet for the political disaffection of the Old World—for social elements which might there have become sources of agitation, but which are here silently and tranquilly incorporated into our system, ceasing to be principles of disturbance as they attain the greater freedom, which was the object of their separation from less congenial combinations in other quarters of the globe." In effect, the United States offered struggling Europeans a refuge on the premise that their struggle would no longer be necessary when they could enjoy the institutions Americans already possessed. Given the opportunity to flee Europe and the opportunity to enter the United States, the aspiring revolutionary foreigner would find that American history had already provided all the liberties that any man could legitimately seek.[32]

Hence the idea of an American asylum was essentially static, like the idea of American example and even the idea of American "intervention": the mission of America would be fulfilled by the extent to which Americans maintained their nation as it was. But better than example (which could too easily be turned to restrictive purposes), better too than intervention (which entailed obvious yet undefined dangers), asylum genuinely promised to help other peoples overcome the burden of their history while still protecting the United States from involvement in the evils Americans had left behind. It could do so, at least, as long as Americans were true to the selves that offered a place to the teeming millions of Europe, as *The Crisis Met* explained in a single hortatory passage that combined national advantages, immigrants' needs, and American mission in a single comprehensive admonition to Democratic voters to support their party as the party of American history:

The emigrants among us have come hither in spite of all the obstacles which an uncomfortable sea-voyage by sailing-vessels has presented. But now that from various parts of Europe commodious steamers of two to three thousand tons burthen constantly ply, how greatly will the number of emigrants be increased! Our own early marriages—productive of an unprecedented rapidity in the natural increase of population—will mingle with this mighty tide of emigration, and give us a people as the stars of heaven for multitude. For these—and for unborn millions of all coming time—we hold in trust the Political System of our country. Herein consists the importance of watchfulness and honesty. [33]

Asylum, then, was limiting in its implications, but it also left room for the inhabitants of the United States to work out a still greater destiny, provided that they kept faith with the fundamental principles of their free institutions. This fact was made immediately apparent by Senator Dix's observation that, in addition to offering discontented elements of the Old World refuge and satisfaction, the territories of the United States were an asset to Europe as well as America. "She is literally going along with us in our march to prosperity and power, to share with us its triumphs and its fruits." He invoked this happy prospect to reinforce his contention that European political stratagems had no place in the United States, but he also portrayed extraordinary accomplishments that American exemption from European evils would make possible: "Political justice demands that in one quarter of the globe self-government, freedom, the arts of peace, shall be permitted to work out, unmolested, the great purposes of human civilization." In these terms, American spokesmen still visualized the American continent as an asylum for all the hopes of mankind.[34]

MANIFEST DESTINY

Dix's argument bore upon one last element of foreign policy that Democrats generally supported and Whigs generally rebuked, territorial expansion of the United States at the expense of other nations. For the subject of his speech was the war with Mexico, to which American aspirations for territory had led, and which American Democrats generally justified. The juxtaposition of topics was no mere coincidence; it exemplified the possibility that enthusiastic liberal democrats might visualize the North American continent as a proper arena for interventions that the European continent precluded. "Manifest Destiny" was the ultimate expression of the Americans' most vigorous hopes for raising the rest of the world to their own level.

It is obvious that it may also have been a cynical rationalization for American economic hopes. American interests in the growing, manufacture, and marketing of cotton played a major part in the annexation of Texas, while clear southern interests in the safety and future of slavery had much to do with both the acquisition of Texas and the events of the Mexican War. But one of the most striking facts about American expansion was the extent to which the so-called slavocracy opposed it, a fact which reminds us that economic motives frequently work at cross-purposes in shaping national policy. More important still, the efforts that proponents of expansion made to defend the measures they advocated by appealing to economic hopes (e.g., a larger market for manufactures) or invoking economic fears (e.g., the power of a British alliance with Texas to destroy the market for southern cotton, if not slavery itself) read today like efforts to find plausible pragmatic grounds on which to justify implausible ideological ventures.[35] Certainly we no longer visualize southern concern for slavery as a merely "economic" interest, just as we have begun once again to recognize that the northern concern for "freedom" was something more than a purely economic commitment. Our growing sophistication in this respect may help persuade us to look to typical American definitions of history to help explain even American expansionism.

To put the matter another way, it seems clear that although American expansionists undoubtedly visualized national economic advantage as one of the primary consequences of territorial aggrandizement, the desire for economic advantage did not lead necessarily and inevitably to an aggressive continental policy. Rather, the advocates and the opponents of American imperialism often shared the same economic perspective.[36] Hence we must look to other kinds of considerations to understand the intellectual motives that conduced to expansion.

One major impulse would seem to have been a growing sense of the intractable disparity between American hopes and world facts, which bothered even the most enthusiastic advocates of peaceful progress on the American model. In effect, the difficulties as well as the opportunities of fulfilling their liberal destiny on this continent seem to have pressed a number of Americans to embrace a continental imperialism.

Certainly one problem Americans constantly confronted was the apparent incapacity of the oppressed peoples of the world to throw off the burdens of their past and imitate the American example. The problem was visible in Europe, where subject peoples repeatedly disappointed naive American hopes, but it was especially marked in Latin America, where the liberated Spanish colonies simply failed (as Americans saw history) to play well the part history had assigned them. Even American writers who sought to speak sympathetically of the Latin American republics were likely to express a gloomy view of their prospects. Describing their colonial wars for independence, the *Democratic Review* held in 1838 that the republics to the south had virtually been doomed to failure by centuries of Spanish rule. "On the character of the [South] Americans," it declared, "the influence of such a government could not but have produced most baleful effects. . . . Are we, then, to be surprised that the struggle for independence was desperate and bloody—and that, when the [South] Americans had succeeded in expelling their tyrants, so few of them were found possessing the habits or the principles requisite for the formation of good citizens, or for the existence of free institutions?" Similarly, American textbooks of the period generally denied that Latin Americans were capable of imitating the American Revolution or American democratic institutions, and indeed the theme of Latin inferiority runs all through the literature of the period. It frequently involved racism, and sometimes also nativism, but the thought was broader than these two modern and invidious terms suggest. Americans had repeatedly witnessed events that cast doubt on the capacity of any other people to duplicate their achievements.[37]

They might react in one of several ways. It was plausible to infer that the circumstances of foreign nations were so hopeless as to be not worth American effort, and this was in fact the position that conservatives of both parties typically took.[38] Alternatively, it was plausible to infer that the desperate situation in which other nations found themselves meant that they required American help of the most constructive sort—not simply action to secure "fair play" in the struggle between rebels and autocrats, which advocates of intervention in the Austro-Hungarian conflict contended for, but direct involvement of a more practical sort, intended to make sure that the subject peoples would somehow learn how to use their freedom if they acquired it. A handful of zealots drew precisely this inference when, during the war with Mexico, they developed the idea that the United States might well absorb all of Mexico in order to guarantee its stability and make sure of its republicanism. According to the *Boston Times*,

The "conquest" which carries peace into a land where the sword has always been the sole arbiter between factions equally base, which institutes the reign of law where license has existed for a generation; which provides for the education and elevation of the great mass of the people, who have, for a period of 300 years been the helots of an overbearing foreign race, and which causes religious liberty, and full freedom of mind to prevail where a priesthood has long been enabled to prevent all religion save that of its worship,—such a "conquest," stigmatize it as you please, must necessarily be a great blessing to the conquered. It is a work worthy of a great people, of a people who are about to regenerate the world by asserting the supremacy of humanity over the accidents of birth and fortune.

Seen in this light, foreign incapacity might lead to extraordinary American efforts.[39]

Still, this was an inference that relatively few Americans reached, and it was articulated during the course of an unexpectedly protracted war; it apparently did not affect initial sentiment for that war so much as capitalize on a sentiment that the events of the war had created. Hence we still have not come to the heart of American attitudes underlying territorial expansion. Far from representing a positive choice of foreign involvement to help other nations imitate the American example, American expansion seems to have been stimulated primarily by an American concern lest the future development of the United States be curtailed by their failures.

Assuredly expansion conducted on this basis would have been compatible with Americans' ideas about their country's place in the history of the world. Progressive (as they thought) beyond every other nation, apprehensive lest they neglect the institutions that had made her successful, hostile to nations and events alike that seemed to threaten her further achievements, Americans tended to view the events of European history in terms of an inexorable confrontation between the forces of liberty and the forces of despotism in which they could ill afford to take direct part lest they subject themselves to its evils. But events that took place on their own continent must have appeared to them in a different light. Here the confrontation between liberty and despotism must be faced because it could not be avoided; and here, too, success was much more likely.

One reason a confrontation could be undertaken was that the North American continent was readily accessible, whereas the European was not; adventures that were impossible overseas were clearly possible at home. By the same token, it could well be assumed that foreign involvements would be less hazardous here than they would be overseas: because intervention in nearby nations' affairs was not likely to involve the country in the same kind and degree of military effort as operations elsewhere, the danger that the United States might imitate European errors diminished. Samuel J. Bayard illustrated both these propositions when he told the graduating class at West Point in 1854 that they must be ready to fight to extend the boundaries of their country, but criticized "unlimited extension" of those territories—by which he said he meant the incorporation of transoceanic nations like France—because of its destructive effect on the institutions of the republic.[40] Under such circumstances, Americans might even seek war in order to achieve their larger historic purposes, confident that it would not entail the evil consequences and create the insupportable burdens that wars in Europe did.

Even so, the central theme of American expansionist oratory was neither the military advantages nor the salutary immunity from history that residence on the North American continent provided. Rather, the main thrust of American arguments in behalf of acquiring Texas and Oregon, which helped shape the national mood before the outbreak of war with Mexico, was that failure to secure both territories would be tantamount to conceding ascendancy to tyranny in the historic world struggle between true and false principles of government.

So far as Texas was concerned, both its spokesmen and its sympathizers labored the proposition that Mexico had forfeited her claims to the territory by infringing on the liberties of its citizens. Obviously the fact that many of those citizens were American emigrants did much to commend them to American eyes, and in fact Texas partisans frequently invoked the American Revolution as a direct precedent for the Texas Revolution. But it was not only ethnic affinity they appealed to in using this argument; it was also the large historic choice between good and evil. American relations with Mexico demonstrated not that the Mexicans needed our help but that they could not be trusted to honor the liberty that free men demanded. "Shall we, who profess to believe in the right of the people to govern themselves, unblushingly adopt, in favor of

Mexico, the exploded doctrines of despotism, and decide for legitimacy[?]" Governor Thomas Ford and his collaborators asked the people of Illinois in 1844. "We think not. We confidently recognize the right of the people of Texas, to revolt against the oppression of Spanish power and cruelty; and to establish Governments and seek alliances to promote their own happiness. It was upon this principle that our fathers revolted from England; and a successful rebellion in our case, as in the case of Texas, became a revolution." [41]

Advocates of the annexation of Texas also made much of the danger that a European foothold there would create for the American republic, a contingency that may only have represented exaggerated military fears but that also seems to have represented a more general fear of the inevitable clash between two contending civilizations. Certainly Andrew Jackson did all that he could to rouse his compatriots to share his anxiety over a potential military descent on New Orleans, and while he undoubtedly both felt and symbolized a technical military concern for the safety of that port, the *entrepot* for the entire Mississippi Valley, his argument as a whole associated the future of the American experiment with its security. Apparently the territories beyond the southwestern frontier of the United States were a necessary pawn in the endless American effort to maintain American freedom, as well as an attractive speculation in real estate and cotton economics. [42]

Oregon occupied the same position in the Northwest, or at least the advocates of acquiring all of Oregon made every effort to represent it in that light. On the one hand, they stressed the horrors of acceding to monarchical influence in the New World; on the other, they hailed the advantages that would accrue to the force of American example from an extension of the area of freedom at home. The *Western Review* was particularly explicit on these points. "We are the depositories of the *democratic principle*," it held in 1846, "and a stern and jealous principle it is, which will admit of no divided empire. It claims for itself this continent, as a rallying ground, from which to move the world; and it will not tolerate the existence of any other political principle in its neighborhood, for the simple reason, that, should it do so, it would aid in its own destruction." [43]

In other words, the accessibility of the territory and the safety of the nation in acquiring it provided a necessary condition but not a conclusive motive for expansion, which seems to have been based as well (as so much of American policy was based) on history viewed as a series of confrontations that could not be dodged, provided they did not jeopardize the history the nation had already achieved. British critics of American policy testified to the thrust of the American position when they commented adversely on President Polk's aggressive message to Congress of December 1845. "Is the whole continent of Europe, teeming with a super-abundant population, to be told that the vast regions of the Western World are henceforward closed against them unless they cast off their national character and adopt the social institutions and the political ascendancy of the United States?" the London *Times* asked in January 1846.[44] Apparently it did not occur to the *Times*, or to other organs making the same protest, that many Americans thought this was precisely what history required.[j]

Giving due weight to this pattern of mind helps to extricate us from what I take to be errors of judgment by the historians who have studied most closely the ideas of Manifest Destiny. Albert K. Weinberg makes much of the paradox implicit in the fact that Americans began by insisting that they were committed to establishing a government based on natural rights and ended by claiming other nations' territories as their own natural right. The paradox largely disappears, however, when we look at American thought as a whole: to the generation of the 1840s, or at least to the enthusiasts, it was quite plausible that loyalty to natural rights in a world otherwise given over to despotism would require Americans to claim territories they might not otherwise demand. Weinberg implies as much in describing two key concepts of Manifest Destiny as "extension of the area of freedom" and "the true title" to the soil, but here too he overstresses their defects as philosophy and so misses their cogency as ideas about America's role in the world.[45]

Similarly, Frederick and Lois Merk point out with implicit sympathy that Whig opponents of annexation and of the Mexican War criticized Democratic expansionists for refusing to concede to European powers the same extraterritorial rights they claimed for their own country. In particular, they note that Democrats misread a phrase used by Guizot in debate in the French parliament as "balance of power," which they then used to discredit all European claims to a role in continental American affairs. But the Merks' interest in discovering exactly what Guizot meant, and their sensitivity to the probability that Democratic enthusiasts deliberately mistranslated him, leads them to underrate the force of the ideas these Democrats appealed to. Seen in its own terms, the major premise of Democratic thought—and, indeed, the premise of Whig thought on other occasions—was that the United States should not be trammeled by the contingencies or even by the proprieties of European diplomacy. To defer to European interests here would have been to accept autocratic powers as equals on a continent dedicated by history to liberty.[46]

In short, a combination of anxiety over threats of European intrusion (however imaginary) and commitment to a policy of expanding the area in which American institutions would be powerful seemingly justified the expansion the Americans attempted. At the same time it exempted them from attempting expansion when they thought it would jeopardize their domestic advantages.[k] In any given case, including the ultimate concession to Great Britain of half of Oregon, expansion was a pragmatic possibility that was governed by a nice balance of historical ideas as well as a nice balance of economic and military considerations.

But it also involved extending the area of freedom. To overlook this element of idealism in American expansionism of the Middle Period is to miss a large part of the American people's motivation, nor can a historical inquiry into their thought be satisfied by the mere reflection that they were mistaken or wrong-headed in their valuation of themselves. Complacent about their role in history they were; ethnocentric and indifferent to the legitimate concerns of other nations as well; but in their own eyes they were engaged in taking an inevitable and even a heroic step toward righting wrongs from which the rest of the world suffered. Quite without recognizing the anomaly of what they said, the enthusiasts for annexation held that it would not only extend invaluable American institutions by conquest but also contribute to the cause of liberty everywhere by reinforcing the power of American example.[47] According to their characteristic vision of history as an effort to realize American standards of liberty and progress, this was an objective that free men everywhere could be expected to respect.

In other words, Manifest Destiny simply carried to their most extreme formulation estimates of the meaning and implications of history that were endemic in American society. The Americans of the Middle Period knew that they had been born free, and they proposed to act in the light of that fact. To be born in the United States or to come to it as an immigrant was to inherit the historic hopes of mankind, and with them a portentous obligation to maintain conditions of freedom that other peoples could only envy and hope to emulate. If means could be found to extend that freedom, so much the better, but it must not be jeopardized in being extended, and there was reason to doubt that other peoples were capable of achieving it for themselves. Hence foreign predicaments were more often a warning to the United States than an invitation to American intervention; but Americans would discharge their obligations to the world by assisting other nations when they could safely do so, while they stood alert at all times to repel even a hint of foreign intrusion on freedom's sanctuary. There was of course a range of opinions on foreign policy as there was on domestic issues, but the degree to which Americans thought alike was extraordinary. Even when they disagreed bitterly on national measures they tended to dispute only how well a given policy would meet the same historic requirements.

A conservative lawyer of Albany (New York) brought together the elements of their common commitment in concluding the Fourth of July oration he delivered there in 1858. "Let us maintain our nationality," Henry Smith urged; "let us endeavor faithfully to discharge our duty as citizens; let us seek to advance the glory, promote the growth and secure the permanency of our institutions: let us behold our rising sun of Empire, and watch that it does not fall, but rises in steady ascent until it attains the meridian, never to go down, but there to stand a light to all the earth, and glory to God." [48] Progressive Democrats put the same basic ideas more succinctly but no more demandingly when they urged their compatriots to "go ahead." By 1858 history had brought the Americans to such a pass that both these injuctions to fulfill their destiny were suspect as evasions of duty, but that is another story. The men who voiced them voiced the characteristic sense of obligation of the Middle Period.

SOCIETY

ᥕ IV ᥦ

EQUAL RIGHTS

Most Americans agreed on the advantages with which history had endowed their country, but they often disagreed over the social order they desired and the measures that were most likely to foster it. Hence the decades of the Middle Period were filled with contentions over domestic policy in which they sought to make sure of the liberty they all claimed. Here the Democratic party was the dominant fact of the age, pressing demands for reforms intended both to vindicate historic liberal hopes and to challenge "aristocratic" residues of Federalism and the European past. Its efforts came to a focus in the party's demand for "equal rights," which runs as a leitmotif through all the debates of the period.

The appeal to equal rights is so common in the literature of the times that we tend either to underrate its importance or to deny its significance, knowing that the clamor was often merely rhetorical and sensing that it helped to produce a society that is far from equal. Yet contemporary European observers clearly took egalitarianism to be the hallmark of American society, a mark many of them deplored and some took pleasure in finding exceptions to, while our own suspicion that the idea of equality may have served special interests or have led to inequality in practice actually testifies to the power it exercised in American thought. In effect, by taking an equality of rights as their primary social objective, the Americans made sure that they would arrive at a social order in which they had no alternative but to practice an undiscriminating liberty.[1]

THE ATTACK ON "ARISTOCRACY"

Democrats began their process of redefining social practices by challenging the premises of the social order into which they had been born. Everywhere they looked they found evidences of "aristocracy," which they visualized as the product of incomplete democrats and "Federalists" who had conspired to defeat the purposes of the American Revolution. Hence the whole thrust of Jacksonian thought was in the first instance negative, an effort to eliminate institutions and practices that an earlier generation had more or less taken for granted.[a]

The "aristocracy" that Jacksonians complained of consisted of selective access to power, prosperity, or influence. At bottom it was a political rather than a social or economic concept: in Jacksonian eyes, an "aristocrat" was someone who was empowered by law to affect the economic and social welfare of his contemporaries, or who enjoyed legal privileges that he could turn to his own account in an otherwise competitive economy. Democrats discerned "aristocracy" in a wide range of traditional republican measures through which the states and the national government had sought to foster public services like banking, transportation, and education by offering wealthy men the means and motives to place their resources where the state judged they would do the most good. The sole result, so far as the Jacksonians were concerned, was a social order in which some men benefited from the labor of others—an order in which, according to the classic Democratic argument, prejudicial laws allowed some men to extract wealth from the pockets of other men by legal rather than economic means.[b]

The classic example of "aristocracy" was the Second Bank of the United States, which would have been vulnerable to Democratic attacks even if it had behaved wholly innocuously, but which confirmed every Democratic suspicion of "aristocratic" influence by seeking to coerce President Jackson into approving its recharter. The events of the Bank War are so familiar that they need no retelling here, but two aspects of the struggle are worth noting as indices to American thought. One is that the advocates of the Bank apparently genuinely believed, either that the President would not dare to destroy it, or that if he did so he would be repudiated by the electorate. Clearly they did not understand the democratic antipathies to which Jackson addressed himself in his veto message. The other aspect is a corollary of the first: no matter what private motives various critics of the Bank may have had, the means they employed to destroy it was a popular concern for "equal rights" understood as the destruction of "aristocracy." [2]

The same concern could easily be extended to banks of issue chartered by the states. "The worst form of political institutions is an aristocracy," the Democratic members of the Massachusetts legislature declared in 1838 at the height of the panic; "the meanest and worst form of aristocracy hitherto known was the aristocracy of wealth, and . . . it remained for the present age to discover a still baser form of government in the oligarchy of bank directors and their pet debtors, of bankrupt speculators making hypocritical pretences to the possession of capital, and distressing the whole country that they may avoid the necessity of paying their debts or confessing their inability." It followed in the eyes of diehard Democrats that any form of legalized banking was intolerable, as Joseph H. Bagg made clear in the Michigan constitutional convention of 1850 when he introduced a resolution calling upon the convention to ban chartered banks entirely. According to the surviving record, "Mr. B. offered the resolution under the full conviction that it expressed the popular will. Our government was based on equality and the principles of equal rights. He believed all banks were based on a doctrine of injustice and unequal rights." [3]

The Democratic interdict also extended to other forms of legislation intended to secure public benefits by creating corporate privileges. The *Charles River Bridge* case became a *cause célèbre* for Democrats everywhere because it destroyed a monopoly of long standing that the Commonwealth of Massachusetts had originally granted in order to ensure that there would be a river crossing between Boston and Charlestown. A number of legal doctrines entered into the decision, but Democrats commonly visualized it in simplistic terms as a victorious stroke in their continuing struggle against privilege. In 1841 the Massachusetts party still sought to capitalize on popular sentiment by declaring that "the struggle of twelve years, with the corporation of the Old Bridge, who had enjoyed a monopoly for half a century, was a test of fundamental Democratic principle, whether the people or a chartered monopoly were sovereign in the State." Four years later, Democratic zealots in the constitutional convention of Texas sought to prohibit all perpetuities and monopolies as well as primogeniture and entailment, while subsequent conventions in other states severely curtailed the right of their legislators to issue charters for any but municipal purposes. [4]

Corporations were intrinsically evil because they rested upon privileges not granted to everyone; in addition, the privileges they exercised—however necessary to their operations—seemed to Democratic doctrinaires to be further proof of their evil character. Here Democratic complaints included not only banking privileges (which had sometimes been extended to canal, turnpike, and manufacturing enterprises in order to expedite their development in the absence of readily available capital), but also the right of eminent domain, which was indispensable both to transportation companies and to manufacturers who required water power, and which derived from the authority of the state to take lands for public purposes. Although it is clear that the corporations often behaved badly toward property-owners whose lands they needed, it is also clear that many Democrats assumed that the owners' rights should automatically take precedence over the companies' needs.[5]

By the same token, the privilege of limited liability of stockholders for the debts of their corporations, which seemed indispensable to mobilizing large capitals in an underdeveloped economy, was in many Democrats' eyes a major argument against them. On the premises of equal rights strictly understood, in fact, a corporation would be next to impossible, as John C. Edwards suggested during the gubernatorial campaign in Missouri in 1843: "I am in favor of repealing all laws which exempt or relieve members of corporations from individual responsibility, and of passing a general law making members of corporations individually responsible for the acts of the corporation. All men should be held responsible for their just debts, no matter in what capacity they may be contracted." Peter D. Vroom offered a broad social rationale for the same policy in the New Jersey constitutional convention of the following year: "If there is any danger to be feared in a republican Government, it is the danger of associated wealth, with special privileges, and without personal liability. It is the aristocracy of wealth we have to fear; and that is the only aristocracy from which danger is to be apprehended." [6]

Democrats extended the same general principles to issues of national policy like the tariff and internal improvements. Here as elsewhere we must note that their enthusiasm for "equal rights" was usually self-serving, focused on destroying economic policies that either hurt them or did not benefit them. But it is also important that the arguments Democrats used took for granted that it was unjust and "aristocratic" to secure public ends by means that did not provide equally for everyone simultaneously, and the form of argument would long survive the occasions on which it first appeared. Senator John Rowan of Kentucky treated it as an axiom in criticizing the proposed tariff of 1828; the *Register of Debates* reported him as saying that "he was opposed to the tariff, as a system of bounties, for the encouragement of certain classes of industry. He considered the protection, which it extended to one class of industry, as a correspondent depression upon other classes. Its professed object was to tax one part of the community for the benefit of another." Not the particular end in view, nor the suitability of the means proposed to secure it, but the very idea of maintaining it at all, was the target of such censures. If it could be shown that any group of individuals would benefit from a given public policy, this fact was enough to condemn it in Democratic eyes. To benefit was to be an "aristocrat" both in the sense of being able to secure privileges and of being able to derive benefits from them.[7]

The proposition was understandable but it was also destructive, and it was extended to other realms in which the argument from deprivation—the argument that a policy is invalid because it deprives other individuals of an equal right to enjoy stipulated benefits—was even less appropriate. On the traditional republican view of society, public office was a public trust to which men of distinction and ability should be elected to conduct the necessary business of government as best they could. Even though radical differences had long since arisen over the policies legislators should adopt, and even though American democrats had increasingly come to look upon their representatives as delegates or agents rather than statesmen to whom they had entrusted the public business, the traditional view of office survived into the 1820s. With the full flush of Jacksonian Democracy, on the other hand, the possession of office became a kind of invidious activity, to be remedied by rotation in office irrespective of the competence the incumbents had acquired or the aspirants could claim.[8]

Here, too, many forces ran together, and here as elsewhere there was much to be said for Democratic criticisms of the established order of politics, but one of the central presuppositions of Democratic reformers was that it would be "aristocratic" not to offer everyone the opportunity to hold office. "If there is a republican principle in our government," the *New York Morning Courier and Enquirer* observed in 1831, when it was still a Democratic organ, "it is rotation in office. If public duties are a burden, all ought to bear it—if a source of profit, the benefit ought to be shared as equally as possible. Nothing tends so much to aristocracy as perpetuity in office." The same principle also served to justify eliminating the age requirement for elective office, while John C. Edwards invoked it in behalf of equal representation in the legislature. "I am in favor of doing full justice to every portion of the State in representing their rights in the legislature of the country," he told the Missouri electorate. "We should give all an equal chance, in legislation as well as in every thing else." [9]

If elective office was not proof against the pressure for equal rights, neither were the professions. One special target of Democratic zealots was the established legal system, which derived all too clearly from British precedents, and which invited charges of "aristocracy" based on the degree of esoteric knowledge that was necessary to make a lawyer competent. Democrats complained about the obscurity of legal principles and the complexity of legal precedent as well as the chicanery of judges and lawyers, all of which resulted in infringements on common sense and common justice. "If there was anything resulting in the most despotic consequences," James C. Zabriskie told the constitutional convention of New Jersey, "it was the privilege of the Bench and Bar of bringing in the provisions of the Common Law. No one but the Bar knew where to find these provisions." In the Texas convention, indeed, Lemuel D. Evans argued that "the whole contrivance of courts of judicature is a fraud upon the community . . . [because] there is no question of right or wrong which a savage is not as competent to decide as the ablest judge in the land." [10]

The Democratic case against the law was one instance of a more general complaint against professional authority. In 1830, dissident medical professors at the College of Physicians and Surgeons in New York City who had petitioned for a charter as a medical faculty condemned the existing licensing system (enacted by the state and administered by the police) as an "odious monopoly" that prevented free competition in medical training. Similarly, the grand jury of the same city implicated its licensing system for pilots in the loss of the ship *Bristol and Mexico*, which had foundered for lack of a pilot. Whatever the merits of their charge, it resulted in a doctrinaire distinction between privilege and equal rights that cast doubt on the concept that competence might best determine who was to be a pilot. On the one hand, the jury held that "after a labor of years" many apprentices "are denied the right of exercising a vocation for which they have been prepared by excessive toil and exertion"; on the other, it called for repeal of the city's restraining law on the grounds that it was "at variance with the principles of a free government." [11]

Institutions of higher learning also became a target for Democratic criticism, both because they made use of public funds and because they allegedly gave the few who attended them advantages over the many who did not. Both contingencies had been willingly embraced by such republican leaders as Thomas Jefferson, who had visualized a system of popular education reaching to the highest academic levels as a necessary instrument of republican welfare, but whose very premises were now called into question as "aristocratic." "In a free government, founded upon the authority of the people, and instituted for their peace, happiness and safety," the Working Men of Philadelphia declared in 1829, "no artificial distinctions or inequalities ought to be tolerated by law, inasmuch as the first principle of nature as well as republicanism, is, that all men are born equally free and independent." In the following year they made clear that higher education at public expense constituted an artificial inequality. [12] Here as elsewhere, democratic efforts to put an end to "aristocratic" distinctions in American society often took shape in what seemed to be an effort to put an end even to learning, to distinction, to prudence, and to competence. [c]

Nevertheless, it was equal *rights* that Democrats contended for—not the leveling of all social and economic distinctions, but the eradication of unwarranted social distinctions that represented the triumph of privilege over equality. According to some contemporary observers, Democrats were seldom able to distinguish the one from the other; conservatives, at least, were sure that the Democrats intended to sweep away all the claims of authority based on merit, while foreign observers like Tocqueville lamented a pervasive leveling spirit that was hostile to both. But Democrats were equally sure that they fought for human rights and against vested interests, and it is an interesting fact that foreign travelers who came to the United States with a disposition in favor of democracy tended to find a society made up of autonomous and self-reliant individualists rather than a mob of democratic automatons. [13] In any event, Democratic agitators took pains to assert that they alone respected true merit. "It is said ours is a leveling system," William S. Balch told the Rhode Island Suffrage Association in 1841. "I admit it. But, thank God, we *level up!* We pull no man down; but carry others as far above as moral right and true merit will permit. We destroy no man's rights; but contend for the rights of the oppressed, the proscribed, the disfranchised. . . . Ours is equality on an eminence!" Other commentators were even more explicit in associating equal rights with universal liberty. "The issue between Bank monopoly despotism, and free trade and equal rights had to be made sooner or later," Samuel Medary wrote in the *Ohio Statesman* in praise of New York's Free Banking Act, "and we are rejoiced that the last stroke has been struck and the standard of freedom has been raised." The difference Democrats envisaged between aristocracy and democracy was not the difference between privilege on the one side and leveling on the other, but between a limited and a complete participation in the rights of man. Robert Rantoul Jr. summed up their case in the *Gloucester* (Massachusetts) *Democrat* when he declared during the middle 1830s, "We go against monopolies, against exclusive privileges, against unequal taxes, against all other usurpations and oppressions on the one side, against disorganization, disunion, and civil war on the other. . . . We go for equal rights, equal laws, equal taxes, equal privileges,—for liberty for the democracy, for the whole people." [14]

The object of Democratic reforms, in other words, was full enjoyment of the rights of man. If Democrats repeatedly attacked traditional social distinctions and existing social authority, it was not because they repudiated every kind of distinction and every source of authority, but because they insisted on putting both to the test of equal rights. (In general, they reversed Federalist and even Republican precedent: whereas Federalist and Republican presumptions had tended to run in favor of the established social structure, Democratic presumptions insisted that the structure be justified by the process that had led to it.) The thrust of their position was evident in the fact that Democrats made no provision to forestall the development of an aristocracy that did not depend on legal privilege. In this sense they may not have been egalitarian enough, for they looked to the processes of freedom to maintain equality of rights once it had been established. The ultimate weakness of their position would prove to be, not the fact that they were hostile to distinction, but that they did not know what to do with it when it had been achieved through equal competition.

THE ECONOMY OF NATURE

The Democrats' view of the free economy had much to do with the situation in which they ultimately found themselves. The destruction of aristocracy was predicated on a definition of free society as an arena in which all men were able to exercise the same natural rights, which rested in turn on the vision of a natural or unspoiled economy in which everyone worked for a living and prospered according to his efforts and his skills. This social ideal was virtually identical with the ideal expressed by John Locke in the first five chapters of his *Second Treatise of Civil Government*, which depicts free men joining together in order to maintain each others' rights to enjoy the fruits of their own labor. The basis of Democratic argument was clearly normative; its source was almost equally clearly empirical, the representation in ethical terms of the experience that seemed "natural" to farmers in an underdeveloped economy. Democrats typically visualized both society and the rights of property in terms of the productive laborer reaping his just reward on a largely physical basis.[d]

Modern commentators and enthusiastic radicals have sometimes been misled on this point by the Jacksonians' reiterated appeals to the "producing classes" to recover rights they had apparently allowed to slip from their grasp after the Revolution. The idea of a producing class that included manufacturers and self-employed mechanics as well as planters and farmers obviously does not correspond to the Marxian or any other modern idea of class. Rather, it was an idea that took its meaning from the experience of a predominantly agricultural country in which almost everyone knew physical labor and in which it was taken for granted that every able-bodied man would put in a full day's work. Although the Democrats of the Middle Period were familiar with a wide range of commercial, industrial, and professional activities, they found it plausible to equate them all with the labor of the farm. Appreciating the steady increase of land values in a prosperous economy, they could even make room among the producing classes for the beneficiaries of what Henry George was later to deplore as the unearned increment in the value of property. But they could not make room for the achievements of a "paper aristocracy" who were by agricultural definition "unproductive" and whose prosperity depended upon legislative fiat. These aristocrats were the enemy precisely because they were created rather than in a literal sense self-made.[15]

We shall have occasion to return to the idea of the self-made man in chapter VI; here it is important to note that in our antipathy toward its long-range consequences in American society we may tend to misconstrue what it meant at the time of Jackson. Its initial egalitarian thrust was unmistakable: to be self-made was to have earned one's position in the world on the strength of one's own capabilities. By the same token, the self-made man was one who had proved himself according to the rules of the natural economy, neither securing artificial advantages nor seeking to protect himself by artificial means against the hazards experienced by other men. Above all, he was a man who inhabited a society of substantial equals in which it could be taken for granted that honest labor would bring only relatively limited rewards. "The planter, the farmer, the mechanic, and the laborer," Andrew Jackson declared in his Farewell Address, "all know that their success depends upon their own industry and economy, and that they must not expect to become suddenly rich by the fruits of their toil." Similarly, when Charles B. Flood and E. Burke Fisher published a series of adulatory biographies of the leading men in the Ohio constitutional convention of 1850–51, the "self-made men" they hailed included a surveyor, a country merchant, and a physician.[16] Democrats did not expect to live in penury, but neither did they think that a truly natural economy would result in grave social distinctions.[e]

This scheme of values very largely determined the perspective in which Democrats saw banks of issue. For one thing, partisans were not wanting to damn them simply because they produced nothing. The *Galena Jeffersonian* expressed this idea succinctly when it declared in 1851, "Banks add not a cent to the sum total of the productive industry of the country.—They produce no wheat, they dig no mineral—but furnish facilities to the speculator to live from the wheat and lead that others have reaped and dug." More significantly, the opponents of banks condemned the very phenomenon that made them serviceable to the economy, the facility of converting investors' obligations into assets that could be loaned at a profit. John D. Pierce repudiated it out of hand during the Michigan constitutional convention of 1850 on the grounds that "This is a system adopted to rob labor of its reward, by enabling persons to bank on a debt and nothing but a debt. Basis it has none." Nor was the animus Pierce expressed limited to midwestern populists. In his *Inquiry into the Principles of the American Banking System* (1832), William Gouge made clear that no form of publicly authorized credit could be legitimate. "In private credit, there is a reciprocity of burdens and of benefits," the economic theorist of Jacksonian Democracy explained. "Substantial wealth is given when goods are sold, and substantial wealth is received when payment is made, and an equivalent is allowed for the time during which payment is deferred. . . . But the Banking system reverses this natural order. The interest which is due to the productive classes that receive the Bank Notes, is paid to the Banks that issue them." [17]

Incorporated banks were only the most egregious examples of sins against the just economy: on the Democratic view, any intrusion of government into the competitive economic process was bound to be evil because it produced a transfer of property from producers to parasites. But the Democratic position was not merely negative—not focused exclusively on the dangers of prejudicial action by government. Rather, Democrats typically beheld "natural" productive activity as a kind of sacred realm to be kept inviolate against any sort of "artificial" behavior, whether political or not. Government was indeed the prime source of economic evils, but the social fact that made it an evil was the prior existence of a "true" natural order based on "real" values and operating according to immutable laws. *The Crisis Met* made this clear in 1840 when it hailed the success of the whaling industry during a period of general business contraction. "While the speculator has been fretting his brief career in the traffic of unreal property," it declared, "the hardy fisherman has ploughed the broad and beautiful Pacific, and drawn from its fathomless abyss the monarch of the sea, and returned to *enrich* his beloved country. For such men there has been a reward, and there ever will be. Industry WILL BE rewarded. This is a law of human condition, established by the Infinite Mind, and when it is trenched upon, be sure that some foul hand hath embarrassed the free action of the social machinery." [18]

Democrats also testified to their underlying ethical perspective by the enthusiasm with which they portrayed ramifying social evils as the consequence of false economic principles. Here too the main danger they had in view was the corrupting effect of political power on the moral character of society, but once again government was only the most likely source of evils, not the center of their concern. "If we give to corporations the power to issue paper money," William Gouge declared in a concise expression of their logic, "we produce other evils. The very act of establishing a money corporation destroys the natural equilibrium of society." His fellow partisans traced the consequences of disequilibrium in every area of social existence. Indiana Democrats blamed the credit system for stimulating habits of paternalism and creating "relations of servility." In Louisiana, George Mayo blamed it for having thrown popular morals into almost irremediable disorder, while the *Democratic Review* attributed trades' unions and the evil they had done to "the most industrious, moral, and frugal of the operatives in Great Britain" to the fact that the same phenomenon had been introduced there.[19]

Other commentators made clear that corruption of government itself followed from abandoning the natural laws of economics because it tempted men to seek gains they were not entitled to, while still others held up a model of political virtue based on their vision of economic morality. In 1840 the Democrats of Indiana warned their countrymen not to imitate the example of Pennsylvania, which had rechartered the Second Bank of the United States when its federal charter expired, in their eagerness to extricate their state from its financial difficulties. "The first step to dishonesty in an individual, is a habit of profuse expenditure not justified by his fortune. The first step to public profligacy in a State, is the incurring of debts beyond the limits of her resources. . . . In public as in private affairs, economy is the surest safeguard of integrity." Four years later, in the New Jersey constitutional convention, Moses Jaques objected to a clause permitting the state to buy out the Camden and Amboy Rail Road, as provided in its original charter, on the grounds that "he did not like the idea of a State entering into speculations. It did not suit his ideas of morality. He had no idea that the State should set up a broker's shop to speculate." [20]

Obviously all these strictures owed a good deal to the influence of laissez-faire economics, but they owed more to "nature" understood as morality. Although Democratic commentators sometimes referred to Adam Smith as their authority, they were more likely to invoke him as a prophet than to employ him as an economic theorist. "It has been well and justly said," Senator William C. Rives of Virginia declared during debate on the Specie Circular, "that Adam Smith had done for the science of political economy what Bacon and Newton had done for physical science, and Sydney and Locke for the science of government, and the fundamental principles of civil and political liberty." Even writers who clearly demonstrated familiarity with formal economic theory were likely to move from technical exposition to moral admonition during the course of a single paragraph. "The comparison some writers are fond of making between paper Banking and steam power," William Gouge declared in his *History of Paper Money and Banking*, "is—only a comparison. It is not an argument, and it is not, in all respects, just even as a simile. Steam power is *essentially good*. Paper money Banking is *essentially bad*. Against accidents in the use of steam, effectual guards may be provided. No checks which can be devised can make paper credit Banks innoxious." The object of economic argument was not to weigh practical alternatives but to reinforce spiritual values.[21]

Certainly most Democratic appeals to "laws of trade" and similar sanctions were exercises in moral exhortation rather than appeals to reasoned judgment. Taking issue with Whig arguments that a national bank would prevent excessive discounts on paper money issued by state banks, the Democratic State Convention of Illinois argued in 1841 that "this matter is governed by the universal laws of trade, and banks can no more regulate it from its very nature, than they can regulate the tides of the ocean. The United States Bank never did regulate them and never can." For that matter, arguments ostensibly derived from experience tended to be accounts of the workings of moral imperatives, not descriptions of actual phenomena even when they were phenomena that might have cast light on public policy. So strenuous was William Gouge's moral bias, in fact, that he argued that corporations *must* fail unless they acquired artificial advantages. While his argument clearly exemplified Democratic antipathies to legislative incursions on the free economy, it also suggested that Gouge was not willing to test his theory pragmatically. Instructed by their experience of an agrarian economy, persuaded by their prejudices against a parasitical "aristocracy," American Democrats typically expected nature to maintain the moral order they valued.[22]

THE ECONOMY OF PRINCIPLE

In general, Democratic theorists took it for granted that the reforms they sponsored would produce the society they desired, but in the last analysis their moral bias was so powerful that they had neither the will nor the capacity to deal constructively with a society that did not answer to their hopes. In their eyes, the economic consequences of economic measures were irrelevant data, if not dangerous temptations, unless they conformed to the moral scheme Democrats adhered to.

Had the economics of that day made provisions for calculations of policy based on the gross national product, for example, Democratic moralists would have rebuked it as a guide to their actions even though the basic idea had been implicit in Adam Smith's equation between the wealth of nations and "universal opulence." Certainly Whig spokesmen made recurrent efforts to portray their economic programs in just this light, and Henry Clay's proposals for an American System clearly rested on the premise that a "home market" would raise the standard of living in the whole nation, but Democratic spokesmen repudiated arguments that sought to override moral economics with immoral facts. Unlike the Whigs, they were committed to an economy of principle rather than an economy of consumption, as Edward D. Barber suggested at Montpelier (Vermont): "By *general good*, I do not mean the promotion of riches, splendor and power in the nation, but the equal protection of every citizen in his rights,—the impartial administration of justice, the supremacy of the laws, in their power of punishment and protection, over all—equal means of wealth, education and advancement to every citizen—the universal diffusion of intelligence and the promotion of honesty, industry and virtue among every class,—and the subordination of all mere pecuniary and temporary interests to the good of man, in all his moral and immortal qualities." [23]

That is, far from seeking to relate their prescriptions to their society, Democrats substituted their scheme of values for experience of its consequences, confident that they already knew what an economy should be, and correspondingly sure that events could only vindicate their moral predilections. At the same time, they held that the policies they advocated would secure every legitimate human objective—not only individual prosperity and substantial social equality, but all the advantages of a higher civilization. Their confidence was quite understandable as an extrapolation from their premises: convinced that moral laws governed the economy, convinced as well that they knew what those moral laws were, Democrats could hardly be expected to anticipate contingencies that ran counter to their predictions. But their theory left them powerless to deal with phenomena that did not accord with their calculations. Their attitudes toward the role of government were only the most evident example of a more basic supposition, to the effect that nothing could be done and nothing should be done to rectify demonstrable social evils when those evils had been produced by "natural" means.[24]

John L. O'Sullivan expressed both sides of their theory in a single essay in the *Democratic Review*, in which he held that the establishment of equal rights "would tend to equalize the distribution of wealth."

Without wholly removing poverty, it would lessen dependence. The strange contrasts created by overgrown affluence and wretched poverty would give place to apportionments of property more equitably adjusted to the degrees of personal capacity and merit; whilst the poor would be raised, the rich would be made better; restless heart-burnings would cease to embitter the intercourse or provoke the deadly animosity of classes feeling themselves to be equals; arrogance on one side would engender no spleen on the other; and destitution, which is the fruitful parent of crime and misery, would occur only as the retributive consequence of ignorance and vice. All ranks of men would begin life on a fair field, "the world before them where to choose, and Providence their guide." Inclination and sagacity would select the sphere, and dictate the mode and measure of exertion. Frugality and vigilance would compel success, and defeat and ruin be felt only as the requital of ill-desert; or, if such things be, as vicissitudes inflicted by Heaven among its inscrutable designs.

Democrats of O'Sullivan's stripe obviously hoped for the best, but they also expected those who did not prosper to be consoled by the consciousness of their own integrity.[25]

The same ambiguous perspective affected discussions even of the fate of equality in the society Democrats projected. On the one hand, they argued that no evils could arise if Americans were true to the moral economy principled men described, explaining that the evils would be at worst transitory. "Leave property to seek its own channels, enact no laws to make it inalienable," George Camp wrote in *Democracy*, "and the natural course of things will direct its transmission to those who have earned it by their industry and frugality; while the largest accumulations will pass rapidly from the prodigal and licentious, and reduce them and their posterity to a condition of want and dependance [*sic*], whence they can only rise by a renewal of those virtues by which the wealth of their ancestors was originally acquired." [26] On the other hand, they could not conceive of interfering with the natural economy to ameliorate its effects. Mindful of the means by which "aristocratic" institutions had been established, but not of the consequences to which morally acceptable institutions might lead if they were allowed to exist without supervision, most Democrats were even prepared to make room for banks as private enterprises after they had repudiated them as public ventures. Although they freely predicted the evil consequences of Whig policies, they could neither predict nor control what would come of their own. At best, they could only hope that equality would survive in a free society. [27]

Within the framework of their moral presuppositions, in short, Democrats tended to be fatalists rather than full-fledged advocates of the good society. Confronted by evils they could attribute to an immoral social order, they would often act like radical reformers, but the defects they noted were finally only symptoms of their country's moral decay, not evils to be rectified by any means that came to hand. If (as some historians have suggested) they sought to live in Arcadia, it was an Arcadia in which there would be human suffering, and in which that suffering would be taken for granted so long as it was "just." True, Democrats predicted that suffering would diminish if men were true to their principles, but the prospective increase of suffering if men did not live up to them was not their primary reason for urging the policies they advocated. They were not Arcadians but Calvinists, figuratively if not literally devoted to doing the Lord's bidding in the world of affairs in the unspoken conviction that the Lord knew better than they what their secular experience should bring them. [28]

This religious metaphor serves partly as an analogy and partly as an index to their thought. Without seeking to settle the question of the extent to which Democratic theory may have derived from Calvinist doctrine, we can recognize that Democrats widely shared a theological cast of mind. For one thing, their theory of the just society involved a deeply pessimistic view of human nature, in that they assumed all men would do evil if they were given the political opportunity to do so. Hence they would diminish men's power to affect the lives of others through politics, while at the same time insisting that everyone confront his own destiny unaided. At the same time, Democratic moralists often mounted their attack on the paper system in terms of a necessary and yet extraordinary purgation of social evil, a triumph over social sin rather than an adjustment of the economy. Their revolutionary zeal ultimately rested upon a theological disdain for the concerns of this world.[29]

More than this, Democratic convictions were to remain consistent in the face of exceptional evils; there was an underlying tenacity to the Democratic position that survived even appeals to human sympathy and liberal sentiments. It is a commonplace of modern American historiography that Presidents Franklin Pierce and James Buchanan vetoed federal appropriations of land for eleemosynary institutions and homesteads, respectively, on virtually the same ethical grounds that Jackson had employed in vetoing the Second Bank of the United States. It is less often remembered that Barnburners as well as Hunkers could invoke the rights of property against conscious efforts to ameliorate the human condition, as Silas Wright and Michael Hoffman did in opposing the Anti-Rent agitation in New York State. Although some excuse can be found for their intransigence in the fact that the agitators had broken the law, the law that had been broken was literally medieval in its origin and clearly unconscionable in its operation. Nevertheless leading Democrats took sides against, whereas liberal Whigs supported, relatively gentle measures intended to eliminate feudal tenures and secure the equal rights that all Democrats ostensibly took to be the basis of a free society. The triumph of Democratic principles did not invariably require a triumph for humanity.[30]

The ultimate outcome of Democratic lucubrations about society, therefore, was virtually to deny its significance. In 1838 the *Democratic Review* epitomized the thrust of Democratic opinion in an incidental remark (here italicized) that it incorporated into a sympathetic account of Locofoco individualism: "It is not our intention, in this paper, either to maintain or to combat the doctrine. Our purpose will be simply to show, that irrational and *anti-social as it may appear, (to use one of the cant phrases of the day,)* it is not original with these much vilified politicians, but has been held by men who would give authority and do honor to any opinion." So, too, the liberal Democrat David Naar explained in the constitutional convention of New Jersey that "the great object of government was to protect property. If it was not for property, it would not be necessary to raise money to support a government. Our social affairs we could regulate among ourselves." Other commentators were more direct in challenging every claim that society had traditionally made of individuals through government. "For what purpose were Constitutions framed, and laws enacted, but to enable every citizen to use his labour honestly to the best advantage—to lay out his earnings to the best advantage—and to be protected in so doing equally with every other citizen?" asked the authors of *Free Trade and the American System* in 1832. Their question was openly rhetorical, intended to elicit "None" as the answer.[31]

Even the measures taken by Democratic legislatures to secure public ends did not seriously challenge this premise of Democratic thought. Purists were always ready to insist that the legislatures had departed from the strict principles of nature, and modern historians have expended considerable energy on cataloguing exceptions to laissez faire that the Jacksonians may be charged with or praised for. Nevertheless, most of the measures they introduced were intended to facilitate public transportation, which was a necessary prop to individual enterprise if also a prolific source of corruption, and the tendency of Democratic politics was to let more and more alone, or at least to take care of less and less, during a period in which we tend to judge that more and more was needed to maintain democratic social values. In any event, the actions that were taken hardly affected the perspective in which typical Democrats saw the social order. Whatever legislatures may have done in defiance of their creed, it did not seriously affect the creed itself, and therefore it left democrats without a truly social perspective in which to view public actions.[f]

Certainly they had no social criterion by which to test the results of their policies; their object was to maintain a self-contained economic process, not to test it by its social consequences. At the same time, they had few criteria by which to judge even the process they hailed, other than what John L. O'Sullivan described as "a fair field" and the absence of "artificial impediments," which again lacked social as opposed to individualistic content. In the long run, they could hold only that self-regarding individual behavior was the criterion of social justice.

The Free Trade Convention of Philadelphia expressed this idea elliptically in 1831 when it declared that "the necessity must be urgent and palpable, which authorizes any government to interfere in the private pursuits of individuals; to forbid them to do that which in itself is not criminal, and which every one would most certainly do, if not forbidden. Every individual, in every community, without exception, will purchase whatever he may want on the cheapest terms within his reach. . . . All men ever have acted, and continue, under any system, to act on the same principle." F. O. J. Smith was more direct when he appraised Maine's legislative policy in *Hunt's Merchants' Magazine* in 1847. "It is an error that supposes republics proceed from the liberality of mankind," he declared. "Exactly the reverse is true. They are the offsprings of individual selfishness, acting upon a large scale, and risen to strength equal to its own protection against the same principle exerted by a few. It is the highest virtue of republican governments, in fact, their esteemed superiority over all other forms, that they exact so little sacrifice—so small surrender of individual liberty, rights, and privileges, to the welfare and protection of the people." In doctrinaire Democratic eyes, there was no way in which society might impinge on the free individual without sacrificing his liberty.[32]

The Democratic position had a long prior history, but Democratic spokesmen brought it to a point beyond anything that had been essayed before, save perhaps in Mandeville's *Fable of the Bees*. Mandeville had deliberately developed a paradox, however, which Democrats were fundamentally unable to recognize as such: they could see no anomaly in the proposition that private vices produce public virtues because they did not describe selfishness as a vice nor public concern as a virtue. "Avarice" was indeed culpable in their eyes, but it could not be met by any measure other than political neutrality—not by legislation intended to influence social behavior, even though social "regeneration" was taken to be at stake.[33] This fact, too, was an aspect of Democratic "Calvinism," not the collective Calvinism of Geneva and the Massachusetts Bay Colony, but the individualistic Calvinism that made each man responsible for his own salvation within a universe governed by divine laws. Democrats substituted equal rights in a competitive economy for every other definition of the good society, and left the inhabitants to face the consequences.[g]

THE DEMOCRAT AS RADICAL

Despite the defects of Democratic social theory, zealous partisans of the Democratic cause often spoke in radical terms of the evils that class privilege had brought to American society, and no estimate of Jacksonian attitudes can be complete unless it takes into account the radical as well as the reactionary thrust of Democratic belief. The resentment of corporate rights sometimes erupted into a strenuous attack on capital itself, not alone when it was powerful but also because it was. John D. Pierce declared in Michigan's second convention that "the spirit of aggregated capital is aggressive. It has no limit, no bounds. Controlling the legislation of the world, it has been resistless in its sway. It never tires, it never sleeps. Soulless, heartless, remorseless, conscienceless, it presses onward, regardless of the dying or the dead. It produces nothing, but watches with an eagle-eye all the products of labor. It taxes all classes. It watches the wheat grower, the wool grower, the cotton grower, the laborer, the spinner and the washer-woman, and is never satisfied except with the lion's portion. Robbing labor of its reward, it reduces to, and leaves the man and his family in, abject poverty; not satisfied, it takes his cot, and turns him, wife and children, out, according to the statute in such case made and provided." [34]

Condemning the power that capital exercised in American society, Democratic zealots also demanded that the law be used to rectify social evils. In Michigan, Pierce castigated opposition to both debtor relief and homestead exemption on the grounds that heretofore legislation had operated upon "the principle of government taking care of the rich, and the rich taking care of the poor." Ireland and Great Britain proved his case: "The rich are taking care of the poor, and the great mass of the legislation of ages gone by has been for the express purpose of providing laws and means to enable the rich to do it most effectually. And they have succeeded to admiration." Citing the same examples, Calvin Britain made much the same point. "Has the legislation of this or any other country been for the people," he asked, "and [for] property only as a necessary support of the people? Sir, it is not so. The legislation of the age and of the world has been for property, not for life; and life, as estimated by the civil institutions of the age, is not worth two-and-sixpence. It is in fact worth nothing in the eyes of the law, when compared with property. Capital and the companies of capitalists have filled your halls of legislation, and have given to the owner of property an individuality of possession which places property entirely above the claims of humanity." [35]

These were typical statements by extreme Democrats who failed to

carry their convention with them, but the Democratic party was primarily responsible for a number of egalitarian reforms. It was widely
successful in passing stay and exemption laws intended to protect
debtors from the effects of financial crises, as well as mechanics' lien laws
to guarantee the unsecured claims of unpaid workingmen. It also succeeded in limiting the inviolability of corporate charters—not simply
prospective incorporations, but in some cases existing charters as well.
On still another level, it contended that property was intended for use,
and in New York State members of its rank and file (as opposed to its
leaders) provided the initial impetus for abolishing feudal tenures, partly
on the grounds that they were inimical to the proper use of the soil. In
other states, moreover, Democrats came close to repudiating state debts
contracted during the great canal-building extravaganza of the 1820s and
1830s. In short, they challenged not simply the privileges but in many
instances the very rights of property, and they cast doubt on the concept
that those rights had a claim to popular respect.[36]

More generally, Democratic enthusiasts succeeded in challenging both
the authority that wealth held in American society and the presupposition that the rights of property took precedence over the rights of society. To this extent they may be said to have subscribed to a vigorously
pejorative theory of class power and class interests which Democratic
reformers sought to neutralize by obliterating the power of property. As
the *Western Review* explained in 1846, "The democracy assert, that man
ought to rule, and are for such action in our legislation, as will be calculated to make their principles speak through the laws, making the
statute-book the record of humanity, and not the volume in which property can look for, with the certainty of finding, the charter under which
it can securely pillage those to whose very action its own existence is at-
tributable."[37]

Yet the same editorial went on to demonstrate the ultimate futility of
the radical Democratic position when it declared,

Hence their advocacy of the right of revolution, of universal suffrage, of freedom
of trade, of the overthrow of banks, and of the establishment of the constitutional
currency—as means to the great ends aimed at,—as steps in the regeneration of
the social system, so that moral worth and human virtue, and not fictitious distinctions, may be evidences of rank in a new world;—of a rank not built upon enjoyments that can exist only through the great suffering of the working classes,

but simply through the practice of the industrial virtues themselves, and the allowing of every member of society to make all legitimate uses of that which is his by the best of all rights, the right of having created it.

Its ultimate target was not wealth but class in the narrow sense—class as an attribute of politics, not of the social order apart from politics— and the *Review*'s strenuous assertions of equality, morality, and reform culminated in an appeal to a literal Lockean freedom.[38]

The same basic pattern was repeated too many times by dedicated opponents of "aristocratic" practices for us to treat it as an incidental quirk in radical Democratic thought. Not only the techniques of reform that Democrats typically appealed to, but also their fundamental assumptions about the good society, made a mockery of their complaints against "class" by neglecting class phenomena that their reforms left untouched. The very fact that Democrats began by invoking "equal rights" as the basis of their complaints against "aristocracy" undoubtedly helped to produce this anomalous result, as William Cullen Bryant's vigorous defense of the rights of trade unions in the columns of the *New York Evening Post* suggests. "Punish by human laws a 'determination not to work,' " he declared, "make it penal by any other penalty than idleness inflicts, and it matters little whether the task-masters be one or many, an individual or an order, the hateful scheme of slavery will have gained a foothold in the land." His editorial justified the right to strike, but his thesis rested on a distinction between liberty and slavery that argued in favor of the right to starve. Honorable and even progressive as his position may have been for its times, Bryant literally insisted that the only class condition that laws could touch was the condition of legal privilege.[39]

Other doctrinaires both acknowledged and willingly acquiesced in distinctions of wealth that would follow from the social process they contended for, insisting only that those distinctions must not arise from political intrusions on the social order. Frequently they reiterated with Representative Alexander Duncan the classic Democratic projection of a more equitable distribution of wealth. "That there will be inequalities in the circumstances of men, under the most free and equal forms of government," the Ohio Congressman declared in a bitter attack on the Whigs in 1845, "all will admit. The inequality in the habits and ability of men to make or collect wealth, or to retain it, will produce inequality of circumstances; but by far the greater inequality is produced by un-

equal legislation in the granting of monopolies, and in the gift of com-
missions with extravagant and profligate salaries." And yet they clearly
refused to criticize wealth as a social phenomenon when it had been
acquired by "just" means. "I am no enemy to wealth when honestly
acquired, either by mental or physical exertion, or even inherited from
those who have so acquired it," Levi Slamm wrote, "[because] it is no
more a crime than virtuous poverty. . . . I would remove every obstacle
in the road to wealth, every act of legislation conferring advantages to
the *few*, and adding unjustly to the burthens of the *many*, and confine
legislation to its purely legitimate object, *protection to person and property.*" [40]

Slamm's words were symptomatic of the fact that doctrinaire Democrats were probably even more likely to accept social hierarchy, as long
as it was purely social, than were run-of-the-mill partisans who fulminated against "aristocracy." (Camp, Gouge, Leggett, O'Sullivan, Rantoul, Robinson, and Sedgwick come to mind, in addition to Bryant,
Duncan, and Slamm.) We may therefore conclude with scholars like
Louis Hartz that the Democrats were diverted by Whiggish temptations
into acquiescing in social inequality, but the fact that their most literate,
articulate, and self-consciously theoretical spokesmen were also least
likely to insist upon achieving democracy in the modern social sense
suggests that events followed a different path. The triumph of inadequately democratic ideas of equal rights among the Democracy was a
triumph of principle over experience, not of temptations Democrats suffered over the theory they enunciated. The Whig ethic of property and
paternalism, which is to be discussed in chapter V, could hardly have
disarmed these zealots as effectively as they disarmed themselves.

Even extreme radicals who attacked Democratic acquiescence in social
class within a clearly democratic framework of belief betrayed some of
the same limitations of vision. Although Orestes Brownson and Thomas
Skidmore both advocated the elimination of private inheritance in order
to guarantee equal rights, the extraordinary nature of their reform was
not matched by the character of the society they looked forward to.
Brownson was so radical in his denunciation of class interests and class
legislation in his essay on the laboring classes (1840) that it is plausible to
think he anticipated Karl Marx, until one recognizes that his ultimate
"solution" to the profound social evils he was clearly aware of was a

species of the secular Christianity Marx clearly repudiated. In addition, Brownson soon abandoned the very concept of equal rights to become a defender of chattel slavery, which even his famous essay maintained was preferable to wage slavery. He may have been right or he may have been wrong; in either case his later opinions suggest that it was virtually impossible to conceive of a genuine reconstruction of society and remain a Democrat.[41]

Meanwhile Skidmore did not contemplate the remaking of human aspirations, but instead depicted a society in which each man would prosper as best he could, secure only in the knowledge that his children would be equally provided for no matter what his success or failure in life. Skidmore's scheme was by any standard visionary, but his vision was surprisingly restricted by the tenets of equal rights in a predominantly agricultural society. It was no mere coincidence that his ideas ultimately achieved recognition and implementation of a sort in the Homestead Act, which undertook to solve American social problems by perpetuating a yeoman society. Even at its most challenging, Democratic social protest was disappointingly theoretical and remarkably obsolescent; it could hardly describe the social problems Democrats reacted against, much less cure them.[42]

THE DEMOCRAT AS LIBERAL

American democratic theory was manifestly inadequate to serve its intended purposes, but it possessed an undeniable vitality, and it spoke to the American condition in ways that its defects did not touch. To compare Democratic social theory of the 1830s with radical theories of social reform in contemporary England (from which American reformers drew much of their information, their indignation, and even their vocabulary) is to recognize the virtues of the American Democrats' defects.[h]

English radical theory also came to a focus in the theory that "class" was the enemy of "justice," but the definitions of both class and justice were different from their American counterparts. In England, class was virtually identical with society, and radicals hardly knew which way to turn in denouncing the evils it had brought. On the one hand, they expressed bitter hostility toward the whole apparatus of aristocracy that stemmed from the Norman Conquest—the monarchy, House of Lords, and landed nobility, as well as the courtiers, privileges, sinecures, and pensions that characterized the English state, society, and church. On the other hand, they were venomous in their hatred for middle-class entrepreneurs who had dragged England into the Industrial Revolution, creating a helpless industrial proletariat out of agricultural laborers and proprietors who seemed at least in retrospect to have enjoyed a comfortable standard of living and the rights of free-born Englishmen. Not least of their reasons for hating the middle class was the fact that it had once toyed with the idea of democratic political reform, only to abandon it in the face of working-class radicalism and after the Great Reform Bill had brought £10 householders suffrage in the towns. So far as the English working class could tell, the victory of 1832 had been exclusively a victory for the exploiters of labor, who promptly undertook to reform the English government by introducing the New Poor Law and other measures intended to remake English society according to the tenets of middle-class liberalism.[43]

Under these circumstances, class was an intractable social phenomenon, and the only way radicals could conceive of dealing with the conditions they discerned was to revolutionize the social order. But their commitment to social revolution presented them with grave difficulties—not because an armed rising was unthinkable in England, although the number and extent of the risings actually undertaken were surprisingly small, but because the kind of society they hoped for was so radically different from the society they experienced that they could not think productively of the ways of getting from here to there. True, a number of writers elaborated schemes for a good society, and Robert Owen (a renegade manufacturer, one might say) even tried to put one into effect at New Lanark; England was not without its panaceas during this time of crisis. But the innovations Owen and others proposed were quite visibly utopian even in their own terms, and one panacea succeeded another in rapid fashion precisely because none solved the problem of means. (Thus Owen's experiments in paternal capitalism gave way to the utopian socialism of A New View of Society, which was succeeded by the Grand National Consolidated Trades' Union, which gave way in turn before the factory movement, which was transformed once again by the campaign against the New Poor Law before coming to a focus in Chartism.) The radical impulse was unmistakable, and it clearly focused on the wish to eradicate the very patterns of English society, but there were no clear theories of society and politics to link the situations men experienced to the solutions they hoped for. Significantly, William Benbow held that the problems of English society would be solved if workers all joined forces in a general strike. He was confident that a convention of popularly elected representatives could devise a new constitution in a month's time.[44]

Chartism escaped some of these deficiencies because its spokesmen did not usually seek to "solve" all the problems of society at once. Instead they demanded six political reforms—essentially, universal manhood suffrage and a reformed Parliament—from which they confidently expected all necessary social reforms to flow. Yet Chartism also suffered from characteristic defects that rather clearly reflected the impossible demands that class put upon English reformers. First, it was often political to the point of being innocuous: many Chartist leaders were so circumspect in their public statements, if not so limited in their private beliefs, as to suggest that possession of the vote would itself solve England's problems. They simply did not provide a social theory. To this extent they hardly departed from middle-class precedents, and as a result they were often repudiated by more energetic leaders like Feargus O'Connor, who advocated radical if undefined social reform, supported if necessary by revolutionary action to secure the vote.[45]

Second, the more radical Chartist spokesmen—even including O'Connor—often seemed to suggest that the grievances workers felt were grievances against social superiors who had not behaved with justice and compassion toward their dependents. It is significant that whereas the moderate Chartism of London and Birmingham was closely tied to middle-class clamor for the vote, the radical Chartism of the North stemmed more largely from passage of the New Poor Law, which substituted punitive incarceration in public workhouses for less restricted relief of the poor in their own houses as a means of combating the evil effects of poverty. In effect, their clamor for manhood suffrage notwithstanding, northern Chartists often implied that the object of their reforms was to hold the possessing classes to standards their predecessors had commonly observed. Apparently the vote was primarily a way of coercing their masters into decency rather than a vehicle for enforcing equality.[46]

Other forms of agitation also tended to reinforce the claims of labor in a class-based society rather than challenge the premises of class itself. Significantly, Henry Hetherington published what he called *The Poor Man's Guardian*, while John Doherty, the leader of the Lancashire cotton workers, established the *Poor Man's Advocate* and organized a National Society for the Protection of Labour. The terms these agitators used and the strategies they employed suggested that the people they intended to serve were a different category of mankind from the rest of society. They also connoted popular claims against that society, which it was the object of reform to secure; we should not overlook its radical thrust. But they did so from a position of tacitly acknowledged inferiority, and they left an ambiguous implication behind them. They testified to a demand for the rights of man; at the same time, they testified to a lurking sense that the problems of English society arose not from the absence of equal rights but from the failures of class.[47,i]

In the last analysis, therefore, English radical thought tended to separate the concept of equal rights from the concept of class, whereas Americans could not distinguish the two; in the United States, one was the obverse of the other, and the problems of "class" could be dealt with by provision for equal rights. (To put matters more succinctly, the Americans made their claims in the name of rights; the English—too often—in the name of poverty.) It is not difficult to see why the English thought as they did, nor would it be legitimate to infer that they should have done otherwise; class was too deeply embedded in their social experience to be eliminated by the fiat of equal laws. Hence they may well have been wiser than the Americans, especially so far as their own society is concerned; but the effects of class on their thought were remarkable none the less. Because class was so much a part of their society they were unable to see their way around it. Some radicals turned to extreme and clearly utopian answers to solve the problem, while others who were more prudent conceded too much to it in their efforts to overcome its effects. Either way, Englishmen were hamstrung by the phenomenon they sought to cure.

In the United States, on the other hand, men started with the belief— illusory or not—that equal rights were possible in a society governed by equal laws. They attacked the evils of "aristocracy" with the same vigor and sometimes with the same phrases English radicals used, yet the fact that they felt able to premise equal rights meant that they were also able to extrapolate a coherent social theory. The theory they extrapolated was close to English liberalism, and it obviously had a middle-class tinge, but it is a mistake to view it simply as an American counterpart of English liberalism, or to imply that American radicals were wholly disqualified as social theorists by the fact of their liberal bias. Rather, they put together a host of miscellaneous elements—the idea of equal rights, hostility to aristocracy, laissez faire economics, Lockean energies, and Calvinistic moral scruples—in a creed that invited them to exploit a continent, secure in the belief that men received their just deserts when the machinations of "aristocracy" were defeated at the polls. They claimed rights, but they could accommodate even poverty in their scheme of values. Given the actual condition of American society (in which there was a remarkable degree of homogeneity and considerable social mobility, evidence of exceptions notwithstanding); given, too, the natural resources of an undeveloped continent, "equal rights" liberated the Americans from the social dilemmas as well as the social obligations that nearly paralyzed English radicalism.[j] For the time being, at least, American democrats held to an optimistic theory of society that enabled them to overcome their most pressing problems.

❧ V ❧

THE CONSERVATIVE
ETHIC

Right or wrong, foolish or wise, American democrats were determined
to establish equal rights as they understood them. The course of American history ran with them, but they succeeded only because they finally
outnumbered and outgeneraled their opposition, not because there was
no opposition to their views. By comparison with Europe, perhaps, the
United States lacked social structure and shared a fundamentally democratic perspective on society, but at home American conservatives of the
1820s and 1830s differed sharply with their democratic compatriots on
the meaning of "equal rights" and the desirability of a "natural" economy. Hence, in a society governed by manhood suffrage, the conservatives' social theory guaranteed their downfall; but for a decade or two
they kept alive an alternative vision of American society that severely
challenged democratic formulas before capitulating to democratic power.
Even in defeat, moreover, the American conservative tradition proved to
be an important element in the deliberations of the Middle Period. Conceding everything but the rights of property, conservative spokesmen
made these rights the touchstone of a conservative social theory that
democrats would find themselves unable to refute.

PROPERTY IN A FREE SOCIETY

Conservatives began by attempting to defend social practices and social values that were already familiar to them.[a] This meant that they
were all too ready to see threats to property and liberty in Democratic
attacks on "aristocracy", but it also meant that they continued for some
time to visualize government as an active participant in the development
of the American economy.

So far as their attitudes toward government and the economy are concerned, it was clear to contemporary Democrats, as it is clear to us
today, that many of the men who advocated public assistance to private
enterprises were interested in those same enterprises. It was not simply

altruism or an abstract concern for the public good that led hopeful investors to seek the privileges of incorporation or the right to conduct banks. They expected to make a profit out of the privileges they acquired, and they felt no particular sympathy for the utopian democratic notion that every man should be forced to make his way in the world unaided.

Nevertheless, the modern view of economic justice has been so much influenced by the success of Jacksonian Democracy that we cannot recognize either the merits or the integrity of the conservatives' position if we say no more about it. For one thing, the distinction we draw between public and private enterprise did not exist so far as they were concerned; instead, their attention was focused on enterprise as such, on unprecedented economic undertakings from which public benefits were expected to flow. (We shall return to this point in chapter VI.) This is not to say that their motives were impeccable. One reason they did not make the distinction was that they took social hierarchy for granted: they felt no reason to doubt that the rich, the wise, and the well-born, together with outstanding individuals who had made their way from obscure beginnings into the ranks of the mighty, should make, implement, and benefit from the major economic decisions of the society. Still, it is important that they insisted on their privileges because it seemed to them that social order was impossible without them, not because they sought to establish unprecedented claims to authority; they also took it for granted that private economic undertakings assisted or protected by the state would in fact produce large social benefits. If they sought to promote their own ends, in short, they also assumed that the profits they made would be earned by the service they provided.[1]

At the same time, they visualized government as a positive and beneficent agency, controlling private actions in order to further the public good. (In effect, they held that in a properly constituted government even selfish men could be brought to adopt constructive social legislation.) Nor was this seemingly visionary hope merely a plausible rationalization for the private economic ventures on which government had bestowed special privileges. Rather, conservatives repeatedly invited democratic assaults by the energy with which they argued that government could and should foster universal prosperity by a selective use of its powers. The point has been made that they ultimately abandoned their principles in order to compete with their Democratic opponents; it might better be said that they clung to a theory of beneficent government long after it had been discredited at the polls.[2]

If government was intended to foster human welfare, so was property. On the traditional conservative view, expressed long before triumphant Democracy seemed to threaten it with expropriation, property was salutary, vested, and privileged: salutary in the sense that it was thought to elicit social virtues and encourage the development of civilization, vested in the sense made famous by John Marshall when he transformed the contract clause of the federal Constitution into a bulwark of existing rights of possession, and privileged in that its advocates succeeded until the 1820s (and to some extent thereafter) in maintaining a restricted suffrage and disproportionate representation in their state legislatures.[3] But it was also conceived as a social instrument, and it might be held to a standard of social utility.

For one thing, its friends clearly visualized property in paternalistic terms, implicitly committing its possessors to perform services for the commonwealth that might not be performed otherwise. The constitutional debates of the 1820s elicited frequent arguments like that of Judge Ambrose Spencer in New York. "To the beneficence and liberality of those who have property," he declared, "we owe all the embellishments and the comforts and blessings of life. Who build our churches, who erect our hospitals, who raise our school houses? Those who have property. And are they not entitled to the regard and fostering protection of our laws and constitution?" Even when we make allowance for the fact that Spencer was pleading a cause, we have no reason to doubt the sincerity with which he and other speakers—Republicans as well as Federalists—argued that property needed to be protected because of the good its owners did. For that matter, orthodox clergymen whose sympathies lay with the propertied establishment often labored the proposition that wealthy men owed society practical demonstrations of their benevolence. It is not too much to say that in the traditional conservative view the obligations of property ran concurrently with its privileges even when there was no thought that society might enforce those obligations.[4]

Property was also legally limited and subordinated to the public good. To an extent that we find difficult to believe in the aftermath of Jacksonian Democracy, the uses to which it might be put were regulated or at least subject to regulation by state courts and legislatures. An elaborate legal tradition grounded in medieval English precedents provided that no one might use his property to the detriment of another man's welfare, while the Americans of the early republic were slow to curtail the right of eminent domain, by which the state might take possession of a given property when the good of the commonwealth required it. Indeed, it was not at all clear on the traditional view exactly how far property may be said to have had rights, in the modern sense of the term. Although its friends had long since begun to visualize it as a kind of social absolute, they also tended to define it as a product of civil society and to imply that its autonomy was justified only by its utility. Hence it is probably legitimate to say that the sanctity conservatives attached to property before the Democratic revolution derived more largely from the fact of social privilege and the premise of public service than from any clear-cut legal right to do what one willed with one's own. Men of property trusted men of their own kind not to infringe on its privileges without sufficient cause, but they did not often claim that it had absolute rights against government.[5]

The success of democratic innovations changed the direction of conservative thought by encouraging its partisans to essay an absolute defense of their possessions. Significantly, they often visualized democratic measures of reform as efforts at "agrarianism," the forcible seizure of property that had been initiated by popular leaders in ancient Rome. Presumably both a taste for classical history and a mistaken belief that they could forestall the march of democracy by equating it with hostility to property in all of its forms played some part in conservatives' use of the term. But it also expressed their sense that popular rule might mean the abolition of property as well as privilege, which necessitated in turn the unconditional defense of an institution that had formerly been subject to management by government. Their fathers had already faced some of the same threats during the 1780s, when they devised a federal constitution and revised some of their state constitutions with an eye to curbing such evils as paper money, infringements on contracts, and other legislative encroachments on property. But the earlier generation had achieved these ends with relatively little difficulty, and in fact their proceedings often suggest that the ends did not loom very large in their minds; rather, security of property was one among many benefits to be expected from the establishment of good government. Confronted, however, with the development of a full-fledged democracy, the conservatives of the Middle Period strove with might and main to protect property against its putative enemies.[6,b]

The pressure on conservative values is apparent in the ambivalent fashion in which leading spokesmen for the cause dealt with incipient pressures for manhood suffrage and the elimination of property qualifications for senatorial office in the constitutional conventions of the 1820s. In Massachusetts and New York, leaders like Daniel Webster, Joseph Story, and Chancellor Kent fought bitterly to retain some kind of protection for property. Yet they also typically visualized it as only one of several interests that required deliberate protection, and if they seemed to say that property alone required special safeguards, it was only because the people seemed well able to take care of themselves. In addition, they argued with evident sincerity that the preservation of liberty depended upon the preservation of property. "Life, and personal liberty are, no doubt, to be protected by law," Webster told the Massachusetts convention; "but property is also to be protected by law, and is the fund out of which the means for protecting life and liberty are usually furnished. We have no experience that teaches us, that any other rights are safe, where property is not safe." In other words, they neither denied their interest in property nor pretended to seek a purely abstract liberty, yet they appealed with apparent candor to a wide range of republican values. Even if property was a paramount concern, it occupied the same ground as other libertarian interests.[7]

At the same time, these spokesmen easily moved from a defense of liberty and property together to a defense of property as if it were alone the embodiment of liberty. In New York, for example, Chancellor Kent first condemned manhood suffrage on the basis of the ancient republics' experience of its "corruption, injustice, violence, and tyranny," went on to hail the landed interest as "the safest guardians of property and the laws," and then elaborated his fears that the poor would dispossess the rich. "There is a constant tendency in human society, and the history of every age proves it; there is a tendency in the poor to covet and to share the plunder of the rich; in the debtor to relax or avoid the obligation of contracts; in the majority to tyranize [sic] over the minority, and trample down their rights; in the indolent and the profligate, to cast the whole burthens of society upon the industrious and the virtuous; and *there is a tendency in ambitious and wicked men, to inflame these combustible materials.*" Webster followed much the same pattern in the Massachusetts convention, invoking Roman history as his evidence for the proposition that "it would be monstrous to give even the name of government, to any association, in which the rights of property should not be competently secured." [8]

Yet this classic position was broader than the position that succeeded it. For one thing, manhood suffrage was relatively untried in 1820, and both Kent and Webster lived in states in which it was plausible to anticipate grave consequences for liberty from the development of a large industrial population. For another, they continued to argue that property was indispensable to liberty—that liberty-in-general was impossible unless it was secured by a social class both interested in and capable of maintaining it. By contrast, the next generation of conservatives could plead no such case. Manhood suffrage and representation by population were now established facts in a good many states, and they had not led to the confiscation or even the limitation of property. Hence there was no good reason to labor its defense. In addition, if liberty-in-general was threatened in the manner that many conservatives complained of, the later advocates of property rights could not show that the institution they defended offered other rights any support. Nevertheless, they continued their clamor in behalf of the rights of property as if the institution were still endangered and as if it were still serviceable to other rights, although the circumstances under which they reiterated their contentions ensured that the rights they defended would exist in a social vacuum. In effect, they treated the rights of property as if they were the summation of liberty. [9]

One of their resources was a theory that property serves mankind by purely impersonal means. Instead of arguing that property-holders were the source of specific benefactions to society, men who sought to contend with Jacksonian egalitarianism tended to describe property as an abstract social phenomenon from which all good flowed. Kent himself developed this proposition in his *Commentaries on American Law* (1826–30): "The natural and active sense of property pervades the foundations of social improvement. It leads to the cultivation of the earth, the institution of government, the acquisition of the comforts of life, the growth of the useful arts, the spirit of commerce, the productions of taste, the erections of charity, and the display of the benevolent affections." Francis Lieber developed much the same argument in his *Essays on Property and Labour* (1841). On this view, property was not a private possession implicitly vindicated by the behavior of its proprietors, but a fact made necessary by the human condition.[10]

Another element in conservative thought was the assumption that property is a natural right. Formally, neither Kent nor Lieber was willing to defend it on that basis, Lieber because he was a German-born scholar educated to European rather than American modes of social analysis, Kent because he recognized that government creates rights, which men may claim but not enjoy without law. Yet both men also treated the status they accorded to property as an indispensable element in a "natural" system of economics, and both invoked the Creator to sanction the rights this system mandated. ("Man was fitted and intended by the author of his being, for society and government," Kent wrote, "and for the acquisition and enjoyment of property.") Hence, despite evident efforts to avoid appealing to natural rights, both men ended by using its concepts even when they repudiated its premises. Lieber held that "private property in land is as natural and unfailing an effect of man's right and duty to appropriate and accumulate, as property in other things," while Kent could escape his dilemma only by arguing that the American people had traditionally believed in natural rights, which therefore commanded the protection of the law.[11]

The practical result was a theory that property should be held without enforceable obligations or legislative limitations. For his part, Kent was careful to say that the right to hold property is subject to a power in the legislature "to prescribe the mode and manner of using it, so far as may be necessary to prevent the abuse of the right, to the injury or annoyance of others, or to the public." But even this formulation made legislative action depend upon infringements on the equal rights of others—not on a general good transcending particular rights—and in discussing the specific applications of his general principle Kent made clear that a legislature could neither limit the acquisition of property by private individuals nor impose burdensome taxes on lands held for speculative purposes by absentee owners. In the same vein Lieber insisted that property might be curtailed if it threatened individuality or hindered social progress, but he criticized all of the measures his contemporaries had proposed to serve these purposes.[12] Although conservative theory might hold that there were circumstances under which property should be restricted, conservative theorists found few occasions for implementing this possibility, or they surrounded it with such severe limitations as to deny its practical significance.

Their bias was clearly in evidence in the second constitutional convention of Illinois, where two Whig delegates condemned the democratic contention that the people have the right to remake their constitutions at will on the ground that it pointed toward the abrogation of private rights, especially those of minorities. The context of the discussion made clear that the rights of property were paramount in these dissidents' minds. The same view influenced the minority report of the Select Committee on the Interference of the Executive in the Affairs of Rhode Island, which held in 1844 that popular sovereignty must be exercised through established constitutional channels. It defended this requirement on the ground that only rigorously controlled constitutional change would protect the natural rights of individuals, among which it identified property as the first and foremost. When a conservative spoke of rights during the 1840s, it was an all but foregone conclusion that he had in mind the rights of property. By now, these were virtually the only rights he felt constrained to protect, and liberty itself had been reduced to a synonym for untrammeled possessions.[13]

This was the context in which conservatives of the Middle Period appealed to the authority of the courts to exempt all forms of property from the authority of the state governments. As Benjamin F. Wright Jr. pointed out many years ago, the contract clause of the federal Constitution had little significance until energetic conservatives employed it, first in the states and subsequently in the Supreme Court, to curtail state legislation intended to restrict or redefine the rights of property-owners even when those rights had originally been established by statute. More generally, Edward S. Corwin has traced a number of ways in which the courts developed a doctrine of vested rights even broader than the contract clause, holding (among other things) that the effect of legislation on existing rights of property was a key test of its validity, that even general legislation clearly intended to serve public ends must not intrude unreasonably upon the rights of ownership, and that any deprivation of property must be fully compensated.[14]

The thrust of these efforts was epitomized in arguments that Daniel Webster invoked before the Supreme Court in *Dartmouth College v. Woodward* (1819) and *The West River Bridge Company v. Joseph Dix et al.* (1847), not to mention *Charles River Bridge v. Warren Bridge*. In the first, Webster argued that any change in the charter of Dartmouth College must be treated as a forfeiture for cause and be adjudicated in court according to previously enacted laws, rather than treated as a legitimate act of the state of New Hampshire, while in the second he held that even eminent domain was a questionable power because it permitted public authorities to legislate property out of existence. (In his view, the fact that eminent domain included compensation did not satisfy the right of possession.) It is true that Webster failed to carry the Court with him in either of the bridge company cases, but his failure was only a temporary setback for the conservative cause. The most significant aspect of all three cases was that a former Federalist who had been born into a society in which governments exercised large powers intended to promote the public good now sought to treat property as an inalienable right subject only to the penalties of criminal law.[15]

AN ECONOMY OF CONSUMERS

The defense of property initiated by the early conservatives and deepened by their successors was essentially static, focused on traditional rights of possession rather than novel rights of acquisition. On the other hand, many conservatives also felt constrained to defend burgeoning economic developments like manufacturing corporations and chartered banks in terms that would meet the clamor of their democratic critics. The result was a systematic conservative justification of economic innovations as beneficent and even popular institutions. It revealed much about the theorists' roots in a hierarchical and paternalistic past, but it also showed how they might yet appeal to democrats against themselves.

One conservative stance was a naive celebration of the advantages of the new economic order. In 1836 Daniel Webster hailed the advent of the machine age on the grounds that technology "multiplies laborers without multiplying consumers, and the world is precisely as much benefited as if Providence had provided for our use millions of men, like ourselves in external appearance, who would work and labor and toil, and who yet required for their own subsistence neither shelter, nor food, nor clothing." Moreover, while Webster spoke before the Society for the Diffusion of Useful Knowledge, where he obviously felt called upon to give modern economic developments a philosophical gloss, Joseph D. Hoag simply took Webster's sense of benefits for granted when he defended manufacturing corporations in the Iowa constitutional convention of 1844. "Manufactories were of unquestionable advantage to a country," the Vermont-born farmer was reported to have said, "and it was to its interest to encourage them. This was an excellent wool-growing country, and woolen manufactories would be desirable to work up the wool." [16]

Nevertheless, either form of argument might have been presented fifty years previously, when the legitimacy of associated wealth was less threatened if also less familiar, and conservatives of the Middle Period typically found it desirable to elaborate their case in ostentatiously democratic ways. One of their chief devices was an explicit ethic of consumption that put aside abstract theories of the public good to emphasize the extent to which the economic innovations they valued satisfied the wants of ordinary men. Webster stressed this point in his lecture: "There has been in the course of half a century an unprecedented augmentation of general wealth. Even within a shorter period, and under the actual observation of most of us, in our own country and our own circles, vastly increased comforts have come to be enjoyed by the industrious classes, and vastly more leisure and time are found for the cultivation of the mind. . . . We may safely take the fact to be, as it certainly is, that there are certain causes which have acted with peculiar energy in our generation, and which have improved the condition of the mass of society with a degree of rapidity heretofore altogether unknown." Nor was he inclined to visualize these developments as imponderable consequences of history; rather, he held that they were inherent in the modern economic system, which depended upon popular satisfactions for its very existence. "The improved condition of all classes, more ability to buy food and raiment, better modes of living, and increased comforts of every kind, are exactly what is necessary and indispensable in order that capital invested in automatic operations should be productive to the owners."

The widest possible enjoyment of consumable goods was a necessity of economics as well as a necessity of man.[17]

Thus far Webster's argument was democratic in the sense that it held up a standard of universal benefits, but it was also significantly at odds with contemporary democratic doctrine. Not only did it pose an economy of consumption against the economy of principle, but it also rested upon paternalistic assumptions about the relationships between corporate endeavor and its social beneficiaries. "There are modes of applying wealth, useful principally to the owner, and no otherwise beneficial to the community than as they employ labor," Webster went on to explain. ". . . Not so with aggregate wealth employed in producing articles of general consumption. This mode of employment is, peculiarly and in an emphatic sense, an application of capital to the benefit of all." His words represented a tolerably accurate reading of contemporary economic theory, but they also clearly suggested that the producing classes should be grateful for a system in which capital so readily answered to their needs.[18]

Other defenders of the factory system also tended to depict its benefits as operating in a society in which men were divided between leaders and followers, benefactors and beneficiaries; the proposition that the system worked impersonally to benefit everyone did not alter, but rather strengthened, the authority of wealthy men. According to the *American Quarterly Review*, the evils of the factory system were as nothing compared with the fact that machinery "places within the reach even of the poorest, a thousand comforts which were unknown to the rich in less civilized ages, and furnishes the humble cottage, if industry, neatness, and sobriety preside over it, with every necessary for substantial enjoyment." Increased consumption was a function of hierarchy held to democratic forms—and of democracy conforming to hierarchical models.[19]

The conservative ethic was in this sense undemocratic, but it is important to note that its alternatives to contemporary democracy were consistent both with each other and with conservative tradition. In addition to hierarchy its advocates took public benefit to be a criterion of social policy, and they justified the privileges they defended by citing the good they were alleged to do. The ethic of consumption was in a very real sense the logical corollary of conservatives' efforts to use government to enhance the general welfare.[20]

This ethic was clearly suspect in its early form, however, if only because ordinary Americans bridled at being conceived of as "the poor," and Whig partisans increasingly turned to consumption without either paternalism or hierarchy to defend their claims to office. In 1840 they made a strenuous effort to equate Democratic rule with short rations. A widely circulated pamphlet entitled *Pictures of the Times* sought by means of both words and pictures to enforce what its subtitle labeled the "Contrast between the Effects of the True Democratic System, as displayed under Jefferson, Madison and Jackson in former times, and the Effects of the Aristocratic Sub-Treasury System, as displayed in Martin Van Buren's Time." Correspondingly, Representative Joseph Underwood of Kentucky turned Democratic sneers at the log-cabin campaign to account, not by harping on Harrison's democracy, but by arguing that

I remember the *log cabin* school house and the *log cabin* church, but I remember all these things coupled with a recollection of the hopes and the prayers then devoutly expressed, that they would, ere long, be superseded by a more prosperous condition. I have witnessed the change, to some extent, so much desired. But, although wonderful changes have taken place, still a large portion of my worthy constituents yet live in *log cabins*. Now, I do not believe that "johnny-cakes," "pumpkin pies," and "new whiskey and brown sugar out of a gourd," are good enough for my constituents who live in log cabins. I think them as much entitled to "enjoy all the good things of the earth" as Mr. Van Buren, or any of those who live in marble palaces.[21]

By 1844, indeed, Whigs were inclined only to condemn Democratic policies for the deprivations they had caused. "Look back fellow citizens to 1830," the Whig State Convention of Indiana insisted. "The country was prosperous. Its currency was safe, cheap and regular. Its trade was profitable and increasing. Its people were contented and happy. Its Government had done for it all that was necessary, and the favorite of the people, and his friends, were intrusted with its offices. One thing only was necessary, 'to let well enough, alone.' " Simultaneously Calvin Colton, always in the forefront of Whig polemics, made an even grosser appeal to materialistic ideals as the criterion of popular politics. "Let every individual calculate for himself what he, personally, has lost, what chances have been sacrificed by him, what he might have done, and what he might have been, if the prosperity of the country had not been arrested by these fatal measures," he wrote in introducing an estimate of the losses the Americans had suffered because of the attack on currency. So much had conservatives conceded to the pressure of democratic beliefs that they could retain their idea of a fostering government only indirectly, as a standard the Democratic party had abandoned, and their ideal of public welfare only in the form of an appeal to individual satisfactions.[22]

AN ECONOMY OF EQUALS

Conservative social commentators were persuaded by contemporary political exigencies to attempt still another version of conservative social theory. Feeling the pressure of democratic antagonism, sensing the weakness of obvious paternalism, and casting about for some broader ethic than consumption, they worked to overcome the undemocratic nature of their position by representing the economy they valued as intrinsically democratic. Try as they would to meet Democratic partisans on their own terms, however, they could not avoid employing traditional hierarchical presuppositions in elaborating their version of equality.

Not consumption but participation was the key to their broader social theory. One of its elements was the claim that capitalists and workers are really identical. On the one hand, conservatives argued in a relatively traditional vein that there is a harmony of interests between workers and proprietors, a contention that was intended to disarm class antagonism by making the rich and the poor allies in a common social endeavor. On the other hand, they insisted that capitalists are laborers in the same sense that their employees are, obviously hoping to deprive class hostility of its force by denying the existence of a distinct working class. In 1844 Nathan Appleton (one of the principal founders of the Waltham mills) argued that the United States was distinguished from Europe by the difference between "labor in action" and "labor in possession," with labor in possession representing claims made on the European economy by privileged idlers. Similarly, in describing the early career of Patrick Tracy Jackson (another of the Boston Associates), John Lowell made much of the fact that Jackson had been a "working-man" all his life, contrary to the "aristocratic notions" of his youth. Hence the friends of less eminent men of business had no difficulty in visualizing them as men of toil. "We are characteristically and distinctly a nation of *workers*," Calvin Colton wrote in 1844. "There are some who do not work; but most people do. Work is the fashion, and the proudest distinction in American society. Nobody looks with respect on those who live in idleness, or who riot in luxurious ease." [23]

In conservative eyes, corporations were also democratic institutions. In Iowa, Joseph D. Hoag defended manufacturing corporations on the grounds that their employees "worked by the week or piece, as they pleased, usually; and the operatives often made more than the owners. Common hands who were stronger and careful, would in a comparatively short time, be able to buy small farms, or otherwise go into business for themselves." A former manufacturer, Hoag may have had some warrant for this happy picture of the experience of the factory population, but even spokesmen for the Boston Associates visualized the factories they knew as instances of democracy in action. In 1841 the manager of one of the Lowell mills told Sir Charles Lyell that the sale of stock to the operatives prevented them from looking on their employers as members of a distinct class, while in 1855 Representative Charles W. Upham insisted corporations were "eminently popular in their nature, and truly democratic in their tendency. . . . Without such a system, the distance between the rich and poor will widen as a country advances in accumulation. With such a system, every industrious man or woman is able to participate in that accumulation. . . . It is, in truth, precisely because such corporate facilities are within the reach of all who may feel disposed to unite their means in the prosecution of any kind of business that there cannot be any serious, or considerable, or lasting oppression of labor by capital in Massachusetts." [24]

Nevertheless, in any of its insistently "democratic" versions the defense of corporations and of the factory system required men of even ordinary perceptions to make an implicit distinction between equality of condition and equality of opportunity. As both Hoag and Upham demonstrated, the basis of such an argument was not a premise that employees and employers are in all respects equals, but that every man can make his way into the class of capitalists. By the same token, conservative apologists for banks tended to hail them as "democratic" institutions but to make clear that their democracy was a democracy of opportunity rather than result. [25] This same distinction also appeared in Democratic invectives against the "paper aristocracy," but never with the same force, for—influenced in part by their agricultural beliefs—Democrats typically assumed that eliminating the paper system would severely diminish the disparity among social classes. For their part, conservative social theorists tended to assume that inequalities were justified by opportunities. Even as they capitulated to democratic pressures, conservatives typically sought to accommodate democratic doctrine to their theory of society as a system of ranks and privileges.

This tendency was evident in two elements of their thought. On the one hand, they often justified their policies on the grounds that a large number of men derived admittedly limited benefits from them. "The workingman, the journeyman, the day-laborer, the apprentice," D. Francis Bacon told a meeting of Clay supporters in 1844, "are aspiring to be master-workmen and employers—as is the clerk to be a merchant, as the poor scholar aspires to an honorable profession." Significantly, however, he went on to argue that "all are hoping if not for wealth, at least for a competence, a comfortable subsistence, not only for themselves, but for others who are yet to be theirs, . . . as becomes the progeny of a race of sovereign freemen." On this view, which was expounded by other Whig apologists as well, the right to enjoy the acquisitions one had accumulated, however modest they might be, took precedence over reforms intended to make sure that they were equally held, while the universal aspiration to a competence was sufficient reason for honoring the prerogatives of men who had acquired more.[26]

On the other hand, conservatives also labored the idea of personal success as a democratic justification for significant social distinctions. We shall trace the complex origins and ingredients of the full-fledged idea of success in chapter VI; here it is sufficient to note that well-known Whig spokesmen employed it in behalf of the established order of society. Daniel Webster appealed to it in 1836, arguing that in America young men who were laborers today would be capitalists tomorrow: "If without moneyed capital, they have a capital in their intelligence, their knowledge, and their good habits." Similarly, the *New-York Review* excoriated trades' unions on the grounds that they sought to penalize men who had earned a high position in society. "In our country," it observed in 1838, "every thing like hereditary distinction or privilege has been abolished. Property can be perpetuated in no family, except by enterprise and virtue; while there is nothing in the theory, and but little in the practical operation of our laws, to prevent the humblest citizen from reaching the highest eminence of wealth or power." The idea of equal competition for unequal rewards served to justify rather than challenge the existing structure of society.[27]

In other words, even in praising the substantial equality Americans enjoyed, conservatives typically slid from praise for equality to praise for mobility in a hierarchical society. The same tendency was apparent in their attitudes toward the "wheel of fortune," the idea that the sons or grandsons of wealthy men revert to the condition from which their wealthy forebears had originally risen. Chancellor Kent expressed an early and essentially egalitarian version of the idea in his *Commentaries:* "When the laws allow a free circulation to property by the abolition of perpetuities, entailments, the claims of primogeniture, and all inequalities of descent, the operation of the steady laws of nature will of themselves preserve a proper equilibrium, and dissipate the mounds of property as fast as they accumulate." But Calvin Colton revealed how little he thought equality of condition was connected with equality of opportunity when he wrote in 1840 that "riches, under the American system, the law of entail being abolished, rarely remain in the same family longer than the second generation. In that time, ordinarily, by the revolutions of the wheel of fortune, those who were poor are at the top, and the children of those who were rich are at the bottom. One would think this ought to satisfy a reasonable sympathy for the poor, who are rather to be envied for the chances of getting up, than the rich in the certainty of going down." On this view, the existence of grave social distinctions was a prerequisite for democratic hopes.[28]

Thus the society of equals that conservatives hailed was a society in which equality was a collective phenomenon, one that characterized it as a whole without sanctioning any of the grievances of particular individuals. Indeed, a number of conservatives argued that the abolition of primogeniture and entail alone ensured that the United States would always enjoy equal rights. We may well suppose that theorists who expressed this view were often disingenuous, but we should probably also suppose that many were very largely sincere, incapacitated by their traditional conception of society as a hierarchical order of merit from comprehending the differences between republican and democratic egalitarianism. It was not only that they sought to protect themselves and their friends against democratic threats; rather, they really could not understand what the democrats were complaining about. Far from representing merely polemical observations, their statements apparently reflected a confused but comfortable assurance on the part of the possessing classes that the problems of social order and social progress had been solved by truly democratic means.[29]

Ivers J. Austin suggested as much in a Fourth of July oration in Boston when he praised "this happy country, where all avenues to office and honor are freely opened, where genius and industry encounter no artificial barriers of birth, rank or wealth, to stay their progress to the highest stations." So did John Aiken, agent for the Lawrence Manufacturing Company, when he differentiated between the American and European condition in a series of letters on *Labor and Wages* in 1848. In Europe, he argued, the facts of social stratification give rise to concepts of social class and lend sanction to radical protests that cannot be justified in the United States. "Where society is entirely homogeneous and without privileged classes; where lands are abundant, cheap, and easily conveyed; where all may be well educated at the public expense; where labor is richly rewarded and competence within the reach of all; where an open and equal field is given to all under equal laws, so that the poorest boy that blows the blacksmith's bellows may become a member of Congress, or the Governor of a State, or it may be the President of the United States, and the poorest girl may qualify herself appropriately to fill the highest station in domestic or social life, . . . what is their truth, or fitness, or decency here?" He moved from the premise of substantial equality to the premise of competitive equality without betraying any sense that they might be distinct.[30]

The thrust of conservative thought becomes even clearer when we compare it with democratic observations on the same themes. Democrats also contended that equality of right was equivalent to equality of result, but their doctrine was far more rigorous, and it did not extend to the same economic practices that conservatives like Aiken defended. In effect, Democrats held that it was necessary to guarantee equal rights in order to justify inequality in society, about which they were then inclined to be fatalistic, whereas the apologists for the new economic order insisted that equal rights were sufficiently provided for by their innovations, and invited men of every condition to participate in their country's advantages. To this extent they were willing to accept the people as equals, but they also implied that equality should be accorded only to those who rose above their neighbors, leaving everyone else to be a beneficiary of the efforts of men who had earned a position at the top of society. In their eyes the object of competitive democratic processes was not to restore equality but to provide an unexceptionable basis for social hierarchy after government had been democratized and deprived of its right to confer favors on the rich. They had not so much abandoned hierarchy as remade it.[c]

THE ABDICATION OF CONSERVATISM

Conservative social apologists remade American conservatism to fit new circumstances, but they also abandoned the most important premises of traditional social thought. As they substituted participation for benefaction as the epitome of social progress, they also diminished the claims that participants in the social process might make of it. More particularly, they held up a right of participation in the economy as the only right or benefit men could legitimately exercise, and they came to suggest that the participants could not even claim the right of consumption unless they could enforce it by exclusively economic means.

This development was illustrated in a small way in the fate of factory paternalism as practiced in the mills of Waltham and Lowell. Initially the founders of these mills had made a point of providing an attractive physical and social environment for their hands, whom they hoped to spare the horrors of the British factory system, and in later years they continued to celebrate the virtues of the American system of industry. As time passed, however, and as the industry became more competitive, they increasingly abandoned their employees to their fate, embracing the dictates of political economy in place of the obligations of "patriotism." Significantly, in 1844 the *Lowell Offering*, the house organ of benevolent capitalism, explained that wages must be governed by the availability of laborers. Meanwhile, of course, the proprietors of the mills continued to justify a protective tariff; they did not reject every form of public paternalism. But they did reject the vision of society as an organic entity in which men who held great privileges also bore great obligations.[31]

Certainly the idea of positive government that conservatives originally took for granted tended to disappear. True, traditionalists continued during the 1840s to visualize government as a constructive force in the economy, much as Richard Rush and John Quincy Adams had during the 1820s. In 1846, for example, Daniel Webster rebuked Democratic hostility to internal improvements at federal expense by invoking the examples of Prussia and Saxony. There, he said, "We behold mountains penetrated by railroads, safe harbors constructed, every thing done by government for the people, which, in the nature of the case, the people cannot do for themselves." By the same token, a "Whig from the Start" urged Webster's candidacy on the party's national convention in 1848 on the ground that he stood for true Whig principles—"improvement and elevation of Man, the promotion of his individual happiness, and his social conveniences and comforts"—while a year later the *American Review* argued that "the Whig Party have been always distinguished from their opponents, by the attribution of a beneficent and protective power to government. And it is in regard of that attribution, that they assert for themselves the name of 'republicans,' believers in the efficacy of law and of the moral and intelligent functions of the government." [32]

Nevertheless, these were confessedly the views of old-fashioned men who were unlikely to win elections or even to secure the support of their own party. Increasingly, Whigs sought to compete with Democrats not by offering an alternative vision of government but by appealing to the same prejudices against government and "aristocracy" that Democrats made so much of. One can hardly blame them—Democrats frequently made political capital out of the fact that conservative spokesman like Rush and Adams had praised positive government[33]—but the effect was abdication of the conservative position. On the one hand, they defended specific powers in government on the ground that they were the best possible safeguard against an aristocracy of wealth; that is, they defended its authority by accepting the premises on which Jacksonians condemned it.[34] On the other hand, they called into question both the integrity and the effectiveness of government and suggested that it could not be trusted with the public business.

Two Whig spokesmen in the New Jersey constitutional convention of 1844 exemplified this second tendency. Charles C. Stratton was willing—as Moses Jaques was not—to see the state acquire the Camden and Amboy Rail Road as a speculation, but he denied that any public works could retain their value if the state were to manage them. His colleague Robert S. Kennedy insisted that the convention limit the pay of state legislators on grounds that were equally invidious: "I believe in the honesty of the People in general but not in particular; that is I believe the people in general are honest in their private dealings with another, but when it comes to Uncle Sam's money, then grab is the game. I hope therefore the amendment will not pass, but that we will permit the people of New Jersey to carry their own keys." Both men may well have been right, but their perceptions were not those of an earlier generation of conservatives.[35]

Even the idea of a protective tariff took on new meanings, or lost old ones, during the course of the Middle Period. Its changing significance was epitomized in the changing meanings conservatives attached to the term and the concept of "free trade." We may best understand what was lost by contemplating Henry Clay's American System, which offered an essentially conservative vision of an organic national economy. The main outlines of Clay's system are well known (he proposed to levy a protective tariff in order to foster domestic industry, and to use revenues from the tariff to finance a network of internal improvements) but the rationale deserves explication. His scheme answered to specific economic interests of his constituents, and he was not above introducing demagogic or at least dubious arguments to support it—for example, the idea that imports "fill the coffers of government, and empty the pockets of the people." At the same time, his argument was usually direct and unambiguous: he praised manufacturing as a better use of the time of women and children than idleness, he criticized southern advocates of free trade for milking the rest of the nation for their own benefit, and he made much of the proposition that a protective tariff would serve specific interests that free trade left to their own devices. More generally, he demonstrated that his underlying assumptions were political rather than economic in any narrow sense by invoking national strength, national independence, national wealth, and the diffusion of wealth to support his cause.[36]

Consequently Clay expressed ambivalent attitudes toward democratic economic theory and economic values. He explicitly rejected the judgments of political economy, which he and his generation identified with British laissez-faire theory, as both irrelevant to the American situation and calculated to open the United States to British manufacturers without securing comparable freedom for American commodities. Free trade, he said, is an ideal economic policy that no country actually practices. Yet he also argued that protection creates a system of free trade within the nation, which has all the virtues that partisans attribute to it among nations. "It may be called a system of real reciprocity," he told the inhabitants of Cincinnati in 1830, "under the operation of which one citizen or one part of the country, can exchange one description of the produce of labor, with another citizen or another part of the country, for a different description of the produce of labor. It is a system which develops, improves, and perfects the capabilities of our common country, and enables us to avail ourselves of all the resources with which Providence has blest us." [37]

In Clay's thought, in other words, free trade connoted a broad range of social responsibilities and a government that actively served them; without sacrificing individual liberty, his scheme stood for liberty on a national scale. During the 1830s, however, domestic free trade came increasingly to signify domestic laissez faire in its most mechanical form. In 1830, for example, New Hampshire's congressional candidates issued a campaign tract that hailed the protective tariff as a means of creating a home market for farmers. Their argument was almost exclusively economic, for it predicted that increased competition would lower the prices of manufactured goods and it held that "if the people on the rich lands of New York, Pennsylvania, Maryland and Virginia, can 'make' wheat cheaper than those of Massachusetts and Rhode Island—and they, of the latter furnish the other with cotton goods cheaper than they can otherwise obtain them, common sense will teach both the value of mutual exchanges." Similarly, the Friends of Domestic Industry, meeting in New York in 1831, hailed "free trade between [New York and New Jersey] and among all the states of the Union" as "the mainspring of general welfare." Significantly, they also spoke well of political economy, and they attributed the evils that some sections of the country allegedly suffered from protection to the effects of free trade among the twenty-four states. It was clear from the context that they thought that such evils were not only irremediable but appropriate. Soon afterward Clay and his party began a long process of accommodation to Democratic dogmas that left only a tariff "for the protection of American industry" as a monument to his original system.[38]

Calvin Colton, Clay's devoted biographer and a dedicated proponent of both the tariff and the national bank, testified to the erosion of conservative principle in his *Junius Tracts*. So far as the tariff was concerned, he made heroic efforts to "prove" that it increased public consumption and raised the standard of living, but he also engaged in semantic acrobatics intended to prove that it really encouraged free trade. "Free trade means *fair* trade," he began a series of "tariff axioms," which culminated in "5. *Reciprocity* in tariffs is a principle of free trade—that is, the same *practically.*" More important, confronted by Democratic antagonism to a national bank, to regulation of the currency, to paper money, and to the factory system, he responded by invoking the laws of trade to prove that Democratic measures were dangerous, superfluous, or despotic intrusions on a sound economy. "Trade is *voluntary*, as between two parties," he argued in one of the tracts, "and cannot be *forced*. It is regulated by the scales, with gold or silver in them. The moment legislation or a despotism says, You shall take *my* currency *for so much*, if it will not bear the *common* test, it is not *trade*, but *force*." His policy remained one of active government—in this instance he was defending paper issue against hard-money zealots—but his expression militated against it.[39]

In short, even conservative theorists whose writings clearly demonstrated that they knew and appreciated the claims of society as an organic entity expressed themselves as convinced advocates of laissez faire. Undoubtedly their shift in position reflected the shift in political power as well as the necessities of practical politics; staunch advocates of a fostering state when men of their own kind controlled its political destiny, they had no recourse but atomism and private rights when their kind lost the power to direct the economy. But their change of position reflected a fundamental reorientation as well as a tactical shift in the categories of American politics. In their theory of society as in their theory of property, conservatives increasingly abdicated every responsibility save the responsibility to self. "Destined as [man] is for society," Francis Lieber wrote in *Essays on Property and Labour*,

he is still conscious that no one can be good or bad, healthy or sick, happy or unhappy, cold or warm, for another. He naturally flies from a state of things in which his individuality would be lost; a situation in whose forced or dull uniformity he would be only distinguished from others, as the prisoner is in a penitentiary—by a number; in which his own gifts, his own exertions, in short, all that may be called his peculiar individuality, could not distinctly imprint itself on his actions and their effects, and in which he should be deprived of his natural and invaluable right to call the product of his own exertions, his own property; to accumulate as he chooses; to exchange it for what he desires, and to dispose of it for the benefit of his individual family.[40]

The upshot was a theory of society that placed human rights in the balance against government and implied that government should have nothing to do with the economy. "It is the great law of liberty to allow things fairly to take their own course," Lieber explained, "and to protect where rights thus grown up demand it." The *Journal of Commerce* employed the same doctrine as a rebuke to French socialists in 1848: "In this country, liberty is understood to be the *absence* of government from private affairs: the social doctrine, on the contrary, demands its most minute interference." But Calvin Colton had already made it a general test of politics in 1840 when he wrote in *The Crisis of the Country* that the true doctrine of American democracy "is this: DON'T GOVERN US TOO MUCH. Another version of the same sentiment is —*Let the people alone.* They may make mistakes, but they will in the end come right of themselves, quicker than any government can set them right. Indeed, any attempts of Government to prevent the transient evils, which result from the action of our free institutions, will only abridge freedom, and aggravate public calamity. Ours is a popular, democratic government, and you cannot touch the primary springs of such institutions, to control them, without embarrassing the whole machinery. It won't do. It is the very destruction of our liberties." [41]

Leading conservative spokesmen even provided a standard by which to measure their abdication. In the same pamphlets in which Colton appealed to natural rights as a weapon against Democratic "despotism" he also reiterated with a kind of fatal schizophrenia that government was intended to take care of the people. "The maxim of Mr. Van Buren, 'Let the people take care of themselves, and the Government take care of themselves,' " he wrote, "is as destructive as it is fallacious. It is subverting the design of Government. . . . The appropriate function of Government is a parental care of the people and their interests; but this maxim destroys this relation entirely. No wonder at the result. If the Government would *let* the people take care of themselves, they would." More philosophically, the professorial author of "Civilization: American and European" in the *American Review* lamented the departure from

American life of both an organic view of society and the corollary willingness to defer to its best men. "We are in danger of forgetting that *society is a system*—a system where all the parts have their proper function and office—and not a mere mass of elements placed in juxtaposition or jostled into a general average." Indeed, American society very truly ran the risk he described, but conservatives as well as democrats were implicated in the fact. All that they left of society in any of its traditional forms was a right of accumulation it was the duty of government to protect.[42]

✣ VI ✣

ENTERPRISE

The struggle between "equal rights" and "aristocracy" occupied most of the Middle Period and helped to obscure the direction in which events were moving. Democrats and Whigs continued to fight much the same ideological battles during the 1840s that they had during the 1830s, or at least to invoke claims and counter-claims that echoed earlier confrontations over Bank and tariff, paper money and corporations. Even the fact that some Whigs consciously sought to accommodate their arguments to democratic dogmas did not obliterate the sense of distinction between the two parties, which remained to arouse loyal followers according to their needs, their prejudices, and their experience. The country as a whole became democratic, while many democrats remained Whigs.

At the same time, there was a process of accommodation going on underneath the surface of American politics that was more important in the long run than either the accumulation of Democratic victories or the residual differences between parties. It is best stated in terms of versions of "enterprise," an expansive economic orientation well in evidence by the 1840s, which involved a national predisposition to increase individual wealth by any acceptable means even if it also meant sacrificing some of the scruples of the past. The paths by which Americans arrived at enterprise, and the measures they took to be acceptable, were key facts in the intellectual history of the epoch.[a]

AN ECONOMY OF DEMOCRATS

One of the paths to enterprise was the cordiality Democrats displayed toward wealth. As the writings of Louis Hartz have shown, it is difficult to describe this phenomenon without at the same time suggesting that Machiavellian Whigs corrupted democratic principles, and indeed there were Democratic purists during the 1830s and 1840s who detected corruption in characteristic Whig appeals. But the economy of principle these purists upheld would have been vulnerable with or without Whig efforts to corrupt it, for democrats were deeply implicated in the quest for riches.

That quest was apparently born of a state of mind variously described by foreign travelers and native dissidents as materialism, individualism, or the passion for wealth. According to these unsympathetic critics, the American countenance was disfigured, the American digestion impaired, and American conversation destroyed by the ceaseless pursuit of money. Obviously this disposition of American democrats comported ill with the yeoman ethic elaborated by Thomas Jefferson and echoed by the advocates of a "natural" economy based on the production of "real" wealth. But it also had features that made it genuinely democratic, raising it above the level of a mere weakness for Whig apologists to exploit.[1]

For one thing, the Americans' pursuit of wealth was fairly clearly a pursuit rather than a possession. This point has often been made, but its full significance has seldom been understood. If the preeminent object of American economic activity was the acquisition of greater wealth, the wealth in view was not an object in its own right but an instrument of each man's growth, just as property was a vehicle of improvement rather than a vested possession. We may well judge that wealth is a poor measure of human achievement on any terms, but we must also conclude that it probably stood for less in American society than it did in European societies in which accumulation was often an end in itself; it was dynamic rather than static, a circumstance rather than a condition in life. A merchant of Boston pointed up the qualities of the American perspective on riches during the 1840s:

> When it is said, as it . . . often is, with scorn, that our conversation, in this country, relates too much to money matters, that we *talk* about dollars, &c., it is but fair to remember that, notwithstanding all that some of our own writers have thought proper to concede, money is regarded here as the *means* of progress, rather than the end in view. It is power in any part of the world; and where difference of rank is abolished, and the highest places are open to the competition of every one, it is *great* power, since it enables a man to raise those who depend on him to the enjoyments and advantages of which he may have felt the want. Probably there is no part of the world where the character of the miser is more uncommon than here; and I have often thought, in noticing the ways of foreigners who come here, that, if we *talk* more about dollars than they do, they *think* more of them than we do, by far.

Nor does the fact that the author was an American defending the American character nullify the force of his observation, for it was confirmed by foreign writers.[2]

In the second place, the American pursuit of wealth was nearly universal, not simply in the sense that white Americans of every condition enjoyed a legal opportunity to try their skill at accumulation, but also in the sense that the pursuit as well as the benefits were apparently widely diffused. If we think closely about foreign observers who commented on the phenomenon, we note that both friends and foes to the American experiment testified to this proposition, albeit from antithetical points of view. Traveling Englishmen whose sympathies lay with the established social patterns of their own country were quick to perceive as evils in the United States the habits that they apparently condoned among their own aristocracy, whereas dedicated critics of English society like William Cobbett found much to admire in the fact that the Americans were self-possessed, self-reliant, and bent on pursuing their own welfare. The difference between such observers was less over what the facts of American life were than how they should be interpreted. Even Mrs. Trollope objected more to the universality of American aspirations for wealth and the nakedness of the Americans' pursuit of it than to the consequences their motives might generate in American society. In effect, she suggested that what American society lacked because of its democracy was a veneer of civility that English society customarily provided even for its most energetic entrepreneurs.[3]

In short, foreign travelers portrayed an economy of maximum participation, and its very democracy gave them their greatest concern. As they pointed out with varying degrees of approval, the main thrust of democratic opinion lay more in the direction of progress understood as individual self-improvement than of ascent in a hierarchical social order, no matter how beneficent or how open to talent. (We shall deal more fully with the democratic idea of success later in this chapter.) Fredrika Bremer captured the Americans' egalitarian spirit when she wrote in 1850 that the typical citizen was "a young man (no matter if he be old) who makes his own way in the world in full reliance on his own power, stops at nothing, shrinks from nothing, finds nothing impossible, tries everything, has faith in everything, hopes everything, goes through everything, and comes out of everything—ever the same. If he fails, he immediately gets up again and says, 'No matter!' If he is unsuccessful, he says, 'Try again!' 'Go ahead!' and he begins over again, undertaking something else, and never stopping until he succeeds."[4]

She also caught the Americans' sense that their individual pursuits defined the national purpose. On one level, their view of their country's destiny was a psychic correlative of "equal rights," a conviction that the United States was great because every man could be self-made rather than manufactured. On another level, it corresponded to their sense of progress as an extrapolation from present felicities. "Wherever he comes on earth," she wrote of the typical American male, "in whatever circumstances, he is sustained by a two-fold consciousness which makes him strong and tranquil; that is to say, he is a man who can rely upon himself, the citizen of a great nation designed to be the greatest on the earth." If history had stopped with American freedom, freedom as the Americans practiced it promised to fulfill human hopes by allowing individual pursuits to bring maximum material returns to both individuals and society. "Look around you," Robert Rantoul Jr. told the Massachusetts legislature on the seventy-fifth anniversary of the Battle of Lexington; "measure the improvement of the condition of the individual denizens of all our towns and villages, and see if it tend not upward and onward in an accelerated ratio, equal, at least, to that of our political greatness." Rantoul, moreover, was a relatively old-fashioned Democrat. Lesser men of a more modern temperament would find few occasions for criticizing material acquisition when their leaders expressed such optimistic hopes.[5]

For that matter, democratic respect for property as an entity with which man had mixed his labor—the "Lockean" democratic tradition—faced in two directions. Sometimes it pointed to limitations on acquisition and forbade the use of paper credit; in this sense, democratic sentiment precluded an expansive economy. Lemuel D. Evans invoked a radical Locke for this purpose in the constitutional convention of Texas when he insisted upon invalidating the gigantic land grants made under the Mexican regime: "The great Locke laid it down that we could rightfully appropriate so much, and only so much as we might need for the plough, or to graze our flock, only so much as we can mix our labor with." At other times the idea that property laboriously acquired was in some sense an extension of the self also pointed toward encouraging universal acquisition as the hallmark of democracy, as Volney E. Howard suggested when he argued that security of property, including security for the beneficiaries of those land grants, was necessary to attract bona fide settlers (rather than speculators) who would "force back the savage and carry civilization into the useless and unproductive wilderness." Despite their differences, these antagonists agreed that the true object of government was to secure the enjoyment of property to those who would put it to use. [6]

Democratic doctrinaires pointed in the same general direction when they made property-in-use a criterion of public policy as against vested rights and property-in-possession. Conservatives were sure that the Democrats intended to despoil them and they protested prospective encroachments on corporate charters as if they were incursions on private rights, but Democratic reforms were intended only to liberate the present generation—not to divest property of its rights, but to make sure that rights established in the past did not interfere with equal access to them in the present, or with the universal diffusion of prosperity that all men could expect to enjoy in a free society. The *Democratic Review* voiced both aspirations in 1838 when it deprecated the fears a Phi Beta Kappa orator had recently expressed. "Our young national Hercules," it declared scornfully, "is to be diverted from his giant sports of subduing the wilderness, founding empires, appropriating a continent, and spreading the triumph of civilization and christianity over every shore, to the more seductive occupation of breaking open the strong-boxes of a few importers of English goods, and manufacturers of cotton!" [7]

In other words, democratic reform clearly made room for exploitation, and even radical Democrats were surprisingly devoted to capitalistic virtues. Isaac T. Preston, whose political sentiments were if anything Jeffersonian, adverted to the heady mixture of Locke, rights, and progress that many democrats imbibed when he told the constitutional convention of Louisiana that it had every reason to encourage immigration from other states. "The hands that nature has given us, and the talents with which she has endowed us, is [sic] capital, and most productive, and constitutes a most valuable accession to the State. For there are vast fields still vacant for all hands that choose to be employed within our State." In these terms, the hinterland of New Orleans invited settlement on the premises of equal rights, and Preston went on to underline the opportunities for manufacturing and commerce as well as agriculture that the free influx of labor would enhance. The capitalism he had in view was insistently democratic, but it was capitalism none the less. If material welfare could be increased without infringing on democratic principles, the most vigorous advocate of those principles would have no reason to quarrel with the gains that exploitation might bring.[8]

Meanwhile other Democrats had taken up the cause of territorial expansion, which corresponded on the international level with the kind of exploitation they preached in the states. Time and again, Democratic proponents of acquiring California, including those who opposed war with Mexico as well as those who supported it, pressed American claims to the region on predominantly Lockean grounds. "Public sentiment with us repudiates possession without use," John L. O'Sullivan wrote in the *New York Morning News* before he had become an advocate of outright imperialism, "and this sentiment is gradually acquiring the force of established public law." Similarly, in describing the annexation of California as an inevitable fact, he observed in the *Democratic Review* that "a population will soon be in actual occupation of California, over which it will be idle for Mexico to dream of dominion. . . . And they will have a right to independence—to self-government—to the possession of the homes conquered from the wilderness by their own labors and dangers, sufferings and sacrifices—a better and a truer right than the artificial title of sovereignty in Mexico a thousand miles distant, inheriting from Spain a title good only against those who have none better." The Americans were destined to occupy the continent because they alone knew how to make use of it.[9]

If the initial premises of Democratic thought were agricultural and restrictive, in short, Democrats who subscribed to them also demonstrated in a number of ways that their impulses were more expansive than the vocabulary in which they expressed them. True, Jacksonian Democrats of the old school, for example most of the men discussed by Marvin Meyers, may well have represented a vision of American society that stood at odds with American practice. By the same token, it is probably significant that Theodore Sedgwick Jr. and the *New York Evening Post* bitterly opposed expansion, whereas O'Sullivan and the *Democratic Review* supported it. But Rantoul and Sedgwick also demonstrated that even Old Republicans could lend themselves to expansive democratic hopes, Sedgwick as an advocate of imperialism by osmosis, Rantoul as an advocate of universal progress who was active in promoting the Illinois Central Railroad. (The theory that Jacksonian Democracy represented a retrogressive faith simply does not account for Rantoul's activities, save as private investments at odds with his principles.) Meanwhile other Democratic partisans like Stephen A. Douglas and the sponsors of "Progressive Democracy" left no doubt of the value they placed upon democracy understood as liberated capitalism, and yet they betrayed no sense that they had departed from the democratic tradition. As they saw matters, their quarrel was with "old fogies" who had forgotten the promise of democracy, not those who maintained its principles. They may have been wiser than we.[10]

THE LOGIC OF FREEDOM

Democracy understood as universal participation in the opportunities the United States held out to all men clearly worked to modify Old Republican theory. At the same time, Democratic doctrinaires of the most impeccable sort helped to produce the same result by the zeal with which they elaborated the principles of equal rights. Far from remaining the instrument of an "Arcadian" past, but equally far from anticipating the "entrepreneurial" future into which they were moving, the theory these enthusiasts articulated furthered the development of a characteristic American economy by its indifference to both loyalties.[11]

This tendency of Democratic doctrine was most clearly expressed by William Leggett in the *Evening Post*. Convinced that selective incorporation was an evil, but unwilling to impose even an Arcadian social ideal on the free economy, he became an advocate of "free banking"—of incorporation according to general rules that permitted any group of individuals who observed standardized legal requirements to qualify as a banking corporation. As he and like-minded Democrats saw matters, banks established according to general laws would have two distinct virtues. For one thing, they would solve the problem of privilege by universalizing it; everyone would have equal access to the business. For another, they would solve the problems of the economy: free competition in banking and the free action of economic laws would cope more effectively with evils like excessive note-issue and injudicious extension of credit than any government could. (Significantly, it was conservative Democrats and Whigs, among them Daniel D. Barnard, who were primarily responsible for the regulatory provisions of New York's Free Banking Act of 1838.) In short, free banking would defeat "aristocracy" and initiate the economy of nature, and therefore it was an innovation that Democrats should support.[12]

Leggett's influence notwithstanding, New York's banking statute was a Whig measure, and for this reason an event that might have taught a shrewder democrat caution. Similarly, when free banking was proposed in the states of the Old Northwest, it was generally supported by Whigs and opposed by loyal Democrats, who succeeded in putting it off for at least a decade. Hence the important point about Leggett's crusade was not its representative so much as its predictive character: an outspoken theorist of democracy understood as equal rights insisted that democratic principles required competitive incorporation of bankers under a minimum of legal restraint. So long as democratic prejudices prevailed, free banking would be postponed; but the triumph of democratic theory would mean the triumph of the corporation.[13]

Furthermore, the man in the street was quicker to see the merits of transportation and manufacturing corporations than those of banks, which offended against a wider range of prejudices. Hence general incorporation laws were widely adopted by the time of the Civil War, although not without opposition from Democrats and not to the exclusion of selective incorporation. (Solicitous of the development of their economies, if not corrupted by the agents of prospective corporations, state legislatures continued to bestow corporate privileges by special charter in spite of the odium that attached to these acts.) Again, the direction and tendency of Democratic innovations were at least as important as legislative practice. Democrats often pressed for general incorporation; they pressed for it as a reform; and they pressed for it on the theory that the way to combat inequality was to prevent state legislatures from exercising their discretion in dealing with the economy. Significantly, even labor agitators, who had most to fear in the long run from liberated capitalism, protested more strenuously at the legal privileges corporations enjoyed than at the working conditions they provided. Workingmen's complaints of the New England textile mills focused on privilege and social prejudice, leaving agitation for health and safety to maverick members of the region's establishment.[14]

Democratic fatalism and Democratic atomism led in the same general direction. We have already noted that the economy of principle required democrats to acquiesce in social class if its origins could not be faulted. This tendency of Democratic doctrine was only symptomatic of a broader kind of acquiescence: in preferring "nature" to society and "rights" to obligations, Democratic theorists minimized the possibility that they would see—much less deal with—phenomena that made men unhappy. On the one hand, when they were consistent with their economic doctrine they could not conceive of interfering with the results of a social process that met their initial premises concerning rights. On the other hand, even their perceptions were likely to be shaped by their premises. Given equal opportunity and open competition, their best theorists contended, the evils that befell men would represent their just deserts. Hence there was no criterion by which to interfere in the economy, not to speak of a moral obligation not to do so, even if the results were intolerable. If evils appeared that could not be ignored, they could always be dealt with by charges that they arose from infringements on equal rights.[15]

Nevertheless, it was still rights that Democratic spokesmen dealt with, and this fact was as important as their fatalism. Their ethic centered upon the right to compete for economic rewards in a society from which adventitious distinctions had been banished, and (whether or not they advocated free banking and incorporation) their reforms were intended to magnify individual freedom. The result was that Democratic theorists pressed the claims of the autonomous individual at the same moment in which they diminished the claims of society on democrats' attention. In the ideal society they depicted, the logical corollary of the evils that befell vicious men was the benefits that came to their virtuous competitors, and society had no right to forestall the one any more than it had a right to prevent the other. Indeed, if "aristocracy" was intrinsically bad because it involved offenses against equal rights, the self-made man was intrinsically good simply because he had made his own way in the world. Hence the just society must treat his acquisitions and his economic advantages as if they were absolutes, claims that were not merely conventional but virtually transcendental, anchored in a moral universe in which material rewards were always objective representations of moral facts. On this basis, every man had an all but unlimited right to exercise his right to property as he saw fit.[b]

But this was what conservatives had also come to maintain, and in fact the two major strains of American social thought coalesced at this point. Starting from different premises, following different paths of development, the doctrines of equal rights and those of property rights resulted in a common definition of freedom.

One element in this shift of conservative attitudes was the substitution of rights without obligations for rights bearing obligations, which (as we have noted) was stimulated by democratic attacks on "aristocracy" and reinforced by conservative fears for property. In spite of the initial distance between them, democratic prejudices and conservative reactions to them actually came to the same end. Buffeted by democratic attacks, attempting to preserve their freedom of action, conservatives gradually abandoned an organic vision of society and adopted an atomistic one in its stead. As we have seen in chapter V, this meant that in a strict sense they were no longer conservatives; but they had found a definition of liberty that would give them a greater rather than a diminished freedom to do what they would with their "own."

In addition, conservatives adopted an expansive attitude toward property that brought them closer than they realized to fulfilling democratic demands that property be put to use. Initially, their conception of property had been static; however boldly wealthy merchants had speculated in public lands, however ingenious some of them may have been in developing trade with Africa or the Orient, they had conceived of the wealth they acquired and the assets they invested as property-in-possession rather than property-in-use, and their defense of their "rights" in the courts had reflected this predilection. Now, however, they began to justify property by its functions in such a fashion as to translate "property" into "wealth" and "wealth" into "capital"; property was not a possession that included obligations so much as a right that produced results.[16]

The eagerness with which avowed conservatives appealed to a Lockean definition of property testified to this shift in meaning. As the exchange in the Texas convention suggests, the Locke who justified property as a product of personal effort was potentially threatening to mere rights of possession but offered an extraordinary degree of support to the active pursuit of wealth. A writer in the *American Whig Review* clearly incorporated this essentially democratic Locke into the conservative justification of property when he wrote in 1846 that

the well we dig, the hut we rear, the clearing we make in the wilderness, the seed which we sow in hope, trusting to the Lord of the harvest for an abundant increase; whatever thing of necessity or luxury we produce, to supply the wants of our physical, or gladden the love of beauty in our moral and intellectual, natures, become [sic] ours, by virtue of the labor which we have bestowed on them.

In obedience to this great law, the ruder productions and implements of art are formed, and with advancing accumulations of property, spring up in all the paths of social life, poetry, painting, sculpture, the higher orders of architecture, and the refinements of civilization.[17]

Obviously their vision was dynamic; the Locke they invoked stood for an expansive economy. This was true in a literal as well as a figurative sense: Whigs as well as Democrats invoked Lockean categories even to sanction American imperialism. In 1846, before the Mexican War had broken out and caused the Whig party to denounce further territorial acquisitions, the *American Review* elaborated American claims to California as a vehicle for exploitation:

No one who cherishes a faith in the wisdom of an overruling Providence, and who sees, in the national movements which convulse the world, the silent operation of an invisible but omnipotent hand, can believe it to be for the interest of humanity, for the well-being of the world, that this vast and magnificent region should continue forever in its present state. Capable of sustaining millions of people, of conferring upon them all the physical comforts of life, and of raising them to the highest point of mental and moral cultivation, if only they have the energy and the ability to use its resources—so long as desolation broods upon it, so long as the shadows of ignorance, indolence and moral degradation hang around it, the manifest designs of Providence are unfulfilled, and the paramount interests of the world lack due advancement.

Even more strikingly, Francis Lieber vindicated American claims to Texas by observing that "if a whole district of land is not used by a nation directly or indirectly, and if the nation has not been able to protect it as its own for a long time, it seems that the essential characteristics of property are really lost, and disimpropriation has taken place. The earth was given to mankind for use; and if it be left wholly unused, it fails to obtain its object." Hence this archconservative defender of the rights of property concluded his essay by saying, "It seems that no mere declaration, 'This belongs to us,' can become a bar against the very destiny of so genial a soil." [18]

Even the vested rights that conservatives sought to defend in the courts gradually took on expansive rather than restrictive connotations. Their initial impulse, expressed by such former Federalists as Webster and Kent and seconded by such former Republicans as Joseph Story, was to protect rights already acquired against rights claimed in the present; hence their appeal to the contract clause of the Constitution. But their more important accomplishment was to create a legal environment that vested current rights in such a fashion that men could count upon pursuing economic opportunities without fear that they might later be curtailed. (The contract clause established that past rights might not be curtailed by present needs; its elaborations guaranteed the right to exploit the continent in the future.) Here was the ultimate significance of the rights the courts accorded corporations—not their exemption from retroactive legislation, important as that may have been to their prosperity, but assurance that even if their charters provided for legislative amendment after the fact, neither courts nor legislatures would infringe on their prerogatives.[c]

This development was far from complete by the end of the Middle Period, but it was at work in the constitutional conventions of the 1840s, where men who would once have been unmistakably conservative worked to surround corporate privileges with all the attributes of private property. In Illinois, for example, a proposal that "the general assembly shall have no power to pass any law, whereby any person shall be deprived of life, liberty, property or franchises, without trial, judgment, or decree in some usual and regular judicial tribunal" failed of adoption by only a single vote, while in Michigan the chief justice of the state's supreme court defended the legal rights of corporations against their democratic critics as if they were identical with those of flesh-and-blood men. "I am utterly incapable of comprehending the force of the argument, founded on the idea that we are dealing with co[r]porations," Charles W. Whipple declared. "This fact cannot influence the judgment of the Convention, unless, indeed, it be contended that the rights secured to our citizens by the Constitution, in their natural capacities, are lost, when the same rights are secured to them by a corporate name. . . . Over all lawful contracts the Constitution extends its protection; it interposes a barrier against State aggression, securing to the humblest citizen an easy victory, though engaged in a struggle with a sovereign power." In the eyes of these latter-day conservatives, the object of a just social policy was to guarantee to individuals and corporations alike an untrammeled right to the pursuit of wealth in an expansive competitive economy.[19]

Given the principle of general incorporation, that is, Democrats and Whigs had relatively little to contend about on any fundamental level of social theory—and Whig leaders less so than nonparty conservatives, because a Whig leader was almost by definition a man who had been forced to abandon conservative premises in his eagerness to cater to democratic opinion. Indeed, except for their bitter disagreements on specific issues of public policy like banks and tariffs, Whigs and Democrats often had common roots that facilitated accommodation between them: traditional Democratic attitudes toward the rights of property and toward social hierarchy were not always distinct from traditional conservative views, as the writings of Theodore Sedgwick Sr. and James Fenimore Cooper attest.[d] But differences had initially existed between the parties, and—more important—they had been bitterly felt, whereas they had largely disappeared by 1850. By then there was far more consensus than the echoes of earlier confrontations revealed.

At the same time, the basis of accommodation was new to both parties. Although the Democrats generally had their way, they had conceded if not actually embraced the exploitative competitive economy, including in many instances innovations like banks and corporations that could be expected to transform American society. Similarly, conservatives had not abandoned their devotion to property, but they had diminished their fears and now tacitly accepted the Democratic insistence that the right of exploitation be made universal. The two parties had never been wholly distinct, but this was not the important point about them. It was, rather, that they had abandoned even the theoretical differences between themselves by uniting—however accidentally, however belatedly—on virtually the same definition of the good society. The very possibility of alternative perceptions and of alternative criteria of the good life had all but disappeared, and nearly everyone took the same step forward into the future.[e]

THE CONSERVATIVE IDEA OF SUCCESS

American ideas of success both exemplified and encouraged this consensus. Originating for the most part in conservative social theory, shifting ground in the face of democratic pressures, the commitment to success became a powerful idea in its own right, reshaping both conservative and democratic thought.

Conservative attitudes toward success were rooted in orthodox moral criticisms of social change. During the 1830s and 1840s, spokesmen for traditional social values attacked American materialism, deplored the passion for wealth, and regretted the deterioration of American character in much the same vocabulary as unsympathetic foreign observers. "We want, as a people, a rounder character," the *American Review* declared in its first number. "Our humanity is pinched; our tastes are not generous. The domestic and social virtues languish." [20] These spokesmen did so, moreover, in the light of a traditional conservative presupposition that the democracy could not be trusted. In their eyes, the passion for gain controverted every principle of righteousness—not only security of property and stability of the social order, which were threatened by "agrarianism," but the religious and moral foundations on which a free society rested. Hence professional moralists flooded the market with didactic handbooks and lectures intended to reinforce ethical principles in a country that seemed well on the way to ruin. Their expressions of concern may have been wholly genuine or they may have been exaggerated; in either case they demanded that Americans live up to a thoroughly traditional moral code.[21]

Three aspects of these handbooks were especially important both in the eyes of their authors and in their implications for the future. One was the stress they put upon the development of individual character. So far as is evident from their admonitions, the object of life was character rather than riches, and the books were filled with specific injunctions as to how to improve one's self by cultivating industry, frugality, and integrity, not to mention avoiding alcohol, tobacco, and sexual vice. (Discussions of the vices tended to be lurid without being explicit.) Significantly, many of the moralists also made a great point of encouraging their readers to cultivate their minds as well as their morals; it was typical of these advocates of character that they should seek to involve aspiring young men in a life-long process of self-improvement that had little to do with their material accomplishments. Even Freeman Hunt, the editor of the *Merchants' Magazine*, offered his readers biographies of eminent men intended primarily to show them how to leave "a fair and untarnished name to posterity" and only very incidentally how to succeed.[22]

Second, it was clear that the obligations the moralists enforced were fundamentally religious duties. William A. Alcott and John Frost, two leading practitioners in the genre, were teachers who had become professional writers, but other authors of young men's guides and similar volumes were often either practicing or former ministers. For that matter, the American clergy had long since made personal conduct rather than theological principle the main burden of their discourses, and the specific standard of conduct the moralists enjoined was virtually identical with the standard that Protestant authors had begun to hold up on both sides of the Atlantic well before the American Revolution. Certainly prominent ministers who preached against the dangers of wealth during the Middle Period might well have been writing handbooks instead, so similar were their injunctions.[23]

Third, the authors of the handbooks obviously took for granted a distinctly stratified society. Several of them went so far as to advise their readers not to aspire beyond their powers or their experience. In *The Young Mechanic* (1843), John Frost explicitly urged mechanics not to be diverted from their calling by vanity or an injudicious zeal for success or distinction, while other authors warned young men engaged in various pursuits that they must not expect to get rich quickly or even to acquire more than a competence.[24] Moreover, even when they dwelt on opportunities for rising in the world, they typically maintained that character was more important than success, or that success should be defined by victory of character rather than the ascent it made possible. Samuel G. Goodrich expressed both points of view in *Lives of Benefactors* (1844), in which he recorded the achievements of eminent men whose character had enabled them to rise to the point of serving mankind. In the traditional conservative view, social welfare depended far less on social mobility than on living up to the demands of one's calling.[25]

Nevertheless, even Goodrich made some obeisances to mobility, and conservative moralists generally praised it as an American advantage although they cautioned against the dangers it brought. (Their object in training character was not to discredit either wealth or eminence, but to make sure that both were respectably achieved and socially beneficial.) Moreover, whereas old-fashioned secularists like Chancellor Kent and Joseph Story tended to describe upward mobility as a social fact assured by the laws against entail and reinforced by the wheel of fortune, some of the moralists put far greater emphasis on the personal achievements that were within reach as a result of equal rights. Significantly, Goodrich praised Benjamin Franklin as a public benefactor on the grounds that "he has contributed more than any other individual in modern times, to teach the working classes to feel their power, and to assert their rights. He has taught them, as well by precept as example, the certain steps by which they can ascend in the scale of society; and hundreds of thousands have been thus led from stations of poverty and ignorance, to the most elevated positions in society." Similarly, Lyman Cobb's *New Sequel to the Juvenile Readers* (1843) instructed the youth of the country that "the genius of our institutions reduces all men to a natural level, where the highest offices and the most dignified stations are legitimate objects for the pursuit of all who choose to compete for them," while Nathan S. S. Beman told the Young Men's Association of Troy, "A man, among us, may choose his own position, if he will submit to the necessary toil. He may pave his own way, and then walk in it. The plough-boy, of to-day, may, in thirty years, be the President of the United States." On this view, social equality was a starting point for attaining honorable distinction.[26]

In addition, the definition of distinction the moralists employed slowly shifted from public to private undertakings and from political or professional to economic pursuits. The traditional view was exemplified by Goodrich's *Lives of Benefactors;* as he said, his book was concerned with benefactors rather than "mere warriors, wits, geniuses, statesmen and millionaires." In addition, traditional writers who stressed upward mobility rather than benefaction typically had in view ascent in the public service. Beman was one example; so was John Todd, who illustrated the advantages of American institutions by pointing out in 1844 that "there is but a single step from the log cabin to the highest office within the gift of a great and free nation; and the orphan child picked up by the Overseers of the poor, may, as I have myself witnessed, rise to great distinction and occupy the most important civil or ecclesiastical stations." Fame rather than fortune, public recognition rather than private wealth, was central to traditional accolades to success.[27]

By contrast, a number of moralists began during the 1840s either to blur the distinction between public and private pursuits or to use private pursuits as examples of success. Richard Abbott has found these crosscurrents of opinion in the agricultural press of the Middle Period, which was devoted to raising the hopes and improving the prestige of farmers without causing them to become disaffected. Similarly, Freeman Hunt's *Merchants' Magazine* hovered between the two alternatives. In the early

years it ran biographies of public men as well as merchants, and it conceived of its merchants as public men, but in later years it tended to
focus on private business and on the individual pursuit of success in a
predominantly economic environment. By 1852, indeed, Timothy Shay
Arthur could write that "American biography has confined itself too
closely to men who have won political or literary distinction." The attitudes of the reading public may have been partly responsible for such a
shift in emphasis, but the effect was the same as if it had been generated
by the moralists themselves. They appealed with ever greater frequency
to images of economic success to reinforce their moral lessons.[28]

So did a number of commentators who depicted purely economic men
as public servants. An apologist for merchants, Hunt had always sought
to portray them in this light, but he was soon outdistanced by writers
who argued that men who pursue their own interests according to a just
scheme of morals will automatically benefit society. Arthur said as much
in 1848, but William A. Alcott had pointed the way in 1834 when he
declared in his *Young Man's Guide*, "There is a class of men who are of
inestimable value to society—and the more so from their scarcity;—I
mean *men of business*." Even William Howard Van Doren, a Dutch Reformed minister whose *Mercantile Morals* (1852) was a series of unusually
strict warnings against the dangers young men confronted, suggested in
his preface that the United States would reach unprecedented heights of
civilization if its mercantile life were guided by religion and morality.
Apparently conservative moralists had fully embraced business, provided that it honored traditional virtues.[29]

Certainly these writers were willing to use the ambiguous concept of
"fortune" to reinforce their moral admonitions. In traditional religious
usage, the fortune men sought was the inestimable blessing of salvation,
and by derivation their fortune lay in the character they acquired. Hence
moralists could plausibly urge their readers to seek a "fortune" that was
no more than a title to self-respect. Yet they did not often exclude the
possibility that great wealth would follow from the acquisition of character, and sometimes they even intimated that it would. Alcott explained
that "there is hardly an employment in life so trifling that it will not afford a subsistence, if constantly and faithfully followed. Indeed, it is by
indefatigable diligence alone, that a fortune can be acquired in any business whatever." In the same vein, the Reverend Daniel Wise, an old-

fashioned moralist in most respects, clearly tied rising in the world to both character and religion. "To be successful in life, to rise above the common herd of mankind," he wrote in his *Young Man's Counsellor* (1850), "a young man requires certain elements of character;—all of which are attainable through the power of religion, and many of which most young men never will attain without that power." He may have meant no more than rising from poverty to competence, but he did not say so, while he obviously held that religion was an economic asset.[30]

Furthermore, the very doctrines the moralists appealed to in order to curb the appetite for mere wealth worked instead to legitimize it. For one thing, their assurance that there was a secure moral universe in which good men were rewarded and bad men were punished helped to undermine their own teachings. Two centuries earlier, when social hierarchy had not been effectively called into question and human concerns still centered on the life after death, their moral scheme would not have affected their purposes; they could have preached the rewards of virtue without looking for them in this world or appealing to images of success understood as rising above one's starting-point, and in fact this was still their initial impulse during the 1830s. By 1840 or 1850, however, they were hard pressed to vindicate their arguments on this otherworldly basis even if they wanted to, and the evidence suggests that they did not want to. Without quite knowing what they were doing, they completed a transformation that had been going on in Calvinist Protestantism for perhaps two hundred years, bringing their religious ethic to a focus in the ethic of material success.[f]

Even if we do not accept the view that Calvinism was primarily responsible for modern capitalism we can see how the doctrines these nineteenth-century moralists employed fed into a cult of success. The more they stressed the young man's ability and obligation to discipline his character, the more they suggested that he could be what he willed to be, a suggestion that transformed their idea of character without depriving it of religious urgency. The Reverend Jasper Adams, New England-born president of the College of Charleston (South Carolina), demonstrated as much in an otherwise traditional lecture on *Laws of Success and Failure in Life* (1833). Citing the lives of eminent public benefactors as examples, he pointed out that "when we observe the series of struggles which they endured amidst poverty, obscurity, and neglect, their disciplined passions, their love of knowledge, their firmness of purpose, and their unconquerable zeal, we perceive that their success has followed in the train of their exertions by the ordinary law of cause and effect." John Frost enforced a comparable lesson in his *Self-Made Men of America* (1848). So did Louisa Tuthill in *Success in Life: The Lawyer* (1850), while John Todd was obsessed with both the obligations and the potentialities of "self-government" in *The Young Man* (1844), and William A. Alcott told his readers, *"You may be whatever you will resolve to be."* The moral universe these writers inhabited was more than merely secure; it actually beckoned men to success, however success might be defined, and the definition was clearly shifting.[31]

Discipline of the will also enabled men to overcome immense handicaps. The moralists portrayed not simply ordinary achievements geared to ordinary efforts, but extraordinary achievements tied to extraordinary efforts, and the calling one originally pursued as best one could in one's initial station in life became instead a commitment to pursue excellence wherever it might lead. Daniel Wise said as much in describing famous English and American lawyers who had achieved great public recognition despite their lowly origins: "Their history shows that the most stupendous difficulties may be defied and conquered by steadily and perseveringly cultivating the mind; and thus fitting it beforehand for the openings of Divine Providence." Similarly, in his discourse at Troy, Nathan Beman held that "our nobility, if we have any, is that of nature. God made it, and not man, and it is not as easily tainted by contact with humanity, as the artificial and spurious! It belongs to the 'inner man,' and is not the creature of human law, statute or common. . . . The mind within—the immortal [mind] of man—is permi[t]ted to expand itself, and throw off the crushing disabilities which may weigh it down, and make and occupy its own level, as graduated by intelligence and attainment, by activity and worth." [32]

Men could be what they willed to be, and an extraordinary man could look forward to extraordinary rewards; this was an essentially religious doctrine that had large implications for secular success. Not only did it argue that great fortune lay within the willing man's grasp; it also suggested that his secular future was in some sense an evidence of his religious estate, and it invited him to affirm his standing in the moral universe by pursuing his secular estate as far as he could. The parallel did not have to be exact for worldly success to take on this religious connotation, for the very fact that discipline of the self was so central to American Protestantism and seemed to be so indispensable in the secular world must have created a predisposition toward assuming the connection even when it was not explicit. Beman, who had been a prominent New School clergyman, demonstrated as much. His language was predominantly secular and the God he invoked was the God of nature, yet the "mind" he portrayed threw off "crushing disabilities" and made its way to its destination by "activity and worth." It does not require much ingenuity to see in these phrases secular equivalents of the soul throwing off the burdens of sin and gaining salvation by being faithful to the promise of works conducted in the light of saving grace.[g]

Certainly many of the moralists kept to basic patterns of Protestant exhortation while praising secular patterns of virtue. Significantly, Alcott warned young men against making use of credit, not for prudential reasons but because credit undermines character. (Apparently it was a sort of secular version of Roman Catholic indulgences.) Praising all the traditional bourgeois virtues, Alcott also urged young men to imitate the example of such secular heroes as Alexander the Great and Julius Caesar, Charles XII and Napoleon Bonaparte, who had risen to extraordinary positions on the strength of their powers of character. His anomalous juxtaposition of industry and frugality with heroic virtues, which also appeared in other writers, can make sense only on the supposition that discipline of the will rather than a practical estimate of what was possible for his readers occupied the center of his mind. Had Alcott been truly a secular writer, he could not have used such examples to illustrate bourgeois virtues; but as a covert and indeed only partly conscious exponent of American Calvinism he literally could not sense the distinction.[33]

So far had the transformation of theological premises advanced by 1850 that the elderly Louisa Tuthill, whose exhortations were for the most part highly traditional, told prospective merchants, "Pleasure is in the race, not at the goal alone. Success is the reward of exertion, yet we play the game of life (serious play!) as we do the game of chess—for conquest; the pleasure is in the contest, the strife, by which the victory is obtained." On a superficial view, her remark would seem to have broken the last surviving connection between religious objectives and secular enjoyments, yet the passage as a whole stressed the rewards of virtue as well as celebrated the pleasures of industry. Hence the remark must have been either a logical aberration or a logical corollary of her moral scheme, and the latter alternative seems much more likely.[34]

Meanwhile clearly secular writers built upon the themes of character, obligation, and calling in much the same fashion as these quasi-religious writers; if the moralists did not directly influence secular thought, they would seem at the very least to have identified its major categories. In 1832 an anonymous editor launched the *Girard Journal of Wealth* in Philadelphia, apparently by way of redeeming the late financier's reputation from the opprobrium of his having been a miser. Significantly, he hailed Girard's prudence in launching commercial ventures, but he also managed to represent prudence as a synonym for the will: "It was not one of the attributes of Stephen Girard to attempt what he could not perform; or to be dispirited by slight obstacles, from the accomplishment of his designs. *Industrious and persevering*, he never remitted his exertions, until he had vanquished and surmounted all intervening obstacles." Similarly, citing the precedent of Demosthenes, B. W. Huntington told the Philomathic Society of the University of Alabama in 1845 that virtually everyone had the capacity to rise in the world if he had the will to undertake the discipline it involved, while in *The American Biographical Sketch Book* (1849) William Hunt labored the personal force and stern endeavor that had enabled humble beginners to reach positions of great eminence.[35]

The effect of religious and secular strains of thought working together was to remake the idea of the self-made man. In democratic eyes, he was someone who had made his own way in the sense of not depending on "aristocratic" favors but prospering by means of "real" rather than "artificial" economic practices; in effect, he had adhered to the calling of the farmer, and his wealth had come to him in the form of a competence he had earned by the labor of his hands.[h] In the new vocabulary of success, however, self-making connoted finding the likeliest vehicle for personal distinction rather than fulfilling the promise of a given calling, and it depended far more upon personal force understood as power of the will than upon force understood as power in the hands. It was still democratic, in the sense that it rested upon equal rights and called upon individual energies. It even connoted a degree of alienation from the establishment, in that some of its proponents suggested for the first time in

conservative discourse that success might have little to do with education.[36] But democracy was only a condition for such success rather than
its criterion. In effect, the moralists held that democracy was necessary
to make individual achievement more significant.

Hence their developed position coincided almost exactly with the
needs of Whig doctrine. Calvin Colton typically recognized as much in
the seventh *Junius Tract*, where he articulated a theory of the self-made
man that has since become famous as an epitome of American conservative doctrine. On the one hand he appealed to sociology: "Ours is a
country, where men start from an humble origin, and from small
beginnings rise gradually in the world, as the reward of merit and industry, and where they can attain to the most elevated positions, or acquire
a large amount of wealth, according to the pursuits they elect for themselves. No exclusive privileges of birth, no entailment of estates, no civil
or political disqualifications, stand in their path; but one has as good a
chance as another, according to his talents, prudence, and personal exertions. This is a country of *self-made men*, than which nothing better could
be said of any state of society." On the other hand he invoked residual
religious ideals when he acclaimed the American laborer as prospective
capitalist on the grounds that "he who can stand up, in the bloom and
vigor of ripening manhood, pure in heart, and determined to prosper,
though he has not a penny in the world, may look abroad, and behold a
large estate within his reach. Within his own skin, and deep down in his
own soul, lies the capital, the productive power, with which he is to
trade. All wealth lies in abeyance to these physical and moral energies,
and comes into hand at their summons." [37] The developed theory of the
self-made man provided both a social and a moral justification for extraordinary inequalities.[i]

THE DEMOCRATIC IDEA OF SUCCESS

In conservative minds, the idea of success retained many of its hierarchical characteristics even after conservative writers had redefined it to
include the ceaseless striving after wealth that many of them had begun
by deploring. Meanwhile spokesmen for democracy—partisan Democrats and their nonpartisan allies—expressed attitudes toward success
that left them vulnerable to Whig innovations.

We have already noted two main elements in democratic thought that modified democratic principles. One was the simple appetite for wealth that offended foreign observers and native conservatives. The other was Democratic fatalism, which taught men to acquiesce in events that a different perspective or a different social theory might have led them to reject. In addition, the self-made man was initially a democratic ideal, at least in the sense that the term necessarily connoted democratic values like equal rights and productive labor before it acquired the more venturesome meanings that writers like Colton attached to it. Hence many democrats were probably readier than they may have realized to fall in with the conservative theory of success.

They could also draw upon a time-honored republican tradition of social mobility, which largely antedated conservative images of self-making. In its pure form, Republican social theory took social hierarchy for granted, but it also insisted that the wealthy should not have exclusive privileges and it pressed them to provide opportunities for virtue. Thomas Jefferson's plan for a state-wide system of education leading from common schools (which everyone was to attend gratis or nearly so) through academies and the University of Virginia (which were to train the ablest graduates of the lesser schools at public expense) epitomized this aspect of republicanism in its most liberal form. As Jefferson explained to John Adams, he sought to find and elevate a natural aristocracy—as much for the benefit of state and society (he did not need to say) as out of any wish to reward meritorious individuals. His view was neither paternalistic nor sentimental but egalitarian, except that his definition of equality was clearly competitive and also clearly elitist. The interests of society and the rights of man coincided in the idea of careers truly opened to talents.[38]

Nathaniel P. Tallmadge, the conservative New York Democrat, appealed to this traditional republican ideal when he defended Martin Van Buren against John C. Calhoun in 1832 on the ground that he was a self-made man. "He is the artificer of his own fortunes," Tallmadge told the Republican legislative caucus; "and often, in the course of his political career, has he been reproached with the humility of his birth. The pride of wealth and of family distinction has sneered at his advancement, and has attempted to frown into retirement the man, whose native energies rose superior to its own exertions." At the same time, Tallmadge also appealed to classic images of success—social rather than atomistic, focused in mobility rather than equality, sentimental rather than philosophical, and demagogic rather than democratic—that would seem to have appealed to much the same motives as the Whig image of Henry Clay. His argument clearly suggested that conservative Democrats were capable of moving from a republican to a Whiggish theory of success without any sense that they were incompatible.[39]

In addition, philosophical Democrats of the Jacksonian era articulated an idea of success that was a corollary of their fatalistic atomism. We have already noted that such Democrats were quick to acquiesce in social hierarchy when it rested upon equal rights; they also embraced success in the same terms. "Let men of talent, enterprise and genius, rest content with the advantages these qualities bestow, and nature has given them for wise purposes," Levi Slamm wrote in 1844. "But men of talent, genius, and enterprise, are, generally, not those who seek the aid of privilege; they are content steadily to pursue the road to competency and eminence, without trampling on the mangled bodies of their fellow-men, on whom nature has been less lavish in her bounties." Robert Rantoul Jr. was more succinct when he urged workingmen to improve themselves through education. "We have a right to have the career kept fairly open to talent, and to be brought equally and together up to the starting point at the public expense; after that, we must shift for ourselves." [40]

Nevertheless, although these statements were modern and "democratic" in the stress they put upon individual achievement in what amounted to a social vacuum, they were also obsolescent in the sense of hierarchy they expressed. The typical democrat probably accepted hierarchy rather than embraced it; the focus of his attention apparently lay in money rather than wealth, if wealth be considered a social phenomenon and money a purely individual achievement. Despite Democratic leanings toward conservative images of success, it is questionable whether ordinary democrats subscribed to an idea that is properly labeled "success." At least it seems clear that their ideas remained significantly different from those that conservatives and Whigs put forward, and that they acquiesced in, rather than shared, Whig sentiments.

Both their attitudes and their idiosyncrasies appear to have been reflected in the biographical pamphlets about wealthy men that enterprising journalists began to compile during the 1840s. These accounts of the rich in New York, Boston, and Philadelphia were democratic in the sense that no matter who compiled them they were apparently widely read, inexpensive, and irreverent. They did not engage in muckraking; they did detail, often in a racy fashion, how the wealthiest citizens of their respective cities had acquired their wealth. (*Wealth and Biography of the Wealthy Citizens of Philadelphia* reported in 1845 that J. B. Barton had "married two good fortunes, and may safely be estimated as worth [$200,000]," and that John Abrahams had "made his money by being inspector of salted provisions under Governor Porter.") That is, their observations were made primarily as statements of fact; the only time their compilers seem to have felt the need to comment adversely on their subjects was when they had been guilty of cant or pretense. *"Our First Men,"* an account of Boston's elite, was especially sensitive to the behavior of wealthy men who had made their money in the liquor traffic and now professed to repudiate it, but this was a compilation that was notably inclined to settle private scores in public. (Its author may have been Richard Hildreth, and its portrait of George Bancroft was a stunning essay in demolition.) By contrast, the other pamphlets usually let the facts speak for themselves.[41]

In effect, the facts of wealth were facts of American life, which the journalists simply recorded. Their efforts suggested that wealth was of universal interest and might even be exhilarating, but they did not labor the proposition that other men could go and do likewise, either as a theory of society or an incentive to self-improvement. In the prefatory note to his second volume on New York's wealthy men, Moses Y. Beach hailed those "who by honest and laborious industry have raised themselves from the obscure and humble walks of life, to great wealth and consideration," but only to use their example as a rebuke to those "whose fortunes have been acquired in a more *equivocal* manner." Furthermore, he very largely ignored social mobility. Instead he paid equal deference to men who had made their own way up and to those who enjoyed well-established fortunes. Similarly, the Philadelphia biographer used the phrases "made his money" and "made his own money" neutrally, as circumstances seemed to require (the proportion of the latter being about one in ten), and even Hildreth described only four extraordinary self-made men, albeit others who had known "humble origins" or "small beginnings." It probably said something about Boston or about Hildreth's Whig sympathies rather than the democratic concept of success that he identified one of the four as an example of "what Carlyle would call 'an heroic money maker.' " [42]

For that matter, the criterion for admission to these pages was simply and solely money, $100,000 in New York and Boston, $50,000 in Philadelphia. Seen in these terms, wealth was more nearly a statistic showing how some men had come out than a comment on what they had been able to do either as a matter of character or as an exercise in freedom. Certainly the accounts bore no resemblance to the biographies published by orthodox moralists. They did not teach any lessons; they did not labor any precepts; and if they made the sort of distinction Beach drew between honest and "equivocal" paths to success, they did not seem to attach great importance to it. (Even Hildreth was more often ironic than sarcastic.) Rather, they suggested that wealth was a fact of life their readers were prepared to live with—in the possession of other men, so far as they could acquaint themselves with it; among themselves, as far as they could obtain it. To make money, not to serve social purposes, transcend humble origins, or demonstrate moral superiority, was the focus of democratic success. [43]

The autobiography of P. T. Barnum, showman and charlatan, said as much in 1854. In it the enterprising Democrat, whose politics had been confirmed by the struggle over disestablishment in Connecticut, re-counted with a sort of picaresque glee the adventures by which he had accumulated his wealth. His perspective was obviously atomistic—he simply did not think about society except as an arena for his accomplish-ments—and it was also resolutely irreverent, a detailed account of how he had sinned against the codes of orthodox morality and emerged richer for that fact. In his eyes, life was a series of manipulative encounters in which every man sought to get the better of his neighbor, and Barnum had succeeded better than most. He had run lotteries, engaged in specu-lation, exploited the theater, and used credit recklessly, as well as pro-moted obvious humbugs, staged fraudulent contests, and turned his hand to anything else that promised to bring a financial return. In effect, he made himself out as anti-hero to New England's traditional codes of heroism. [44]

Yet Barnum also viewed himself as a moral figure, and he was ap-parently delighted to be able to offer advice to his readers; he did not eliminate, but rather redefined, social virtue. He records instances of genuine religious feeling; he makes a good deal of his role in the struggle for religious liberty in Connecticut; and he insists that he never really did evil, or that the good outweighed the evil even in his frauds. More significantly, it is obvious that he labored over his rules of success, which appeared first as a section of his book and later in the form of a lecture he delivered in England in 1858. But while most of the rules are familiar, he introduces one that puts all the others in a novel perspective: *"Advertise your business. Do not hide your light under a bushel."* For him, publicity was a kind of alternative to living by the traditional moral code, a simple technical practice involving no moral misgivings and most effective when not inhibited by calculations of its possible side effects. It was, in short, a wholly acceptable means of making money precisely because it was effective; and yet it was also innocuous—part of a game one played in a world in which everyone else played the same game.[45]

To put matters another way, Barnum refused to take his career as seriously as the moralists proposed; instead, he recorded a process that he had enjoyed. Significantly, he entitled his lecture in England "The Art of Money-Getting." Even more significantly, his autobiography as a whole expresses no sense that the path he has followed will exclude anyone else; his book is an invitation to imitate him if one can, being ever mindful that there are always Barnums around to contend with (and enjoy) if you do. Indeed, in the absence of a sense of society there is also no social mobility and no implication of success, except in the sense that success is a synonym for the effective pursuit of wealth, and mobility among callings is indispensable to it. Barnum has thrown off the codes of his childhood the better to pursue the main chance, which is all the success that a democrat can want. There can hardly be anything wrong (every page seems to say) with a pursuit that brings the rewards he has experienced.[j]

In short, democrats who read Beach's biographies and Barnum's account of his own life were left with success as an epitome of society, but the success they honored was not identical with the success that conventional moralists described. It was egalitarian rather than elitist, democratic rather than paternalistic, and moral in its own terms rather than those of the Protestant ministry. It really obliterated both society and the social ethic as a context in which one strove, as a source of norms while striving, and as a criterion of the consequences of striving. The quintessential democrat moved with confidence into a future that left everyone to his own devices.

AN ECONOMY OF ENTREPRENEURS

Democrats like Barnum really depicted a society devoted to enterprise—not to success in the classic sense, still less to a puritanical implementation of either the conservative or the Democratic creed, but to the activity of making one's way according to broadly democratic standards. Moreover, Barnum was hardly unique, however unusual his candor may have been. Political disagreements notwithstanding, the idea or the fact of enterprise united men of virtually every political faith in an effort to make use of the opportunities they saw before them.[46]

The history of the term "enterprise" itself helps to point up the evolution of this characteristic American perspective. Initially the noun conveyed two basic meanings: it was a synonym for "undertaking" or "project," and it suggested that the activity in question was either bold or hazardous. Thus the original connotation of the adjective "enterprising": to be bold and even lofty in one's vision, aspiring to the completion of measures that were beyond the reach of ordinary men. (Hence the adjective also occasionally bore an invidious meaning.) Frequently, "enterprise" in its original sense was applied to efforts in the public interest such as the exploits of heroic kings, and it continued to bear such connotations when it was applied by early republican writers to projects like the building of the Erie Canal. By the same token, the adjective retained much of its original meaning when it was employed in the young men's guides to describe an indispensable trait of character: to be enterprising was to have a penchant and a capacity for undertakings beyond common men, whose vision and capabilities were less expansive and whose ability to propel society forward was less marked. Public or private, "enterprise" was in its traditional manifestations a corollary of society conceived as an organic whole and led by extraordinary men whose will was the key to its destiny.[47]

Men of the Middle Period radically altered these meanings. Conservatives who praised success carried forward the connotations of public service—this was one indication of their conservatism—but they also shifted the locus of that service from the public to the private arena, just as they limited the obligations that property owed society and maximized the authority of material success. Under these circumstances, "enterprise" increasingly connoted a private trait of character that bore a large public significance without bearing a direct public responsibility. Hence in the long run it came to be conceived on a gigantic scale and to be linked with the Romantic celebration of what Emerson typically labeled "representative men," meaning men who had risen head and shoulders above their contemporaries.[48]

Meanwhile democrats tended both to assert the private rather than the public meaning of the term and to diminish the scope of the efforts to which it might be applied. So far as private and public meanings are concerned, the *New English Dictionary* records the appearance of the phrase "private enterprise" in 1844, when it was used by H. H. Wilson to describe economic activities that the British East India Company had left to others. (We must remember that the company had been, in effect, the government of India.) Here the addition of "private" to "enterprise" made a distinction that was significant but also neutral, for it implied only that there were two ways of accomplishing public ends, and that the company had chosen one over the other in certain instances. When William Leggett used the same phrase in 1835 to describe the ideal postal service, however, it represented an invidious distinction in favor of the private method of serving public ends. It had the same effect when the Democratic members of the constitutional convention of Wisconsin invoked it in 1846 to curb the authority of government. Spokesmen for Jacksonian Democracy insisted even more strenuously than conservatives, although for very different reasons, that private enterprise precluded public control.[49]

Once private had been distinguished from public enterprise, "enterprise" tended to become a synonym for "business." Whigs as well as Democrats used it in this sense. In 1832 James K. Polk used it in a restricted sense, speaking of "trade and commercial enterprise" as partners of agriculture and manufacturing. Similarly, the Antimasons of Massachusetts complained in 1836 that Democratic policies threatened "every enterprise of commerce." In 1840, however, Massachusetts Whigs repudiated Democratic attacks on corporations on much the same grounds; by now—and not surprisingly, given the origins of the state's textile industry—they had extended the categories of commerce to cover manufacturing corporations. So, too, the sponsors of general incorporation laws in New York's constitutional convention of 1846 advocated "legal facilities in enterprise" open to all, while in 1852 the *Democratic Review*, now the voice of George Sanders and Young America, hailed the Democratic party as the party of "freedom in trade, freedom in mind, and freedom in enterprise." Even the critics of American materialism accepted the term as a definition of what they criticized. In 1844 the *New York Observer*, a Presbyterian organ, noted unhappily that "within the last year or two, there have been most evident tokens of another general rush toward riches. Almost every department of enterprise has gathered new life and energy." Taken together, such usages clearly isolated enterprise from public obligations and also diminished its stature by universalizing it. The formula invoked by the *Democratic Review* closely parallels Barnum's ethical code, while even the Whiggish advocates of Massachusetts corporations insisted that enterprise lay within the reach of everyone.[50]

Nevertheless, the evidence suggests that Whigs probably employed the term more frequently than Democrats. The reason is not far to seek: influenced by a tradition that linked enterprise to heroic achievements, seeking at the same time to defend essentially privileged endeavors against democratic reformers, they had every reason to equate their activities with qualities that even democrats might be expected to defer to. Under these circumstances "enterprise" would have seemed to them both a title to popular respect and a claim on popular sympathy, as it clearly was when the Massachusetts Whigs praised corporations because they offered opportunities "for men of moderate property to engage in enterprises beneficial to themselves and the public, which otherwise could be prosecuted only by the very rich." By contrast, democrats apparently preferred "business" to "enterprise" to describe the activity they pursued. Certainly party spokesmen who referred to enterprise tended to be either old-fashioned Republicans, who may have retained some sense of the tradition of public enterprise epitomized in the Erie Canal, or philosophical commentators whose tastes remained elitist in spite of their doctrine.[51]

The difference was more than verbal. As long as enterprise connoted either heroic aspirations or forms of social obligation, it would stand at odds with democratic attitudes toward the economy. Business was more plebeian—less pretentious, less elitist, and ultimately less egocentric, in the sense that although the typical democrat willingly pursued the main chance he did so without any protestation that he was also serving some larger end. (Tocqueville gave this basic attitude what he intended to be a pejorative label when he dubbed it "individualism"; in his essentially aristocratic perspective, individualism connoted a blanket indifference to social needs and traditions.) In the typical democrat's view, such services as he performed for society were performed in a completely secular marketplace, in which character itself appeared to be an asset to a career but not a moral title to wealth.[52]

Certainly this was the lesson that Edwin T. Freedley taught in his *Practical Treatise on Business* and other volumes compiled during the 1850s. Although Freedley was in fact a liberal Whig, his work pointed up the ultimate tendencies of democratic social thought by its contrasts with that of Freeman Hunt, who published a handbook for success and two volumes of mercantile biography during the same decade.[53]

Freedley was twenty-three years younger than Hunt, a native of Pennsylvania rather than Massachusetts, and an apologist for industry rather than commerce; in all three respects he was a representative of the future whereas Hunt was an honored spokesman for the past. Freedley was also insistently practical, and his treatise stood in about the same relationship to Hunt's *Worth and Wealth* as Barnum's autobiography to the laudatory biographies Hunt published in *Lives of American Merchants*. Although both authors' handbooks were potpourris of anecdote, advice, and "philosophy," Freedley's stressed the actual workings of the world of business (albeit in rather general terms) whereas Hunt's was "a collection of maxims, morals and miscellanies for merchants and men of business." Freedley did incorporate a good deal of hortatory advice, some of it highly traditional, but he also described how to make money in a variety of undertakings, which included both speculation and banking, and he expressed a striking ambivalence toward the traditional moral code of success. Although he paid homage to agriculture and the prudential virtues, he complained that traditional moralists had devoted too much time to admonitions respecting the getting of wealth and too little to its spending, and he argued that business was the real test and therefore the real source of morality. Even when he introduced familiar moral injunctions, the suffocating piety that traditionally accompanied them was missing, as the inclusion of a sanctimonious chapter on "The True Men of Business" by Horace Greeley demonstrated by its contrast with the rest of the book. As if to make sure that no one would take Greeley seriously,

Freedley followed his effusion with an anonymous Boston merchant's discussion of "How to Get Rich by Speculation." [54]

Freedley clearly honored millionaires, and to this extent he may seem to have echoed the traditional deference for men of extraordinary talents that Hunt and others expressed. But here, too, Freedley was a Barnum rather than a proper Bostonian. He valued the millionaire *as* millionaire—as a possessor of more of what most men wanted, not his wealth as a symbol or a surrogate for something else—and he surrounded him with techniques of success that bore little resemblance to the orthodox techniques. They included familiar preliminaries like industry and frugality, but they also included a large admixture of luck, and Freedley was at some pains to point out that the rules do not always work—that the best one can do is abide by them in order to be ready for an extraordinary opportunity if it should arise, settling meanwhile for the assurance of a competence. In these terms the pursuit of wealth was neither a test of character nor an occasion for the display of one's virtue, and the millionaire cannot be said either to have occupied or to have exemplified a secure moral world. Least of all did he exemplify "mastery" in the sense in which Hunt used the term to describe the outstanding personal qualities and the highly personal success of the most eminent merchants.[55] In Freedley's book the object of making money was neither more nor less than making money, with the hope of making more by any means that came to hand.[k]

Nevertheless, success as Freedley described it was closely tied to providing goods and services, implicitly in the *Practical Treatise* and explicitly elsewhere. In *Opportunities for Industry and the Safe Investment of Capital* (1859), he opened his remarks by discussing the millionaires of the ancient and recent past in his usual factual manner, continued by explaining how a man could obtain a start toward great wealth by ordinary industry and frugality, and then proceeded to describe in considerable detail hundreds of profitable ways of employing the capital so acquired, by finding new markets, developing new resources, inventing new technologies, and serving new needs. By the same token, his *Leading Pursuits and Leading Men* (1856) was a factual if overenthusiastic account of the major manufacturers of the United States; Freedley portrayed not paragons of private virtue but practitioners of useful production—industrious, intelligent, enterprising men who had made their money by producing goods for other men to consume, and whose aim in life might better be stated as success in business than as success for its own sake. Undoubtedly the kind of volume Freedley compiled directed his attention to some of these characteristics, but he had made the occasion in the first place by sensing the need for the volume. (So, too, he later helped to produce J. Leander Bishop's *History of American Manufactures*, the first study of its kind in the United States.) In effect, he invited his countrymen to take pleasure in the enterprise of American industry. Neither dreams of success nor zeal for the public service, neither deference to an elite nor sentimental ideas of mobility, but Americans' common experience in business created the market for his volume.

In short, Freedley preached *to* the Americans rather than *at* them, while the problems he sought to advise them about were practical problems of business rather than theoretical problems of character.[1] The object of industrious effort was not to rise to the point at which one might benefit one's country, but to enjoy the advantages the country provided, secure in the knowledge that freedom would benefit everybody. Hence Freedley lavished praise on enterprise, but in clearly democratic terms. If Americans would only capitalize on their opportunities, all his works implied, they could expect to provide for the world.

In part this was a familiar democratic hypothesis, for classic Democratic theory had always held that laissez faire was warranted by its effects in the world as well as its legitimacy at home. But the classic theory also held that the Americans should feed Europe and provide the raw materials for its industry, receiving in turn its finished products at the cheapest possible rates, and Freedley had no idea of acquiescing in such a one-sided distribution of the world's wealth. Neither he nor other northerners, Democratic or Whig, Pennsylvanian or New Englander, felt that Americans should restrict themselves to agriculture and commerce when there was a world of manufacturing to enter at a profit. Only in the South, which was dependent on agriculture for its income and tied to the European economy by its markets, would Americans remain faithful to laissez faire when they had sensed the opportunities for economic expansion that governments might create.

Hence the more active they became in business the more likely the Americans were to return to "enterprise" after it had been purged of its invidious connotations. Northern purists aside, even loyal Democrats made exceptions to their party's interdict against a fostering government when they conceived of it as an asset to democratic undertakings. This was the case in the Middle West when they demanded improvement of rivers and harbors; in Pennsylvania and other industrial states when they clamored for protective tariffs; in the North as a whole when they agreed to commit public lands to a transcontinental railroad. It was the case even in banking, when midwestern Democrats supported national banks in order to overcome the defects of local institutions. Once equal rights seemed firmly established, once government sponsorship introduced no obvious infringements on "natural" economic patterns, nearly everyone in the United States could join in exploiting the continent with such public assistance as he needed or could muster.[m]

At the same time, in reopening the door to government intervention in the economy, democrats did not become advocates of government participation in its planning, development, or regulation. Instances like the so-called national banks (which were a far cry from the Second Bank of the United States in both their genesis and operations) and the tariff (which was intended at least in theory to produce the benefits of free trade at home) are only apparent exceptions that confirm the general rule. Rather, democrats became advocates of enterprise as a universal American phenomenon—the advocates of "liberated capitalism," if you will, except that American capitalists had always been remarkably free in the absence of effective popular controls. (The controls they had experienced in the early years of the century were for the most part controls they themselves had sponsored.) Under the auspices of democratic government, capitalism was freed from hierarchy, freed from paternalism, and freed from responsibility. Enterprise now connoted the practice of exploiting the continent by private means grounded in public assistance but lacking even gestures of deference to aristocracy, to government, or to society.

Hence it was only natural that by the late 1850s many Democrats should increasingly find themselves in the Republican party as they discovered that the southern wing of their own party stood in the way of their aspirations. Right or wrong, fortunate or unfortunate, this circumstance said more about the dynamics of democratic thought than about the machinations of the Whigs. The Republicanism of the 1850s did not represent the substitution of a new creed so much as the transformation of an old one, at which only purists and southerners demurred.[56]

POLITICS

❧ VII ☙

THE POLITICS OF
DEMOCRACY

Democratic demands for equal rights took for granted that the good society was one in which every man was left alone to exploit his economic
opportunities as best he could. The demand for rights so defined also
helped to produce a characteristically American concept of politics, one
that corresponded in many respects to the theories of European liberalism but that incorporated distinctly American elements and assumptions
as well. In effect, American liberal democrats so far identified democracy
with freedom as to call government itself into question. Their theory of
politics reinforced their theory of society.

THE PROBLEM OF POWER

The most significant element of democratic political doctrine was a
predisposition to visualize political power as an incubus on popular liberty.[a] Instead of viewing the governments they had grown up with as in
some sense an extension of themselves, Democrats commonly conceived
of them as an external and potentially hostile force, an agency that might
indeed be necessary for their safety, but one that constantly threatened
to encroach on the freedoms they valued.[b] M. A. Richter articulated
their sentiments lucidly in 1847 when he explained, in an idiosyncratic
essay on self-government, that "the less the inhabitants of a town are
able to govern themselves, the more constables, jailors, sheriffs, police-
men, night-watches, prisons, lawyers, judges, courts, law-makers, governors, and finally, soldiers, and guns, and cannons, will be wanting to
govern and rule them." The antipolitical premises of his utopian tract
were well established in American democratic thought; John Calhoun
employed them without apology when he wrote to Andrew Jackson in
1826 to apprise him of his loyalty: "An issue has been fairly made between *power* and *liberty;* and it must be determined in the next three
years, whether the real governing principle in our political system be the
power and patronage of the Executive, or the voice of the people." In

1839 John D. Freeman invoked the same basic prejudice without partisan intention during the course of a Fourth of July oration at Natchez, in which he capped a series of invidious comparisons between Europe and America by declaring, "If they have GOVERNMENT, we have LIBERTY." Even when American democrats spoke up for democracy, they were all too likely to treat government and liberty as antithetical.[1]

Their protracted campaign against the "money power" was both occasion and evidence of their preoccupation with power as the key issue of public policy. Certainly the attack on the Second Bank of the United States came to a focus in political considerations, as Jackson's veto message suggested in criticizing the Bank's power far more than its performance. For one thing, the chief magistrate portrayed investment in the Bank by foreign stockholders as a permanent threat to "the purity of our elections in peace and . . . the independence of our country in war." Here power was literally an alien force, and the more threatening because of that fact. Second, Jackson devoted a considerable part of his message to refuting the doctrine of implied powers that Alexander Hamilton and John Marshall had employed to legitimize a national bank; in effect, he placed himself in the constitutional balance against their extension of public authority. Finally, he treated the admitted ability of the Bank to make or break banks in the states as *prima facie* evidence that it should be destroyed, although in point of fact there would not have been much justification for such a bank had it not exerted a powerful influence in the economy. In short, it was less the consequences than the capabilities of the Bank that Jackson chose to attack, and his message proclaimed that no such capabilities were tolerable in a free society.[2]

Democrats also kept up a drumfire of protest against the power of the Bank long after it had ceased to exist. Jackson adverted to its evils in a long passage of his Farewell Address that was crowded with metaphors of unholy coercion. In much the same vein, loyal Democrats throughout the country sought to portray each successive election as a renewed struggle between power and popular liberties. "In the political contest approaching," the party's convention in St. Lawrence County (New York) predicted in 1837, "it is now quite certain, that the opponents of the present administration, will seek to establish a National Bank. The scheme of a great irresponsible monied power, to regulate the business of men, and to control the action of government has always been a favorite object with our political opponents, with that party which now styles itself whig. Aristocracy looks to such a power, as the basis upon which its principle may be incorporated in the government, and permanently fastened upon the country." In the following year a Maine state senator told his colleagues that he saw "in the late movements and manifestations of the designs of the MONEY-POWER, which had recently, more markedly than at any former period, upreared its hydra-head to contend with the PEOPLE, a determination . . . to rivet on this country the manacles of Bank Despotism, and to bind up in its iron chains the dear-bought liberties of this now free and happy people!" During the 1840s Democratic spokesmen recounted past victories in much the same vocabulary. In 1842, for example, James K. Polk declared that, had the Whigs succeeded in creating a national fiscal bank, "it would have soon become an immense political engine of deadly hostility to the purity of elections and to the liberties of the people, and would have been wielded by a corrupt faction, as was the late bank of the United States, and for the worst of purposes." [3] Democrats clearly identified their party with the eradication of an intolerable power.

They invoked the same considerations against banking in the states. William Gouge devoted the opening chapter of his *Inquiry into the Banking System* to extracts from a great many authors who had criticized the power of banks to do evil even when they were in fact behaving well, especially the power to ruin honest men and to "enslave" a people by corrupting their legislatures. In 1837 Thomas Hart Benton invoked the same specter when he spoke in behalf of Martin Van Buren's proposal to create an Independent Treasury in lieu of placing federal funds in the "pet" banks: "The power of a few banks over the whole, presents a new feature of danger in our system. It consolidates the banks of the whole Union into one mass, and subjects them to one fate, and that fate to be decided by a few, without even the knowledge of the rest. An unknown divan of bankers sends forth an edict which sweeps over the empire, crosses the lines of States with the facility of a Turkish firman, prostrating all State institutions, breaking up all engagements, and levelling all law before it." Midwestern Democrats pressed the same case against state-chartered institutions during the constitutional conventions of the 1840s. "Besides all financial reasons there are most weighty political objections against banks," the *Racine* (Wisconsin) *Advocate* declared in 1847.

"Money is power, and a great power; and the concentration of the money power in banks creates a great political power. Pennsylvania was corrupted by the presence of one vast monster monopoly; New York was controlled in its politics for years by the association of safety fund banks; and the United States Bank waged equal war for years with the whole power of the United States, in which it was ultimately foiled only by the indomitable purpose and universal popularity of one man. . . . Great as are the financial evils of the banking system, the political dangers are infinitely greater." [4]

Theoretically it was possible to infer from such charges against the power of banks and bankers that popular government must be strengthened to control them. In one sense this was what Democrats contended for: Jackson vetoed recharter of the Second Bank, Martin Van Buren proposed the Independent Treasury partly in order to extricate government from the clutches of the state banks, and Democratic legislators and convention delegates sought to counteract the financial evils they described by preventing the incorporation of additional banking institutions in their states. But the signal domestic achievements of the national Democratic administrations between 1828 and 1860 consisted of vetoes and negations rather than exercises in governing the economy. Jackson's fame as a powerful president rests primarily upon his vetoes of the Maysville Road Bill and of the Second Bank, together with the actions he took to exempt government from the machinations of the "money power." Even the Nullification Proclamation and the Force Bill resembled vetoes in the sense that they denied certain powers claimed by South Carolina without asserting any novel authority in the national government, and yet they alienated a good many southern Democrats who were for various reasons unwilling to concede to the federal government even the power of self-preservation. As William Leggett explained in 1834 in defending Jackson against Whig charges of executive despotism, "All his 'tyranny' has consisted in successfully interposing the Constitution of the United States in defence of the EQUAL RIGHTS of the people; and . . . all his 'usurpations' have been confined to checking those of the advocates of consolidation, disunion, monopolies, and lastly a great consolidated moneyed aristocracy, equally dangerous to liberty from the power it legally possesses, and those it has usurped." [5]

So far as banks and other corporations were concerned, moreover, many democrats argued that their very existence demonstrated the dangers rather than the promise of governmental activity. We must remember that an act of incorporation was originally clearly understood to be an exercise of sovereignty, one bestowing essentially political privileges like limited liability and eminent domain in return for anticipated public benefits. Hence it was all too easy for doctrinaire Democrats to equate charters with the "tyrannies" practiced by "despotic" governments. Predicting that the newly elected Whig Congress would seek to incorporate a third national bank for a fixed span of years, Benjamin F. Hallett asked in 1841, "What is this but the monarchical principle in government?"

For whatever form or administration of government establishes in the state, directly or indirectly, a sovereignty independent of the people, is essentially monarchical. It is immaterial whether this sovereignty, this exclusive and irrepealable power, is held by a single man or by a privileged few—by a king or an aristocracy—by nobles or by corporations—by a divan or a bank. Whenever it is irresponsible to the people which it governs, whether it be guarded by the divine right of kings, by hereditary succession, by tenures of office for life, or by special charters which the people cannot reach, it distinctly embodies the monarchical principle.

Alternatively, they contended that the measures conservatives advocated might indeed be liberal in Europe, but that they were unmistakably tyrannical in the United States. Isaac Crary developed this argument in Michigan's second convention during the course of an attack upon American judges for being too much disposed to follow English precedent in construing American law. "Take for example the grant of a charter," he declared. "Here it is an infringement of liberty; a restriction upon the rights of the masses. In Great Britain it is an extension of liberty and an enlargement of the privileges of the many." On this view, corporate charters were as incompatible with political liberty as they were with economic equality.[6]

But corporate charters were only the most visible and most egregious examples of tyranny, which Democratic spokesmen attributed to virtually every act of governing understood in the traditional sense of selecting particular means to achieve general public ends. To them it was axiomatic that such choices infringed on the natural order of society. In addition, they insisted that discretionary behavior in government was not only unequal and impolitic but also coercive and evil. In 1839 James K. Polk recalled to the people of Tennessee the struggles he had engaged in as a freshman representative of democracy, contending with the "latitudinarian doctrines" of President John Quincy Adams. "It was publicly proclaimed," he reported with obvious hostility, "that the wholesome restraints of the public will on the action of the servants of the people were to be disregarded, and that the 'Representative was not to be palsied by the will of his constituents.' It was declared by that Chief Magistrate to be ineffably stupid to suppose that the Representatives of the people were deprived of the power to advance the public weal, thereby substituting the unrestrained discretion of Congress and of the Federal Government for the specific grants of power conferred by a Constitution of limitations and restrictions." By 1843 Martin Van Buren took it for granted that the issues Polk pointed to had been settled by public opinion. "Not only is power much more liable to abuse than to beneficial exercise," he wrote to the Democratic State Convention of Indiana, "but . . . with the purest intentions it can do far less good, than it can perpetrate mischief when perverted to evil. The people of the United States have repudiated despotic or discretionary power, in all their political institutions, because of its propensity to abuse." [7]

The Democratic indictment extended well beyond the evils that the federal government had perpetrated under the National Republicans. "The Democratic Republican, Jacobin, Radical, Destructive (*quocunque nomine gaudes*)," the *History of the Federal and Democratic Parties* declared in 1837, "believes that no more power should in any case be delegated than the circumstances imperiously require to produce the good intended, because history clearly shows the tendency of all power to exceed its proper limits, that the holders of all power should be responsible for the use of it, to those who gave it; that if any excess be excusable on either side, it is better to concede rather too little than to[o] much, as it is much more easy to add than to diminish." In the constitutional convention of Texas, Robert E. B. Baylor justified the right to bear arms on the grounds that "it is the policy of governments to disarm the people, that they may have the opportunity to oppress them," while William B. Ewing urged the New Jersey convention to make constitutional amendment difficult because "Heavier bodies do not more certainly descend or lighter ones arise, than does the mind of man grasp after power when the opportunity occurs. If this principle did not exist in the United States or in this State, what is there to prevent the evils of consolidation?" [8]

Similarly, the portrait Democrats typically drew of executive power was unflattering and apprehensive except where they were able to visualize an incumbent as the tribune of the people. During the early 1820s they made much of what Polk described in 1826 as "the alluring and corrupting influence of Executive patronage." "I may have fears upon this subject, which firmer minds can, and do repel," Representative William Cabell Rives of Virginia declared in 1828; "but it has long been my opinion, that there is a decided tendency in our Government to a dangerous and disproportionate accumulation of power in the Executive branch, and that *Monarchy* is the euthanasia of our political system." Advocating an elective rather than an appointive judiciary, James F. Brent told the constitutional convention of Louisiana in 1845 that "the patronage of the executive is a remnant of the monarchial principle, and it is the fountain from whence have issued copious streams of demoralization, that have flowed over the land." In 1847 the *Racine Advocate* contrasted the proposed constitution of Wisconsin, which provided for popularly elected executive officers without substantial rights to patronage, with those of less progressive states: "The great evil of the executive department of most of the states, as every person at all conversant with politics well knows, has been the congregation at the seat of government of an associated band of officeholders, who have assumed a species of political regency and exercised a vast control over the government of the state beyond their appropriate delegated authority. This constitution forever emancipates Wisconsin from this adventitious power." [9]

Undoubtedly the evils the *Advocate* pointed to were real, as were many of the evils democrats imputed to selective incorporation. To recognize that they were genuine, however, is to miss the thrust of democratic thought. Right or wrong, democratic doctrinaires carried their antipathy toward power to the point of casting opprobrium on the whole range of activities traditionally associated with governing. In effect, they denied the legitimacy of government even under democratic auspices. John L. O'Sullivan gave classic expression to their logic in the introductory number of the *Democratic Review*, where he defended democracy as a surer guarantee of the general good than aristocracy but went on to point out that even democratic government could be expected to infringe on the rights of some of the people as long as it exercised power over their lives.

It is under the word *government*, that the subtle danger lurks. Understood as a central consolidated power, managing and directing the various general interests of the society, all government is evil, and the parent of evil. A strong and active democratic *government*, in the common sense of the term, is an evil, differing only in degree and mode of operation, and not in nature, from a strong despotism. This difference is certainly vast, yet, inasmuch as these strong governmental powers must be wielded by human agents, even as the powers of the despotism, it is, after all, only a difference in degree; and the tendency to demoralization and tyranny is the same, though the development of the evil results is much more gradual and slow in the one case than in the other.[10]

Hence Democratic leaders typically demanded that government be "divorced" from the affairs of society—above all from banking, but also from other areas in which it had traditionally played a major role. In 1830, for example, Jackson defended his veto of a bill appropriating federal funds for the purchase of stock in the Maysville and Lexington turnpike company on the grounds that he objected to "mingling the concerns of the Government with those of the States or of individuals"; it was "inconsistent with the object of its institution and highly impolitic." By the same token, the Democrats of Indiana declared in 1838 that "it is not . . . the question in debate between the two present political parties, whether the numerous family of Banks shall exist, but only whether Government, out of that family, shall select one as a Bride. The Whig Party contends that such a marriage is suitable and expedient; while the Democrats assert, that the proposed union is a virtual divorce of our Republican Government from its early love—from its first fair bride, LIBERTY." [11]

Two other political concerns accompanied this clamor for a separation between government and economy. Democratic spokesmen repeatedly expressed fear for the autonomy of governments and the purity of elections if wealthy men felt that they had reason to seek power or look for political favors. Speaking in this vein, they often sounded like secular moralists whose sole concern in government was to isolate it from the corruptions that infected other human institutions. They also insisted, however, that the intrusion of economic interests of any kind on the processes of government was sure to destroy popular liberty. C. C.

Cambreleng incorporated both fears into a single appeal when he told the House of Representatives in 1835 that "if these abuses are persisted in; if corporations are to be multiplied throughout the land; if the credit of the State is to be abused for banking purposes, and the dignity of Government degraded by partnerships in trade; if a perpetual annuity of millions is to be thus indirectly collected for the benefit of banks established under the authority of Government—then may we anticipate, before many generations shall have passed away, the thorough corruption and revolution of every Government in the Union. Perpetuate these legislative abuses, and the time is not distant when your Representatives will volunteer their services to your thousands of powerful corporations, and when avarice will control every Legislature in the land." [12] Democratic partisans' most characteristic response to the problems of power, like their response to the problems of poverty, was to prevent government from governing.

THE RIGHT OF THE PEOPLE TO RULE

Diminishing government, Democrats also sought to subordinate it to the will of the people, pressing one innovation after another intended at least in theory to extend popular sovereignty. But they conceived of their innovations primarily as resources against power—as devices by which the people could prevent their governors from exceeding their authority. In this sense they treated politics as a problem to be overcome rather than a vehicle to be employed, and they ended by substituting the popular veto for the exercise of popular power.[c]

One of their reforms was democratization of the state and national legislatures, which had for many years been considered the bulwarks of American liberties, but which had not yet fully succumbed to the egalitarian spirit. Convention after convention in the states eliminated residual qualifications for elective office, opened the suffrage to adult white males, and eradicated all but the most trivial restrictions upon voting even by newcomers and aliens. (True, there were heated controversies over how many years aliens must have resided in the United States before they could vote, but even conservative critics of quick enfranchisement commonly demanded no more than several years' residence, while Democrats typically clamored for an almost instantaneous extension of the privilege.) Simultaneously, Democrats made a fetish of the right of instruction—the right of a given electorate or its spokesmen to direct how a state's delegation in Congress should vote on controversial issues, more generally the right of the people to control the actions of their representatives everywhere. Congressmen were not always responsive to public opinion, and some went so far as to refuse to accede to political pressure, but it is significant that they usually chose to do so on the grounds that the clamor they heard did not represent the true will of the people. In effect, almost everyone accepted the premise that that will should be honored if known, while a number of distinguished senators actually resigned or lost their seats because of their unwillingness to take direction.[13]

There were many precedents both for extending the suffrage and for instructing a state's representatives, but the reasons the Democrats advanced spoke volumes about the meaning they attached to democracy. We shall deal with their ideas about the suffrage as such in dealing with their theory of natural rights; here it is important to note that they equated instruction with popular liberty rather than popular power. "The right of instruction is a sovereign right," a committee of the Michigan constitutional convention held in 1835. "It lies at the foundation of representative government; and, without it, liberty, in such government, is but a name. . . . It is the essence of representative government, the shield of civil liberty, the most effective and harmless prerogative retained by the people to check abuses in government, and to preserve their own freedom and interests from destruction." James K. Polk echoed these sentiments in his gubernatorial campaign of 1843, while both Solomon Downs and Zenon Ledoux argued that the Louisiana constitutional convention could not propose novel measures of constitutional reform without infringing on popular rights. Apparently even the fact that proposed changes must be submitted to the electorate for its approval seemed an insignificant security for the freedoms the convention was intended to safeguard.[14]

The thrust of Democratic thought becomes even more apparent when we recognize that the same generation of reformers who subordinated legislative deliberations to the authority of the people also struggled (and with considerable success) to place curbs on the very legislatures they had democratized. They managed to secure biennial legislatures in most of the states, and frequently to limit the number of days even a biennial legislature might sit. In doing so they abandoned one of the axioms of Old Republicanism, "Where annual elections end, tyranny begins," but it can hardly be said that they intended thereby to treat liberty lightly. Rather, they conceived that more frequent sessions of the legislature created too many opportunities for misgovernment, which they sought to prevent by diminishing the power to legislate. At the same time, they often required that legislative action on such controversial measures as banking, incorporations, and internal improvements be considered void unless approved in a popular referendum, which some state constitutions required even of general laws touching on these matters. The more democratic a state's constitution was, the more likely it was to incorporate this recourse to the people. Theoretically, of course, the referendum might have served as a vehicle for innovations the legislature opposed—it was to be employed for this purpose during the 1890s—but both the provisions made and the arguments offered by delegates to the conventions of the 1840s demonstrate that its purpose during the Middle Period was negation.[15]

Democratization of the executive branch had the same significance. Qualifications for the governorship were diminished, the electorate was extended, and reformers even toyed with the idea of establishing direct election of the president in order to remove both the inequities and the temptations to corruption that indirect election created. Democrats also made a good deal of the chief executive in both state and nation as tribune of the people, answerable to the whole electorate rather than to particular sections of either political unit, and effective for the general good rather than special interests. This was the basis on which they vindicated Jackson's presidency and justified strengthening the executive veto in the states, where Republican precedent had made legislatures powerful and governors weak, and where Federalist precedent had discredited a strong executive. But it was a veto that they justified, and they rejected with a persuasive show of evidence Whig efforts to equate the power to nullify legislation with the power to rule. In 1843, indeed, Martin Van Buren took special pains to point out that the presidential veto was innocuous whereas the power of appointment was "peculiarly adapted to the sinister purposes of ambitious and selfish aspirants." "It is therefore by diminishing this executive power, and not that of the veto," he added, "which is least liable to abuse, and has been thus far uniformly exercised for the public advantage, that our statesmen can render the most essential, and, I doubt not, the most acceptable service to the cause of the people." [16]

Democratic efforts to curb the judiciary were equally paradoxical. On the one hand, a number of Democrats recognized that judicial review was incompatible with the sovereignty of the people. In 1828, Senator John Rowan of Kentucky, incensed by the federal courts' actions in setting aside a number of his state's laws, pointed out that "if you accord to the judges the power of making laws, you do by that very act surrender to them the sovereign power of the Government. If you permit them to carry into effect, by their own judgment, the laws which they shall have made, you transform the Republic into an Oligarchy; and if, in addition to the power of making and interpreting the laws, you permit them to execute them, you substitute despotism for republicanism, and oppression and slavery for freedom." Invoking similar arguments, a number of Democrats pressed for an elective judiciary in the states. "No man can arise upon this floor, in the face of the assembled representatives of the people," James F. Brent stated in the constitutional convention of Louisiana, "and deny that the people, from whom he holds his trust, are . . . in full possession of all the rights and powers inherent in the sovereignty of the State. That question, then, I shall regard as settled, and I will hereafter hold the right of the people to elect their judges as indisputable and undisputed." [17]

On the other hand, many of these same Democrats also made clear that the only good reason for asserting the preeminence of the people over the courts was to prevent an autonomous judiciary from becoming despotic or an accessory to despotism, not to secure full popular authority over the conduct of government. Rowan said as much; so did Brent, who appealed to the Declaration of Independence and the Bill of Rights to support his assertions. "As for myself," he added, "I had rather the judiciary should be a thermometer, to indicate the rise and fall of popular excitement, or that it should be a weathercock, to designate which way the winds of popular feeling blow, than that it should be constituted into a court of record, to register the edicts of the executive mansion, or the mandates of legislative usurpation." Here as elsewhere the declared object of increasing popular participation in government was to provide surer defenses for popular liberties. [18]

This was also the declared object of the Democratic party as an organization, which its leaders repeatedly hailed as a vehicle of the popular will, but which they also persisted in describing as an agency of popular freedom doing battle against the machinations of the aristocracy. Significantly, they often deplored the effects of party and implied that their main purpose was to eradicate its baleful influence. At other times, they claimed that they embraced the Democratic party because it was the party of democratic principles, and they suggested that it would be needed as long as aristocrats sought to pervert governments to their own illiberal ends. In either case they treated the problems of politics as problems of power that democrats must find means to control. In 1832 the Democratic Republican State Convention of New Hampshire explained to its constituents that the party disputes of the day reflected an eternal conflict between "love of power, and a disposition to abuse it, on the one hand, and a regard for the rights of the people on the other," while William Leggett wrote in 1834 that "in common times, the strife of parties is the mere struggle of ambitious leaders for power; now they are deadly contests of the whole mass of the people, whose pecuniary interests are implicated in the event, because the Government has usurped and exercised the power of legislating on their private affairs." Rhetorical or not, such statements pointed to a strong Democratic antipathy toward politics in the ordinary sense of the term.[19]

The increasing tolerance that Democratic spokesmen displayed toward the two-party system worked in the same direction. As Richard Hofstadter has pointed out, relying heavily on the evidence Michael Wallace accumulated for New York State, during the 1830s and 1840s leading Democratic politicians came to accept permanent competition between parties as a necessary and indeed a salutary feature of democratic politics, whereas the conventional wisdom of their day frowned on parties as exercises in "faction" if not compromises with evil. Nevertheless, the Democrats' change of heart on this difficult point can have worked only to weaken popular sovereignty understood as implementation of a positive popular will. To the extent that Democrats valued the existence of an effective opposition, that is, they implied that politics were intended primarily to prevent misgovernment. In this sense their views were entirely compatible with those of John L. O'Sullivan, whose introduction to the *Democratic Review* had sought to marshal both the electorate and the intelligentsia in the Democratic party as the party of truth, but whose theory of politics reduced to finding some sort of substitute even for government by the people.[20]

In one way and another, in short, Democrats testified to the general proposition that their primary objective in democratizing American politics was to counteract the encroachments on popular rights that the traditional political process had created. Their position was significant whether or not they were candid and whether or not they were faithful to their declared principles. Even if all of them invoked democracy in this restrictive sense only to facilitate their own rise to power, the fact remains that they ran on a platform of restriction and that restriction was the legacy they left to subsequent generations. Indeed, it seems entirely plausible that one of the reasons American democratic politics so rapidly degenerated into the pursuit of private emoluments through illegitimate maneuver and dishonorable manipulation of the powers of government was that Democratic ideologues had so discredited traditional definitions of politics as to leave aspiring politicians no other definition of their role. If this be true, their actual behavior in office can only have reinforced the negative image the electorate had of government, and thus may be presumed to have strengthened its disdain for a constructive reading of democratic politics.[21]

In any event, the work of democratic innovation came to a focus in a theory that democracy was the common man's first safeguard against the authority of government. In part, the theory represented a continuation of classic Republican theories of politics, for example the views of Nathaniel Macon, whom the *Democratic Review* eulogized in its first issue for his belief that "a tendency to usurpation and corruption was the nature of all human institutions; and the only palliative, a frequent recurrence to the fundamental and absolute authority of the popular voice." In part, however, it represented a more general theory, a belief that democracy was an exercise in prohibitions. "If democracy triumphs in our land, if equal rights and a fair field be continued," *The Working Man Defended* declared in 1840, "we, and our children, and our children's children to the latest generation, will enjoy the fruits of their labor, and rear up their descendants in respectability and independence[.] If, on the other hand, democracy do not prevail[,] the rich and the influential will slowly, though certainly, make one after another inroad on equal rights, until a political system shall in time exist that will make the rich richer and the poor poorer, *precisely as is the case in the old countries*. If like causes produce like effects, the evil must happen unless democracy triumph." [22]

Ely Moore attributed comparably prohibitory purposes to the organization of the working classes. "In order to mitigate the evils that ever flow from inordinate desire and unrestricted selfishness," he told the General Trades' Union of New York City; "to restrain and chastise unlawful ambition, to protect the weak against the strong, and to establish an equilibrium of power among nations and individuals, conventional compacts were formed." He also found that compacts so formed had never been able fully "to stay the march of intolerance, of mercenary ambition, or of political despotism," but the inference he drew was that the labor movement might succeed where compacts had not. Even the radical democratic attack on the privileges and immunities of chartered corporations was often grounded in a theory of popular sovereignty that equated it with retaining power to prevent evils rather than retaining authority to promote the general good. Democrats of a liberal persuasion agreed that the people's power to rule was above all a power to prevent the evils that government might otherwise bring.[23]

THE RIGHT TO VOTE

Democrats typically represented the collective authority of the people as a resource against power, and not surprisingly they represented the right to vote in the same terms. Hence although it is true that most of the states enjoyed an extended suffrage well before Andrew Jackson became president, it does not follow that the aggressively democratic agitation of the 1830s and 1840s labored a foregone conclusion so far as voting was concerned. Rather, democrats attached such great importance to the right of suffrage that they would not be satisfied with traditional republican limitations on it.

In one sense, democratic theories of the suffrage only carried forward established republican doctrines. Even republican theory had presupposed a large-scale popular participation in government and had tended to equate suffrage with liberty. Nevertheless, republican theorists also drew lines of distinction that democratic theorists were to abandon. For one thing, they supposed that representative government was necessary not only to protect liberty but also to raise the level of political delibera-

tions. Joseph J. Daniel echoed their views in the constitutional convention of North Carolina when, defending the choice of governor by the
legislature, "He said there was a great difference between Mobocracy
and Democracy. If the people were in a body to undertake to pass their
own laws, this would be Mobocracy; but when they elect Representatives for the purpose of forming their laws, this is Democracy." [24]

Similarly, republican advocates of manhood suffrage often took for
granted a standard of popular political behavior that was incompatible
with the actual practices even of their own day. In 1820 *Niles' Register*
declared editorially that "in looking at some of the state constitutions, we
have much cause to wonder that in this enlightened day, so many barriers should be placed between the people at large and their local governments—as though it were necessary to have a body of patricians to stand
between the plebeians and power!" Yet it also went on to say that "the
right of suffrage is so common in other states that it is not valued as it
should be. . . . The inestimable right is exercised with indifference, or
from favoritism. The choice of a sheriff, to execute the law, produces ten
times the bustle of the election of an officer who is to make the law. This
should not be so. We may have our *friends* at elections, but never ought
to forget that our first duty is to serve ourselves, in a serious selection of
persons best qualified by their wisdom to discern the wants and wishes
of the people of a state, and vested with virtue sufficient to pursue its interests to their consummation, in defiance of the intrigues of party or the
clamors of unworthy men." In republican eyes, the right of the people to
rule did not obliterate their obligation to rule wisely. [25]

Typically, Republicans also presupposed that the right to vote should
be limited to men who could make some claim to competence on the
basis of a demonstrated stake in society. As heirs of Jacksonian democracy we are inclined to equate all arguments from the stake in society
with reactionary challenges to popular rights, and it is clear that some of
the most insistent advocates of the principle—Chancellor Kent in New
York, for example—invoked it in intransigent antagonism to democracy.
But liberals as well as conservatives often assumed that some kind of interest must be established by anyone who aspired to the vote. In New
York State's convention, John Z. Ross embraced two versions of the
democratic principle. On the one hand, he declared that "in every free
state, the electors ought to form the basis, the soil from which every

thing is to spring, relating to the administration of their political concerns. Otherwise it could not be denominated a government of the people." On the other hand, he went on to say that "consequently all, at least, who contribute to the support or defence of the state, have a just claim to exercise the elective privilege, if consistent with the safety and welfare of the citizens. It is immaterial whether that support or defence of the state be by the payment of money, or by personal service, which are precisely one and the same thing, that of taxation." Even if we recognize that circumstances may have compelled him to temper his argument to the prejudices of the times, we must also acknowledge that those prejudices included at least a diminished version of the stake in society.[26]

Advocates of an extended suffrage who repudiated these implicit limitations were also prone to employ prudential calculations about the probable behavior of democratic voters to support their case for the vote. In New York, Nathan Sanford asked, "How is the extension of the right of suffrage unfavourable to property? Will not our laws continue the same? Will not the administration of justice continue the same?" Obviously, his argument was intended to discredit the fears that conservatives employed to defend a propertied senate, but even as a rebuttal to them it was strikingly insensititive to the changes popular rule might bring. (In effect, he simply assumed that the democracy would continue to act like a republic.) Similarly, the nonfreeholders of Richmond who petitioned the Virginia constitutional convention of 1829 for an extension of the suffrage insisted that "the generality of mankind, doubtless, desire to become owners of property: left free to reap the fruit of their labours, they will seek to acquire it honestly. It can never be their interest to overburthen, or render precarious, what they themselves desire to enjoy in peace." They were of course correct in their predictions, but the most striking thing about their argument is the fact that it left democracy to be vindicated by its performance even if it also tended to take that performance for granted.[27]

By contrast, democratic advocates of popular rule simply assumed the people's capacity for self-government. In doing so, of course, they drew upon the fortunate experience of the American republics, implying thereby that competence remained a criterion for the suffrage. Nevertheless, their view readily metamorphosed into an article of faith, as the *Democratic Review* demonstrated in celebrating Democratic victories in the 1838 elections: "The *people* have justified our trust in our political faith, and our confidence in them—in one of the greatest and finest of party triumphs ever obtained, under such a heavy combination of disadvantages—let us never be false to the people. A *principle* has proved its own indestructible vitality and its own invincible power, and has saved us out of the jaws of destruction—let us never be false to a principle. On these two commandments hang all the law and the prophets." Hence when they invoked experience in support of popular claims it usually took the form of self-evident truths vindicated by history. James Davis adopted this view in defending an elective rather than an appointive Secretary of State in the Texas convention: "It was a prevalent notion before the formation of the government of the United States, that the people are incapable of self government; that they should be ruled by something like an aristocracy. But, sir, have the fears then entertained been realized? No, sir. What has been the result of the experiment? It has made the United States equal to any country on earth: its improvement has been more rapid than that of any other: it has satisfied the lovers of freedom throughout the world, that the people are capable of governing themselves, and capable of selecting their own officers." [28]

More generally, democrats simply substituted rights for competence.[d] In 1844, the Select Committee of the House of Representatives on the Affairs of Rhode Island, dominated by Democrats sympathetic with the Dorr Rebellion, held that "the right of suffrage is a *natural*, not a *conventional* right, which attaches to the *man*, independent of the accidents of birth or fortune; of which right he cannot be divested, except by usurpation or force." In Louisiana, Isaac T. Preston went so far as to argue that the right existed in defiance of legal qualifications for voting: "I cannot consider it . . . a penitentiary offence," he declared during debate on voting frauds, "for an American citizen to attempt to get his right of suffrage. I would as soon think of prosecuting Promotheus [*sic*] for stealing fire as I would think of punishing a man for attempting to exercise a right which is implanted in the human soul." [29] On this view, manhood did not testify to competence so much as make it irrelevant, and such reservations as these enthusiasts still acquiesced in could legitimately be justified by failure to qualify as a man.[e]

To notice the residual deference Democrats expressed toward competence as a justification for the vote is, indeed, to scant their fundamental political commitment. Time and again, they said plainly that men retain their full range of natural rights on entering government and that the object of government is to preserve those rights intact. Philosophical Democrats like George Camp and Robert Rantoul Jr., who may be presumed to have derived elements of their political faith directly from Thomas Jefferson, held (in Rantoul's words) that "by our Constitution, perfect freedom is a natural, essential, and unalienable right. . . . The end of the institution, maintenance, and administration of government, is to secure the existence of the body politic, to protect it, and to furnish the individuals who compose it with the power of enjoying, in safety and tranquillity, their natural rights and the blessings of life." [30] Democratic agitators of a more modern persuasion subscribed to the same view. In New York City, the Equal Rights Party stated that "the rightful power of all legislation is to declare and enforce only our *natural rights and duties*, and to take *none of them from us*. . . . The idea is quite unfounded that on entering into society, we *give up any natural right*." In the same vein, the Democratic legislators of Massachusetts rebuked their Whig counterparts in 1840 for subscribing to a contractual theory of government that set limits on the natural right of self-government. So, too, Moses Jaques sought to persuade the New Jersey constitutional convention that men do not surrender any rights on entering into society, while Volney Hascall argued in Michigan that the people fully reserve their right to govern themselves. [31]

Seen in these terms, voting was not simply a natural right like other natural rights; it was also the indispensable guarantee for those rights. That is, it was a negative resource against power in the same sense that the rest of the democratic apparatus was a resource against power, and it was a natural right because democrats assumed that every man needed protection against government, not because every man had some sort of claim to competence in matters of public policy. "FREE SUFFRAGE is a subject of absorbing interest," the Democrats of Bristol County (Massachusetts) declared in 1842 apropos the Dorr Rebellion. "The right of voting is the basis of liberty. It distinguishes the SLAVE from the FREEMAN. In Rhode Island THREE-FIFTHS of the men are deprived of this right because they do not own REAL ESTATE." In Louisiana, Isaac T. Preston defended easy qualification for the legislature on similar grounds. "He who has but his industry to invest in the productive labor, and in the rich rewards of enterprise which our State presents," he declared, "has his person, his liberty, his character, and his prospects to be protected and advanced by government. These are as invaluable to him, and even to the State, as property to the rich: and therefore he should have a voice in enacting and executing the laws on which all that is dear and invaluable to him depends." The vote was priceless because it protected each man in the pursuit of his private interests.[32]

For that matter, it seems likely that one of the reasons Democratic partisans were so tolerant of an alien suffrage was that they conceived of the right to vote as a protective rather than a constructive function. Certainly some of its advocates pressed it as an agency of greater liberty. "We have now free suffrage, let us retain it," David L. Gregg argued in Illinois in 1847. "Do not let us follow examples of other states who have bound up this inestimable franchise by restrictions, until by lessening the right of suffrage, they have lessened the liberty of their people, have lessened their rights." Similarly, Walt Whitman attacked Native Americanism in 1842 on the ground that "we could see no man disfranchised, because he happened to be born three thousand miles off. We go for the largest liberty—the widest extension of the immunities of the people, as well as the blessings of government." Our supposition has plausibility even if we make large allowance for the fact that the Democrats expected to gain additional votes for their party by advocating only the barest of restrictions on alien voting. Significantly, conservative Democrats— those who continued to think that governments might usefully foster banking, internal improvements, or other public undertakings—were also much more likely than their "radical" counterparts to rebel at admitting aliens to the vote.[33]

In any event, the right of the people to decide public issues, which democrats of virtually every persuasion treated as an axiom of politics, commonly meant the right of the people to vote against intrusions on their autonomy. A radical agitator like Seth Luther articulated the theme in his *Address to Workingmen:* "We wish to injure no man, and we are determined not to be injured as we have been; we wish nothing, but those equal rights, which were designed for us all. And although wealth, and prejudice, and slander, and abuse, are all brought to bear on us, we have one consolation—'*We are the Majority.*' " The *Democratic Review* invoked the same right more temperately when it sought to define its party's creed in 1838: "The democratic creed may be summed up in this brief formula. As little government as possible; that little emanating from, and controlled by, the people; and uniform in its application to all." [34]

Otherwise, democracy meant an expansion of rights at the expense of government. In 1846, assessing contemporary constitutional reform, Theodore Sedgwick Jr. wrote in the *Democratic Review* that democracy meant "restoration of every citizen to the enjoyment of every liberty or privilege not inconsistent with the enjoyment of a corresponding liberty or privilege by every other." Democratic stalwarts in the conventions bore out his statement. In Iowa, Stephen Hempstead defended an elective judiciary on the grounds that "we were elected by the people to save to them all the rights that they could rightfully and properly exercise," while in Louisiana both James F. Brent and Cyrus Ratliff argued (in Brent's words) that "our mission is to give the people greater liberties; not to restrain the liberties which they already enjoy." "Give to every man in the community the greatest amount of liberty consonant with the safety of society," Isaac Preston urged. "Place all your citizens upon a footing of perfect equality as to their political rights, and you will promote the well-being and happiness of all." In the context of democratic doctrine, even the restrictions such spokesmen apparently put upon the extension of liberty were necessitated by the rights of the people.[35]

THE RIGHT OF SELF-GOVERNMENT

In democratic eyes, all power was dangerous, and democracy would be safe only insofar as it made superfluous the positive exercise of power even by the people. Hence the ultimate tendency of democratic thought was to turn to self-government as a way of avoiding the necessity of government.[36] The logic of democratic doctrine was amply expressed in a number of essentially philosophical attempts at a theory of democracy. In conservative doctrine, as we shall see, self-government tended to follow from the claims of character. On this view, men of a suitable disposition were entitled to govern themselves politically because they were already able to govern themselves as individuals.[37] By contrast, Democratic philosophers often seemed to suggest that freedom came first and character was irrelevant.

George Camp said as much in *Democracy*. On one level, he argued in a vein of democratic self-denial that "we are not made for authority over our fellow-beings. That moral nature, by virtue of which alone we could claim it, has evidently been given us for the regulation and government of ourselves alone. . . . Nature has made each, for himself alone, the executor of her laws, and she qualifies no man to prescribe and act for another." ᶠ On another level, he insisted that any plausible definition of liberty must include an individual's freedom to obey only his own will. "Our passions prompt us to action, our moral and deliberative powers regulate us in our choice of actions, and the will sets the whole machine in motion," he declared in the vocabulary of contemporary psychology. "But what tends all this machinery but to *action?* and, if we are not *free* to *act,* to what purpose are we *free* to *will?* If, the instant we begin to act, we must be subjected to some external governing power, the whole man is nonplused at once; and those exalted powers, that liken us to the image of God himself, are made superfluous lumber in the human breast." On this basis self-government was identical with throwing off external authority: "Man has no right, by nature, to make laws for another. . . . [He] enjoys by nature, in relation to other men, the right of repulsion, and not the right of direction. The difference is, that the exercise of the former right is confined exclusively to one's self, the latter extends to and arrogates the direction of the affairs of third persons." [38]

Other theorists largely agreed in ignoring the possibility that there might be intellectual or moral conditions American citizens must meet in order to qualify for self-government. True, John L. O'Sullivan clearly believed that they had further progress to make in the course of civilization before they could be fully exempted from government in the traditional sense, and M. A. Richter went so far as to argue that a self-governing man must be not only a "perfect man, but also a perfect member of human society, who does not permit himself to be guided by others, as they please, either by the sword or by any other force, because he is able, and always ready to guide himself personally alone, and, of course, will respect the same qualities in others." But Richter began his little treatise on *Self-Government* by declaring that "The word, Self-Government, is of American origin. Its meaning is,—*Rational, candid and manly conduct and independence in our concerns, which does not admit the interference of others. It is the fruit of Liberty in America, and is but very little known in Europe and Asia.*" In addition, he tended like O'Sullivan to attribute contemporary failures of self-government to the destructive influ-

ence of governments on human capabilities, a view that obviously placed
the responsibility for undermining liberty on government rather than
mankind.[39]

To the extent they suggested that self-government depended upon morality, moreover, these same writers often took for granted that the necessary morality would follow from freedom. In this sense they placed
morality in the balance against authority by making the one the antithesis of the other: it was not a condition to be met but a consequence
that could be expected to follow from democracy as they understood it.
"The same mind that adopts religion for its truth, its purity, and its simplicity," the *Democratic Review* declared in 1838 in a revealing analogy,
"would be inclined, for the same reasons, to adopt the principles of democracy. The same mind that discovers the necessity of the penal sanctions of the law, to give adequate moral force to religion, is inclined to
discover the necessity of some external, physical, independent power, to
control man's moral conduct." During the 1840s George Camp and William S. Balch echoed the idea that self-government produces morality,
and in 1853 Michael Doheny summed up "The Principle, Progress, Tendency, Obligations and Destiny of Democracy" by declaring, "Here
popular government has nearly reached perfection. It has, in fact, ceased
to be the *government* and become the REIGN of the people. This is the
nearest approach possible to the laws of providence and nature, and the
best exemplification of free-will." [40] Democracy demanded in the name
of morality that men throw off every trace of subordination to political
institutions.[g]

Doheny also argued that it was not necessary for the people to interfere with the courses of action their delegated functionaries took because
they could leave any infractions to the punishments the law provided.
His expression was cloudy but his sentiments were clear and also rather
familiar: demeaning power, politics, and government, Democrats who
denied that men must be moral before they could be free turned to the
law as an all-pervading instrumentality that would make free society
habitable. Sometimes they had specific constitutional arrangements in
view when they invoked it; we shall examine their attitudes on this score
in chapter IX. But frequently they looked to law in its generic sense to
maintain the freedoms they described. Even when they criticized the
American judiciary for cleaving too closely to English legal precedents,

they still bore clearly in mind the vision of a society in which "justice" would do the work of legislation, in which the administration of legal rights by the courts would constitute virtually the whole domestic work of government. "We are among the most steadfast friends of a government of law," the *Democratic Review* held in 1838.

There can be no good government without its supremacy. While law is wisely and impartially administered, other operations of government may almost stand still, without much private wrong or public suffering. Let justice be faithfully administered . . . and the entire apparatus of Presidents, Secretaries, Generals, Post-captains, Foreign Ministers, Members of Congress, and other functionaries, with armies, navies, fortifications, appropriations, &c. &c. may almost be dispensed with; and we confidently believe that a century hence will exhibit such an approximation towards this state of things, and with it a yet-unknown degree of social well-being and improvement, as would astonish the present generation.[41]

On this view, the law could safely be substituted for government because, unlike government in the more active sense, it guaranteed rights without encroaching on freedom.[h]

Even the lawlessness that less philosophical Americans notoriously displayed seems paradoxically to mirror the respect their philosophers had for law as the matrix of society. To understand the paradox we must recognize that their much lamented tendency to ignore the law when it did not coincide with their wishes was a plausible corollary of self-government understood as the right to regulate one's own conduct. In effect, the lawless citizen held that laws were needed to restrain evil men but not to disadvantage good ones like himself. At the same time, the Americans' equally notorious tendency to press retribution for crimes beyond the provisions of their own legal code was also a plausible corollary of self-government in the sense that it represented actions taken by ordinary citizens to enforce minimal standards of self-government against villains who took advantage of freedom. Inasmuch as American democrats visualized law primarily as a protection of their own rights, not a securing of others', they had little reason to be aware of the extent to which they sinned against the very principle they enunciated.

This, at least, was the thrust of an otherwise incomprehensible argument that Representative John A. Quitman of Mississippi put forward in 1856 in condemnation of the nation's neutrality laws, which President

Pierce had invoked to suppress filibustering expeditions to Central America.

The government is responsible *to* the citizen, but not *for* him. He may commit, without responsibility to any earthly power, many deeds which the government cannot so commit. The latter is always responsible. The American citizen sits enthroned within the charmed circle of his reserved rights, the monarch of his own actions. The reservation of these individual rights is the noblest feature of our system; and he is its worst enemy who, by legislative usurpation or judicial construction, would seek to impair them. The true patriot should watch and guard them from secret as well as open foes.

  Even if the penal laws which I have arraigned were strictly constitutional, I would still oppose them as unwise, impolitic, and against the genius of our free institutions. They are founded upon the false assumption that the government should direct the morals and control the sentiment of the people. It is sheer political hypocrisy, or, at least, self-stultification, to crown with honor the memory of the good man Lafayette, . . . if we are by legislation to stigmatize as criminal the efforts of our own citizens, to bear assistance to a neighboring people, groaning under the yoke of an iron despotism—a despotism to which the condition of our ancestors was almost a state of freedom.

Few men who heard Quitman agreed with him completely, but he was typical of his generation in refusing to make a fetish of law in the sense of limitations, on the ground that he was attached to law as the vehicle of rights.[42]

❧ VIII ❧

THE POLITICS OF
WHIGGERY

In general, the success of democratic innovations in politics also meant the success of Democratic candidates, and men who wished to compete with Democracy were forced to adopt a theory of politics they had often begun by denouncing. This was the origin and significance of Whiggery, which emerged from a long process of political accommodation that may be said to have begun with the younger Federalists, continued with the National Republicans and Antimasons, and culminated in the candidacy of William Henry Harrison. Although the line of descent was by no means as direct as this classic exercise in genealogy suggests, there is no reason to cavil over it so long as we remember that we are dealing with ideas rather than biographies. During every decade, leading figures in one major party or political faction aligned themselves with their erstwhile opposition, but the ideas they employed or the rationalizations they invoked had a long and fairly consistent history.

The general pattern is so familiar that, sensing the insubstantiality of many Whig fears and recognizing the cynicism of many Whig politicians, we often neglect to examine it in detail. Yet the doctrines and tenets of Whiggery deserve examination not only because they were widely held and demonstrably effective on particular occasions, but also because in the long run they helped to divide democracy against itself. Whiggery as well as Democracy was part of the American political tradition.[1]

THE WHIG STANDARD OF POLITICS

Much Whig argument began with a declared wish to secure election of the best men to office. The premise was especially prominent in presidential politics, where many conservative spokesmen held that both the candidacy and the election of Andrew Jackson represented a gross distortion of traditional republican standards of politics. Here as elsewhere we must attempt an act of historical imagination in order to recognize the basis of conservative fears. We may know better, but Jackson's opponents thought they had reason to doubt his competence and to look askance at his military temperament. As Senator David Barton of Missouri observed in defending the action of members of the House of Representatives who had voted for John Quincy Adams in the election of 1824, "We conscientiously believed Mr. Adams the better qualified of the two principal candidates. . . . Our devotion to the civil over the military was sincere. We perceived no essential difference in their political principles. Their construction of the great charter of our rights and powers was the same; their great leading principles of policy were the same. We saw no difference then; we see none now." [2]

Opposing Jackson, conservative spokesmen often also criticized the party machinery that helped to place him in office. On the one hand, they reprobated the very idea of party, which they associated with "faction" and blamed for the corruption of the political process. By the same token, they also condemned Democracy as an instrument of political oppression, imposing its will even on its own adherents. In *Quodlibet* John Pendleton Kennedy has Abel Brawn say "Thank God! the democracy I've larnt in my time . . . has imbibed in to my mind the principle that I am a freeman, and have a right to think for myself, to speak for myself and to act for myself, without having a string put through my nose to lead me wherever it suits a set of scheming, lying, cunning politicians to have me for their benefit. Democracy's not what it used to be, or you would never find the people putting up with this eternal dictation from the President and his friends, to Congress and to the nation, what he will have, and what he won't have:—that's what I call rank monarchy, and I will fight against it to my latest breath." [3]

Nevertheless, the principle of nonpartisan politics was self-defeating, and for every thoughtful conservative who truly hoped to exclude party loyalty from politics there were several who sought to attract popular support for a new opposition party. Governor James Barbour of Virginia exemplified a transitional stage in this development when, at the "Democratic Whig National Convention" of 1839, he invoked the surviving soldiers of the Revolutionary War as aides in the work of redeeming American liberty from the demagogues who controlled American politics. The very name "Whig," which conservatives adopted during the late 1830s, betokened the same kind of effort to equate contemporary political efforts with the heroic tradition of the past. So did the appeal to a "revolution" at least in opinion, which dominated Whig polemics in 1840.[4]

By 1844, however, leading Whig spokesmen simply acquiesced in the existing party structure and sought to turn it to account by equating the Whig party with a timeless liberty. In Rhode Island, William R. Watson drafted a defense of the party in which he demonstrated (at least to his own satisfaction) that "the Whig party, at all times and in all lands, has raised high the banner of Freedom. Under its broad, bright folds patriots have ever battled bravely against the abuses, the encroachments and the tyranny of power—whether wielded by a monarch on his throne, or a ferocious and despotic party in the halls of legislation. It is a glorious party—the party of the free—the liberal—the patriotic every where." Calvin Colton demonstrated even more clearly the extremes to which Democratic successes ultimately forced Whig apologists when he explained in *The Crisis of the Country*, and reiterated in the *Junius Tracts*, that one of the principal reasons for supporting the Whigs was the fact that "the two great parties of this country will always remain nearly equal to watch each other, and every few years there must be a change. This is essential to the preservation of our liberties. If power stays always in the hands of one party, the leaders would ruin us. This accounts for the fact, that we are nearly ruined now." On this view, party loyalty was indispensable not only when but also because it was a loyalty without specific content.[5]

At the same time, Whig partisans elaborated their original doubts of Jackson's suitability for high office into a systematic attack on "executive despotism" that radically altered the principles they initially espoused. To some extent their fears were genuine and reflected legitimate issues of constitutional structure and practice, but to an ever-increasing extent they seem to have represented a cynical effort to discredit Democratic candidates by appealing to popular fantasies about power encroaching on liberty.[a] In 1835, for example, Senator Joseph Kent of Maryland sponsored a constitutional amendment to limit the veto power of the president on the grounds (among others) that he holds office for a long time, is a single figure, can plot in private, and is as chief executive especially susceptible to the lust for power, not to say singularly able to control the action of Congress through use of the patronage. Similarly, in a letter to the *New York American* that was subsequently reprinted in the *Cincinnati Daily Gazette*, a Whig partisan declared that Martin Van Buren intended "a war on the currency of the country, . . . a war on the merchants and mercantile interests, . . . linking together of the monied institutions of the country, to support the power of the general government," ruthless treatment of the Indians, dismissal of all office-holders who disagreed with him, and "an assumption of all doubtful or questionable power by the Executive." These were not concerns peculiar to the 1830s but standard Whig complaints, equally serviceable in other campaigns, and useful even to explain why John Tyler had proved so unsatisfactory a successor to William Henry Harrison. "The will of one man triumphed over the expressed wishes of a nation, and the spirit of the constitution," the Democratic Whig Young Men of New York City explained in 1841. "With grief and shame we saw our own elected officer so dazzled with the glitter of the presidential office, that he could not surrender the unjust acquisitions of his predecessors." [6]

The logical effect of such diatribes was to discredit not only the presidents Democrats named but the office they filled. Significantly, the Whig party of Missouri committed itself, in its *Address to the People* (1840), to diminishing the "vast power" of the presidency irrespective of who exercised it: "We flatter ourselves that we have demonstrated its dangerous and corrupting tendency, and we leave it with our fellow republicans of the State to decide whether, IF MR. VAN BUREN HAD DONE EVER SO WELL, THE INTERESTS OF THE UNION AND THE UNCORRUPTED PRESERVATION OF ITS INSTITUTIONS, DO NOT REQUIRE THAT THE EXAMPLE SHALL BE NOW SET, THAT NO MAN, OR SET OF MEN, SHALL HAVE CONTROL OF THE GOVERNMENT BEYOND A SINGLE TERM?" Similarly, Harrison's inaugural address was in many respects an abdication, a state document suggesting that he intended to reign but not to rule in order to redeem liberty from its Democratic enemies. [7]

Clamoring against executive despotism, Whig spokesmen also called into question the very concept of an effective national government, which their conservative predecessors had held to be an indispensable political objective. Their shifting values were particularly evident in their attacks on the Independent Treasury, which the Van Buren administration advocated as an alternative to placing federal deposits in the so-called pet banks. Sometimes they invoked a "divorce" between bank and state at least as complete as anything the Democrats had proposed, albeit with a different perspective on how that divorce was to be effected. On other occasions they insisted that a government active in banking must be a coercive and illiberal institution, wholly threatening to popular freedom. "It is Government stepping aside from its appropriate functions," Calvin Colton wrote in the *Junius Tracts*, "and setting up in trade; for banking is nothing more or less than trading in money. It is, so far, laying aside the proper uses of Government, and usurping the rights of citizens—commercial rights. . . . No Government ever went into trade, in money or any thing else, without injury to the rights of citizens; or with gain to itself, except in the augmentation of its power, which is always its object." [8]

Above all, they equated the power government might exercise over and through the Treasury with the power the Bank of the United States had exercised as a private corporate enterprise. Far from distinguishing between the two kinds of power, the one politically responsible and subject to popular control, the other politically irresponsible and protected by charter against public interference, they acquiesced in Democratic fantasies about power in order to turn them against Democratic policy. "A national Government Bank, to answer the purposes of such an institution," Colton insisted, "aims to regulate and control the currency of the country, and in doing that, it—that is, the Government—brings within its power, to deal with at pleasure, every possible commercial or trading interest of the country, from that of banking in general, down to the vocation of a grinder of knives or a retailer of brickdust. It would be a supreme commercial power, in the hands of the supreme political power, controlled by none, but controlling all, itself master in trade, and master of the authorities under which all trade is carried on." So, too, they portrayed the proposed sub-treasury as an effort to "divorce the Government from the people" for the greater aggrandizement of the government. "Of all schemes of policy I can conceive," Senator William C. Rives of Virginia declared in 1837, employing polemical categories that would echo through the next three years, "that which proposes a permanent distinction between the Government and the people in their pecuniary interests—one currency, and that the *better* one, for the Government, and another, and inferior currency, for the people—such a system of discrimination is, to my mind, of all others, the most injurious and revolting in principle, the most heartless in character, and the most despotic in its tendencies. It is like quartering the Government, as a foreign enemy, on the heart of the country." [9]

Their tactics were understandable but the consequences were deplorable for anyone who still thought that government might be employed to foster the public welfare; if these protestations were to be believed, the party was committed to a career of masterly inactivity in office, as well as insistent obstructionism when out of it. Henry Clay exemplified the destructive tendencies of Whig doctrine during a campaign speech in 1840, in which he remarked, "Do not mock us with the vain assurance of the honor and probity of a President, nor remind us of the confidence which we ought to repose in his imagined virtues. The pervading principle of our system of Government—of all free governments—is not merely the possibility, but the absolute certainty of infidelity and treachery with even the highest functionary of the State; and hence all the restrictions, securities, and guarantees which the wisdom of our ancestors or the sad experience of history had inculcated have been devised and thrown around the Chief Magistrate." [10]

Even so, this was ostensibly only an attack on executive tyranny; but the party's presidential candidate converted it into a general rule of politics. "Under Jefferson, Madison, and Monroe," Harrison declared at Fort Meigs (Indiana), "the eye of the people was turned to the right source—to the administration. The administration, however, now say to the people, 'You must not watch us, but you must watch the Whigs! Only do that, and all is safe!' But that, my friends, is not the way. The old-fashioned Republican rule is to watch the Government. See that the Government does not acquire too much power. Keep a check upon your rulers. Do this, and liberty is safe." As the Whigs now defined it, their object in seeking power was to prevent the government from exercising it, which they now claimed they were better able than the Democrats to do. [11]

THE WHIG STANDARD OF RIGHTS

The Whigs first developed their argument against power in government in relation to national politics, where Democratic propaganda had been most successful and where there was a long tradition of suspicion to draw upon. *Mutatis mutandis*, however, many of the same forces were also at work in state politics, where conservative spokesmen began by debating the theory of democracy only to capitulate to it finally in its most egregious form.

The standard the Whigs abandoned was sharply dramatized in the constitutional convention of Louisiana, where conservative delegates contended bitterly against both democratic dogmas and democratic pretensions. On the one hand, they protested the theory that government is intrinsically inimical to liberty; on the other, they denied that the people have either a God-given competence or a God-given right to decide complex public questions. W. C. C. Claiborne spoke to both points when he declared, during debate on proposals to establish a longer residence requirement for alien voters, "If every reasonable restraint in government is to be considered a harsh restriction, we had better abolish the government at once, and resolve society into its original state of individual independence and anarchy." [12]

The debates in Louisiana were unusual in that the conservative politicians who spoke there apparently had no fear that they might be penalized at the polls for their reactionary views, but Whig spokesmen in other areas also expressed such grave reservations with respect to both popular rights and popular competence as to warrant the conclusion that Whigs in general had a lively sense of the anomalies implicit in theories of politics based on natural rights. In Massachusetts, the party's legislative delegation replied to Governor Marcus Morton's inaugural address by denying that paupers and other citizens who paid no taxes deserved to vote and by insisting that the suffrage was not and could not be a natural right. Likewise, in the constitutional convention of Illinois, Whig opponents of an alien suffrage denied that men had a natural right to vote, while the minority members of the Select Committee appointed by the federal House of Representatives to investigate affairs in Rhode Island went out of their way to disavow Democratic claims based on such "rights." Not surprisingly, therefore, Chancellor Kent's *Commentaries on American Law* criticized a number of state constitutions because their bills of rights proclaimed the right of the people to instruct their representatives: "This would be repugnant to the theory of government, which supposes that the representatives are to meet and consult together for the common welfare, and to have a regard, in the making of laws, to the greatest general good, and to make the local views and interest of a part of the community, subordinate to the general interest of the whole." [13]

Outspoken conservatives denied not only the natural rights of the people but also the theory that government is authorized simply to protect the rights they may surrender. The Whig legislators of Massachusetts explicitly developed this point in 1840: "The natural right of man is to be governed by himself alone; but this natural right is to be abandoned the moment he enters into a state of civilized society." Similarly, in 1848 Henry W. Warner of New York argued in the *American Review* that the people cannot reserve rights against government because they neither create it nor determine its powers; rather, he pointed out, their right to vote and their other rights are themselves created by that government. Moreover, in reviewing E. P. Hurlbut's *Essays on Human Rights and their Political Guaranties*, in 1845, the Whig monthly condemned the author for treating society as a mere aggregate of individuals and government as a mere instrument for protecting individual rights. When they thought about politics systematically, Whigs—or at least Whigs who lived in the older portions of the country—were as repelled by the Democratic theory of rights as by the Democratic fear of power.[14]

Despite these clear evidences of their hostility to democratic doctrine, the Whigs ended by insisting that they alone were faithful to it. This effort was particularly apparent in Calvin Colton's sixth *Junius Tract*, in which he attempted much the same verbal magic with respect to "democracy" that he practiced with the "money power." On the one hand, Colton charged the Democrats with being the advocates of monarchy and insisted that the Whigs had always been the advocates of popular government. On the other hand, he launched a brief inquiry into the essential character of the American government, in which he deprecated attempts at "a nice scrutiny of the constitutional structure of our Government, as compared with an original and pure theoretical democracy, sitting and governing themselves in primary assemblies of the people." The object of this maneuver was clear: to define away the advantages that Democrats gained by the very name of their party. With it, however, he also defined away distinctions between republicanism and democracy that had been important to American conservative writers for well over fifty years.[15]

Identifying themselves as the only true democrats, Whig spokesmen also substantially altered the conservative theory of rights. The nature and import of this transaction are apparent in their insistently repeated claim that (in the words of the minority of the Select Committee) "if the majority of a whole people associated under government are supreme, above law and constitution, [and] their will is the only limit of their act— natural rights have no existence, because the supremacy of this will may decree their destruction; [and] minorities are slaves, to whom obedience becomes sacred duty." Given its premises, the statement could not help but be true, but we need not labor the point that its authors did not offer it as an exercise in tautology. Rather, they intended to place rights in the balance against power to the detriment of power, and they invoked natural rights because those rights offered the greatest possible potential for resisting the evils of majority rule.[16]

Their argument was understandable, but it amounted to an abdication of traditional views. Chief Justice Joseph C. Hornblower of New Jersey demonstrated how far most Whigs had come when he criticized the idea of incorporating a bill of rights into that state's revised constitution. Echoing a number of Federalists who had thought that a bill of rights was superfluous in a popular government, he argued that "we have now arrived at a period when we should discard the lesson which we have learned from our ancestors, who were compelled to ask crowned heads for a bill of rights. What do we want them for? Although I was born in revolutionary times, at the first dawning of my reasoning powers, I imbibed the doctrine that these rights were our own. They are written on our hearts. Why shall we tell ourselves what our rights are, or protect ourselves against ourselves?" But he was admittedly in a minority, repudiated by his immediate colleagues and by most Whigs elsewhere. "If I understand what eminent writers say upon the subject," John C. Ten Eyck declared, citing Kent and Story as his sources, "they say that a bill of rights is more necessary and called for in a republican government, than under a crowned head—that as all power springs from the people, they should declare that the great fundamental doctrines of civil liberty should not be interfered with in any way, but that minor matters should be left with the Legislative." [17]

The object of such appeals was obvious, their utility in forestalling contemporary radicalism no less so. For that matter, some conservative spokesmen made no attempt to disguise their intention of restraining the popular will. "It is not questioned that in all republican governments majorities must rule," Judah P. Benjamin declared in Louisiana; "but it is no less true that the constitutions of all the States are made for the purpose of protecting the rights of the minority from being trampled upon by the majority; and that the only reliance the minority can have, is the measure of restriction thrown into the constitution by which they are to be governed. Without the constitution be framed in such a way as to accomplish both these ends, it will be an useless instrument." The content of the conservatives' argument was no less significant because it was invoked to protect vested interests. For whatever reasons and with whatever candor, political commentators who had reason to know better sought to restrict the authority even of the state governments, which they had at one time considered agencies of the common welfare.[18]

Moreover, conservatives often advocated constitutional restrictions in the name of rights they would once have scorned, had they been invoked by democrats against the fostering hand of a republican government. Francis Lieber exemplified the thrust of their thought in distinguishing invidiously between the principles of ancient and modern liberty. The first, he wrote in *Essays on Property and Labour,* required the equal partici- pation of everyone in government, "no matter how this was effected," whereas "modern liberty consists essentially in guarantees of the individ- ual rights of man, and, consequently, in checks upon power, and the protection of the minority against aggressions by the majority. Hence our constitutions, binding even overwhelming majorities." Thomas H. Lewis demonstrated even more clearly than Lieber the shift in conserva- tive assessments of politics during the course of a single speech in the Louisiana constitutional convention. There he supported requiring five years' residence of legislators on the clearly conservative ground that the representative is the ruler of the people. "The truth may be unpalatable to the ultra democracy, the ultra democrat, and the jacobins. They may not relish the idea of submission in the sovereign people, but relish it or not, to get rid of it, they must destroy the very essence of government." Yet he also went on to cast doubt on the premises of his argument when he asked rhetorically, "Whence proceeds . . . so much improper legisla- tion? It is because men are actuated too often by their sudden impulses, and go to extremities without weighing the consequences! Hence, the necessity for hedging our liberties with proper guards and restrictions: to limit the power and the possibility of doing evil, as far as human sagacity can prevail." [19] If he fell short of invoking natural rights against government, he left no other criterion by which to test a government's performance.[b]

Seeking to curtail the power of government when they could not control it, the Whigs also turned to constitutionalism—the deliberate invocation of complicated checks and balances and other mechanisms of political limitation—to serve their political ends. In doing so they drew on a well-established tradition in American conservative thought, but the fact that the tradition was well established does not fully account for their doctrines. Rather, they made a clearly selective use of the constitutional tradition, and they also elaborated it in ways their predecessors could not have anticipated. The outcome of their deliberations was a constitutional mystique that went far toward challenging the tenets of the democracy.[20]

Conservative constitutionalism was most clearly apparent in the state constitutional conventions of the 1830s and 1840s, in which Whig leaders retreated before aggressively democratic innovations but continued to insist that the fundamental constitutional apparatus of their states be preserved. The logic of their course was especially apparent in their treatment of the upper house, which some spokesmen visualized not as a coordinate branch of the legislature but as a superior branch intended to curb the aberrations of the more popular house. "It is right and proper," Peter I. Clark declared in the New Jersey convention of 1844, "that the impulses of the people should be gratified, should be wasted, should be exhausted Sir, in the House of Assembly. And in that portion of our representatives I am quite willing to see such a body of men, who represent the impulses, the excitement, the feelings of the people. But, Sir, I want to feel assured that notwithstanding all this exists in that body, there is another body above them who will not be alarmed by these storms, who will not be swayed by these feelings." In the following year Charles M. Conrad and André B. Roman developed the same argument in the Louisiana convention, where leading Whigs were outspoken in their hostility to democracy.[21]

Even so, the attempt to subordinate democratic impulses to the authority of the upper house was far from being the characteristic feature of latter-day Whiggery. Although the attempt had a good many precedents, illustrated in part by the conventions held in Massachusetts and New York in 1820 and 1821, it had been doomed in practice by the democratization of American politics, which simply pushed aside extraordinary qualifications for office, the representation of special interests, and a restricted suffrage, in favor of the direct election of senators by the same means and on the same basis as representatives. Under these circumstances it would have been logical to abandon the upper house, but in practice Whig partisans not only took its necessity for granted but also strove diligently to maintain some sort of distinction between it and the lower house. "If the members of the two branches of the legislature were to possess like qualifications, to be vested with like powers on all subjects of legislation, to be elected upon precisely the same basis of population, by the same electors, in the same manner, and for the same term," Abner C. Harding asked in Illinois in 1847, "why should they be divided into two branches? It was not enough to be told that one branch was intended to be a check upon the other, unless by their different characters and constituency this desirable result was to be secured." In effect, they declared that they would retain bicameralism because it promised to make governing more difficult.[22]

We tend today to take this point of view for granted and so to miss its significance. In one sense, the theory of a distinctive bicameralism only echoed earlier constitutional doctrines, which had made deliberate use of complexity in the governing process to forestall political evils. Nevertheless, the constitutionalism that earlier conservatives embraced had been intended more to protect society against the effects of ill-considered legislation than to throw obstacles in the way of governing. Appeals to a representation of disparate interests had initially had much the same force. The North Carolina convention of 1835 provides useful examples of the thrust of traditional beliefs. There, William Gaston insisted that "government is formed for the purpose of protecting property and persons, and would be inadequate to its end, if [it] left either at the mercy of the other." Similarly, Hugh McQueen argued that it was as necessary to protect liberty as to protect property in the composition of the legislature, while David Outlaw defended a powerful senate on the grounds that the proposed constitution was intended to represent both sections of the state. (Here as elsewhere in the South, numerical representation favored the upcountry and property representation the lowlands.) Even if some of these arguments were disingenuous, motivated by the hopes or fears of particular segments of the society, the constitutional model they took for granted assumed a kind of watchful collaboration in government, checked but not forestalled by the balance they hailed.[23,c]

By contrast, typical Whigs tended to call for a constitutional balance that would virtually prevent governing. Recalling Benjamin Franklin's comparison of bicameralism to a wagon with one horse hitched in front and another in the rear, one of their number in the Illinois convention complained of Democratic efforts to strengthen the executive veto: "Gentlemen here, are not only for putting a horse before, and a horse behind, but for putting so great a weight upon the wagon, that it cannot be moved." But his sentiments were obsolete, and although many of his fellow partisans joined him in opposing an executive veto, it was not because they objected to restricting the efficiency of government. Significantly, Abner Harding urged that the two houses must be grounded in real differences in order to overcome their natural tendency to align themselves with the executive, while William A. Minshall advocated both a large representation in the legislature and an effective executive veto: "I entertain a desire to see a full and fair representation of the people in the popular branch of the Legislature, because this is the department which most closely and intimately reflects the wishes and interests of the people; but for the very reason that this branch also represents the passions and prejudices of the mass, . . . the executive should therefore be invested with this negative, this counteracting power. In this consists the beauty, harmony and science of our system." In effect, both men suggested that the veto would be desirable if it could be used to restrain popular enthusiasms, but undesirable if it were used to implement them.[24]

More generally, Whig spokesmen embraced the whole apparatus of constitutionalism as a mechanism for controlling popular government. This, too, was a time-honored position; but again the tenor of conservative opinion had changed. On the classic view, constitutional mechanisms were necessary to curb aberrations of every sort: of legislatures and executives, of majorities and minorities. On the modern view, they were explicitly intended to restrict popular majorities. As a result, the conservative argument that restrictions are inevitable in any government metamorphosed into an argument that constitutions are intended to restrict popular power for the sake of minorities. "Allow me to ask for what pu[r]pose we are here?" Judah P. Benjamin inquired in Louisiana. "Is it not to make a constitution? And what is a constitution except a system of rules and *restrictions* intended to secure a permanent government, which shall be unaffected by the changing views and passions of the hour; which shall *restrict* majorities and protect minorities? If the people are to be governed without *restrictions* at all, as some honorable members would seem to insist, what a farce are our proceedings?" [25]

Exploring the possibilities of constitutional limitation, Whigs also labored to endow established constitutional arrangements with a prescriptive authority. In commenting on affairs in Rhode Island, for example, they argued repeatedly that the Dorr government was not only revolutionary but illegitimate because it had sought to alter the existing constitution of the state by means not provided in it. The fact that the constitution against which the Free Suffrage movement had rebelled was in reality a slightly modified version of the original colonial charter, which had not been revised like other states' instruments of government at the time of the American Revolution, did not affect their judgment of the issues. Neither did the fact that Benjamin Hazard's *Report* to the state legislature in 1829 had denied it the right to extend the suffrage on the grounds that such changes belonged to the constituent people. "We understand the report of the majority to contend," the minority members of the Select Committee on Rhode Island declared with obvious incredulity, ". . . that a majority of the male adult citizens of any State have the right, in their original sovereign unlimited capacity, without sanction of law, and against the will both of the minority and existing authorities, to change or destroy a government they themselves may have formed, or which had been formed even prior to their becoming citizens under its provisions." In the eyes of these spokesmen, the antiquity of the charter obviously justified rather than condemned it. [26]

Elsewhere, Whig leaders commonly sought to prevent any easing of the amending process they themselves engaged in. Meeting in constitutional conventions mandated for the most part by popular referenda, elected by popular suffrage, and dependent on additional referenda to legitimize their proposals for constitutional change, they could hardly deny the right of the people to alter their fundamental laws. They could, however, deny them the right to do so easily, on the grounds expressed by Richard S. Field in the New Jersey convention. According to the surviving account, "Mr. F. said he might have incorrect ideas about constitutions but he thought they should be in a degree, out of the power of majorities. I regard constitutions as one of the noblest inventions of modern times. The ancient republics were without them—and the consequence is, that the plains of Marathon are now trodden by the slave, and the once proud mistress of the world is now only celebrated for the ruins which shadow forth her ancient glory—and it has been reserved for us in modern time to invent constitutions, by which the people may be protected against themselves." [27,d]

Here their behavior suggested that constitutions were to be restrictive whether or not they were vested, and in fact Whigs often appealed to the mystique of a fundamental law to support the provisions they desired. One of the elements in this mystique was a portentous appeal to history—not to the historic origins of specific constitutional provisions, although these attracted some attention, but to the future of freedom embodied in the document they were drafting. "Sir, what are we called together to do?" asked William Woodbridge in Michigan in 1835, turning to constitutional longevity to discredit Democratic party efforts to extend the suffrage to aliens,

To fix upon a fundamental law—to settle upon and adjust those great principles which are to constitute the shield and the safeguard of the public liberties—to form a constitution of government, the influence of which is to be felt for ages. And is it wise, sir, and prudent, and philosophical to fashion and graduate that constitution, with a view to the operations of party? Of party, sir? All parties are and ever have been, creatures of a day; mutability is stamped upon their very front: that which is in the ascendant one day, is prostrate the next! It is for that very reason that *constitutions* are formed—and are necessary. They are necessary expressly to guard against the despotism of party; minorities must be protected, and protected against the excesses of a majority, carried into ephemeral power perhaps by the force of party, and made delerious [*sic*] in the effervescence of recent conflict—lest at any time their rights and their liberties should be swept away! Sir, constitutions are made for minorities; and I say it with emphasis, majorities have the whole power of the state in their own hands, and what need have *they* of constitutional protections?

In Louisiana, Charles M. Conrad employed similar images in behalf of seating two Whig members from New Orleans: "We were delegated to establish a constitution which would subsist when we were numbered with the dead: a constitution which would entitle us to the blessings or the curses of posterity, when the exciting differences that now divided our political parties would pass into oblivion. He had hoped and believed that political animosities would have been obliterated, and that all considerations not directly connected with the object that brought us here, would have been cast aside." Whig spokesmen sought in the figurative as well as the literal sense to make constitutionalism an obstacle to democracy.[28]

Appealing to the future, they also appealed to the idea that a constitution was an organic development combining the qualities of vested inheritance with those of an obligation to posterity. In this sense their position was reminiscent of Edmund Burke, implying the existence of a relationship binding together the past, the present, and the future, except that Burke would hardly have understood the mechanical contrivances they valued, and they did not invoke Burke. Rather, they sought to inculcate a sort of disembodied reverence, a deference to law that would be equally applicable to any particular instrument so long as it was effective. Woodbridge approached this form of argument in Michigan, as Conrad did in Louisiana, but it was left to the *American Review* to articulate it most directly. Criticizing the proposed new constitution of New York for the haste with which it had been drafted, the *Review* observed in 1846:

Indeed, indeed, "this is a sorry sight." The reconstruction of the Constitution and political society of a great State; the fundamental law of property and life for millions of men for a quarter of a century; in theory, *the work of the people;* is to be puddered over for a few days, and huddled through; done in hot and indecent haste, without deliberation or scrutiny, or an eye to the careful adjustment of its parts, so as to secure a symmetrical and perfect whole, which a work of such vast magnitude and fraught with such tremendous consequences so imperatively demands. This is to be hereafter cited against us, and, we fear, cited with resistless force, as one of our examples of our boasted capacity for self-government. A Constitution of government is to be struck out by the people at a single heat—cut out and finished as quick as a tailor could make a decent suit of clothes! Doubtless, it deserves to last about as long; and the people will be wise to begin to think of having a whole wardrobe of constitutions, that they may be the more conveniently cleansed and repatched, as they, from time to time, grow seedy and threadbare.[29]

"In theory, *the work of the people*"—the *Review* also sought to equate any true constitution with the will of the people, and this was the final element in the conservative constitutional mystique. Stressing again and again that constitutions are intended to restrain majorities, Whig leaders also insisted that the constitutions that did restrain those majorities were the apex of popular self-government. "We, the people, are liable to err, and to be led astray," Thomas H. Lewis argued in Louisiana. "We are liable individually and collectively to be swayed by our passions, and our interests; and it is wise and prudent that we should be under some of those wholesome restraints which are dictated to us in our cooler moments, as necessary and indispensable to keep us within the bounds of discretion. . . . The mino[r]ity must be protected from the majority, and the majority protected against themselves." [30]

Lewis's argument was in one sense preposterous, made so not only by his obvious attempt to equate popular rule with popular restraint, but also by his valiant attempts to curb popular authority in practice. Yet it was also most persuasive if understood in the context of the moral philosophy of the day, which equated self-government with deference to an objective moral order. In 1848, the *American Review* published a philosophical essay in which the Reverend John W. Nevin of Marshall College argued that human freedom consists not in exemption from Christian obligations but in voluntary acceptance of them. The *Review* applied the same argument directly to politics in 1846: "Self-government is not, as has been acutely but sophistically maintained by a late writer in the Democratic Review, a self-contradiction: Rather it is, morally and politically speaking, the highest problem of civilization—for it is, in these respects, the proper self-development of man. It by no means implies the rejection of an external rule, a law and an authority emanating from a source above us, and revealed to us as well as in us—it only rejects such a rule and authority as emanating from a source which is not above us. Self-government begins with a reverential recognition of a supreme law: its process is a constant endeavor to render that law objective, real [and] operative." [31]

Under these circumstances, it was entirely possible for conservative spokesmen to link obedience to constitutional restrictions on democracy with the fullest development of self-government. Benjamin F. Porter articulated the logic of the Whig position when he declared at Tuscaloosa in 1845, "The largest amount of liberty consists in the most extensive obedience to good laws. The restraints imposed by such, are not restraints upon natural rights, but upon natural tendencies to do wrong." [32] At the moment, Porter was discussing the general obligations of law rather than the particular obligations of constitutions, but his formula clearly extended to them as well. Thanks to the moral philosophy of law, conservative spokesmen were able to unite natural rights, constitutional restraint, and "self-government" in the service of Whiggery.[e]

WHIG CONSTITUTIONALISM: THE FEDERAL COMPACT

Refining the meaning of constitutional government, the Whigs may also have facilitated a redefinition of the federal Constitution. It was already a sort of ark of the covenant, both a symbolic expression and an institutional guarantee of the liberties the American nation had achieved; but it was also subject to a variety of sectional and polemical interpretations that worked to prevent its details from having the emotional force of supreme law. Conservatives of the Middle Period labored to transform the constitutional arrangements they preferred into immutable principles of freedom.[f]

The tendency of their thought was the more striking in that they began with an essentially pragmatic view of the national document, comparable in many respects to the classic view of state constitutions as arrangements for accommodating disparate interests in a coherent political system. The Friends of Domestic Industry appealed to one version of this pragmatic view in 1831 when they rejected Democratic claims that Congress was forbidden to enact protective tariffs: "As a constitutional question, the inquiry is not whether the laws are wise or unwise, whether in their operations they are always equal, or sometimes unequal, or whether individuals may not think them so wide a departure from a just administration of the powers of the government, as to be, in an indefinite and loose sense, inconsistent with the spirit of the constitution. The true and real question is, do they exceed the power of the lawgiver; and do they, for that reason, fail to be obligatory?" By the same token, in 1842 Daniel Webster protested the constitutional niceties that were invoked to prevent effective national government. "The constitution was intended as an instrument of great political good," he declared at Faneuil Hall; "but we sometimes so dispute its meaning, that we cannot use it at all. One man will not have a bank, without the power of local discount, against the consent of the States; for that, he insists, would break the constitution. Another will not have a bank with such a power, because he thinks *that* would break the constitution. A third will not have an exchequer, with authority to deal in exchanges, because that would increase executive influences, and so might break the constitution. And between them all, we are like the boatman who, in the midst of rocks and currents and whirlpools, will not pull one stroke for safety, lest he break his oar." Both arguments obviously took for granted a flexible fundamental law geared to the constructive use of government for public economic ends.[33]

At the same time, partly because the Constitution they described generated Democratic opposition, partly for other reasons, Webster and his colleagues also sought to endow it with another kind of authority. For Webster himself, the great occasion arose during his second reply to Hayne, where he rebuked southern theories of nullification with a combination of pragmatic appeals to the utility of the federal document and transcendental appeals to its mysteries. On the one hand, he argued that separate state interpretations of its meaning were insupportable, that the "liberty" South Carolinians clamored for reduced to anarchy, and that the federal document itself provided a means for settling internal disputes. To this extent he simply echoed the proposition that it was a rational and necessary instrument of government, no more hostile to liberty than was government itself. On the other hand, he insisted that the Constitution had been established by the people, that it had been maintained by the people, and that it could be amended by them, from which he inferred that it was in every sense an extraordinary vehicle of popular rule. In effect, he worked to separate the theory of nullification from the ideal of popular liberty by locating liberty in the authority of the federal document.[34]

Still, the authority Webster invoked in 1830 was authority to conduct a positive government, whereas the political experience of the Whigs increasingly suggested that popular authority must be curtailed if liberty was to be preserved. In particular, their struggles with Andrew Jackson encouraged them to invoke a severely restrictive mechanism, a document that guaranteed liberty by counteracting the unholy alliance President Jackson had created between himself and the people. In 1834, during the struggle over the right of the executive to dismiss the secretary of the treasury, Representative George Poindexter of Mississippi praised the federal Senate in much the same terms that conservatives applied to the upper houses in the states: "The Senate, by its peculiar organization, is well calculated to preserve and perpetuate the great fundamental principles of public liberty to the latest posterity. Removed from popular impulses, which sometimes arise in the convulsions incident to freedom of opinion, and of discussions of great political questions, it may look with calmness on the misguided multitude, misled by some popular demagogue, and thereby save the state from the deleterious consequences of errors which are the inevitable result of passion or precipitation." Similarly, Senator Peleg Sprague of Maine insisted that the checks and balances of the Constitution must either overcome or be destroyed by the alliance between executive and democracy: "The people are the fountain of all power; they are politically omnipotent. They can make and unmake constitutions at pleasure. But they cannot have moral incompatibilities. Omnipotent as they are, they cannot have an elective monarchy and a constitutional republic at the same time. Let it then be distinctly understood, that these two tremendous powers, the Executive and the people, cannot meet, and in their coming together, crush the legislature, the judiciary and the Senate between them, and still leave a constitutional republic." [35,g]

Conservative spokesmen also turned to the Constitution as it was to nullify innovations sponsored by the democracy. In 1826, for example, Edward Everett argued during the Congressional debate on a proposal to elect the president by electoral districts that radical changes in the established frame of government were beyond the pale of constitutional liberty. In effect, he anticipated the case that other Whigs would make against the Dorr Rebellion, distinguishing constitutional government from revolutionary change in order to forestall even measures that had a large popular following. Similarly, Caleb S. Henry spoke for a number of doctrinaire conservatives when, in a commencement address at the University of Vermont, he invoked constitutional checks and balances as an apparatus intended to check the popular will. For his part, William Henry Harrison criticized the executive veto in his inaugural address but also declared that it should be employed to protect minorities against political combinations hostile to them, while Henry W. Warner came close, in the columns of the *American Review*, to equating constitutional government with irreducible limitations on the people. Men of a conservative temperament clearly hoped that the federal document would counteract a whole range of popular innovations.[36]

These were ritual expressions of no great moment, moreover, when compared with the campaign that the Whig party mounted in the name of constitutional liberty against the presidential veto. The path the campaign followed as it developed was as important as the fact of its existence. Initially, National Republican spokesmen contended against the actions of the president on the grounds that a headstrong and highly partisan chief executive had misused his office to nullify desirable measures and abuse his political enemies. They often invoked the Constitution, but the Constitution they invoked was at least in part a document that sanctioned what they took to be constructive public policies.[37] As time passed, however, they increasingly invoked the elaborate apparatus of constitutionalism as a rebuke to Democratic presidents. The result was a series of electoral campaigns predicated on a relatively undifferentiated constitutionalism—a constitutionalism that was clearly restrictive and at the same time remarkably empty of content. Earlier Whig clamor against the veto power had had the virtue of being, at least by implication, a defense of the authority of the national legislature to shape the national economy. The clamor of the later years came close to being an attack on authority itself.

Whig polemics during the campaign of 1840 demonstrated as much. "We are in the midst of a revolution!" the Whigs of New York began their election address. "Your Federal Government, which was established with limitations, checks and balances, to preserve the principles of civil liberty, is undergoing a change fatal to its republican character. . . . The limitations of the constitution are explained away, by new readings adapted to the understanding and conformable to the wishes of the President for the time being." Governor Barbour invoked the same specter at the party's national convention, while Henry Clay very largely avoided discussion of the measures Jackson had opposed in order to condemn his unconstitutional pretensions.[38]

The same charges echoed during the mid-1840s, when both Clay and Calvin Colton made it seem that one of their party's main functions was to restore American liberty by defeating Democratic innovations in constitutional law. "To secure the exercise of the powers of Government by the people, in all that the Constitution prescribes and warrants," Colton wrote in the *Junius Tracts*, "has been the undeviating aim of Mr. Clay, in all his public life and labors; and in doing this, for many years past, he has been found in uninterrupted conflict with the Executive and the Locofocos. These facts are signs, indexes, and infallible proofs of *democracy* in those who thus take the side of the people; and no less are they conclusive evidence of the *lack* of democracy in those who take the side of the Executive *against* the people." By now Whigs appealed to the Constitution not so much because it vindicated their policies as because their policies reduced to constitutionalism.[39]

But they also appealed to democracy; if their claims were to be believed, the Constitution they defended represented the deliberate will of the American people, who were bound by that fact to uphold it against the Democracy. "In a country, where a free and self-government is established," Clay declared at Raleigh (North Carolina),

it should be the pleasure as it is the bounden duty, of every citizen to stand by and uphold the Constitution and laws, and support the public authority; because they are *his* Constitution—*his* laws, and the public authority emanates from *his* will. Having concurred, by the exercise of his privileges, in the adoption of the Constitution, and in the passage of the laws, any outrage or violation attempted of either ought to be regarded as an offence against himself, an offence against the majesty of the people. . . . With a free people, the fact that the laws are their laws, ought to supply, in a prompt and voluntary rally to the support of the public authority, a force more peaceful, more powerful and more reasonable, than any derivable from a mercenary soldiery.

Empty as it may have been, the vacuous constitutionalism the Whigs now sponsored in the name of democracy was also their most obvious resource against the authority Democrats apparently clamored for.[40]

THE GUARDIANS OF THE LAW

Whig constitutionalism was vacuous but it was not impotent, for it rested upon a supposition that means could be found outside the democratic process to maintain the law Whigs described. Beyond constitutional complications and inhibitions they looked to the judiciary to protect the values they honored. If in their eyes the essence of democracy was constitutionalism, the essence of their constitutionalism was an autonomous judiciary.

Here, too, developments in the states were at least as important as those at the national level, which bore an immense long-range significance but which would not be fully realized until the federal Supreme Court extended its jurisdiction over an ever-increasing range of legislative activities. (As of 1850, it had nullified only one act of Congress, and although it dealt more firmly with the antebellum legislation of the states, it did so as much to vindicate federal authority as to prohibit social change. Even the acts it overruled on the grounds of the contract clause were relatively few and relatively insignificant as statements of social policy, Democratic clamor against them notwithstanding.) By contrast, Whig partisans in the states moved with immediate effect from constitutionalism as a complex of structures vindicated by time and liberty to constitutionalism as a juridical process.[41]

One thing was clear before the Whigs started: judges had both the right and the duty to nullify legislation that contravened the constitutions they had sworn to uphold.[42] In this sense the conservatives' battle was already won, and they needed only to invoke the authority of the judiciary whenever they were confronted with unacceptable public measures. Nevertheless, spurred by attempts to substitute an elective for an appointive judiciary, they articulated a clearly defined theory of the role and functions of the judiciary that more than compensated for their defeat on the specific question of its election. In effect, they defined the ideal judge in such a fashion as to make him a sure antagonist to popular pressures.

Their theory was grounded in an apolitical and indeed antipolitical vision of the judge as an impartial figure who conducted any business that came before him with a single-minded attention to the merits of the issues, uninfluenced by either personal interest or partisan allegiance. Chancellor Kent expressed this ideal in classic terms when he wrote in his *Commentaries on American Law,*

The just and vigorous investigation and punishment of every species of fraud and violence, and the exercise of the power of compelling every man to the punctual performance of his contracts, are grave duties, not of the most popular character, though the faithful discharge of them will certainly command the calm approbation of the judicious observer. The fittest men would probably have too much reservedness of manners, and severity of morals, to secure an election resting on universal suffrage. Nor can the mode of appointment by a large deliberative assembly, be entitled to unqualified approbation. There are too many occasions, and too much temptation for intrigue, party prejudice, and local interests, to permit such a body of men to act, in respect to such appointments, with a sufficiently single and steady regard for the general welfare.[43]

Thus far there was relatively little to criticize in Kent's perspective, but he also extended his vision of the impartial judiciary to include the role of judges as referees in constitutional questions, whereupon it acquired more portentous connotations: "An independent judiciary, venerable by its gravity, its dignity, and its wisdom, and deliberating with entire serenity and moderation, is peculiarly fitted for the exalted duty of expounding the constitution, and trying the validity of statutes by that standard." Nor did he stop with this seemingly innocuous pronouncement; he went on to say, "It is only by the free exercise of this power that courts of justice are enabled to repel assaults, and to protect every part of the government, and every member of the community, from undue and destructive innovations upon their chartered rights." In effect, he held up the criterion of an apolitical judge as a model for the judge acting in a clearly political capacity to resolve controversial public questions.[44]

Even so, his point of view was Olympian in its detachment rather than unambiguously hostile to democracy. Lesser men invoked similar sentiments to describe a judiciary that would clearly prove an obstacle to popular wishes. In North Carolina, for example, John Giles declared that he particularly favored election of the governor and both houses of the legislature by the people, but added that "he did not wish them to have any thing to do with the Judiciary Department. An enlightened and independent Judiciary is all important, and he wished, therefore, to see them free from any influence that might bias their judgments." The *American Review* was less direct but no less dogmatic when it criticized popular election of the judiciary on the grounds that "the judge is emphatically the Aegis of the Constitution and the rights of the people. He stands aloof from the contentions of parties; instead of representing a faction, he represents the whole people; with a placid dignity he surveys the wide fields of human action: the rich man and the poor, the widow and the fatherless, the oppressed struggling against power, and legitimate authority struggling against popular excess, all appeal to him with confidence. With a voice unmoved by passion, and a heart which renders a perfect allegiance to the law, he interprets the sacred charter, and stands a ministering priest at the venerable altars of the Nation's justice." [45]

Confronting democratic pressures for change, in short, spokesmen for the conservative cause depicted an autonomous judiciary as an indispensable element in republican government precisely because it was beyond the reach of popular power. Chancellor Kent spelled out their beliefs in a footnote to the fourth edition of his *Commentaries* in which he took issue with Tocqueville's fears of the tyranny of the majority. "If there was no check upon the tyranny of legislative majorities, the prospect before us would be gloomy in the extreme. But in addition to the indirect checks of the liberty of the press, and of popular instruction, and of manners, religion, and local institutions, there are fundamental rights declared in the constitutions, and there are constitutional checks upon the arbitrary will of majorities, confided to the integrity and independence of the judicial department." Thomas J. McKean was less circumspect in defending the role of an appointive judiciary in the Iowa convention of 1844:

We had adopted a bill of rights, the object of which was to secure and perpetuate the rights of the individual citizen.

The rights therein guaranteed were to remain forever inviolate. They were never to be curtailed by any modification of our form of Government or change in our Constitution. They were not to be infringed upon, either by any department of the government, or by the people themselves. But there was an end to all security for those rights, if these propositions were adopted; the constitutional guarantee was of no force. He, said Mr. McK., was in favor of protecting the people in all their rights and privileges; but he wanted to effect that object in a different manner, than that proposed by some gentlemen. He would not effect that object by destroying all constitutional guards, and removing from the machinery of Government all the checks and balances that have been found to be salutary and wise. He would protect the people by securing the individual—protect the individual, and the people were all cared for.

On this view, expressed here by a civil engineer, the courts stood as the final arbiters between popular liberty and popular excess. [46]

It followed for many conservatives that an elective judiciary was incompatible with free government. Kent said as much; Giles made no bones about his belief; McKean was adamant on the question; and the *American Review* exclaimed regarding the proposed constitution for New York State, "Our judges are to be chosen directly by the people! and that serene and elevated region, which the winds and waves of political excitement have, till this time, respected, is to be thrown open to their utmost violence." (For that matter, its articles on the proposed constitution dealt almost exclusively with the judiciary.) To judge by such laments, the gradual substitution of an elective for an appointive judiciary marked the end of effective liberty.[47]

In the long run, however, the critical issue was not how judges might be chosen but how their role would be defined. At first glance, popular election threatened judicial autonomy, but Whig spokesmen could afford to concede the mode of election if they did not have to abandon the ideal of judicial independence. In a sense, this point may have made the difference between a strictly conservative and a more generally Whiggish position. In any event, the *American Review* itself recognized the direction Whigs must ultimately take when it explained in a prefatory note to one of its essays on the new state constitution that "as the writer of this article conclusively argues, it is not so great a matter that the highest judges should be chosen by popular election as that *when chosen* they are to be *turned out again in eight years*, thus subjecting what *no nation* has yet subjected, the high seats of Justice to all those temptations to corrupt action, all the miserable caballing and strife which now pertains to the most petty political office, whose incumbent may desire a re-election. How different would it be, if, when once chosen, in the tumult of a popular election, they could settle down into that calm atmosphere which invests a judicial office whose term is to cover nearly the residue of life?" In effect, if they could be sure of how judges would behave, they had no reason to stick at how they were to be chosen.[48]

Elsewhere Whigs were less intransigent, but no more than the *American Review* did they give up the role they had prescribed for the judiciary. In Illinois, for example, they struggled with the Democrats over the manner rather than the fact of election—it was to their advantage as a minority party to defend the election of judges by district rather than general ticket—but they did so on the grounds that the mode they sponsored would make the state's highest court more effective as a bulwark of liberty. In Iowa, moreover, Joseph S. Kirkpatrick actually advocated an elective judiciary against the advice of his more conservative colleagues on the grounds that election would strengthen them against the corrupting influence of politics. The decisions they must make, he insisted, had been "blazed out by the decision of courts in past times, those decisions were published to the world, and inside of those blazes they must travel, or otherwise be censured. Through the freedom of the press their decisions would easily be contrasted with former decisions, and corruption ferreted out. The circumstances of the judges being elected by the people, was [sic] surely the greatest safeguard against corruption." In short, he argued that the people themselves were the best guarantee that the courts would be faithful to their trust.[49]

In doing so Kirkpatrick took for granted an amenable people, which more conservative Whigs hardly felt able to do. They clearly doubted that the people could ever be trusted to abide by a law they did not make, whereas more perceptive men like Kirkpatrick realized that they had long since declared their loyalty to a sort of involuntary self-government in the courts. Even the *American Review* gave implicit recognition to this fact while condemning an elective judiciary. "Hitherto," it declared, "the people, justly suspicious of themselves and their own hasty and impulsive action, have voluntarily put it out of their power to disturb the sacred scale of justice with their excited hands. . . . This noble self-restraint was one of the most beautiful illustrations of the temperance that may belong to freedom, and, while it continued, answered a thousand sneers which the foes of liberty directed at our licentious institutions." [50] To this sort of lament Kirkpatrick confidently replied that the courts would still function like courts when they were secured but not controlled by the importunities of democratic politics.

Most of the same doctrines were also applicable to the federal Supreme Court, to which conservatives increasingly came to ascribe salutary functions. The very nature of the federal compact required them to do so; if they would assert the preeminence of national authority they must also encourage reverence for the agency that maintained it. This was Webster's course during his debate with Hayne; significantly, he made much of the "trust" the people had reposed in the judiciary, whereas his Senate colleagues stressed the proposition that the Supreme Court was a necessary alternative to anarchy. However, although Webster was to appeal to the Court again and again to invalidate acts that infringed on vested rights in the states, he continued to think of it as a prop to active government on the national level. Speaking before a Whig audience in Philadelphia in 1846, he hailed the federal Constitution, "fairly expounded, justly interpreted," as the "bond" of the American Union. "It was not, then, fair for those who had opposed the adoption of the Constitution, to come in under it, afterwards, and attempt to fritter away its provisions, because they dislike them. The people had adopted the instrument, as it stood, and they were bound by it, in its fair and full construction and interpretation." If he appealed to the authority of the Court in the name of the authority of the people, he had in view powers the Court had sanctioned, not those it had denied.[51]

His political allies also insisted, however, that the Court was an indispensable agency of government in the more ambiguous sense of equating autonomous judicial deliberation with popular freedom. Joseph Story applied a temperate version of this familiar theme to the federal government when he wrote in his *Commentaries on the Constitution* (1833), "Where there is no judicial department to interpret, pronounce, and execute the law, to decide controversies, and to enforce rights, the government must either perish by its own imbecility, or the other departments of government must usurp powers, for the purpose of commanding obedience, to the destruction of liberty. The will of those, who govern, will become, under such circumstances, absolute and despotic; and it is wholly immaterial, whether power is vested in a single tyrant, or in an assembly of tyrants." Kent was more explicit in advocating a Court that would be independent of popular authority. "By the constitution of the United States," he wrote in his *Commentaries*, " 'the judges both of the supreme and inferior courts are to hold their offices during good behaviour; and they are, at stated times, to receive for their services a compensation which shall not be diminished during their continuance in office.' The tenure of the office, by rendering the judges independent, both of the government and people, is admirably fitted to produce the free exercise of judgment in the discharge of their trust." Formally, both men addressed themselves only to a structural defense of the judiciary—Story against the other departments of government, Kent against any encroachments on impartial justice—but it is clear that both also visualized it as a last resort against the errors of democracy.[52]

We need not condemn the result in order to be sensitive to its logic. Proclaiming the ideal of impartial justice, building on the necessity of the federal system, the advocates of judicial review elaborated a scheme of judicial authority that extended beyond the voiding of legislative aberrations to the defeating of popular errors. At the same time, they attempted so far as they could to equate the power of the Court with the protection of popular liberties, which democratic theory might plausibly have left to the people themselves. The outcome of their deliberations on both the state and national levels was a political ethic of self-denial: self-denial for the electorate very largely defined by the deliberations of the judiciary, whom conservatives identified with the deepest values of American society. "Revere and support the Judiciary," Theodore Romeyn exhorted his countrymen in 1847. "This is the civilized and christian institution, which has taken the place of an appeal to arms. The submission of our citizens to law, their identification with its administration, and the potency with which it works, through the support of enlightened public opinion, without the aid of a strong police or soldiery, are among the most remarkable and creditable traits of American character." In the federal courts in particular, he added, where the judiciary repeal the enactments of states and suspend the activities of federal officials, "we behold the highest evidence of christian civilization, and the best result and surest protection of peace and liberty." In conservative eyes, the American experiment in self-government culminated in reverence for the one agency of government that might be expected to withstand popular urgencies. [53]

✤ IX ✤

THE CONSTITUTION
OF DEMOCRACY

Whig spokesmen often posed constitutionalism as an alternative to democracy, looking to the mechanisms of constitutional inhibition and the authority of the judiciary to prevent popular infringements on the rights they sought to protect. Hence they also supplied liberal Democrats with motives, if they did not already feel them, to repudiate both constitutions and courts as obstacles to popular sovereignty. The outcome of Whiggish responses to Democratic assertions of power might well have been the collapse of American constitutionalism.

Instead it flourished, for reasons that are an important comment on American democratic thought. To some extent constitutional loyalty was habitual, and inertia probably had much to do with the result. Again, the Democrats were never a monolithic party, least of all with respect to constitutional principles, and their internal divisions undoubtedly helped to preserve the practices Whigs hailed. But the mental processes of democratic reformers also had much to do with the success of the constitutional creed, and in this sense their behavior made a most significant contribution to the consolidation of a common faith. Thanks to democratic ideas of liberty, men who might have led the opposition proved in the long run to be among the most stalwart defenders of constitutional orthodoxy.[a]

THE DIVIDED MIND OF DEMOCRACY

In the states, liberal democratic constitutionalism began with a fairly explicit recognition of the theoretical problems that constitutional structures pose for democratic government. To a degree surprising to us today, who tend to view both state and national constitutions as nearly immune to popular protest, progressive democrats in the state constitutional conventions deplored the obstacles that existing instruments of government put in the way of popular sovereignty. Hence they mounted a sustained attack on most of the devices conservatives typically advocated.

For example, they often took issue with the assumption that popular government requires numerous restrictions on popular power. In the New York convention of 1821, Erastus Root went so far as to ask why his colleagues wished to set government against itself by dividing and separating its functions and emphasizing the differences among the branches. "I agree that in a monarchical government, where little liberty is left to the people, it is necessary to have such checks as gentlemen have described. In such governments there are different *orders*, as lords and commons in England; different *estates*, as in the diets of Sweden, Denmark, and Germany. But the necessity in those governments bears no analogy to ours.—We have no different estates, having different interests, necessary to be guarded from encroachment by the watchful eye of jealousy.—We are all of the same estate—all commoners; nor, until we have privileged orders, and aristocratic estates to defend, can this argument apply." Nathaniel P. Tallmadge echoed the same complaint in 1824 when he defended direct popular choice of presidential electors on the ground that the founding fathers had repudiated checks and balances in favor of equal rights and popular self-government. His history was bad, but his antipathy to constitutional structures was unmistakable.[1]

Later commentators sometimes developed a comparable attack on constitutional limitations. In the Michigan convention of 1835, John Norvell denounced those who would create substantial restrictions on the people's authority in order to protect the rights of minorities. "He had himself been in minorities. He did not, for that reason, suppose that he was peculiarly entitled to have the protecting shield of the constitution thrown over him. He had supposed that constitutions were established for the benefit and protection of the rights of all, whether of the depressed minority, or the ascendant majority. The contrary idea, advanced by the member from Wayne [William Woodbridge], was the vision of a morbid imagination." In Louisiana, moreover, Isaac Preston rebuked his colleagues for their tendency to "fall into minute legislation" intended to prevent prospective evils. "Why waste our time with this ordinary legislation," he asked during debate on measures intended to regulate voting districts in New Orleans. "He hoped the new constitution

might not last ten years, and conceiving this matter to be purely legislative, was adverse to placing it in that instrument." [2]

Criticizing the apparatus of constitutional restriction, Democratic partisans also insisted that the separate branches of government be visualized as agencies of popular power rather than obstacles to popular rule.
"In the Constitution of our government," Preston declared in Louisiana,
"the legislature represents the *will* of the people, the executive their
power, and the judiciary their *reason* or justice. The executive officers, the
members of the legislature and judges of our courts, are therefore the
mere agents and servants of the people. And it is the right, the duty, and
for the interest of the people to appoint these agents personally, if possible, and if that cannot be done [,] by the means that may be most convenient to the whole people." Similarly, the Democratic convention of Jo
Daviess County (Illinois) resolved in 1839, "That the persons filling the
Executive, Judicial, and Legislative department of the government of the
United States and of this State, are only trustees for the people. That
they have no power or authority whatever beyond what is given by the
people *in express terms,* set forth in the people's constitutions." [3]

It followed for many Democrats that the people must control the constitutions under which they lived. Hence they insisted that no constitution could be binding unless it had been adopted by a majority of the
people, and on occasion they also held that it must have been drafted by
a truly representative deliberative body. [4] They also argued that obstacles
to amendment were intolerable in a free government. Again Preston was
most eloquent in defending popular authority: "To make an organic law,
or any other law, we must have some spontaneous expression of popular
will; and if either is to result beneficially to the people at large, why
should we restrain it? Why should we say that in ten or twenty years
hence, those who then may be desirous of changing their senatorial representation, should be debarred from doing so, although the senate may
have become like so many rotten boroughs?" Preston was not alone; in
New Jersey, for example, David Naar was equally testy with those who
sought to make amendment difficult. He "regretted that extraneous considerations had been introduced. The question was simply whether the
people should have the right of amending the Constitution or not. . . .
Mr. N. would take the present Constitution with this means of future

amendment, rather than the best devised system of checks and balances tied up against future reform." [5]

Finally this line of thought pointed to the conclusion that the people have a right to do what they will in defiance even of established constitutional provisions. In Louisiana, Cyrus Ratliff ventured an early version of the doctrine of popular sovereignty, later to be articulated on a national level by Stephen A. Douglas, when he argued that constitutional restrictions on eligibility for office were fruitless. "If the people are disposed to observe these restrictions, why, then, they are useless; if they are not disposed to observe them, they are still useless, and there is no power to enforce them against the will of the people." In Texas, moreover, Lemuel D. Evans moved to eliminate from the state's proposed Bill of Rights a section sanctioning the right of peaceable assembly. Significantly, he defended his motion on the grounds of popular sovereignty rather than natural right: "He objected to the clause, as altogether anti-republican in its spirit. It represents the functionaries of the government as a superior order of men, and the people as their inferiors. It secures the right of the people to assemble in a *peaceable* and *respectful* manner, so as not to offend the functionaries of the government; it secures the right of the people to do certain things, *provided* they are respectful. Now he held that the people are the sovereigns, and the functionaries of the government their servants. He held that the people had the right to assemble, whether peaceably or not, provided it were for the public good, and no functionary could interfere with them. He wanted the people to stand out in their full and ample majesty." [6]

These were mere rhetorical flourishes, however, by comparison with the doctrines liberal Democrats developed in dealing with events in Rhode Island. There, George Turner, Thomas W. Dorr's defense attorney at his trial for sedition, developed the argument that existing constitutional provisions simply could not bind the majority of the people when they chose to exercise their right to alter the fundamental law. The Democratic members of the state legislature employed much the same argument when they appealed to the Congress to repudiate the actions of President Tyler, who had given federal assistance to the established government, and the Select Committee of the House of Representatives echoed it in 1844 by invoking "THE INHERENT SOVEREIGN RIGHT OF THE PEOPLE TO CHANGE AND REFORM THEIR EXISTING GOVERNMENTS AT PLEA-

SURE." So, too, an anonymous Bostonian defended the Dorrites in 1842 on the grounds "that the only supreme power is the people; and that this power towers above all charters, constitutions, or antiquated parchments, whether they be signed by the crowned or the uncrowned," and sympathizers in other states insisted that the people's right to establish new forms of government superseded all legislative limitations on their authority.[7]

In all these respects liberal Democrats challenged the premises of conservative constitutionalism—its bias in favor of a restrictive instrument, its predisposition to elaborate checks and balances, its obstacles to easy amendment, its devotion to a contractual theory of obligation vested in an existing document. Yet in other respects they testified to its hold on their imagination, at least to the extent of sharing many of the premises on which conservatives based their characteristic structures. Rebuking conservative constitutionalists, they failed to question constitutionalism itself, and they ended by accepting far more than they rejected.[b]

The very case the Democrats made against specific constitutional practices implicated them in the constitutional apparatus they criticized. It is not without significance that the loudest clamor for the rights of the people arose in state constitutional conventions or in connection with Rhode Island's belated effort to establish a legitimate frame of government. In another country the demand for a recognition of popular rights might well have betokened more radical intentions; in the United States it betokened no more than an attempt to perfect familiar schemes of government.

Certainly Democratic convention delegates who clamored for change in the name of popular sovereignty also sought it in the name of constitutional liberty. In Michigan, for example, John Norvell concluded his criticism of conservative constitutionalists by declaring that "in a majority or minority, . . . he was desirous to see a liberal constitution, extending its beneficent influence over all that came within the sphere of its operation, adopted and submitted to the people of Michigan." Similarly, Preston urged his colleagues in Louisiana to avoid excessive constitutional legislation because he expected their successors to devise a more perfect constitution in later years, while the Democrats of Jo Daviess County stipulated that the people's agents were limited by the people's constitutions. Again, all arguments that the separate branches of govern-

ment must effectively represent the people clearly presupposed a continuation in nearly identical form of the existing structures of government;
even Erastus Root sought only to rebuke the advocates of a propertied
senate, not to eliminate the second house of the legislature. Similarly, all
of the Democrats who asserted a constituent right of the people obviously asserted it as a right to devise and amend constitutions, and even
Lemuel Evans did not seriously contemplate eliminating constitutional
limitations on government. The object of these constitutional reformers
was to make sure that the constitutions they would live under were faithful to liberal principles, not to explore the possibility of doing without
them.[8]

The case they made for the rebels in Rhode Island exemplifies their
ambiguous perspectives. Here, where revolution was apparently necessary to complete the work of democratization that other states had begun
during the War for Independence, Democratic reformers repeatedly
argued that the constituent right they claimed for the people of Rhode
Island was a right peculiar to the American constitutional structure. Far
from asserting the right of revolution *as* revolution, they inveighed against
it in the ordinary meaning of the term. "The fathers of the American
Revolution," declared the Select Committee on Rhode Island in 1844,

> when they asserted the great right of the people 'to alter and abolish' the existing
> government when it was perverted to the purposes of tyranny, or failed to an-
> swer the ends for which it was instituted, . . . could never have intended that it
> was nothing more than the right which the oppressed people of England, the
> serfs of Russia, or the slaves of Turkey enjoy, and may exercise whenever they
> have the power and will to do it. They could never have contemplated any such
> absurdity; but they intended to assert that it was an inherent right in the people,
> which they could at all times *peaceably* exercise, whenever it became necessary for
> their security and happiness.

So, too, in pleading the case of *Luther* v. *Borden* before the Supreme
Court, Benjamin F. Hallett argued in 1848 that the traditional right of
revolution was a merely natural and physical right, available equally in
monarchies and republics. "But in the American system, in opposition to
the European," he held, "the *moral* was first combined with the physical
and natural right to resist oppression. It became a voting as well as a
fighting right." [9] In effect, Democratic partisans came close to arguing

that the Dorr Rebellion had been legitimate because American constitutional practice sanctioned it.[c]

Hallett appeared before an established constitutional tribunal, while the Select Committee had every reason to look for constitutional sanctions: in this sense their arguments may be evidence rather of their ingenuity as lawyers than of their ultimate commitment to constitutionalism. But even if we make allowances for these circumstances we must also acknowledge that the same constitutional argument runs through the literature on the subject, and that the literature in turn corresponds to the actual behavior of the Free Suffrage movement. (In practice, the Rhode Island rebels simply constituted a new government parallel to the old one and began to exercise the powers provided in their new constitution. In addition, they proceeded with apparent confidence that when the two governments existed side by side, the Supreme Court would accept the new one as legitimate.) At most, these advocates of revolutionary change insisted upon their constituent right to draft new constitutions that would secure manhood suffrage, after which they were apparently content to be bound by the document they had created.[10,d]

Beyond this, liberal Democrats clearly deferred to most of the constitutional prejudices that conservatives typically respected. Significantly, they took the separation of powers for granted. "In a pure despotism," James F. Brent observed in Louisiana during debate on an elective judiciary, "all power centres in the monarch. He is at once legislator, judge, and executive. Just in proportion as you divide and separate these powers, you advance from monarchy to republicanism." John E. Fletcher made the same point in the same cause in Iowa: "Delegated authority was always liable to be abused; and as was said by the gentleman from Jackson the system of proxy voting marred the beauty and symmetry of our form of government. We elected Legislatures to make laws, Judges to administer them, and an Executive to enforce them. These departments should all be kept separate and independent." [11]

Furthermore, the separation of powers they described was clearly intended to function as part of a mechanism of checks and balances; it was not merely a protection thrown around distinct offices, but a device to curb the activities of government. In Michigan, Thomas B. Church opposed adoption of a bill of rights on the grounds that the enumeration of certain rights might be taken to disparage others, whereas the same ends might better be served by assigning the necessary authority to each of the branches of government and then "closing in each by the necessary checks and balances." The *Racine Advocate* expressed a similar faith when it declared in 1846, "We should like to know what a convention was called for if not to place restrictions on the executive, the judiciary, and the legislature. The very definition of the powers of each is a restriction from other powers, and if we are to have no restrictions, of course we can have no constitution." [12]

Formally, of course, Democrats upheld checks and balances as restrictions on *government,* and to this extent they obviously dissented from the constitutional arrangements conservative Whigs invoked to curb the *electorate.* Nevertheless, the line between the two versions of constitutionalism was remarkably thin, as Louisiana's most outspoken Democrats demonstrated. There James F. Brent protested that "he could not conceive on what just principle" the process of amendment he supported could be resisted. "It cannot be the intention of the gentlemen," he declared in remarks aimed primarily at Thomas H. Lewis and Bernard Marigny, "to assert that the constitution of the State is to be placed beyond the will of the majority." Yet the rest of his argument suggested that it was, indeed, a very deliberate majority that he would raise to power. "If the amendment [on the floor] prevails surely there are yet sufficient checks against any haste or improvident action. It will require two votes of the legislature and one of the people before amendments can be embodied in the constitution. What more would gentlemen have?" Isaac Preston made the same case in more temperate language. "It is far wiser and better . . . to leave to a majority the power to act, when you have placed all proper checks to prevent haste in legislation, and to leave them then free to act as to them may best seem fit." The people were the only legitimate source of authority, but democracy was intended to take shape through the channels of constitutional inhibition. [13,e]

It might even be limited in other ways; at any rate, the Democrats' concern for the rights of man would seem to have increased Democratic pressures for actual prohibitions on the power of government. Their intellectual ancestors, the Antifederalists, had very clearly contended against the federal Constitution because it made no provision for inalienable rights; with rare exceptions the Democrats of the Middle Period strove to maintain those rights in the constitutions they drafted. For every confident Democrat who insisted, like Tallmadge in New York, that the people could best maintain their own rights on their own initiative, there were several who thought that only a constitutional protection would suffice to guard them. James C. Zabriskie took issue with Joseph Hornblower on this very point in the New Jersey convention:

Although I have no objection to the adoption of the article proposed by the Hon. the Chief Justice, I differ essentially from him in his remarks on the subject and the necessity of a bill of rights. He says that the day has gone by when declarations of rights are necessary to protect the people. That where despotism prevails, such contrivances might be of service. Sir, I look upon them as designed to subserve another and a greater purpose. Despots grant only bills of *privileges*, not declarations of rights. Such is magna charta. *There*, power resides in the despot: *here*, in the people. Although the people may know their rights, to maintain them unimpaired, it is necessary to have them frequently before the mind. In addition to that, Sir, declarations of rights contain a restriction upon legislative action. They exert in this respect a most salutary and conservative purpose. How dark are the evils that unbridled legislation has inflicted upon the community. We are called upon in the exercise of the high and responsible duties that devolve upon us to guard all the avenues by which the people's rights may be invaded. By adopting the declaration of rights, we will circumscribe the action of the legislature within its legitimate and proper sphere, as well as proclaim those great and fundamental truths which lie at the foundation of civil liberty.[14]

Here, too, we must acknowledge that the prohibitions the liberal Democrat hailed were intended to circumscribe the legislature rather than the people, but it is difficult to believe that Zabriskie did not intend to protect popular rights even against popular majorities. Certainly this was the practical effect of any constitutional declaration of rights. In addition, Democrats as well as Whigs invoked the rights of minorities against possible depredations by the majority. Charles Stokes articulated the logic of their position when he sought to require an extraordinary majority of the legislature to initiate constitutional amendments. He advocated the motion, the surviving report explains, "on the ground that Constitutions were designed to protect the rights of minorities and that therefore a mere majority ought not to have the power to unsettle them at any time; that if we were to depend on mere majorities there would be no reason in establishing a constitution but that every thing might be left to ordinary legislation; [and] that the constitution now protects certain rights against the legislature, but if amendments are to be made by majorities, those rights will be completely at their mercy." In some Democratic eyes, at any rate, the right of the people to rule extended only as far as constitutional barriers established in the name of individual rights. Democrats differed from Whigs on which rights most needed protection, not on the idea of protecting them.[15]

THE LOGIC OF CONSTITUTIONAL REFORM

It seems fairly clear that liberal Democrats were committed to constitutional processes and even to constitutional prohibitions as necessary concomitants of democratic self-government. At the same time, they sponsored a number of constitutional innovations that served to reinforce their dedication to the complex apparatus of government that many conservatives increasingly favored. In effect, in seeking to impose limitations on the authority of governments they developed a democratic constitutionalism that was in its way as restrictive as the conservative version.

We have already discussed the negative bias of Democratic reformers, who sought to exclude government from the economy and to make that exclusion permanent by controlling the actions of their state legislatures. These developments profoundly affected Democratic constitutionalism in a subtle as well as a self-evident sense. The changes Democrats introduced plainly involved technical changes in the structure and content of their states' constitutions, but they also involved the translation into structural terms of prescriptions that derived originally from considerations of policy. Quite apart from pressing for specific injunctions on government, in other words, Democratic reformers turned to the constitutional process as a whole to deal with issues of policy that earlier constitutions had left to legislative discretion. In effect, they substituted constitutional balances for legislative deliberation and sought to secure the future they desired by putting the major decisions they had arrived at beyond the reach of subsequent generations to alter.

The restrictive tendency of their thought is strikingly illustrated in the debates among convention delegates over incorporating excessive "legislation" into their proposed constitutions. As we have seen, leading liberals occasionally protested their colleagues' obsession with forestalling every evil and circumscribing every future legislature. Isaac Preston did so in Louisiana, as did Charles P. Bush in Michigan. But it may be relevant

that most of these men tended to speak in the accents of Old Republicanism, no matter how sympathetic they were to the tenets of Progressive
Democracy, and in any event it seems clear that conservatives were far
more likely than liberals to insist upon leaving important issues to the
discretion of future legislators. Bush complained about his liberal colleagues' enthusiasm for restrictions, not of conservatives' devices.[16]

By contrast, liberals typically held that it was necessary for the conventions in which they were engaged to spell out their intentions against
the notorious tendency of legislatures to exceed their proper authority.
In the Michigan convention of 1835, John Norvell insisted that its
members could not afford to imitate the example of Ohio, which had left
the legal definition of the term "inhabitant" to its legislature, only to find
it restricting the term and the suffrage to United States citizens. "What
right had the legislature of Ohio to alter or repeal any part of the constitution of that state?" he asked. ". . . It warned us to guard against the
occurrence of any pretext for any legislative interpretation of the elective
franchise in future times." Walter B. Scates was equally adamant in the
Illinois convention of 1847 in rejecting the idea that the legislature might
be trusted with the power of special legislation. "The people had called
this Convention to remedy that evil, and their representatives should be
heeded when they asked that these things should be done. If everything
was to be left open for the patriotism, discretion, and purity of future
legislatures, it would be better to have no constitution. But the people
required a constitution and that in it the powers of the Legislature
should be limited, and the evils of past legislation remedied." [17]

Again the restrictions these Democrats proposed were theoretically
only restrictions on legislation, but—given the difficulty of subsequent
amendment, which Democrats generally eased but did not eliminate—
they were also restrictions on the electorate. Sometimes, indeed, Democrats took credit for that fact. In Illinois, Scates acknowledged that one
objection to a total prohibition on banks was that "it forever binds the
people who may hereafter desire a bank," only to add that "if we were to
recognize the principle that we must act, in framing this constitution,
with due regard to the changes of the popular mind, we had better go
home at once, for that would defeat the ends of all constitution." Similarly, in 1843 Theodore Sedgwick Jr. launched a series of articles on contemporary constitutional reform in the *Democratic Review* in which he

declared that a constitution "is intended to operate both as a guarantee against encroachment by the Legislature upon the rights of the people, and against the political caprices of the people themselves." He also defended frequent revisions of the states' constitutions to accord with new discoveries in the science of government, but he saw in them no threat to his principle of limitation because he clearly visualized each successive convention as an occasion for "final legislation" on points previously at issue.[18]

In addition to specific prohibitory clauses, Democrats championed structural innovations intended to have the same effect. Chief among them was the increased weight of the executive veto, which we have already noted as a deliberately adopted negative influence, but which also had constitutional implications in the special sense of representing a change in constitutional structure intended to add complications to the already complicated processes of self-government. "Our government is one of checks and balances, and this is one of those checks," David L. Gregg argued in the Illinois convention. "If we abandon them and let the government go without these checks and balances it would fast run it to ruin and destruction for want of the proper means to preserve its several departments, to preserve their independence and proper functions. He was in favor of keeping those checks and restrictions upon each department of the government by the other, which were first introduced by the framers of the constitution of the United States to preserve the government, and this veto power was one which in their wisdom they had incorporated in that constitution." Thomas G. C. Davis also drew on the experience of the national government to prove that bicameralism was an insufficient although a necessary safeguard for liberty. "The Senate is a check upon the House of Representative, and *e converso*, but all experience has shown that these checks, wholesome as they are, great as they are, are not sufficient to restrain men in the enactment of injurious laws. All experience has shown that something more is needed, and that is the placing in the hands of the executive, the power to arrest unwise and unwholesome exactments, before they inflict upon the country, the irremediable evil of their blighting influences." Even as they democratized their legislatures and diminished the other differences between the two houses, Democrats increased the power of the executive to curtail the operations of government.[19]

The language they used is sometimes confusing because they invoked the concept of representation to justify the veto, but they were clear in their own minds that they were increasing obstacles to governing. That is, they honored the representative character of the governor because they were convinced that no public official should lie beyond the power of the electorate; but the fact that he was representative simply made the internal balance within government more complete. The *Racine Advocate* expressed their perspective on all three departments of government when it held in 1847 that "to cut off the patronage of the executive and to restore to the people the choice of their own servants is a simple and easy duty. To free our system from the abuses and usurpations of a life tenure of the judicial power is also a duty of comparative facility. But to restrain the legislature, so as to leave in their discretion all proper and sufficient power and at the same time to strip them of all capacity of great political and economical abuse—this is indeed a duty of great difficulty, and one never yet fully discharged by any constitution of any country." So far as the executive veto was concerned, the object of constitutional revision was not to aggrandize the executive but to make him a more effective antagonist to legislative evils within a more effective system of checks and balances.[20]

Hence democracy culminated in a constitutional apparatus that was in many respects more hostile to governing than anything Old Republicans had contended for at the state level. It is true that southern Republicans like Nathaniel Macon had placed an interdict on active government even at the state level, but they were slow to urge constitutional structures that would curb popular power. In the Middle Period, however, the democratization of politics encouraged an elaboration of structural obstacles to the exercise of political power at the instant the people made it their own. Paradoxical as this development may seem to us, it accorded with the preoccupations democrats expressed in contending for "equal rights." In effect, they sought power to nullify power, and the constitutional changes they introduced served directly to secure that end. "It has been remarked, Mr. Chairman, that power is dangerous," Isaac Van Zandt declared in the Texas convention during debate on the executive veto. "According to my impressions there is no maxim more correct; and the only way to disarm it, and free it from a dangerous tendency, is to divide it. If you vest the two Houses of the Legislature, as proposed by the committee, with the sole unchecked power of enacting laws, it occurs to me that this power becomes dangerous; and that it is calculated to produce more disorganization and confusion in the country than any power which you are likely to bestow upon the Governor." A constitution was a way of seeing to it that power would always be mustered against power for the greater protection of liberty.[21]

Other considerations pressed loyal Democrats in the same direction. Chief among them was the acknowledged fallibility of the popular intelligence, which they were particularly inclined to note on occasions when the Whigs won elections, but which was compatible with their broadly Calvinist view of human nature and especially of human nature in politics. In one sense the political competence of the people was irrelevant to Democratic doctrine, inasmuch as they participated in government to protect their rights and not to shape positive policies. But they might still be misled, as the *Democratic Review* observed more than once, and this fact apparently taught Democrats to look to constitutions to secure wiser deliberation. "We should not calculate too strongly upon human reason," the *Review* declared in 1838 in commenting on the ways in which Whig partisans had distorted the issues of the day. "In the long run, in an enlightened community, its dictates will always prevail, and the 'sober second thought of the people,' in the philosophical language of President Van Buren, is perhaps 'never wrong.' But in the passion or delusion of the moment, evils may be inflicted which time cannot repair; and there are some maladies of sudden origin which are incurable." From this point it was no very long step to looking to constitutional processes rather than democracy to secure sober second thoughts and prevent incurable evils.[22]

Hence liberal Democrats ended by embracing virtually the whole of the constitutional apparatus that the Whigs also honored. They did so for somewhat different reasons, and they never fully identified popular government with restrictions on popular sovereignty, but they clearly abandoned the kinds of pretension to popular authority that men like Root and Tallmadge had articulated, however temporarily. They retained the idea of a constituent people, which Whigs often sought to circumscribe by theories of vested right or organic law, but the right of the people to rule reduced rather oddly to their right to re-*constitute* governments, whereupon (it was assumed) the electorate would be bound by its own handiwork. "The people do not any the less govern," George Camp wrote in *Democracy*, "by thus governing in a certain mode which they themselves prescribe, and which they reserve to themselves the liberty at any time to alter." In many respects he was correct; but it was also true that these same people constituted governments so that they *would* the less govern.[23]

To put matters another way, their fear of being governed led them to identify their ability to govern themselves with the restrictions they placed upon their own freedom to make mistakes. Theodore Sedgwick Jr. explained matters in just this fashion in the pages of the *Democratic Review*. The pressure of competing interests for legislation hostile to the general interest, he wrote, results in powerful, despotic, and corrupt governments, and of all the possible means of curbing it "the constitutional check is the only one which the people voluntarily assume, and is the only one known, that is based upon a liberal representation of the popular will. It is likewise the one which admits of the largest liberty to the individual man." For Democrats as well as Whigs, the solution to the problem of self-government required the aid of an apparatus that might take issue with any specific act of the people's government.[24]

It even required the services of an independent judiciary. In liberal Democratic theory the judiciary must be elected by the people in order to prevent it from becoming an "aristocracy," but the judges so elected corresponded to the constitution popularly adopted: once installed in office they were to be defenders of the law, not agents of public opinion. (To employ Rousseauean language, they were to represent the General Will; but American democrats did not expect their courts to force men to be free so much as to guarantee them against political aberrations.) The fact that Democrats typically demanded written constitutions to safeguard popular rights had the same consequence. The law the people had adopted became the law as their judges interpreted it, not only in the straightforward sense that the judges were responsible for applying it in specific instances, but also in the less plausible sense that the law the judges found became the law the people were bound by.[f]

This tendency of events was the more striking in that liberal Democrats clearly recognized the dangers of an autonomous judiciary. "That much lauded independence of the judiciary," Sedgwick wrote in one of his essays on constitutional reform, ". . . covers, we fear, a grave political fallacy. To have efficiency in a public officer, as a general rule, there must be a different, though it be, a baser sense of accountability than that which the incumbent experiences in communing with his own conscience." In Louisiana, moreover, the *New Orleans Jeffersonian* pointed directly to what was at stake for democracy in the convention's debate over an elective judiciary. "The necessity of electing judges becomes absolutely imperative, in our minds, when we approach the consideration of the functions they fulfil. Judges not only decide controversies between individuals, but they interpret and construe the constitution and the laws, which is nothing less than the equivalent of making constitutions and laws. . . . That such a power as this should be placed beyond the controlling influence of public opinion, which is public knowledge and public virtue, is clearly incompatible with free government." [25]

It is significant, however, that Sedgwick invoked "efficiency" and the *Jeffersonian* "public virtue"; somehow not even these outspoken arguments came down to an unlimited assertion of popular sovereignty. Moreover, the most vigorous advocates of democratic institutions often clearly embraced the theory that the judiciary must be strengthened to make it more effective in the constitutional system of checks and balances. In the first Michigan convention, John Norvell insisted that judges should be appointed by the governor rather than the legislature and be installed for a period of seven rather than four years, the better to guarantee their independence of the legislature, while Isaac Crary took it for granted that an independent judiciary was necessary to protect popular rights against "the manifest disposition of the different powers, Legislative and Executive, to trench upon the constitution." Ten years later James F. Brent demanded popular election of the judiciary in Louisiana on the grounds of popular sovereignty—and of the balance of the constitution. "The Judiciary is the balance wheel of our political system," he declared. "As the balance wheel in the machinery of a steamboat, regulates the stroke of the piston, the movement of the valves, and the harmonious action of the engine, even so is it the office of the judiciary, to steady the movements and working of our system, by giving force and proper direction to the other powers of the government." [26]

Otherwise, liberal Democrats concerned themselves primarily with preventing judges from becoming an engine of aristocratic influence. To this extent they equated an elective judiciary with popular power, but even here their assertion of power was largely negative and betokened an effort to maintain the integrity of the judiciary rather than the authority of the people. "We want no part of our government independent of the people," Frederick Robinson told the Trades' Union of Boston in 1834. "Those, who are responsible to nobody, ought to be entrusted by nobody. But to whom are the judges responsible? The aristocracy always centre around power placed beyond the reach of the people; and until we can fill the bench with men of learning, good sense, and sound judgment, who do not belong to the secret fraternity of the bar, all attempts to simplify the laws, and the practice of the law, will be in vain." By 1845 Brent had moved the argument no further. "No principle hostile to our republican institutions, can ever creep into the government, unless it is through a department, that does not connect directly with the people. If a monarchical or aristocratic principle is to find a lodgment any where, it will be in that branch of the government that is not responsible to the popular authority." So far as the courts were concerned, the triumph of democratic principles produced a climate of opinion in which it seemed that popular election of the states' highest courts was sufficient to make self-government secure.[27]

THE DEMOCRACY OF THE CONSTITUTION

One major consequence of liberal democratic belief was to bring its adherents surprisingly close to the doctrines conservatives espoused. In particular, it brought them closer to conservative Democrats, who occupied a position somewhere between the liberals of their own party and the Whigs who opposed it. (There was also a small number of liberal Whigs who shared vigorously democratic attitudes toward the suffrage, the constituent authority of the people, and the judiciary.) Were we interested in achieving a statistically precise rendering of American constitutional belief we would be compelled to explore these mediating positions, but the fact that the two more extreme patterns of thought tended to meet on a common ground makes such exploration unnecessary here, where we are more concerned with the tendencies of American thought than with its details. Although conservative Democrats were an important force in American politics, and although they may have had distinct ideological characteristics, they contributed relatively little that was either new or striking to the constitutional debates of the period. Hence it seems legitimate to put them aside as a not very illuminating segment of American constitutional opinion.[g]

It *is* important, however, to examine the ways in which Democrats of various descriptions responded to the federal Constitution, both because their attitudes were intrinsically significant and because they had important consequences. Generally speaking, Democrats of different persuasions shared a common perspective that was to have a large bearing on the confrontations of the 1850s.

The existence of a broadly felt Democratic commitment to the federal Constitution was the more significant in view of the origins of so much Democratic opinion in the fears of the Antifederalists. It is relatively easy to understand Democratic constitutionalism in the states, where governments were close to hand, constitutions were repeatedly amended, and the electoral process increasingly brought government under the sway of the people. In effect, constitutional structures at the state level offered no irreducible obstacle to popular rule but existed by virtue of a kind of suspended animation of the popular will, however much that will was inhibited by the idea or the fact of constitutional checks and balances. By contrast, the federal government was relatively inaccessible; its constitution was almost beyond the reach of amendment; and even the political reforms of the Jacksonian era (among them the substitution of party conventions for the Congressional caucus, the development of the powers of the presidency, and the rise of the second American party system) left large areas of constitutional machinery untouched by democratic innovations. Above all, the Supreme Court remained a largely alien force, dominated in the early years of the period by the arch-Federalist John Marshall, in later years by many of the precedents he had established. If logic alone commanded events, it should have caused the victorious Democrats to overturn the limitations the Constitution placed on them, precisely as Whig conservatives charged they would.

Occasionally Democratic commentators did reveal a sensitivity to the obstacles that the federal constitutional structure placed in the way of popular self-government. "Do the vast body of the people need an independent power to oppose and assail their interests and their wishes?" George Camp asked in *Democracy*. "Compromises do sometimes take place in human affairs; but these, when wise, are the results of necessity, not of choice. The only proper checks and balances in a constitution are those that necessarily and naturally arise out of the rights and interests to be protected." Similarly, in 1826 Representative James K. Polk criticized the opponents of presidential election by districts who, like Edward Everett, urged their contemporaries to be extremely cautious in changing the existing provisions of the federal document, while Michael Doheny insisted, in *The Principle, Progress, and Tendency of Democracy*, that "when the people delegate certain powers and functions, and abdicate the right of resumption, the living and operative principle of Democracy ceases to be. Herein is the distinction between a republic and a monarchy. In the latter there may be more practical and general freedom; but yet the vital principle of Democracy must be extinct, for it consists not more in the power to confer than in the power to resume authority. This latter is the essence of republicanism." [28]

In addition, the decisions of the Supreme Court repeatedly antagonized Democratic spokesmen, who replied by fulminating against its authority. Given their premises, the case they made against the Court was powerful and tended at least by implication to call the whole constitutional structure into question. For one thing, they were incensed by the fact that the Marshall Court nullified state legislation and overturned state courts' decisions, primarily on the strength of the contract clause. They were also incensed by the sympathy the contract-clause cases showed to vested interests in maintaining the rights of creditors against debtors, of corporations against their critics, and of the holders of property against the authority of state governments. Above all, they were alarmed by the apparent tendency of the Court's decisions—its aggressive assertions of federal supremacy, its appeals to the doctrine of implied powers, and its habit of resolving clearly problematical issues in favor of its own jurisdiction and authority. They were sure, not only that the Court had made many mistakes, but that it would continue to favor the consolidation of national power at the expense of popular liberties.[29]

Democratic criticisms of the Court extended beyond the content and effects of its decisions to its role in the constitutional process. Senator John Rowan of Kentucky argued during debate on the Foot Resolution that the federal judiciary must be made responsible to the people if the people were to be truly free and truly self-governing. In 1838 the *Demo-*

cratic Review renewed Rowan's charges against the irresponsibility of judges in both state and federal courts and decried popular veneration of the federal Court as an "abject mental subjection to authority and [an] assumption . . . unworthy equally of our country and age." "It is our opinion," it declared, "that the judiciary system of the United States is based on false principles." More generally, Democrats refused to concede the power of the Court to decide public issues. In his Bank veto message, Andrew Jackson denied that the Court's opinion in *McCulloch* v. *Maryland* could bind the President to affirm the constitutionality of the Bank of the United States, and in 1840 M. Hall McAllister argued before the Democratic Convention of Georgia that no Court decision could bind the government or the people beyond the disposition of the case immediately before the Court: "A contrary principle would assimilate the decisions of the Supreme Court of the United States, to the Constitutions of the Roman Emperors, and prostrate the liberties of the people at the footstool of the Federal Judiciary." [30]

In short, a number of Democrats presented reasons for throwing off the authority of the Court, and in this sense at least they betrayed a good deal of skepticism about the legitimacy of American constitutionalism. Had they persevered in their antagonism they might have reshaped both, but in practice they were remarkably restrained. One reason presumably is that they won office, and with it control of all three branches of government, whereupon the constitutional arrangements they deplored tended to work for Democratic ends. Still, the change in administrations did not eliminate the problems they pointed to, and (as the *Review* and McAllister indicated) the Court in particular continued to present obstacles to popular authority. Hence their restraint also suggests that they were more committed to constitutionalism than their stated premises should have let them be. In effect, they would seem to have taken the theoretical possibility of amendment as evidence that the Constitution the Court expounded was an acceptable mode of self-government.[h]

Certainly Democrats continued to take the power of the judiciary for granted: although they fulminated against specific decisions and questioned the legitimacy of judicial review, they ended by arguing that the Court must return to the true interpretation of the Constitution. Far from pressing their criticisms of the fact of judicial review to its logical consequence in some alternative mode of deciding disputed issues, they accepted the practice and objected to the practitioners.[i] The *Democratic Review* ended the same article in which it castigated popular veneration for the Court and deplored the irresponsibility of the judiciary, by appealing to the Court to void every law that *truly* impaired contracts or operated *ex post facto*, as it held the recent session of the Taney Court had done. "We are in the midst of a revolution," it declared, only to describe the satisfaction with which it contemplated Court, president, Congress, and states carrying forward "the great and glorious cause of reducing government and enlarging freedom as much as possible." Six months later the same magazine acknowledged that judicial annulment of laws in conflict with a written constitution was "an entirely new thing in the practice of the world" as well as an imposing and possibly dangerous spectacle, only to remark that "we are not, however, among those who entertain a very exaggerated opinion of the political importance of the judiciary department of the Government, whether for good or evil." Other Democrats seemingly welcomed the authority the *Review* chose simply to accept. "States will deviate sometimes, legislatures likewise," said Pierre Soulé during a heated debate in the Louisiana convention on the qualifications for governor; "but judges are still left to bring them back 'nolens volens' to the supreme laws of the land." Obviously leading Democrats counted upon the Court to play a significant role in maintaining popular liberty.[31]

Democrats also deferred to the federal Constitution apart from the Court as an apparatus of self-government. Frequently they invoked it to enforce policies they valued. In 1840 Col. Benjamin Faneuil Hunt of South Carolina rebuked the constitutional arguments of Daniel Webster in favor of a national bank by recounting the largely legendary history of a democratic constitution that the Federalists had hoped to pervert to the ends of a consolidated national government.

The democratic character of the constitution of the United States, the strict enumeration of what powers the people of the several states were satisfied to confide in the general government, the cautious reservation of all power not granted to the 'states respectively or to the people,' the popular tone given to the electors of the chief magistrate, all emanated from the democracy that had struggled through toil and blood to shake off the trammels of a transatlantic monarchy, and erect on these western shores a proud democracy, based upon the eternal truth that the people possessed the ability for self-government, and that equality of right would always enable honest industry to reap a sure reward.

So, too, Democratic delegates to state constitutional conventions often appealed to federal precedent to justify specific constitutional measures like checks and balances. If they remade history on a Democratic model, the history they wrote tended to glorify a Constitution that was only dubiously democratic.[32]

They also invoked the Constitution in a purely mystical sense. A seemingly radical commentator like Robert Walker took pains to reassure a gathering of workingmen of New York, "Think not, fellow-citizens, I wish to urge you to overthrow our constitution, as based on the declaration of independence; far from it: those evils I have hinted at are but excrescences fastened by the interested on our glorious constitution, and which require but the caustic of reform, efficiently applied, to remove them from the glorious edifice they contaminate and deface." Other commentators simply equated the Constitution as it was with the highest achievements of democracy. Celebrating the passage of the Independent Treasury Bill in 1840 as a second Declaration of Independence, Hugh A. Garland of Virginia hailed the founding fathers for having created a Constitution "precisely adapted to the circumstances of the country and the condition of the people, limited to those functions only which are indispensable to the common good, imposing no unequal duties, conferring no especial benefits on any class or section." George Bancroft portrayed the events of the 1780s even more enthusiastically when he wrote in introducing the fourth volume of his *History of the United States*, "The equality of all men was declared; personal freedom secured in its complete individuality; and common consent recognised as the only just origin of fundamental laws, so that the people in thirteen separate states, with ample territory for creating more, each formed its own political institutions. By the side of the principle of the freedom of the individual and the freedom of the separate states, the noblest work of human intellect was consummated in a federative union. And that union put away every motive to its destruction, by insuring to each successive generation the right to better its constitution, according to the increasing intelligence of the living people." In such statements partisan advantage took second place to national necessity; to be a Democrat (its spokesmen indicated) was to be an American constitutionalist.[33]

Even so, these enthusiastic expressions may have been exercises in popular macrohistory rather than expressions of political belief; but the mystique that Democrats invoked supported a complex constitutional structure as well as a heroic retelling of American constitutional history. In 1836 the Democratic-Republican convention of Indiana rebuked Whig plans to throw the presidential election into the House of Representatives on the grounds that legislative choice of the president would constitute an infringement on constitutional checks and balances intended "to guard against intrigue, treachery, and corruption." Similarly, the *Democratic Review* asserted in 1838 that "the distribution of power is unquestionably one of the essential principles on which, in connection with the kindred one of frequent responsibility to the sovereign source of all, the healthy action of free institutions depends," an assertion that apparently overrode its earlier complaint that the Constitution drafted in 1787 had embraced monarchical and aristocratic features intended to check popular authority. (In effect, it declared that these checks were salutary when democratic and evil only when they provided a refuge for "aristocracy.") So, too, discussing constitutional changes in Europe in 1848, Oliver C. Gardiner compared the American constitutional structure with European practices, to the detriment of the European: "The incomparable value and strength of the American confederacy, is found in the wise distribution of all its powers,—not only in the form of the national legislature, but in the operation of the power by which this body is to be perpetuated. Every state sovereignty is but a miniature of the national, as perfectly adjusted in its legislative system, and also in the method of the renewing power. Its crowning glory is its moral strength, which binds all parts together—the strongest and most delicate machinery—thus guarding it against foes without, or enemies within." [34]

Democrats defended the executive veto in the same ambiguous terms. Significantly, in its rebuke to Whig charges of "executive usurpation," the *Democratic Review* made plain that it viewed the president as a tribune of the people, but it also argued that the legislative and executive branches of government represented the people in different ways, and it expressed the hope that the time would never recur when it would be necessary for the chief magistrate to assert the full measure of executive power. "We are no friends to strong governmental action," it declared. "We are no friends to powerful executive influence." The Democratic

State Convention of Illinois was, if anything, more explicit in its contention that the veto power was an essential element in a complex system of checks and balances,

one house of Congress being a check upon the other, and the Executive, the representative of the whole people, a check upon the excesses of both. . . . To take this power away, would bring the Executive and every other department of the government under the control of Congress, and would destroy the symmetry and beauty of a system, fashioned by the fathers of the Republic, and which has extorted the admiration of the world. Yet, fellow citizens, [it] is seriously designed by the party in power so to change the constitution as to get rid of this clog upon Congressional action, in order that a bare majority may enact such laws as they please—in order that they may rule with undivided empire, and without let or hindrance, arbitrarily dispose of all your constitutional rights.[35]

The case these Democrats made was undoubtedly polemical in the sense that they chiefly sought to defend the actions a Democratic president had taken, but its polemical character does not seriously diminish its significance as a statement of Democratic belief. For one thing, the Illinois Democrats actually came to the defense of John Tyler; for another, those who criticized Jackson's vetoes tended to move into the Whig party, leaving behind others who apparently genuinely supported the president's actions. More important, Jackson himself presented a strikingly restrictive view of his constitutional role on the very occasions on which he seemed to the Whigs to be most threatening. Contending with critics who invoked the authority of the Supreme Court to support recharter of the Bank of the United States, he argued that each of the three departments of government must be free to cast its vote against a controversial measure. Contending with the Senate over its efforts to censure him, he appealed to the constitutional separation and distribution of powers to sanction the removal of the deposits. Contending with both sets of opponents, he invoked a magisterial public document to which the people of the United States had knowingly committed their lives, their fortunes, and their liberties. Far from challenging the authority of constitutional limitations, he maintained them against what he took to be the enemies of the people.[36]

It seems quite likely that he would have come to a different conclusion had he conceived of democracy in a positive sense as a vehicle for satisfying popular needs through activities intended to serve them constructively. But in fact he conceived of it primarily in negative terms, and therefore he never really confronted the disparity between popular authority and constitutional restrictions. As a result, conservatives had little to fear and much to respect in the Constitution as Jackson defined it. In the nation as well as the states the Democratic creed came down to the prevention of evil through constitutional mechanisms intended to magnify the popular veto of political errors. The highest aspiration of the Democracy was to maintain the Constitution inviolate.

Only in dealing with nullification in South Carolina did Jackson invoke a more affirmative instrument, and even then it remained more nearly a document that restrained illegal behavior than one that asserted the authority of the people. The point has often been made that for the moment Webster and Jackson collaborated; it might better be said that Jackson virtually conceded the Constitution Webster had described in his debate with Hayne. He disputed the logic of nullification; he also invoked a people's document that took precedence over the rights of the states because the people had ordained it as the preferred instrument of their self-government. If in some sense he asserted the power of the federal government, he did so on the grounds of the Constitution as it was, and he concluded by equating that Constitution with both liberty and democracy.[37]

THE RIGHTS OF THE STATES

During the nullification controversy, Jackson rallied the nation to the support of the Constitution and postponed for a generation the South's tragic effort to remake it. In doing so, however, he alienated many of his followers and took issue with a key principle in the Democratic creed. Confronted by the threat of anarchy, he virtually repudiated states' rights, which was the final element in Democratic constitutionalism.

To the modern eye his assertion of federal authority was indispensable and his opponents were thoroughly wrong-headed. On this view, the very fact that they engaged in a protracted and often tedious legal argument about the contractual rights of the states only confirms their irrelevance. So, too, the fact that at one time or another every major party and virtually every American state has invoked states' rights has made the doctrine seem a mere rationalization for special interests. Nevertheless, the frequent reappearance of the argument should teach us that it has been a critically important part of American democratic thought. Its particular formulations may well have been arid or tendentious, but they rested upon profound convictions about the requirements of popular liberty.[38]

Unlike the original doctrine of the rights of the states, which was advanced in the Philadelphia convention by the representatives of small states like New Jersey, who feared the nationalistic tendencies embodied in the so-called Virginia Plan, the doctrine that prevailed during the Middle Period was grounded in a theory of popular freedom. Its advocates often engaged in historical discourses about the origins of the federal government, but the compact they described was really a legal fiction intended to protect the ends they had in view. In essence, they associated liberty with local self-government and oppression with the concentration of power in Washington. "Consolidation will be the euthanasia of our Constitution," Thomas Addis Emmet argued before the New York Court of Chancery in 1824. "Make that consolidated government as democratic and free as you please, make its base as broad and its principles as liberal as philanthropy and philosophy can devise; it will still be a single government over a vast extent of territory; it will follow—it will surely and speedily follow—the course of all the governments of ancient times and modern Europe, which began with elective rights and free institutions but have silently sunk into despotisms." So, too, in his Bank veto, Andrew Jackson deplored the efforts of consolidationists to invade the autonomy of individuals and the rights of the states in a misguided pursuit of national power, while in 1853 Governor Joseph A. Wright of Indiana looked forward to the day when, faithful to the autonomy of the states, Americans would be truly able to govern themselves:

When we shall live up to our privileges as members of our happy form of State government, and discharge our whole duty in the small circle in which we move; when we shall adapt our laws and institutions, which affect us every day in all the relations of life, and in all our intercourse with each other, so as to make each man feel that upon *him* rests a portion of the responsibilities of life; when we shall come up to that full standard of State *pride*, State *ambition*, State *rights*, that our forefathers designed we should occupy, it will make but little difference what three hundred men at Washington do, or whether this or that act of Congress shall pass. *The top may tremble and agitate, but the base will be immovable—the foundation will be secure.*[39]

The general thrust of Democratic opinion was clear enough; the difficult position in which South Carolinians found themselves vis-à-vis the tariff of 1828 gave it a particular direction.[j] At first they appealed to a general theory of constitutional liberty to check what they took to be infringements on their economic rights. "To prevent the frequent resort to revolution," the inhabitants of the Abbeville District declared in 1828, "governments are instituted with limited powers, checks and balances: and a written constitution (although very liable to metaphysical subtleties in its construction) is best adapted to express the precise forms and limits which the parties to the social compact would prescribe for their government." So, too, spokesmen for the Richland District declared that "the peculiar excellence of a written constitution, is, that it affords protection to the minority of the nation, which it governs. The majority can protect themselves without a constitution. We, a minority—the party oppressed, and standing in need of protection, seeking not to exercise, but to restrain power—we look up to and invoke the constitution." Particularly in the early stages of the tariff controversy it seemed plausible to believe that southerners would be able to bring their oppressors to reason simply by affirming the theory of constitutional limitation.[40]

As time went on, however, spokesmen for the South increasingly feared that existing constitutional limitations would not serve to protect their interests. Witnessing the perserverance of the federal government in the tariff they abominated, they had no alternative but to descry a consolidating national authority encroaching on their liberties. They were also easily persuaded that the evils they described resulted from a deliberate corruption of the legislative process, whereby men who should have known better were bribed by sectional advantage to adopt unconstitutional measures. "In short, Gentlemen," former Representative James Hamilton told the State Rights Celebration in Charleston in 1830, "during the last four years of my service in Congress, I witnessed enough to convince me, that, practically, the government of this confederacy was nothing more or less than an organ of indefinite power, admirably used (if not contrived) for the purpose of taxing one portion of the Union, with the view of distributing its exactions in another." [41]

In addition southerners insisted that the Supreme Court must necessarily fail to maintain the balance of the Constitution. The South Carolina

Exposition and Protest of December 1828, written for the most part by John C. Calhoun, developed this point with unusual clarity. Although the Court is often described as a bulwark for the rights of the states, Calhoun's argument ran, it must take the stated intention of legislation at face value, and therefore it cannot be expected to overrule unconstitutional enactments such as protective tariffs. More than this, it is part of the federal government, and—far from serving as an impartial judge of competing claims to authority—it inevitably takes sides with the government to which it is attached. Finally, it is beyond the reach of its creators and beyond the reach of correction. Hence the liberty of the people is in jeopardy, for the division of powers mandated by the Constitution is made nugatory by the Court's bias and irresponsibility.[42]

More generally, the *Exposition* appealed to a whole range of Democratic principles to sanction southern resistance. For example, it held that irresponsible power is incompatible with liberty and requires "judicious contrivances" to keep it in check. Among these it listed frequent elections, but it also insisted that "power can only be met by power, and not by reason and justice, and that all restrictions on authority, unsustained by an equal antagonist power, must forever prove wholly insufficient in practice." It inferred from these observations the necessity of checks on the federal government, which it justified by the history of liberty, and it also stressed the proposition that such limitations are not only compatible with the authority of government, but actually necessary to curb its abuses.[43]

Thus far the *Exposition*'s argument accorded with the tenets of Democratic constitutionalism, but it laid greater stress on the protection of minority interests than did Democratic orthodoxy. Nevertheless, the minority it defended was at least in theory a majority of southern agriculturists, to whom Democrats normally deferred, and a good many Democratic leaders were prepared to argue that even a democratic majority will be tyrannical if it exercises discretionary power. (Certainly the tariff was discriminatory. The issue it raised was whether its evils were justified by their results, not whether it discriminated against some producers in favor of others.) Hence the real novelty of the document lay in the lucidity with which it confronted the question of what was to be done if the established constitutional machinery failed to serve the purpose for which it was intended. In substance, the *Exposition* proposed nullification as a new means to secure free government.[k]

Not everyone in South Carolina espoused Calhoun's remedy, and northerners generally repudiated it as a monstrous innovation; to this extent we must concede that it was un-Democratic if not undemocratic. Before we conclude that it lay outside the mainstream of American democratic thought, however, we should note other ways in which the *Exposition* in particular, and the southern case for nullification in general, corresponded to beliefs that liberal Democrats expressed.

For one thing, many advocates of nullification clearly sought constitutional means to secure liberties that were not protected by the existing constitutional structure. Far from claiming a right of revolution through which they might create a constitution more to their liking, they insisted that because the checks and balances they honored did not work as intended there must be some means within the framework of the Constitution to augment them. "We do not choose in a case of this kind," the Convention of South Carolina declared in its *Address to the People*, "to recur to what are called our natural rights, or the right of revolution. We claim to nullify by a more imposing title. We claim it as a CONSTITU-TIONAL right, not meaning as some have imagined, that we *derive* the right from the Constitution, . . . but we claim to exercise it as one of the PARTIES to the compact, and as consistent with its letter, its genius and its spirit." In this sense they anticipated the argument of the reformers in Rhode Island who were to lay claim to a constitutional right of revolution, available in the United States but not in Europe. They also resembled the Rhode Islanders in that their circumstances may well have compelled them to adopt a constitutional form of argument; but it is equally pertinent that they found the form at hand and employed it in full measure.[44]

It is also significant that the Convention appealed to the right of the constituent authority to alter an existing constitution. Classic Democratic theory identified this constituency with the electorate, whereas the theory of nullification identified it with the states, but the fundamental contention was the same: the powers that create a constitutional government reserve the right to alter it. Given the attachment that the men of that generation felt to their states, in fact, it is not at all implausible to suppose that the contractual legalists we criticize actually voiced a wide-spread conviction. In any case it is important to remember that the South Carolinians sought to improve a constitutional apparatus that was dominated by the Marshall Court, and that the improvement they proposed took the form of referring disputed constitutional issues to the same authority that had adopted the Constitution. Unless we are to accept Webster's history and revel in Webster's mystique, it is difficult to see how they could have been more faithful to the traditions of American Democracy.

Finally, although South Carolinians were deeply divided over the merits of nullification, they were largely agreed upon the need for some form of protection from northern "avarice." They agreed, that is, that they were oppressed, and they protested northern innovations in constitutional practice, but they disagreed over the means most appropriate for restoring self-government. In this sense they may be said to have subscribed to competing versions of the same constitutional principle, the optimists holding either that less strenuous remedies would produce the desired results or that it was better to suffer some evils than to jeopardize the whole constitutional structure. John Calhoun's reply to critics who complained that nullification was tantamount to anarchy demonstrated the extent to which proponents and opponents disagreed over means rather than ends: nullification poses no threat to the public welfare, he argued, because it is only a check on government, which retains all of its unchallenged powers. In effect he held not only that nullification was necessary to protect liberty but also that it would be employed only when needed.[45]

The theory of constitutional nullification thus rested upon Democratic shibboleths and built upon Democratic arguments. The *Address to the People of Mississippi* drafted by John A. Quitman and six other delegates to the State Rights' Convention of 1834 demonstrates this fact in remarkably explicit terms. As these die-hard dissidents described matters, the main problem of politics is the conflict between power and popular freedom, which hung in the balance even during the Philadelphia convention of 1787. For the moment, they said, the advocates of liberty were aroused to protest against Federalist schemes of consolidation, which they succeeded once again in curbing in 1800, but the history of the United States since has been a history of continuing encroachments, culminating in Andrew Jackson's proclamation to the people of South Carolina. Meanwhile, they added, the Supreme Court has demonstrated that it will not curtail the federal government, and in any event its authority is incompatible with democracy because it assigns despotic power to a handful of federal officials. They concluded that there must be a remedy, which they associated with strengthening the political powers of the states against federal authority: "No man will deny that the interposition of a proper and efficient check to usurpation, is essential to liberty. The checking power, we admit, may be abused as well as the usurping power. No system yet devised by human frailty, is perfect. If we must make a choice of evils let us choose the less. . . . The course of free governments has not been so smooth, but with every shock of opposing power, and with every collision of opposing interests, liberty has been better secured." Like many other Democrats, in other words, they began with popular liberty and ended with an elaboration of constitutional machinery.[46]

They also lost their argument, not only in the North but even in the South, where no other state joined South Carolina, and where South Carolina herself abandoned the cause. Northern Democrats took comfort from the fact, but they might better have regretted it. They would find in time that events in South Carolina had so discredited the rights of the states as to jeopardize many of the liberties they claimed. In addition, southerners had lost a desperately needed resource against power. The next time they sensed that their rights were in danger they would have no real alternative but to choose between liberty and union.

FREE INSTITUTIONS

❦ X ❧

RELIGION AS A FREE
INSTITUTION

By 1850 most Americans believed that the history of liberty had come to fruition in the United States, which enjoyed the benefits of a free society because it had thrown off European traditions of aristocracy and adopted equal rights under constitutional limitations. But complacent as they may have been about their nation's achievements, they sensed that the advantages they enjoyed depended in some sense upon their society's circumstances as well as came to a focus in its political institutions. Even zealous Democrats who refused to let suffrage wait upon competence were aware that a vicious population could hardly be expected to maintain liberty, while more conservative observers were quick to perceive evils that untrammeled freedom might bring. Hence many commentators reflected at some length on the provenience of free institutions—the specific institutional arrangements that would protect them and their descendants against "European" evils without curtailing American liberties. In essence, they looked to free religion, free schools, and free land to guarantee the privileges they had been born to.

Religion was the first of the guarantees they invoked, not only because its concerns were central to their lives, but also because they were heirs to a long tradition of evangelical effort. At the same time, the fact that they shared a complex religious heritage meant that they were compelled to work out a fresh conception of their faith in its relationships with society. Had they persevered literal-mindedly in their traditions, they might well have had to choose between democracy and religion. By conceding free religion, however (taking that term in its voluntaristic rather than its anticlerical sense), they converted it into the first bulwark of their liberties.

THE RELIGIOUS VALUES OF CONSERVATISM

We may best comprehend the thrust of these commentators' thought by recognizing the extent to which men of a generally conservative temperament assumed that religious convictions were necessary to maintain social order. There was no real difference on this point between those who were orthodox and those who were heterodox in their own religious opinions. However they may have felt about the cardinal points of American Protestantism, they sensed the important role that religion played in the lives of ordinary men, and they often sought to turn it to account for the better preservation of the republic. The Reverend Jasper Adams, President of the College of Charleston, expressed their essentially utilitarian intentions with unusual clarity when he spoke in 1834 to its society of graduates on the moral causes of the welfare of nations:

> The problem presented for solution to those who, in any form, are called to the difficult undertaking of governing others, is, to secure the requisite obedience, and the greatest good of the greatest number, at the least possible expense of restriction, and especially of punishment; and when punishment is necessary, to select that, which of all others, is most salutary in its tendency, and otherwise least exceptionable. That government is most wise in its principles and salutary in its effects, which, with the fewest possible penalties and restrictions, furnishes the greatest number of encouragements (motives) to good conduct in the citizen. Under our institutions, we partially govern ourselves, and mutually aid in governing each other;—and consequently, our encouragements are as many, and the penalties and restrictions imposed on us, are as few, as slight, and as unexceptionable, as our passions and tempers will permit them to be.[1]

Its utilitarian cast aside, two aspects of this statement are especially significant. Although it apparently divided mankind between those who govern and those who are governed, it was neither cynical nor manipulative. Rather, it reflected understandable fears lest the proliferation of democratic institutions divest American society of its props to virtue, which Republicans as well as Federalists had thought necessary to the maintenance of freedom. At the same time, it evinced a clearly felt wish to minimize the coercive functions of government by finding voluntary motives for virtue. Far from calling liberty into question, men like Adams held that the greater the liberty a society enjoyed, the greater was its need for some kind of purely moral influence that would protect it against disintegration without requiring the use of force. "On the morality and intelligence of a people," wrote Adams's counterpart at Brown University, "will greatly depend the freedom of its civil constitution; that is, the accuracy with which it limits the power of the society, that is, of the government, over the person and property of the individual."

So, too, the Chief Justice of Kentucky explained to the Deinologian Society at Centre College in 1834 that "as a free moral agent, man in the social and civil state, must be regulated by moral principles," and John Todd made a special point in *The Young Man* of describing the role a sound public opinion played in maintaining American freedom. Europeans, he declared, "cannot conceive of a condition where every man is on the side of law, and every man is the guardian of law and a maker of law, and where every man helps to create public opinion—the most powerful of all kinds of law." [2]

Taken at face value, these pronouncements had no specific religious implication, yet every appeal to moral principles presupposed some kind of religious influence, and many spokesmen who skirted the question of what form that influence should take were none the less certain that it was indispensable to liberty. Speaking at Dartmouth College in 1832, George Kent exhorted college graduates everywhere to persevere in their fostering care for government lest it be undermined by religious infidelity or political corruption, be destroyed by popular ignorance, intemperance, or lawlessness. Eleven years later Nathan S. S. Beman announced at Hamilton College that "the only problem which remains to be solved in relation to our continued existence and progressive prosperity, as a nation, is, whether we have moral principle enough for the nature of our institutions. . . . We make our own laws, and execute them; and should the time ever come when freemen will legislate in favor of their own vices, or stay the execution of the law from a deep consciousness of their own moral delinquencies, no government could be as inefficient and baseless as ours." Consequently "scholars" everywhere declared that their kind must enter "politics" to promote the moral redemption of democracy. [3]

So strenuous were the fears some conservatives felt that they toyed with the idea of a "national religion," which alone might suppress human frailties and make possible an ordered liberty. In 1826, commenting on the deaths of John Adams and Thomas Jefferson, the *Christian Examiner* stated, "There is danger . . . that in separating church and state, we should separate the ideas of *religion* and the state. Now it is true, indeed, between the state and religion, *considered as an establishment*, there is no necessary connexion. Our own example has proved it. Our government needs no hierarchy to support it. But at the same time, let us never forget, that between a state *like ours,* and religion considered as a *principle,* there is the most necessary, the most indissoluble connexion." Twelve years later a writer in the *New-York Review* contended that the American government had no choice but to foster religious principles: "To maintain religion in honor—and by religion we mean christianity—is, beyond doubt, among the primary obligations of those who are called upon to administer a government that is founded upon it. How to do this without offence, it may be, is not easy; but many things are not easy in government which yet are necessary, and this is one. The state has cast off the church, but it cannot cast off religion; that is its vitality, and without it, it would soon sink into ruin." [4]

The *American Review* adopted much the same position without the excuse of a declared religious allegiance. In 1845, reviewing E. P. Hurlbut's *Essays on Human Rights,* it explicitly argued that enlightened self-interest was a contradiction in terms, which could be redeemed only by a "national conscience." "And if a national conscience, then likewise a national religion," it added; "a term which we cannot be deterred from using, because some shallow demagogue, who knows no better, may confound it with something so widely different as an established church." Five months later it returned to the cause, acknowledging the difficulties but insisting that the nation as nation must have a publicly acknowledged conscience, which was dependent in turn upon an explicit religious orientation. Legislation should not regulate religion, but religion must regulate legislation. [5]

In other words, typical conservative commentators often conceived of religion as a social necessity, important less for its intrinsic qualities than for the moral influence it might exercise. Nevertheless they were foolish in their hopes, which were weakened rather than strengthened by their concessions to religious freedom: they wanted the functions of an established church without retaining its structure, at a time when the democracy had repudiated both as offenses against popular liberty. Hence it was left to other men, of a more narrowly religious temperament, to explore the ways in which free churches might still save the republic.

THE CONSERVATIVE VALUES OF RELIGION

Whereas the utilitarian approach to religion lacked efficacy, the theological approach to American politics produced important practical results. Thanks partly to their own preoccupations and partly to their critics, American religious leaders whose social attitudes were conservative moved from defending the religious establishment of the past to conceiving of religion as a free institution.

This development was facilitated by two characteristic features of American Protestantism. One was that it was unmistakably devout: whatever the positions its leaders might take on matters of theology, morals, or politics, they would be grounded in deeply felt religious sentiments. The other was that American clergymen habitually visualized religion as a social force, a temporal as well as a spiritual phenomenon. Although many orthodox Protestants clearly demurred at confusing the undertakings of this world with the obligations of the next, they often shared the conviction that worldly behavior must defer to religious principles, while a surprising number of highly regarded preachers actually labored for the millennium.[6]

These two facts meant, in turn, that as soon as the ticklish question of relationships between church and state had been settled, religious leaders of virtually every denomination would seek to redeem American society by means compatible with freedom. In this respect, events in New England bore a significance out of all proportion to its size and population. Established churches in other colonies had disappeared during the Revolution, and they were never instituted in the new states across the mountains, but they survived in modified form in the key states of Connecticut and Massachusetts. Their existence there prompted widespread resentment and helped to create a democratic opposition that might have been excused if it had repudiated all forms of civil religion when it finally pushed through disestablishment in 1818 and 1833. Instead, the destruction of the Standing Order led to a great moral crusade to make Americans worthy of the liberty they had inherited. Moreover, although many dissidents remained suspicious of this new religious impulse, the freedom they had fought for prevented them from suppressing it as they had the established churches.[7,a]

The career of Lyman Beecher epitomizes these developments. In his early years Beecher was a die-hard Federalist, a last-ditch defender of the established church in Connecticut, and a bitter critic of innovations in church and state. Hence he condemned exclusion of the Bible and the catechism from the common schools, and criticized changes in the law that provided public support for the ministry: "The practical effect has been to liberate all conscientious dissenters from supporting a worship which they did not approve—which the law intended, and to liberate a much greater number, without conscience, from paying for the support of the Gospel any where—which the law did not intend." At about the same time he initiated a Society for the Suppression of Vice and the Promotion of Good Morals, which was intended primarily to encourage Sabbath-keeping and temperance, but also to "produce such freemen as were [once] formed by early habits of subordination and the constant influence of the fear of God." After he had moved to Boston he continued his labors in the Hanover Association of Young Men and *Lectures on Political Atheism* (1829), both devoted to combating the spread of false principles in religion and politics.[8]

Despite these political views, Beecher was always a moderate on purely theological issues. As he recalled in his *Autobiography* (1864), the main purpose of his ministry had been to unite devout men in the service of God, and the growing strength of religion in American public life seems to have reconciled him even to the disestablishment of the church. At any rate, he insisted that the separation of church and state had been "*the best thing that ever happened to the State of Connecticut*," because it freed the churches from their dependence on secular power, removed the complaints of persecution that had beset religious authorities, and strengthened the work of the ministry. "By voluntary efforts, societies, missions, and revivals," he declared in that volume, "they exert a deeper influence than ever they could by queues, and shoe-buckles, and cocked hats, and gold-headed canes." His *Lectures on Political Atheism* implicitly expressed the same point of view, for they attributed both religious skepticism and political infidelity to the union of church and state and the attempt to secure religious faith by force.[9]

Yet the fact that Beecher embraced the separation of church and state did not mean that he had abandoned his moral principles. Both the clergy as an institution and the voluntary associations clergymen sponsored still seemed indispensable to civil liberty; the divorce of church from state was tolerable only because it extended no further than the elimination of legal support. "Christianity is the world's last hope for civil liberty," he declared in 1829; "if this will not diversify the results of national prosperity, then are we with rapid strides making for the precipice, and preparing to bid a long farewell to all our liberty." [10] But it was significant that he adopted freedom in religion as a necessary condition of religious vitality as well as pointed to religious vitality as a condition of political freedom. The churches he preached in were now entirely free, yet they remained in his eyes a foundation for national liberty. They were a "free institution" in the sense that they would serve institutional purposes and respect the requirements of freedom at one and the same time.

To put the matter somewhat differently, when Beecher accepted the idea of a voluntary religion he apparently recognized that in most ages and most countries formally organized institutions like the church, the nobility, and the army had been thought necessary to maintain social order. But he also increasingly recognized that those institutions had been both illiberal in themselves (hierarchically organized, exclusive, and grounded in force) and illiberal in their consequences (imposing their often dubious will on a reluctant people). Hence he became increasingly willing to abandon the alliance between church and state, which was in any event discredited in America, and which bore the added disadvantage for a Protestant of eliciting only outward compliance with religious or social values.

At the same time, as a clergyman he could hardly look with equanimity on the decline of religious influence and the destruction of religious organization; he continued to bear in mind the purposes that the institutional structure had been intended to serve, and therefore he sought means, compatible with religious freedom, to retrieve the institutional force of religion. In this sense the free institutions he spoke for were not simply churches understood as voluntary agencies to which devout Christians might turn for spiritual instruction, but social agencies through which the conditions of secular freedom could be voluntarily maintained. They might be institutional in their internal structure and in their consequences without sharing the institutional defects that European religious establishments entailed.

Even so, Beecher's acquiescence in religious liberty was belated and perhaps also conditional, whereas many of his contemporaries embraced it without reservation. In 1835 Stephen Chapin, the Baptist president of Columbian College in Washington, echoed his denomination's long campaign against an establishment in any form when he told the Evangelical

Society of the college that "most of the present forms of government, are corrupt and oppressive, presenting strong barriers against the prevalence of civil freedom, and the diffusion of Christianity." Andrew Wylie, the Presbyterian president of Indiana College, argued in much the same vein in 1830 that Christianity did not need the state, being superior to it, independent of it, and powerful without it; and in 1838 Solomon Southwick, a Methodist theocrat speaking before the Albany County Temperance Society in the Dutch Reformed Church of Bethlehem (New York) insisted that the Reformation would not be complete until the church was entirely divorced from the state. "The REFORMATION has not yet done its work; and the reason is, that though intended for a thorough purging both of church and state, LUTHER was driven by necessity, or a mistaken policy, to avail himself of the aid of political power. . . . But still the undying principles of regeneration and reform were planted, took strong root, and will eventually spread, and triumph in the universal destruction of all King-craft, Priest-craft, and TYRANNY and MONOPOLY of every kind." [11,b]

Nevertheless these same men also insisted that religion alone could maintain secular liberty. Chapin said as much in Washington, while Wylie argued in Indiana that the very existence of free government depended upon religious influences because "to be capable of governing themselves mankind must be raised above the level of their ordinary attainments; and, to prevent their sinking back again to this level, the application of sundry moral causes is constantly and indispensably requisite." So, too, Southwick devoted his oration to a long catalogue of the moral evils that threatened the republic—not only intemperance and usury and profaning of the Sabbath, but natural religion and other departures from Bible Christianity. "Were I on a dying bed," he announced, "I would conjure you, with my last breath, and from the bottom of my heart, to trust no man with the guardianship of your laws and liberties, who is not the faithful and the fast friend of the Christian Religion." [12]

Men who anticipated the near approach of the millennium had additional motives to promote Christian morality. Because they were postmillenarians, they were deeply concerned with the quality of American life, which would largely determine how and when the great day arrived. Hence a good many clergymen worked insistently to promote

temperance, Sabbath-keeping, and similar reforms, which they understood as both private obligations and public necessities. Frequently they
moved from a belief that voluntary efforts would secure the necessary
degree of morality to the belief that only legal prohibitions (as on alcoholic beverages and Sunday mails) would suffice for their purposes. But
other men moved in a contrary direction, from suppression to conversion, and in any event their disagreements over tactics did not cause
them to abandon their basic principle. The secular achievement they
hoped for came to a focus in religious effort.

Similarly, while a good many of these zealots were extremely conservative in their political and social attitudes, their conservatism seems to
have been less important than their religious zeal in stimulating their
mission to the republic. The key point about millenarian orthodoxy was
not that it was sometimes constrained by reactionary prejudices, but that
it embraced a heartfelt religious effort to further the cause of freedom by
enabling the men of that time to live up to it. Solomon Southwick exemplified the range of religious faith when he explained without any apparent sense of contradiction that the demise of tyranny and monopoly
throughout the world would bring a time when "pure DEMOCRACY and
pure CHRISTIANITY, twin-sisters born of Heaven, will yet bear universal
and permanent sway: Not, however, by the agency of mercenary speculators, calculating 'small-ware politicians,' caucus managers, and their
trained bands of hireling and corrupt writers, whether Newspaper Editors, or unprincipled Infidel Novelists and Political Pamphleteers: But by
the divine agency of a sound Christian Education, and of such statesmen
as are described by the graphic pen of the immortal WILLIAM JONES." [13]

Nor did one have to anticipate the millennium to demand moral reform in a society that hoped to be truly free. In 1842 Nathaniel T. Bent,
an Episcopalian minister of Taunton (Massachusetts) was one of dozens
of clergymen who devoted his Fourth of July oration to describing the
ways in which intemperance and alcoholic beverages threatened the
safety of the republic. Other clergymen, expressing doubt that temperance reform would be enough to save it, pressed a comprehensive Christian education as its only true support.[c] In *Our Country's Evils and Their
Remedy* (1843), Benjamin P. Aydelott urged that only a Bible commonwealth could combat mercantile dishonesty and populist egalitarianism,
lax enforcement of the law, and slavery; philanthropic societies were in-

adequate to the task, which required *"a larger measure of* BIBLE CHRIS-
TIANITY. . . . Despotism may stand without it. A limited monarchy may
get along tolerably well with the paralyzed and effete christianity of an
established church. But a BIBLE CHRISTIANITY IS THE ONLY PALLADIUM OF
A FREE GOVERNMENT." [14]

Even clergymen who clearly demurred at imposing moral principles
by means of legislation testified to the force of contemporary belief. One
of them was Mark Hopkins, the president of Williams College, who took
the occasion of the Massachusetts election sermon of 1839 to admonish
state officials that all moral reform must be accomplished by voluntary
means because government is intended to reflect rather than dominate
society. His commitment to individual freedom notwithstanding, Hopkins was a prominent advocate of the Christian Sabbath, which he described in 1847 as an indispensable support for free institutions. Meanwhile Edwin H. Chapin, a Universalist clergyman born in Washington
County (New York), had told the Massachusetts authorities in 1844 that
"all human power is dangerous, and should be as limited as is consistent
with the well-being of each and of all. Yet, without interfering with a
single private right, without assuming any censorship over private opinions, or unlawfully restraining private conduct, a moral influence may
breathe out from every institution and be embodied in every law, that
shall infuse life and purity and power into individual souls." Libertarians
as well as latter-day theocrats looked to religious virtue to serve public
ends. [15]

Despite great differences in theology, politics, and even temperament,
in short, a number of prominent clergymen insisted both that religion
must have primacy in the American society and that it was an indispensable element of secular welfare. Although many of their compatriots took
issue with this echo of Puritan theocracy, others clearly accepted it without question. The extent of the nation's agreement was apparent in the
ways in which clergymen of significantly different persuasions hailed the
influence of religion as a prop to opinion that automatically dispensed
with the props of force. Benjamin P. Aydelott expressed their belief in a
distinctly conservative context when he wrote in 1843 that "either we
must be kept in order by the iron hand of despotism, or at least restrained by such a police power as will greatly impair our liberty, or, we
must have a larger infusion of Bible Christianity." But the same proposi-

tion might serve equally well as the expression of a moderate or even a liberal spokesman for religion as the guarantee of American liberty. In Alexandria (Virginia), Father William Sparrow told the parishioners of Christ Church in 1852 that, thanks to the nation's pure Christian faith, its use of force had been reduced to a minimum. "Society has not needed to be governed much, because individuals have largely governed themselves." Similarly, the *New York Recorder* proclaimed, and the *Home Missionary* repeated in 1846, that "thus far the advancement of popular liberty in the Anglo-Saxon race, has been regulated by the more than equal progress of the Gospel, and hence its triumphs have been more those of opinions, than of swords. . . . Our churches and our schools are the true conservators of American liberty, and the best friends of progress. The triumph of Christianity is the triumph of popular liberty, and the school teacher, the tract distributor and the home missionary will do more for liberty than troops of vaunting politicians." Liberty had fostered religion and religion would take care of liberty.[16]

So insistent was the connection Americans drew between religion and social welfare that even Horace Bushnell avowed it, although he often took issue with doctrines that seemed to subordinate religion to secular ends. In 1840, for example, he rebuked his contemporaries for paying too much attention to political controversies, and he went so far as to suggest that the fall of the republic might be a blessing in disguise. In 1860, moreover, he rebuked both the abolitionists and the defenders of slavery for the "low conceptions of Scripture and its authority" they had displayed in their pamphlet warfare over the Biblical justification of slavery. Yet he also argued that "it is to be, in fact, the glory of Christianity, that it prepares a growth in ethics and evens up the world to those higher conceptions of duty and beneficent practice, which are necessary to the well-being of society." Paying homage to the fathers of New England in 1849, moreover, Bushnell put two centuries of religious change into perspective by saying that "as Church and State must be parted in the crumbling and disintegrating processes of freedom; so, in freedom attained, they will coalesce again, not as Church and State, but in such kind of unity as well nigh removes the distinction." Visionary, transcendental, and theocentric as his judgments may have been, they also demanded a truer form of Christianity for the sake of society as well as salvation.[17]

Thus, too, had Lyman Beecher argued, and in this sense at least the two men held remarkably similar views as spokesmen for an establishment that must work by other means. But the day of establishments had passed, and the similarity between their positions testified less to the survival of the earlier tradition than to the success with which religion had been transformed into a free institution. Edward Beecher, the second son of Lyman, indicated the change that had taken place when, in 1865, he described the Congregational polity as a sure means to the millennium because it rested entirely on the "universal indwelling of God," unimpeded by the hierarchy or the authority of an external source of belief: "A Congregational church is a school for all those traits of character which fit a people for self-government. Relying not on authority and forms, and sacraments, but on truth, and holiness, and the fear of God, it demands and encourages popular education, and the highest standard of practical morality. It trains men to reason and think, and to bear responsibility. Thus it creates the elements of free, intelligent, God-fearing, self-governed people." [18]

By the same token, in 1863 Mark Hopkins revised his earlier discourse on *The Sabbath and Free Institutions* to make it less doctrinal and less obviously theological but no less insistent on the importance that religious observances held for the welfare of the American republic. Significantly, he even essayed a definition of free institutions. They are, he said, society both organized and made free by the voluntary choice of social ends; and they are an alternative to government, which is necessary only because men are not always able or willing to do what is required of them. The travails of Lyman Beecher had led to a religious enterprise that put all thought of an establishment aside, the better to secure the American republic. [19]

THE RELIGIOUS VALUES OF DEMOCRACY

Separating church from state, abandoning even a residual theory of ecclesiastical authority, orthodox Protestant clergymen moved ever closer to a universal theory of freedom. At the same time, their efforts to redeem the republic from sin met with unmistakable hostility from Democratic sources. American party loyalties have never coincided exactly with religious commitments, but for a variety of reasons Democratic spokesmen were far more likely than Whigs to take issue with freedom understood in the clergymen's terms. Hence we may usefully describe a Democratic view of religion. No matter how devout they may have been in their private lives, many Democrats looked for other ways to serve freedom than by tying it to Protestant morality.[d]

Their hostility to religious requirements was rooted in two very different reactions to the colonial establishment. For one thing, it reflected the long history of strife between the churches that the founders had introduced and the sects that had grown up in opposition to them. In New England the establishment had been Puritan; in the South it had been Anglican; and nothing could have been more natural than to find Baptists and Methodists, not to mention Scots-Irish Presbyterians and German pietists, uniting against both. Impelled by their dissidence, most of these outsiders gravitated into the Republican party, which stood even in its earliest days for the rights of the people against the rights of religious "aristocracy." [20] Obviously Republicans of this persuasion were devoted to their religion, so deeply devoted that they could not tolerate existing connections between church and state.

At the same time, many of the leaders of the party were either Deists or skeptics, to whom struggles for religious supremacy and measures of religious oppression were deeply distasteful. Hence they formed a marriage of convenience with the dissidents that was really a marriage of principle: both adopted the "voluntary principle" to avoid the evils of a state church.[21]

The arrangement they reached carried over into the nineteenth century. Although the line of descent from the Republicans of the 1790s to the Democrats of the 1840s was by no means direct, the Republican tradition seems to have borne very heavily on the ways in which Democrats conceived of religion in its relationship to government. In particular it accommodated two otherwise contradictory perspectives. Whereas Democrats might well split over banking and currency reform or express conflicting views of constitutional liberty, they had no real reason to divide over applying the voluntary principle to religion. It answered to skepticism and it answered to religious zeal without pitting either against the other.[e]

As a result, most Democrats were already predisposed to demand "freedom" when the advocates of Protestant orthodoxy renewed their efforts to subordinate democracy to religion. They had not forgotten the clergy who branded Jefferson an infidel, and the evangelism of the 1830s revived their fears because it was seemingly calculated to assert the primacy of clerical values over the preoccupations of the people. The *Democratic Review* epitomized its party's hostility in the second of its purported "Extracts from the Private Diary of a Certain Bank Director," where it made out the banker's son, who had already demonstrated his skills at note-shaving, log-rolling, and similar "aristocratic" practices, as simultaneously an advocate of moral reform and a hypocrite in his professions. In the eyes of many liberal Democrats, moral reform was a partisan conservative device for curbing the people's will.[22]

The effect of all these factors together was to turn Democratic theorists toward predominantly secular explanations of the strength of American institutions, in lieu of the quasi-religious explanations many clergymen insisted upon. Chief among them was the proposition that freedom was its own best safeguard, which they apparently extrapolated from their religious beliefs.

This proposition appeared in several versions. One held simply that history had already provided the Americans with the institutions all men aspired to. James K. Polk developed this idea most clearly in his annual message for 1848, in which he congratulated the American people on their exemption from the revolutionary turmoil through which Europe was passing.

> In reviewing the great events of the past year and contrasting the agitated and disturbed state of other countries with our own tranquil and happy condition, we may congratulate ourselves that we are the most favored people on the face of the earth. While the people of other countries are struggling to establish free institutions, under which man may govern himself, we are in the actual enjoyment of them—a rich inheritance from our fathers. . . .
>
> To our wise and free institutions it is to be attributed that while other nations have achieved glory at the price of the suffering, distress, and impoverishment of their people, we have won our honorable position in the midst of an uninterrupted prosperity and of an increasing individual comfort and happiness.

On this happy view, Americans needed only to be true to their existing political institutions to maintain the full range of their freedom.[23]

Writing on other occasions, Democrats argued that the openness of democratic politics provided the most powerful support for the democracy. In 1838 the *Democratic Review* rebuked Whig complaints of contemporary "radicalism" by declaring that it was "fortunate for our republican system, and for the interests of freedom, that some ardent spirits exist who carry their ideas to the verge of extravagance." As a result of their freedom, it held, they are able to "invigorate and preserve the sacred flame which otherwise might become dim, or even extinct. Their enthusiasm animates those whose devotion might become sluggish from their absorption in sordid pursuits and material occupations. Their too ardent zeal serves as a check to restrain and counterbalance the opposite tendency to anti-liberal opinions which, under every form of government, exists in the very nature of many men. These opposing impulses, like the centripetal and centrifugal forces, keep the body politic in its true and invariable orbit." Similarly, George Camp looked to the freedom Americans enjoyed to overcome any evils that immigration might bring. "Give men their rights, make education accessible and property attainable," he wrote in *Democracy*, "and you make a different people of them. They become orderly and friendly to government, because they are a part of the sovereignty; they respect the right of property, because they are proprietors themselves; and, to be qualified for the exercise of the prerogatives which property and self-sovereignty confer, they zealously apply themselves to the lights of education, and make every exertion to secure its benefits to their families. They become respectable men, because they are free citizens." [24]

Democratic enthusiasm for freedom as its own best security fed into still another Democratic contention, that the processes of democratic politics educate men to their responsibilities as citizens. Camp made the connection explicit when he wrote, "The liberty that republics accord to all men of every rank of governing themselves, elevates their characters, and qualifies them for self-government. . . . Deprive a man of influence, let him become of no account, and consequently pass unobserved in society, and he loses one of the highest inducements to acquire character, or to preserve his integrity; but add to his weight and respectability, let him feel that he and his children are integral parts of the nation in the midst of which they live, parties to its laws, and equal partakers of its rights and privileges, and you increase, as much as human means can, the force of his moral motives and the energy of his active powers." So, too, in *Considerations upon the Nature and Tendency of Free Institutions* (1848), Frederick Grimke defended the election of postmasters by the people of each neighborhood on the grounds that "there is no possible way of making free institutions succeed but by training the popular mind to the habits of self-government, to make it feel and realize the consequences which ensue from any mistake in the management of public business." Both men predicated the success of free institutions upon establishing the full measure of democracy, whereas political and religious conservatives typically insisted that men must be qualified to rule before democracy could be safe.[25]

Praising the virtues that democracy elicited, Camp and Grimke also laid great stress on the material support it provided for American institutions. On the one hand, they described a claim to popular loyalty; on the other, a guarantee of popular liberty. This was a familiar Democratic argument, one that Representative Silas Wood had voiced during debate on the electoral college in 1826. Before free governments can succeed in Europe, the conservative New Yorker told the House of Representatives, "society must be reorganized; rank must be abolished, or some means adopted to countervail its influence; the restraints against the alienation of real property must be removed, and the People admitted to an equality of political rights, and instructed in the elements of freedom, to render them capable of self-government." Self-government seemingly waited upon abundance; but Wood also held that civil liberty depended equally upon "the organization of society, the moral character of the People, and a free Constitution." Perhaps the fact that he was a conservative Democrat led him to require virtue as well as prosperity.[26]

In 1838, however, the *Democratic Review* suggested that democracy need have nothing to do with virtue. Significantly, it developed this point of view in criticizing Alexis de Tocqueville, who had argued that the American democracy rested upon religion. Conceding that religion and morality were assets to the republic, the *Review* argued that its political institutions were far more important because of the material advantages they produced:

From the first establishment of the colonies up to the present day, there has always existed a general equality of condition and property, broken, no doubt, by exceptions in practice and theory of a greater or lesser extent, but still sufficiently real to furnish a proper basis for a government founded on the principle of political equality among the citizens. This adaptation of the form of the government to the substantial condition of the people is the real cause of the existence and maintenance of democratic institutions; and the circumstances which tend to keep up the equality of condition among the people,—such as the abundance and cheapness of land and the laws for the equal division of intestate estates among all the children,—are the most important of the subsidiary causes that concur in producing this result.

Lest this challenge to clerical convictions not be pointed enough, the *Review* added that religion might be useful chiefly to compensate the victims of a bad government by offering them motives for good conduct when their worldly prosperity did not. In effect it repudiated orthodox morality in the name of equal rights.[27]

The burden of many Democratic polemics thus was an appeal to secular values. Sometimes the appeal was explicit, sometimes only implicit, but in either of its versions it excluded the teachings of theology from the conduct of public affairs. Yet Democrats did not repudiate religion. It was religion understood as a deliberately contrived social institution that they feared, whether in the form of a church that was an adjunct of politics or a church that made politics its arena. The *Review* underlined this distinction between an institutional church and undefiled religion in rebuking Whig claims to the effect that religion, wealth, and learning were all enlisted in the Whig cause. At one time, it declared in 1838, American politics had indeed tended to divide on these lines: "The clergy, as a class, had, in all countries, at the time our experiment of government commenced, showed themselves not exempt from the desire of power; indeed, it may be said, that a love of temporal authority as an adjunct of ecclesiastical prerogative, was their besetting sin, if not their ruling passion." That is, it blamed any antagonism between democracy and religion on the ambitions of an established clergy, and it went on to stress that it was the clergy rather than the people who had been false to religion:

Men were so accustomed to consider the Church as an establishment constituting a part of the State, and they had so little confidence in men's moral qualities, they did not conceive it possible to sustain religion without the patronage, protection, and coercion of the civil power in a government. It is no wonder that the clergy, who were then considered the representatives of the religious feelings of the country, with such passions and prejudices, attached themselves politically to those who were of congenial sentiments with them, who had the same deep distrust of man's moral fitness, in a free and unshackled state of mental existence, to establish and maintain that order which constitutes good civil government. The case is far different at this day. The success of the voluntary system for the support of religion and religious institutions, is complete. The political connexion of religion with government, by those who wish to see it flourish "pure and undefiled," is no longer desired,—nay more, they would consider it pollution.

In effect, the *Democratic Review* claimed religious faith for the voluntary principle, and corruption for any establishment.[28]

To put matters another way, in pointing to men's moral qualities under conditions of freedom the *Review* suggested that as soon as religion was treated as an end in itself it was bound to serve the purposes of liberty. To this extent it accepted the importance of religious principle while denying it institutional standing; it implied that the purer religion was, the more effective it could be in serving social as well as private ends. Hence, while religion could not be in the traditional sense an institution, it was one of the glories of free institutions, their safeguard as well as their object. More briefly, the *Review*'s remarks suggested that if freedom was the surest guarantee of freedom, free religion was both its highest achievement and its most significant asset.[f]

Certainly liberal Democrats expressed a degree of loyalty to Christianity that seems surprising in view of the extent to which they also equated democracy with freedom from religious institutions. In 1838, for example, the same magazine observed that "the American Government is founded on no paper constitution, although it was manifested and declared thereby. It is a tree which grew up, in all its fair proportions, amidst a storm which would have torn up any superficial growth. It existed in the souls of men, in the habits of the people, long before it showed itself in the high places of power. It was the ultimate fruit of the Christian seed, when it was at length planted in the wild soil of nature." So, too, John L. O'Sullivan asked in 1838, "What, indeed, is Democracy but Christianity in its earthly aspect—Christianity made effective among the political relations of men. Christianity, in which it accords with every design of Providence, begins with individual man, addressing its lofty persuasions to him, and makes his full development its chief solicitude and care. The obstacles reared by artificial life its throws aside; the rubbish heaped by centuries of abuse upon the human spirit it removes, the better to unfold man's inward beauty, and bring forth man's inward might." [29]

These writers not only identified democracy with Christianity but treated moral character as one of the advantages that democracy bestowed on mankind. George Camp pointed out that freedom had brought a general well-being to the United States, encouraging the development of Christianity and education as well as material prosperity and careers open to talent: "Let those who think the picture exaggerated and overcharged look at the condition of the great *mass* in other countries. . . . What proportion of them are beggared? What proportion of them know of the protecting arm of government except in the experience of the punishments it inflicts? of the mild, consolatory, and reforming influences of Christianity, except in the exaction of tithes and penances? of the importance of education, except in the frowning aspect of their colleges?" Similarly, O'Sullivan observed that "if we apprehend it, civilization consists in the establishment of elevated social relations, upheld by lofty and refined personal character; or, in other words, the development among men of the best powers of the mind and heart. . . . It supposes a condition of prosperous trade, intellectual elevation, and moral development; but literature, science, politics, and morals, must have reached a considerable progress, and physical comfort, commercial ease, and mental attainments, be generally possessed by the people." Democracy meant universal intelligence as well as equal rights, universal morality as well as religious freedom.[30]

It also meant that government itself could be free because its citizens were moral. The proposition led some Democrats of a clearly conservative orientation to treat existing religious institutions as a bulwark of the republic. One such spokesman was Joel R. Poinsett, who took the occasion of an address on nullification to complain of the ill treatment he had received in Mexico at the hands of a "bigotted priesthood." "For the character of the regular clergy throughout Spanish America," he observed in a footnote to his discourse, "see *Noticeas Secretas*, by Jorge and Ulloa. They differ widely in character and conduct from the clergy of this country, to whose enlightened zeal and virtuous example we are indebted for the moral and religious character which distinguishes the people of the United States, and on which the safety and permanency of republican institutions must rest." Eighteen years later a self-professed "Hunker" told the constitutional convention of Michigan that it must not forbid the state's legislature to appoint paid chaplains lest it seem thereby to condone infidelity. "Take away moral restraint, sir," J. Van Valkenburgh declared "—remove those safeguards which have been kindly thrown around society by the great law-giver, and the language of the poet is true—'Man's greatest enemy is man.' Remove these kindly influences, and the hand of every man is against his brother, and this world becomes a scene of anarchy and of blood; an Acaldema; a field of blood, over which angels would weep, could tears be shed in heaven." [31]

Yet liberal as well as conservative Democrats clearly testified to this central belief. They might not lend their sanction to publicly supported chaplains, but they obviously counted upon popular morality to sustain popular freedom. Significantly, George Camp developed two different versions of the classic argument that "all governments are either governments of force or governments of opinion; governments of usurpation, or governments of consent." The first was this simple secular statement, which made no reference to morality. The second was equally libertarian, but tied at the same time to an essentially religious definition of freedom: "There are but two ways in which government can be upheld: either on the voluntary principle, appropriate to all the complicated agencies of rational and moral beings, or by coercion, exercised through the passions, and subjecting men, like brutes, to force. The least abridgement of one of these methods induces the necessary application of the other." [32]

James C. Zabriskie appealed to much the same principle in the constitutional convention of New Jersey when he took issue with conservatives who wished to restrict the people's power to amend their own constitution: "All the gentlemen who had spoken placed the security of our rights and interests upon the wrong basis.—They do not rest upon written constitutions, but upon the virtue and intelligence of the people. Of what avail to the people of South America were their written constitutions? Did they enjoy the rights which were written on their parchments?" According to the newspaper account, "He further argued that the 'plains of Marathon were not trodden by the feet of slaves,' for the want of written constitutions, and that the ancient republics were destroyed because the people were corrupt—and became, first, the slaves of vice, and then of despots." [33] In liberal Democratic eyes the great advantage of free government was that it encouraged men to adopt virtue voluntarily. Democrats substituted the voluntary principle for coercion, the better to maintain freedom.[g]

THE LIBERAL VALUES OF RELIGION

Democrats often put freedom before morality, whereas Protestant clergymen typically put morality before freedom, but they had in common a commitment to religion as a basis of social order. By contrast, a small handful of liberal philosophers pressed contemporary concerns for religious freedom to the point of rebuking Protestant orthodoxy. They were far from being representative, but their urge to transcend the ordinary canons of morality points up the extent to which most Americans still proclaimed loyalty to some form of religious institution.

One of these commentators was William Ellery Channing, the Unitarian elder statesman who was active both in promoting a wide variety of humanitarian reforms and in inculcating the fullest possible measure of individual self-reliance. In 1830 he declared in the Massachusetts election sermon that spiritual freedom is the highest interest of mankind and he emphasized that free institutions are indispensable to give men scope and teach them self-government. Yet the freedom Channing described did not exclude religious obligation nor deny the legitimacy of political authority. Rather, he insisted that religion is necessary to advance spiritual liberty ("We possess improved fabrics, but deteriorated men," he complained) and he also held that government is an ordinance of God. Profoundly conservative in this respect, he held that government had not been created as a matter of convenience but as an agency of spiritual fulfillment, in that it exercised its authority over objects like property that elicited spiritual attitudes. Hence while he criticized all forms of established religion, he did so only to insist that its traditional objectives must be reached by wholly liberal means, and he rebuked his contemporaries for idolatrizing the mechanics of free institutions when they should be seeking their spirit.[34]

Channing applied the same general principles to all of the institutions that might be thought to serve virtue. In particular, he criticized voluntary associations of both a conservative and a radical sort for infringing on the liberty of individuals who joined them. "Let no error be suppressed," he wrote in 1829, "by an instrument, which will be equally powerful against truth, and which must subvert that freedom of thought on which all truth depends." Rather, he held that associations of any kind should be conceived as purely educational institutions intended to elicit innate powers and cultivate innate virtues. As a result he brought all of his social criticism to a focus in the demand that those who heard him speak should develop their own moral resources. This was what true religion taught, and it was also the best hope of American society. "Awake! Resolve earnestly on Self-culture," he exhorted the working-men of Boston in 1838. "Make yourselves worthy of your free institutions, and strengthen and perpetuate them by your intelligence and your virtues." Neither church nor state nor private association, but the self made moral through freedom, would fulfill American liberty.[35]

Theodore Parker went much further than Channing toward demanding social reform, but he was almost equally devoted to a definition of liberty that militated against institutional changes. There is sin in a society that permits some men to work sixteen hours a day in order that others may live in idle luxury, he wrote in the *Dial* in 1841, and five years later he charged the mercantile classes that "I think there is no nation in Europe, except Russia and Turkey, which cares so little for the class which reaps down its harvests and does the hard work." Hence he invoked the ideal of a "church militant" that would teach mankind to weed out "licentiousness, intemperance, want, and ignorance and sin" and "turn all the nation's creative energies to production—their legitimate work." More than this, he demanded significant social reform on the grounds that the existing economic order destroyed the manhood of its victims. "In a society where the natural laws of the body are constantly violated, where many men are obliged by circumstances to violate them," he declared in another sermon, "it follows unavoidably that many are born little by nature, and they transmit their feebleness to their issue." It followed that Christianity must be made effective in the solution of social problems.[36]

Nevertheless even Parker typically presupposed that the problems he described would be amenable to moral effort. Significantly, the reforms he espoused in his sermon to the mercantile classes came down to help and encouragement for those who were victimized by society. Similarly, his sermon on "The Perishing Classes" proposed to remedy the evils of Boston's ghetto by providing (in addition to temperance reform) separate schools for Roman Catholics, farm schools for juvenile offenders, jobs for released convicts, an improved standard of living in the city's poorhouses, and the hope of better pay—when it was financially possible. At bottom, Parker intended chiefly to remedy the evils of society in order to make it more effective as a vehicle of personal growth; the ultimate object of reform was not so much justice as it was opportunity for self-culture. "We all know there are certain things which society owes to each man in it," he told the American Institute of Instruction in 1841. "Among them are a defense from violence; justice in matters between man and man; a supply of comforts for the body, when the man is unable to acquire them for himself; remuneration for what society takes away. Our policy, equally wise and humane, attempts to provide them for the humblest child that is born amongst us; and in almost every case these four things are actually provided. But there is one more excellent gift which society owes to each; that is, a chance to obtain the best education the man's nature will allow and the community afford." Given such a start, he implied, it was up to the working classes to cultivate their moral and religious natures as time and opportunity presented themselves.[37] Parker was both a conservative who had become a radical for impeccable conservative reasons, and a radical who remained a liberal out of his concern for religious growth.[h]

For his part, Ralph Waldo Emerson never troubled himself about social problems because he was so dedicated to individual liberty. His criticisms of his contemporaries came down to charges that they had not freed themselves from the tyranny of mind and the tyranny of the past, the tyranny of books and the tyranny of conformity. As a result he denied the relevance of institutions in his enthusiasm for Self-Reliance, and he obliterated the traditional claims of religion because of his pursuit of transcendental perceptions. To this extent he fell in with democratic liberalism, but the individualism he prescribed bore only a superficial resemblance to the atomism democrats honored. (Significantly, it was Channing rather than Emerson who attracted praise from Democratic partisans.) Emerson repudiated all mediocrity because he challenged men to become giants; he repudiated all institutions because they diminished individual achievement. Hence the liberty he proclaimed was a liberty against society, which few contemporaries hailed, and he defined the common sentiment by the zeal with which he condemned it.[38]

❧ XI ❧

THE USES OF
EDUCATION

During the Middle Period, American Protestantism was an effective national creed, a widely shared commitment that had regained its public
authority as it put aside ecclesiastical controversy. Nevertheless the freedom on which it rested, not to mention the denominational differences
within it, militated against its utility as a vehicle of social control. Although it held up a standard of virtue to its adherents, it had relatively
little power over men who had not been converted. The attempt to
legislate Prohibition testified to its weakness in this respect: it was an effort to secure morality in spite of the wishes of the immoral, and it
generated extensive opposition because it intruded on popular liberty.
In addition, whereas Protestants might well unite to belabor Roman
Catholics or to intimidate religious skeptics, when they took issue with
each other they had neither authority to guide them nor motive to control their speculations. The proliferation of religious utopias demonstrated the problems Americans faced. Widespread though they were,
they were also sectarian rather than inclusive, and they lacked the necessary means to make their teachings universal. When Americans agreed
on theological matters, they could visualize their common beliefs as a
prop to their social order. When they could not agree on these fun-
damentals, they were forced to treat their faith as a merely private belief.[1]

Partly for these reasons, partly for reasons having little to do with
religion, Americans sought to reinforce their liberties by improving popular education. Acting with clearly defined social ends in mind, they
worked to enlarge educational opportunities, to revise pedagogical techniques, and to systematize public instruction. In doing so they clearly
thought of education as an instrument of social control; but they also
came to perceive it as a vehicle of liberation. It constituted, in short, a
second free institution, more efficient than the Protestant churches but
still substantially free, for it escaped many of the hazards that religious
efforts ran.

THE CONSERVATIVE IMPULSE TO EDUCATE

The first major effort to ground democracy in education was conservative in origin and conservative in conception. Spurred largely by their fear of social change, men who deplored Jacksonian democracy and looked askance at contemporary materialism set out to "revive" American schools. As a result they also tended to rewrite American history. They exaggerated the educational achievements of the New England colonies and deprecated those of other regions; they also exaggerated contemporary ignorance and reduced the meaning of popular education to the activities of public schools. Unfortunate though this development may have been for the historiography of American education, it betokened the social purposes most educational reformers shared. They turned to the common school because it seemed that only universal education administered by public authority and supported by public funds could serve the needs of public order.[2]

They began with a republican truism: the safety of free government depends upon the education of the people. Calvin Stowe appealed to this proposition in 1837 when he reported to the legislature of Ohio on educational practices in Europe: "Republicanism can be maintained only by universal intelligence and virtue among the people, and disinterestedness and fidelity in the rulers." George Holley invoked the same principle two years later at Peru (Illinois) when he rebuked democratic complacency over the strength of free government. "It does not necessarily follow that, because a nation is free and prosperous, it will therefore be enlightened and virtuous. But it does necessarily follow that, if a nation is enlightened and virtuous, it will, sooner or later, be free and prosperous." So, too, De Witt C. Walker told the constitutional convention of Michigan in 1850 that "if we refuse to adopt the principle that all the children shall be educated, we undermine the basis upon which our government is instituted. Can a Republican government be sustained without intelligence? It may be attempted, but the pyramid is resting upon its apex, and the first political convulsion will overwhelm it into ruin." In the West quite as much as in the East, conservatives looked to education to make sure that liberty was safe.[3]

If they adopted a republican truism, however, they often burdened it with unprecedented anxieties. In 1837 William H. Seward told an audience at Westfield Academy (near Chautauqua, New York), "It is a fearful truth, that we are rapidly approximating towards the maximum of population and maturity of national character, wealth and power, and yet have made no corresponding advance in moral and intellectual cultivation." Five years later, commenting on a plan to devote the proceeds of the public lands to the improvement of popular education, the *New-York Review* remarked,

> We are stern republicans, disowning all authority, and recognising no laws but those which the will of the people enact [*sic*]. The people are sovereigns. Now a little plain truth ought to do us good; it should provoke resentment from no one. On examination, it will be found that, as a nation, we are very ignorant and very depraved, and the misfortune is, that this mass of ignorance and depravity enters into the law-making power, and controls the execution of the laws. . . . Any one can see that we require a system of education so broad and so deep, as to reach through, and bind together, all the elements of society into one solid, consistent mass, with intelligence to know, and rectitude to do, every duty which rests upon a citizen, and to execute every trust with which he may be honored.

Similarly, Horace Mann held as late as 1848 that "nothing would be easier than to follow in the train of so many writers, and to demonstrate by logic, by history, and by the nature of the case, that a republican form of government, without intelligence in the people, must be, on a vast scale, what a mad-house, without superintendent or keepers, would be on a small one,—the despotism of a few succeeded by universal anarchy, and anarchy by despotism, with no change but from bad to worse." [4]

The more directly they confronted the changing patterns of their society, the more strenuous their appeal to education was likely to be. In 1835, for example, Calvin Stowe admonished the Western Literary Institute and College of Professional Teachers that "unless we educate our immigrants, they will be our ruin. It is no longer a mere question of benevolence, of duty, or of enlightened self-interest, but the intellectual and religious training of our foreign population has become essential to our own safety; we are prompted to it by the instinct of self-preservation." Horace Mann developed an equally apprehensive portrait of contemporary dangers at Boston in 1838: "Our institutions furnish as great facilities for wicked men, in all departments of wickedness, as phosphorus and lucifer matches furnish to the incendiary. . . . Through the right,—almost universal,—of suffrage, we have established a community of power; and no proposition is more plain and self-evident, than that

nothing but mere popular inclination lies between a community of power
and a community in every thing else." So, too, Judah P. Benjamin told
the Louisiana constitutional convention of 1845 that "he considered the
only safety for this State and for the United States, was the establishment of public schools, to diffuse the blessings of universal education
among the people. We were fast diverging into the extremes of democracy. Unless means were taken to enlighten the masses, in order that
they may be enabled to exercise political rights, with the extreme opinions which now prevail, it requires no great foresight to predict that we
shall soon reach a state of complete anarchy." [5]

The fears that conservatives expressed pointed to the kind of education
they would demand. During the early years of the century, before their
sense of urgency mounted, men who were fearful of social change had
looked to the activity of college graduates to counteract untoward developments. This was especially the case in New England, where Phi Beta
Kappa orators and other college spokesmen celebrated both the claims
educated men had on their country and the responsibility they had acquired to lead it. Sometimes these celebrants expressed liberal sentiments and sometimes they were optimistic; more often than not they
criticized modern innovations. In any event they appealed to educated
men to act as the conscience of the republic and described a political elite
whose influence would depend less on their scrabbling for votes than on
their power to sway the multitude. Chancellor Kent voiced their political
theory in uncharacteristically hopeful terms when he told the Phi Beta
Kappa Society of Yale College in 1831, "Artificial distinctions and exclusive privileges are gradually losing their hold on society, by the operation
of the knowledge and spirit of the times. The masses of free and enlightened human beings are constantly enlarging, and they all lie under the
dominion of moral force, and are capable of being swayed by argument
and eloquence flowing from intellects of superior cultivation." They took
elementary education for granted and rested the hopes of the republic on
the authority that college training commanded. [6]

By contrast, the leaders of the educational awakening recognized the
futility of such achievements. The authority claimed by scholars in politics depended upon a deferential attitude among the voters, who proved
increasingly intolerant of hierarchy in education as well as leadership in
politics, and this authority all but disappeared in the upsurge of Jack-

sonian democracy. Significantly, many of the most energetic advocates of educational innovation came from states in which literacy was widespread and schools were most abundant, as if to dramatize the proposition that circumstances an earlier generation had not foreseen demanded an education it had not been able to accomplish. Meanwhile the deepening of contemporary problems such as the influx of non-English immigrants and the growth of an urban proletariat presented ever greater obstacles to the ends conservatives sought. The common-school awakening was born as they acknowledged their political difficulties.[a]

The columns of the *North American Review* document the evolution of conservative attitudes in New England. In 1817 Edward T. Channing appealed to the leaders of the republic to raise the level of political discussion, while in 1821 Jared Sparks advocated using funds from the public lands to help enlighten public opinion. In 1823 and 1824 J. L. Kingsley and George Ticknor, respectively, praised contemporary interest in improving the common schools, but they also took issue with aggressive democrats who denounced public assistance to academies and colleges. By 1826, however, Orville Dewey had published the first of a series of articles in which the *Review* was to clamor for improvements in elementary education as the very basis of public liberty. It never wholly abandoned its interest in higher education, but it increasingly focused its attention on reforms that would make popular instruction effective.[7]

The path by which conservatives became educational reformers was even more apparent in the activities of the Western Literary Institute and College of Professional Teachers. Founded in Cincinnati in 1831 to promote western culture and encourage western education, the Institute devoted its annual meetings to deploring modern evils and urging educational innovations. In 1836 Albert M. Picket opened its proceedings by lamenting the "degeneracy" of youthful morals and rebuking youthful resistance to authority, while Alexander Campbell brought them to a close by appealing to its members to promote the education of immigrants. Simultaneously, members who were no less conservative in their social attitudes pressed for improvements in western pedagogy. Picket, their president, demonstrated the potential limits to their enthusiasm when he decried "all short methods, all easy methods," but Calvin Stowe read them an abbreviated version of his report on educational innovations in Prussia and Wurttemberg, while Samuel Lewis proselytized for a new system of public schools adapted to the needs of the community. Despite obvious hesitations, these dedicated conservative reformers moved with ever greater zeal toward generating public schools that could cope with modern problems.[8]

The hesitations some of these westerners expressed about the value of nonsectarian instruction added point to their developing convictions. Sensitive to theological differences, the Reverend Joshua Wilson argued in 1836 that there could be no substitute for parental instruction, while other speakers insisted that any education the schools provided should be identifiably religious rather than perfunctorily Christian. To this extent they declared their allegiance to orthodox religious principles, and in 1839 they were to hear Benjamin P. Aydelott deliver an "Address on the Duties of American Citizens" in which he described both a political duty to maintain constitutional liberty and a religious duty to promote Bible Christianity. More characteristically, they skirted divisive issues in religion to proclaim the authority of Christian ethics. In 1835, summarizing unpublished proceedings, one of their officials developed the proposition that teachers must be made more effective because all men had the vote. "There is no safety but in God and the People: ONE GOD and the WHOLE PEOPLE. And hence arises the necessity for Education: we must know God, the relation in which we stand to him, and to one another: and the acquisition of this knowledge is Education,—true, practical, useful Education, ramifying and distributing itself into all those branches of science and literature, which are commonly comprehended under the name. It is through this means that 'Universal Suffrage' must act as the great cementing law of human society,—the law of mutual love and kindness, not of terror and alarm." [9]

Elsewhere spokesmen for orthodox Protestantism moved with surprising ease from treating education as a function of religion to visualizing it as a function of the state. Although some prominent leaders continued to protest that the common schools were "godless" and to call for parochial institutions, by far the greater number accepted the necessity of non-denominational instruction in a society of many denominations.[b] Presumably they would have done so anyway as they confronted the consequences of their diversity; in addition they were influenced by the proliferation of Roman Catholics, who seemed to threaten Protestant values and to require systematic acculturation.[c] The very fact that Catholics often criticized the common schools can only have reinforced conservatives' devotion to them, as Horace Bushnell demonstrated in 1853. "We can not have Puritan common schools," he declared in Hartford (Connecticut) "—these are gone already—we can not have Protestant common schools, or those which are distinctly so; but we can have common schools, and these we must agree to have and maintain, till the last or latest day of our liberties. These are American, as our liberties themselves are American, and whoever requires of us, whether directly or by implication, to give them up, requires what is more than our bond promises, and what is, in fact, a real affront to our name and birthright as a people." [10]

Confronted with untoward developments, in short, conservatives who occupied a variety of religious positions turned to systematic public instruction as their ancestors might have turned to an established church, to promote popular morality and obliterate threatening evils. They met with inevitable opposition as they enlarged the responsibilities of education, for some men were bound to deplore even an educational establishment while others were bound to condemn it for its indifference to theology. In the long run, however, the common schools were a reassuring alternative to an institution that conservatives had not been able to maintain. They were, indeed, a free institution, in that they promised to bolster the status quo without infringing on religious conscience, to serve traditional social purposes without inviting religious strife. [11]

The terms in which conservative publicists made their case for common schools reinforce this reading of their thought. One of the most striking phenomena of the Middle Period was the legend of the Puritan past—the tendency displayed by the inhabitants of a variety of states to embrace the New England common school as if it had been part of their own history. Far from repudiating New England's colonial example as provincial and outmoded, conservatives throughout the republic tended to invoke it in their cause, as if to suggest that even though Puritanism was clearly dead its purposes might still be served by the institutions it had introduced.[d]

Chancellor Kent introduced a preliminary version of the legend into his Phi Beta Kappa discourse at Yale: "This system of free schools, sustained and enforced by law, has been attended with momentous results, and it has communicated to the people of this state, and to every other part of New England in which the system has prevailed, the blessings of order and security, to an extent never before surpassed in the annals of mankind." Other men developed Kent's formula without sharing his rostrum. In 1836 Frederick A. Packard, a Pennsylvanian who was secretary to the American Sunday School Union, hailed the historic Yankee system of education for its devotion to God and the Bible; in the constitutional convention of New Jersey, Richard S. Field denounced opposition to the common-school "experiment" by engaging in historical legerdemain:

Our common school system an experiment! A novelty! A novelty, sir, in this quarter of the world, of which this system has been for the last hundred years our pride, our glory, and our boast. An experiment, sir! Why sir, the pilgrim fathers landed on the rock of Plymouth in 1620, and in 1647, only 27 years after, the foundations of a common school system were laid in Massachusetts. The school house and the church were built up side by side and their spires pointed together to Heaven; and if there is one thing to which Massachusetts is indebted for her superior intelligence and superior virtue, it is her common school system.—It is this that makes her an object in this country and in Europe of imitation and emulation.

Considering that Field was an Episcopalian who had been born in New Jersey, his words were a remarkable testimony to the perspectives conservatives shared.[12]

Their attitudes toward tax support of common schools also demonstrated the esteem in which conservatives came to hold public education. For well over fifty years the historians of American education, echoing the polemics of the educational reformers, have pointed out that spokesmen for the well-to-do classes fought bitterly against having to pay for the education of the poor while sending their own children to academies and private schools that cost many times as much. But they have also exaggerated this opposition, and have overlooked the fact that the common-school awakening coincided with a deepening of conservative concern to protect the rights of property. It is true that some men conceived of public education as tantamount to "agrarianism"; for others, however, it was the most efficacious safeguard that could be thrown around rights of possession. Even the most adamant defender of property could recognize the logic of this case. "Let any man, dwelling in the United States, consider this fact," an anonymous writer declared in 1839 in the *North Amer-*

ican Review; "that he is living in the midst of some millions of human beings, having strong bodies, strong wills, clear heads, and mighty
passions; let him consider, further, that these millions suffer him to pursue his business, and sleep quietly at night, because they see it to be
their interest, or feel it to be their duty, to do so, but that, as soon as
they cease to see their interest, or feel their duty, they may pull his
house about his ears and hang him upon the nearest tree;—and he will
feel, to his heart's core, the necessity of wide-spread moral and religious
education *to his own safety.*" If property was the first right many conservatives respected, public education might be its most indispensable support.[13]

It followed that the conservative commitment to public schooling was
often essentially illiberal, a means of coming to terms with modern evils
that was intended primarily to curb popular aberrations rather than in-
form popular discussion. Yet it was also intrinsically liberal in that it
substituted right opinion for force as the bulwark of the republic. Daniel
Webster said as much in the constitutional convention of Massachusetts
when he described popular education as a "wise and liberal system of
police" that inhibited crime and served as a political safeguard "as well
against open violence and overthrow, as against the slow but sure undermining of licentiousness." So, too, in 1836 Albert Picket told the Western Literary Institute, "We know, that our free institutions are not to be
secured by armies, and that intelligence must stand in the place of *bayo-
nets* and *bulwarks*. We know the people will uphold their liberties, if their
knowledge is of the right kind." From the aggressively modern point of
view, perhaps, conservatives visualized a restrictive kind of education intended to serve a coercive social order. Taken in the context of their
times, however, they sought to reconcile liberty with order by substituting an institution that was compatible with freedom for the coercions
other countries required.[14]

In addition, many of the educational reformers held out the hope that
truly public schools would rectify social injustices by equalizing economic opportunity and diffusing universal prosperity. Undoubtedly this
hope was in part polemical, an effort to overcome the clamor against "aristocracy" by opening its advantages to all. Certainly it was in keeping
with the conservative idea of success, which stressed opportunity rather
than equality and treated improvements in the standard of living as a suf-

ficient form of compensation for the existence of social distinctions. But the advocates of educational reform also insisted with apparent candor that only through education could the egalitarian values of American society be preserved. In 1846 Horace Eaton, Vermont's first superintendent of schools, wrote in his first annual report,

Experience proves that as society advances in age, there is ever growing up a tendency to wide disparities of rank and condition. And what means can be devised that shall be so effectual in guarding against them as the general diffusion of knowledge? Here is an equalizing power—a levelling engine, which we may rightfully and lawfully employ. Its operation will not undermine, but consolidate and strengthen society. Let every child in the land enjoy the advantages of a competent education at his outset in life—and it will do more to secure a general equality of condition, than any guarantee of "equal rights and privileges" which constitution or laws can give. And if we would preserve this life giving spirit, as well as the form, of our republican institutions, we must rely mainly upon popular education to accomplish our purpose.[15]

Two years later Horace Mann was to argue that Massachusetts as well as England was threatened with industrial feudalism, which only universal education could counteract. "If one class possesses all the wealth and the education, while the residue of society is ignorant and poor," he wrote in his *Twelfth Report*, "it matters not by what name the relation between them may be called: the latter, in fact and in truth, will be the servile dependants and subjects of the former. But, if education be equably diffused, it will draw property after it by the strongest of all attractions; for such a thing never did happen, and never can happen, as that an intelligent and practical body of men should be permanently poor."[16] Such arguments suggested that when conservatives adopted educational reform they also found means to embrace liberal social values. In presenting the widest possible diffusion of knowledge as the great instrument of equal rights, they transformed the traditional conservative conception of a hierarchical social order supported by institutions that were geared to its complexities, into the more generous vision of an open competitive order sustained by the universal practice of education. The effect of their changing vision was to make education the institutional embodiment of American freedom—not simply a check on popular vagaries, nor yet a diversion of popular energies, but an act of public authority that would guarantee liberty to everyone.

THE DEMOCRATIC IDEA OF EDUCATION

Confronted with the efforts of educational reformers to curb popular aberrations, antagonized as well by many of the innovations they wished to introduce into the schools, a majority of American democrats probably looked with some disfavor on the common-school awakening. Their doubts were often reinforced by the historic democratic hostility to both public authority and public expenditure, and they resulted in a fairly consistent party division on the merits of educational reform. Nevertheless the educational revival went forward in Democratic as well as Whig states. This fact suggests that, their initial antipathy notwithstanding, democrats as well as conservatives looked to the public schools to serve their social ends.[17]

One source of democratic antipathy was the conviction that the educational reformers wished to improve upon institutions that were already perfectly adequate. In 1838, discussing Amos Kendall's boyhood in rural Massachusetts, the *Democratic Review* argued that the district school Kendall had attended for two abbreviated sessions every year until he was ten was preferable to the continuous or "hot-house" system common to the cities, which was physically injurious as well as enervating to the mind. Eight years later Stoddard Judd, speaking in the constitutional convention of Wisconsin, took issue with the idea that the state required a superintendent of schools to make its educational system work. As the *Madison Express* reported his remarks, Judd "took the ground (as it appeared to us) that no improvement could be made, or, indeed, was necessary in our common school system; that the plan of superintendence advocated by gentlemen was not adapted to this territory; that it would be a mere frittering away of the school fund to appropriate any of it to the payment of a salary to a state superintendent; and that all that was wanted to have good schools was money to pay teachers and erect schoolhouses." [18]

In addition, Democrats often contended that efforts to systematize public instruction were modeled on European innovations that befitted monarchical governments. This was the substance of Governor Marcus Morton's charge against the Board of Education in Massachusetts in 1840, to which a compliant Committee on Education of its House of Representatives responded with a sustained attack on the Board for attempting "a system of centralization and of monopoly of power in a few hands, contrary, in every respect, to the true spirit of our democratical institutions, and which, unless speedily checked, may lead to unlooked for and dangerous results." So, too, in 1838 a commentator writing in the *Democratic Review* tempered his praise of educational reform in Michigan by observing,

A plan of popular education forming part of the public administration of a State, enjoying the highest possible degree of political and civil freedom, presents some problems of deep importance, and no small difficulty; the chief of which must always be to combine, in due proportion, the principle of central control and the unbending authority of official ministration, with the freedom of popular coöperation, and that diffusive vitality which voluntary effort, moved by reasonable inducements, can alone produce. . . . The centralizing system recently adopted in France, in which the government strives at omnipresence, and to dispense with the coöperation of the people except as a physical instrumentality, we need not say, is wholly unadapted to the spirit of a free community, as well as to the best and highest ends of education.[19]

Nevertheless, these statements demonstrate only that Democrats who criticized the educational revival quarreled with its alleged perversions of the democratic principle, not with universal schooling. Certainly the most vigorously democratic critics of contemporary education commonly attacked it for its inadequacies and its defects rather than its pretensions. The agitation of the early workingmen was especially significant in this respect: far from challenging the legitimacy of educational reform, they typically insisted that it embraced too little and served too few.[e] In Rhode Island, Seth Luther complained both that the school fund was drawn from the pockets of the poor by means of a state lottery and that the factory system prevailing in that state deprived thousands of children of the opportunity to benefit from it. Meanwhile the workingmen of eastern Pennsylvania fulminated against the pauper system of education that had been established there in 1809, arguing that only a truly common education would answer to republican needs, while New Englanders as well as Pennsylvanians pressed for manual labor schools on the grounds that they would make universal education financially practicable and overcome the class bias implicit in a merely literary training. Everywhere workingmen visualized truly democratic schools as an indispensable basis for a truly democratic society.[20]

Even the self-proclaimed radicals who took issue with education as a panacea testified to the importance it had in their thought. Thomas Skidmore has become famous for denying that education could reach the needs of a starving proletariat, and Orestes Brownson equally so for challenging William Ellery Channing's comfortable assertion that self-culture would elevate the proletariat above poverty and deprivation. So, too, the *Voice of Industry*, the organ of the New England Labor Reform League, deprecated the claims New Englanders made for the education of the people. "It offers, professedly, what is called, as if in mockery, an *education* to all," it declared in 1848. "What avails this offer to the thousands whom the stern necessities of life debar from its acceptance? What boots it that the world offers one Education, Wealth, or Fame, while it denies him the power to reach it? Of what benefit are our Schools to the hoards [sic] of ragged, filthy and obscene children of sin, who throng the perlieus [sic] of Ann and Cross streets?" But Skidmore and Brownson clearly deprecated educational reform only because it was substituted for more radical changes—not because they despised it intrinsically—and Brownson went so far as to imply that the elementary schooling that philanthropists had already provided for the factory children of England would ultimately rouse the masses to overcome their capitalist oppressors. Similarly, the *Voice of Industry* criticized the education New England offered, only to demand that it respect the full range of human faculties: "We are entitled, by virtue of our threefold organization—Physical, Intellectual and Affectionate, to a threefold development—to an Integral culture. We are entitled to an Industrial, a Scientific and a Social Education." It was a rare critic of American society who did not visualize improved schooling as a vehicle for democratic principles.[21]

Critics on the left also tended to place great stress upon equating equal rights in politics with equal rights in education. A committee of the workingmen of Philadelphia articulated their position with unusual clarity when it wrote in 1829 that "the original element of despotism is a monopoly of talent, which consigns the multitude to comparative ignorance, and secures the balance of knowledge on the side of the rich and the rulers. If then the healthy existence of a free government be, as the committee believe, rooted in the will of the American people, it follows as a necessary consequence . . . that this monopoly should be broken up, and that the means of equal knowledge, (the only security for equal liberty) should be rendered, by legal provision, the common property of all classes." Several years later, compiling a history of the Workingmen's party, Hobart Berrian pointed up the extent to which its demands had come down to education as a vehicle of liberty. "These reform men broached neither novel nor startling doctrines; they were not disorganisers, nor were they fanatics. They were composed of mechanics and workingmen, who, from principle as well as circumstance, were in favor of the largest latitude of liberty. Universal education, abolition of all monopolies, and equal taxation, were the desire of their hearts, and upon the accomplishment of these reforms they were zealously intent." [22]

Taken all together, in short, democrats of a radical persuasion were more likely to complain that the schools served them badly than to renounce public education in its entirety.[f] Meanwhile prominent Democrats pressed hard for public schools as one of the few indispensable functions of government. "The people cannot be intelligent and moral unless they are educated," Robert Rantoul Jr. declared in 1833, "and free institutions cannot sustain themselves, except where the people are intelligent and moral; a system of free education, therefore, is an indispensable auxiliary to free institutions." In the same fashion, when Levi Woodbury took up the cause of educational reform during the 1840s, he argued that the dangers the United States experienced because it was a self-governing republic must be rectified through popular education. The primary means of improvement, he explained, must be "free schools every where," and he insisted that they must be reformed in order to impart "increased intelligence in the community at large, to elevate, expand, and purify; next, a more thorough discipline, or, in other words, training to follow implicitly the dictates of that intelligence; and after these, as difficulties arise too formidable for them to overcome, a more constant reliance on moral and Christian principles for direction, rather than on the blinder impulses of passion, prejudice, or appetite. These, more than any other instruments, can aid to form correct national habits of thinking and action." [23]

Hence the ultimate outcome of Democratic deliberations was a sense that even the informal processes of education upon which Democrats often relied to maintain popular liberties depended in no small measure on effective public schooling. On one level, it is true, spokesmen for the party often seemed to argue that the existence of popular deliberation was itself a sufficient guarantee of popular competence. Isaac T. Preston implied as much when he told the constitutional convention of Louisiana that "the people are ever ready to glean all the information they can, in order to act understandingly. The consequence of discussion is that the people obtain information, and the humblest citizen who retires to his simple cottage, carries with him and treasures up some of the important facts that may have been elicited in that discussion. It is this interchange of thought and facility of hearing every public question discussed, that disseminated so much general information among the people, and gives them a decided advantage over the people of other countries." John L. O'Sullivan was more succinct in making the same point: "The halls of legislation and the courts of law in a Republic are necessarily the public schools of the adult population." [24]

In comparing these institutions with the public schools, however, O'Sullivan inevitably implied that the schools served a similar purpose. By the same token, other Democratic spokesmen suggested that popular education and not simply popular deliberation was necessary to make democracy work. Preston apparently took schooling for granted; so did John R. Williams when he defended extending the vote to aliens in Michigan on the grounds that—unlike the citizens of Rome—the citizens of the United States were already enlightened. For that matter, although the *Democratic Review* contended in 1840 that the people were intelligent without formal training and explained that they were also blessedly exempt from the dangers of learned sophistry, it concluded its discussion of their powers by arguing that they required only "the simple elements of learning, *with the means of educating themselves*" to achieve their full capabilities. In 1838, moreover, it linked the advance of democracy to the spread of popular education: "Our principles strengthen in the light of knowledge, and are nourished and diffused as education develops the length and breadth and depth of the popular mind. Let other systems pervert the faculties of mind, and facilities of knowledge, to mystify, and disguise with the logic of artful theories, principles at war with the interests of the mass; be it the glory of Democracy that it courts investigation, that it shuns this luxury of concealment; that the truths of religion, and the inquiries of philosophy, and the achievements of learning in every branch of knowledge and of art, constitute the best friends of its principles." [25]

It followed that when Democrats sought to strengthen popular government against incursions on popular rights they were likely to visualize public schooling as an indispensable support for their values. J. Van Valkenburgh offered the second Michigan convention a Hunker version of their faith when he advocated adopting a constitutional provision for public schools, in defiance of critics like Joseph H. Bagg who wished to leave education to the legislature.

We live under a republican government—we have no law of primogeniture, no hereditary titles—but the road to wealth and distinction is open to all. What do we propose in the bill reported by the committee? To render education accessible to all the children of the land, and that the government shall be accountable for the education of its youth, and that the money spent in education will be saved by the less demand for penitentiaries, alms houses, and the expenses of holding courts. We believe that we are called upon to establish a system of free schools— free to all—that the youth may be educated and prepared for the responsible situation of citizens of a free republic. I care not how this is attained, if the object is brought out; but I am unwilling to leave it to the Legislature. We are bound to ourselves, to our children, bound to posterity, to see that the Legislature shall provide a system of free schools that shall afford the facilities of education to all.

Lorenzo Bevans, a Whig recently turned Democrat, developed much the same argument in Wisconsin in 1846. Pressing that state's first constitutional convention to adopt both public schools and a state superintendency, he announced that "the safety of the state and the perpetuity of our free institutions are absolutely dependent upon a faithful discharge of this duty, since, as ignorance and vassalage are inseparable, so are the liberties of the people and the permanency of our loved institutions dependent upon intelligence and virtue." [26]

But it was not only conservative Democrats and renegade Whigs who relied upon public schools to secure democratic institutions. "Our safety is not in constitutions and forms of government," declared John D. Pierce in his third report as superintendent of public instruction in Michigan, "for no constitution within the power of man to devise can provide such security, but in the establishment of a right system of general education, [in] the development and culture of [the] moral, and intellectual powers implanted in the nature of man." Beyond this, liberal Democratic spokesmen also looked to the common schools to guarantee an egalitarian social order. In the second Michigan convention, Edward S. Moore argued:

Free schools have a powerful influence in disseminating the principles of true *democracy*. Where on earth is there such a practical demonstration of the doctrine that "all men are born free and equal," as in the school house under a free school system—where every barefooted urchin may have the same teacher, the same books, and set [*sic*] on the same seat with the most fortunate heir in the town— may stand at the head of his class and take the precedence over all that wealth and rank can array against him, if only God has given him the better mind, or the more diligent disposition? It ennobles and encourages the poor boy, and fires him with such thoughts of the dignity of a human soul that tyrants can never after oppress him with impunity. It corrects, too, the thoughtlessness of the rich by the standard of mind, and teaches them to reckon rank by the Roman rule of merit.[27]

Thus Democratic advocates of popular education often joined with self-consciously radical workingmen to proclaim that the fulfillment of American democracy depended upon the widest possible diffusion of knowledge. In doing so they were probably less inclined than either the workingmen or Whiggish conservatives to proclaim the material advan- tages that education would bestow, but they were no less inclined to define public schools as safeguards of the republic. Whereas Whigs tended to see education as a vehicle of social betterment, Democrats tended to see the protection of individual rights. Whereas Whigs tended to visualize it in positive terms, as a corollary of internal improvements, Democrats tended to visualize it negatively, as a means for defeating power.[28] But when Whigs came to see education as an institution that would protect all the values of American society without employing co- ercion, Democrats heartily concurred. "It is the illumination of the uni- versal mind that is the sure foundation of democracy," Marcus Morton told the legislature of Massachusetts in 1840. "It is the elevation of every rational soul into moral and intellectual consciousness and dignity, that is to carry onward improvements in our social and civil institutions. To this end should be directed the highest aims and efforts of the legisla- ture." Even among Democrats who suspected the apparatus Whigs built up to administer it, the common school was the palladium of American liberties.[29]

Still, the residual differences of emphasis between Whig and Demo- cratic ideas of education admonish us that the ideas the two parties held were neither interdependent nor derived from each other; Americans ar- rived at their consensus on the common schools by coincidence rather than imitation. This fact makes the terms in which they saw their educational institutions even more striking. In very broad terms, conservative and Whig thought began with the wish to moralize the nation lest it lose sight of both morality and liberty in its headlong pursuit of equality. In equally broad terms, democratic and Democratic thought began with an anxious concern for the fate of popular rights, which depended upon but could not be made contingent upon popular morality. Nevertheless, both parties concluded by visualizing every individual's possession of intelligence and virtue as the best safeguard American liberty could know. In doing so, conservatives implicitly conceded the democratic contention that every man must be empowered to defend his rights, while democrats implicitly conceded that those rights must be morally conceived and morally exercised. Beyond this, the two parties increasingly concurred in assigning responsibility for American freedom to the success of the common schools. The schools seemed an inestimable support to free institutions because they promised to serve both liberty and democracy without encroaching on either.

THE CONSERVATIVE AS LIBERAL PEDAGOGUE

Spokesmen for conservative values who interested themselves in public schooling were typically far less willing than their democratic critics to leave freedom to its own devices. At the same time, some of these same men developed a vision of popular education that was at least as liberal as any that democrats advanced. In effect, they looked to education to free men as well as elevate them, and they puzzled out the circumstances under which it would be truly liberating.

Their thinking had two main elements, the pedagogical and the political. The pedagogical element was implicit in the fact that a number of political conservatives were also educational reformers, and it was made most explicit in their defense of Prussian innovations. Seen in a narrowly conservative perspective, these innovations represented an efficient modern process for shaping the American character. As seen by some reformers, however, their efficiency was a neutral quality, desirable in the construction of any social institution; hence, the greater the degree of democracy a country enjoyed, the more effectively democratic its schools must be when they were reformed. More important, the reformers insisted repeatedly that the more widespread education was, throughout, the world, the more surely it would work to liberate mankind. We may suspect this argument today because we have witnessed the failures of educational reform, but we should not read back our skepticism into the Middle Period. As heirs of the Protestant Reformation who were sometimes also heirs of the Enlightenment or proponents of evangelical Christianity, the conservatives of that earlier day looked to schools to make men free because they believed in the power of the word.[30]

In addition, they often saw devices to free the human spirit in the specific improvements they proposed. The writings of William Ellery Channing demonstrate the ultimate tendencies of much reform thought. Although Channing was not a partisan of educational reform in the sense that Horace Mann was—he could not lend himself to the proliferation of governmental apparatus that Mann clearly counted upon—he repeatedly described education as a process through which the mind, soul, and character of the child would be developed. He was at some pains to point out, moreover, that no child should be brought to a pre-established standard of behavior; rather, he looked to education "to call forth power of every kind, power of thought, affection, will, and outward action; power to observe, to reason, to judge, to contrive; power to adopt good ends firmly, and to pursue them efficiently; power to govern ourselves, and to influence others; power to gain and to spread happiness." As a result he declared that the office of the teacher was more important even than that of the statesman, and he concluded by urging his contemporaries to adopt educational practices that would be sure to liberate the rising generation.[31] Channing was clearly a conservative when he described the role education might play in promoting social harmony and discouraging unmanly coercions, but equally clearly a liberal when he contemplated how it must be made to work.[g]

Other spokesmen for educational reform embraced a less demanding but no less significant devotion to pedagogical innovation. Because they were less intent than Channing on the primacy of spiritual freedom, they went well beyond him in introducing changes into the actual practice of the schools. In a real sense the common-school awakening began with expressions of concern about the dangers to be feared from popular illiteracy but moved toward an investigation of the manner in which children should be taught. This development was already clearly at work during the 1830s in the columns of the *North American Review* and the

proceedings of the American Institute of Instruction and the Western
Literary Institute, but it remained tentative and limited in character
there, as if to suggest that so long as traditional republican standards of
politics and learning remained influential the discussion of pedagogical
changes would be curtailed by an essentially elitist concern to improve
the intellectual and moral capacities of the lower classes. William H.
Seward expressed the traditional point of view when he argued in his
discourse at Westfield that "our government is emphatically a democratic
republic. Our people ought, therefore, to possess a measure of knowledge, not only as great as is enjoyed by the citizens or subjects of other
states, but at least as much superior as their power and responsibilities
are greater." His prescriptions for reform were correspondingly restricted: far from stressing the need for innovations in the actual practice
of teaching, he took the largest interest in improving the state's machinery for supervising its educational system and for holding its graduates to a high standard of performance.[32]

By contrast, the educational reformers of the 1840s began to examine
the processes of instruction in some detail, seeking to discover whether
they were compatible with the demands of a free society. Horace Mann
exemplified this tendency of their thought when he argued in his *Ninth
Report* (1845) that children must be permitted to practice self-government
in the schools if they were to be capable of it in adult life. Mann never
adopted the most advanced pedagogical views of his times, and he was
indifferent if not hostile to the ideas of freedom the Transcendentalists
espoused, but he was far more sensitive than most of the reformers who
had preceded him to the ways in which the processes of education were
themselves the key to liberty. Moreover, he was not alone; the wish to
ensure popular morality and the wish to make public schooling more effective culminated in the country's first significant effort to make the
schools themselves free.[33]

The other liberal departure in conservative social thought involved the
growing conservative belief that, given a people who had some modicum
of formal training, American political institutions guaranteed that the
people would be sufficiently educated to maintain American liberty.
This doctrine undoubtedly owed something to republican statesmen who
had portrayed popular government as a spur to popular intelligence, and
it paralleled Democratic claims that a free people could be trusted to pro-

tect their own rights. But it also represented a clear conservative discovery of the possibilities of American freedom. During the Middle Period a number of men whose views were in most respects rooted in an organic vision of society and a hierarchical sense of government came to visualize American politics as a liberal educational institution.[34]

Putnam's Monthly expressed a challenging version of this perspective in 1855 in an essay defending the political rights of immigrants. "The American is not of a better nature than the European—for he is often of the same stock—nor is there any charm in our soil and climate unknown to the soil and climate of the other hemisphere; but there is a difference in institutions. Institutions, with us, are made for men, and not men for the institutions. It is the jury, the ballot-box, the free public assemblage, the local committee, the legislative assembly, the place of trust, and, as a result of these, the school and the newspaper, which give such a spur to our activities, and endow us with such political competence." Speaking of the contemporary agitation of social questions, Henry B. Stanton carried the same proposition to the point of restating the role that the "scholar" might play in American life. "America is a great lyceum," he wrote in 1850, "a grand debating society, a mass convention, sitting permanently, and courting the utmost freedom of discussion. The press and the forum, the pen and the stump, rule the republic. Being all of the nobility, all of the blood royal, all heirs to the throne[,] all sovereigns, in no other country can a speech or an essay be heard and read by so many who have a direct influence upon public affairs. Would our scholars instruct and lead the national mind? Let them not strive to become an isolated class, an 'order' of society, but fused with the body of the people, giving an impulse to and receiving an impress from the mass around them." On this view, free institutions were a way of guaranteeing education that would in turn guarantee freedom.[35]

These spokesmen were enthusiastic converts whose statements were so optimistic that they cannot be presumed to have represented the attitudes of more hesitant conservatives. What makes their views particularly significant is that they were shared, albeit rather tentatively, by manifestly conservative contemporaries. One of them was an anonymous writer in the *American Review* who concluded a list of dangers and safeguards to the Union by pointing to the advantages of manhood suffrage. Deprecating party spirit and the theory of states' rights, rebuking territorial aggrandizement and the institution of slavery, he announced that he had changed his former opinions about the dangers to be expected from an injudicious exercise of the vote. "The unwise and often reckless exercise of the right," he conceded, "is the great evil that attends it. But this evil is only temporary; for our early experience will assuredly ascertain its unfortunate application in a given case, and administer a lesson of wisdom for the future which shall more than compensate for the mistake that has occasioned it. But more by far than this, the sense of merely self-respect and the feeling of personal responsibility implied in the possession of the right, are of the very gist of freedom, and belong permanently to the very life of free institutions." [36]

Taken at face value, such an argument might even make public schooling seem unnecessary, as Joseph C. Hornblower demonstrated in the New Jersey convention. But it was also fully compatible with the principles of educational reform, as Henry Barnard showed when he held, in his eighth annual report as superintendent of common schools in Connecticut (1853), that the magnificent educational systems some European countries had established could not compete with American institutions, which might fall short in formal training yet subjected American youth to the uniquely liberating influences of a free press, town meetings, unlimited social intercourse, and individual self-reliance. Nathan S. S. Beman appealed to the same liberal vision in addressing the Young Men's Association of Troy (New York) in 1846: "A free people form a national academy, in which the process of self-education is carried on, by the spontaneous action of its own essential elements. Every thing which relates to agriculture, manufactures and commerce, to our domestic and foreign relations, to peace and war, to internal improvements, to taxation and expenditures, to freedom and oppression, to the safety, protection and happiness of the Republic, comes before the nation, and must interest every individual. . . . Here, then, we have a kind of national education of itself." This was the ultimate advantage of the American republic over its European competitors, he explained, for he equated the claims of American freedom with cultivation of the popular mind. [37] In the eyes of conservatives like Beman, freedom and education were identical, mutually reinforcing assurances that the United States would remain true to its destiny. [h]

❦ XII ❦

THE FRONTIER WEST
AS IMAGE OF
AMERICAN SOCIETY

E ducation offered the opportunity to every American to be an effective citizen in a free and prosperous republic. Nevertheless, despite its democratic advocates and despite the hopes of liberal reformers, it remained a conservative moral instrument, a means by which clerks who no longer aspired to public authority might still inculcate lessons in political and social morality. Even the democracy of success that many educational reformers clamored for was highly selective and at best tangential to ordinary democratic aspirations, which tended to run toward universal prosperity rather than meteoric careers in business. The idea of popular education answered more closely to the needs some Americans felt for moral guarantees of their well-being than to the demands others pressed for material advantages, and many secular democrats were prepared to say that freedom required a more tangible support than the promises either schools or churches held out.[1]

The gap they might otherwise have felt was filled by the frontier West, which reassured at least two generations of Americans that free institutions were inviolable. Here we must distinguish between the idea and the fact of the West, as we have already distinguished between the idea and the fact of an American mission or the idea and the fact of the Second Bank of the United States. Whatever influence the actual frontier may have had on American life, it presented itself to most Americans in the form of an imagined phenomenon—an intellectual event compounded in unequal parts of fiction, fact, and pious hope—that had large consequences in American thought and behavior. As a fact it may have been insignificant; as an idea it became the ultimate recourse for American hopes of liberty.[a]

DEMOCRATIC IDEAS OF THE WEST

The West that Americans embraced was essentially a democratic phenomenon, a source of Democratic strength and a vehicle for Democratic innovations. The historic debate between Daniel Webster and Robert Y. Hayne reflected something more than competition between the New England states and those in the Southeast for the allegiance of western voters: it symbolized conflicting visions of the character of western settlement. New Englanders, who were predominantly National Republicans and would in time be Whigs, hoped for an orderly progression westward in which the economic interests of the East and the level of culture in the West would both be protected against the evils of uncontrolled migration. Conversely, the men of the Southeast, which was already predominantly Democratic, were committed at least for the moment to economic opportunity rather than good order, to freedom rather than civilization. Meanwhile the western settlers themselves, eager to develop their country, were torn between a desire for internal improvements (which the National Republicans supported) and a desire for a liberal land policy (which leading Democrats promoted). In the end they turned to the states to foster improvements and to the Democrats to give them land.[2]

Western Democrats often justified their region's land hunger on the ground that a wide distribution of property was indispensable to the health of the republic. In 1828 Senator Richard M. Johnson of Kentucky argued that a progressive reduction in the price of the public lands would benefit the whole nation:

The country will be enriched by the industry of a class whose misfortunes will otherwise render them a burthen rather than a blessing to the country. The refuse lands, which will otherwise lie waste, only to increase the distance betwixt improvements, and so render more inconvenient all useful business, will be rendered fruitful by cultivation. The settlers will escape many temptations to vice and dissipation. They will form a bulwark of defence to the nation. Their patriotism, and the republican simplicity of their manners, will be a protection to our liberties. They and their families will be virtuous and happy. Manufacturing towns and villages will grow up spontaneously among them, equal at least to the wants of their own settlements, and requiring no other protection than what the produce of these refuse lands will be certain to afford.

Easterners as well as westerners were disposed to see the West in this light. In 1852, advocating early homestead legislation, Representative

Charles Skelton of New Jersey rebuked a hostile colleague who had insisted that the public lands already constituted "the balance-wheel that regulates the labor of our country." "Now, Mr. Chairman," he argued, ". . . if this is the balance-wheel which regulates the liberty of our country—if this is the asylum to which the oppressed are to flee for refuge—if this is the place where the intelligent, the industrious, and worthy may go to get themselves homes, I would like to know why every man, a citizen of this country, should not have a plat of ground which he may call his home? . . . Let each man have a plat of ground to live upon, and a house to dwell in. Then you will have built up there a population of intelligent and independent freemen, who will defend our country in the day of need and the hour of danger." [3] Democrats of both regions clearly visualized a West that was indispensable to democratic politics and a key to national prosperity.[b]

Thus far the Democratic case was addressed chiefly to the public good; it was a necessary form of reply to the objections opponents raised against dissipating the nation's resources. But it also merged almost imperceptibly into a different kind of claim, to the effect that the welfare of individual democrats depended upon the availability of free land. Senator Johnson suggested as much; so did Representative Skelton. So, too, did Senator Hayne, who announced during his first speech on Foot's Resolution, "I can conceive of no policy that can possibly be pursued in relation to the public lands, none that would be more 'for the common benefit of all the States,' than to use them as the means of furnishing a secure asylum to that class of our fellow-citizens, who in any portion of the country may find themselves unable to procure a comfortable subsistence by the means immediately within their reach. I would by a just and liberal system convert into great and flourishing communities, that entire class of persons, who would otherwise be paupers in your streets, and outcasts in society, and by so doing you will but fulfil the great trust which has been confided to your care." [4]

Other Democrats argued even more insistently that the West was the "poor man's country." Significantly, Senator Benton sought to discredit Foot's Resolution by associating it with Richard Rush, who had observed two years earlier that low prices for western land constituted a subsidy to western agriculture at the expense of eastern industry.

The manufactories want poor people to do the work for small wages; these poor people wish to go to the West and get land; to have flocks and herds—to have their own fields, orchards, gardens, and meadows—their own cribs, barns, and dairies; and to start their children on a theatre where they can contend with equal chances with other people's children for the honors and dignities of the country. This is what the poor people wish to do. How to prevent it—how to keep them from straying off in this manner—is the question. The late Secretary of the Treasury could discover no better mode than in the idea of a bounty upon non-emigration, in the shape of protection to domestic manufactures! [5]

Eight years later the *Democratic Review* invoked the same vision of western opportunity to discredit the Whig party, which it charged with denying the right of preemption to "the poor man who is willing to reclaim his quarter-section from the wilderness, on condition of being suffered to dig from it an honest livelihood by the sweat of his own brow." In 1852 Representative Andrew Johnson of Tennessee defended the Homestead Bill against its southern opponents—southerners now feared free land—on similar grounds. "Gentlemen say here that you will by this bill take away the laboring man from the old States," he argued, only to urge them, "Look at his condition. Do you not see, under the circumstances that surround him there, that his condition is unalterably fixed, and that he can never extricate himself from the iron grasp of poverty? Where is the man, abstractionist, North Carolinian, Virginian, or citizen of any other State, who has a heart that beats with love for his kind, and patriotism for his country, that could say to him, Do not go away; stay here in your poverty; do not go and settle upon the new, rich, and fertile lands of the West, but stay here, linger, wither, and die in your poverty, and where the only inheritance which you can leave to your children is your poverty." [6]

The idea that the West could or would benefit the poor man blended in turn into the proposition that it offered every worthy American an opportunity to prosper. George Bancroft incorporated one version of this attitude into the fifth volume of his *History of the United States*, where he asserted that "nothing could restrain the Americans from peopling the wilderness. To be a freeholder was the ruling passion of the New England man. Marriages were early and very fruitful. The sons, as they grew up, skilled in the use of the axe and the rifle, would, one after another, move from the old homestead, and with a wife, a yoke of oxen,

a cow, and a few husbandry tools, build a small hut in some new planta-
tion, and by tasking every faculty of mind and body, win for themselves
plenty and independence." In the same vein, in 1841 Senator Perry
Smith of Connecticut defended the preemption bill on the grounds that
"pre-emption rights will enable a great many worthy citizens to move
into a new country, where they will soon rise with the country, from
poverty to wealth; they are there enabled to take rank among their neighbors, and in society which is gratifying to their ambition, and to give full
scope to useful talents which otherwise might have lain dormant, and
been smothered and stifled by the cold chills of poverty." Both the object
and the result of emigration would be a perfected liberal society.[7]

Spokesmen for western interests reinforced democratic hopes by the
enthusiasm with which they described western accomplishments. In
1830 Representative Dixon H. Lewis of Alabama upheld the new states'
claims to the lands lying within their boundaries by citing many of the
same circumstances that Smith was to invoke.

What was the value of these lands before they were reclaimed and subdued by
the enterprise of the first settlers? To quote the language of the mover of these
resolutions, (the honorable gentleman from Vermont,) they were "waste and un-
cultivated deserts." Sir, their value has been imparted to them by the industry,
enterprise, and sufferings of that hardy population who precede the comforts and
conveniences of a more advanced condition of every newly settling country. Who
levelled the forests, who opened the roads, who established the towns, who gave,
in fact, a determinate value to all the lands in the country, by converting a wilderness into a country possessing all the comforts of cultivated life? The people
of Alabama. The labor and hardship was with them; and shall they be placed on
no better footing than the old states?

So, too, in 1841 Senator Richard M. Young of Illinois reassured the
critics of preemption by pointing to its salutary effects: "Let any man go
and look at these Western settlements; let him travel through them and
mingle with the people; let him see what sort of people were on this national domain, and who they were that were actually benefited by our
pre-emption laws, and they would soon have all doubts as to the expediency and utility of the system done away. Men who went into that
region on a pack-horse, carrying their worldly all upon his back, had
now become respectable farmers, and were able to give their children a
good education. Should not the law give a preference to such men as

these over mere land speculators?" Self-seeking as these arguments were, they also described a frontier condition that answered to democratic needs.[8]

It followed that eastern democrats should prove increasingly sympathetic to land reform: to graduation of the price of land, to preemption, ultimately to giving the lands away to bona fide settlers. At the same time, so widespread was the idea that the West served liberal values that social critics who did not press these specific measures tended none the less to think of the region as an asset to equal rights. Significantly, William Gouge argued in his *Inquiry into the American Banking System* that the banking monopoly was evil because it controlled finite assets, whereas the abundance of land in the United States prevented it from being monopolized. Similarly, the *Democratic Review* argued in 1839 that the country suffered from "the only kind of privileged order which can, in the nature of things, exist in the United States." "Where the supply of land greatly exceeds the demand for cultivation," it held, "it is impossible to have a landed nobility, unless the tillers of the soil can be reduced to the condition of serfs, and chained to certain estates, as in Russia." Reviewing other possibilities, it rejected them on appropriate grounds before bringing its analysis to a climax with the observation that "a paper nobility is the only one that could be established here." Democrats might well demand "radical" reform, but they also made obeisances to the West as a resource for American liberties.[9]

Even the opponents of homestead legislation sometimes invoked the same vision. In 1852 Representative Thomas J. D. Fuller of Maine criticized the proposed reform on the grounds that

our present land system operates like a great balance-wheel upon our political institutions. It regulates the value of real property; it controls the wages of labor; and so long as one day's work will purchase an acre of productive land, and secure a certain and sure title, directly from the Government—eastern manufactures can never control the wages of labor. . . . As our population increases and becomes more dense, they will emigrate to this broad domain, occupy and cultivate the soil, establish schools and churches, and form settlements, and thereby avoid those evils incident to a more dense and thickly-settled country. But offering extraordinary and unusual inducements for settlement will not increase the number of good and reliable settlers. Such settlers multiply only by time and the natural course of events. I trust, sir, that our public domain may be long so held, and that our children, and our children's children, may always have the privilege

of resorting to it for settlement and support, and at an unvarying price, with a
certainty of title, until the almost countless acres of our unoccupied domain shall
be covered with a virtuous, industrious, and happy people.

In 1847, moreover, a States' Rights Democrat with obvious southern
sympathies turned the same vision to account in criticizing the Wilmot
Proviso. "That which constitutes the strength of the Union, the wealth
and independence of its people," he wrote in the *Democratic Review*, "is
the boundless expanse of territory laid open to their possession; and the
more rapidly it is overrun by needy settlers, the greater is the security,
that it will be equally and extensively distributed, and the more impossible it becomes for any section or clique to exercise 'control over them,' or
to encroach upon the rights they enjoy under our constitution." Differences over land policy notwithstanding, Democrats characteristically
relied upon untrammeled access to western lands to bolster equal rights
and reinforce popular liberties.[10]

It is of course true that some insistent radicals made a point of denying
the region's beneficence. In an odd way, however, they too confirmed
the common opinion—not only by their manifest need to refute it, but
also by their need to ground their case against the Americans' complacency in a denial of the value of the West. In Massachusetts, Samuel C.
Allen argued that the workingmen of the United States must ultimately
experience the same course of degradation as their counterparts in
Europe. "The unsettled lands in the West," he noted in 1830, "may re-
tard its celerity here, and there may be several generations before it will
reach the goal, but this is an accidental circumstance, and does not affect
the certainty of the results." So, too, Robert Barnwell Rhett told the
House of Representatives in 1838 that the country's free institutions
were already close to destruction. "It is the accident of our situation
alone, having a continent to people, which has enabled us so long to
maintain them. But the time will come,—is rapidly approaching, when
the way to the West will be blocked up." [11] To be radical as these men
were was to deny the promise of the West along with most of the other
values that ordinary men shared.[c]

Southern proslavery critics played a comparable role. Although many
southerners were initially sympathetic to democratic aspirations in the
West, as antislavery sentiment spread and the sectional crisis deepened

they came to see in the filling up of the region the decline of their own political authority. Hence they repudiated policies they had previously condoned and fought bitterly against the Homestead Bill. In doing so, they were forced to repudiate the hopes that northern liberals expressed; as Henry Nash Smith notes in one of the most striking chapters of *Virgin Land*, they could neither tolerate the fact of westward expansion nor acquiesce in the images of frontier democracy that drew free men westward. They challenged the nation's commitment to free land because it seemed to be a vehicle for liberal institutions; but the grounds on which they challenged it can only have worked to reinforce democratic belief.[12]

It seems clear, therefore, that despite the skepticism some Democrats expressed and the hostility others betrayed, a majority of American democrats thought of the West as an asset to democratic liberties. They also clearly conceived of it as a free institution in the sense in which we have used that term to describe props to American liberty that were themselves free. For one thing, they visualized it as an alternative to education and a substitute for religious effort, a support for democratic institutions that avoided the difficulties Democrats often detected in demands for a purer morality and clamor for educational reform. Representative Fuller portrayed western settlement as an occasion for the spread of schools and churches; George H. Evans linked ignorance to poverty and oppression, implying that land reform would end them; and John D. Pierce fought for homestead exemption in the second Michigan convention on the grounds that "free religion, free schools, free trade, and a free home, are the essential elements of liberty. The home must be inviolate, or liberty is but a name, and freedom a mockery." Representative Cyrus L. Dunham of Indiana expressed a still more expansive view of the West as the essence of free institutions when he invoked homestead legislation as the characteristically American alternative to measures intended to involve the United States in the defense of Hungarian liberty:

Sir, if this measure will add to the revenues of the Government, and to the wealth of the country; if it will add to the happiness of our citizens; if it will add to the prosperity of the people; if it will augment the power and glory of the nation, shall we not do more by adopting it to diffuse the spirit of liberty throughout the world than you will by going forth, sword in hand, to accomplish such a result? Our mission is one of peace. . . . If we would keep the fires of liberty burning brightly upon her altars, we must cultivate the arts of peace, we must add to the prosperity, the virtue, the intelligence, and the happiness of the people. You will thus give an influence to the cause of freedom that armies and navies cannot restrain.

Democrats did not deny the utility of virtue and intelligence so much as supplant the school and the church with the western family farm.[13]

They did so, moreover, on expressly liberal grounds. Far from visualizing distribution of the public lands as an example of active government that might be taken to rectify the economy of nature, they perceived it instead as an exercise of freedom that made further reforms unnecessary. In 1844 William Kirkland explained in the *Democratic Review* that the nation's liberal land policies were "a practical corrective of the evils caused by the tendency of property to accumulate in large masses." "It is the aim of good government," he added, in classic Democratic accents, "to lessen these evils without encroaching upon the rights of individuals. Our happy position enables us to strike at the root of the difficulty, and by the virtual gift of a freehold to every poor man who is disposed to take possession of it, to prevent that excessive inequality of property which, in the countries of the Old World, is the worst enemy alike of individual happiness and national prosperity." The West could serve as the ultimate prop for democratic institutions because it promised to secure popular freedom by reinforcing individual rights.[14]

CONSERVATIVE HOSTILITY TOWARD THE WEST

For the most part, Democrats readily embraced the West, honoring both the measures it demanded and the values these measures represented. Partly by reaction and partly for other reasons, conservatives who lived in the East—and in a sense there was no other kind—often looked at the same region with a combination of antipathy and fear. Their antipathies reflected its innovations, their fears its growing power. Far from promising to redeem free institutions, it seemed to threaten their very destruction.[15]

The tradition of eastern hostility had been born with the republic. For one thing, conservatives were quick to deplore the existence of western territory because it threatened eastern interests. At the constitutional convention in Philadelphia, Gouverneur Morris observed that "the Busy haunts of men not the remote wilderness, was the proper school of political Talents. If the Western people get the power into their hands they will ruin the Atlantic interests. The Back members are always most averse to the best measures." Federalist Congressmen opposed the Louisiana Purchase on the same grounds. Representative Roger Griswold of Connecticut spoke for them when he declared in 1803 that "the vast and unmanageable extent which the accession of Louisiana will give to the United States; the consequent dispersion of our population, and the destruction of that balance which it is so important to maintain between the Eastern and the Western States, threatens, at no very distant day, the subversion of our Union." Hence there was a long history behind the antagonism many eastern Whigs expressed toward the annexation of Texas and the acquisition of Mexican territory. "The annexation of Texas forms a new era in the history of our country," Representative James Pollock of Pennsylvania declared in the House in 1845. "They were told the people demanded it. But he asked what reasons were assigned for it? Was it the acquisition of territory? Already we had a vast territory, extending from the Atlantic to the Pacific—from the seas of the north to the Sabine on the south. The wilds of the West alone would provide a home for millions for ages yet to come. He said emphatically, we needed no more territory." [16]

Other conservative commentators who would not declare themselves so flatly against expansion maintained none the less insistently that the West must undergo an orderly development if it were to be an asset to the country. This point of view, which reflected the idea of an organic society that conservatives were wont to press, placed its advocates in opposition to most of the measures western democrats demanded. Benjamin Rush expressed it in 1787 when he wrote that the chief threat to American well-being was a too-rapid expansion into the West, and his son Richard reiterated it forty years later when he observed that cheap lands in the West provided an incentive for migration that served only to depopulate the East. Horace Greeley continued to hold to this idea in 1841 when he spoke out against Democratic party measures like preemption and graduation:

The direct object and effect of the Loco-foco propositions now pending before the Senate, is the spoliation of the Old States. . . . [The] thriftless, industry-hating adventurer who shall first pounce upon a section at the junction of two rivers, or at a head of navigation, or in the midst of valuable timber—worth probably fifty to five hundred dollars an acre before his foot touched it—shall be entitled to purchase it whenever he gets ready at a dollar and a quarter an acre. What justice, what policy, can there be in this? . . . We feel and know that the triumph of preemption and graduation will rob the Old States of an incalculable property, at the same time that it will debauch and demoralize the New, plunging the whole country into another whirlpool of delirious speculation like that from which it has just emerged.

Eleven years later, Whig spokesmen in Washington charged the Democratic party with having betrayed the national heritage. "The truth is," they declared, "the public domain is gone hook and line. The demagogues have got hold of the subject, and within the next half dozen years this inheritance, richer than any other God ever bestowed on a free people, will be scattered to the four winds of heaven." [17]

Greeley's words also suggested that, thanks to unchecked migration, the West had become an arena in which the worst men triumphed. This too was a conviction of long standing among conservative easterners, nowhere stated more explicitly than in Timothy Dwight's *Travels in New-England and New-York* (1821–1822). There the Congregational clergyman and erstwhile president of Yale College excoriated the early settlers of Vermont, whom he took to be typical of pioneers everywhere. "These men cannot live in regular society," he complained, going on to develop a catalogue of their defects as men and as citizens. "They are too idle; too talkative; too passionate; too prodigal; and too shiftless; to acquire either property or character. They are impatient of the restraints of law, religion, and morality; grumble about the taxes, by which Rulers, Ministers, and School-masters, are supported; and complain incessantly, as well as bitterly, of the extortions of mechanics, farmers, merchants, and physicians; to whom they are always indebted." On the classic conservative view, frontiersmen not only abandoned themselves to their weaknesses but also repudiated both the organic society and the institutional props that conservatives took for granted, and the West gave them an opportunity to do so with impunity. [18]

Later writers expressed comparable fears. In 1848 the Reverend Charles T. White, a New England clergyman who had become president of Wabash College, associated western behavior with traits his kind deplored. "All who have become acquainted with American society," he said in the *Biblical Repository and Classical Review*, "have observed that its most marked feature, is restless activity. Enterprise is more characteristic of us than a high civilization; a passion for the glitter and parade of wealth, more than a tendency to substantial, unostentatious investments and solid comforts. It has now become a universal statement and opinion, that a spirit of adventure and advancement, as also an actual forward and ascending movement, are no where in the country more apparent than in the Valley of the Mississippi. This ardor and progress, as is always the fact in new countries, respect the physical more than the intellectual; fortunes and honors more than facilities of knowledge and achievements of mind. All education is in a depressed condition." [19]

Speaking in Portland in 1838, John Neal was even more hostile to western influences, for he equated loyalty to the American republic and loyalty to the state of Maine with "strengthening our own borders, and saving the best of our population from the vices and vicissitudes of the West." "On this one thing it depends after all," he told his Fourth of July audience, ". . . whether this day shall be celebrated for ever and ever among the nations of the Earth." In 1846, indeed, an anonymous writer in the *American Review* congratulated eastern voters for their nearness to Europe, which had taught them well-established principles of politics, and simultaneously condemned the inhabitants of the western states for their isolation, which led them to repudiate state debts and persecute the Mormons. In the eyes of such commentators, the West remained an open invitation to the practice of moral degradation. [20]

To such men the West appeared finally as an untamed force in American society that threatened the integrity of the republic. In 1828 the *Quarterly Register and Journal of the American Education Society* and in 1842 the *Home Missionary* reviewed current census statistics and calculated their electoral implications in essays that clearly expressed a fear of western growth. "Before the present generation shall have passed off the stage," the *Quarterly Register* observed editorially, "the 'star of empire' will have taken 'its way westward,' and the consequence will be either a blessing or a curse, just in the degree that virtuous or vicious principles prevail among the people." The *Home Missionary* was even more explicit:

It will be obvious to everyone, that this rapid transfer of political influence will in ten years more, at the same rate, give a clear majority in our national councils, to western men. This will indeed be a matter of trifling importance, if those men, and the constituents by whom they are elected, are intelligent and virtuous; for in that case, the East, and the country at large, will have no reason to dread their influence. But if that predominance of political power is to be wielded by men over whose hearts no divine principles have sway, who are chosen for their subserviency to transient and party interests, whose affinities are with the boisterous blasphemer, the duellist and the assassin, then may the East, now resting so securely, tremble for its cherished institutions. The wave of ruin will roll over all that is fair in the land of the Pilgrims, quenching the fire on their altars, and sweeping away the monuments reared by their fathers' piety and toil.[21]

Anti-Catholic prejudice and hostility toward immigration, common among eastern conservatives, reinforced this apprehensive vision. In 1826, assessing Timothy Flint's euphoric *Recollections of the Last Ten Years* for the *North American Review*, James Flint wrote that the West "presents a fruitful theme of anxious contemplation and prophetic conjecture to the statesman and philanthropist, as the destined theatre of future events and exhibitions of human character, of the most solemn import to the welfare of mankind; as the scene of the future trial of those broad principles of freedom in governments, and of toleration in religion, assumed as the basis of our national constitution, never before put to the test of actual experiment in any country." Two years later the *Quarterly Register* warned its readers,

Let the sabbath breaking, the intemperance, the profaneness, the practice of fashionable murder, and the licentiousness of manners so generally prevalent at the West, as well as in some other portions of our country, proceed unchecked by any counteracting influence for a few years to come, and the moral condition of these States will be truly deplorable. . . . Over this mighty mass of unsanctified intellect, either the "unsleeping spirit of popery" will attempt to erect its dark spiritual dominion, or infidelity will infuse the fiery elements of discord among all classes, till the whole mass will swell, and heave, and be as terrible as the breaking up of the great deep.

In the eyes of many conservatives, the West was an arena in which the forces of Protestant liberty had already joined battle with the Antichrist for the future of mankind.[22]

The result of all these concerns was a campaign to save the American republic by suppressing western aberrations. To some extent it was purely religious, a mission to the poor who happened to live in the West. Inevitably, however, even missionary effort acquired large social implications, while men who had no particular sympathy with evangelical religion were as energetic as any revivalists in seeking to raise western standards. The *Princeton Review* exemplified the broadening reach of missionary zeal when it argued in 1836 that the mingling of people in the West had produced a society of characterless individuals that was at war with the best interests of the nation. "It is evident," it declared during a discussion of the western ministry, "that we cannot be a mixed people and prosper. The permanency of our civil and religious institutions, and the happiness of all, demands that this mass of heterogeneous and discordant materials, be formed into one consistent and harmonious whole." [23]

Meanwhile Edward Everett had offered an audience of Boston philanthropists a secular version of the same dubious campaign. On the one hand, he argued that the settlers who had moved westward required eastern help if their increase in numbers and prosperity were to be matched by their moral and intellectual growth. "The individual settler," he pointed out during an address in behalf of Kenyon College, "can fell the forest, build his log-house, reap his crops, and raise up his family, in the round of occupations pursued by himself; but he cannot, of himself, found or support a school, far less a college; nor can he do as much toward it, as a single individual, in older States, where ampler resources and a denser population afford means, coöperation, and encouragement, at every turn." On the other hand, he also explicitly asserted that that help must be bestowed in order to maintain New England's influence. "The real government, in this Country," he declared in a familiar formula, "is that of opinion. Toward the formation of the public opinion of the Country, New England, while she continues true to herself, will, as in times past, contribute vastly beyond the proportion of her numerical strength. But, besides the general ascendency which she will maintain, through the influence of public opinion, we can do two things, to secure a strong and abiding interest in the West, operating, I do not say, in our favor, but in favor of principles, which we think sound and salutary." [24]

He proposed two main measures. The first was "to let the West know, by experience, both in the halls of Congress and the channels of commercial and social intercourse, that the East is truly, cordially, and effectively, her friend; not her rival nor enemy." Beyond this, he explained, "We can put in motion a principle of influence, of a much higher and more generous character. We can furnish the means of building up institutions of education. We can, from our surplus, contribute toward the establishment and endowment of those seminaries, where the mind of the West shall be trained and enlightened. Yes, sir, we can do this; and it is so far optional with us, whether the power, to which we have subjected ourselves, shall be a power of intelligence or of ignorance; a reign of reflection and reason, or of reckless strength; a reign of darkness, or of light. This, sir, is true statesmanship; this is policy, of which Washington would not be ashamed." [25]

Confronted with western developments, in short, conservatives of various descriptions tended to fear western successes; they held that the region threatened American institutions and must be redeemed by eastern energies. The greater the hopes that they expressed for the nation, the more strenuous were their plans for remaking western behavior. "Engaging with our utmost ardor to save the wilder portions of our country," Horace Bushnell wrote in 1847, "we shall carry on thus our own noble beginnings to completion, and finish out a character, as earnest in its sacrifices and catholic in its charities, as it is firm in its original elements. . . . We will measure our strength by the grandeur of our object. The wilderness shall bud and blossom as the rose before us; and we will not cease, till a Christian nation throws up its temples of worship on every hill and plain; till knowledge, virtue, and religion, blending their dignity and their healthful power, have filled our great country with a manly and a happy race of people, and the bands of a complete Christian commonwealth are seen to span the continent." History, piety, and politics required that conservatives turn the West against itself. [26]

THE CONSERVATIVE REDEFINITION OF THE WEST

As conservatives initially perceived it, the West was an epitome of the dangers democracy had brought and was the antithesis of free institutions. Hence their effort to redeem it was often as hostile to its special qualities as the more general efforts they made to preserve American liberty were hostile to democratic pretensions throughout the country. Nevertheless, just as these general efforts to curb democratic innovations sometimes worked to reshape conservative attitudes, the idea of redeeming the West led to surprisingly liberal conclusions. Before the Middle Period ended, conservatives embraced a West they had begun by rejecting and conceived of the frontier itself as a free institution. [27]

Experience of the western character apparently had something to do with their change of heart. In 1829 the *American Quarterly Review* of Philadelphia published an anonymous but seemingly first-hand account of the West that was striking for its sympathies. "The pioneers are a people peculiar to our country," it declared, going on to explain that

they live of choice in the forest, and are unwilling to submit to the restraints of society. When others follow and settle around them, they still recede, keeping ever in advance of the permanent population. They are brave, patient of fatigue, and capable of enduring wonderful hardships. They lodge in the open air, and live for whole days without food, without any apparent inconvenience. Their cabins afford but little protection from the climate, and all their domestic arrangements show them to be a migrating people, unaccustomed to provide for any day beyond that which is passing, or to foresee any emergency more pressing than that which is present. They are honest, and very generous. Crimes of magnitude seldom occur among them; and it is a singular fact, that at those remote points, where the *law* is almost unknown, travellers enjoy a degree of security which is scarcely known in any other part of the world. . . . Like the uncivilized races, they are indolent, improvident, and careless of the comforts of life; sagacious, and fertile of invention, and capable, when excited, of powerful bodily exertions.

Seven years later, James Freeman Clarke, a Unitarian minister who lived in Kentucky, attempted an unusually balanced estimate of the western character in the *North American Review*. "Of force and impetus," he concluded his account, "there is enough in the western character; all that is lacking is direction. . . . Religious restraint is needed, moral principle is needed, wise guidance is needed. A deep reverence for truth, a profound respect for law, a ready submission to right, a loyal allegiance to duty, these will make the western character as perfect as humanity can ever hope to become." Meanwhile the Baptist missionary John M. Peck had come to characterize western manners in terms normally reserved to western enthusiasts. "The rough, sturdy habits of the backwoodsmen, living in that plenty which depends on God and nature," he wrote in 1836 in direct imitation of Timothy Flint, "have laid the foundation of independent thought and feeling deep in the minds of western people." To judge by these instances, men whose first impulse had been to redeem westerners from their sins were also sensitive to western virtues.[28]

Simultaneously, leading members of the New England establishment began to see great hopes for redemption where their predecessors had seen obstacles. Lyman Beecher demonstrated the thrust of their thought when he declared in *A Plea for the West* (1835) that "the West is a young empire of mind, and power, and wealth, and free institutions, rushing up to a giant manhood, with a rapidity and a power never before witnessed below the sun. And if she carries with her the elements of her preservation, the experiment will be glorious—the joy of the nation—the joy of the whole earth, as she rises in the majesty of her intelligence and benevolence, and enterprise, for the emancipation of the world." In 1851, moreover, Noah Porter expressed a comparable enthusiasm for western prospects without sharing Beecher's millenarian vision. "At the West," the president of Yale University stated in a prize essay written for the Society for the Promotion of Collegiate and Theological Education at the West, "society is yet to be formed. There, in the process of being united into a great empire, are minds of astonishing energy, and hearts of fire, that need to be taught, and guided, and restrained. The rapidity with which this empire is rushing up into an organized structure can find no likeness in the history of man. Old habits, old institutions, old laws, and old manners present but few hindrances to new impressions and new influences. Never was the need of education so pressing, never was its power for good so full of promise." Concerned as these essayists may have been to secure the West from its vices, they were also clearly exhilarated by the promise of their success.[29]

Hailing the religious potential of the West, spokesmen with impeccable credentials also discovered that it generated social virtues. To some extent their discovery merely reflected their missionary zeal, as when Horace Bushnell argued in 1847 that much of the decline that civilization suffered in the West could be attributed to settlers from the South, who were well on the way to being elevated by the institutions that New Englanders had established. Bushnell also noted, however, that "if the emigrants from New England lose ground, in manners, piety, and habits of intelligence, they also gain in spirit, freedom, self-reliance, and other qualities that are certainly desirable." Other writers were equally enthusiastic in describing western influences. In 1846 an article in the *New Englander* pointed out that "men who in the circles where they had their origin, would have ever stood back, relying upon others' opinions, are not unfrequently, in a new settlement, thrown upon their own resources, and compelled to think and act; and hence, by the same law of necessity, they are forced to read, observe, and resort to all available sources of information. Hence it is that the West abounds with what are sometimes called self-made men—men who have fitted themselves for the emergencies into which they are thrown."[30]

What seemed good for American society might also seem good for American politics. In 1842 Cornelius C. Felton, professor of classics at Harvard and a former visitor to the West, described western politics as an exercise in equal rights.

A bold but not over-educated population is growing up there [he wrote], with none of the restraints which fetter the characters of the working classes in other countries. No feudal feeling tempers the natural overflowings of passion, and restrains the growth of original humors. The sentiment of loyalty to any thing except a political party, does not exist to bind them in respectful obedience to a head and representative of the sovereignty of the nation. Each man is himself a sovereign by indefeasible right, and has no idea that another is his better in any one respect. Manners are, therefore, of the most unrestrained sort, and one accustomed to the conventions, and deferences, and distinctions, that have grown up even in our republican cities, is apt to find himself annoyed and embarrassed, when he gets into a circle of these tree-destroying sovereigns. But there are compensations for these things. There is more activity and stir in one of these new communities, than in the ancient towns. Public affairs more engross the minds of men, and are more discussed, within doors and without. Poetry and art,—music, sculpture and painting,—the last new novel, to-morrow evening's concert, last evening's "Lowell Lecture," are things unheard of; but political disquisitions, not always of the wisest, stump speeches, the affairs of the town, county, or State, and the pretensions of rival candidates, are vehemently argued.

After a visit to the West, one cannot but be struck with the comparative apathy of the New England people. We look with wonder on communities of men who attend to their own business, and seem to care but little who is made President of the United States, or even County Commissioner.

So far had conservative perspectives shifted by the end of the Middle Period that in 1850 the *American Review* found merit in western settlers' recourse to lynch law. If conservatives were not prepared to approve, some were at least ready to condone, behavior that they would once have rejected out of hand.[31]

Above all, conservatives began to see the West as an economic asset to eastern society. In part, they visualized it as a refuge for the industrious poor (rather than a vehicle of individual degradation); in part, as a guarantee of good wages (rather than a threat to eastern manufacturers). More generally, they turned their original fears upside down and described a support for eastern institutions. Edward Everett demonstrated their vulnerability to the West's material advantages when he wrote in 1829 that "many of [our] youthful republics, as we are all rightfully called, are in that state of overflowing population, which characterizes the oldest countries in Europe; although the abundance of vacant lands, and the facility of effecting a settlement upon them, have placed that point with us much lower than it stands abroad. The young men, who have emigrated from the Atlantic coast to the West, did not, like the emigrants from Ireland and the Palatinate, leave potato-fare and six pence a day behind them. On the contrary, they left a country of high wages and hearty diet. If emigration be the safety-valve of states, ours is calculated to open at a very low pressure." [32]

Caleb Cushing depicted the effect of western lands in even happier terms during the course of a Fourth of July oration in Boston in 1839. "Emigration to the West is the great safety-valve of our population, and frees us from all the dangers of the poverty, and discontent, and consequent disorders, which always spring up in a community when the number of its inhabitants has outrun its capacity to afford due recompense to honest industry and ambition." For his part, William H. Seward saw in western expansion an even more comprehensive guarantee of American felicity. "A rapid increase of population in newly explored districts," he told the Phi Beta Kappa Society of Union College in 1844, "maintains labor at higher prices, the interest of money at higher rates, and science and skill in higher estimation, here than elsewhere. From these causes, as well as from the reverence of weary, down-trodden men, to our free institutions, we derive a perpetual influx of emigrants from Europe, with talent and capital in just proportion." [33] So far as conservatives like these were concerned, the West that attracted so many easterners also promised to guard American institutions against the evils of other lands.[d]

Described in these terms, indeed, the unoccupied lands of the region became an asset to conservative politics, a powerful polemical tool as well as a source of conservative confidence. In 1820, advocating a protective tariff, Henry Clay argued that the existence of vacant lands would prevent all the evils that his critics associated with manufacturing. Representative Tristam Burges of Rhode Island invoked much the same principle in behalf of the Distribution Bill of 1830. "In what other country," he asked, ". . . is freehold and inheritance so acquired as it is in the United States? Young men in the old States, who 'work out' from sixteen to twenty-one, and whose fathers receive one-half their wages for their clothing, their home, and subsistence while not employed, can then go to the West, purchase a farm, and, with labor and economy, they are, in a few years, independent and prosperous. . . . Our country, sir, is bountiful to all her children. She takes from the common inheritance a portion, and as much, too, as he may desire, for each." Similarly, the *American Review* appealed to the western experience in 1850 to discredit contemporary social agitation. "This, then, this teeming soil has done or will do for humanity," it declared, combining a refutation of radical politics with an exhortation to aggressive individualism. "It shew us that never before has man held destiny so completely in his hands. That from the working men of America must come development, if development really lies before us in the world. It tells the Fourierist raving about conventional distinctions, that distinctions are the work of nature's hand; that the strong arm is lord of the weak one, and that he who can search the depths of his brother's soul, can turn that soul to his own will." [34]

The West not only justified Whig policies but promised to solve American problems. The *American Review* suggested as much, while the prospect helped lead Horace Greeley to change his mind about national land policy. In 1846 he wrote in the *Daily Tribune*, "Every day's reflection inclines us more and more to the opinion that the plan of holding and settling the public lands of our Union proposed by the little band who have taken the name of 'National Reformers' is the best that can be devised. . . . This system, with such modifications and safeguards as wisdom and experience may suggest, would rapidly cover the yet unappropriated public domain with an independent, substantial yeomanry, enjoying a degree of equality in opportunities and advantages such as the world has not seen." [e] So, too, in 1851 Representative George W. Julian of Indiana argued that passage of a homestead bill would retrieve "the degraded vassal of the rich" from both poverty and weakness. "Humanity to the poor thus unites with the interest of the nation in making the public domain free to those who so much need it; taking gaunt poverty into the fatherly keeping of the Government, and giving it the home of which land monopoly has deprived it; administering to it the blessings of existence, and at the same time using it as an instrumentality for building up the prosperity and wealth of the Republic." Given the appropriate national policy, both men suggested, the ends of radical reform could be solved by western geography. [35]

As conservatives became reconciled to the American democracy, in short, they were also reconciled to western development; but the promise of western development apparently helped reconcile them to the democracy. James H. Lanman, a persistent western booster from Connecticut, demonstrated as much in a paean to western republicanism. "If, as has been remarked by a distinguished statesman," he wrote in *Hunt's Merchant's Magazine* in 1841, "cities are the sores of the political body, where the bad matter of the state is concentrated, what healthful habitudes of mind and body are afforded by agricultural enterprise! . . . The agriculturist, removed from the pernicious influences that are forever accumulated in large cities, the exciting scenes, which always arise from accumulations of large bodies of men, passes a quiet and undisturbed life, possessing ample means and motives thoroughly to reflect upon his rights and duties, and holding a sufficient stake in the soil to induce him to perform those duties both for himself and his country." [36]

This was time-honored republican doctrine self-consciously applied to the needs of a commercial nation. In 1850, however, William H. Seward suggested that democracy as well as republicanism would be secured by western lands. His comment, made during debate on the admission of California to the Union, was the more significant in the light of fears he had once expressed that the education of the people did not meet the needs of the republic.

> Sir, those who would alarm us with the terrors of revolution, have not well considered the structure of this Government, and the organization of its forces. It is a democracy of property and persons, with a fair approximation toward universal education, and operating by means of universal suffrage. The constituent members of this democracy are the only persons who could subvert it; and they are not the citizens of a metropolis like Paris, or of a region subjected to the influences of a metropolis like France; but they are husbandmen, dispersed over this broad land, on the mountain and on the plain, and on the prairie, from the ocean to the Rocky Mountains, and from the great lakes to the gulf; and this people are now, while we are discussing their imaginary danger, at peace and in their happy homes, and as unconcerned and uninformed of their peril, as they are of events occurring in the moon.

The Reverend William Sparrow was even more outspoken in cataloguing the advantages the nation derived from its expanse of unoccupied territory. Our history, our politics, and our society are all assets to our liberties, he declared in 1852, but they are of relatively little significance when compared with the influence of our morality and the effects of our vacant lands. Conservatives had not abandoned their concern for free institutions so much as found them redeemed by the West they had begun by fearing. It promised to stabilize democratic politics, to guarantee equal rights, and to extend the history of liberty.[37]

THE FRONTIER WEST AS IMAGE OF AMERICAN SOCIETY

The outcome of conservative deliberations was a vision of western felicity that virtually duplicated democratic enthusiasms. Despite lurking anxieties, irrespective of residual doubts, Americans of various persuasions joined in the belief that the West would reinforce their freedoms. Harriet Martineau noted this tendency of American opinion as early as 1837, when she wrote in *Society in America,*

> The pride and delight of Americans is in their quantity of land. I do not remember meeting with one to whom it had occurred that they had too much. Among the many complaints of the minority, this was never one. I saw a gentleman strike his fist on the table in an agony at the country being so "confoundedly prosperous:" I heard lamentations over the spirit of speculation; the migration of young men to the back country; the fluctuating state of society from the incessant movement westwards; the immigration of labourers from Europe; and the ignorance of the sparse population. All these grievances I heard perpetually complained of; but in the same breath I was told in triumph of the rapid sales of land; of the glorious additions which had been made by the acquisition of Louisiana and Florida, and of the probable gain of Texas. Land was spoken of as the unfailing resource against over manufacture; the great wealth of the nation; the grand security of every man in it.

"On this head," she added, "the two political parties seem to be more agreed than on any other." [38]

Furthermore, such differences of attitude as survived tended rather to express other kinds of disagreement than to challenge the common sense of the region. To some extent, Democratic advocates of western expansion persisted in visualizing it as an arena for the extension of American agriculture, whereas Whigs were more likely to see it as an opportunity for a wide variety of enterprises. Nevertheless, Democrats also tended to enlarge their vision of its possibilities as they learned to develop the economy, just as Whigs came to value its politics as they learned to live with democracy. The transition between the older and the newer Democratic view was apparent in the overlap between Senator Richard M. Johnson's picture of the West as a refuge for the poor and his vision of western prospects. "We have a virtuous and industrious population among us," he declared in 1828, "who are willing to cultivate these lands, if they may be permitted to call their labors their own; and if the wealth and resources of the nation in any degree consist in the improvements of the country, only speak the word, and they will raise the nation to opulence unexampled. The forest will bow to the husbandman, and your wilderness will smile like Eden. Their habits urge them to the work, and a waste domain, almost boundless, invites them to its banquet." Far from representing limited hopes, the West seemingly invited aggressive exploitation.[39]

Much the same thing was true of the range of attitudes Americans expressed toward the ultimate significance of the region. Democrats tended to be insistently pragmatic in their outlook, describing a West that would minister to their material needs, whereas Whigs often perceived even the economic prospects it held out in terms of their spiritual promise.[f] Yet Whigs as well as Democrats clearly projected a future devoted to material expansion, while Democrats were also sympathetic to a vision of spiritual "empire." Oliver Wendell Holmes testified to the first point in reviewing an exhibition of Washington Allston's paintings. "For all the declamation about the sources of inspiration to be found in the grandeur of nature in our Western world, and the influences to be exerted by our free institutions," he wrote in the *North American Review* in 1840, "they have hitherto impressed a tendency to the useful, rather than the beautiful, upon the national mind. The mountains and cataracts, which were to have made poets and painters, have been mined for anthracite and dammed for water powers." Amos Kendall testified to the second point in 1843: "As a man of the West we say to the General Government, *clear out our Rivers, protect us from piracy and war on the ocean, and give us the world for a market.* Do this, and in half a century, we will show you results never surpassed in earthly beauty and protectiveness, since God planted the first garden among the four rivers of Eden." [40,g]

In other words, the West as Americans perceived it made room for their disparate hopes, while the resources it made available may have reconciled their conflicting visions of society. Certainly the idea of homestead legislation, which played a large role in the reorientation of American politics during the 1850s, answered to a combination of impulses. Democratic liberals tended to look to it to reinforce their atomistic economy, whereas the Republican successors of the Whigs were at least equally bent on serving collective needs. Yet these alternatives were compatible in the West even though they might well conflict in the East. According to their various supporters, homesteads promised to guarantee democratic equality while securing the rights of property; to promote equal opportunity while encouraging universal prosperity; and to safeguard popular freedom while promoting public order. The exploitation of western lands became a focus of national hopes not only because it fulfilled agrarian dreams but because it promised to serve a wide range of purposes without requiring any victims.[41,h]

More generally, the West was a vacant domain on which Americans could project their most cherished values, and conservatives as well as democrats found scope for their social aspirations. But it was also an unexploited reality in which they could perceive an expansive future. The aggressively Democratic journalist, Francis Grund, expressed their expectation of future achievements in relatively reserved terms when he wrote in 1837 that "every new colony of settlers contains within itself a nucleus of republican institutions, and revives, in a measure, the history of the first settlers. Its relation to the Atlantic states is similar to the situation of the early colonies with regard to the mother country, and contains the elements of freedom." Representative John Perkins Jr. of Louisiana expressed no such reservations when he addressed the House in 1854. "To my mind," he declared during debate on the disposition of the public lands,

the grandest spectacle of the age is the gradual growth of the colonies along the Pacific Coast into free and independent States, received into this Union on an equality with those on the Atlantic. On looking back a little more than a century, to the first feeble settlements on our eastern shore, and then, from the standpoint of our present national greatness, forward into the future, at the spread of civilization and art, and the growth of towns, cities, and commerce, along our western shore, the mind is by turns awed and dazzled by the vision. The Roman poet, taking his hero to a point from which he could view the successive generations of his nation spreading out into all the greatness of the Roman empire, describes him as shedding tears over the ills that he saw were to befall them. In our case, if we are wise, there is no such cause of sadness.[42]

Meanwhile conservatives came to value the West in almost the same terms. They had always been sensitive to the changes that western expansion might bring; slowly they began to visualize them as prospects that challenged the imagination rather than threats that counseled despair. In 1834, for example, the *Quarterly Christian Spectator* prefaced a typical hortatory essay on the religious needs of the West with a remarkably ambiguous testimony to its economic and political importance. "The immense extent, the unequalled fertility, and the future overwhelming influence of the west, are trite subjects. Every school-boy is by this time familiar with topics which have formed so large a part, not only of the epistolary eloquence and anniversary declamation of those who live there, and who may be viewed as interested; but of the more sober statements of judicious and unprejudiced observers. Yet the triteness of the subject renders it not the less true or important; and it would be inexcusable in the christian, to overlook the practical lesson which is thus taught." [43]

Seven years later, speaking at Union College, William Kent looked forward to a time when the valley of the Mississippi would be subdued by labor, covered by civilization, proud of its cathedrals and lyceums and universities, and famous for its painters. In 1839 the *New-York Review* described the same area as

the region where those principles which have always marked the Anglo-Saxon race, should be most perfectly developed in action. The physical characteristics of that valley, its fertility, its commercial advantages, its manufacturing capabilities, and its climate, all these promise a dense, wealthy, and working population: and when we consider the parentage of the people that will fill it, the circumstances under which they are going thither, their government, religion, literature, and other forming influences, we cannot but feel, that the prospects of what we call "the West," are wonderful beyond all precedent, and too interesting, even now, to fail in riveting the attention of every true man, and faithful christian, whose mind is once directed to the point.

Conservative fears notwithstanding, the West seemed an extraordinary national possession. [44]

So powerful were the region's attractions, in fact, that the projection of eastern expectations ultimately merged into an identification of national hopes. Whatever the United States may have been in the past, various commentators suggested, its future lay in the West. Westerners were quick to hail the fact: in 1847, Theodore Romeyn told the graduates of Rutgers College that "most assuredly in the central valley are to be the abiding place and the elements of the mighty people that are to possess and control the North American continent. Here the work of colonization and settlement is going on, with a rapidity inconceivable by those who have not witnessed it." So, too, in 1853 Jessup W. Scott, a prolific western booster, wrote in *DeBow's Review* that "the west is no longer the west; nor even the *great* west. It is the great centre. It is the body of the American eagle whose wings are on the two oceans." [45]

Easterners as well as westerners embraced this happy vision. One of them was William Kent, who observed at Union College that "if ever the hand of nature visibly pointed to the seat of empire, it will be on the continent of North America." Another was Jesse Olney, author of *A Practical System of Modern Geography*, who informed American schoolchildren that "if we glance an eye over this immense region, connected by navigable rivers—if we regard the fertility of the soil, the variety of its productions, and if we combine those advantages offered by nature, with the moral energy of the free and active people who are spreading their increasing millions over its surface—what a brilliant prospect opens upon us through the darkness of future time!" Clearly the geography of the western territories promised to enlarge the nation's destiny. [46]

In the same vein, some eastern Democrats insisted that the occupation of western lands was the key fact of American history. In 1852 Representative Galusha Grow, born in Connecticut, educated in Massachusetts, and representing northeastern Pennsylvania, equated westward migration with the nation's highest traditions. "During the two and a quarter centuries since Jamestown and Plymouth Rock were consecrated by the exile," he admonished the House during debate on the Homestead Bill, "trace the footsteps of the pioneer, as he has gone forth to found new States, and build up new empires. In these two and a quarter centuries, from an unbroken forest, you have a country embracing almost every variety of production, and extending through almost every zone. . . . In these two and a quarter centuries, a whole continent has been converted to the use of man, and upon its bosom has arisen the noblest empire on the globe. True, the united energy, enterprise, and industry of the entire American people have produced this vast result." [47]

Governor Horatio Seymour of New York developed an even more expansive vision of the West as the focus of American history. Compared with the great movement of population across the Atlantic Ocean, he declared in 1855 in a speech at Tammany Hall,

the subjects of European diplomacy are trivial. This is the great combat which is to tell upon the destinies of nations, and the history of the world. No Alexander or Caesar in the height of their conquests, ever made such acquisitions of power as immigration brings to us.

But those who are against the cause of their country in this contest, contend that immigration brings with it destitution, poverty and crime. Trace these hands of strong-limbed but poor foreigners until they plant themselves upon the hitherto useless land of the West, and see how wealth is evolved by their very contact with the soil. They were poor, and the fertile land was valueless, but combine these two kinds of poverty and the wealth which alchemists dreamed of, is the magical result.

The West as these men perceived it not only protected American institutions but constituted their unique significance.[48]

Hence the West was also the chief arena for fulfilling the American mission. Representative Dunham of Indiana argued as much in denouncing aid to Hungary in 1852: "If we take too much of your population from the old States, supply yourselves from those daily seeking homes upon our shores; and, in doing this, we shall be accomplishing the great mission for which we were sent—to relieve mankind, and restore to them liberty and happiness." Representative John L. Dawson of Pennsylvania urged the same visionary hope, untainted by Dunham's isolationism, during debate on the Homestead Bill:

The American Government is the great pioneer in the cause of freedom. By the force of republican principles and of unexampled success, it has advanced in nationality until it is now hailed as a beacon-light for every continent, and a star of hope for every people. With a population of but three millions, at the close of the Revolution, we now have twenty-three millions: with but thirteen States, we now have thirty-one, and territory enough for fifty more—a Union stretching across a continent from one great ocean to the other. All that is wanted to develop its great resources and fulfill its destiny, is a population commensurate with the fertility of its soil and the extent of its territory.[49]

The West defined American history and it would also renew American liberty. A number of western Democrats made this plain in their state constitutional conventions. Isaac Crary spoke for them when he declared in the Michigan convention of 1835–36 that "he was not willing to accede to whatever had been incorporated into the constitutions of the older states without giving the same a severe scrutiny. Their condition was different from ours. Many of their constitutions were made and adopted when they were in the full vigor of manhood—while we are the creatures of yesterday. They were fettered by long established customs and habits—we, though not entirely free from them, have more of the spirit of the uncaged eagle. Our habits as a whole people are many of them yet to be formed—our institutions are yet to be built up." [50]

This may have been western hyperbole, but it was echoed in an eastern source. In 1841 the *Democratic Review* hailed the coming of age in the West in much the same terms:

We of the Atlantic shore have not yet recovered from a certain paralyzing influence produced on the free development and movement of our national mind, by that colonial relation toward the mother-country, which the Revolution destroyed only in its political point of view. The West stands more free from those impalpable moral trammels of English dependance, which we sometimes think have sadly dwarfed the growth of our intellectual stature. . . . We look to see yet in the West a bolder and a manlier action of the American mind, which will scorn that emasculate imitativeness of England and English things that yet holds us in an unworthy thraldom, which will surrender itself more freely to the guidance of the genius of American democracy, and will find an inspiration stimulating it to achievements worthy of itself, in all those vast sublimities of nature, ever young in her most hoary age, that are there spread out before it as though for this very purpose.

More briefly, the organ of the Democratic party looked to western settlement to fulfill the pattern of history and perpetuate its liberal values.[51]

To this extent the West remained Democratic and a vehicle for democratic ends, but conservative spokesmen demonstrated that it answered to their purposes too. One of them was James S. Allan, who suggested to the literary society of Centre College in 1835 that the United States could not have reached its present eminence without the experience of westward migration. On the one hand, he paid tribute to the colonists of New England, who had occupied a new land; on the other, he eulogized western settlers, who had brought the nation to its present condition: "The spirit infused into the west by our pioneer fathers is no less to be applauded. The ardent, impulsive, buoyant character of their children, is suited to the growth of generosity, enterprize, elevated pride, boldness of original conception; in a word, all that constitutes the *soul* of a state."

Thirteen years later Thomas M. Foote took comfort from the same phenomenon as he contemplated the uncertain future of the region. "The great danger to be apprehended," he explained to the literary societies of Hamilton College,

is, that a people so abounding in enterprise and energetic action may, in their pursuit of the material, lose sight of the spiritual. But even in this regard, I would cherish a sanguine and hopeful spirit. The great West, that in its growth and developement, its restless enterprise and the heterogeneous elements that make up its population, may be taken as a somewhat exaggerated type of the whole country, will warrant the trust that throughout the land, as we have witnessed there, will grow up among our people, without any detraction from their high hope, self-reliance and untiring energy, a more perfect civilization, more extended intellectual culture and a purer moral development.[52]

These were carefully balanced estimates by comparison with the assessment of western influence that some western enthusiasts developed. In 1840 James H. Lanman reported in *Hunt's Merchant's Magazine*, "The people of the west are generous, though crude, unmindful from habit of the luxuries of life, endowed with great boldness and originality of mind, from the circumstances under which they are placed. They are, from the various elements of which they are composed, in a state of amalgamation, and from this amalgamation a new and valuable form of American character will spring up." John M. Peck went further still when he climaxed a long career of writing hopeful accounts of the West, intended to elicit missionary effort, by arguing in the *Christian Review* that the blending of "Puritans" and "Cavaliers," not to mention a host of foreign nationalities, had produced a new American character, which the West had further developed. As a result, westerners displayed "great energy, and the spirit of enterprise," intense patriotism, "strong social feelings," "high-toned republicanism, or strong democratic tendencies," a zeal for education, a universal spirit of improvement, and an "increasing influence of pure Christianity." In short, they were very nearly paragons of American manhood; and "the feelings of honor, the abhorrence of falsehood, and entire frankness of Western Character only need to be animated by deep, ardent, and intelligent piety to make us what we ought to be." If missionary effort was still required, his analysis suggested that it would be a mission to the heart of America.[53]

In this sense the missionary impulse conservatives felt was finally transformed by the region it was applied to; by the end of the Middle Period even New Englanders tended to perceive the region across the mountains as an image of their hopes. In 1858 Representative Eli Thayer of Massachusetts, a founder of the Emigrant Aid Society, announced to the House of Representatives that the United States had solved the problems of territorial expansion by providing its newest settlements with the advantages of churches and schools. "Sir, in years gone by, our emigration has ever tended toward barbarism. But now, by this method, it is tending to a higher civilization than we have ever witnessed. Why, sir, by this plan, a new community starts on as high a plane as the old one had ever arrived at; and leaving behind the dead and decayed branches which incumbered the old, with the vigorous energies of youth, it presses on and ascends. Sir, such a State will be the State of Kansas, eclipsing in its progress all the other States of this nation, because it was colonized in this way." Thayer was typical of his kind in his concern for replicating eastern institutions, but he looked to a West that enjoyed them to be a pioneer for American liberty.[54]

Meanwhile Charles W. Upham, reviewing histories of the Nebraska Territory and the Emigrant Aid Society for the *North American Review*, had rewritten the history of the world to bring it to a focus in the West. On the one hand, he saw in the peopling of the American hemisphere an act of social and political "regeneration" of which no man knew the outcome. On the other hand, he argued that the same developmental process was now at work on the American continent, defining the national character and establishing a new course for humanity. At one time, he held, the continent as a whole had been the refuge of human liberty, but the West had inherited its mantle and represented the future of the American experiment. Moreover, if he hoped for eastern policies that would preserve western freedom, he also looked to western liberty for the salvation of mankind:

From that central heart will flow influences, for good or ill, that will reach each ocean shore and extend from the equator to the pole. If society is built up there upon the eternal basis of right and liberty,—if freedom and education illuminate and bless all classes and all employments,—if every being within its limits, bearing the lineaments of a man, partakes of the common sovereignty and shares in the common lot,—then we may be sure that from it a light will irradiate that will kindle with its beams the elements of social progress and regeneration in all the surrounding regions, and throughout the world.[55]

Ever hopeful of eastern influences, in short, conservatives came to embrace a West that nearly duplicated democratic visions. As a result they were to discover a hero who would in time be as significant as Andrew Jackson. The *American Review* demonstrated the ultimate thrust of their thought in May of 1850 when, in an essay on the western prairies, it adopted a picturesque West to which it attributed "perfect social equality," asylum for those who needed it, a powerful social ethic, and unprecedented opportunities for success and personal distinction. It continued by saying,

Little wonder is it then that individuals in the West so often rise from the lowest vocations to celebrity. One is now before our mind, who, in his youth, swung the axe for fifty cents a day, and whom early manhood found spelling over his a, b, c's. But the best of all educations for the battle of life, the knowledge of men, this bounteous land had given him in common with all its sons. He is now an accomplished lawyer, and a whig representative in Congress. Such men know the value of the institutions under which they grow up, and not one jot or title [*sic*] of their well balanced conservation [*sic*] would they abate. We hope shortly to be able to present our readers with a portrait of this gentleman. "Long and lank and brown, as is the ribbed sea-sand," ungainly in figure, and attenuated in face, its knightly lines impress, and its frank conciliation wins. His warm blood flames in his eye, but his *bonhommie* is irresistible by crowds or individuals.

For conservatives as well as democrats, the West most men could only imagine had become the image of American society.[56]

CONSEQUENCES

✛ XIII ✛

CONSEQUENCES

A history that culminated in America, society reduced to its individual atoms, a polity devoted to maintaining popular rights by minimizing the scope of government, institutions that would preserve social order by means compatible with liberty—these were the beliefs that dominated American social thought by the close of the Middle Period. Not only were they the rationalizations men appealed to in order to vindicate their public measures; they were also the intellectual categories through which those same men increasingly perceived their experience. The politics of Whiggery were a classic demonstration of the power they acquired: however conservative typical Whigs may have been at the start, whatever the disingenuousness with which they first adopted Democratic rhetoric, they ended by embracing most of the ideas their fathers had condemned. By 1850 it was difficult for most Americans to think in other terms.

Needless to say, Americans did not always behave as their doctrines said they should; the activity of state legislatures in bestowing selective charters well into the 1860s was only one of many ways in which their practice ignored their prescriptions. Nevertheless, the doctrines remained in force as a test of the practices men actually adopted. When Americans acted in their private capacities or when they felt a public need, they might well take measures that their theory could not condone. But when they acted in the public eye, or when they sought to remedy public evils, they felt a constant pressure to come to terms with the beliefs they said they held.

The policies they adopted demonstrated the latent force of those beliefs. Americans were expansionists at home and isolationists abroad, as their historiography taught them they should be; they diminished the authority of government and encouraged economic exploitation, in keeping with "equal rights"; they democratized their politics while they strengthened constitutional government, as their fear of power suggested; and they "solved" their problems of order by disestablishing the churches and developing public schools, as their idea of free institutions required. Their failures as well as their successes were controlled by these same perspectives. Their economy was unstable and it developed rampant evils, but they persisted in freeing it from controls when they might better have worked to shape it.[1] Their liberties were imperfect and they earned true liberals' scorn, but the Americans held fast to their coercions as the basis of their freedoms. Even the aberrations modern historians have decried were frequently instances of doctrine that had overridden common sense. Anti-masonry was preposterous, but it reflected widespread fears; nullification was intolerable, but it built upon democratic constitutionalism; nativism was obscene, but it answered to national ideals. The Americans were clearly committed to the dogmas they pursued as well as to the successes they enjoyed.

Above all, the doctrines they developed and made into a system of belief during the 1830s and 1840s shaped their thought and experience during the decade of the 1850s. Acting out the roles that their sense of history had provided them, encouraging economic growth within the framework of their hopes, exercising their authority as they thought their polity permitted, and grounding their freedom in the liberal institutions they had developed, Americans discovered that they faced a number of unsolved national problems and looked for means of solving them within the intellectual framework they had acquired. More briefly, the ideas of the Middle Period were the agenda of the republic as it approached the Civil War, and the war was the preeminent consequence of the ideas it had developed.

The evidence for this proposition forms the substance of this chapter, but we may anticipate its main elements here. In brief, the chapter argues that the Civil War took place because of various intellectual phenomena that bore a largely fortuitous relationship to each other. One was the moral imperative to eliminate slavery, in the first instance a conservative commitment to moral reform that flourished during the 1830s and broadened during the 1840s, but that was limited by its origins and largely ineffective among democrats. Another was the deepening of northern concern for the preservation of American liberties—economic and political, institutional and historical—which had little to do with slavery but much to do with its extension. Still another was the role Democratic doctrines played in producing Republican victories by dismaying northern voters and reinforcing northern fears. Last was southern intransigence, which challenged northern values and invited northern attack. All played major parts in the confrontations of the 1850s, and the interactions among them touched off the final disaster.*

THE DEVELOPMENT OF A MORAL IMPERATIVE

The initial steps toward war were taken by religious reformers who invoked divine antagonism toward human slavery as an ineluctable command to conscience. Neither their numbers nor their influence was sufficient to precipitate the conflict, but they developed a social theory that contributed to that event. The history of their efforts is only partly included in the history of the abolitionists, who have attracted a good deal of attention from historians because they were the radicals of the antislavery cause. The radicalism of the abolitionists, however, was something like the radicalism that Emerson and Theodore Parker displayed when they dealt with contemporary religious issues: it elaborated doctrinal innovations at the expense of more common values, and it often ended by antagonizing the audience to whom it was ostensibly addressed. The sentiment we are concerned with here was a widespread conservative position; the sentiment of aggressive abolition was an extrapolation that relatively few men were willing to adopt.†

The basic position was conservative in the same sense that most clerical moralists remained conservatives during the decades of democratic growth. Both moralists in general and antislavery spokesmen in particu-

---

* My account here is intended to be an interpretive essay rather than a treatise, although its topic deserves at least a volume; it is focused on the ways in which the ideas of the Middle Period precipitated civil war, not on all the causes that may have contributed to that catastrophe. Therefore I do not make any systematic effort to deal with the immense amount of information that has grown up about the war, although I have obviously used some of it for my purposes and have been influenced by particular studies. Readers who are interested in learning which works I have found most useful or suggestive should consult note 2 for this chapter.

† Another cautionary note seems necessary here: I do not seek to trace all the currents of thought that may have entered into the antislavery crusade, but to establish the main outlines of antislavery sentiment as a given in order to assess its role in the confrontations of the 1850s. By the same token, I shall not pursue the sectarian intricacies that divided the antislavery agitators. For our purposes I think I am better advised to look for the common premises that informed their moral crusade, inasmuch as the influence they achieved clearly depended upon the attitudes they shared rather than the principles that divided them. Readers who wish to know what secondary works I have found most useful in dealing with antislavery thought should consult note 3 for this chapter.

lar tended to assume an organic society in which all men had their place, and both also presupposed social hierarchy, which assigned authority to religious leaders because they represented spiritual values. As we have seen, the manner in which they sought to exercise their appointed role had changed, but the role itself survived: the clergy and their allies functioned as critics of secular error who spoke for divine obligation, and they devoted their public careers to elevating the nation's behavior to the level of its religious standards. No secular activity was immune to their strictures, and if they were more likely to condemn Democratic errors than to reproach Whig policies, they also applied their moral indignation to any evils they could see. In this sense the antislavery agitators were the conscience of American conservatism—men who stood fast by virtue while the Whigs abandoned their responsibilities. They were reformers because they were moralists, and opponents of slavery because they were reformers.[a]

They began with the premise of moral order that most Protestants took for granted, but they converted it into an injunction that devout men were hard put to evade. William Ladd, the founder of the American Peace Society, articulated the fundamental faith common to most reformers when he wrote in 1840, "It is an incontrovertible axiom, that *every thing of a moral nature which ought to be done, can be done.*" Charles G. Finney put the same idea more forcefully when he told the businessmen who came to his revivals, "Only make it your invariable rule to do right, and do business upon principle, and you control the market. The ungodly will be obliged to conform to your standard. It is perfectly in the power of the church to regulate the commerce of the world, if they will only themselves maintain perfect integrity." For moralists of an active disposition, at any rate, the truths of Protestant theology came to a focus in secular obligation.[4]

It went without saying that the obligation the moralists described was personal in the sense that it was addressed to conscience, while the fact that it came home to individuals meant that it did not point to an agreed-upon solution for the evils they became aware of. Nevertheless, as Stanley Elkins has pointed out, the personal nature of the obligation created immense pressures on the men who felt it; if the character of their action might vary, its necessity was overwhelming. Finney clearly assumed as much when he announced that "Christians can no more take neutral ground on [slavery], since it has come up for discussion, than they can take neutral ground on the subject of the sanctification of the Sabbath." Similarly, John Greenleaf Whittier exhorted his countrymen to recognize their immense moral responsibility to overcome slavery every time they went to the polls. "Freemen, Christians, lovers of truth and justice!" he charged them in *Justice and Expediency* (1833),

Why stand ye idle? Ours is a government of opinion, and slavery is interwoven with it. Change the current of opinion, and slavery will be swept away. Let the awful sovereignty of the people—a power which is limited only by the sovereignty of Heaven, arise and pronounce judgment against the crying iniquity. Let each individual remember that upon himself rests a portion of that sovereignty; a part of the tremendous responsibility of its exercise. The burning, withering concentration of public opinion upon the Slave system is alone needed for its total annihilation. God has given us the power to overthrow it;—a power, peaceful, yet mighty—benevolent, yet effectual—"awful without severity"—a moral strength equal to the emergency.[5]

Both arguments also suggested the extent to which the reformers held individual Christians responsible for the evils other men practiced. This, too, was a long-established principle in the American religious creed, nowhere more evident than in clerical appeals to universal conversion as a prelude to national redemption. Finney demonstrated its specifically reformist connotations very clearly when he admonished his faithful hearers, "I believe the time has come, and although I am no prophet, I believe it will be found to have come, that the revival in the United States will continue and prevail, no farther and faster than the church take right ground upon this subject. . . . Let the churches of all denominations speak out on the subject of temperance, let them close their doors against all who have any thing to do with the death-dealing abomination, and the cause of temperance is triumphant. A few years would annihilate the traffic. Just so with slavery." Operating on the same assumptions, Angelina Grimké Weld told the abolitionists of Philadelphia in 1838 that "the great men of this country will not do this work; the church will never do it. A desire to please the world, to keep the favor of all parties and of all conditions, makes them dumb on this and every other unpopular subject. They have become worldly-wise, and therefore God, in his wisdom, employs them not to carry on his plans of reformation and salvation. He hath chosen the foolish things of the world to confound the wise, and the weak to overcome the mighty." [6]

The pressure of all these injunctions clearly threatened the sectional peace. By the close of the 1830s, Christian moralists had not only indicted the American republic for its tolerance of southern practices but also laid an obligation to eradicate them upon the shoulders of all true believers. They had also minimized the obstacles to the moral reform they championed. Assuming that the divine economy made every measure possible, they held that the intractable institution of slavery was as amenable to moral persuasion as were lesser evils like intemperance and Sabbath-breaking, which clearly depended upon individual dispositions. To this extent they had articulated a moral imperative against slavery that was subject to practical failure, but they had also described the institution's survival as evidence of national sin. Hence future debates over slavery were likely to take place within a framework of extraordinary urgency: a blight on the American conscience, slavery might also come to seem the occasion of the ultimate battle between the forces of Good and Evil.

Certainly prominent religious spokesmen represented the territorial disputes of the 1850s as occasions for moral effort. In 1850, replying to critics who had condemned it for meddling with political questions, the *Independent* argued that it kept aloof from parties; but it also made a point of asserting that Christians must stand for principle and that they could not compromise with sin. Such moral obstinacy was widely diffused, as the Reverend Ezra S. Gannett, the Unitarian minister of the Federal Street Meetinghouse in Boston, demonstrated in 1854. A man of irenic disposition who acknowledged that the advocates of slavery in the territories might be honest and respectable even if they were mistaken, he insisted nevertheless that the North must either forestall them or contemplate secession. Two years later Philip S. Cleland, the orthodox pastor of the Presbyterian church of Greenwood (Indiana), used the occasion of a Thanksgiving sermon to reassert the authority of the higher law. "If God's law is higher than man's law," he declared in accents reminiscent of Timothy Dwight,

it is the right and duty of those who are appointed to declare that law, to preach against the sins of government, and of all who are in authority. . . . If the government violates and virtually abrogates the Sabbath by running the mail and opening the post offices on that holy day, the pulpit must not keep silence because it is a political measure. If ungodly politicians trample down the plighted faith of the Nation and the sacred principles of liberty, in order to extend the wicked, cruel, blighting system of slavery, the ministers of righteousness can not connive at such enormity by cowardly holding their peace.[7]

Meanwhile clergymen of a more strenuous disposition equated the politics of national liberty with the theology of national salvation. In 1851 D. F. Robertson, speaking at the Broadway Tabernacle in New York, delivered a classic jeremiad on the theme of national decay. Deploring Protestant dissidence and condemning Roman Catholicism, attacking secular instruction in the public schools and irreligion in public office, he also indicted American slavery as a devastating national sin. "The Constitution of the United States may hold together the various States in federal unity. I hope it may. But the curse will fall and strike what is more precious to every man and every family, than even the National Constitution. Alas, the curse is already out and doing its work. The general obtuseness of the public conscience, north and south, and at the seat of government, respecting the *present* operations and tendencies of slavery, is a demonstration of this curse, to any man whose moral sense remains to control his thinking and his opinions." Five years later the Reverend Asahel Brooks asked his Presbyterian congregation in Chicago, "Do we fully realize that with the enthroning of slavery over the land we utterly subordinate the gospel of our Lord and Saviour, and deprive ourselves of the power to perform the great commands of our supreme authority, to go and preach the gospel to every nation? Let slavery have the reign in our government, and she will unite Church and State, and take the control of the christian pulpit in an hour." [8]

The upshot was often a vision of the western territories as the scene of an apocalyptic confrontation between Liberty and the Devil. It was significant that the Reverend Robertson equated slavery with the threat from the Catholic Church; his juxtaposition of these deadly evils not only documented his fundamentalist bias but reinforced his sense of crisis. So, too, in 1856 the Reverend M. K. Whittlesey told the First Congregational Church of Ottawa (Illinois) that the same two evils portended the final battle for God's kingdom. Even more important, however, was the fact that whether or not they were dedicated anti-Catholics, the most vigorous religious spokesmen for antislavery expressed the same kind of fervor that Lyman Beecher had tried to enlist in his *Plea for the West*. According to Whittlesey, for example,

The elements opposing here can never be quieted or reconciled. They are in their own nature conflicting and mutually exterminating. The battle begun about slavery, in the forming of our Federal Union, will never cease till slavery or liberty is subjugated and vanquished. Every year adds fuel to the flame. All attempts to smother it out make it burn the fiercer. Endeavors to quiet agitation fail. God is against them. The battle must be fought through. Christ's gospel is engaged in it. Strong must that man be who shall plant himself against the advancing cause of christian [sic] freedom, and say to Jesus Christ, "Thy truth, liberty and love, shall never enter this domain of mine." [9]

Three years later the Reverend Daniel Rice of Lafayette (Indiana) demonstrated the ultimate thrust of religious antislavery when he greeted the news from Harpers Ferry with an even-handed criticism of northern as well as southern "phillipics" [sic], only to point out that "after you have set aside the equally wild and half crazy fanaticism of both sections, . . . yet remain the deliberate utterances of the advocates of slavery, and the advocates of freedom. This hostility is so radical and essential that it deserves special attention in this discussion.—Mark—not a hostility between the North and the South, the slaveholder and the non-slaveholder, but between the very spirit of freedom and of slavery." Although Rice was careful to make a distinction between sectional and philosophical struggle, his argument virtually obliterated it: the confrontation he described between slavery and freedom quickly metamorphosed into a quasi-religious confrontation between competing sections:

On a goodly soil they have grown to be giants in stature, and now rock the continent with the weight of their tread. The eye of each is fixed on empire, and unsatisfied with the boundaries of a Continent is looking out for stepping stones to other realms in the isles [o]f the ocean. The one, with [t]he eye of an eagle, looks out for territory where she may multiply free men, the other with the eye of a hawk, for territory where she may multiply slaves. In infancy side by side they might sleep together.—In childhood, their fallings out might be deemed only the short-lived quarrels incident to this period of life. But not so with the fully developed contrarieties and hostilities of their mature and independent manhood. Their strongest dislike, their bitterest hatred, their intensest hostility is and ever must be that which they feel towards each other.

Even clergymen who did not preach a war of liberation responded to the deepening crisis of the 1850s by condoning national strife as an evil that had been necessitated by national sin.[10]

Nevertheless the question still remained how far their clamor would be effective, and the efforts they made to enforce it suggest that it was only partly persuasive so long as it was tied to morality. The core of the clergymen's difficulty lay in the fact that many democrats as well as Democrats remained obdurate in their hostility toward humanitarian reform. So far as slavery was concerned, they deprecated the reformers' motives and took issue with their premises; they challenged their ways of thinking and denounced their moral zeal. More generally, good Democrats rebelled at the conservative assumptions that underlay most appeals to conscience and repudiated the reformers' prescriptions because they threatened popular freedom.

Senator John B. Weller of California articulated one of their characteristic reactions to antislavery agitation when he attacked the Independent Democrats who had aligned themselves against the Kansas-Nebraska Bill. Inconceivable though it may seem in retrospect, he argued that the "abolitionists" of Ohio would never again control the actions of its legislature or return another senator like Salmon P. Chase. His reasoning was as interesting as his prediction was mistaken. "In a social point of view," he told the Senate in 1853, "I should be sorry, sir, to lose the Senator from Ohio; but unless he abandons his errors and renounces his heresies, his political days are numbered. It is not probable that a contingency will ever occur again when a great political party will be willing to throw itself into the hands of a few Abolitionists, and sacrifice principle in order to obtain place." [11] In the eyes of this typical Democratic politician, the clamor over slavery in the territories was the device of a factious minority to achieve public office in defiance of the people's best judgment.[b]

Presumably one reason many Democrats took Weller's view of antislavery was that they could not credit the reformers' attachment to the rights of Negro slaves. In modern terms they were racists, but the term partly misses the point: rather, they were often populist democrats who could not embrace social reform except in terms of equal rights, which they could not imagine extending to black men, and therefore they were persuaded to read antislavery agitation as a perverse attempt to under-mine democratic principles. Senator James Shields of Illinois expressed their fundamental sense of racial limits in dignified and even humane terms during debate on the Compromise of 1850: "All I have seen, and heard, and read, convince me that when there are two distinct races in the same community, one inferior and the other superior, like the negro and the white race, a state of mild and gentle slavery is the safest and happiest condition for the inferior race. Equality of rights and equality in the hard struggle of life, result in the insensible but certain extermination of the inferior race. You may give the slave liberty if you please, but that very liberty is his destruction." [12]

Democrats also repudiated antislavery as an expression of the reform-ers' "fanaticism," a term they commonly used to describe almost any moral effort to intrude on secular freedom. Calvin Britain articulated their deeply grounded hostility to the premises of conservative reform when—although an advocate of temperance himself—he opposed legisla-tive prohibition in the constitutional convention of Michigan.

We are here making a constitution to be submitted to the people for their appro-bation or disapprobation. I desire to so submit it that it shall be entirely discon-nected with any question that would embarrass their judgment and action upon it. I wish to save it from the operation of several fanaticisms. I desire to save it from the fanaticism produced by men who lecture upon temperance as a trade, because it is easier to support themselves in that way than by labor. I desire to save it from the fanaticism produced by the reformed drunkard, who, instead of "repenting in sackcloth and ashes" for his crimes, justifies himself, and, Adam-like, charges the whole fault upon the "rum-seller." I desire to save it from the fanaticism of those moral reformers who, possessing a "zeal which is not ac-cording to knowledge," and forgetting the divine injunction "to be subject to the higher powers, for the powers that be are ordained of God," weaken the con-fidence of the people in the wisdom and integrity of your most patriotic and enlightened statesmen, slander and degrade your laws, and through the license of a temperance lecture, invade the temple of human liberty, and attempt to enthrone therein a tyrant more intolerable than Nero himself.

Six years later Orestes Brownson employed the same kind of argument to discredit the Republican party, and although he spoke with a Catholic bias it corresponded to many Protestants' antipathies: "The views the anti-slavery men and the Maine Liquor Law men hold may be very wise and very just, and it may be their right and their duty to carry them out by argument and moral suasion; on that question we offer here no opinion; but they have no right to attempt to carry them out politically, and to get them embodied in civil enactments. To do it were to enter upon a course of political agitation and civil legislation as fatal to all personal freedom and independence as that sanctioned by John Calvin at Geneva, or attempted by the New England Puritans in early Colonial times." Democrats who took issue with antislavery were insensitive to the claims of blacks, but they were often insistent defenders of the liberties that whites had gained.[13]

They remained, in short, enemies of the very substance of moral reform, the hope of enforcing moral principle by appeals to public authority. Horatio Seymour summed up their position in speaking at Tammany Hall, where he invoked self-government, individual autonomy, and a policy of laissez faire against a battery of modern enthusiasms that included nativism, prohibition, and attempts to interfere with slavery. "We reject legislative legerdemain," he concluded, employing a familiar Democratic epithet to belabor his many targets. "We have but one petition to our law makers—it is, to be let alone. We have one reliance for good government, the intelligence of the people; one source of wealth, the honest, thinking labor of our country; one hope for our workshops, the skill of our mechanics; one impulse for our commerce, the untrameled [sic] enterprise of our merchants; one remedy for moral evils, religious education; one object for our political exertions, the common good of our great and glorious country." In the following year the Democratic State Convention, representing both factions of the party, lumped all of its opponents together as advocates of intrusive reform. (Significantly, it also charged them with hypocrisy, as the *Democratic Review* had done two decades earlier in condemning contemporary conservatives for trying to appeal to religious sentiments to serve their partisan ends.) Its allegations were obviously polemical and its politics were clearly misguided, but they echoed Democratic principles that condemned conservative reform.[14]

Meanwhile, partly conscious of Democratic resistance and partly moved by democratic ideals, some of the antislavery reformers sought to enlist the American public in their cause by appealing to human rights. We are inclined to honor these agitators for their devotion to universal liberty, but we must also note the ambiguities of their position, which tended to nullify their efforts. Either they advocated complete equality for the blacks and antagonized most of the nation, or they campaigned in the name of lesser liberties that marked only an incomplete accommodation to democracy.

Their dilemma was broadly apparent in the uncertain way in which they insisted upon rights for blacks. Although radicals like William Lloyd Garrison fully embraced the blacks as equals, moderates who were no less opposed to slavery as an institution could not bring themselves to adopt that extreme position. For one thing it was not politic, but its politics were hardly central; rather, these moralists perceived the claims of the blacks in terms that befitted their needs as men but missed their rights as citizens. In effect, as Albert Barnes demonstrated in his judicious *Inquiry into the Scriptural Views of Slavery* (1846), they declared that slaves were deprived of privileges that belonged to men as moral beings—those of marriage and parenthood, of worship and the avails of one's labor—but they ignored their potential claims as democrats. Even the more zealous reformers often made the same ambiguous case. In 1839 Theodore Weld compiled *American Slavery As It Is* to prove the evils of slavery by extracts from southern newspapers. His account was most telling because it was highly circumstantial, but the circumstances it documented invited sympathy for a downtrodden people rather than dedication to equal rights. So did Charles Sumner's famous indictment of "The Barbarism of Slavery," delivered in the Senate in 1860, which was a catalogue of moral infringements that characterized the peculiar institution and came to a focus on the master class for its complicity in social sins.[15,c]

To the extent that Sumner believed in racial equality, moreover, his argument against "barbarism" was deliberately tangential, an attempt to sway public opinion by appealing to emotions that had little to do with his principles. Similarly, Weld made no bones about his wish to reach the public mind by the manner of his presentation. "Reader," he prefaced his anthology, "you are empannelled as a juror to try a plain case and bring in an honest verdict. The question at issue is not one of law, but of fact—'What is the actual condition of the slaves in the United States?' A plainer case never went to a jury." Other dedicated agitators also appealed to essentially tangential concerns in order to enlist popular sympathies. Chief among them was the right of free speech, which they asserted whenever possible against southern efforts to control it. In Illinois, Elijah Lovejoy courted martyrdom in his zeal for abolition, and the fact that he quickly attained it became one of the rallying points of the cause. Similarly, the congressional opponents of slavery sought to broaden their moral influence by campaigning against the "gag rule" that southerners had invoked to cut off their flow of petitions. More generally, spokesmen who were committed to ending slavery made every effort they could devise to equate its continued existence with infringements on northern rights.[16]

They clamored for northern rights to bolster their moral reform, but they faced oppressive difficulties because of the idea of rights they expressed. For one thing, as Tocqueville clearly noted, ordinary American democrats were not devoted to free speech understood as a philosophical absolute. He might well have added that the ideal was predominantly conservative, in that it was most often invoked by Whiggish sources, and that its association with such spokesmen must have diminished its claims on the public.[17] Moreover, whether or not American democrats were committed to free speech as a general principle, many of them were apparently convinced that the needs of public order required the suppression of antislavery radicalism. Their conviction on this score was compatible with their idea of freedom as it was expressed in "free institutions," and it acquired additional force as they came to fear for the nation's survival.

Representative Daniel E. Sickles, a Democratic party stalwart from New York City who was to achieve an uncertain fame at Gettysburg, demonstrated this conviction in an address of 1859 in which he moved almost unconsciously from mocking the moral reformers to denouncing their claims to freedom, the mockery expressing Democratic complacency and the denunciation Democratic fears.

Meetings, they say, . . . have been held in the State. I observed the proceedings of the most noticeable one at Syracuse. It was the only considerable gathering, I think, in New York. Now, sir, anybody who knows New York, could not be astonished at any assemblage that might be seen at Syracuse. Syracuse is to my State what I might call a city of refuge. Everybody can go there and hold meetings or conventions, for any purpose under heaven. There is no revolution in society so radical, there is no extravagance in politics or philosophy so repugnant to reason or experience, there is nothing which can attract the human intellect so erratic or so absurd, which may not collect together its admirers and advocates at Syracuse, and nobody will disturb them. They have no theatres there, and the people rely upon such things for their amusement. . . . Men and women meet there in grave convention, and resolve that the salvation of the country and the peace and good order of society depends [sic] upon conceding the ballot and the Bloomer costume to all women in the Commonwealth.

Suddenly, however, his mood turned, and he went on to say,

These strange meetings are held in almost all northern cities. They denounce the Bible; they denounce the Church; they denounce our social system, as well as the social system of the South; they meet and discuss and resolve the downfall of everything that we hold precious, as well as menace the peace and safety of remote portions of the Confederacy. They are tolerated, because toleration is northern sentiment—I will not say peculiar to the North: but which we have, in common with others, who regard toleration to be expedient or right. When, however, it is found that such meetings have for their objects movements and designs of a seditious character, they will not be tolerated.

Even Democrats who were loyal to liberty drew a line at abolitionists' rights.[18]

THE SHIFTING BASIS OF ANTISLAVERY:
SOCIETY AND POLITICS

Given Democratic principles, there was little that conservative moralists could do to sway democratic opinion. Hence the specifically moral agitation of the 1830s tended to weaken during the 1840s and remain ineffectual during the 1850s. In its place, however, another kind of sentiment arose to condemn the peculiar institution; the moralists' efforts faltered, to be redeemed by democratic anxieties. By 1860 a good many northern democrats had been converted to antislavery.

The primary ground of their conversion was the threat of southern rights. Pragmatically, legally, even philosophically, it should have been possible for a majority of northern democrats to accept the events of the 1850s and wait out southern demands; they had little to fear from southern expansion and much to gain by temporizing. In practice, however, the recurrent debates on territorial expansion worked to rouse democratic apprehensions and deepen the democrats' antipathies toward the South. In this respect their ideas clearly outran their experience. Although practical economic issues like the development of western rivers and harbors and the location of a transcontinental railroad undoubtedly helped to intensify sectional animosities, only fears for the nation's future can explain northern democrats' behavior. At bottom, they could not live with slavery because they perceived in it a still more threatening enemy to democratic values than the enemies they had feared over the course of the previous thirty years. Not every northern democrat shared this apprehensive perspective, for reasons we shall consider later, but the Republican victory of 1860 demonstrated its influence on the rank and file of the party.[d]

The victory of 1860 also demonstrated the democrats' influence on the persuasions of American conservatives, who abandoned most of their traditional premises in favor of essentially populist arguments against slavery. To some extent their conversion was undoubtedly polemical, a deliberately manipulative effort to find new ways of attracting popular support for their candidates for office. (In this respect it was clearly reminiscent of earlier conservative efforts to weaken Democratic loyalties by pretending to democratic values.) To a large extent, however, the conversion was probably genuine, a true shift of opinion stimulated in part by the political confrontations of the 1830s and 1840s, but both facilitated and accelerated by the growing democratic clamor against slavery. In any event the motives that impelled it were less important than the enthusiasm with which conservatives embraced an insistently liberal vision of American society: Whigs metamorphosed into Republicans in order to celebrate their devotion to democracy, which they expressed in their theories of history and institutions as well as those of economy and politics.[e]

So far as convinced Democrats were concerned, the primary threat from slavery lay in its social consequences in the West. The response the liberal Democrats of New York State accorded the Mexican War epitomized northern democrats' fears and helped to prepare the way for the confrontations of the 1850s. At bottom they favored the war, but they also insisted that it be devoted to the ends of economic democracy. Hence they demanded that any territories the nation acquired be reserved for exploitation by free men. In March of 1847, for example, Senator John A. Dix defended the Wilmot Proviso on the grounds that it protected the rights of all whites who wished to labor for themselves, whereas opening the West to slavery would deprive them of their property in their own persons. So, too, a dissident delegate to the Democratic state convention at Syracuse proposed to exclude slavery from the territories on the grounds that "we believe in the dignity and rights of Free Labor; that free white labor cannot thrive upon the same soil with slave labor, and that it would be neither right nor wise for the general government to devote to slave labor, the temperate climate and fertile soil of any territory now free, to the exclusion of the free labor of all the States." The West as these Democrats perceived it was intended to be a vehicle for their own kind.[19]

In addition, the fact that Democrats hoped to reserve the West for themselves invested the question of its disposition with the same significance as the major issues of the 1830s. In 1848, protesting the way in which the party's conservative leaders had abandoned democratic principles, its liberal members in the New York State legislature argued that the American government owed a special obligation to the "toiling masses" of the world, who could not migrate to the territories if they were populated by Negro slaves. "From the first institution of government to the present time," they declared in justifying their hostility toward Hunker policies, "there has been a struggle going on between capital and labor for a fair distribution of the profits resulting from their joint capacities. In the early stages of society, the advantage was altogether on the side of capital; but as education and intelligence are diffused, the tendency is stronger towards that just equality which all wise and good men desire to see established." Similarly, reporting a series of resolutions to the Herkimer convention of 1847, David Dudley Field revived the whole apparatus of liberal democratic economics as a charge against the Hunkers, insisting in the name of Democratic traditions that the territories be kept free of slavery. In the eyes of these northern Democrats, at least, the first object of democratic politics remained the achievement of white equality, which made the encroachments of slavery on the territories into an assault on equal rights.[20]

The issue these dissidents raised was resolved by the Compromise of 1850, which promised them the substance of their demands even if it fell short of guaranteeing their principles. As a result, the reopening of the territorial question in the Kansas-Nebraska Bill had the effect not only of challenging democrats' expectations but of intensifying their fears; threatening to introduce slavery into the rest of the territories the nation had acquired in 1803, it roused popular antipathy as no efforts at merely moral persuasion could. Salmon P. Chase, the insistently libertarian opponent of slavery, demonstrated the force of democratic concern for the whites' economy in his famous *Appeal of the Independent Democrats:* "From the rich lands of this large Territory, . . . patriotic statesmen have anticipated that a free, industrious, and enlightened population will extract abundant treasures of individual and public wealth. There, it has been expected, freedom-loving emigrants from Europe, and energetic and intelligent laborers from our own land, will find homes of comfort and fields of useful enterprise. If this bill shall become a law, all such expectation will turn to grievous disappointment." George Law justified his support for Frémont on the same grounds: "I intend to go for the man who most nearly represents the American sentiment, and the sentiment in relation to Slavery of the freemen of the North, which declares that Slavery is sectional and that Freedom is national. At the same time I desire to have the best representative of the progress of the age in which we live. I want a man who has done something for the great material interests of the country." Democrats enlisted in the opposition because they feared for northern opportunities.[21]

Even Democratic dissidents who were morally repelled by slavery suggested that Democratic loyalties were most vulnerable to alleged infringements on whites' rights. In 1858, for example, Senator Hannibal Hamlin of Maine celebrated his recent departure from the Democratic party with an insistent criticism of its territorial policies. Comparing its support for the Lecompton Constitution with its support for the *Dred Scott* decision, he charged that the party's present leaders "affirm that majorities of white men in the Territories have no rights that the Democratic party are bound to respect. That is the conclusion. It is the logical conclusion from your acts. . . . I say it is historically incorrect. But improving on that doctrine, that black men, for a century before the Constitution, had no rights that a white man was bound to respect, modern Democracy claims that a majority of free white men in your Territories have no rights that it is bound to respect." Similarly, Anson W. Burlingame had long since addressed himself to the thrust of Democratic opinion when—well before the Kansas-Nebraska Bill—he advocated western expansion and development while opposing the Fugitive Slave

Law and the extension of slavery into the territories. "We have no more to do with slavery at the South," he told a Free Democratic Meeting at Faneuil Hall in 1852, "so long as it behaves itself, and minds its own business, than we have with bigamy in Turkey, or with cannibalism in the Feejee Islands." Morality might be a problem for missionaries; Democrats were concerned for their rights.[22,f]

Meanwhile obvious conservatives embraced the same egalitarian concerns, adopting these secular complaints but incorporating them into a larger scheme of values. Even when their intentions were clearly polemical they achieved a powerful effect, and as their charges broadened they acquired ever greater significance. In 1854 Senator Benjamin F. Wade of Ohio taunted Stephen A. Douglas with the fact that Senator Archibald Dixon of Kentucky had defended the Kansas-Nebraska Bill by arguing that northern whites could go elsewhere if they did not wish to work alongside slaves. "Is that the democracy of the Chairman of the Committee on Territories?" Wade asked. "Let him tell the yeomanry of Illinois—the hard-fisted laboring man of that great State—that this is the principle upon which he acts; that this Territory is to be covered over with slaves and with masters, and that his proud constituency are to go out there and work side by side, degrading themselves by working upon a level with your miserable slaves. Let him do so, and it is a declaration which I think will tingle in the ears of Democracy, and the people will come to understand that you are legislating for the privileged aristocracy of the South, to the exclusion of the whole North." [23]

Wade's attack was narrowly partisan; Senator James Dixon of Connecticut demonstrated that the principled defense of free labor was likely to metamorphose into a critique of southern institutions. "Do you ask why we are unwilling to extend slavery, to add more slave States to this Union?" he asked in 1859 in a carefully modulated speech on the bill to acquire Cuba,

Not because we desire to gain, or to keep political power. It is for a higher and nobler reason. Slavery, wherever it exists, must, necessarily, disgrace and degrade free labor. The opinions expressed at the last session of Congress by an honorable Senator from South Carolina, on this floor, and by other Senators on other occasions, though severely animadverted upon at the time, are the logical result of the system of slave labor which prevails in our southern States; and which the Senator from Louisiana proposes by this bill to perpetuate in Cuba.

They are the legitimate consequence of a policy permitting the existence of a servile class in a community, subjected to the actual ownership of those for whom they labor.

Significantly, Dixon also went on to distinguish between the complaints of humanitarian reformers and the views he was now elaborating, and he reinforced his secular concerns by invoking the dignity of labor against the perversions of aristocratic sentiment. Thus, although he nominally dealt only with territorial questions, he also repudiated southern society in the name of equal rights.[24]

Conservative antagonists of slavery in the territories also broadened their economic indictment by invoking natural law understood in substantially democratic terms as the teachings of economic justice unencumbered by human contrivance. Loring Moody demonstrated how the economics of democratic liberalism might supplement moral injunctions when, in *A Plain Statement addressed to all Honest Democrats* (1856), he challenged southern editors to explain why Virginia should not be a great manufacturing state:

Why not, *Mr. Virginian?* For the simple and plain reason that SLAVERY has made you too proud and too lazy to go to work, like honest men, and develop the rich agricultural, mineral, and manufacturing resources which a kind Providence has bestowed upon you in such "prodigal abundance." It is *slavery*, with its concomitants, pride, arrogance, and laziness, which has dilapidated your plantations, converted your fertile plains into "mullen and pine barrens," and sent such "blighting and mildew" throughout your borders that even the bondmen might stand up and laugh in his [sic] chains to see how slavery has smitten the land with ugliness.[25]

Other conservative spokesmen applied the same argument to the weaknesses of the southern economy as a whole, belaboring southern deficiencies as grounds for northern intransigence. In 1860, for example, Samuel H. Hammond announced that "the line between the Free and the Slave States is as traceable in the difference in the thrift of the people, and the value of their lands, as it is by the monuments erected to divide them. Kentucky is a Slave State as prosperous as any, but her lands, equally productive with those of Ohio, are not more than half equal in value to those of the latter to-day. Missouri has a soil rich as that of Illinois, but the value of the land of the latter is, on the average, more than twice that of the former." The concern for the national welfare that conservatives had traditionally embraced now came to focus in freedom, while the problems the slave-based economy experienced, far from inviting their sympathetic consideration, only condemned the South for its departure from liberty.[26]

In this fashion, conservatives not only turned to economic arguments to bolster their charges against the South but invoked economic liberty as a criterion by which to measure southern claims. The speeches of Abraham Lincoln document the reorientation in conservative values. On the one hand, he repudiated southern slavery on typically conservative grounds, demanding rights for Negroes although denying them social equality. On the other hand, he criticized southern policies because they encroached on white men's freedom, and he was later to describe the Civil War as a struggle "to elevate the condition of men—to lift artificial weights from all shoulders—to clear the paths of laudable pursuit for all—to afford all, an unfettered start, and a fair chance, in the race of life." These words did not deny antislavery, nor did they deprecate its moral concerns, but they emphasized the extent to which the Republicans' vision had incorporated democratic rights. Only in his image of competitive success did Lincoln recall his conservative origins, and it came close to the popular conception of the rights of the self-made man.[27]

Embracing a democratic society, Republicans also embraced the politics that went with it, complaining of southern infringements on the integrity of popular government. Their anxieties were often polemical and they sometimes merely echoed traditional fears, but they committed themselves to democracy to the detriment of southern power.

Their views were the more striking in the light of the stand-pat constitutionalism with which their Whig predecessors had sought to prevent the annexation of Texas in 1844.[g] Acting as they had on previous occasions when western expansion seemed to threaten the stability of the republic, Whigs had hoped to bar the new territory because of the troubles it might cause. Although they failed to secure their objective, they helped to create a barrier to further expansion that was to bear great significance during the 1850s. Calvin Colton defined it with unwonted moderation when he noted in one of his *Junius Tracts*, "It should be well considered, that, while the people of the free States, naturally and generally averse to slavery, will feel bound to defend the Constitution for the whole republic within its present limits, they would as naturally be reluctant to aid in employing the powers of the Federal Government, which were professedly set up to give and secure freedom to mankind, to extend yet farther, and farther to fortify the domain of slavery." [28]

Given this attitude, the war with Mexico inevitably encouraged even ordinary conservatives to look with deepening suspicion on the conduct of the national government. Hence many of them adopted or at least condoned the allegation, first popularized by dedicated abolitionists, that the events of the late 1840s demonstrated the existence of a carefully contrived conspiracy to extend the influence of slavery. Thurlow Weed, ever sensitive to currents of northern opinion, expressed an early version of the new conservative doctrine when he wrote in the *Albany Evening Journal* in March 1847 that "with one-fourth of the wealth, and less than that proportion of free representation, the South has gradually acquired the control of the Senate, and transformed the people of the North into mere 'hewers of wood and drawers of water' for Slavery. But they can go no farther. The last foot of slave territory has been acquired; and if the issue is to be more Slave territory or no Union, the sooner the issue is tried the better. We have no fears of the result. Freedom will triumph, and the glory of our beloved country will be maintained." Two years later Representative James Wilson of New Hampshire treated the charge as almost a commonplace of legislative debate when he characterized "the acquisition of territory, out of which to form slave States" as only "the most palpable instance of the overweening determination of the slave power to extend and perpetuate itself, and govern the country according to its own sovereign pleasure." [29]

The Compromise of 1850 confirmed the drift of conservative thought. Although it was patched together by moderates of both sections who hoped to avoid secession, and although it led Daniel Webster to suppress his previous criticisms of slavery and to abandon his previous opposition to its extension, it attracted the support of relatively few northern Whigs.[30] Moreover, even the labors that conservative spokesmen subsequently undertook to rally northern opinion to the Compromise could be effective only so long as it seemed to have settled the issue of slavery in the territories. Hence the events of the 1850s virtually destroyed their hopes for peace, as the pressure of southern expansionists undid the constitutional arrangements that the conservatives had given up so much to maintain.[31]

The bill to organize Kansas without a prohibition on slavery served as the point of departure for most Whigs' conversion into Republicans. Although it was clearly modeled on the Compromise of 1850 and therefore had some color of plausibility, it also nullified the Missouri Compromise and thereby threatened the status quo. At the same time, by establishing legal conditions under which slave-holders might enter new territories, it encouraged northern conservatives once again to associate the measures of the Democratic party with a conspiracy of dedicated aristocrats. As in other matters, it is difficult to say how much Whig spokesmen were genuinely influenced by the fear of a southern conspiracy and how much it represented only a calculated partisan effort to elicit popular sympathies. The answer to this question is less important than the fact that in invoking the specter of a "slave power" dedicated to undermining the nation's liberty they deferred to both the abolitionist sentiment they had once deplored and the democratic sentiment they had once criticized. Senator William H. Seward pointed up this tendency of conservative belief when he declared during debate on the bill that "one slave-holder in a new Territory, with access to the Executive ear at Washington, exercises more political influence than five hundred freemen. It is not necessary that all or a majority of the citizens of a State shall be slaveholders, to constitute a slave-holding State. Delaware has only 2,000 slaves, against 91,000 freemen; and yet Delaware is a slave-holding State." His argument begged the question whether southerners might not have rights in the territories that any administration was bound to respect; instead, it equated southerners' claims as slaveholders with infringements on free government.[32]

Passage of the Kansas-Nebraska Bill consequently unsettled conservative opinion, which the policies of the national government further dismayed by legitimizing the most exaggerated fears. Conservatives complained with apparent justification that the Democrats in Washington failed to protect the free settlers of Kansas against marauding bands from Missouri; they also accused the national administration of complicity in the designs of the slavocracy. In 1856, for example, a Select Committee of the Vermont House of Representatives proposed to appropriate $20,000 for the relief of migrant Vermonters who had settled in the new territory. In its report on the subject it insisted that affairs in Kansas infringed on constitutional rights by denying Vermonters their right to migrate and by penalizing them for their devotion to free institutions. In addition, however, it charged that the spread of slavery was itself an unconstitutional act that had come about because "those, who enjoy the benefits of free institutions, have, from time to time, acquiesced in and compromised with Slavery, in its bold, rapid and aggressive strides towards unlimited and irresponsible power. This, and this only, has brought on the crisis which we deplore, and for which Vermont and her sister States are now seeking a remedy." In effect, they nerved their constituents to repudiate southern rights in the name of northern liberties.[33]

At the same time, contending against Democratic policy in Kansas, some conservatives weakened the authority of the Constitution by clamoring for popular rule. Although many of them were dedicated to preventing the extension of slavery under any circumstances, they often argued, instead, that the influence of the slave power challenged the right of self-government. Early in 1856 a preliminary convention of the new Republican party, meeting in Pittsburgh, told the American people: "We proclaim our belief that the policy which has for years past been adopted in the administration of the General Government, tends to the utter subversion of each of the great ends for which the Constitution was established; and that, unless it shall be arrested by the prompt interposition of the people, the hold of the Union upon their loyalty and affection will be relaxed, the domestic tranquil[l]ity will be disturbed, and all constitutional securities, for the blessings of liberty to ourselves and our posterity, will be destroyed. The slaveholding interest cannot be made permanently paramount in the General Government, without involving consequences fatal to free institutions." [34]

The more they berated southern power the more exaggerated their demand for freedom became. The idea that deference to southern claims would mean the imposition of slavery everywhere was a favorite theme with moralists, who increasingly identified slavery with the Antichrist, but it also influenced secular agitators, who introduced it into politics. In 1856, for example, Deodatus Wright rebuked former Governor Washington Hunt of New York, who professed to be opposed to the extension of slavery, for refusing to participate in forming a new antislavery party. "The Republican party," Wright explained in the second of two public letters, "does not owe its existence to a desire, or a design, to 'ameliorate the condition of the negro,' but to a firm, fixed and resolute purpose to relieve themselves, the people of the North, from an oppression similar in character, and from a proscription as intollerant [*sic*], as those to which our fathers were subjected." In the following year an anonymous pamphleteer brought his *Address to the Voters of Indiana* to a close by insisting that "Slavery may yet steal its way into Indiana. The Old Liners may, if they succeed in gaining power, push Slavery into universal dominion—they may yet make it national—then would be realized the prophecy of Senator Toombs, that he would yet call his slave roll from the shade of Bunker Hill Monument, but God forbid it. Now, sovereigns of Indiana, the facts are before you for your choice—for your response to these facts, God and your country will hold you responsible." Clamor against the southern slavocracy as an agency of sectional interests culminated in hints of a democratic revolution to limit southern power.[35]

The shift of conservative opinion was carried still further by the *Dred Scott* decision, which confirmed slaveholders' rights in the territories in defiance of existing legislation. Under ordinary circumstances most conservatives would probably have counseled acquiescence in the Court's decision, but a decade of sectional controversy perceived as the result of southern aggressions ensured that many of them would see it instead as a crime against popular rule. Abraham Lincoln expressed this point of view during his debates with Stephen A. Douglas, in which he appealed to constitutional formulas to invalidate popular sovereignty yet insisted that a constitutional decision must not frustrate the popular will. William M. Evarts, already a well-known constitutional lawyer, demonstrated the thrust of conservative opinion even more clearly in a speech at Auburn (New York) during the presidential campaign of 1860:

Now, gentlemen, look at the unsleeping eye of Slavery—that great powerful interest which, while we, a free honest people, have been minding our own business, satisfying ourselves by sending John Jones or John Smith to Congress, has been seizing upon the power of the government; and the slave interest, with six millions of white people, and we with thirteen millions of white people—they have got the Supreme Court of the United States, and they have got the Circuit Courts, too. Yes, oddly enough, it turns out that six millions of men have five Judges, while thirteen millions have but four. . . . But, furthermore, whenever the organization of the Supreme Court shall be adjusted, according either to the claims, or the pressure of business, or the amount of population, there will be at least six of the nine judges representing the Free States, and three only representing the Slave States; then we will agree that the Supreme Court of the United States of America is the place to settle the question of Liberty and of Property.

For many men of a conservative persuasion, the Court's action in invalidating the Missouri Compromise apparently weakened their long-standing commitment to the authority of an autonomous judiciary.[36]

More generally, the sequence of national events during the 1850s increasingly involved conservative spokesmen in the celebration of liberal democracy. The position they ultimately arrived at was undoubtedly facilitated by their original prejudices against the South, which their concern for the nation's morality may also have served to confirm. Similarly, their indignation at southern oligarchy was clearly heightened by their political interests. Nevertheless, the long-range thrust of their arguments carried them beyond their original views, and they ended by revolutionizing American politics in the name of popular rights. De Witt C. Leach, one of the early Republican leaders in Michigan, expressed the novel tendencies of their faith during a speech in the House of Representatives, in which he sought to deny the Democratic party its claim to democratic principles. The Republican party, he asserted in 1860,

holds the political faith of the fathers of the Republic. We believe that all men have an inalienable right to "life, liberty, and the pursuit of happiness." We believe—nay, we *know*—that slavery, socially, morally, politically, is a blighting and a withering curse. We know that its influence is deleterious upon both the oppressor and the oppressed. We know it retards the development of the material resources of the country. We know it checks the onward march of civilization. We know it impedes the progress, as it corrupts the morals and perverts the doctrines, of the Christian religion. We know it is surely, and with fearful rapidity, undermining the very foundations of our Government; and that if its onward course is not speedily stayed, our country will soon be a Republic only in name.

The political struggle over slavery in the territories firmly enlisted many northern conservatives in the liberal democratic cause.[37]

Meanwhile, the fear of southern power also roused northern Democrats, whose antipathy toward moral crusades remained unbroken only as long as their own autonomy was not challenged. Once their anxieties were aroused, the main tenets of democratic belief closely resembled conservatives' fears, to the extent that conservative polemics undoubtedly influenced democratic opinion. Even before this development took place, however, powerful democratic traditions pointed in much the same direction; the only step that many Democrats were not immediately prepared to take was to apply their fear of power to the slaveholding elements in their own party, and the events of the 1850s might well have accomplished this result without the efforts of antislavery conservatives.

Certainly liberal Democrats expressed much the same sense of dismay at southern "innovations" in constitutional interpretation as many conservatives did. In 1847 Senator Dix spoke for many of his compatriots when he defended the Wilmot Proviso on the ground that whereas territories added to the Union on previous occasions had already been committed to slavery, it could be extended to the Mexican Cession only by positive action of the federal government. More generally, he complained that southerners had changed their constitutional beliefs to enforce their territorial demands: "Our southern friends have heretofore stood upon the ground of defence: of maintaining slavery within their own limits against interference from without. The ground of extension is now taken, and of extending slavery upon free territory. I cannot believe this position will be sustained by the southern States. It is new ground, and it is taken with avowals which are calculated to spread surprise and alarm throughout the non-slaveholding States." Three years later Senator Shields demonstrated Democrats' vulnerability to antislavery sentiment in the same speech in which he argued that slavery was the only viable solution for the coexistence of the races. Asserting white supremacy, urging reconciliation between North and South, and rebuking northern efforts to agitate the territorial question, he nevertheless opposed the extension of slavery as an infringement on natural rights and denied there were constitutional sanctions for the rights that southerners claimed. "The Constitution of this country only tolerates slavery where it exists," he declared, "but neither extends nor establishes it anywhere." Increasingly, Democrats as well as Whigs appealed to a constitutional stasis to repudiate southern claims.[38]

Thus far, Democratic dissidence remained relatively temperate although pregnant with future disasters, but the Kansas-Nebraska Bill caused more critical members of the party to elaborate classic Democratic fears of power into a major indictment of its southern wing. The author of the Wilmot Proviso pointed the way in an address to the

Herkimer Convention in which he attributed divisions among northern Democrats to "malign influences" that had silenced the press and suppressed the voice of the people: "Powerful indeed must be that magic, that can divide friends, and in the midst of freemen raise up an army to fight the battles of slavery. Its charms seem to have a peculiar influence over men in high places and those who, through the press, sway popular opinion. . . . I warn the people to beware of the subtle and powerful influences at work to betray them. Every firm advocate of their rights will be crushed if the strong arm of power can crush him." Hence it was natural for Salmon P. Chase to repudiate Senator Weller's contention that the Independent Democrats represented a small minority of abolitionists, by declaring in 1853 that "the great body of voters who compose this organization, and whose numbers increase from day to day, claim to be Democrats, because they hold in good faith all the cardinal maxims of the Democratic faith, and insist on their impartial application to all questions. They call themselves Independent Democrats because they reject the dictation of the slave power." [39,h]

The settlement of Kansas simply broadened this development. In 1856 the Free Soil Democrats of New York, meeting at Syracuse to condemn the national administration, appealed to loyal Democrats to abandon their party on the grounds that "that party of glorious memory, which once spoke and acted for Freedom, has fallen into the hands of office holders and political adventurers, serving as the tools of a slaveholding oligarchy. For more than ten years the measures of the General Government have been directed mainly to the increase of Slave States. One measure has followed upon another, each bolder than the last, until we have violence ruling in the Federal Capitol, and civil war raging in the Territories." Two years later Colonel William M. McCarty was to repudiate the Buchanan administration's heavy-handed efforts to gain the admission of Kansas under the Lecompton Constitution, declaring to the Democratic State Convention of Indiana that "the question to-day for us to solve, is whether we shall protect and preserve the liberties of the people of Kansas, by adhering with fidelity to that principle of self-government, which enshrines our liberties as well as theirs—a principle which attaches to all distinct political societies in their several spheres, and absolves them from obedience to any rule or domination, except that to which they voluntarily yield allegiance." [40]

The same liberal democratic sentiment also served to place in an ominous light the administration's efforts to enforce party regularity. According to Colonel McCarty, "To say that we should defer to the will of a President, is to inaugurate absolutism. If the co-ordinate branches of the government and the people are to be the mere echoes of the President, the state of rule would be the same if the echoes should be blotted out and he be clothed with dictatorial powers." So, too, Representative William Montgomery of Pennsylvania repudiated both the Lecompton Constitution and President Buchanan on the broadest possible grounds. "The issue between us and those who contend for the admission of Kansas," he told the House in 1858, "is radical and fundamental. We contend that the constitution must be the work of the people, express their will, and speak with their authority. On the other side it is contended, that a convention, no matter how constituted, binds the people by its action. . . . For the first time in the history of our country has the great principle of self-government been openly attacked; for the first time we are called upon to stand up in the Halls of Congress to defend the right of white men to frame their own institutions and regulate their own government." [41]

The fear of aristocratic rule also shaped the reactions that Democrats expressed to the *Dred Scott* decision. Hannibal Hamlin appealed to a historic Democratic contention when he told the Senate in 1858 that the Supreme Court "had no more authority to decide a political question for us, than we had to decide a judicial question for them. Keep each branch of the Government within the sphere of its own duties. We make laws, they interpret them; but it is not for them to tell us what are the limits within which we shall confine ourselves in our action; or, in other words, what is a political constitutional right of this body, any more than it is for us to tell them what is a judicial right that belongs to them. Of all despotisms upon earth, the despotism of a judiciary is the worst. It is a life estate." [42]

In sum, the pressure of southern demands worked to revive Democratic fears of power, which the events of the 1850s served to clothe with a new semblance of plausibility. As a result, many Democrats adopted much the same diagnosis of the nation's problems that conservatives also propounded. They were vaguely watchful lest the "conspiracy" of southern slaveholders threaten northern freedom as well as western rights.

They also perceived the electoral issues of their times in a mood of confrontation; if they repudiated didactic morality, they acquiesced in a moral choice. Finally, they concluded that the Union was threatened only by slavery, with consequences that were equally drastic: their bias in this respect not only deprived them of the normal political motives to compromise but actually encouraged them in their intransigence. They opted for liberty and union, almost unmindful of the chasm between them.

THE SHIFTING BASIS OF ANTISLAVERY:
HISTORY AND INSTITUTIONS

Northerners were concerned for liberty in both the economic and the political senses, but their feeling of crisis went deeper, to the heart of the American experience. As the sectional quarrel developed, they came increasingly to believe that southern slavery challenged not only liberty understood as specific popular rights, but the underlying structure of free institutions. As a result, slavery came to seem a monolithic social entity against which its northern opponents were required to marshal all the resources of a free society, as Americans understood that phenomenon.

So far as northern conservatives were concerned, their anxiety over the future of free institutions began with characteristic conservative apprehensions over the degradation of western politics. The fears they typically expressed identified a familiar evil and proposed a familiar cure: they declared that the introduction of slavery into the territories threatened the happy combination of virtue and intelligence on which the American republic rested and required heroic efforts to save the region for freedom. Representative James Wilson, the Whig son of a Federalist father, summed up their redemptive impulse in a speech on the political influence of slavery. "Sir," he declared in 1849, "let Congress give to those Territories free institutions and equal and just laws—institutions and laws that will improve, enlighten, educate, and elevate those who are now there, those who may hereafter go there, and the generations that may be born there in all after time. Those are the institutions and laws, and those only, that I am willing to be instrumental in sending into that comparatively new country." John A. Wilstach took issue with the Kansas-Nebraska Act on much the same grounds. "The people of the

North and of the peopled West are the natural guardians of their unoccupied sister territories," the Indiana attorney declared in 1855, "and if they suffer them to be poisoned with the bad principles of political quacks, they might as well leave their wards to grow up with diseased constitutions and premature feebleness." Didactic, moralistic, and intrusive, conservatives proposed to save the West for liberty by introducing their own institutions there.[43]

At the same time, conservatives increasingly expressed their concern for virtue and intelligence in the South itself, comprehending the patterns of slavery as threats to republican freedom. Protestant reformers had long made the moral and intellectual condition of the blacks a ground for religious execration, inasmuch as it deprived them of opportunities for salvation; during the 1850s secular figures came to indict white illiteracy in the region as an illustration of southern hostility to the premises of free government. This development was especially apparent in the political commentators who began to reproach the South for depriving its poor whites of schools; on their view, its failure to educate its people damned its other institutions out of hand. Senator Dixon of Connecticut demonstrated the larger significance many northern critics attached to southern illiteracy when he told the Senate in 1859,

Negro slavery does, in truth, not only enslave the African race, but, in every community where it exists, it also includes, in the chains of its bondage, the labor of the white man. For him I now speak. Let those Senators who consider what they call hireling labor degrading, visit the North, and a new vision will greet their eyes; intelligent, free-labor, with its ample rewards, its happy firesides—the homes of education and refinement; its hours of leisure, for the studies which fit freemen for their political duties; its means of educating the children, who, while the father bends in cheerful toil over the plow, the bench, or the anvil, are laying the foundations of that learning, which is preparing them to become your authors, your inventors, your teachers, your Governors, your Senators, and the Presidents of your Republic.

Reports of southern "backwardness" such as we have already noted in discussing economic objections to slavery went to prove the same point: institutions as well as economics confirmed the error of southern ways and invited northern inflexibility.[44]

More generally, in the eyes of many northern conservatives the confrontation that developed between the North and the South over their rights in the territories took on the characteristics of a struggle between freedom considered as an inclusive social policy and slavery considered as its equally inclusive and therefore totally reprehensible antithesis. As a result, men who were unwilling to embrace abolition outright nevertheless introduced much of its absolutism into political discourse by clamoring against the extension of slavery on the grounds that freedom was "national" whereas slavery was "sectional," a proposition that ultimately became one of the slogans of the Republican party. William H. Seward expressed this idea in its classic form during debate on the Compromise of 1850 when he argued that slaveholders could not expect to enjoy the same constitutional guarantees in the territories as other men because their peculiar institution was intrinsically inferior to freedom. He applied this key distinction even to the state of South Carolina: "*Slavery* is only *one* of many institutions there—freedom is equally an institution there. Slavery is only a temporary, accidental, partial, and incongruous one; freedom, on the contrary, is a perpetual, organic, universal one, in harmony with the Constitution of the United States. . . . You may separate slavery from South Carolina, and the State will still remain; but if you subvert freedom there, the State will cease to exist." [45]

Thus far Seward argued only that the nation's commitment to freedom precluded opening the territories to slavery, but his words also pointed toward a conclusion that was to influence ever greater numbers of conservatives as the sectional controversy deepened. The more they conceived of freedom as a comprehensive social condition, the less able they would be to conceive of satisfying its requirements by securing liberty in the territories. More simply, freedom could not be "national" so long as slavery existed—least of all for thinkers who retained some sense of society as an organic entity—and although many conservatives were deeply troubled by the abolitionists precisely because they proposed to do something about slavery in the South, they were also pressed by the logic of their own position, in conjunction with events that tended to reinforce it, to move ever closer toward accepting the abolitionists' sense of the nation's obligations. The degree to which the Republicans broke with their conservative past was nowhere more evident than in the difference between the idea of an "irrepressible conflict" between two distinct civilizations, put forward by Seward at Rochester (New York) in 1858, and the moral neutrality the *American Review* had claimed for the

Whigs nine years earlier. "They have conceded to the people of the territories," it had declared, "the liberty of shaping constitutions according to their sovereign will and pleasure; and have refused to sanction the affixing of political conditions to a State charter. They would not allow a factious or a fanatical party to interpose their 'peculiar institutions,' or their moral usurpations, during the formation of a State." In 1849, the *Review* had repudiated antislavery "fanaticism" in the name of constitutional liberty; Seward clamored for "freedom" even at the risk of union.[46]

The attitudes many conservatives took toward the South as an inferior republic apparently also helped to minimize their sensitivity to the possible consequences of the confrontation they insisted upon forcing. Some men clearly anticipated disunion but contemplated it with equanimity, as if to suggest that they concerned themselves with slavery primarily as a sin of northern complicity. This point of view was quite common among dedicated reformers like Wendell Phillips, but it also clearly influenced run-of-the-mill politicians like Samuel H. Hammond of New York, who declared in 1860 that he would see the Union dissolved rather than allow slavery to "march forward into territory consecrated to freedom." Others denied that the Union could be dissolved, as if unaware that southerners might insist on rights that differed from their own. Later in the same year, William M. Evarts dismissed the threat of disunion with the observation that it represented "Mexican politics—not ours," while Hammond insisted grandiloquently that his state's commitment to the "conservative" principles of justice and right would inevitably enlist her in opposition to any attempt at secession. Either way, northern conservatives expressed a commitment to freedom that simply pushed aside southern complaints.[47]

The outcome of all these developments was a tendency to embrace "freedom" defined in northern terms as a fundamental national commitment that must be honored as the basis of union. Abraham Lincoln demonstrated both its power and its implications when he addressed the Republican state convention at Springfield (Illinois) that had just nominated him for the Senate.

> If we could first know *where* we are, and *whither* we are tending [he declared], we could then better judge *what* to do, and *how* to do it.
> We are now far into the *fifth* year, since a policy was initiated, with the *avowed* object, and *confident* promise, of putting an end to slavery agitation.

Under the operation of that policy, that agitation has not only, *not ceased*, but has *constantly augmented*.

In *my* opinion, it *will* not cease, until a *crisis* shall have been reached, and passed.

"A house divided against itself cannot stand."

I believe this government cannot endure, permanently half *slave* and half *free*.

I do not expect the Union to be *dissolved*—I do not expect the house to *fall*—but I *do* expect it will cease to be divided.

It will become *all* one thing, or *all* the other.

Either the *opponents* of slavery, will arrest the further spread of it, and place it where the public mind shall rest in the belief that it is in course of ultimate extinction; or its *advocates* will push it forward, till it shall become alike lawful in *all* the states, *old* as well as *new—North* as well as *South*.

Subjected to careful scrutiny, Lincoln's formula neither accurately described the problems the nation confronted nor offered a plausible solution to them. (It is difficult to believe that slavery genuinely threatened the free states, and equally difficult to believe that Lincoln truly regretted the antislavery agitation. In any event, he proposed only to adopt policies that would put the public mind at rest—not to solve the large social and economic problems that slavery had created—and he insisted that he saw no threat to the Union.) Seen as a political statement, however, the speech clearly summarized contemporary conservative belief: it insisted upon a commitment to liberty, in full confidence that the results would all be advantageous. Two years later, nearly two million northerners voted for Lincoln as if his declaration in favor of principle had sufficed to guarantee both liberty and union against a South that repudiated both.[48]

The conservatives' sense of history also helped to bring about this result. Sharing a long tradition of exhorting the American people to live up to their moral responsibility for the success of their nation's experiment, they increasingly perceived southern institutions as an evil they were bound to eliminate. Charles Hammond, the principal of Lawrence Academy in Groton (Massachusetts), applied classic logic to the problem of slavery when he addressed a Fourth of July celebration at Union (Connecticut) in 1853. He hailed the founding fathers for seeking liberty "that they might use it for nobler designs than were ever before contemplated by the founders of great states"; he criticized contemporary evils that threatened to frustrate their hopes; and he observed that "the perpetuity and perfection of our American Institutions, depends [*sic*] upon the termination, and that too at not a very remote period, of American Slavery, or else the oppressor and the oppressed will be involved in a common destruction." The further history of the American republic must be governed by northern traditions of freedom.[49]

Hammond's argument also suggests how the historical consciousness of many conservatives may have made them vulnerable to the claims of religious obligation. Certainly the advocates of observing the "higher law" in politics succeeded in blending the tradition of religious effort with appeals to the requirements of history.[i] William H. Seward clearly fused them in his speech on the admission of California, but a Conscience Whig from Massachusetts probably reflected the thrust of conservative opinion more accurately during an exchange with a New York Democrat in 1853. Speaking in the House of Representatives, Horace Mann challenged Josiah Sutherland's contention that there is no higher law than the Constitution "or than any interpretation which any corrupt Congress may put upon it." "I know it is said," Mann added, "that if the doctrine of the 'Higher Law' is admitted, all laws will be set at naught, and civil Government be overthrown. All history refutes this; for, of all the men who have ever lived, those who contend for the higher law of God have universally been the most faithful and obedient, when human laws were coincident with the divine. That identical principle in our nature, which makes us true to the will of God, makes us also true to all the just demands of men." In effect, the higher law as Mann described it not only addressed itself to the conscience in defiance of secular error, but guaranteed that the exercise of conscience would produce secular good. With God's help, his words implied, a nation that held fast to righteousness need have no fear for its future.[50]

Secular as well as religious in its origins, the idea of an American mission also influenced Republican opinion. In 1856, for example, an anonymous pamphlet for Frémont appealed to international history to vindicate his claims to the presidency: "In bygone times, loud hurrahs were uttered when Greece and Hungary triumphed; and the pulse of the nation beat more feverishly as the thrones of despots reeled and tottered before the wrath of an outraged people; and shall a tyranny be permitted to remain in our midst, more rampant than either the Moslem or the Austrian, without an effort being made for its removal?" Other political tracts adopted a more typically conservative stance, investing the domestic struggle with the significance of a universal cause. Four years later William H. Fry concluded his party handbook with the admonition, "We have either to succumb to, or to triumph over, the slave-power. There is no middle course. We must either have the black flag of Slavery, or one scintillating with freedom, to symbolize our home and country. Our irreversible word, then, should be for Liberty—circling our lakes and seas; traversing our mountains and prairies; covering our cities and villages; going forth in many ships over many waters: liberty for the poor, the exiled, and the oppressed; liberty of sense and soul, of thought and speech, of aspiration and action." [51]

The Americans' idea of microhistory clearly worked in the same direction, as the fear of political apostasy led directly to the Republican cause. Not only did the members of the new northern party deliberately adopt the name "Republican" and appeal to Thomas Jefferson as their patron saint; they also reconceived the history of slavery as a departure from the intentions of the founders. In this respect they followed the lead of earlier reformers, who had insisted that they sought only to redeem the founders' expectations that slavery would die of its own accord. In addition, they echoed typical conservative charges to the effect that the South had acquired an improper influence in the republic by extending the three-fifths clause to new states. But they also addressed themselves to the more basic American conviction—religious in its origins but clearly secular in its outcome—that the object of American politics was to preserve the founders' government against the machinations of its internal enemies. The objective facts of expansion and the bitterly fought issues of the 1850s simply converted slavery into an enemy that had to be purged from the land, and the Republican party acquired power as it identified itself with this aim. [52]

Abraham Lincoln demonstrated both the polemical character of their historiography and the fundamental commitments that made it plausible in his challenge to Stephen A. Douglas. On the one hand he invoked the Declaration of Independence to bolster Republican claims; on the other he clearly rewrote it to discredit Douglas's argument that it had never been intended to apply to Negro slaves. In this respect it seems fairly clear that he was compelled to manipulate the history of the Revolution to fit his partisan needs, but it is at least equally clear that he expressed a widespread conviction that the United States had been false to its history when it tolerated the extension of slavery. "The assertion that 'all men are created equal,' " he said at Springfield in 1857, "was of no practical use in effecting our separation from Great Britain; and it was placed in the Declaration, not for that, but for future use. Its authors meant it to be, thank God, it is now proving itself, a stumbling block to those who in after times might seek to turn a free people back into the hateful paths of despotism. They knew the proneness of prosperity to breed tyrants, and they meant when such should re-appear in this fair land and commence their vocation they should find left for them at least one hard nut to crack." The campaign he now launched for freedom was a mandate from the Americans' past.[53]

For their part, northern Democrats were slow to embrace either history or freedom understood in these essentially conservative terms; atomists and secularists, or at least advocates of the separation of church from state, they were often hostile to moral injunctions and antagonistic to social reform. At the same time, their very devotion to a secular definition of freedom made them even more vulnerable than many conservatives to threats to the democratic West, in that southern claims to the territories not only challenged their economic aspirations but seemed to threaten the institutional basis of their liberties. Because they conceived of the West as the key to their nation's history, they were increasingly constrained to act to protect it against its domestic enemies.[j]

The liberal Democrats of the New York legislature demonstrated the critical effect of democratic ideas of the West when they complained that southern expansionists' attempts to send Negroes into an area previously reserved for white labor were a threat to democratic society: "Where labor is to a considerable extent committed to slaves, to labor becomes a badge of inferiority. The wealthy capitalists who own slaves, disdain manual labor, and the whites who are compelled to submit to it are regarded as having fallen below their natural condition in society. They cannot act on terms of equality with the masters for those social objects which in a community of equals educate, improve and refine all its members. In a word, society, as it is known in communities of freemen—with its schools and its various forms of voluntary association for common benefit, and mutual improvement, can be scarcely said to exist for them or their families." Obviously the West these commentators depicted was more significant than any merely economic asset; it was their emblem of social equality and the ultimate recourse of their freedom.[54]

Liberal Democratic spokesmen displayed the same exaggerated loyalty to the West conceived as a political asset; in their eyes it not only suffered from the encroachments of the slave power but threatened to involve the whole country in its decline. In 1848 Martin Grover told the Barnburners of New York, meeting in Utica after their withdrawal from the Baltimore Convention, "If the schemes of the South succeed, farewell to liberty. He would as soon live under a monarchy as under the rule of 300,000 slave-holders. This question affects the future fate of a territory equal to fourteen states like New-York. It was a question which involved the fate of liberty on the whole continent. No matter what others might do; for himself, sink or swim, live or die, survive or perish, he went for the Flag of Freedom." The report of the convention adds that "Mr. Grover concluded amidst tumultuous cheers"; apparently his rhetorical flights spoke to the concerns his hearers felt. The antislavery wing of the party appealed to the same expansive images in 1856 when it asked the electorate forebodingly, "What shall we say of the future? Kansas lost to Freedom, and as a home for the oppressed of all nations; free labor driven across her borders, and that noble dominion of the New-World, broader and fairer than many a realm of the Old, made, not prosperous and rich like Wisconsin and Iowa, but half barbarous, like Western Missouri." [55]

In short, the thrust of democratic opinion apparently pressed many northern Democrats to perceive the struggle for the West as a profound moral confrontation, a challenge not only to their private hopes as individuals but also to the survival of free society. By the same token, it represented a challenge to the nation's place in history. Grover and the dissident New Yorkers suggested as much; so did Oliver C. Gardiner in his campaign tract for the Free Soil Party. "The crisis has come for the trial of our fidelity," he wrote in 1848. "The time is at hand when at the seat of our sovereignty—the ballot-box—we are to say whether or not, in view of her recent struggles for freedom, we will continue the bright example of republican government to Europe,—when we are to say whether or not a vast territory, just added to our limits, shall be the soil of freedom or slavery. In the double light then of late foreign events, and of our example, as a model of government to the world, the question of free soil becomes one of the most important of the present time." The historic accomplishments of the Union seemed to be at stake in the western territories, and Democrats as well as Whigs girded for battle to redeem their nation's future.[56]

Their sense of historic obligation may also have made liberal democrats more sensitive to charges of southern apostasy. Interestingly enough, apparently only adamantly Free-Soil Democrats pressed the conviction that the very existence of slavery in the West demonstrated the extent to which the nation had strayed from the principles of the founding fathers. Democrats of more varied persuasions repeatedly protested, however, that members of their party's "doughface" oligarchy had abandoned the historic principles of the party. This was clearly a polemical charge, but it was evidently thought sufficiently persuasive to be employed on many occasions. It was invoked by the dissident Democrats of New York in 1848; by Democratic critics of the Lecompton Constitution, who charged the Buchanan administration with reverting to "ancient federalism" in its hostility to popular sovereignty; and by the State Rights Democrats of Pennsylvania, who charged it with conspiracy as well as apostasy. Indeed, the very devotion many Democrats had traditionally shown to their party as a historic vehicle of liberty may well have influenced their reaction against it when they repudiated its alliance with the slave power. To the extent that "doughface" was a term of opprobrium applied by Free-Soil Democrats to members of their own party, it suggested that loyalty rather than conscience was at stake in the Democratic mind.[57]

In any event, the thrust of Democratic historiography generally anticipated Republican ideas; if Democrats were less tolerant of abolition, many of them shared the same sense of national crisis and the resolution to do something about it. Hence the large-scale opposition between Slavery and Freedom, which may well have appealed to their religious convictions as well as their sense of history, undoubtedly helped to lead many of them into the Republican party in spite of its questionable origins. So, too, their sense that they must intervene to protect the West against the influence of the slave power clearly reflected their more general belief in expanding the area of freedom on this continent, where it could not involve the evils of a foreign war or suffer from an uncertain mixture of foreign races. But they also apparently felt a more general sense of obligation to the world, which the territorial question sharp-ened. In 1858, at any rate, Hannibal Hamlin repudiated both the Bu-chanan administration and the Lecompton Constitution by declaring in the Senate,

I have no laudations to bestow on this Union. It needs none. Its eulogy is written in the history of the past. I choose that my acts shall speak for me, rather than the words I utter. I would, sir, that it should remain a monument forever to guide the nations of the world. I would, sir, that this Government should be per-petuated for all coming time; and no act of mine, no instrumentality of mine, shall be exerted or given except for that perpetuation. I would that our nation should stand a moral monument to enlighten other nations; but I cannot resist the conclusion that if we are to bow to the unlimited power of party despotism, if we are to do acts which in our judgments and in our hearts we reprobate, the day, the hour, of our downfall is as certain as that of other nations which have preceded us. . . . That act which is before us, that bill upon which we are to vote, is one of the measures which is calculated, if not designed, to produce that event.

In addition to domestic liberty, the calculations of a historic mission called a halt to southern power.[58]

Meanwhile conservative spokesmen invested the disposal of the West with much the same significance as these uneasy Democrats, reinforcing their fears for the future with a fear for the nation's Utopia. Samuel H. Hammond demonstrated how their anxiety over the incursions of the slave power might take on added meanings because the West was at stake when he asked in 1860, "Shall Slavery be nationalized? Shall it be an outspreading and progressive institution, marching forward, always un-der the protection of Federal law and shielded by the Stars and Stripes? Is there to be no limit to its expansion? Shall all the broad territory of the Great West—territory large enough to make ten New Englands—territory reserved by the patriotism, the wisdom, the humanity of our fa-thers as an inheritance to the generations of freemen to come after them, consecrating it to free labor, free enterprise, and free institutions—be given over, through all time, to the blight and curse of Slavery?" The ul-timate charge against slavery in the territories was that it would deprive the nation of its place in history by destroying its opportunities for ex-panding liberty.[59]

The tenor of this exhortation also suggests how effectively Republican concern over the territories incorporated the same kind of fear that

Lyman Beecher had once invoked against the Roman Catholic Church. Seen in this light, the region was not only a battleground for liberty but the ultimate hope of the American republic, and through the republic the world. Even men who spoke in a predominantly secular vein often expressed an essentially religious sense of responsibility for its fate. One of them was William H. Seward, who in 1850 appealed to the higher law to reinforce constitutional requirements that committed the region to freedom. "The territory is a part—no inconsiderable part—of the common heritage of mankind, bestowed upon them by the Creator of the universe. We are his stewards, and must so discharge our trust as to secure in the highest attainable degree, their happiness." Another was Charles W. Upham, who wrote in the *North American Review* in 1855, "It is obvious that no issue can possibly arise, more important in its bearings upon the future of America or of mankind, than that which determines the character of the people who are to occupy the region just described and the institutions of government and society to be established there. It cannot but decide the destinies of the continent, and the last great experiment of humanity." [60]

Their words also suggest how their focus on western institutions may have served to distract conservative spokesmen from the probable consequences of their enthusiasm for curbing southern expansion. Had they confronted the peculiar institution on its own ground with the same quasi-religious zeal, they might have seen better where their enthusiasm for freedom led. (It is clear that many abolitionists, not to mention an increasing number of religious intransigents, were at least half prepared for war to enforce their moral demands; it is less clear why so many secular conservatives fell in with their drastic measures.) Confronting an open West, however, in which the existence of slavery could be treated as a remediable incursion on freedom, they persevered largely unconsciously in their pursuit of sectional strife. (In this respect the exhortations of Beecher's imitators must have possessed the emotional force of anti-Catholicism without its attendant difficulties: Catholics already lived in the West when Beecher began to preach, whereas slaves might still be excluded from it.) Misled by their hopes as well as influenced by their fears, many conservatives could not understand why southern Democrats insisted that the exclusion of slavery from the territories was intolerable as well as unconstitutional. All they knew was that saving the West would also save the Union as they understood it.[k]

Be that as it may, conservatives as well as democrats clearly clung to an imagined West as the guarantee for American liberties. There were significant differences between them, but there was also significant agreement: slavery could not be tolerated in the territories because the West was too important to the nation. In this sense the imagined West was at least as important as its actual existence in promoting civil war. It not only offered social and economic opportunities to the American people but imbued them with spiritual attributes. Its development represented, in addition to a competition for political power in the ordinary numerical sense, a confrontation between good and evil in which liberty and democracy were both at stake. The West also expressed the Americans' sense of their freedom—not only the proliferation of schools and churches, untrammeled by alien institutions, but the essential conditions of American liberty, which would either contract or expand with their fate in the unoccupied territories. Finally, it was the Americans' future incarnate and the main realm of their liberal mission, the focus of their historic example and the unquestioned arena for their expansion. The West as northerners imagined it had become the West they insistently pursued.

THE DEFECTS OF DEMOCRATIC POLITICS

If concerns for secular freedom made many northern democrats into Republicans, the expressions of Democratic leaders also contributed to that unexpected result. Sometimes these expressions were deliberately provocative, sometimes simply blind, but in either case they worked to destroy the moral authority the party had long enjoyed. The defects of Democratic politics led directly to the loss of 1860.

One Democratic flaw consisted of being true to political principles that had won friends during the 1830s but were obsolete during the 1850s. Again and again, prominent Democrats reiterated their traditional beliefs in an environment they did not fit, giving evidence by their exhortations that they failed to understand the spirit of the age. The more august the Democratic champion, the more likely he was to misconstrue the era, as Thomas Hart Benton demonstrated in 1851 when he commiserated with

Charles Sumner (no less) on his having missed the age of heroes. "You have come upon the stage too late, sir. Not only have our great men passed away, but the great issues have been settled also. The last of these was the National Bank, and that has been overthrown forever. Nothing is left you, sir, but puny sectional questions and petty strifes about slavery and fugitive slave-laws, involving no national interests." [61] In this sense, many leading Democrats of the 1830s had simply outlived their time.

Old men lived in the past while young men looked to the future, but the manner in which they perceived it could still contribute to Democratic difficulties. As late as 1860, Daniel W. Voorhees of Indiana told a Fourth of July gathering at the University of Virginia that "if this Union shall escape its perils, if the constitution shall survive its enemies, our future will be to our past as is the meridian sun to the gray struggling dawn of the morning. There is a destiny in the pathway of this Union such as the eye of man never beheld, nor the heart of man conceived." Moved by a traditional Democratic vision of progress as an extension of existing institutions, Voorhees also anticipated further territorial expansion as a law of national development. "The expansion of the Republic is a natural law of its healthy existence," he declared, as if unmindful of the confrontations expansion had already brought. "That principle is now paramount to all other questions of national policy which remain to be developed, except the question of the preservation of the Union itself. In the past, it has steadily met the requirements of the age; but the future of this government, if it shall happily have a future, is to be one wide theater of expansion. Opposition has always stood in the way of this doctrine; but we have only to look at the map of the United States to vindicate it in its former practical results." Not only did he persevere in expansionist daydreams that could only exacerbate northern fears, but he invoked the prospect of fulfilling them as a palliative to sectional strife. [62]

As Voorhees's remarks suggested, Democrats were also handicapped by their devotion to the Union when they confronted the crises of the 1850s. On the one hand, they clung to it with a passion that almost equaled the passion the reformers had for "freedom." Samuel S. Cox of Ohio demonstrated how their passion might overcome their sensitivity to the evils their contemporaries clamored against when he told the House of Representatives in 1861 that "Regarding our NATIONALITY as more than a life, as the association of many lives in one, as an immortality rather than a life, the people of this country will cling to it with a tenacity of purpose and an energy of will, as the very cross of their temporal salvation, and revere it as the impersonation of their sovereign upon earth, whose throne is this goodly land, and whose mighty minstrelsy, ever playing before it, is the voice of an intelligent, happy, and free people." In effect, a religion of Democratic Union, of which Andrew Jackson was the patron saint because of his actions during the nullification controversy, helped blind its northern adherents to the sense of crisis other men felt.[63]

Other Democratic spokesmen held that threats to the nation's survival were manifestly absurd, a heresy against history that was clearly outlawed by its results. Representative John Tibbatts of Kentucky voiced this more complex persuasion in dealing with northern opposition to the annexation of Texas: "The simple fact that no State can better its condition, and that any State must put itself into an infinitely worse one, both in regard to its foreign and domestic relations, by a separation from the Union, will prevent it in all time to come." The events of the 1850s should have shaken this pragmatic faith, but Representative Daniel E. Sickles still invoked it in 1859 to rebuke a Pennsylvania Republican for agitating the question of slavery in the territories. "I think it would be impossible," Sickles declared with resolute indifference to the tenor of contemporary affairs, "in the compass of a single proposition, to embrace more of injustice to northern opinion, more inaccuracy of statement, and more inconsistency of political action, than is embodied in these declarations of the gentleman from Pennsylvania. Sir, the North does not stand upon any such ground; the North does not desire to enter a political contest upon any such question; the North is practical, as well as loyal to the Constitution of the country; it would prefer to see the next presidential contest decided upon other and more useful issues." Democrats persevered in thinking impossible the very developments that were most clearly before them.[64]

The blind spots such men showed were reinforced in turn by the traditional Democratic antagonism to intrusions on popular liberty, which led latter-day spokesmen like Caleb Cushing to perceive antislavery agitation as an offense against free government. "These acts of aggression, on the part of some Northern States as against those of the

South," the erstwhile Whig declared at Tammany Hall in 1858, "have been perpetrated under the shelter of our common government, when they would have been just cause of war as between foreign governments; and occasionally reach to such a point, that some States and Statesmen of the North, in the extremity of their blind zeal, apply to their fellow citizens of the South, language of political and personal denunciation, fit only for the case of declared national enemies. And then, if, goaded by the sense of wrong, a State or a Statesman of the South recurs to defensive acts or words, there is another outcry of the 'slave power.' Meantime, all these aggressive acts at the North are undertaken, we are continually told, in order to repel the aggressions and overthrow the domination of the 'slave power.' " [65]

It followed in such minds that the moralists who spoke against slavery were enemies to the republic, their clamor a mark of their corruption rather than a warning to loyal Democrats. "Never, in the worst days of the worst factions of Greece or Rome, of England or France," Cushing insisted, "was there a more gross effort to inflame the popular passions by false appeals to prejudice—never a more wanton abuse of the freedom of republican speech—never a more miserable and contemptible party cant—never a more abominable attempt to gratify personal ambition at the expense of a country's welfare and peace. Slave power! It is the cry of 'stop thief' on the part of the burglar fleeing from the pursuit of the officers of justice." Although many Democrats who denounced antislavery had plausible reasons for deprecating its moral stances, the antagonism they so clearly expressed worked equally clearly against their political ends.[66]

Hostility to an intrusive government also worked to discredit Democratic leaders when they tried to deal with the nation's economy. In general they succeeded in defeating Whiggish measures like the Bank and the protective tariff, yet the successes they enjoyed called their principles into question. This was the case not only in Pennsylvania, which remained a Democratic state that was also a stronghold of protection, but in the Middle West as well, where the vetoes by Democratic presidents of legislation providing for the development of rivers and harbors roused a vigorous reaction among Democrats who were devoted to enterprise. Ignoring these signs and portents, Presidents Pierce and Buchanan persevered in their destructive policy, confident that their principled vetoes maintained the Democratic tradition. The extent to which they erred was demonstrated in their treatment of homestead bills as infringements on equal rights. As the *Nashville Union and American* reported unhappily in 1860, "It is the opinion of a distinguished Northern Democrat, who is cool and calculating in his language, that any opponent of the Homestead policy would lose 200,000 votes in New York, 100,000 in Pennsylvania, and he couldn't touch bottom in the Northwest." The tenets of economic liberalism helped to destroy the Democratic cause.[67]

The main source of Democratic weakness, however, was probably the party's devotion to constitutionalism, which incorporated these various stances into a persuasive political delusion. On the familiar Democratic view, the Constitution properly construed would protect all popular rights against the encroachments of unacceptable evil; hence the solution to the gravest problems lay in referring them all to the Law. Horatio Seymour appealed to this vision of political order in his address at Tammany Hall. "At this time many speak lightly of constitutional law," he said, in derogating the political agitation of moral questions.

They are impatient that their peculiar views are checked by its barriers, not bearing in mind that it is their only safeguard against unjust or hasty legislation, affecting their lives, their liberties and their rights of conscience. We are not made [free] merely by putting power into the hands of the people, but by written constitutions restraining majorities and protecting minorities, and forbidding the legislators from touching a single right of a single citizen. In these days of legislative encroachment and legislative corruption, it is the duty of every citizen to uphold constitutional law.[68]

Their faith in constitutional liberty led them in turn to appeal to constitutional obligations as if they had the authority of the higher law. Representative Josiah Sutherland of New York voiced one version of this Democratic doctrine during his exchange with Horace Mann, in which he declared with every semblance of sincerity, "I ask the gentleman if every American citizen does not obey the higher law of God when he obeys every part of the Constitution? . . . Is not the spirit of the Constitution in accordance with the higher law? Can you point to a clause in the Constitution which, when fulfilling to the best of my ability, would make me violate the higher law of God?" Samuel Medary, president *pro tem* of the Democratic National Convention of 1856, expressed the same misplaced confidence in the authority of the country's secular institutions when he proclaimed that "in this Convention delegates are present from the Atlantic slope and the shores of the wide Pacific—thus manifesting in an unmistakable form, the progress of Democratic institutions and constitutional government. These are the institutions and this the government which it is our mission to defend and maintain. I repeat, that as long as we are governed by written constitutions and written laws, we should observe that deportment both personal and political, which will justify the expectation that we are capable of self-government." In either version, these Democrats' faith in the Constitution as an agency of free government apparently blinded them to the concerns that other men felt. In effect, they appealed to a political morality that dated from the 1830s to obliterate ideas of government that a new morality dictated.[69]

It followed that Democrats were often blind to the weakness of their position: because they sought to deal with contemporary issues in narrowly constitutional terms, they could not assess their situation with the wisdom it required. In 1850, for example, Representative Alexander W. Buel of Michigan defended the Fugitive Slave Law on the grounds that it was self-evidently constitutional as well as entirely compatible with previous legislation on the subject. Similarly, President Buchanan sought to legitimize the Lecompton Constitution in 1857 by appealing to the Supreme Court's opinion in the *Dred Scott* case. Hence it was easy for Representative Sickles to conclude in 1859 that "the pervading sentiment which now seems dangerous to the general peace and safety, is held bound in the grasp of the Constitution, and will yield to the duty which patriotism imposes. When that hour comes to the people of the North— 'the sober second thought'—as come it will and come it must, they will yield to the mandate of conscience, and all can repose with safety and confidence in their justice and honor." [70]

Finally, the constitutionalism Democrats embraced not only misrepresented contemporary issues and obscured contemporary events; it also invited negative reactions by its quarrels with democratic values. Although Democratic constitutionalists had good reason to think of the federal Constitution as a claim on the electorate's political loyalty, they tended to forget other political assumptions that many Americans took for granted. For one thing, while leading Democrats' insistence on following constitutional processes represented a clear philosophical perception that the legitimacy of the policies any constitutional government adopts depends upon their conformity to the prescribed norms of political behavior, it also overlooked the fact that American democrats had consistently viewed the federal document as a vehicle of "justice" rather than as a means of accommodating conflicting interests. Even on the purely practical level the federal document was deficient, for its ambiguities in dealing with such controverted areas as territorial policy apparently encouraged men to differ just when a consensus was most needed. Hence every Democratic appeal to restless northern democrats to stand by the constitutional process required a greater degree of self-denial than the democrats were likely to adopt, not to say convicted its proponents of complicity in the evils their critics sought to curb. Also, these same democrats typically viewed constitutions as agencies of popular government, binding so long as they were popular, but alterable on popular demand, whereas the Democratic constitutionalists of the 1850s sought to persuade them to abide by constitutional arrangements that they had already begun to repudiate. In short, the Constitution and the Union could not compete with Liberty and Union, which many northern democrats thought they served, and they set out to secure both by curbing southern rights.

The *Dred Scott* decision deepened all these problems and pressed toward their inevitable result. In it a Supreme Court made up chiefly of Democrats sought to settle outstanding issues between the North and the South by ruling on controverted points that were not formally before it. Far from settling the public mind, the Court's revocation of the Missouri Compromise stimulated northern fears of the power the slaveholding South possessed to pervert the fundamental law and invited renewed attacks on the authority the Court sought to exercise. Historians still contend over the legitimacy of the Court's action; it seems more appropriate here to note that whatever legitimacy the decision may have had, it was also bound to exacerbate sectional tensions precisely because it sought to impose a constitutional solution on a democracy that was not prepared to acquiesce in legal formulas. In one moment of understandable blindness the Court revived every fear of judicial legislation that democrats had ever expressed and split the Democratic party between its legalists and its libertarians.[71,1]

In doing so, the Court also undermined the only other solution to contemporary issues that Democratic traditions made possible. This was the device of "popular sovereignty," which George M. Dallas first sponsored during the territorial debates of the 1840s, but which reached its greatest fame at the hands of Stephen A. Douglas. Northern concern over western freedom and northern antipathies toward southern institutions might well have produced the same result, but the action of the Court in outlawing Douglas's panacea clearly doomed his hopes for the presidency and guaranteed the failure of the Democratic Union.[72]

The concept of popular sovereignty represented an effort to employ Democratic values to avoid sectional strife. When Douglas introduced it into the Kansas-Nebraska Bill, it had the clear practical purpose of facilitating territorial development by opening the region to both sections, but it also answered to Democratic traditions that had nothing to do with slavery. It connoted self-government in the sense that it sanctioned local authority against the claims of an external government; it negated congressional authority less on the basis of the constituent right of the people than on the ground that men in any geographical location are better able to choose their own policies than to have those policies chosen for them. At the same time, it expressed the familiar democratic idea that the object of popular government is liberty—not only liberty of economic enterprise, which was clearly a prime consideration in Douglas's mind, but also freedom from sumptuary intrusions, which federal regulations affecting slavery must necessarily create. On this view, moral indifference was a virtue, and local popular rule was the best way to secure it.[73]

Still further, the idea of filling the territories with an autonomous self-governing people corresponded with the Democratic vision of history, which depicted horizontal expansion as a corollary of American progress and which tended at the same time to exclude the millennial expectations that conservative reformers shared. (Democrats might well anticipate the millennium, but they tended to do so as individuals, rejecting conservative clergymen's efforts to dragoon the whole nation into a special relationship with God.) In addition, the idea of popular sovereignty expressed the western Democrat's sense of his region as the apex of American civilization; in repudiating eastern sovereignty it also repudiated the traditional conservative view that the West must conform to eastern standards before it would be ready for self-government. Finally, popular sovereignty reflected a classic Democratic reaction to conservative ideas of property: the territories were there to be exploited, if necessary in defiance of eastern prescriptions, and neither the rights of southern slaveholders nor the anxieties of northern moralists should be permitted to inhibit western democrats in their destined use of the soil.

These were the intellectual premises that must have made popular sovereignty seem plausible to Douglas, but instead of reassuring northern opinion it revived northern fears. In addition to its defects in stirring up familiar anxieties over the threat of southern expansion, it appeared, not as a way of solving a sectional impasse, but as a deliberate Democratic effort to open the territories to slavery when everyone thought it had been excluded. In this sense the device Douglas had chosen produced a political effect that was contrary to his plain intentions: far from subordinating the debate over slavery to the claims of popular rights, it equated the occupation of the territories with the destruction of democratic values. Here as in so many other instances the pressure of Democratic traditions served chiefly to disarm Democratic spokesmen in the face of northern concerns.[74]

Even so, the idea of popular sovereignty might have proved an acceptable response to slavery had the Court not burdened it with its opinion in the *Dred Scott* case, which had two destructive consequences that Douglas could not hope to avoid. In the first place, it duplicated the effect of the Kansas-Nebraska Act in opening still further areas of freedom to the incursions of southern slaveholders, whereas Douglas had clearly supposed that his bill would effectively bar slavery from most of the territories. It also made Douglas vulnerable to Abraham Lincoln, who challenged him in their famous debates to bring his favorite doctrine to the test of constitutional interpretation. As Lincoln well knew, Douglas could not do so; but this was not the main consequence of Lincoln's lawyerly stratagem. It was, instead, that he helped destroy all hope for Douglas's moderate solution to the strife between sections by appealing to constitutional consistency to make Douglas's position seem unacceptable to the democratic conscience. In the last analysis, he maneuvered even democratic constitutionalism into a weapon against the Democratic Union.[75,m]

THE INTRANSIGENT SOUTH

While Democrats like Douglas unintentionally weakened their party's authority, southerners of the same political persuasion did almost everything that could have been done to further the sectional crisis. This was plainly not their intention, and it is doubtful whether many of them recognized the ultimate tendency of their actions, but they too contributed to the disaster that finally overtook the Union by the intransigence with which they clung to their rights and institutions.

The loyalty that southerners felt to Democratic principles undoubtedly had much to do with the inflexibility they ultimately displayed. Motivated by relatively clear-cut economic interests, probably motivated as well by deep-seated fears that any kind of active national government threatened to put an end to slavery, southerners were often exceedingly doctrinaire in articulating the laissez-faire principles that characterized Jacksonian Democracy. Their attack on the protective tariff, which led to the nullification controversy of the early 1830s, was in some sense a paradigm for all later confrontations. In southern eyes, at any rate, the tariff demonstrated that the North would abandon principle when its interests conflicted with its professed ideals, and its actions in later decades simply renewed southern efforts to restore true liberty.

The starting point for southern agitation of the tariff question was the familiar Democratic proposition that any legislation that redirects the economic activities of the nation also deprives the producing classes of the hard-earned rewards of their labor. This was the economic heart of John C. Calhoun's *Exposition and Protest* in 1828; it was reiterated at some length in South Carolina's *Address to the People of the United States* in 1832; and it ran through the harangues that characterized other southern documents. As the Jackson and Barbour Convention of North Carolina explained in 1832, "The majority may lay taxes on you not only to defray the expenses of the government, (a power which all admit,) but also for the purpose of conveying a part of the profits made by one portion of the community into the pockets of another portion—of regulating the employment of capital and the pursuits of individuals, and of distributing as they may think proper the fruits of every man's industry." [76]

Undoubtedly this doctrine was polemical and might have varied in the course of time, but the South's peculiar position as a predominantly agricultural economy with major markets overseas ensured that its fundamental economic prejudices would not be easily abandoned. In addition, the declared loyalty of northern Democrats to the principles of liberal economics meant that southerners were bound to feel betrayed when they witnessed national measures that conflicted with them. Congressional legislation that protected northern manufactures or promoted internal improvements was not only an infringement on the economy of nature and an offense against the economy of principle; it was also an evidence of oppression that warranted talk of revolution. Anomalous as the argument may seem to us today, southerners who were exercised over the tariff could say with perfect aplomb that (in the words of the South Carolina *Address*), "it is a question of liberty on the one hand, and slavery on the other." "The broad principle in which the American people have cast the foundations of all their institutions," argued the citizens of the Richland District in their own *Address* of 1828, "is that every man is free to pursue his own interest according to his own judgment. Government is instituted not to direct man what is his interest, but to protect him in the pursuit of it. To surrender this great principle, would be to give up the achievements of the revolution." [77]

The southerners' sense of politics followed from these beliefs. They clung to constitutional structures as a remedy for political evils; in effect, they declared that only if northern legislators were curbed by constitutional devices could the authority of the national government be compatible with their own freedom. Hence they adopted the constitutional innovations we have already discussed in chapter VI, seeking to protect their rights against the changes that time had brought. Yet they were also profoundly aware of the extent to which the constitutional provisions they valued had been corrupted by the pressure of "aristocratic" interests and the compliance of northern voters. Again it hardly matters whether their perception of northern corruption was wholly polemical or partly genuine, for in either case it pointed toward the ultimate failure of any constitutional measures to solve southern problems. Nevertheless, the style of southern argument suggests that principle lent added strength to what polemics clearly expressed, a puritanical sense of indignation at the treachery of unworthy men. If Old Republicanism understood as a quest for pristine virtue had any hold on the American imagination, it was clearest in the South Carolina that propounded nullification. [78]

The nullification controversy brought the nation to the verge of a sectional confrontation from which all but the most zealous advocates of southern liberty drew back, and in this sense neither the concern for southern rights nor the attempt to modify the Constitution survived the counterpressures that southern agitation created. It seems fairly clear in retrospect, however, that only the disappearance of practical issues overcame southern doctrine: the relative success of national Democratic leaders in reducing the tariff and discouraging public expenditures meant that for the time being only purists like Calhoun felt the need to ponder the structure of the American government and its relationship to popular liberty. On the other hand, the very success the South experienced in securing its practical ends meant that it would be vulnerable to an extraordinary despair when its prerogatives were threatened a second time. In the long run the trend of national politics would not only convert most southern Democrats into followers of John Calhoun but destroy the southern Whigs because of their former sympathy with northern rule.

The conversion of southern politics was undoubtedly hastened by the fact that the territorial controversies of the 1840s and 1850s were explicitly controversies over slavery rather than disputes over the tariff. We shall return to the question of slavery in a moment; what is important here is that, confronted with what seemed to be unmistakable northern intrusions on their rights, southern spokesmen strove valiantly to redeem their section's position by an appeal to constitutional protections such as other Democrats had frequently maintained. In return they increasingly discovered that the Constitution as northerners perceived it did not protect the rights they insisted upon claiming, and they found themselves in a position in which they could afford to tolerate the Union only so long as some constitutional agency—the president, the Senate, or the Supreme Court—promised to maintain their equal rights against the aberrations of democratic politics. Langdon Cheves exemplified the agonizing position in which even Union Democrats were placed in his *Letter on Southern Wrongs*. Published in 1844 in response to northern attacks on the annexation of Texas, it deprecated the agitation for secession that some South Carolina hotheads had revived and rebuked other measures that these same men had proposed. Throughout the discourse, however, Cheves testified to his hatred of the wrongs done the South, and he left the unmistakable implication that the South must ultimately act to protect itself if the North would not abandon its aggressions.[79]

The reception that the North accorded the Wilmot Proviso clearly deepened southern fears. On the typical southern view, the whole nation had participated in the Mexican War and deserved to benefit from its rewards, while northern attacks on the slave power for precipitating an immoral war made unthinkable southern acquiescence in any formal measure to bar slavery from the new territories. Even more important, the proviso seemingly amounted to a distinct sectional perversion of the meaning of the Constitution, which had made explicit provisions for extending the nation westward. Whatever the legal or historical defects in their constitutional analysis, southerners could reasonably ask, as Representative Isaac Holmes of South Carolina did in 1845, "Must they suffer the construction to prevail which would confine the guaranties of the constitution to those limits, and none others, which existed at the time the constitution was adopted, and which utterly denied to the institution of slavery all power to expand itself in proportion to the progressive wants of the South?" Beyond this point, equal rights in the economy vindicated what the Constitution might not require. During the 1850s it was a commonplace of southern argument that every white man in the United States had a right to take his property into the territories under the equal protection of the laws. The ethic of economic exploitation determined the direction that constitutional interpretation must take, and the failure of northern Democrats to abide by their own ethic only proved to southern critics how desperate their situation was.[80]

In addition, northern agitation against slavery as an institution represented a clear political intrusion into an area supposedly reserved from the exercise of national power. On the classic Democratic view, the moral concerns of mankind had no place in the federal document, which in any event legitimized slavery by acknowledging it as a political fact. Calhoun explicitly developed the logic of this laissez-faire position in 1837 when he argued that the precedent of the Force Bill had stirred abolitionist zealots to try to capture the federal government in order to enforce their moral doctrines. Whether or not his sense of their motivations was accurate, it anticipated the inferences other southerners would soon draw from the hearing the North gave to antislavery doctrine in spite of constitutional limitations on the power of the federal government to deal with the domestic institutions of the South. In 1850, for example, a steadfast opponent of the Compromise of 1850 rebuked William J. Grayson for having supported it in spite of his previous record of resistance to the evils of federal oppression. In particular, he deprecated Grayson's argument that abolitionism was insignificant because it was only a social prejudice; rather, he insisted, Congress had repeatedly acted to apply the social lessons of abolition to the resolution of political issues.[81]

Even so, the confrontation of the 1840s came to a halt in the Compromise of 1850, in which the most vigorous advocates of southern rights were once again outvoted by the moderates of both sections. Had the compromise remained unchallenged, therefore, they might have lost their following; but the reopening of the territorial controversy in 1854 virtually guaranteed their ultimate success. The very raising of old issues in substantially the same form was bound to lend support to the zealots' interpretation of events. In addition, the clear tendency of northern agitators to question the domestic institutions of the South along with southern rights in the territories could only reinforce southern desperation. Northern reactions to the *Dred Scott* decision inevitably produced same effect. Frail as it might seem as a guarantee of southern rights, the Constitution as it had been interpreted by the Taney Court remained the last major means by which the South might be reconciled to the Union, and northern threats to override the decision clearly demonstrated how little faith might be placed in that vessel of national unity.[82]

But even northern antagonism toward the *Dred Scott* decision was not enough to undo southern loyalty completely. That depended instead upon the election of Abraham Lincoln—to which southerners themselves had contributed by rejecting Stephen A. Douglas—which apprehensive southerners perceived as an irrevocable challenge to the only remaining bulwark for their rights. Representative Humphrey Marshall of Kentucky summed up this widespread southern view when he attacked Representative Israel Washburn Jr. of Maine for having declared that the nation must elect a Republican president in order to stop the spread of slavery. On the one hand, he argued that because the status of existing territories was legally settled and further expansion was unlikely, the South could only infer that continued agitation of the issue was part of an implacable northern plot that might force the South to secede. On the other hand, he summarized William H. Seward's recent speech on the "Irrepressible Conflict" to bear witness that the real purpose of the Republicans was to destroy constitutional rights. Had southerners been more pragmatically inclined, perhaps, they might have recognized the futility of seceding in order to protect their practical interests, but their devotion to constitutional order helped drive them to their fate.[83]

This was the intellectual route by which the South moved toward secession. At the same time, convinced that they were wronged, and increasingly convinced that they were wronged because of unjustified antipathies toward their peculiar institution, southerners also undertook to defend it by rebuking northern ideals. In doing so they not only facilitated a more rapid development of their own willingness to secede but also fed northern antagonisms that made their situation intolerable.

The first premise of their attack was an argument that every white man in the South enjoyed a full measure of liberty because he was exempted from possible oppression through the slavery of an inferior race. "So far from this institution being uncongenial with a Republican Government," Representative John Campbell of South Carolina declared in 1842, "it is more useful in such a Government than in any other; for, as paradoxical as it may appear on a superficial view, it is nevertheless capable of demonstration that domestic slavery produces equality and nurtures a spirit of liberty among the citizen population of a country." Where it does not exist, "The poor and the rich . . . become divided into classes; and the free-born and laboring poor, although perhaps more virtuous than their rich neighbors, are treated as inferiors." Representative Henry A. Wise was more succinct. "The principle of slavery was a levelling principle," the Virginia Whig contended; "it was friendly to equality. Break down slavery, and you would with the same blow destroy the great Democratic principle of equality among men." [84]

Thus far the defenders of slavery stood on fairly familiar ground, but their argument from racial rights necessarily involved the corollary proposition that any society in which all men are legally equal must in fact deprive some of them of their freedom. This might have remained a merely sociological observation, a recognition of social facts that northern agitators had ignored. The pressures southerners felt, however, increasingly caused them to transform it into an attack on northern values. Instead of resting content with the theory that they were advantaged by their own situation, they insisted upon praising slavery as a way of life that rebuked northern pretensions to liberty. In effect, and sometimes even in actual speech, they insisted on treating their peculiar institution as a cure for northern freedoms.

The details of this proslavery argument are sufficiently familiar to require no further analysis here. What is important for our purposes is the thoroughness with which its partisans sought out and rebuked northern hopes. They took issue with the northern economy and denounced northern politics; they denied northern institutions and scoffed at northern reforms. George Fitzhugh exemplified the ultimate thrust of their thought in two extraordinary books in which he condemned beneficent capitalism and ridiculed liberal economics, defended aristocratic privilege and denied equal rights, criticized free governments and deplored constitutional liberty, laughed at free society and mocked the idea of progress. Virtually the only northern commitment he did not subject to a withering attack was universal education for the poor, which he sought to promote in Virginia, and other southern intransigents more than made up for this deficiency. "We have got to hating everything with the prefix free," one of them wrote during the 1850s, "from free negroes down and up the whole catalogue—free farms, free labor, free society, free will, free thinking, free children, free schools—all belonging to the same band of damnable isms." The final outcome of northern agitation was southern secession from northern rights.[85]

Such extraordinary challenges could only feed northern antagonisms, and as the sectional crisis deepened the opponents of slavery extension made ever greater use of the materials with which these southern zealots had provided them. The most important fact about proslavery theory was not the extent to which it may have expressed a conviction that was not widely felt in the South, but the way in which it entered into the sectional controversy with results that could only be disastrous. Whatever role it may have played in southern politics, it provided authentic texts with which northerners could justify repudiating southern claims. The final outcome of southern agitation was northern indifference to southern rights.[86]

Other southern expressions clearly reinforced this inexorable tendency. One involved western homesteads: not only did Democratic leaders defeat successive bills, but southern opponents of the prospective measures subjected them to the same kind of scathing indictment that other southern polemicists had applied to other northern hopes. Simultaneously, southerners' insistence upon claiming their rights in the territories, understandable as it may have been, clearly served to deepen northern anxieties by its implicit challenge to the values they attached to the West.[87] Still another form of intransigence was the proslavery invasion of Kansas. Here as elsewhere the question of who was "right" is less important than the consequences southern intransigence invited: a handful of armed slaveholders seeking to maintain their legal privileges in Kansas destroyed popular sovereignty and engendered northern retaliation. So, too, the intermittent agitation of other controversial questions that many northerners had supposed were settled intensified northern hostility at the expense of southern rights. One was the acquisition of Cuba, with its analogies in Central America: even the mention of annexing further slave territory, not to speak of the activities of southern filibusterers, was bound to cause reactions that could only damage southern influence. Another was the idea of reopening the slave trade, which some zealots demanded as a legal privilege while others put it into practice by smuggling Negroes into the country. In both cases, men who acted outside the law only served to convince apprehensive northerners that the law itself must go.[88]

The ultimate southern expression was an appeal to the right of secession, which southerners increasingly invoked. From their point of view this was a logical and even a necessary measure to protect their constitutional rights. From the perspective of their northern critics, on the other hand, it was the final proof of southern sin. Indeed, the fact that many northerners only half believed the southern threat probably served to intensify the hostile attitude with which they perceived southern grievances: had they taken the threat of secession seriously, they might have sensed the force of southern fears, but instead they took offense at the clamor southerners made. In any event, the ultimate recourse southerners invoked served paradoxically as a final guarantee that the North would ignore their rights.

ARMAGEDDON

The roads the Americans took led to civil war. For the reasons we have explored, a generation that had very little sense of where it was going and virtually no prior intention of carrying out the measures it finally adopted entered into a war that few men believed was desirable for ends that were only vaguely defined. If either party to the war really knew what it was doing it was the South, which literally took its own life into its hands when it withdrew from the American union and defied it to do its worst. Hence the events of the 1860s depended in a very real sense on how the North reacted to secession, while the attitudes that region took toward history and politics determined the actions it would ultimately take. Like the controversies of the 1850s and the schism of 1861, the war as it finally developed was an act of the American faith.

The war was also an extraordinarily complex event, which we cannot examine here. Nevertheless, we can sketch out some of its most basic preoccupations as an outgrowth of earlier opinion. In essence, secession elicited predictably ambivalent reactions among both conservatives and democrats, which they resolved in favor of war because their traditions gave them no other choice. As various scholars have pointed out, Abraham Lincoln contributed a good deal to this result, and for this reason we might conclude that this conservative Whig lawyer, whose views had been formed during the Middle Period, determined the pattern of events by his devotion to liberty and union. Important as he may have been to the outbreak of hostilities, however, in his initial acts as president he neither invoked his section's most fundamental commitments nor fully articulated northern concerns. Rather, he helped to precipitate a war for the Union in the course of which the values his people adhered to ultimately reshaped his rather limited social faith.

Among conservatives, the most significant opinions were essentially religious, or at least tinged with religious concern. On the one side stood those whose initial reaction to secession was summed up in Horace Greeley's famous injunction, "Let the erring sisters depart in peace." Such a position had various origins but resulted in a common stance: whether because its proponents wished primarily to absolve themselves of sin, because they recognized that slavery was too deeply embedded in the Constitution to be overcome without war, or for other kinds of reasons, they put the truth as they perceived it before the claims of union. On the other hand, some few conservatives who were devoted to religious truth were willing even in 1860 to enforce their ways on the South, and the fighting as it deepened clearly added to their number. Moralists in their politics and intrusive to a fault, they gained a growing following as the struggle in which the North was engaged took on the characteristics of a holy war that might even be the prelude to the millennium. Their motives as moral reformers combined with the bitterness of the northern experience to transform their region's perspective on the war as it proceeded.[89]

The conservative point of view, so understood, reached its classic expression in the "Battle Hymn of the Republic," in which a northern humanitarian reformer triumphantly articulated her kind's vision of struggle and destiny during a dark period of the war. Two elements of the hymn are especially relevant here. One is the theme of divine retribution that dominates the opening stanza and extends through the three that follow it:

> *Mine eyes have seen the glory of the coming of the Lord:*
> *He is trampling out the vintage where the grapes of wrath*
>   *are stored;*
> *He hath loosed the fateful lightning of His terrible*
>   *swift sword:*
>   *His truth is marching on.*

The other is the theme of holy sacrifice that characterizes the final stanza:

> *In the beauty of the lilies Christ was born across the sea,*
> *With a glory in his bosom that transfigures you and me:*
> *As he died to make men holy, let us die to make men free,*
>   *While God is marching on.*

The war as this abolitionist ultimately perceived it was a war for all mankind conceived in the highest image of Christian benevolence.[90]

For their part, the great majority of northern democrats probably continued to look with suspicion on northern moralists' exhortations in spite of their own demonstrated susceptibility to those moralists' characterization of the struggle between slavery and freedom as a confrontation between evil and good. Devoted as they may have been to liberty, devout as they may have been in their private religious beliefs, they were predisposed to see both in the perspective of laissez faire. In addition, many of them—not only doughfaces and prospective Copperheads— seem to have felt with Alexander H. Stephens that force could not preserve the Union as Americans understood it. (In his letter to Abraham Lincoln saying as much, the future vice president of the Confederacy appealed to a classic Democratic conviction that the government of the American republic was grounded in the voluntary loyalty of its citizens—in "opinion" rather than "force," as so many writers had expressed it.) In 1860 as well as 1830, one part of the democratic mentality thought that freedom precluded force even in the best of causes.[91]

On the other hand, the Union probably meant more to democrats than it meant to many moralists: while the moralists owed their ultimate loyalty to a higher law to which it was the duty of their generation to respond, democrats shared a secular commitment to their nation as an embodiment of human freedom. Force could not legitimately be employed to coerce dissident opinion except when it jeopardized the survival of that nation, whereupon all of the secular values of democracy were infused with a spiritual meaning that transcended individual interests. During the crisis of the 1860s, northern democrats generally came to feel that their equal rights as individuals, their political rights as citizens, and their very identity as Americans must be maintained by public authority. They might sing "John Brown's Body" or they might use Julia Ward Howe's more stirring words; they marched off to war in behalf of their established ideals.

The ultimate grounds of their actions were expressed in four symbolic events. One was the fact that, far from sulking over the fate to which his political enemies had brought the nation, Stephen A. Douglas rallied his followers to the Union during the early days of the war. The second was that Senator Andrew Johnson of Tennessee, always a vigorous Democrat, cast his lot with the Union in part (as he declared) because he opted for the "great experiment" of self-government rather than the evils of southern "monarchy." [92]

The third was Abraham Lincoln's second inaugural address, in which the wartime president acknowledged the anguish of the conflict in terms of religious zeal—not the facile zeal for righteousness that so many moralists proclaimed, however, but the zeal to abide God's purposes even when their logic was partly obscure: "Fondly do we hope—fervently do we pray—that this mighty scourge of war may speedily pass away. Yet, if God wills that it continue, until all the wealth piled by the bondman's two hundred and fifty years of unrequited toil shall be sunk, and until every drop of blood drawn with the lash, shall be paid by another drawn with the sword, as was said three thousand years ago, so still it must be said 'the judgments of the Lord, are true and righteous altogether.' " [93] This was an essentially democratic statement in the sense that it presupposed neither the moral authority of a religious establishment nor the existence of an organic social order in which that establishment might influence the conduct of government. It suggested, instead, that the war had come because men had not been wise enough to prevent it, and that it could end only with the eradication of a grave social evil that had made liberal democracy impossible.

So, too, the fourth incident demonstrated that the democratic heritage had reached its highest expression in the war. Sixteen months earlier the president had articulated a vision of the struggle in the terms in which we still perceive it. Speaking of it as history rather than theology, of politics rather than morality, he portrayed the nation's agony as the ultimate test of the American experiment. "Four score and seven years ago," he said,

our fathers brought forth upon this continent a new Nation, conceived in Liberty, and dedicated to the proposition that all men are created equal. Now we are engaged in a great civil war, testing whether that Nation or any Nation so conceived and so dedicated can long endure. We are met on a great battle-field of that war. We are met to dedicate a portion of it as the final resting-place of those who here gave their lives that that nation might live. It is altogether fitting and proper that we should do this. But in a larger sense we cannot dedicate, we cannot consecrate, we cannot hallow this ground. The brave men living and dead who struggled here have consecrated it far above our power to add or detract. The world will little note nor long remember what we say here, but it can never forget what they did here. It is for us, the living, rather to be dedicated here to the unfinished work that they have thus far so nobly carried on. It is rather for us to be here dedicated to the great task remaining before us, that from these honored dead we take increased devotion to that cause for which they here gave the last full measure of devotion; that we here highly resolve that the dead shall not have died in vain; that this nation shall, under God, have a new birth of freedom; and that Government of the people, by the people, for the people, shall not perish from the earth.[94]

ABBREVIATIONS USED IN APPENDICES AND NOTES

AHR	*American Historical Review*
Am. Nat. Preacher	*American National Preacher* and *National Preacher*
Am. Rev.	*American Review* and *American Whig Review*
Ann. Cong.	*Debates and Proceedings in the Congress of the United States* (Annals of Congress)
AQ	*American Quarterly*
Cong. Globe	*Congressional Globe, Containing the Debates and Proceedings*
Dem. Rev.	*United States Magazine and Democratic Review*
Hunt's	*Merchants' Magazine and Commercial Review* and *Hunt's Merchants' Magazine*
Ill. C. C. (1847)	Arthur C. Cole, ed., *The Constitutional Debates of 1847*, Collections of the Illinois State Historical Library, vol. 14 (Springfield, Ill.: published by the Library, 1919)
Iowa C. C. (1844) *Iowa C. C.* (1846)	Benjamin F. Shambaugh, ed., *Fragments of the Debates of the Iowa Constitutional Conventions of 1844 and 1846* (Iowa City: State Historical Society of Iowa, 1900)
JAH	*Journal of American History*
Ky. C. C. (1849)	*Report of the Debates and Proceedings of the Convention for the Revision of the Constitution of the State of Kentucky. 1849*, R. Sutton, official reporter (Frankfort, Ky., 1849)
La. C. C. (1844)	*Official Report of the Debates in the Louisiana Convention.* N.p., n.d.
La. C. C. (1845)	*Proceedings and Debates of the Convention of Louisiana. Which assembled at the city of New Orleans January 14, 1844*, Robert J. Ker, reporter (New Orleans, 1845)
Mass. C. C. (1820–21)	*Journal of Debates and Proceedings in the Convention of Delegates, Chosen to Revise the Constitution of Massachusetts, Begun and Holden at Boston, November 15, 1820 and Continued by Adjournment to January 9, 1821*, new ed., rev. and corr. (Boston, 1853)
Mich. C. C. (1835)	Harold M. Dorr, ed., *The Michigan Constitutional Conventions of 1835–36. Debates and Proceedings,*

University of Michigan Publications in History and Political Science, vol. 13 (Ann Arbor, Mich.: U. of Mich., 1940)

Mich. C. C. (1850)   *Report of the Proceedings and Debates of the Convention to Revise the Constitution of the State of Michigan. 1850* (Lansing, Mich., 1850)

MVHR   *Mississippi Valley Historical Review*

N.J. C. C. (1844)   New Jersey Writers' Project, Works Progress Administration, *Proceedings of the New Jersey State Constitutional Convention of 1844* ([Trenton, N.J.]: New Jersey State House Commission, 1942)

No. Am. Rev.   *North American Review*

No. Car. C. C. (1835)   *Proceedings and Debates of the Convention of North-Carolina, Called to Amend the Constitution of the State, Which Assembled at Raleigh, June 4, 1835* (Raleigh, N.C., 1836)

N.Y. C. C. (1821)   *Reports of the Proceedings and Debates of the Convention of 1821, Assembled for the Purpose of Amending the Constitution of the State of New-York . . . .* Nathaniel H. Carter and William L. Stone, reporters (Albany, N.Y., 1821)

N.Y. C. C. (1846)   *Report of the Debates and Proceedings of the Convention for the Revision of the Constitution of the State of New-York. 1846,* reported by William G. Bishop and William H. Attree (Albany, N.Y., 1846)

N.-Y. Rev.   *New-York Review*

Ohio C. C. (1850–51)   *Report of the Debates and Proceedings of the Convention for the Revision of the Constitution of the State of Ohio, 1850–1851,* J. V. Smith, official reporter, 2 vols. (Columbus, Ohio, 1851)

Reg. Deb.   *Register of Debates in Congress*

Texas C. C. (1845)   *Debates of the Texas Convention,* Wm. F. Weeks, reporter [Austin, Tex., 1845]

U.S. Rep.   *Reports of Cases Argued and Adjudged in the Supreme Court of the United States*

Va. C. C. (1829–30)   *Proceedings and Debates of the Virginia State Convention of 1829–1830. To Which Are Subjoined, the New Constitution of Virginia, and the Votes of the People* (Richmond, Va., 1830)

West. Rev.   *Western Review*

Wisc. C. C. (1846)   Milo M. Quaife, ed., *The Convention of 1846,* Publications of the State Historical Society of Wisconsin, Collections, vol. 27 (Madison, Wisc.: The Society, 1919)

APPENDICES

Short titles of works are used throughout. Full titles will be found in the Bibliography, except for works listed in Abbreviations Used in Appendices and Notes.

CHAPTER I: MACROHISTORY

a. These generalizations about European thought would require considerable amplification if I were concerned with that thought for its own sake, or with tracing the origins of American belief. They are sufficient for my present purpose, which is to identify certain special characteristics of American thought that the rest of this chapter examines in detail. I have argued my general case in a somewhat different form in "The Idea of Progress in America: An Essay in Ideas and Method," *Journal of the History of Ideas* 16 (1955), 401–15, which also comments on some of the literature, including Arthur A. Ekirch Jr.'s *Idea of Progress in America*. See also Robert L. Heilbroner, *The Future as History*, ch. 1.

In *Redeemer Nation*, Ernest L. Tuveson argues persuasively that the American idea of progress was religious rather than secular in origin, a product of the millenarian tradition stemming from the Reformation rather than the perfectibilist ethos derived from the Enlightenment. He also implies that there was no possible meeting-ground between secular and religious conceptions of progress, but here I think that even if he is correct in differentiating the two strains he misconstrues the ways ordinary Americans thought. I shall deal with these religious doctrines more extensively later in this chapter; suffice it to say here that, having identified a bona fide millennial vision of progress, Tuveson associates it exclusively with Federalist writers and their New England successors, to the exclusion of the many devout Protestants who came to follow Thomas Jefferson, and whose ideas apparently influenced latter-day Democrats.

b. Here and elsewhere I differentiate writers into "conservatives" and "democrats" because I wish to examine the way men of different political persuasions or temperaments employed the ideas current in their time. Although these terms are far from satisfactory, they seem preferable to others that I might use, and they enable me to explore the range of American beliefs on key issues. In general, I associate what I characterize as "democratic" beliefs with the Democratic party, and what I characterize as "conservative" beliefs with the National Republicans and Whigs; where there is no other basis of distinction I am content to use the party affiliation of a writer (when it is known) as my clue to his intellectual allegiances. Nevertheless, I am well aware that there were conservative Democrats and liberal Whigs, and I qualify my two gross political categories where it seems appropriate to do so. Hence I sometimes distinguish liberal Democrats from their conservative collaborators, the better to assess the thrust of American thought. I make a comparable distinction among Whig spokesmen, dividing them (as I think they divided themselves) between those men who were loyal to an essentially organic vision of society and social order, and those who adopted a more modern view of society as a collection of atomistic individuals. (In such cases, I tend to believe that the differences between social perspectives rather than the similarities in party affiliation deserve closest attention.) In any event, I judge that the categories I use are the most effective way of getting at the patterns of thought I am interested in elucidating, and I hope that readers who bear with them will agree that they have meaning in the analysis of American thought.

c. I make large use of Fourth of July orations and similar set pieces in part 1 of this study because they provide the most succinct statements of Americans' attitudes toward history. They may seem dubious sources to modern eyes because they were so obviously rhetorical and because they were soon to pass out of fashion, but we should not underrate their importance as clues to the thinking of the Middle Period. So far as their deliberately rhetorical qualities are concerned, they represent no more than a heightened version of contemporary rhetorical practice, while the abstractness, allusiveness, and insistent spirituality we find so offensive were qualities much admired by contemporary audiences. In addition, as Richard M. Weaver has pointed out, speakers who employed what seems to us an artificially heightened mode of expression did so in the knowledge that they were invoking overriding moral principles and a heroic vision of history that their auditors fully shared. When, subsequently, oratory of this sort deteriorated and disappeared, it was not because it had been insignificant in its prime but because American tastes and attitudes had changed.

It is also worth noting that the ceremonial nature of the Fourth of July oration testifies to its importance. If, as various writers have suggested, the American people of the Middle Period sought to establish a national identity, which their newness and diversity made difficult, the only truly national ritual in which they participated offered them an unusual opportunity for expressing fundamental beliefs about their history—beliefs that might well be pushed aside in the bustle of daily affairs yet that surrounded and gave larger meaning to their daily activities. Howard H. Martin has very suitably compared the whole Fourth ceremony to a religious observance, in which the Declaration of Independence (customarily read at the start of the day's festivities) served in lieu of a religious text, and the oration in lieu of a sermon. For that matter, even the burlesque orations that first appeared during the 1850s and flourished during the 1870s gained their force from the contrast they exhibited between high-sounding principle and actual contemporary practice.

For penetrating discussions of the rhetoric of the Middle Period in general and of the Fourth of July in particular, see Richard M. Weaver, *The Ethics of Rhetoric*, ch. 7; Howard H. Martin, " 'Style' in the Golden Age," *Quarterly Journal of Speech* 43 (1957), 374–82; and Martin, "Orations on the Anniversary of American Independence, 1776–1876" (Ph.D. diss., Northwestern University, 1955), ch. 6. Chapters 3–5 of the dissertation could also be cited as partial confirmation of many of the specific attitudes I discuss here. Barnet Baskerville describes "19th Century Burlesque of Oratory" in *AQ* 20 (1968), 726–43, beginning with "Mr. Pepperage's Fourth of July Oration," in *Putnam's Monthly Magazine* 6, no. 1 (July 1855), 91–98, which is worth reading in its own right. See also Daniel J. Boorstin, *Americans: The National Experience*, pts. 6 and 7, and James W. Hall, "Concepts of Liberty in American Broadside Ballads 1850–1870," *Journal of Popular Culture* 2 (1968), 252–77.

d. Common American attitudes toward the period of time between the first colonial settlements and the achievements of the 1770s and 1780s tend to confirm the general expectation that the future would resemble the past. For the most part, conservatives and radicals alike linked discovery and colonization of the North American continent to the Revolution, as part of the same epochal event. At first glance such a practice may seem perfectly natural, inasmuch as Americans still tend to view their national past in terms of a comprehensive "American heritage." For that matter, it was logically consistent with the Jacksonian generation's sense of European history as a series of signal achievements punctuated by epochs of stasis or even momentary decline. But it was also an anomaly in their historical consciousness (if carried to its ultimate significance it would have deprived of importance the very achievement their Fourth of July orators sought to commemorate), and in any event it tended to deny the significance of historic time on this side of the Atlantic. The belief in an undifferentiated past was both striking in itself and predictive of an undifferentiated future, at least so far as history on the large scale was concerned.

Wesley F. Craven discusses American attitudes toward the colonial and revolutionary past in *Legend of the Founding Fathers*, in which ch. 1 is particularly relevant to my analysis. In *Genius of American Politics* and in other essays, Daniel Boorstin stresses the attitudes of "seamlessness" and "givenness" the Americans brought to their past, which I shall return to in chapter II of this study.

e. In a justly celebrated essay in the *American Quarterly*, as well as in other essays and his doctoral dissertation, Major L. Wilson has argued cogently that prominent Congressional Democrats of the Middle Period conceived of American freedom as something already completed, whereas Whigs saw it as a condition still undergoing development and reaching its full flowering only with the development of a corporate rather than an atomistic society. (See particularly "The Concept of Time and the Political Dialogue in the United States, 1828–1848," *AQ* 19 [1967], 619–44, and "An Analysis of the Ideas of Liberty and Union as used by Members of Congress and the Presidents from 1828 to 1861" [Ph.D. diss., University of Kansas, 1964].) It is impossible to do full justice to Wilson's argument here, but it is legitimate to indicate various reasons why I hold to my own reading of the sources.

First, it seems to me that the differences Wilson describes were differences of emphasis within a general position that can be described in fairly homogeneous terms. Despite their differences, Americans do not seem to have disagreed significantly when compared with contemporary Europeans. In addition, Wilson himself points out a general tendency of American commentators, especially in the North, to arrive at a consensus substantially like the "Democratic" belief he begins by viewing as only one among several competing beliefs, and it is worth noting that many of his citations to archetypal "Whig" thinkers are citations to men who remained aloof from many contemporary developments (e.g., John Quincy Adams) or who took different positions at different times (Daniel Webster). Under these circumstances it is difficult to credit his basic dichotomy.

Second, Wilson is primarily interested in tracing American attitudes toward the Union, and although he points out ways in which ideas of union reflected ideas about other aspects of American society, it remains true that he takes a special case to demonstrate a general proposition. Furthermore, in all of his work he is concerned to pursue an overriding thesis or question, one that amounts to a single key to American history. For better or worse, I hold that while historic secrets may often be unlocked by such keys, historic patterns of thought may not. To understand the American mind of the Middle Period we must approach it with greater willingness to sense its complexity.

In this connection, it is interesting to note that other analyses of American thought during the same period come to significantly different conclusions. For example, while the work of Marvin Meyers makes out the Jacksonian Democrats as dedicated adherents of an outmoded republic of virtue who consciously left innovation to their Whig opponents, Fred Somkin documents the ways in which conscious conservatives sought to celebrate a mythic past in order to counteract unwanted changes in their society, especially those engineered by democrats if not Democrats. (See Meyers, *The Jacksonian Persuasion*, and Somkin, *Unquiet Eagle*.) Each of these studies has great merit—and others might be cited to the same effect—but their disagreements cast doubt on any schematic historical formula, whether single-minded (as these tend to be) or elaborate and complex (as Wilson's is). At any rate, I find my own rather more eclectic reading of the sources more satisfactory in getting at what I take to have been the operative levels of American thought.

Most important, I find Wilson's argument implausible because he makes Jacksonian Democrats defenders of the status quo and Whigs proponents of significant long-range changes in the character of American institutions. Even if we grant the retrospective character of much of Jacksonian thought, it is difficult to see appeals by such men as Daniel Webster to the vision of a future freedom different from the present as being anything more than rhetorical flourishes intended to protect their clients against Democratic attacks. Wilson seemingly forgets how often conservatives have appealed to a vision of society perfecting itself through time in order to defeat any present measure of reform. In this sense, it was quite possible for Whigs to invoke continuous change and still revere the institutions established by the founding fathers—as in fact they were more inclined to do than Democrats, so far as any difference existed between the two parties. There is something perverse as well as provocative about identifying Webster primarily with the proponents of change.

Nor am I being inconsistent with my own dependence on rhetorical statements for evidence when I dismiss these conservative effusions as "rhetoric." To declare that some expressions of belief were merely rhetorical is not to deny the significance of thought generally; but if we accept all expressions as equally significant or representative, we are as foolish as if we accept none. Conservatives may indeed have felt a theoretical attachment to future change, but they clearly also felt an operational loyalty to established modes of conduct. If we are to treat their ideas as functional elements of their behavior—as shaping their perceptions of the world about them and controlling their responses to it—we must focus on their apparent practical convictions, inferring them as best we can from their statements, but proceeding with caution in our use of their formal theories.

In any event, there are many indications that conservatives embraced an essentially static view of American history. See, for example, John Neal, *Oration, Portland*, passim; [Calvin Colton], *Junius Tracts* no. 7, p. 10; Rufus Choate, "The Position and Functions of the American Bar, as an Element of Conservatism in the State" (1845), as found in Perry Miller, ed., *Legal Mind in America*, p. 262; [Charles Brooks], *Remarks on Europe*, p. 36; and H. W. Warner, "The Republic. No. 1," *Am. Rev.* 9, no. 4 (April 1849), 404b, as well as my discussion of conservative constitutionalism in chapter VIII. See also Norman Jacobson, "The Concept of Equality in the Assumptions and the Propaganda of Massachusetts Conservatives, 1790–1840" (Ph.D. diss., University of Wisconsin, 1951), for clear evidence that Massachusetts conservatives subordinated their private beliefs to the needs of propaganda.

f. In *The Jacksonian Persuasion*, Marvin Meyers has rightly identified a Jacksonian wish to affirm the past but has visualized it, I think erroneously, as a predominantly retroactive or retrogressive impulse. The Americans clearly believed that their forefathers had already established freedom and the institutions to maintain it; they sought to recapture a liberty that had been corrupted and suffered to degenerate. But it is only the modern historian who sees their search as nostalgic; in Jacksonian eyes, the problem was to be true to themselves, not true to some golden age. Chapter II and parts 2 and 3 of this volume deal more extensively with this belief and its implications.

g. My view here conflicts with that expressed by a number of scholars who see Thomas Cole's painting, "The Course of Empire," which portrays ascending and then descending stages in the history of a composite classical people, as a literal pictorial representation of the Americans' sense of history. It seems to me that they have misread this and other examples of the familiar appeal to cyclical history; it is at least questionable whether the people who flocked to Cole's exhibitions—the literati aside—did not see a series of events that it was within their power to avoid. Perry Miller suggests as much in "The End of the World," in *Errand into the Wilderness*, p. 236.

h. Godwin's hostile judgments help to put Whitman's insistently progressive perspective into context. However much Whitman looked forward to "new experiments in liberty," he remained faithful to the very political and social arrangements that Godwin repudiated.

i. Technically, of course, postmillenarians believed only that the Second Coming would follow rather than precede the thousand years of preparation for the Day of Judgment. Nevertheless, they also tended to believe that the thousand years had already begun and that it would come to fruition in their own country if not their own time. Thanks in part to the hopes Jonathan Edwards had expressed for the New World, this view was well established in American religious thought, but it had remained narrowly theological and highly speculative during the eighteenth century. During the early nineteenth century, however, it became a popular and a quasi-secular belief. On this point, see in particular J. F. Maclear, "The Republic and the Millennium," in Elwyn A. Smith, ed., *Religion of the Republic*, pp. 183–216, esp. pp. 194–200.

j. It goes without saying that many Protestants and several Protestant denominations, especially those of an Old School persuasion, rebelled at both the arrogance and the reformist proclivities that millenarian enthusiasts displayed. They objected not to the zeal for virtue but to the sense that perfect virtue was possible for fallen man and that it would be rewarded in historic time and geographic America. In doing so, however, they testified to the extraordinary nature of the Americans' faith in their country's destiny; although they demurred on unmistakably orthodox grounds at the heresy and the presumption in locating the millennium there, their dissent, respectable as it was, did not dissuade their compatriots from equating the country's prospects with final realization of the most cherished hope of mankind.

The prevalence of a sense of millennial expectation that apparently affected even secular writers helps confirm my judgment that most Americans did not visualize their history as one event in an ever-recurring cycle. It also helps explain why I tend not to credit interpretations of the Age of Jackson that represent typical Americans as seeking a return to Nature or to the Garden of Eden. Although literary figures expressed both sorts of ideas, I am convinced that they did so primarily to express their wonder at the opportunities that lay before the American people, not to anticipate a retrogression in time, and I find few invocations of either idea outside of literary circles. Chapter 1 of Roger B. Stein's *John Ruskin and Aesthetic Thought in America*, a subtle assessment of literary and philosophical views in the United States before the Civil War, reinforces my sense that "nature" was a literary and aesthetic convention that had little to do with the way Americans viewed their material experience; and see chapter XII of this study.

k. At this point I depart from Tuveson's interpretation. Tuveson insists, quite appropriately, that the two traditions were distinct and even disparate, but he ignores the possibility that American writers may not have been so scholarly as to keep them apart. Significantly, in his famous Phi Beta Kappa address at Union College in 1848, Charles Sumner made a point of distinguishing between indefinite improvement (a secular phenomenon) and perfectibility (an aspiration reserved to divinity). But he also predicted that with continuous improvement mankind would ultimately fulfill the law of God, and by gradual means (see Sumner, *Law of Human Progress*, pp. 12, 28f., 34f.).

l. To the modern eye there may seem to be an inconsistency in announcing that history has favored the Americans, only to wonder whether they are capable of living up to its demands, but in the religious perspective of the times the two propositions were virtually interchangeable; the answer to all doubts was unceasing effort. Here too Perry Miller's work is most suggestive; see particularly "From the Covenant to the Revival," in *Nature's Nation*, pp. 90–120.

CHAPTER II: MICROHISTORY

a. It seems highly probable that Democrats who spoke in these terms appealed (whether they knew it or not) to religious urgencies initially stimulated by Jonathan Edwards and Gilbert Tennant. In *Religion and the American Mind*, Alan Heimert repeatedly intimates that Democrats of the 1830s and 1840s inherited a religious commitment to social virtue that he traces to the years between 1740 and 1789. I think that much of his case remains to be proved—certainly it is questionable whether Whigs were exclusively "legalists" and Democrats all loyal followers of Edwards—but it suggests a good deal about Democratic beliefs as distinguished from Democratic facts. In effect, Democrats consistently tried to *identify* Whigs as "legalists" in a community of believers.

b. My reading of the sources also suggests that Democrats who cited the Alien and Sedition Acts against the Whigs may have done so more often because the Acts had been allegedly pro-British than because they had been manifestly illiberal, although Democrats could hardly be expected to distinguish between these alternatives because their predecessors, the victims of the Acts, had been anti-British.

c. Conservatives' rejection of the Old World is the more striking because many of the founding fathers had anticipated that the United States would one day find itself imitating its social patterns. Maurice Klain develops this point at some length in his Ph.D. dissertation, "Property in a Free Society: A Study of Early American Political Thought" (Yale University, 1949), pt. 1, ch. 5. It also conflicted with the affection and respect conservative writers often bestowed on British and even European precedents. Perhaps, indeed, conservatives secretly honored European traditions; on the hustings, however, they made more of the distinctions between Europe and the United States than the similarities. For typical public statements by unmistakably conservative Whigs, see John K. Porter, *Address at Albany*, pp. 20–21, and Daniel Ullmann, *Address delivered in the Tabernacle*, passim.

d. It is also worth noting that this version of history must have commended itself to immigrants to the United States, in that it presented them with much the same national history as native-born Americans. The act of migration was comparable to the American Revolution as an affirmation of liberty that every American shared, while the focus of immigrant effort—like the focus of native effort—was to perfect the enjoyment of that liberty. Indeed, in compressing the colonial settlements and the Revolution into a single event, native Americans implicitly equated their ancestors' immigration with attainment of the blessings of liberty. Although the proposition is speculative, it apparently helps solve a problem that has troubled sensitive historians, By what means did a nation of immigrants acquire identical founding fathers? It did so, apparently, by focusing their attention on present aspirations secured by having emerged from the European past. Treatments of American loyalty and American nationalism typically point to the zeal with which disparate ethnic groups adopted American heroes, but they do not satisfactorily explain the logic that made such adoptions possible.

CHAPTER III: THE MISSION OF AMERICA

a. A third school of thought has visualized American foreign policy as a product of American capitalism, and has devoted considerable ingenuity to showing how domestic economic pressures generated "imperialism." I find its explanations of events provocative but essentially irrelevant, for reasons I hope this chapter demonstrates. Suffice it to say here that even if economic considerations often shaped American policy, the frame of reference within which Americans took note of foreign affairs, and within which they sought to identify their interests and develop their policies, had a large bearing on how they conducted themselves. Only a historian who assumes there is a single law of necessity (and one that he is somehow privy to) can afford to ignore the recorded intellectual transactions of any given generation in assessing its behavior.

For that matter, my reading of the sources suggests that on the occasions when Americans most explicitly invoked economic interests as reasons for adopting given foreign policies, they did so largely in vain and out of a wish to appeal to their otherwise indifferent compatriots by associating measures they valued for reasons of "mission" with material interests that they thought most Americans pursued *in place of* it. This is not to say that economic interests were irrelevant to foreign policy nor to deny that particular men and particular groups clearly visualized the rest of the world as a vehicle for the nation's economic development. The question, rather, is what role such men were able to play in American society and what actions American attitudes toward the rest of the world made possible. The evidence suggests to me that the most far-sighted or expansive proponents of American capitalism dominating the world were prophets without honor in their own country.

b. In part, my distinction between secular and religious obligation is artificial and heuristic. As I have suggested in discussing religious elements in the Americans' ideas of macrohistory during the 1830s and 1840s, it is difficult to know where religious ideas ended and secular ideas began. On the other hand, the fact that many early advocates of a specific national mission were men whose other judgments were distinctly conservative in politics as well as orthodox in theology suggests that Ernest L. Tuveson and Yehoshua Arieli are correct in seeking to dissociate an orthodox religious tradition of mission from the secular agrarian tradition of example expressed by Jefferson and his followers. Still, mission and example were often blurred, or if distinct did not remain true to their putative origins, as this chapter indicates. (See Tuveson, *Redeemer Nation*, ch. 4, and Arieli, *Individualism and Nationalism in American Ideology*, chs. 7, 12 passim.)

c. The fact that so many advocates of American example—or, rather, of limiting American policy to example—were conservatives helps to explain why I do not share the view (expressed by Arieli and Tuveson) that two distinct traditions survived in the foreign-policy attitudes of the Middle Period. In broad terms, New England conservatives and spokesmen for political as well as religious orthodoxy quickly abandoned their region's peculiar commitment to a providential mission, or at least converted it to a mission of example, whereas (as we shall see) liberal democrats from other parts of the country were much more likely to insist that the example be vigorous, if indeed example were enough. It may well be that leading New England spokesmen for orthodoxy raised more clamor than their liberal counterparts about the need to evangelize the world, but the operative effect on foreign policy was minimal. Indeed, as Tuveson himself suggests, it seems likely that their missionary zeal was easily satisfied by the preaching of the word, and certainly they were insistent on the need to regenerate the United States before they could hope to regenerate the world. The sermons, homilies, and career of Lyman Beecher exemplify these patterns of belief, as does the example of Horace Greeley, who proposed to fulfill American obligations to European revolutionaries by sending them revolutionary tracts in lieu of more tangible assistance (for Greeley's proposal, see Arthur J. May, *Contemporary American Opinion of Mid-Century Revolutions*, p. 50). For typical religious expressions of an obligation to evangelize the world, see William Allen, "Freedom Conferred Only by the Gospel," *Am. Nat. Preacher* 7, no. 5 (October 1832), 65–80; Lyman Beecher, *Plea for the West;* John W. Fowler, *Society: Its Progress and Prospects*, p. 41; and John G. Bergen, *Discourse on Providence of God*, pp. 10–11.

d. In focusing on these late developments, we pass over an earlier event that also elicited American enthusiasm and seemingly threatened American neutrality, the Greek War for Independence that began in 1821 and entered into Congressional debate in 1823–24. But Greek independence was distinctly a minority cause, in a sense that later causes of a similar nature were not. Whether because they had not yet felt the challenge of Jacksonian democracy, because they still visualized the American nation as a chosen people with a providential mission to the world, or because they habitually thought in terms of religious missions to foreign lands, men who would one day become vigorous Whig opponents of the whole range of Democratic policies made their only major gesture toward an assertive foreign policy during the early 1820s.

Nevertheless, the position Greek sympathizers assumed and the arguments they adopted were strikingly similar to those that appeared during the 1840s, although the Greeks also benefited in American eyes by being latter-day exemplars of the classical heritage of liberty, as well as a Christian people locked in mortal combat with the forces of the antichrist. For a close study of American attitudes toward the Greek struggle for independence, see Myrtle Cline, *American Attitude toward Greek War of Independence*. The Congressional debates are reported in *Ann. Cong.*, 18th C, 1st S, cols. 1085–1213 passim. Edward M. Earle surveys "American Interest in the Greek Cause, 1821–1827" in *AHR* 33 (1927), 44–63, while Stephen A. Larrabee chronicles the attitudes and activities of zealous Hellenophiles in *Hellas Observed*.

e. Much the same thing may be said of other improprieties the Americans committed, such as sending Andrew Jackson Donelson to Frankfurt as an official emissary before the Frankfurt Assembly had established its authority, permitting German agents to fit out ships at the Brooklyn Navy Yard, and William H. Stiles's offer (while chargé d'affaires to Austria) to mediate the Austro-Hungarian conflict, not to mention Daniel Webster's gross treatment of the Chevalier Hülsemann, the Austrian chargé in Washington. The point is not that the Americans did nothing out of the ordinary, but that they offended European courts without affecting their course of action.

f. The extreme proponents of "Young America" probably form an exception to this generalization. This small group of outright interventionists, some of whom combined a financial interest in supplying arms to Hungary with advocacy of direct support for revolutionary regimes, helped to keep the issue of intervention before the public. But apparently they succeeded only in pressing Congressional Democrats to insist more strenuously than they might otherwise have done that one day the United States would be compelled to take up arms in Europe.

My remarks reflect my reading of the Senators and Representatives commonly identified as sympathizers with Young America, and especially those identified by Siert F. Riepma in " 'Young America': A Study in American Nationalism before the Civil War" (Ph.D. diss., Western Reserve University, 1939); but I leave out of account the aggressively antislavery agitators, especially John P. Hale and Joshua R. Giddings, who sought to convert popular sympathy for liberty abroad into a weapon against slavery at home. Hale's speeches in particular are striking exercises in a disingenuous logic, but their very skill casts doubt on the extent to which he took foreign policy seriously in formulating them. (See the speeches of 10 January 1850 [*Cong. Globe*, 31st C, 1st S, *Appendix*, pp. 113–15] and 3 December 1851 [ibid., 32nd C, 1st S, pp. 23–24].)

g. Strictly speaking, Democrats invoked liberty whereas Whig interventionists might also invoke righteousness as their goal. The difference was probably emblematic of residual differences between liberal and conservative versions of mission, but it would be difficult to maintain that the policies envisaged, or the objectives they were intended to serve, were significantly different because of this fact. (For Whig statements, see Seward, 9 March 1852, *Cong. Globe*, 32nd C, 1st S, *Appendix*, p. 247c, and Rep. John Wells, 2 July 1852, ibid., p. 790b.)

h. Clearly asylum was not offered to representatives of nonwhite races, but our modern tendency to decry what was wrong with American ideas of that earlier period will cause us to miss the thrust of American belief if we focus on this flaw. What we now call racism was so basic to the Americans' vision that it is an exercise in philosophy rather than historiography to tax them with it.

i. The idea that immigrants exercised a choice in coming to the United States, and (more broadly) that everyone was a resident by choice, may also help to explain why the idea that the Americans were a "chosen people" survived into the Middle Period without retaining the connotations that had initially attached to it. In effect, Americans would seem to have confused the original concept of *having been chosen* to carry out the Lord's work with the different concept of *having chosen* to do so. For that matter, such a shift in emphasis was quite compatible with the shift in Protestant theology from a vision of men dependent upon divine grace for salvation to a prospect of men enabled to choose salvation if they wished to. Perhaps this explanation is another way of conceiving the shift of values that Perry Miller points to in describing the metamorphosis of a Puritan people from "colonists" into "provincials" and ultimately into cultists of "Nature." (See particularly Miller, *Nature's Nation*, pp. 197–207.)

j. The characteristic thrust of American aspirations is made more apparent by the language of the *New York Herald*, which invoked typical fears of European intrusion as an excuse for outright imperialism. "This question of the unwarranted interference of the powers of Europe with the people of this continent," it held in January 1846, ". . . is destined to be the absorbing question in the politics of the age. It will swallow up Oregon and all other minor questions, which, in a momentary excitement, may appear of paramount interest. It appears to us that the true policy of the United States consists not in irritating these powers by idle demonstrations or by throwing at them paper bomb-shells of declarations of resolutions—not in seeking, or in clamoring for war with any of them, for that will come in its time—but our own true policy is to go on strengthening the Union—carrying out the annexation policy—to drop all small questions and boldly grasp the larger one. In fact to annex the whole of Mexico, instead of California—to merge the two republics in one, instead of taking a slice for breakfast today and another for dinner tomorrow. We shall be compelled to do this. The movement of the European powers will force us to take this important step, as a means of protection to our free and happy institutions" (*New York Herald*, 20 January 1846, as quoted by Frederick and Lois B. Merk, *Monroe Doctrine and American Expansionism*, p. 82).

It is also worth noting that various enthusiasts for expansion described territorial aggrandizement in terms also employed in describing the American mission to the world. Riepma notes with some dismay that Douglas Democrats typically took "intervention for non-intervention" to mean intervention in the Western Hemisphere to exclude British or other foreign influences in Cuba and elsewhere, but—given Democratic assumptions—this use of the term was quite understandable. By the same token, the *Democratic Review* developed its enthusiastic picture of immigration into the American asylum (described on page 62) during the course of an essay on the hazards and opportunities of territorial expansion; clearly its editor thought of expanding the area in which asylum would be possible. So did Benjamin F. Porter, a prominent Alabama Whig, in his Fourth of July oration at Tuscaloosa in 1845 (*Outlines of Oration of Judge Porter*, pp. 22–23). And it is not merely a fluke of history that William H. Seward should have conceived of reuniting the republic in 1861 by contriving a war of liberation against the French in Mexico. A Unionist and a bitter opponent of the expansion of slavery, he had also been an advocate of "intervention" and a friend to immigrants. (See Henry W. Temple, "William H. Seward," in Samuel Flagg Bemis, ed., *American Secretaries of State*, 7:29–36; but also note Henry Blumenthal, *Reappraisal of Franco-American Relations*, ch. 1.)

k. The fact that a handful of zealots, among them Senators Robert F. Stockton and Sidney Breese, continued to press for war over Oregon is an exception that proves the general rule. Extremists thought it was necessary to risk American liberty, as other extremists thought it was necessary to acquire all of Mexico, but they only identified the points to which even the typical expansionist would not go.

CHAPTER IV: EQUAL RIGHTS

a. Jacksonian measures plainly involved important political considerations as well as those of a predominantly social nature. Given the Jacksonians' definition of democracy, in fact, it is almost impossible to disentangle these two strains of thought, but we can understand the generation's thinking better if we make an analytical distinction here, returning to their theory of politics in part 3 of this study.

It should also be said that in associating the attack on "aristocracy" with the Democratic party I do not intend to imply that Democrats had a monopoly on either the ideal or the rhetoric of equal rights, which also informed the Antimasonic crusade and other contemporary developments, not least of them the opposition to Martin Van Buren's "Albany Regency." Nevertheless, the Democrats largely succeeded in identifying themselves with equal rights to the political detriment of National Republicans and Whigs, and to the extent that there was a philosophical difference between parties it lay in the difference between the principles of equal rights and traditions of hierarchy, deference, and an organic view of society.

It is also true, of course, that the Democratic party was far from monolithic and that it was often sharply divided against itself. In general, however, even when it divided over specific public measures it retained its nominal allegiance to equal rights, and in the long run it tended to impose its more systematic doctrines even on party members who had initially opposed them. For particulars of Democratic politics, see James R. Sharp, *Jacksonians versus the Banks;* Herbert Ershkowitz and William G. Shade, "Consensus or Conflict? Political Behavior in the State Legislatures during the Jacksonian Era," *JAH* 58 (1971), 591–621; David J. Russo, "The Major Political Issues of the Jacksonian Period and the Development of Party Loyalty in Congress, 1830–1840," *Transactions of the American Philosophical Society*, n.s., 62, pt. 5 (1972), as well as the more extended studies by Lee Benson, Thomas B. Alexander, and Joel H. Silbey (Benson, *Concept of Jack-*

sonian Democracy; Alexander, *Sectional Stress and Party Strength;* and Silbey, *The Shrine of Party.*

b. Democratic theory owed much to Thomas Jefferson's economic liberalism, but the fact of Jefferson's long hostility to "Hamiltonian" measures of national policy has tended to obscure the extent to which he and his sympathizers sanctioned positive government at the state and local levels. We will understand Jacksonian Democracy better if we recognize that it challenged Republican as well as Federalist practices.

The developments of the Middle Period are extraordinarily complex, but they seem to have involved the following elements:

(1) A basic democratic antipathy toward social class, and especially toward the superior pretensions of a social, political, or economic elite. This antipathy stemmed from the Revolutionary epoch if not before, and may well have involved a fundamentalist "Calvinist" hostility to the authority and practices of "Arminians" as well as a secular hostility to an elite that had no discoverable basis in birth, breeding, or any of the other qualities of European aristocracies. This phenomenon is explored sensitively by Alan Heimert in *Religion and the American Mind,* and exemplified in Samuel Eliot Morison, ed., "William Manning's *The Key of Libberty,*" *William and Mary Quarterly,* 3d ser., 13 (1956), 202–54.

(2) A genuine sense of dismay at the changes apparent in American society, which was just entering its period of economic "take-off," experiencing simultaneously a host of novel phenomena, among them the development of manufactures, commercial banking, intensive national or at least regional competition, a permanent labor force, technological innovation, and unfamiliar (not unprecedented) patterns of social distinction. The economic developments are lucidly sketched by George Rogers Taylor in *The Transportation Revolution,* although not in the language of take-off, while Marvin Meyers provides the best single estimate of democratic dismay in *The Jacksonian Persuasion.*

(3) A history of political innovations intended to enable the young nation and its separate states to cope with the problems and take advantage of the opportunities of independence. The electoral victory of the Jeffersonian Republicans in 1800 and their continued successes at the polls had made it possible for the country to adopt public economic measures like the Second Bank of the United States and a protective tariff, and for the states to charter corporations for banking, transportation, and manufacturing, that would probably have been politically impossible had the Federalists survived as an effective alternative party responsible for originating most of these measures. In any event, the needs of the economy, and above all its shortage of capital, pressed republican leaders to embrace economic innovations they would once have condemned. So did their elitist traditions of politics, which permitted them to look to a combination of public and private enterprise (exemplified in such ventures as corporate charters and public subscriptions to private undertakings affected with a public interest) to achieve public ends. These developments are discussed, so far as the states are concerned, in a series of studies that began with Oscar and Mary Handlin's *Commonwealth: Massachusetts;* the most relevant here is probably Nathan Miller's *Enterprise of a Free People.*

(4) The convergence of these phenomena in times of crisis, whether real or imaginary. True, there had always been voices in the wilderness like that of John

Taylor of Caroline, who repeatedly cried out against deviations from what he took to be the true principles of democracy; but Taylor had remained ineffectual, a doctrinaire theorist without a substantial following, until circumstances gave him an unprecedented hearing. The exact nature of these circumstances remains a puzzle in spite of all that has been written about Jacksonian Democracy. Their nature is not central to our concern here, however, which has to do with the ideas men employed and the way they employed them rather than with the circumstances that intially led to invoking them; we need say only that democratic ideas were available for use when untoward phenomena needed explaining, and that at the same time they apparently helped to determine what would seem untoward.

Certainly the same general pattern of reaction against previously accepted policies and practices was to recur again and again during the Middle Period. The history of the newer states is a history of underdeveloped societies introducing economic innovations like banks and corporations, which neither they nor anyone else fully understood, in order to accelerate economic growth, and of their people's reacting with increasing dogmatism against the innovations, the economic developments they had sought to foster, and the political agents and structures that had fostered them, when their defects became apparent. Under these circumstances, it was all too easy for midwestern democrats to turn to questionable and often obsolescent theories of society to "explain" their problems and "cure" their evils, and they were most likely to find support in the egalitarian Democratic tradition, if only because Whigs initially sought to justify positive government in spite of its incidental evils. The shifting attitudes of the midwestern states are nicely illustrated in two doctoral dissertations, Bayrd Still's "State Constitutional Development in the United States, 1829–1851" (University of Wisconsin, 1933), and William G. Shade's "The Politics of Free Banking in the Old Northwest, 1837–1863" (Wayne State University, 1966), which has recently appeared as *Banks or No Banks: The Money Issue in Western Politics;* and see ch. 17 of Richard E. Ellis, *The Jeffersonian Crisis.*

c. I have felt free to use the workingmen as spokesmen for democratic ideas because, despite their distinct party affiliation and sometime collaboration with National Republican managers, they clearly embraced and even more clearly articulated ideas that were less plainly stated but no less firmly held by a great many Democrats. For more general discussions of the patterns of American belief about education, see pt. 2 of my *Popular Education and Democratic Thought* and ch. 12 of Richard Hofstadter's *Anti-intellectualism in American Life,* which fails, however, to differentiate sufficiently between hostility to unwarranted aristocratic pretensions and hostility to learning and intelligence. For an illuminating discussion of workingmen's politics, see Walter Hugins, *Jacksonian Democracy and the Working Class.*

d. Yehoshua Arieli discusses the theoretical components and refinements of "free society" as it was visualized by Jeffersonian Republicans in ch. 8 of *Individualism and Nationalism in American Ideology.* I find his account persuasive as a study in the history of ideas but somewhat too philosophical to explain the attitudes ordinary Democrats held during the Middle Period. Marvin Meyers discusses many of the same phenomena in *The Jacksonian Persuasion,* but his analysis is so clearly governed by the hypothesis that Jacksonian thought came to a focus in the conscious reaffirmation of "Old Republican" values that it falls short of perceiving the ideas the Jacksonians held as a working system of belief. These remarks are at best a very quick rendering of the two books, which deserve an extended analysis that cannot be attempted here, but they may serve to indicate why I go over the same ground again.

In *The Liberal Tradition in America*, Louis Hartz has made much of the "Lockean" tradition in American thought, which, as Daniel Boorstin points out, was often Biblical rather than Lockean. Yet there was a secular tradition that is more properly associated with Locke than with the Bible, provided we take into account the thrust of Locke's argument rather than read all American history as an exercise in "Lockeanism." In the early chapters of his *Second Treatise of Civil Government* (1689), Locke insisted that men living in a state of nature could rightfully acquire no more than what they could consume, and that all further acquisition was against the law of nature because wasteful. In one of the least satisfactory chapters of the treatise, Locke went on to declare that men living in society might create other forms of property by convention, which would permit them to acquire and preserve wealth beyond their immediate needs, but the power his book had as an argument for liberty against tyranny rested on its image of the productive laborer retaining a modest reward, not on its ingenuity in extending that image to cover all forms and degrees of wealth, and this was the sense in which the Americans were Lockeans. Part 2 of Maurice Klain's Ph.D. dissertation, "Property in a Free Society," traces the development of radical ideas of property in America from their colonial origins into Jeffersonian thought, where they became part of the doctrine that Jacksonian Democrats inherited.

e. The further ramifications of Democratic ideas about success and self-making remain to be traced and compared with Whig ideas on the same subjects, but it is worth noting here that the vision of a competitive society of equals that most Democrats took for granted helped them to escape being torn apart by the contradictory visions recent historians have tended to discover in their thought, as for example "enterprise" and "Arcadia," "liberated capitalism" and "Old Republicanism." Certainly these disparate tendencies existed, and certainly the Democratic party was often split into factions that emphasized the one or the other, but the very fact that both factions tended to see themselves as the "true" Democratic party suggests that they had more in common than either faction had with the Whigs, and that what they had in common was a primary commitment to economic virtue rather than economic privilege as the basis of the good society.

f. Two celebrated Supreme Court decisions further exemplify the defects of Democratic logic. In the *Charles River Bridge* case, Chief Justice Taney appealed to an image of the social advantages to be gained by facilitating novel developments in transportation in order to support his action in setting aside the charter of the original bridge company. But his argument went no further than justifying strict construction of corporate charters in cases involving such public interests; by implication, at least, no social necessity could have overcome a clearly assigned right to exclusive control over the river crossing in question. In addition, Taney invoked constitutional precedents that clearly sanctioned his interpretation of the law; if anything, his opinion testified to the leeway constitutions had once given public authorities to promote the public good, not to the leeway

Democrats now demanded. (See *Charles River Bridge* v. *Warren Bridge, U.S. Rep.*, 11 Peters 536–54.)

Much the same thing may be said of *West River Bridge Company* v. *Joseph Dix et al.* Counsel for the defendants, who had appropriated the West River Bridge in Brattleboro under the provisions of a Vermont statute authorizing towns to establish public thoroughfares along the routes of previously established turnpikes and similar facilities, argued that the right to take private property for public use required no more justification than public interest or convenience. But Justice Daniel, speaking for the Court, held only that an incorporated body had no greater claim than a private individual to exemption from seizure by eminent domain. In other words, he ruled against a corporation but not in favor of extending the rights of the state, and in any event he found that the rights of the corporation had not been infringed upon inasmuch as compensation had been paid the plaintiffs. (See *U.S. Rep.*, 6 Howard 507–50.)

The *West River Bridge* case is also discussed in chapter V of this book; and see Wallace D. Farnham, " 'The Weakened Spring of Government': A Study in Nineteenth-Century American History," *AHR* 68 (1963), 662–80, for a provocative discussion of postbellum economic policies as a reflection of democratic hostility to the use of government for public purposes. Harry N. Scheiber deals at some length with the legal context of both the *Charles River Bridge* case and *West River Bridge* in "The Road to *Munn:* Eminent Domain and the Concept of Public Purpose in the State Courts," *Perspectives in American History* 5 (1971), 327–402. In stressing the existence of antebellum precedents for *Munn* v. *Illinois*, however, he tends to overemphasize the scope granted governments by the courts of the 1830s and 1840s.

g. In abandoning society for individuality, Democrats did not wholly abandon the possibility that government might be used to foster individualism, as the discussion in chapter VI argues in greater detail. They were not literal anarchists, and they had residual uses for government that might even grow, provided that the criteria of equal rights and the natural competitive processes were also met. But they did abandon other criteria by which the actions of government might be judged; this was their achievement and also the source of their ultimate weakness.

h. A more direct comparison might be drawn between English radicals and their American counterparts, social reformers like John Commerford and John Ferral, who were closely linked to English movements. But it would largely deprive us of additional perspectives on the American scene, for it would simply document the fact that a few American writers depicted their society in precisely the same terms as the English. This is the primary weakness in Edward Pessen's *Most Uncommon Jacksonians*, which is a convincing demonstration that some American writers bitterly rejected the social order in which they lived, but which can only hail them for their perceptions, not document their relevance. (That is, they may have been "relevant" in pointing to overriding evils, but a statement of this fact does not enable us to understand the Jacksonian mind any better, as Pessen's title and conclusion suggest.) At best, they were "right" rather than representative or influential.

I have essayed another kind of comparison between English and American ideas in the introduction to my anthology, *American Writings on Popular Education*, which deals primarily with middle-class attitudes toward democracy in the two countries. Robert Kelley approaches some of the same issues in *The Transatlantic Persuasion*, a sort of transatlantic extension of Marvin Meyers's work.

i. Typical radical attitudes toward personal success further confirm the residual effects of class in English social thought. Memoirs of leading agitators depict a constant process of self-making focused on rising in the world by acquiring the equivalent (or better) of a university education on one's own initiative. We have reason to sympathize with such aspirations to self-improvement because they did not involve grinding the faces of one's competitors and because they held up higher learning as a measure of personal worth, but we should not overlook the fact that these aspirations not only did not exclude, but actually embraced, a hierarchical vision of society. (Even today, the obverse of the anti-intellectualism of the United States is the intellectual elitism of Great Britain.) For a typical autobiography, see Thomas Cooper, *Life of Thomas Cooper*, and note the discussion of popular education in J. F. C. Harrison, *Learning and Living*.

j. The fact that Robert Owen's son Robert Dale Owen became a prominent Democratic doctrinaire and a Congressman from Indiana, whereas British radicals like William Lovett and Feargus O'Connor were persistently critical of American imperfections, epitomizes in a startling way the differences between the two societies.

CHAPTER V: THE CONSERVATIVE ETHIC

a. As will become apparent, the conservatives I discuss sought to justify substantial innovations in the American economy, including the expansion of paper credit, the development of corporations, and the encouragement of manufactures; they were by no means conservative in the sense of standing pat on the existing economy. But their vision of society, their concept of government, and their sense of the role wealthy men should play in both, were distinctly old-fashioned as well as conservative in the theoretical sense of offering a coherent social alternative to democratic atomism. However much they may have sought to innovate, they wished to do so on their terms and not on those of the egalitarian democrats who criticized them.

b. Even the famous *Essex Result*, drafted by Massachusetts conservatives who were frightened by the authority the proposed state constitution of 1778 bestowed on the state legislature, lacked the narrowness of later protests. Although it clearly came to a focus in the protection of property, which it represented as a natural right, it did not preclude effective government by suitably chosen representatives of the people. By the same token, it is worth noting that later fears of "agrarianism" probably depended in some degree on the conservatives' traditional expectations of active government. Had governments never held power over property, the substitution of popular rule for mixed government might not have seemed to threaten it. Given the precedents for active government, however, the prospect of universal suffrage and untrammeled access to office was understandably unsettling.

Beyond this, we may add that although the American colonists' controversy with Great Britain undoubtedly did much to alert conservatives to the threat of an intrusive government, it was probably the democratic rather than the conser-

vative critics of British policy who went farthest toward making property an inalienable natural right. Gentlemen of property and standing clearly invoked
Lockean principles in defense of their accustomed rights and privileges as colonists, but (as Alan Heimert insists to their discredit) they apparently read Locke
with implicit understanding of the limits both of his appeal to natural rights and
of his corollary appeal to popular sovereignty. By contrast, it was Thomas Jefferson who converted Lockean categories into a full-fledged expression of the right
to life, liberty, and the pursuit of happiness, as of the corollary right of revolution. The fact that Jefferson did not himself visualize property as an inalienable
right did not commit his followers to the same limited view of its claims.

For the *Essex Result*, see Theophilus Parsons Jr., *Memoir of Theophilus Parsons*,
pp. 359–402. Heimert's discussion of the limits of Whiggish radicalism is to be
found in his *Religion and the American Mind*, ch. 8. Wiley E. Hodges briefly traces
Democratic-Republican appeals to the natural rights of property in "The Theoretical Basis for Anti-governmentalism in Virginia, 1789–1836," *Journal of Politics*
9 (1947), esp. pp. 325–28, and see Richard Schlatter, *Private Property*, pp.
187–200. For a belated expression of the traditional conservative expectation that
property must contribute to the general welfare, see "Proposed City Loan," *Cincinnati Daily Gazette*, 2 January 1837, p. 2a, and contrast it with Noah Webster,
Instructive and Entertaining Lessons for Youth (1836), as found in Ruth M. Elson,
Guardians of Tradition, p. 280, and John P. Kennedy, *Quodlibet*, p. 129.

c. In this connection it seems significant that the defenders of corporate
charters freely invoked the needs of widows and orphans as a reason for maintaining the rights of property. Here as elsewhere they expressed a concern for
the welfare of dependent classes as the hallmark of their democracy. See particularly *Facts for the People* (1832), pp. 4b, 5a, and [Calvin Colton], *Junius Tracts* no.
7, p. 3.

CHAPTER VI: ENTERPRISE

a. Here as elsewhere I am pressed by what I take to be the weight of the evidence to emphasize ways in which Americans of the Middle Period reached a
consensus on public issues despite a tradition of disagreement. Again I find that a
number of fascinating studies of American thought have emphasized the disparate origins of American belief to the detriment of their understanding of the
direction in which it moved. Yehoshua Arieli in particular stresses two distinct
traditions, the Jeffersonian idea of "free society" (which corresponds to what I
have described under "equal rights"), and the New England idea of "individualism" (which I shall discuss in connection with the conservative idea of success),
as the background for American individualism more broadly considered. Yet his
study is so largely concerned with the philosophical origins and elaborations of
these two disparate positions that it undervalues their interactions and ultimate
conjunction. As will become apparent, I tend to see neither a complete resolution
of the differences between traditions nor a victory for one over the other, but a
partly unconscious process of accommodation that actually restated the issues of
American politics.

b. Be it noted that I am describing a logical tendency, and one grounded in
considerations of individual rights rather than those of "success" in any well-
developed sense. I deal with the extent to which Democrats adopted the idea of

success in a later section of this chapter. For clear Democratic expressions of devotion to property, see William Leggett, 30 December 1834, in *Political Writings*, 1:144; David Naar, in *N.J. C. C.* (1844), p. 400; Thomas M. Wadsworth, in *La. C. C.* (1845), p. 548a–b; and C. P. Bush, in *Mich. C. C.* (1850), p. 67a, as well as notes 6 and 7 to this chapter.

c. Readers who are familiar with James W. Hurst's studies of the American legal tradition will note that I adopt most of Hurst's general conclusions but that I do not accept his happy interpretation of American law as a constructive vehicle of national development. Taken as a social phenomenon, of course, the law did provide a friendly environment for economic expansion, but its practitioners can hardly be said to have played so conscious and consciously positive a role as Hurst implies. Even Leonard W. Levy, who documents the important role played by Lemuel Shaw in the modernization of the common law, has difficulty in maintaining his thesis that Shaw was a creative and resourceful jurist, and Shaw was admittedly unusual. For these matters, see Hurst, *Law and Conditions of Freedom;* Levy, *Law of the Commonwealth;* Corwin, *Liberty Against Government*, ch. 3; and Commons, *Legal Foundations of Capitalism*, esp. ch. 2, a neglected study that demonstrates with remarkable persuasiveness the long-range tendency of the courts to expand the rights of property at the expense of the rights of society.

d. Partisan microhistory aside, the overlap between democratic and conservative attitudes toward property and society probably helps explain why so many Federalists gravitated into the Democratic party and so many Republicans into the ranks of the Whigs. The constitutional convention of Louisiana provides a stunning confirmation of the grounds of similarity: the conservatives who defended property representation in the state senate to the bitter end were more often Democrats than Whigs. (Their views are discussed at some length in appendix g to chapter IX.) Nevertheless, the confusion of party principles should not be permitted to distract us from the fact that in Louisiana as well as elsewhere there was a distinct clash of opinion between democrats and conservatives, or that even in Louisiana Democrats who sought to defend property representation generally acceded in other respects to the same views as their more radical fellow-partisans. American attitudes toward politics and social policy may have been confused but they were not homogeneous, although they moved toward homogeneity as the Middle Period wore on.

e. Two writers of impeccable conservatism document this shift of perspective. Although Freeman Hunt continued to hold the mercantile class to traditional social obligations in the columns of his *Merchants' Magazine*, the essays and editorials he printed there increasingly described an atomistic social universe rather than the organic universe of the past. Hence, for example, his publication of various essays by F. O. J. Smith. Similarly, although Francis Wayland clearly subscribed to conservative views of both property and society, his formal economic theory could not have been more atomistic or more antagonistic to theories of social obligation.

f. Richard Weiss provides a fresh insight into the character and effects of the so-called Protestant ethic in ch. 1 of *American Myth of Success*, which stresses the importance of a secure moral order over other elements of the creed. Nevertheless, I think he has so far differentiated the Protestant ethic in America from its European versions as to miss the internal logic of the doctrine.

Much the same thing may be said of other studies that seek to refute Max Weber by demonstrating that Calvinism in its original form was far from giving its sanction either to atomistic individualism or to zeal for upward mobility. Although they provide a necessary corrective for vulgarized renderings of Weber's hypothesis, they also fail to acknowledge the extent to which the secularization of religion worked to transform the theological concepts they describe. It is quite true, for example, that the idea that every man has a calling in this world originated in a purely religious sentiment (the priesthood of the individual believer) and took the world as it was for granted (rather than challenging the individual to prove anything about himself by his role in it); hence the individual played his assigned role as an act of faith rather than works. But the very concepts of faith and works were radically altered by developments within Calvinism, most particularly by the covenant theology, which tended to make faith a work and work a means to salvation rather than an expression of one's holy estate. On one level, this development apparently introduced an irresistible pressure to visualize secular activities as expressions, signs, and (ultimately) means of grace. On another level, it apparently tended to dissolve the bonds of society by increasing each man's responsibility for his own salvation. It was not just that no one else could provide salvation for him, but that he alone held it within his grasp, if only he mastered himself. The first development tended to promote republicanism understood as acquiescence in social hierarchy, provided the needs of upward mobility were met; the second to promote democracy understood as the equal rights of individuals to pursue their own paths.

Here, at least, is the main outline of what I take to have been the evolution of characteristic American attitudes. It remains unproven here, but it suggests how it was possible for Protestantism to metamorphose into a secular faith that would have been disowned by its founders. As usual, Perry Miller's works provide stimulating clues to the transformation of American theology. In addition, I have found three doctoral dissertations most useful in assessing the origins and significance of the ethic: Robert S. Michaelsen, "The American Gospel of Work and the Protestant Doctrine of Vocation" (Yale University, 1951); Ruth Douglas See, "The Protestant Doctrine of Vocation in the Presbyterian Thought of Nineteenth-Century America" (New York University, 1952); and Marie Ahearn, "The Rhetoric of Work and Vocation in Some Popular Northern Writings before 1860" (Brown University, 1965).

g. Obviously the idea that the soul is able to throw off the burdens of sin represented theological heresy (Arminianism) as well as a potent source for ideas of upward mobility. But the heresy was widespread in nineteenth-century America. Beman had been an ally of Charles G. Finney in the controversies that rocked the Presbyterian Church during the 1830s, and other writers expressed similar ideas even though they did not engage in theological polemics. Louisa Tuthill, who was the widow of the editor of the *Christian Spectator* and who had turned to writing didactic literature to make ends meet, drew a direct analogy between farming and a successful career that obviously stemmed from the same voluntaristic theology. Success depends on Providence as farming depends on rain, she wrote, only to add that the result in either case is assured if one does the right things (*Success in Life. The Merchant*, p. 8).

h. Conservative writers occasionally invoked the agrarian idea of success when it suited their purposes. In 1838 John Neal drew a parallel between national and personal independence in his oration at Portland, and the Whigs of Pennsylvania sought to identify their gubernatorial candidate as a self-made yeoman in their address to the people of the state (Neal, *Oration, Portland*, pp. 23–24; *Proceedings of Convention of Democratic Young Men for Ritner*, p. 8). See also Henry Clay, Speech on the American System, 2 February 1832, in which he describes the manufacturers of Kentucky as "enterprising and self-made men, who have acquired whatever wealth they possess by patient and diligent labor" (*Works* 5:464).

i. The conservative idea of the self-made man also involved a combination of Romantic and sentimental attitudes that cannot be dealt with at length here. The Romantic idea was exemplified above all by Emerson, who converted self-making into a cosmic obligation and cosmic obligation into self-making. The sentimental idea was epitomized by Henry Clay, whom Whig apologists depicted as a barefoot boy living in the "slashes," working for his widowed mother, wending his way West as a helpless orphan, and rising to great distinction by virtue of his peerless intellect. The Romantic version would deeply influence postbellum American thought; the sentimental version naturally appealed to Whig partisans, not only because it seemed to fit Clay's career, but also because it offered a synthesis of elitism and egalitarianism that corresponded with Whig visions of society. For a stunning expression of the Clay legend, see the advertisement an anonymous author wrote for *The Life of Henry Clay* by Horace Greeley and Epes Sargeant, which appears in the appendix of Greeley's *An Overland Journey*. For other examples, see [Calvin Colton], *Junius Tracts* no. 4, p. 2 (under the heading of "The self-made man"), and "Hamilton" [W. R. Watson], *The Whig Party*, p. 38. Daniel Webster tried to achieve much the same effect by his famous claim to log-cabin origins (see A. B. Norton, ed., *Great Revolution of 1840*, p. 233).

j. Still another evidence of Barnum's essentially naive celebration of the art of money-getting is his ingenuous expression of pleasure in his achievements as an entrepreneur. His museum was clearly a business—not a lugubrious didactic undertaking, but a good show. His "Persian" villa at Bridgeport had some of the same qualities—it might in fact be said to have been designed according to the specifications of Middleton Flam, whom John Pendleton Kennedy satirized in *Quodlibet*—and even his patent fire extinguisher was a useful gadget that Barnum talks about as a worthy achievement without offering any cant about its utility. It should also be said that Barnum was clearly gratified by his reception in England, where he was honored by the Queen and entertained by the nobility. But even here he seems not to have lost his buoyant sense of self-esteem; he was pleased to be recognized as an American rather than as an aspirant to the equivalent of a title or an order of merit.

k. Hence the pursuit of success that Freedley took for granted was not so obsessive as the pursuit enjoined and at the same time monitored by orthodox moralists. Freedley's approach left his readers with little else to think about but the pursuit of the main chance; in this sense it made success a paramount aim. But it did not require money-making in the same sense as the developed Protestant ethic, for prosperity rather than salvation was at stake.

Alternatively, it might be said that Freedley remained faithful to traditional versions of salvation rather than the Arminian heresy. Certainly his description of the extent to which the aspiring businessman can wrest a fortune from circumstances seems to echo traditional religious injunctions touching on preparation for salvation: "Independence is certainly attainable by adhering to the laws of trade; a reasonable degree of happiness is attainable by the right management of business; but all that can be done by any one towards acquiring wealth is to place himself in the way of favorable junctures, and make himself ready for their approach; to descry opportunities at a distance, and keep his eye steadily upon them . . . ; and, secondly, not to turn aside the favorable train of circumstances that may have been laid for him, by his own wilfulness, imprudence, or unskilfulness" (*Practical Treatise on Business*, p. 34, and cf. pp. 230–31). Freedley's unpretentious perspective on wealth was also demonstrated in the appendix to *Opportunities for Industry and Investment*, which offered his readers advice on such matters as the composition of alloys, the manufacture of ice-cream, breaking a horse, and making soup.

l. Freedley's use of Hunt's statistics on the failures experienced by merchants illustrates this difference. In 1846 Hunt published in his *Merchants' Magazine* an address by Gen. H. A. S. Dearborn on "The Chances of Success in Mercantile Life," and he returned to the theme in 1847 and 1848, whereupon Freedley reprinted all three articles in his *Practical Treatise on Business*. In the *Merchants' Magazine*, however, they appeared to be backhanded testimony to the challenge of mercantile pursuits as well as admonitions to lesser men not to run such risks. (All three agreed that the odds were better than 25 to 1 against achieving lasting success.) By contrast, Freedley used the statistics to launch a discussion of how bankruptcies might be *avoided*. Compare *Merchants' Magazine* 15, no. 5 (November 1846), 475–77; 17, no. 3 (September 1847), 324–35; and 19, no. 2 (August 1848), 233, with Freedley, *Practical Treatise on Business*, ch. 14.

m. The paradox of Democrats who insisted upon laissez faire only to demand the benefits of subsidized transportation or even of a protective tariff is sufficiently familiar to need no documentation; my point here is that it was plausible rather than paradoxical. William G. Shade's "Politics of Free Banking" is especially illuminating on midwestern attitudes toward banks, as is ch. 16 of Fritz Redlich's *Molding of American Banking*.

The process of accommodation was already at work in the 1840s, at least so far as use of the word "enterprise" was concerned. It seems significant that the term appears repeatedly in Democratic arguments for territorial expansion, where American enterprise is contrasted with Mexican sluggishness; it is apparently a corollary of Lockean economics. But the usage in these instances bears none of the burdens of earlier usages, for enterprise is now a national characteristic (not a characteristic shared by different men in unequal quantities), and it also legitimately connotes heroic acts undertaken with a view to national needs (rather than connoting either unacceptable social distinctions or an illegitimate use of government). Hence use of the term in this context tends to confirm the proposition that "enterprise" became palatable to democrats when it was universalized and stripped of its connotations of conscious paternalism.

CHAPTER VII: THE POLITICS OF DEMOCRACY

a. The sequence of my analysis here reflects what I take to be one of the key facts about American political attitudes: that in many respects popular claims to rights followed rather than preceded the popular antipathy toward power. In any theoretical system, of course, it is both easier and more plausible to begin with a definition of rights and derive a system of government or a system of limitations from it, and in dealing with political thought we are all too prone to look for such a definition and assume that opinions were based upon it. Nevertheless, it seems to me that anyone who observes the characteristic patterns of American democratic thought without such theoretical presuppositions in mind must acknowledge that rights are paramount only in the sense that Americans appeal to them to justify exemptions from authority. Historically, this was the pattern they had followed during their dispute with the British Crown, and it was also the pattern of their responses to "monopoly," "aristocracy," and the other evils of positive government in both Jeffersonian and Jacksonian times. Although they articulated a general theory of rights, and bills of particular rights to protect them, they did not set about extending rights to all men so much as cataloguing the things they would not permit governments to do to themselves.

This was especially true of the political as distinct from the economic realm. Although democratic economic theory centered on equal standing before the law and repudiated intrusions on the order of nature, the very fact that democrats visualized society as a body of individuals pursuing their own economic interests probably helped them to conceive of economic rights in both a positive and a universalistic sense: every man qualified for, and was entitled to, a range of rights best described as natural and extending equally to everyone. By contrast, looking with disdain on government and its officers except as expressions of popular sovereignty, they had little occasion to project rights as a positive claim on society. True, they could easily perceive voting as a natural right, for the reasons I shall indicate: in effect, it gave every man the necessary power to protect himself. In other respects, however, their expressions of rights came down to assertions of the limited authority of government, and when they universalized them (as, for example, in barring an established religion) it was only to the extent of securing the same right for everybody against public authority—not to that of protecting every dissident enthusiast in the pursuit of his own idiosyncratic beliefs.

Neither European liberals nor thoughtful American democrats fully understood this bias in American thought, which understandably seemed to them a betrayal of the liberty Americans particularly prided themselves on. Hence Tocqueville's strictures on the tyranny of the majority, and hence also the recurrent popularity among American intellectuals of Tocqueville as historian of the American democracy. One need not agree with Tocqueville's criticisms in order to appreciate the thrust of his observations. The idea of liberty that Americans adhered to was neither grounded in philosophical premises about human rights nor shaped by philosophical perceptions about the extent to which any true theory of liberty must provide for the rights of others with whom one is not sympathetic. Rather, it came close to being each individual's assertion that no one else might govern him, from which he tended (logically enough) to infer that government itself must be diminished to a minimum.

Implicit patterns of thought like this are difficult to demonstrate with any certainty, but they are surprisingly apparent even in the relatively philosophical statements about self-government that Americans occasionally drafted. (Unphilosophical Americans simply ignored the philosophical issues and clamored for their "rights.") We shall turn to these systematic expressions of belief after examining more prosaic and more typical statements.

Meanwhile it may be helpful to speculate why American democrats generally held such a restricted view of political freedom. In essence, I suspect it arose because so many of them were religious dissidents, in America as well as Europe. (I do not intend to deny the influence of the Enlightenment, especially on someone like Jefferson, but it is difficult to see where the Enlightenment was permanently domesticated in the United States.) Antagonism arose between dissidents and established churches in the colonies, where it took the form of an understandably absolute and irreconcilable hostility to authority because any act by that authority tended to threaten conscience rather than mere convenience. Hence the chief lesson of religious dissent was that, however well-intentioned, efforts to promote the good of society by controlling individual behavior are intolerable exercises of power. This derivation of democratic attitudes seems to me the more plausible in view of the tendency Jacksonian social theorists displayed to equate the separation of bank and state with the separation of church and state. (See note 12 to this chapter, and also the pronouncement by the St. Lawrence County Convention [New York] in 1837: "In a republic, where the government is essentially democratic, as in ours, the grand fundamental principle, is equality; in such government, a great regulator of the business occupations, or consciences, of men, not only, is not required, but should not be tolerated. The blessings of such government, like the dews of heaven, should be dispensed, alike to all, and should be felt only, in the security which every citizen enjoys, in the possession of his own property, the produce of his own industry and skill, the safety of his person, and the enjoyment, of 'life, liberty, and the pursuit of happiness, rights inestimable, and unalterable' . . ." [*St. Lawrence Republican, Extra,* July 1837, p. 2a]. Democratic invocations of the "voluntary principle" in economics had the same force; see, for example, [John L. O'Sullivan], "Introduction," *Dem. Rev.* 1, no. 1 [October 1837], 7, and "Glances at Congress," ibid., p. 70.)

Obviously this democratic perspective had ancient roots, most particularly in the English libertarian tradition. But American democrats of the Middle Period carried the original principle far beyond the point to which either English political theorists or their own revolutionary forebears had carried it. English liberals and English republicans had visualized a politics of virtue as a counterbalance to the politics of corruption practiced by a number of British monarchs, but they had not implied that governments established according to their specifications would be almost as dangerous as those maintained in defiance of them. Similarly, American revolutionary leaders had challenged the legitimacy of hereditary monarchical rule and had elaborated a number of reasons for fearing the effects of power, but they had not demurred at establishing an effective republican government. It is true that English radicals like the Levellers, and American opponents of consolidation who made up the bulk of the Antifederalists, came close to insisting that every act of government must have the sanction of the electorate, and it seems probable that democratic doctrines were influenced by these contentions. Still, both the English radicals and the Antifederalists clearly took the role of government for granted except in those areas to which they were particularly sensitive, whereas American doctrinaires increasingly called its very existence into question, as my further discussion of this point is intended to demonstrate. I shall discuss what might be called theories of government here, and theories of rights in the third section of this chapter. For an overview of the origins of American political beliefs, see Bernard Bailyn, *Ideological Origins of the American Revolution;* Gordon Wood, *Creation of the American Republic;* Richard Hofstadter, *America at 1750,* ch. 8; Gilman Ostrander, *Rights of Man in America;* Yehoshua Arieli, *Individualism and Nationalism in American Ideology;* and Cecelia S. Kenyon, ed., *The Antifederalists.*

b. As before, I am trying to establish major patterns of thought, not achieve immediate statistical precision in describing "Democratic" (and, later, "Whig") beliefs. In general, Democrats leaned toward the positions I shall describe here; Whigs toward the positions I shall describe in Chapter VIII. There were, of course, numerous exceptions—and some of these men ultimately changed party because of their ideas.

c. Lest it should seem from my expression here that I am totally insensitive to modern complaints that the electorate cannot do what it wants with the American government, let me add that the issue democrats drew in the Middle Period was different from the issue modern dissidents draw. By 1845 it was abundantly clear that democratic views were in the ascendant in the United States and that alternative visions of government were no longer viable. That is, Democrats felt able to do what they wanted to do; but what they wanted to do may well have been inadequate or irrelevant to their declared purpose of creating a just and equal society. At the risk of embroiling myself unnecessarily in modern controversies, I will add that in my opinion the inability of modern democrats to do what they say they want to do derives in large part from a fear of power that they have inherited from the Middle Period, as well as from economic and social practices that largely originated in that period.

d. For reasons of economy, I have simplified the pattern of the arguments for an extended suffrage. Some Republicans demanded the vote on the basis of rights; some democrats continued to invoke the traditional prudential arguments. *Niles' Register,* the non-freeholders of Richmond, N. G. Howard in his address to the people of Rankin County, and Thomas W. Dorr in his *Address to the People of Rhode Island* (1834) all appealed to both categories at once. Nevertheless, the general pattern was clear; these were clearly transitional expressions, and (so far as white manhood suffrage is concerned) the Americans moved from competence to rights.

e. The democratic definition of rights could even accommodate the fact that the vote was restricted to men, inasmuch as most men held that women were clearly disqualified by nature for participating in politics. Conversely, it is instructive that the first major effort to extend the vote to women was mounted in terms of the doctrine of natural rights. Indeed, it is an interesting speculation how far the initial flowering of the feminist movement in politics depended upon the substitution in nineteenth-century political discourse of a theory of natural rights for a theory of competence as a basis for extending the vote.

Some of the same questions may be raised with respect to Negro suffrage in the North. Typically, Democrats opposed extending or even retaining the suffrage for Negroes, and they tended to argue that the right of suffrage was only a conventional right. On the other hand, the proponents of Negro suffrage tended to be Whigs, who frequently appealed to the Declaration of Independence and other natural-rights sanctions to defend their position. In effect, the two parties tended to reverse positions when they turned from whites to blacks.

It would be plausible to conclude from this reversal that the doctrine of natural rights was merely a rhetorical device or a plaything of political advantage. Yet it is entirely possible to account for the apparent inconsistency of its partisans without conceding that the doctrine was insignificant. At least in part, Democratic appeals to the conventional origins of rights in order to exclude Negroes from the suffrage suggest that the Democrats felt compelled to escape the consequences of their loyalty to natural rights; that is, they were compelled by their racial prejudice to find reasons why Negroes should not enjoy political power. (In addition, being racists, they could well conceive both that Negroes had no title to political rights and that their enjoyment of political privileges must be controlled by its probable social consequences.) To this extent, the theory that rights are conventional, but not the theory that rights are natural, was a political rationalization.

By the same token, although most of the Whigs who espoused Negro suffrage on the basis of natural rights were undoubtedly candid in their statements of belief, their sincerity is less important for our purposes than the fact that it was only after conservatives had accepted a full-fledged theory of natural rights that they could apply it to Negroes. If their commitment was sincere, it represented a substantial concession to democratic theory. If it was largely polemical and designed primarily to embarrass Democrats, their behavior testified no less forcefully to the power of the democratic dogma. For that matter, the idea of natural rights not only survived the vagaries of contemporary politics but in the long run controlled them. The main political issue that remained to be settled as the Middle Period drew to a close was not the importance of natural rights but freedom for Negroes—and incidentally for women—to enjoy them.

For an unusually detailed argument against both Negro suffrage and female suffrage by a prominent liberal Democrat, see the remarks of Isaac T. Preston in *La. C. C.* (1845), p. 150 a–b, and cf. the report of a select committee of the Iowa constitutional convention on the same subjects (*Iowa C. C.* [1844], pp. 52–55). There is a classic debate on Negro suffrage in the Michigan convention of 1850 (*Mich. C. C.* [1850], pp. 284–96), and see ch. 8 of Eric Foner's *Free Soil, Free Labor, Free Men* for a discussion of the major parties' positions on the subject.

f. In stating the theory of democracy so that it included limitations on the self, Camp demonstrated the need that philosophical writers felt to articulate a complete theory of rights. The other writers I discuss in this section felt the same need and provided comparable formulations. Nevertheless, I reiterate what I suggested in appendix a to this chapter, that these theoretical elaborations of rights on a universal philosophical basis were far more characteristic of self-conscious political theorists than of ordinary democratic advocates of liberty.

g. My rendering of democratic thought here further differentiates my interpretation of American attitudes from that of Yehoshua Arieli. He points to a tradition, derived from leading British moralists, which held that a "free society" as Americans understood it would automatically provide for the social ends that other men left to the action of government to secure. I do not think that he is mistaken but that he overstresses the Americans' commitment to serving social purposes and consequently overstresses their insistence on secular virtue as a condition of freedom. I have somewhat the same reactions to John William Ward's brilliant essay, cited in note 1 to this chapter, which focuses on Democrats' attitudes toward power but which also implies that they treated virtue as a prerequisite of liberty. For a further discussion of the connections Democrats made between morality and popular government, see the third section of chapter X.

h. I trust it is clear that I am seeking to represent characteristic American attitudes even when they were not thought through. Obviously any body of law is in some sense derived from legislation, and American democrats often complained that their law was in fact judge-made or even English-made when it should have been restricted to measures adopted by their own legislatures. Nevertheless they continued to visualize the product they desired, not as a body of injunctions subject to continuous legislative amendment, but as a system of justice the legislature would perfect. By the same token, although they recognized and even demanded that the law be administered by competent democratic lawyers rather than the lackeys of "aristocrats," they apparently had little sense that the guild of lawyers might become a sort of professional corporation distinct from the common man. Given truly American law and truly American practitioners, they implied, justice would be done and popular rights would be secure.

CHAPTER VIII: THE POLITICS OF WHIGGERY

a. The campaign against Jackson also had roots in the Antimasonic movement, which Whig tacticians such as Thurlow Weed sought to attract into the Whig fold. In some instances the Antimasons leaned to the Whigs, in others to the Democrats, and in still others they resisted being incorporated into either party. It does not matter here, however, whether they were essentially conservatives in populist clothing (as the traditional interpretation suggests) or democrats opposed to Democratic party machines like the Albany Regency (as more recent interpretations indicate); the Whigs did all they could to enlist Antimasonic fears of power in their cause. For the classic account of the movement, see Charles McCarthy, *The Antimasonic Party*, 1:365–574. Arthur Schlesinger Jr. calls its democracy into question in ch. 23 of *The Age of Jackson*, while Lee Benson vouches for it in chs. 1–3 of *Concept of Jacksonian Democracy*. David Brion Davis treats Antimasonry as one of several characteristically American political aberrations in "Some Themes of Counter Subversion: An Analysis of Anti-Masonic, Anti-Catholic, and Anti-Mormon Literature," *MVHR* 47 (1960), 205–24, but Ronald P. Formisano treats many of the same behavior patterns more sympathetically in "Political Character, Antipartyism and the Second Party System," *AQ* 21 (1969), 683–709. For contemporary examples of Antimasonic hostility to power, see *Brief Report of Debates in Anti-Masonic Convention of Massachusetts; Free-Masonry*, p. 27; *Proceedings of Second United States Anti-Masonic Convention*, p. 29; and William Slade, *To the Public*.

b. In addition, of course, men like William Ellery Channing, Emerson, and Thoreau pursued their idiosyncratic religious convictions to the point of breaking with established values in both theology and social theory. They would appear to have given relatively little impetus to conservative thought, however, until more

pedestrian thinkers found their way from an organic to an atomistic theory of society and politics—whereupon Channing and Emerson (at least) became conservative sages. There is a further brief discussion of these writers in chapter X; see
also Yehoshua Arieli, *Individualism and Nationalism in American Ideology*, chs.
12–13.

c. In this connection it is worth noting that Daniel Webster's famous argument before the Massachusetts convention of 1820–1821, defending the senate as
a check upon the lower house rather than the people, may well have been
straightforward. Although we tend to see in it a disingenuous effort to maintain a
property-based upper house as a control on popular aberrations by disguising it
as a check on legislative error, Webster probably had in mind the need to filter all
legislation through a complex representation of divergent interests, the better to
arrive at a general good. There is no doubt that he also sought to protect property; but his wish to defend it need not be taken as proof that he deliberately
misrepresented the role of the senate for that reason (see Webster in *Mass. C. C.*
[1820–1821], p. 307).

d. It is interesting that Joseph Hornblower, who demurred at a bill of rights,
also demurred at the difficulties his colleagues sought to put in the way of
amendment: "If the people of New Jersey have submitted for sixty years to a colonial charter—which is no constitution at all—they may be safely trusted with
the power to change their constitution whenever the majority of the people shall
desire it" (*N.J. C. C.* [1844], p. 55, and cf. pp. 57–58). His dissent on the two
points together served both to mark him off from his colleagues and to underline
the direction in which they were moving.

e. Inasmuch as Democrats also looked to the law to serve their political purposes, it may be advisable here to underline the distinctions between the democratic and the conservative visions of the phenomenon of law. We have already
noted that democratic reformers sometimes attacked the common law on the
grounds that it was foreign, vested, and judge-made even though they often also
upheld the political ideal of a government of law rather than men. We have also
noted occasions on which progressive Democrats took issue with constitutionalism understood as reverence for an organic vision of law in which the
present was bound by the past and the future would be similarly bound. (We
shall return to Democratic constitutionalism in chapter IX.) Finally, we have
noted that the law as some democrats embraced it seems to have accommodated
lawlessness as well, the only rule of law democrats respected being a form of self-
government not amenable to external authority of any kind. By contrast, conservative advocates of law as a social instrument clearly visualized the phenomenon
they hailed as an authority external to its subjects and superior to their natural
motives. In effect, common law and constitutional law would work together to
prevent any generation from taking government into its own hands.

f. Discussions of the place the federal Constitution occupied in American
thought tend to argue that it was not fully established until after the Civil War,
which settled the outstanding issues of federalism and invited business interests
to discover an economic version of the higher law in the due process clause of the
Fourteenth Amendment. (See, for example, Wesley F. Craven, *Legend of the
Founding Fathers*; Paul C. Nagel, *One Nation Indivisible*; and James W. Hurst,
Growth of American Law, pp. 202–4.) Nevertheless it is clear that Fourth of July

orators and other celebrants frequently combined the drafting of the Declaration of Independence, the Revolution, and the drafting of the Constitution as a single breath-taking event that had changed the course of history by creating the American experiment. (See Howard H. Martin's "Orations on the Anniversary of American Independence," as well as chapter 1 of this study.) My own reading of the sources suggests that disagreements over issues like federalism and the scope of the judicial power did not diminish the Americans' reverence for the Constitution so much as intensify their effort to establish it in its true significance. That is, American publicists typically took it to be a part of their heritage, labored mightily to combat others' errors with their own truths, and quarreled most bitterly precisely because so many of them viewed it as the basis of their liberties.

g. Clearly, conservative arguments owed much to earlier statements of constitutional theory such as the *Federalist Papers*. The significant thing about them is not that they were unprecedented but that they were invoked when they were and for the purpose of combating democracy; they represented a clearly understood conservative strategy that increasingly subordinated popular government to political restrictions in the name of constitutional liberty.

CHAPTER IX: THE CONSTITUTION OF DEMOCRACY

a. In ch. 3 of *Liberal Tradition in America*, Louis Hartz argues that American constitutionalism was engendered by applying European categories of thought to American political conditions in such a fashion as to deprive American democrats of their proper claims to authority. Edwin Mims Jr. argues in a similar vein, in *Majority of the People*, that the Americans were persuaded by clever polemicists (chiefly Alexander Hamilton) to adopt external limitations on their power in the form of constitutional checks and judicial review. As these pages will demonstrate, I tend to see democratic constitutionalism instead as a product of popular attitudes toward power and liberty that were much more closely associated with the native American tradition than with the dialectic of European history, and that might well have arisen had Hamilton never collaborated in the *Federalist Papers*. (Indeed, it is a nice point whether Hamilton's arguments could have carried weight with typical democrats, given the way in which they usually treated his memory.) It is also worth noting that Thomas Jefferson, the Democrats' patron saint, anticipated many of the arguments that Mims develops against the canon of American constitutionalism, yet failed significantly to alter it. For a provocative discussion of constitutional limitations and Jefferson's attitudes toward them, see Henry Steele Commager, *Majority Rule and Minority Rights*, and consult ch. 2 of Oscar and Mary Handlin, *The Dimensions of Liberty*, for a more general treatment of American constitutionalism.

b. It is not my purpose here to assess the advantages and disadvantages of American constitutionalism, but it may be desirable to point out the problems that it has helped to create in American politics. Whether or not it was necessary or desirable in other respects, the American habit of looking to constitutional structures and processes to guarantee free government has had the effect of converting issues of political practice and public policy into issues of constitutional law and legal precedent. The role of the courts in frustrating popular wishes is only the most visible and in some senses the least significant consequence of our constitutional preoccupations, which have often prevented us from paying attention to what we were doing because our attention was so narrowly focused on how we were doing it—either in conforming to the constitutional structure or in finding ways to circumvent it. Although it is to be used with caution, the Progressive literature on constitutional government and judicial review has a good deal to say about the predicaments in which we have placed ourselves; see esp. chs. 1–3 of Herbert Croly, *Progressive Democracy*.

c. An exchange in the constitutional convention of Illinois reinforces this proposition. There Curtis K. Harvey, a young Democratic lawyer, ridiculed the idea that a revolution might be conducted under constitutional forms, but he was rebuked by Albert Gallatin Caldwell and Thompson Campbell, prominent members of the same party, for his skepticism. Although it is not clear from the surviving text whether Caldwell and Campbell intended specifically to sanction a constitutional right of revolution, it is clear that they sympathized with the Dorr rebels as legitimate revolutionaries. Furthermore, the very fact that Harvey saw fit to attack the idea suggests that it was current at the time. (See *Ill. C. C.* [1847], pp. 847–49.)

In this connection it is also worth noting that a number of state conventions sought to accomplish more than their enabling acts authorized and that in Michigan and New Jersey they met without strict constitutional authority. Clearly, Americans were used to taking constitutional law into their own hands—the better to implement their constitutional prejudices. Even Thomas Skidmore, the most consistently radical reformer among American radicals, presupposed that his agrarian innovations would be adopted by a popularly elected constitutional convention, which would simply set aside existing economic arrangements by a constitutional mandate. On the one hand, his device obviously represented an appeal to the constituent people to remake their constitutions; on the other hand, it is striking that he proposed to act through a quasi-constitutional process. For a discussion of events in Michigan, see Harold M. Dorr's introduction to his edition of *Mich. C. C.* (1835), pp. 3–18; for New Jersey, John Bebout's introduction to *N.J. C. C.* (1844), pp. xxxix–l. Skidmore explains his scheme in *Rights of Man to Property!* pp. 137–44.

For that matter, leading liberal Democrats habitually condemned European revolutions for their violence even when they sympathized with their aims. See, for example, John D. Pierce in *Mich. C. C.* (1850), p. 736a; and see "The Canada Question," *Dem. Rev.* 1, no. 2 (January 1838), 218–19, and "Annexation," ibid. 17, no. 1 (July and August, 1845), 5–10, where the authors clearly hope to see the results of revolution without its travails.

d. There were other instances in which democratic reformers claimed a constituent right of the people to alter their constitutions. The most dramatic occurred in North Carolina, where the advocates of reapportionment, blocked by the legislature from securing a legitimate convention, met extralegally at Raleigh in 1822 to draft a new constitution, which they submitted to the electorate at the next general election. Their campaign came to nothing, however, both because the proponents of reform were divided and because the electorate demurred at so radical a step. (On this point, see William K. Boyd, "The Antecedents of the North Carolina Convention of 1835," *South Atlantic Quarterly* 9 [1910], 83–93, 161–76.)

One aftermath of this event was that liberal Whig delegates to the constitutional convention of 1835 insisted that the constitution they were drafting be easily amendable, arguing that the people have a constituent right to alter their governments. The fact that they were Whigs rather than Democrats is relatively unimportant—in North Carolina, as in Virginia, sectional antagonisms tended to produce atypical political alignments, and in any event the domestic politics of the state bore little resemblance to national patterns—but it is still interesting, inasmuch as it suggests how little the constituent right of the people was thought to challenge constitutional principles: the Whigs asserted the *constituent* right of the people to justify an easy *amending* process. (See the remarks of Burges S. Gaither and John Giles, in *No. Car. C. C.* [1835], pp. 347, 369–70.)

Meanwhile radical reformers in Maryland had threatened to rebel if the legislature continued to obstruct equalization of the state's representation and limitations on its own power (see Bayrd Still, "State Constitutional Development in the United States," pp. 142ff.).

e. Clearly these liberal democrats of the 1840s departed substantially from the precedent of their immediate precursors in the early state conventions. The shift of opinion is puzzling until we realize that many advocates of popular power were in some degree Democratic-Republicans rather than Democrats in their thinking. That is, they represented a vision of politics geared to active government, competent public officials, and an informed electorate able to hold both in check, whereas latter-day Democrats tended to give up all three criteria in favor of democracy understood as limited government, rotation in office (the spoils system, not frequent recourse to the electorate), and an unrestricted suffrage. Their constitutionalism was an attempt to secure these conditions of politics, which were by traditional republican standards painfully restricted. Significantly, both Root and Tallmadge, not to mention a number of other Democratic-Republicans who did not sympathize with the extreme atomism of the Virginia school of politics, became Whigs or Whig supporters in their later years. We may put this fact down to apostasy, as "progressive" Democrats were wont to do, or we may suppose—I think more plausibly—that they originally embraced democracy understood in relatively elitist terms because they assumed that the populace would continue to honor both their leadership and their principles, but that they turned against it when it proved to be hostile to paternalism, to elitism, and even to competence in government. Chapters 16 and 17 of Richard E. Ellis's *The Jeffersonian Crisis*, are especially suggestive on this point.

f. Again it may be appropriate for me to point out that one need not oppose an independent judiciary in order to be aware that the view most Democrats held of the judiciary stood at odds with the declarations some of their liberal spokesmen made in favor of popular sovereignty. The clearest expression of the view they might have taken is Isaac Preston's remark in the Louisiana convention, to the effect that "judges are but the servants of the people. The government is distributed among three departments—the legislative, the executive, and the judiciary. The legislative is to express the will of the people, the executive is to execute it, and the judiciary to interpret it" (*La. C. C.* [1845], p. 700b). Significantly, however, Preston had in mind an elective *parish* judiciary, and he did not extend this argument to the state's highest court.

We gain a further sense of the position liberal Democrats took when we realize it would have been logical for them to demand that the determination of questions of constitutional law be referred to juries rather than judges, on the ground (implicit in the English origins of the jury) that twelve worthy laymen could say what the law of the community was. Obviously there are many historic reasons why Democrats did not propose such a system of popular review; one of them surely is that they were not effectively motivated to find a substitute for the judiciary. (Significantly, with more at stake, they developed a variety of proposals for curbing the federal Court, including measures intended to refer constitutional disputes to the Senate or to the constituent states.) Instead, popular election of judges sufficed to serve the purposes they had in view—and strengthened the effective power of the courts over the electorate.

g. It is a nice question whether conservative Democrats occupied a distinct position of their own or simply shared Whig opinions. Certain recognizably conservative statements by known Democrats suggest, however, that (especially in the South) conservative Democratic constitutionalism echoed typical Old Republican beliefs rather than approached the values of Whiggery. That is, while conservative Democrats often felt compelled to join their Whig counterparts in challenging democratic dogmas, their arguments remained in a real sense Democratic, although hostile to democratic enthusiasms.

Certainly one of their values would appear to have been a passionate commitment to inalienable rights, viewed less as an obstacle to a government they could not dominate than as a phenomenon any government must defer to. Volney Howard developed one version of this commitment during debate in the Texas convention when he took issue with the claim that the convention possessed unlimited authority to devise any constitution the people wanted: "Whatever may be the brute force of the majority, I deny its power as a question of right, under the pretence of governing, to adopt such measures as tend to the dissolution of society and the destruction of social order. I maintain, that government, whether the ultimate sovereignty be lodged in the hands of a few, or the whole people, has no right to violate the laws of nature or the social compact. When man submits himself to the laws of society and government, he surrenders so much of his natural liberty as the legitimate ends of society and government require; but he does not yield that which would be destructive of all society and his own existence." Similarly, in Louisiana, Thomas M. Wadsworth opposed easy amendment of the proposed constitution on the grounds that "the doctrine that majorities can do no wrong, and that they may substitute at their will and pleasure their say-so as the irrevocable law of the land, without consulting the minority, is one of the most aristocratic notions that can be conceived." (*Texas C. C.* [1845], p. 639; *La. C. C.* [1845], p. 845b.)

It followed that the rights of a minority must be afforded special protections, not simply because its property was jeopardized by threats of "agrarianism," but because any minority was self-evidently vulnerable whereas the majority could look after itself. Whigs knew this too, and perhaps only an excessively sensitive eye would seek to differentiate conservative Democratic statements from the commonplace Whig position. However, it seems to me that Democratic statements were distinctive, based upon the premise that individual rights are so sacred as to require special provision for minorities, whereas Whig statements that invoke the same general principle nevertheless convey a sense that their authors are more attached to some rights than others, and less concerned for minorities in general than for the special minority they represent. Certainly Cyrus Ratliff was much preoccupied with minorities in the Louisiana convention, and Wadsworth coupled vigorous assertions of Democratic doctrines with a defense of the minority principle. "The gentleman has asked me," Wadsworth declared in rebutting James F. Brent's latitudinarian views of the amending process, ". . . to give him a reason, why the constitution should not be placed at the whim and caprice of a temporary majority? I will tell him why. It is because the constitution is not made alone for the majority, it is made to protect the minority, the majority can very well take care of themselves. But the minority must be protected—they must be guaranteed against the ebulitions [sic] and outbreaks of majorities" (La. C. C. [1845], pp. 282b, 845a; and see the report of debates in the first session, La. C. C. [1844], p. 63b).

Even when Democratic conservatives explicitly sought to protect the rights of property, their statements sometimes suggested that it was not property as an institution or even property as a vested right but property as an extension of personality that must be protected—a right that corresponded with, rather than stood superior to, other rights. In Louisiana, Wadsworth urged a property basis for apportioning the state senate on the grounds that "all our exertions are to secure property. The representation of taxation and property, therefore, should be a vital principle in the formation of the senate. You have universal suffrage the basis of the house of representatives—for the sake of justice, then, let the senate stand by to prevent the State from being flooded with ruin by a prodigal waste of the treasury funds." By the same token, Bernard Marigny insisted that the convention had "a sacred obligation, to protect the rights of property in our courts of justice." "Where," he asked, "shall we, in fact, place the guarantees for property, if after establishing the executive and the legislative departments upon the unqualified rights of suffrage, we do not consecrate a place of refuge for property in the temple of justice[?]" Wadsworth's statement in particular recalls the hostility many Democrats felt toward active government as an engine of deprivation; conservative as it may be, it is not typically Whiggish, and in fact Wadsworth played a prominent role in the convention as a Democratic enemy to Whig economic measures (La. C. C. [1845], pp. 503a, 731b; and see James F. Brent and John R. Grymes, in ibid., pp. 110a–b, 722b–23a; also Charles W. Whipple, in Mich. C. C. [1850], p. 589b).

If these distinctions are valid, they also help to support the proposition that even when conservative Democrats expressed a most vigorous commitment to bicameralism or other forms of checks and balances they did so for somewhat different reasons from the Whigs. In Louisiana the line of distinction is so fine in the case of the most adamant conservatives as to be virtually if not actually invisible, witness John R. Grymes's statement that "in republican governments, which in one sense are essentially the governments of the people, we should establish certain definite principles, which while they secure the expression of the popular voice, and give to us all the benefits of republican institutions, will restrain any outbursts of sudden passion, or any abuses which the majority, under temporary excitement, may be disposed to commit; and which will maintain the vested rights of the minority." Still, it is interesting that Grymes advocated a "conservative power," which Democrats of less egregious conservatism also took to be a necessity even in popular constitutions, and that he sought to forestall the effects of "temporary excitements" within a specifically republican scheme of government. In addition, the vested rights he defended were probably those of slaveholders, which caused many southern Democrats to seek absolute prohibitions on legislative authority without sharing the whole Whig theory of vested rights in a corporate state (*La. C. C.* [1845], p. 122a; also Grymes, pp. 104a–b, 621b–23a; George Eustis, p. 545a–b; Marigny, p. 693b; and Robert E. B. Baylor, in *Texas C. C.* [1845], pp. 471–72).

Certainly conservative Democrats in other states expressed an explicitly "conservative" fear of the abuse of power understood more nearly as a political than an economic phenomenon. "The design of a Senate," Robert McClelland argued in the second Michigan convention, "is to act and operate as a check upon the House, and to preserve the conservative character of the Legislature. Hence the necessity of its members representing a larger territory and different constituents and interests from those of the House. . . . When the Representatives and Senators represented different territories, different constituencies and different interests, the measures proposed by one house were generally severely scrutinized by the other, and thus much hasty and immature legislation was prevented." So, too, John Clark declared that he "had always supposed that the object in creating a Senate was to make it a conservative body, so that it should operate as a check on the hasty and immature legislation of the more popular branch. That object was proposed to be accomplished by electing the members for a longer time, and making them the representatives of more general interests." In short, the explicitly "conservative" Democratic position seems to have originated in an antipathy toward active government, whereas the typical Whig position was fairly clearly a stance adopted to curb the authority of government after it had passed out of conservative hands. (*Mich. C. C.* [1850], pp. 112a–b, 348b; and see Robert E. B. Baylor, in *Texas C. C.* [1845], p. 137.)

Under these circumstances even the idea that a constitution binds subsequent generations took on somewhat different overtones from those that characterized it in Whig expressions. In general, Whigs seem to have sought to bind the future against predictable democratic aberrations, whereas conservative Democrats reacted more broadly against unwonted infringements of any kind on the public good. A delegate to Michigan's first convention as well as its second, McClelland rebuked his liberal colleagues for their carelessness in proposing to admit aliens to the suffrage. "Gentlemen urged that if the people were not pleased with the operation of this amendment, it could easily be amended. But were gentlemen disposed to act from such expectations? Were they satisfied with framing a sort of ephemeral constitution (if he might use the expression,) a constitution to exist for a day, and then to pass and be forever blotted out of existence? or were they prepared to establish it for the public good and guaranty and ensure its permanency to posterity? If the latter were their object, then he would inquire whether the step they were about to take, was not counter to all the precedents adduced and alluded to, and contrary to reason and prudence? Did they not endanger the existence and perpetuation of their most wholesome institutions by the introduction of a foreign influence? For the sake of illustration, suppose that in a presidential election, the event depended upon a single state, which was about equally divided, in such crisis might not alien votes, thrown into either scale, determine the election, and their influence in fact regulate and direct the destiny of our

country? Thus they might exercise over all our most important elections an un-
controllable influence: For if the principle were a good one, then every state in
the Union should adopt it, and then who could foresee the consequences." (*Mich.
C. C.* [1835], p. 190; and see Whipple in *Mich. C. C.* [1850], p. 588b; also p.
589b.)

A comparison between McClelland's remarks and those of William Woodbridge, which appear on page 204, reinforces the differences. McClelland employed the same formal argument in the same cause; perhaps there is no basis on
which to choose between them. Furthermore, the incomplete state of the contemporary record, the different origins and ages of the two speakers (Woodbridge
had been born in Connecticut in 1780; McClelland in Pennsylvania in 1807), and
the possibility that differences in rhetorical style may mask similarities in position, admonish us to be cautious in comparing them. Still, the two statements
were different, and the difference seems to lie between an essentially elitist sense
that constitutions must be kept sacred primarily in order to protect a well-
defined minority against prospective democratic tyrannies, and a more "democratic" sense that they are sacred because democrats as well as "aristocrats" will
benefit from prudent restraints on the conduct of the people.

Finally, there was the matter of judicial independence, which conservative
Democrats typically defended with the same tenacity and even the same phrases
as conservative Whigs. Yet it is a striking fact that George Eustis, the chief justice of Louisiana, sought to dissuade his colleagues from adopting a clause voiding illegal elections on the grounds that it would be an invitation to judicial
meddling, and it may also be significant that other very conservative Democrats
dwelt on the rights that the judiciary protected rather than the evils they might
forestall. "I look upon it as the sheet anchor of our rights," Thomas J. Rusk
declared in the Texas convention. "If we have an intelligent, honest, and correct
judiciary, your position is safe; the rights of persons and property are safe. If, on
the contrary, we have one which is swayed about by popular clamors, you are
upon a sea without a compass; your rights of person are not safe; your property
is not safe; the reputation of your country is endangered; all is anarchy and confusion." So, too, in Illinois, Onslow Peters argued that "the history of the judiciary throughout the country shows, that in no single state has it escaped from
the effects of a feverish excitement against the higher judicial tribunals, which in
many instances had forced them to submit to popular clamor and legislative control. This fact was known to all, and he called upon gentlemen to place at least
the highest courts of the state above all these influences, and then the people, in
case the inferior tribunals of the country do them injustice, will always have one
tribunal to protect their rights, property and liberties, and one conservative
power on which they can depend." (Eustis, in *La. C. C.* [1845], pp. 655b–56a;
Rusk, in *Texas C. C.* [1845], p. 288, and see James S. Mayfield, in ibid., p. 284;
Peters, in *Ill. C. C.* [1847], p. 450.)

In short, the evidence presented here seems to suggest that although conservative Democrats clearly differed from their more liberal colleagues, they also differed from the Whigs with whom they often collaborated. The proposition is
hardly conclusive, but it may still add something to our perception of liberal
Democratic thought. The existence of a conservative Democratic position that
shared key positions with liberal Democrats would help to explain why liberal

Democrats accommodated themselves so readily to constitutionalism; it was not just political necessity, but philosophical sympathy too, that worked to bring them together. It may also help to explain the hold that a remarkably conservative and even legalistic constitutionalism came to have in Democratic thought generally during the 1850s. But this is a development that we may better pursue at the conclusion of this study.

h. During the 1820s irate members of Congress pressed a number of proposals for constitutional reform aimed at limiting the power of the Court, as by repealing the Judiciary Act of 1789, requiring an extraordinary or an absolute majority of its members to override state legislation, or establishing the Senate as a court of last resort. (So, too, they debated reforming the Electoral College because of the "corrupt bargain" of 1824.) All of these proposals came to naught, however, and by 1835 (the historians of the Court tell us) its power was not seriously questioned. Charles Warren suggests that its authority was enhanced by the nullification controversy and by the publication of Kent's *Commentaries;* if so, we need to ask why these events should have been so persuasive. I would argue that democrats were largely prepared to accept the authority of the Court once it was as Democratic as the rest of the government, judicial review being incompatible with Democracy only as long as it was in the hands of "Federalists." Democratic party victories at the polls, together with the slight diminution of federal authority initiated by Chief Justice Roger B. Taney, undoubtedly helped to dispel Democratic fears, but the fact remains that the party of popular sovereignty, with leaders clearly sensitized to the anomalous role of the Court, hardly lifted a finger against it when they achieved power. See Charles Warren, *Supreme Court in United States History,* chs. 17–22; Charles Grove Haines, *Supreme Court in American Government and Politics,* chs. 13–17; and Commager, *Majority Rule and Minority Rights.*

i. Of course it should be added that some Democrats, most noticeably those in South Carolina, did press their criticisms to the point of proposing alternative constitutional devices, especially nullification (state interposition followed by amendment) and the idea of a concurrent majority. But these proposals centered more closely on the rights of the states against the federal government than on the rights of the people against constitutional obstacles to their authority. We shall return to the issues of states' rights in the next section of this chapter; here we may simply note that if states' rights had any effect it increased rather than diminished the existing obstacles to the exercise of popular power at the national level.

j. William W. Freehling makes a persuasive case, in *Prelude to Civil War,* for the proposition that slavery rather than the tariff was primarily responsible for South Carolina's fears and hence for the nullification controversy. I shall continue to treat the tariff as the center of the southerners' attention because this was what they *said* they were struggling over and because—once Freehling's point is conceded—it is simpler to do so rather than persevere in correcting their language. My argument holds, no matter what we take their primary grievance to have been: they appealed to constitutional rights, and were forced by northern attitudes to consider what they would do to maintain those rights in the face of external pressures. In this connection it may be necessary to point out that most southerners who clamored for "liberty" thought only of white men's needs. We will be less able to understand either southern defenses of slavery or Democratic attitudes toward it if we persist in the modern habit of confusing our own standards of politics and social order with those of an earlier day.

k. We can perceive the Democratic aspect even of Calhoun's minoritarian theory if we state his argument schematically: The people of any given state must be able to protect themselves against the inevitable encroachments of political power, but they cannot do so when they are in a permanent minority or when the national authority is enabled by its very infringements on the Constitution to persuade the electorate of other states to support its unconstitutional actions. Therefore any distinct minority must have some means to protect itself against the central government, and the population of every state must have some recourse against bribes that circumvent the fundamental law. If the Constitution does not provide these means, it makes liberty impossible. Therefore South Carolina is justified in sponsoring measures that are not specifically provided in the existing document. (As Calhoun himself observed, they are implicit in it in the same sense that judicial review is.)

CHAPTER X: RELIGION AS A FREE INSTITUTION

a. In general, there seem to have been two different moral crusades, which overlapped but were not identical. One was the effort, mounted by conservative Protestants who tended to be Federalists in their politics, to organize voluntary associations like those introduced by the Evangelical Movement in England and Wales, devoted to home and foreign missions, a domestic and foreign bible society, the distribution of evangelical and social tracts, and the introduction of religious training into secular Sunday schools, all intended to maintain traditional if not conservative standards of social order. The historians of this movement, which flourished in New York as well as New England, agree that it more or less lost its influence during the 1830s, handicapped by an ill-judged effort to restore the Christian Sabbath through legislation and by the Panic of 1837, which severely curtailed the funds that rich laymen like Arthur and Lewis Tappan could devote to the cause.

The second crusade would seem to have been more specifically rooted in New England and more clearly a theological development, an unraveling of the logical implications of Christian freedom by men who often began as the organizers of moral associations but who worked their way through to a more expansive vision of the power of religious opinion to redeem the national conscience. Many men were active in both camps—Lyman Beecher for one—but this New England tradition (if such it may be called) survived the difficulties of the 1830s and flourished in new environments like the Burned-Over District of western New York, where it helped to generate a vast outpouring of religious effort quite independent of any establishment. In effect, the greater the freedom an individual enjoyed, the less he could count upon established institutions to secure divine ends, and the greater the obligation he felt to secure them by his own actions.

In short, the first, or theocratic, tradition was almost bound to disappear, whereas the second, or revivalist, tradition had a long and useful life as a prop to free institutions. For further discussion of both traditions, see not only notes 6 and 7 to this chapter but also Whitney R. Cross, *The Burned-over District*. The first section of chapter XIII of my own study traces their involvement in the antislavery movement of the 1830s and afterward.

b. I have chosen these examples simply because they illustrate a point of view that increasingly characterized men of very different theological and social persuasions. Obviously Baptists and Methodists were more likely than Congregationalists and Presbyterians to espouse complete religious freedom, as they were also more likely to be democrats if not Democrats. But Chapin was a former Congregationalist; Southwick exemplified the peculiar come-outer strain in New England Puritanism; and Wylie represented the Scots-Irish Presbyterianism of western Pennsylvania, where his father had settled after migrating from Ireland. In effect, many devout Americans simply declared their independence of the ecclesiastical tradition that men like Beecher had sought to carry forward into the nineteenth century.

Because I am interested in exploring patterns of social thought (ideas about social structure, social change, and social obligation) I have not dealt with the specifically religious character of the concept of freedom that so many Americans expressed at this time. Nor is the question of its fundamental character easily solved, as is attested by persistent disagreements over its origins in the writings of leading historians of American religion. There can be no doubt, however, that most American denominations adopted the principles of "voluntaryism" during the Middle Period if they had not done so previously. That is, they declared that only religious authority voluntarily accepted by the individual had any validity, and they insisted upon separating the church from the state in order to make conviction truly free. (Even their zeal for moral reform often presupposed converting individuals to their truth, not coercing them into morally acceptable behavior.) At the same time, they adopted this religious vision out of respect for religious truth, not out of indifference to it. Hence they had no reason to build a wall between church and state once they had purged the relationships between them of every last vestige of impropriety and coercion. The struggle for religious freedom was not a struggle to eliminate religious values, but to make sure that they would prevail on their merits.

For suggestive discussions of the idea of religious freedom, see Perry Miller, "The Location of American Religious Freedom," in *Nature's Nation*, pp. 150–62; Wilber G. Katz, "Religion and Law in America," in James W. Smith and A. Leland Jamison, eds., *Religion in American Life*, 2:53–80; Winthrop S. Hudson, *American Protestantism*, passim; Mark DeWolfe Howe, *The Garden and the Wilderness*, passim; Timothy L. Smith, "Congregation, State, and Denomination: The Forming of the American Religious Structure," *William and Mary Quarterly* 25 (1968), 155–76; and William G. McLoughlin, *New England Dissent*, 2:1277–82.

c. Sometimes their demand for a truly Christian education was heightened by their hostility toward the homogenized Protestant morality that educational reformers like Horace Mann sought to introduce into the common schools. More often, it was motivated by the fear and hatred with which they witnessed the attempts of Roman Catholic leaders to acquire a share of public funds for parochial schools, or to drive the King James Bible out of the schools their wards attended. But the real point about this bigotry, as far as their ideas about free institutions are concerned, is that they thought religious training was indispensable to liberty, not that they wished to infringe on the true claims of conscience. For a classic statement of their position, see Horace Bushnell, *Common Schools*.

d. A number of scholars have suggested that the division of American politics corresponded closely with the division between advocates of an established church and advocates of complete religious freedom, or between "legalists" and revivalists in theology. I find these distinctions exaggerated, but significant as long as they are not taken literally. The most important thing about them is not their implied contention (as it were) that a revivalist could not be a Whig, nor a theocrat a Democrat, but that there was a recognizable relationship between religious and political ideas, which had much to do with the ways party spokesmen thought about religious issues. For brief discussions of the parallels between religious beliefs and American politics, see Lee Benson, *Concept of Jacksonian Democracy*, esp. chs. 7–9; William G. McLoughlin's introduction to his edition of Charles G. Finney's *Lectures on Revivals of Religion;* Perry Miller, *Life of the Mind in America*, bk 1, ch. 2; and Alan Heimert, *Religion and the American Mind*, passim.

e. This explanation for Democratic acceptance of the "voluntary principle" is at best tentative, but it makes sense out of otherwise incomprehensible circumstances. It seems fairly clear that most Democratic voters were inclined to be fundamentalists in their religious beliefs, whereas Whigs were more likely to be religious liberals, yet the outright advocates of secularism clearly gravitated into the Democratic party—in which Roman Catholics also found a home. The only plausible way to explain this otherwise baffling alliance is to assume that the party's position accommodated very different kinds of religious belief. Of course other factors were also influential, but it seems doubtful that they could have overriden deeply felt religious differences if no common ground had existed.

f. These observations serve to refine, and in this sense to reinforce, Stanley Elkins's brilliant insights into the anti-institutional character of American thought, which have received less than their due because of the overenthusiastic way he presented them in *Slavery*. As his critics have contended, American democrats clearly counted upon a whole variety of institutions (churches, schools, and the family, not to mention political parties, banks, and municipal corporations) to support the conditions of life they valued; hence they were far from being the transcendental anarchists Elkins describes. But it is equally clear that they sought to purge most of these institutions of their traditional coercive functions, so as to prevent them from encroaching on individual freedoms through their connections with the state. Even if they were not Transcendentalists, they were much concerned to assert the sovereignty of the individual under the sovereignty of God.

g. In general, the Democratic attachment to virtue may seem to have arisen out of the Republican tradition that Yehoshua Arieli discusses in *Individualism and Nationalism in American Ideology*, but it also changed it in significant respects. As we noted in chapter VII, Democrats rebelled at making virtue a *condition* of rights. At the same time, they may be said to have modified Republican hostility to an established church to the extent at least of acknowledging a prevailing religious sentiment. This development gives us more trouble than it gave them, however, for as long as rights were not threatened Democrats perceived no reason to deny the authority of Christianity. At this point their secularists naturally demurred; but they had nowhere else to turn, and insufficient numbers to challenge common opinion.

h. Parker's underlying allegiance to conservative ideas of social responsibility is apparent not only in his own writings but in their many similarities with the injunctions of conservative reformers like Joseph Tuckerman and Charles Loring

Brace. See, for example, Tuckerman's *Principles and Results of Ministry at Large*, esp. pp. 158–93 and 286–327, and Brace's "First Circular of the Children's Aid Society" (1853), as found in *Life of Charles Loring Brace*, pp. 489–92.

CHAPTER XI: THE USES OF EDUCATION

a. Naturally the shift of conservative efforts was gradual, and at least two major attempts to educate the American people by informal means continued into the 1830s. One was the campaign to establish denominational colleges in the West, through which the people of the newer states might be brought to share the Christian and republican virtues prevalent (so it was thought) in New England. The other was the American Lyceum, which began as an effort to encourage popular learning by means of voluntary associations devoted to self-culture and public benefaction. For an example of the former, see Edward Everett, "Education in the West" (1833), in *Importance of Practical Education*, pp. 162–71. For the plan of operation of the latter, see Josiah Holbrook, "Considerations," in *American Lyceum of Science and Arts*, pp. 5–7, and cf. Amasa Walker, *Address before Young Men of Boston*. See also John Ware, "Address delivered on the First Anniversary, Nov. 1823," in *Addresses before Association for Religious Improvement*, pp. 3–10, which exemplifies the religious bias of most early attempts to elevate the poor through charitable associations.

b. Timothy L. Smith challenges the idea that public schooling depended primarily upon governmental efforts; instead, he finds that philanthropic individuals and benevolent societies initiated the education of the poor, in the West as well as the East, by means of nondenominational Protestant schools (see Smith, "Protestant Schooling and American Nationality, 1800–1850," *JAH* 53 [1967], 679–95). Smith's point is well taken, but the fact remains that many conservatives could not be content with voluntary efforts at popular education as their sense of crisis deepened, while as soon as the states undertook to develop it they confronted opposition from orthodox religious leaders who resisted the idea of nondenominational instruction. Hence there *was* a problem of religious accommodation, which was resolved at least in part because no viable alternative existed.

c. Our modern tendency to decry all nativism as reactionary and all hostility to Catholicism as illiberal sometimes causes us to forget that a large Catholic population, located primarily in urban centers, and seeking to act as a balance of power in municipal politics, could well have been perceived as a threat to American institutions even before it demanded the elimination of the King James Bible from the schools. There is no question but that some conservative leaders tried to capitalize on anti-Catholic feeling, which was often hostile to the Democratic party, but it is equally clear that others were genuinely concerned lest an influx of unreachable immigrants undermine Protestant liberalism. In any case, conservatives tended to rally to the common schools when they were threatened with Catholic opposition. For a general treatment of American nativism that synthesizes much monographic material, see Ray A. Billington, *The Protestant Crusade*. For a close study of the struggle in New York, see Vincent P. Lannie, *Public Money and Parochial Education*.

d. This was true even in the South, until growing sectional antagonism, created primarily by southern reactions to northern antislavery sentiments, caused southern advocates of education to repudiate northern examples. For an example of a transitional southern statement, see Henry A. Wise, *Address to his Constituents (1844)*, in my anthology, *American Writings on Popular Education*, pp. 121–32. William R. Taylor discusses shifting southern attitudes in "Toward a Definition of Orthodoxy: The Patrician South and the Common Schools," *Harvard Educational Review* 36 (1966), 412–26.

e. Here as elsewhere I find it appropriate to treat the early workingmen as democrats if not Democrats. Although the literature on the subject demonstrates fairly clearly that at least in New York and Philadelphia they tended to ally themselves with the Whigs, their own statements of principle unmistakably anticipated the attacks that Democrats were to press against banking, chartered monopolies, and other forms of privilege that the Whigs were inclined to defend. Furthermore, when they supported the Whigs, they apparently did so as much to punish the Democrats for abandoning equal rights as to express any sympathy for the positions Whigs commonly adopted. Edward Pessen provides a useful summary of their politics in "The Workingmen's Movement of the Jacksonian Era," *MVHR* 43 (1956), 428–43.

f. Somewhat the same thing may be said of spokesmen for the Roman Catholic Church, who held that no public school was tolerable when it encroached on religious freedom. From their point of view, neither nondenominational Protestantism nor purely secular instruction was compatible with Catholic principles. In this sense they repudiated the common school and denounced public education; yet the primary object of their efforts was to secure public funds for use in their own schools. It was only after this measure failed because of overwhelming Protestant opposition that they gave up on public education. See Lannie, *Public Money and Parochial Education*, for a case study of New York.

g. Theodore Parker, Ralph Waldo Emerson, and Bronson Alcott demonstrated the further extremes to which philosophical minds might carry the search for liberation through education. Parker, whose thinking was far more sensitive than Channing's to the social problems of liberty, repeatedly expressed the belief that public education must be provided for all in order to counteract contemporary social inequalities. He was also deeply concerned that it educate the man rather than a socially useful automaton, and he looked to formal education to prepare children for the education that life in society would afford them. Hence he took an even greater interest than Channing in the actual practice of educational reform, although he too remained a philosopher who addressed himself to contemporary needs rather than an organizer of educational improvements. (See esp. "The Education of the Laboring Classes" [1841], in *Social Classes in a Republic*, pp. 72–102, and "The Public Education of the People" [1849], in *Sins and Safeguards of Society*, pp. 91–138. Both addresses were delivered before educational gatherings.)

Emerson's thinking on the subject began with his fundamental conviction that experience must elicit all true perceptions of manhood and self. "The use of the world is that man may learn its laws," he declared in his essay on education. Hence his views of contemporary educational practice focused on the ways in which it failed to generate autonomous individuals who would be able to rise above established conventions. "Our culture has truckled to the times,—to the senses. It is not manworthy," he charged. "If the vast and the spiritual are omitted, so are the practical and the moral. It does not make us brave or free. We teach boys to be such men as we are." It followed that education should respect the pupil—that it should "keep [a boy's] nature and arm it with knowledge in the very direction in which it points." "Our modes of Education aim to expedite, to save labor," he declared; "to do for masses what cannot be done for masses, what must be done reverently, one by one: say rather, the whole world is needed for the tuition of each pupil." Nevertheless, he explicitly denied that he had specific reforms to suggest to teachers. "No discretion that can be lodged with a school-committee, with the overseers or visitors of an academy, of a college, can at all avail to reach these difficulties and perplexities, but they solve themselves when we leave institutions and address individuals." In the last analysis he left educational reform as well as education to the ministrations of the cosmos. (Emerson, "Education," in *Works*, Riverside ed., 10:125, 133–34, 142, 151, 153–54.)

For his part, beginning with many of the same philosophical assumptions but pursuing them in the actual conduct of a school, Bronson Alcott developed a whole series of observations about how education must be conducted. On the one hand, he repeatedly stressed the role of the teacher in developing moral and even religious perceptions; on the other hand he described pedagogical devices intended to encourage the pupils themselves to arrive at philosophic truths. In this sense he was the preeminent practitioner as well as the preeminent theorist of a Transcendentalist pedagogy based upon the free individual. Freed of adult impositions, encouraged by sympathetic teaching, each child would embrace the highest values of mankind. (See particularly Alcott, *Essays on Education*; Elizabeth P. Peabody, *Record of a School*; and Odell Shepard, *Pilgrim's Progress*.)

h. The hold this idea acquired over essentially conservative minds was further exemplified by the fact that self-proclaimed "scholars in politics" like George William Curtis consciously worked to illuminate the public mind on the slavery question by eliciting the liberal principles thought to lie within it, and that they prided themselves after the Civil War on their success in having done just that. For an early explicit statement of their claims, see Henry Ward Beecher, "The Success of the American Democracy" (1862), in *Freedom and War*, pp. 248–69.

CHAPTER XII: THE FRONTIER WEST AS IMAGE
OF AMERICAN SOCIETY

a. The general proposition that American ideas of the frontier West represented a crucial element in its historic significance has been demonstrated beyond any plausible doubt in Henry Nash Smith's *Virgin Land*. My approach differs from his in focusing on sociological rather than literary images of the West and in attempting to assess the role these other images played in shaping the Americans' sense of their history, society, and polity. In particular, while American publicists frequently drew upon images of an agrarian utopia populated by hardy yeomen to embellish congressional debate and vindicate disputed policies, most of them seem to have visualized a much more comprehensive West as the focus or the climax of the American experience. The region they described embraced cities as well as villages, mines as well as farms, and in most respects these commentators could hardly wait until the transportation networks they projected and the economic resources they praised had created a new society modeled after the old but triumphing over its difficulties and surpassing its expectations.

These remarks are intended only to differentiate what I argue here from the case already made by Smith, not to make light of the immense debt every intellectual historian of the nineteenth century owes him. If we have reservations about his book, they should attach to the fact that it was such an extraordinary achievement as to encourage a host of largely imitative studies that have ignored other kinds of questions.

b. Of course, not all Democrats subscribed to the idea that the public good could best be served by the occupation of western territories; both eastern conservatives and southern planters found flaws in rapid settlement. Nevertheless, prevailing Democratic opinion in the North and West held to this happy vision, and (as we shall see) the men who criticized it increasingly brought opprobrium upon themselves.

The argument from the public good undoubtedly derived in large part from Thomas Jefferson, who had equated the existence of available lands with the perpetuation of a yeoman republic. However, the important fact about Democratic attitudes toward the West was not that they had roots in Jeffersonian dogma, but that the existence of a vast unsettled territory gave additional meanings to Jefferson's vision. We are concerned here with the whole range of possibilities that Americans perceived in the frontier West, of which the Jeffersonian was only one.

c. In addition, it is worth noting that these critics' arguments manifestly failed to persuade the agitated workingmen who joined George H. Evans in the struggle for land reform. A committee of the National Reform Union demonstrated how readily their radicalism might be satisfied when it declared in 1844, "We are the inhabitants of a country which for boundless extent of territory, fertility of soil, and exhaustless resources of mineral wealth, stands unequalled by any nation, either of ancient or modern times. We live under a Constitution, so just and so equal, that it may well lay claim to a divine origin. As a People we are second to none, in enterprize, industry, and skill. Thus it is clear, that we are in possession of all the elements of individual and national prosperity. And, yet, we allow those elements to lie dormant, that labor which ought to be employed in calling forth the fruitfulness of Nature, is to be found seeking employment in the barren lanes of a city, of course, seeking it in vain." (*Working Man's Advocate*, 6 July 1844, as found in John R. Commons et al., eds., *Documentary History of American Industrial Society*, 7:297–98; also *Young America*, 11 September 1847, as quoted by Joseph G. Rayback, "Land for the Landless: the Contemporary View" [Master's thesis, Western Reserve University, 1936], pp. 17–18. See also Helène S. Zahler, *Eastern Workingmen and National Land Policy*, passim.)

d. Meanwhile, of course, eastern migrants to the West often sought to counteract eastern criticisms by praising western prospects. See in particular the writings of James H. Lanman: "'The Progress of the Northwest," *Hunt's* 3, no. 1 (July 1840), 22–40, "Agricultural Commerce of the United States," ibid. 5, no. 3 (September 1841), 201–20; and *History of Michigan*, passim.

e. Citing Greeley as a conservative may seem anomalous in view of that worthy's long career as a champion of social reforms. Yet—quite apart from his initial apposition to a liberal land policy—it is important to note that Greeley's frontier doctrine was conservative in at least two key respects. For one thing, it addressed itself to a society still conceived in organic terms. The West would help to make an individualistic solution of social problems possible, but Greeley did not begin by denying their existence as *social* problems. Second, the entire thrust of his doctrine was to vindicate established institutions once his measure had been adopted. In effect, western lands provided terms on which eastern conservatives could well afford to adopt democratic individualism.

f. To this extent, Major Wilson's characterization of the established political parties' attitudes toward the future has real point: in effect, Democrats frequently conceived of the West as an arena for the replication of existing institutions, whereas Whigs tended to anticipate substantial changes. See particularly "Analysis of Ideas of Liberty and Union," ch. 4, and "The Free Soil Concept of Progress and the Irrepressible Conflict," *AQ* 22 (1970) 769–90.

g. Kendall's invocation of the Garden of Eden, which was duplicated in other writings of the period, also underlines the extent to which the "paradise" the Americans sought differed from the nostalgic and often pastoral version of paradise that contemporary literary figures often invoked in commenting on American life. Quite possibly the West acquired additional significance in American thought because it somehow fulfilled the religious, millennial, and even paradisaical expectations that some Americans expressed. (See, for example, George Holley's *Oration at Peru*, p. 11.) But its significance was hardly restricted to these categories: the West that enthusiasts described as if it were God's country was not simply transcendent, but immediately accessible; not simply spiritual, but highly tangible. (See Benjamin F. Tefft, *The Far West*, p. 31; Abram P. Maury, *Address on Advantages of the United States*, p. 12; and John A. Wilstach, *Imperial Period of National Greatness*, p. 6.)

h. There were, of course, victims—the aboriginal Indians, whom the whites virtually destroyed. By now, however, not even the Whigs were much concerned over the Indians' fate, and to a great extent most Americans had come to believe that the destruction of the Indian tribes was a necessary step in human progress. For discussions of shifting attitudes toward the Indians, see ch. 3 of Albert K. Weinberg, *Manifest Destiny*, and the more comprehensive treatment of the topic in Roy H. Pearce, *The Savages of America*.

CHAPTER XIII: CONSEQUENCES

a. Leaving aside the insistent moralism of the Protestant clergy, it seems likely that one of the reasons conservative spokesmen (both secular and religious) adopted one or another version of antislavery was the fact that they were readier than many liberal democrats to notice and to seek a remedy for the plight of men and women who could not claim full standing in the society of equals that Jacksonian democracy presupposed. The very fact that conservatives continued to honor an organic and hierarchically divided society freed them to be paternalistic and benevolent toward slaves and blacks, as they also were toward disadvantaged whites. In the long run their benevolence would also make room for blacks and women as equals; as they accommodated to democratic dogmas they were far readier than the original sponsors of democracy to make those dogmas universal. In this sense conservative attitudes were to play a large role in establishing the categories in which all Americans ultimately perceived both slavery and the subjection of women; but for the moment they were largely restricted to the influence that specifically religious injunctions could achieve. For some discussion of these currents of thought, although it is focused on different issues, see John L. Thomas, "Romantic Reform in America, 1815–1865," *AQ* 17 (1965), 656–81, as well as the studies of religious influence considered as a form of social control, cited in note 7 to chapter X.

b. If we think such Democrats' suspicions peculiar, we need only remember the extent to which they thought they detected a conspiratorial wish on the part of conservative leaders to exert social control over the democracy—the same wish so belabored by modern historians who do not otherwise admit to Jacksonian prejudices. Much the same attitude reappeared after the Civil War among the professional politicians of both major parties who, beset by clamor for the elimination of political corruption by means of civil service reform, literally could not understand the complaints of the mugwump reformers except as a way to acquire office for themselves or their friends.

c. The paternalistic concerns of antislavery leaders were entirely appropriate not only to conservative traditions of benevolence but also to traditional conservative solicitude for morality. The evils these commentators discovered in slavery answered to familiar anxieties over the insidious power of vice and were close to conservative anxieties over the moral health of the republic. It is a nice question how far the conservative moralists imposed their particular intellectual concerns on slavery, how far the peculiar institution represented the kinds of evils to which they were already most sensitive.

d. This general proposition, which is to be developed here in greater detail, both bears a relationship to and seeks to rectify gaps in two familiar explanations of American behavior during the 1850s. One is the "revisionist" interpretation of the coming of the Civil War, which generally recognizes the importance of ideas and emotional biases in bringing the war, but which also tends to denigrate these attitudes because of their results; the effect is to make the perceptions northern democrats employed into "distortions" of democratic principle. The other familiar explanation is the "paranoid" theory of American democracy, popularized by Richard Hofstadter and brought to a focus on the war by David Brion Davis. I find this psychological diagnosis one-sided, but even if we grant its general relevance we cannot allow it to suffice as an intellectual explanation of the war, any more than of the other events it has been applied to. Despite its attractive qualities, the explanation does not account for the specific beliefs that entered into the psychosis the Americans suffered from.

e. Some historians will object that the Republicans clearly remained loyal to positive government as exemplified in a national bank, a protective tariff, and a transcontinental railroad built at public expense. Even if we concluded that these were insistently Whiggish measures adopted in defiance of Democratic values—a view many southerners shared, but many northerners did not—we would still have to say that the Republicans of 1860 or 1870 differed most distinctly from Federalists and National Republicans both in the specific character of their measures and in the general attitude they bore toward the part that government might play in shaping the economy and the society. In effect, they sought to facilitate exploitation of the nation's resources by means that were undoubtedly prejudicial to certain segments of the population but that did not even masquerade as benevolent or organic most of the time. The subsequent failure of Reconstruction illustrates this feature of American conservatism. Although modern historians are wont to conceive it as an occasion on which the federal government intervened in the affairs of the society in order to secure desirable social ends, they find little persuasive evidence that the Republicans either understood the issues that were at stake or sought to do anything significant about them. Rather, they depict a party that dealt uncertainly with even the legal ramifications of emancipation and that largely ignored the social and economic problems good conservatives would have been sensitive to.

f. Obviously there were some liberal Democrats whose hostility to chattel slavery rested directly upon their belief that all men—blacks as well as whites—were entitled to a full range of democratic rights including the vote. (For a classic statement of their political theory, see the remarks made by Norton S. Townshend in the Ohio constitutional convention of 1850–1851, *Ohio C. C.* [1850–1851], 550–51.) Nevertheless, the evidence seems overwhelming that northern Democrats were slow to concede even nominal equality to members of the Negro race and that the efforts extreme liberals made to do so produced widespread antagonism. Therefore it is necessary to look to other factors to explain why many rank-and-file Democrats came to join the Republican party, or at least to support its candidate in 1860. As the Lincoln-Douglas debates indicate, the appeal extreme liberals often made to the principles of the Declaration of Independence to sanction their egalitarian beliefs tended chiefly to alienate Democratic stalwarts who had no sense that the Declaration applied to Negroes; hence the principles of the Declaration cannot be taken to explain northern Democratic hostility to the practice of southern slavery.

g. Despite the sharp disagreement that exists between historians who see conservative opposition to the annexation of Texas as an echo of conservative concerns over the proliferation of predictably Democratic states and those who hold that Whig opposition to territorial expansion was grounded primarily in northern hostility to slavery coupled with southern Whigs' reluctance to precipitate sectional controversy, it seems to me that the two points of view are generally compatible. On the one hand, northern Whigs clearly and repeatedly criticized the South because it benefited politically from the numerical representation accorded three-fifths of its slaves in the House of Representatives; obviously they felt a practical political grievance. On the other hand, the very fact that they increasingly criticized a provision that had been introduced into the Constitution to protect property suggests that they were also motivated by novel principles. In any event I know of no law of psychology that requires men to adhere to only one of two possible motives that lead in the same direction, especially when the problems they are dealing with are extremely difficult to resolve satisfactorily. Most of the contemporary sources seem to suggest that conservatives opposed the extension of slavery both intrinsically and because it would further strengthen the southern wing of the Democratic party. More briefly, the extension of slavery seemed "unjust" on several levels simultaneously. For a detailed account of the controversy in one state, see Kinley J. Brauer, *Cotton versus Conscience;* also a less detailed study by Norman E. Tutorow, "Whigs of the Old Northwest and Texas Annexation, 1836–April, 1844," *Indiana Magazine of History* 66 (1970), 56–69.

h. The Democrats' fear of power and aristocracy probably also helps to explain why they proved susceptible to conservative clamor for the protection of free speech despite their initial hostility to antislavery agitation and their otherwise incomplete dedication to civil liberties. In effect, their concern for "free speech" along with "free soil" and "free labor" expressed their fears that power might encroach on freedom, not a concern for securing the cosmic give and take of liberty described by someone like John Stuart Mill.

i. Conversely, the confrontations of the 1850s probably helped convince many hesitant clergymen that politics was a suitable and indeed a necessary arena for their activities. Not only did the rampant evil of slavery (as they saw it) justify a departure from their hard-won position of political neutrality, but the confrontation between good and evil in the territories undoubtedly suggested to some of them that the day of reckoning was at hand, hence that there was an occasion for them to enter into secular politics. For some discussion of the ways in which religious imperatives found their way into the politics of the 1850s, see pp. 201–3 of Timothy Smith, *Revivalism and Social Reform*.

j. Although Democrats began with a widespread prejudice against the intrusion of secular authority into areas they assigned to conscience, their commitment to religious principle may well have made them vulnerable to moral anxieties about the spread of slavery. It was one thing to seek to cure other men's vices in their own neighborhood; it was another to open the West to the evils of slavery. In addition, the slavery issue probably tended to isolate the essentially secular Democrats who had long been heavily represented in the leadership of the party from its much more religious rank and file, who had been content to follow Jefferson and to tolerate religious skeptics but who could not be expected to abdicate all responsibility for the sins of their times. As Avery Craven has argued in *Coming of the Civil War*, many of them proved susceptible to both temperance reform and antislavery. It is even worth asking how far Democratic leaders' clear hostility toward moral reform may have helped to discredit them in the eyes of their followers. At some point their intransigent concern for their own moral autonomy must have served to identify them as "aristocrats" who were too irreligious or too corrupted by their secular position to oppose the spread of an institution that almost all northerners agreed was an evil.

k. William H. Seward's invocation of the "higher law" during debate on the admission of California affords still another evidence of the importance that conservative opponents of slavery apparently attached to the West. In effect, Seward declared that the divine injunction applied *only* to the territories, a proposition that was intrinsically illogical and that increasingly alienated staunch antislavery moralists, but one that was quite compatible with a vision of the West as somehow the key to the nation's identity. Had the West stood for nothing more than unexploited territory, Seward would have found difficulty in discussing it in any but constitutional and legal terms, which an appeal to a higher law would simply have set aside. Because of the way Americans viewed the West, however, he could remain a constitutionalist with respect to the rights of the existing states yet speak as a moralist with respect to the territories. Once he had adopted such a position, of course, he was the more vulnerable to arguments in favor of a complete liberation of the American republic, as his speech on the "irrepressible conflict" subsequently demonstrated.

l. Almost needless to say, there was a countertendency among northern voters: a number of conservative Whigs shared many of the constitutional premises Democratic legalists held and repudiated many of the moral enthusiasms they rebuked. The similarity of their views helped to further the realignment of northern parties, but inasmuch as explicitly conservative Whigs had almost no standing in the democracy, their sympathy with Democratic constitutionalism cannot have lent it much strength. In 1860, moreover, conservative constitutionalists were moved to form a Constitutional Union party, which presumably did more damage to Stephen A. Douglas's candidacy than to that of Lincoln or Breckinridge.

m. Modern readers may look askance at the disapproval of Lincoln's tactics implicit in these remarks. Nevertheless, I find Lincoln's behavior on this point irresponsible. If the true test of the Lincoln-Douglas debates is their conformity with moral principle, it is difficult to reconcile the image of Lincoln as a profound democratic moralist with this shabby forensic trick of doing Douglas in by condemning him for pointing out a plausible way around the *Dred Scott* decision when Lincoln himself opposed the decision and proposed to circumvent it whenever he could. If the test of the debates is who scored a point on his opponent, of course, Lincoln clearly demonstrated his superiority; but perhaps that is a comment on the defects of legal argument as a way of resolving deep-seated national controversies.

NOTES

Short titles of works are used throughout. Full titles will be found in the Bibliography, except for works listed in "Abbreviations Used in Appendices and Notes" (p. 393).

CHAPTER I: MACROHISTORY

1. *Albany Argus,* quoted in *Baltimore Republican,* 8 November 1828, p. 2f.
2. Ker, *History of Liberty,* p. 28; Porter, *Address at Albany,* pp. 18–19; also Peter J. Shand, *Oration at Charleston,* pp. 7, 13; M. Augustus Jewett, *Oration in Vigo County,* p. 3; Samuel Milroy, *Address before the "Hickory Club,"* p. 11; [Charles Brooks], *Remarks on Europe,* p. 36; and George Upfold, *The Distinguishing goodness of God,* passim.
3. Walker, in Myer Moses, *Full Annals of the Revolution in France* (second pagination), p. 109; Balch, *Popular Liberty and Equal Rights,* p. 5.
4. Sparrow, *The Nation's Privileges,* pp. 10–11; Allan, *Oration at Centre College,* p. 13; Rantoul, *Memoirs,* pp. 184–85; also John A. Dix, *Address at Geneva College,* pp. 65–66; and Sen. Robert F. Stockton, 2 February 1852, *Cong. Globe,* 32d C, 1st S, pp. 438c–439a. See also Paul C. Nagel, *One Nation Indivisible,* which argues that the Americans of the period came to venerate the Union as a unique and transcendent product of history (chs. 4–6 passim). In ch. 1 of *American Nationalism,* Hans Kohn points out that the Americans were unusual in combining assertions of the rights of man (which are universals transcending history) with respect for established traditions of liberty they associated with the British constitution.
5. Bent, *National Jubilee,* p. 10; also Horace Bushnell, "An Oration, Pronounced before the Society of Phi Beta Kappa, at New Haven, on the Principles of National Greatness, August 15, 1837," in Clark S. Northup, ed., *Representative Phi Beta Kappa Orations,* p. 2; Jewett, *Oration in Vigo County,* p. 12; and Benjamin F. Tefft, *The Far West,* p. 8; and see Robert P. Hay, "Providence and the American Past," *Indiana Magazine of History* 65 (1969), 79–102.
6. Kent, *Address at Union College,* pp. 10–11; also Abram P. Maury, *Address on Advantages of the United States,* p. 5; and James C. Conkling, *Oration in Springfield,* p. 3a.
7. Brown, as quoted by Frederick Jackson Turner, *Frontier in American History,* p. 355; Lindsley, *Address at Nashville,* p. 17; also "The Canada Question," *Dem. Rev.* 1, no. 2 (January 1838), 217; "The Great Nation of Futurity," ibid. 6, no. 23 (November 1839), 427; Ker, *History of Liberty,* p. 32; Alfred H. Hanscom, in *Mich. C. C.* (1850), p. 65a; John A. Wilstach, *Imperial Period*

of *National Greatness*, p. 9; Martin Van Buren, *Inquiry into Political Parties*, pp. 17–18; and cf. Frances Trollope, *Domestic Manners of the Americans*, p. 134.

8. Porter, *Address at Albany*, pp. 22–23; Webster, 14 April 1826, *Reg. Deb.*, 19th C, 1st S, cols. 2262–63; also Calvin Colton, *Thoughts on Religious State of the Country*, p. 169; Jewett, *Oration in Vigo County*, p. 3; Abraham Lincoln, "Address to the Springfield Washington Temperance Society" (1842), in *Collected Works*, 1:278; Horace Mann, Report for 1843, *Life and Works*, 3:406–14; and Jesse Olney, *History of the United States* (1851), as quoted by George H. Callcott, *History in the United States*, p. 166. See also J. Merton England, "The Democratic Faith in American Schoolbooks, 1783–1860," *AQ* 15 (1963), 191–99. The attitudes of conservative writers receive further attention in the third section of this chapter.

9. Channing, "National Literature," *Christian Examiner* 7, no. 36 (January 1830), 288; Hallett, *Oration at Oxford*, p. 35.

10. See G. D. Lillibridge, *Beacon of Freedom*.

11. Gilpin, *Speech at the Democratic Celebration*, p. 27; New York Republican State Convention, September 1836, as quoted in *St. Lawrence Republican, Extra*, July 1837, p. 3a; *The Crisis Met*, p. 2; also *Address in relation to National Policy* (Indiana), pp. 3–4.

12. Barnard, *Address at Amherst*, p. 7; Mann, Report for 1848, *Life and Works*, 4:261; Bushnell, *Discourse on the Sea*, p. 9.

13. "Radicalism," *Dem. Rev.* 3, no. 10 (October 1838), 103, and see "How Stands the Case?" ibid., no. 9 (September 1838), 4; Cambreleng, 11 February 1835, *Reg. Deb.*, 23d C, 1st S, col. 1318; Whitman, *Gathering of the Forces*, 1:9–10.

14. For Bushnell, see not only *Discourse on the Sea* (note 12) but "American Politics," *Am. Nat. Preacher* 14, no. 12 (December 1840), 203. The fact that Barnard invoked a plane rather than a ladder or staircase of improvement is also significant evidence that the American vision of progress involved no discontinuities. Theodore Parker used the same image in *Lessons from the World of Matter*, p. 307.

15. [John L. O'Sullivan], "The Course of Civilization," *Dem. Rev.* 6, no. 21 (September 1839), 211; also the review of William H. Prescott's *History of the Reign of Ferdinand and Isabella*, in ibid. 2, no. 2 (May 1838), 161; [Levi D. Slamm], *The Tariff, No. 1*, p. 8a; and note the full title of Stephen Pearl Andrews's anarchistic tract, *Science of Society: The True Constitution of Government in the Sovereignty of the Individual as the Final Development of Protestantism, Democracy, and Socialism*.

16. Rayner, in *No. Car. C. C.* (1835), p. 261; Quinton, in *Iowa C. C.* (1844), p. 107; Downs, in *La. C. C.* (1845), p. 114b; also James Sullivan, in *Mich. C. C.* (1850), p. 90b; De Witt C. Leach, Joseph H. Bagg, and Calvin Britain, in ibid., pp. 285a–b, 467a, 488b–489a; and *Address of Democratic Central State Committee of Massachusetts. 1845*, p. 4.

17. Beardsley, in *Mich. C. C.* (1850), p. 84a; Pierce, in ibid., p. 736a.

18. Resolutions at a Mass Meeting in Providence, 5 July 1841, in *Report of Select Committee on Rhode Island*, pp. 407–8. It must be acknowledged that both the specific occasion and Rhode Island's peculiar constitutional situation probably encouraged the meeting to adopt decidedly conservative arguments. (The state's constitution was its colonial charter, which had not been renounced or even significantly remodeled in 1776.) Nevertheless, the advocates of constitutional change in both North Carolina and Maryland, which had adopted new constitutions during the Revolution, invoked the same principles to overcome resistance to the holding of constitutional conventions. See chapter IX and appendices c and d to that chapter for a fuller discussion of these developments.

19. Preston, in *La. C. C.* (1845), p. 565a; Downs, in ibid., p. 411a; also John Norvell, in *Mich. C. C.* (1835), p. 206; and James S. Mayfield, in *Texas C. C.* (1845), p. 529.

20. For radical commentators, see George H. Evans in *Young America*, 29 March 1845, as quoted by Siert F. Riepma in " 'Young America': A Study in American Nationalism before the Civil War" (Ph.D. diss., Western Reserve University, 1939), p. 8, and also *New York Tribune*, 16 August 1852, as quoted in ibid., p. 245. For congressional spokesmen, see Lewis Cass, 21–22 January 1850, *Cong. Globe*, 31st C, 1st S, *Appendix*, p. 58a; Cass, 10 February 1852, *Cong. Globe* 32d C, 1st S, *Appendix*, p. 165b; Pierre Soulé, 22 March 1852, ibid., pp. 351–53; and Edward C. Marshall, 11 March 1852, ibid., pp. 383–86.

   For other examples, see *New York Herald*, 14 April 1852, as quoted in Riepma, "Young America," pp. 194–95; *Cleveland Plain Dealer*, 6 August 1852, as quoted in ibid., p. 245, n. 64; and Stephen A. Douglas, in *Proceedings at Banquet of Jackson Democratic Association*, pp. 10b–11a. In this connection, it is worth noting that New York's Hunker Democrats were quite willing to adopt the slogans of Young America. In 1847 they challenged the Barnburner faction's claim to state office on the grounds that it represented "old fogeys" too long retained in power. See Herbert A. Donovan, *The Barnburners*, ch. 10.

   Merle Curti presents a useful summary of "Young America" in *AHR* 32 (1926), 34–55.

21. Kent, in *N.Y. C. C.* (1821), p. 222; and see John T. Horton, *James Kent*.

22. Williams, in *Mich. C. C.* (1850), p. 88b; and see H. W. Warner, "The Republic. No. 1," *Am. Rev.* 9, no. 4 (April 1849), 399–406. Interestingly enough, Joseph H. Bagg, the aggressive spokesman for "Progressive Democracy," made the same point in the Michigan convention (*Mich. C. C.* [1850], p. 225a).

23. *Address of Whig State Convention [of Indiana]*, p. 2a; Kennedy, *Quodlibet*, p. 65; also Warner, "The Republic. No. 1," p. 404b. At first glance, Flam's remarks may seem to vindicate Major Wilson's contention that the typical Whig conservative visualized history as a continuous process of develop-

ment, but the text as a whole clearly underlines the static orientation of Whig thought.

24. "Introductory," *Am. Rev.* 1, no. 1 (January 1845), 3a. (Although dated 1845, this first issue actually appeared in 1844.)

25. "The Progress and Destruction," ibid. 2, no. 1 (July 1845), 90–99; "Civilization: American and European," ibid. 3, no. 6 (June 1846), 611–24, 623b, 624a; "Democracy in France," ibid. 11, no. 1 (January 1850), 1–16, esp. p. 3a; also "The True Progress of Society," *Biblical Repertory and Princeton Review* 24, no. 1 (January 1852), 16–38. It should be added that the second part of "Civilization: American and European" (*Am. Rev.* 4, no. 1 [July 1846], 27–43) withdrew much of the praise the first had lavished on the country; being a conservative was difficult in the United States. See also the last section of this chapter.

26. Joel Parker, *Progress*, pp. 20ff.; Headley, *The One Progressive Principle*, p. 30.

27. Everett, *Discourse on Progress and Limits*, pp. 17, 39ff.; *Oration at Request of the City Government; Oration at Holliston.* In the 1839 oration, delivered after his conversion to the Democratic cause, Everett expressed satisfaction with American institutions on the grounds that they had proved themselves to be truly democratic in elevating a friendless youth named Martin Van Buren to the presidency. "After all the various experiments in government that fill up the history of the world," he added, ". . . the time has at length come in the order of Providence when the People are permitted to make, for once, the grand and final experiment of their own capacity for self-government" (*Oration at Holliston*, p. 31).

28. [Slamm], *Injustice of the Tariff*, p. 6; also Baynard Hall, *Righteousness the safeguard of nation*, p. 11; "European Views of American Democracy," *Dem. Rev.* 2, no. 8 (July 1838), 353, 356; Daniel D. Barnard, "Commerce, as connected with the Progress of Civilization," *Hunt's* 1, no. 1 (July 1839), 3–4; [Calvin Colton], *Junius Tracts* no. 3, p. 15; and Sen. James Shields, *Speech on the Territorial Question*, pp. 6–8.

29. Address of Whig members, as found in Jabez D. Hammond, *Life of Silas Wright*, p. 436; also "Reformers and Reforms," *Ladies' Repository* 11, no. 8 (August 1851), 287–88.

30. Thoreau, "Civil Disobedience," in *Writings*, 10:169; Emerson, "The Young American," in *Complete Works*, 3:372.

31. [Ripley], "The Fourth of July," *Harbinger* 1, no. 2 (21 June 1845), 32a, and see [Ripley], "Tendencies of Modern Civilization," ibid., no. 3 (28 June 1845), 33a; Godwin, *Democracy*, pp. 10–23.

32. Ernest L. Tuveson analyzes American millennialism in *Redeemer Nation*, but I have also learned from Shirley J. Case, *The Millennial Hope*. Perry Miller casts light on the phenomenon in various essays, esp. "From the Covenant to the Revival," in *Nature's Nation*, pp. 90–120, and "The End of the World," in *Errand into the Wilderness*, pp. 217–39. See also Ira V. Brown,

"Watchers for the Second Coming: The Millenarian Tradition in America," *MVHR* 39 (1952), 441–58, and J. F. Maclear, "The Republic and the Millennium," in Elwyn A. Smith, ed., *Religion of the Republic*, pp. 183–216.

33. Fowler, *Society: Its Progress and Prospects;* also Lyman Beecher, *Plea for the West,* ch. 1; and John Todd, *The Young Man,* pp. 17ff., 34–37. For useful discussions of both kinds of millennial fervor, see Whitney R. Cross, *The Burned-over District,* ch. 17, and Timothy L. Smith, *Revivalism and Social Reform,* ch. 14.

34. See, for example, Thomas H. Skinner, "The Signs of the Times," *Am. Nat. Preacher* 6, no. 8 (January 1832), 305–20; Charles G. Finney, *Lectures on Revivals of Religion,* esp. chs. 1, 15; Samuel H. Cox, *Bright and Blessed Destination of the World,* esp. p. 27; George B. Cheever, *The Century of Preparation;* and see chapter X.

35. Tefft, *The Far West,* p. 35; Jewett, *Oration in Vigo County,* p. 11; also "The Moralist," *Universalist and Ladies' Repository* 4, no. 6 (December 1835), 247b.

36. Drake, *Duties of American Citizens,* pp. 27–28; Stiles, *Connection between Liberty and Eloquence,* p. 30; also Joel Parker and Joel T. Headley as in note 26; Robert Walker, *Oration at Clinton Hall;* George W. Holley, *Oration at Peru;* Benjamin F. Porter, *Outlines of Oration of Judge Porter;* and Asahel Kendrick, *Ancient and Modern Civilizations Contrasted.*

37. See Noah Webster, *An American Dictionary of the English Language,* and cf. *A New English Dictionary on Historical Principles,* s.v. "experiment."

38. Camp, *Democracy,* p. 21; also Sen. James Shields, *Speech on the Territorial Question,* pp. 8–9, and [Theodore Sedgwick Jr.], *Constitutional Reform,* pp. 3a–4a. Roger A. Brown describes American attitudes toward the War of 1812 as a test of American institutions in *The Republic in Peril,* while Paul C. Nagel points out, in *One Nation Indivisible,* that American attitudes shifted from an experimental to an "absolute" assessment of the Union between 1800 and 1860.

39. Sparrow, *The Nation's Privileges,* p. 9; also Chester Dewey, "Permanence of Free Institutions," *Biblical Repository* 8, no. 24 (October 1836), 257; and Ezra S. Gannett, *Thanksgiving for the Union,* p. 8. J. Earl Thompson Jr. finds clear expressions of this sense of experimentation in New England sermons dating from about 1800; see "A Perilous Experiment: New England Clergymen and American Destiny 1796–1826" (Ph.D. diss., Princeton University, 1966), passim, and cf. Fred Somkin, *Unquiet Eagle,* ch. 1.

40. Clay, in *Proceedings of National Republican Convention of Young Men,* p. 9; Duane, in *Account of the Great Whig Festival,* p. 17; also George Robertson, *Address on behalf of the Deinologian Society,* pp. 12, 19–20; Allan, *Oration at Centre College,* p. 12; William H. Seward, "Discourse at Westfield" (1837), in *Works,* 3:136; William Slocomb, "Address on Education," *Transactions of the Western Literary Institute* 8:242; Nathan S. S. Beman, *Claims of Our Country,* p. 33; John Todd, *The Young Man,* pp. 32–33; and Edwin P. Whipple, *Wash-*

ington and the Revolution, pp. 47–49. See also chapter X, the first section, as well as John R. Bodo, *Protestant Clergy and Public Issues,* ch. 8, and Charles C. Cole Jr., *Social Ideas of Northern Evangelists,* pp. 232ff.

41. Butler, *Representative Democracy in the United States,* p. 16; Jackson, in James D. Richardson, ed., *Messages and Papers of the Presidents,* 3:308; also Lewis Cass, *Address before Alumni of Hamilton College,* p. 39; William H. Welch, in *Mich. C. C.* (1835), p. 177; [Robert Dale Owen], *Address of the Democratic Convention,* p. 20; and Shepherd Leffler, in *Iowa C. C.* (1844), pp. 8–9.

42. These attitudes are more fully discussed in chapters VII, VIII, X, and XI; and see Paul C. Nagel, *This Sacred Trust.*

CHAPTER II: MICROHISTORY

1. Daniel Boorstin recognizes that time did not completely stop on this side of the Atlantic, but many of the writers who follow him do not. (Compare ch. 1 of *Genius of American Politics* with ch. 2 of Fred Somkin, *Unquiet Eagle,* or chs. 1–2 of David W. Noble, *Historians against History.*) Henry Steele Commager has developed a provocative overview of American attitudes toward history in "The Search for a Usable Past," *American Heritage* 16 (1965), 4–9, 90–96.

2. For examples, see Amasa Walker, *Oration at Stoughton,* p. 3; *Address and Proceedings of Ohio State Convention,* p. 16; Benjamin F. Hallett, *Oration at Oxford,* p. 5; and chapter I, n. 40.

3. *Summary of Proceedings of a Convention of Republican Delegates,* p. 10; also *Voice from the Interior;* [Robert Dale Owen], *Democratic Address;* John A. Dix, *Address in Herkimer County;* and Hugh A. Garland, *The Principles of Democracy.*

4. Dix, *Address in Herkimer County,* p. 4a; also Edward D. Barber, *Oration at Montpelier,* p. 10; and M. Hall McAllister, *Address to Democratic Republican Convention of Georgia,* p. 3.

5. *Proceedings of Democratic Republican Convention of Indiana,* p. 5; also *Address to People of Connecticut,* pp. 6–7; "Address Of the Republican State Convention to the Democracy of the State of New-York," *Democratic State Convention,* p. 4; McAllister, *Address to Democratic Republican Convention,* p. 6; Thomas L. Smith et al., *To Democratic Citizens of Floyd County,* cols. a–b; James F. Brent, in *La. C. C.* (1845), pp. 111b, 246a; and Martin Van Buren, *Inquiry into Political Parties,* pp. 214–15.

6. For attacks on the Whigs as "Federalists," see *Address to Republican People of Tennessee* and *Proceedings of Convention of Republican Delegates in Fredericksburg.* For imputations of conspiracy, see *Proceedings at Dinner to Isaac Hill,* p. 3b; *Proceedings of Democratic Republican Convention of Indiana,* p. 6; and Solomon W. Downs, in *La. C. C.* (1845), p. 75a–b. Other typical attacks include [Joseph Worrell et al.], *Letters addressed to John Sergeant; Address of Jackson Convention of Missouri; Address of Democratic–Republican Central Committee of New-Hampshire;* [Charles G. Greene], *Identity of Hartford Convention Federalists with*

Whig Party; To Democratic Electors of Second Congressional District [of Indiana], col. b; and Harry Hibbard, *Letter to Stephen Pingry.*

7. See *History of Federal and Democratic Parties; Compilation of Political Historic Sketches; Proceedings and Address of Democratic County Convention at Galena,* pp. 4a–5a; *Voice of the Southwest; Address in relation to National Policy,* p. 3; Smith et al., *To Democratic Citizens of Floyd County,* col. c; Joseph H. Bagg, in *Mich. C. C.* (1850), p. 487a–b; and Van Buren, *Inquiry into Political Parties,* pp. 166, 267–68, 423–24; and see Richard Hofstadter, *Idea of a Party System,* and Michael Wallace, "Changing Concepts of Party in the United States: New York, 1815–1828," *AHR* 74 (1968), 453–91.

Sometimes Democrats even sought to evade the invidious connotations their historiography attached to George Washington as a Federalist, for example by denying that he had been one; see *Address of Democratic-Republican Central Committee of New-Hampshire,* p. 4a, and [Owen], *Democratic Address,* p. 4a (note). Their efforts underline the fact that I am dealing here with the history that Democrats (and Whigs) propounded, not with the question of who was correct. Richard P. McCormick and other modern writers have shown with great clarity that many Jacksonian leaders were in fact former Federalists. In this respect historical scholarship only emphasizes the extent to which ideological considerations compelled both Democrats and Whigs to misconstrue their past. (See in particular McCormick, *The Second American Party System.*)

8. See, for example, Charles Miner, *Address at Wilkes-Barre.*

9. "The Position of Parties," *Am. Rev.* 1, no. 1 (January 1845), 5–21; "Origin of the Two Parties," ibid. 9, no. 1 (January 1849), 6–20; and "A History of Parties," ibid. 10, no. 4 (October 1849), 331–39, and no. 5 (November 1849), 524–31.

10. Underwood, *Speech on the Sub-Treasury Bill,* p. 25; *Facts for the People* (1840), p. 3a; [Calvin Colton], *Junius Tracts* no. 6, p. 16; and see "The Position of Parties," pp. 5–6.

11. Miner, *Address at Wilkes-Barre,* p. 4a; Burnet, in *Proceedings of Democratic Whig National Convention,* p. 35; [Colton], *Junius Tracts* no. 4, p. 3. According to George R. Poage, in the fall of 1844 the Democrats and Whigs of Tennessee actually debated whether James K. Polk's *grand*father had been a Tory or a signer of the Mecklenburg Declaration of Independence (*Henry Clay and the Whig Party,* p. 150). See also the amiable satire by "Christopher Quandary," *Some Serious Considerations on Present State of Parties.*

12. Miner, *Address at Wilkes-Barre,* p. 4a–b; [Colton], *Junius Tracts* no. 2, p. 15; *Proceedings of Convention of Democratic Young Men for Ritner,* p. 15; *The Cass Platform; James Buchanan, His Doctrines and Policy;* also Willis Green, *Address before Alexandria Clay Club,* pp. 3–4. The fact that the charge against Buchanan was true and elicited a disingenuous reply from his supporters only underlines the seriousness with which Americans of both parties took their

microhistory. Cornelius P. Van Ness, a nationally prominent Vermont Democrat, expressed the logic of the generation with unerring eye if also partisan zeal when he told the state's Democratic convention in 1840, "It ought to be particularly observed that the course pursued by the federal party in this State, in claiming to be the real Jeffersonian Democrats, carries with it two distinct and important admissions. First, it amounts to a confession that the Democratic principles proclaimed and acted upon by Jefferson are right, and, consequently, that the opposite doctrines should be rejected as being wrong. Secondly, it confirms what we have steadily declared, that the two parties are divided upon the old grounds of Republican and Federal, since if each claims to be the Republican or Democratic party, and charges the other with being the federal party, both necessarily admit that those are the two existing parties. Considering the subject upon this ground, the whole dispute between us and our opponents is reduced to a single question of *fact*, and that is, which of the two parties is actually the Democratic, and which the Federal party. In short it is a mere question of *identity*." (Van Ness, *Speech at Woodstock*, pp. 3b–4a.)

13. For examples of Whig hostility to "experiments" in government, see *Proceedings of Convention of Democratic Young Men for Ritner*, p. 14; [Jacob B. Moore], *The Contrast: or, Plain Reasons why William Henry Harrison Should be Elected President*, p. 16; [Calvin Colton], *Crisis of the Country*, p. 11; and *Whig Songs for 1844*, p. 7.

The appeal to "revolution" runs all through the campaign literature of 1840. For a useful compendium, see A. B. Norton, ed., *Great Revolution of 1840*, which reprints Clay's statement at p. 211, and similar appeals by other speakers and writers at pp. 52, 59, 61, 225, 241. See also Miner, *Address at Wilkes-Barre*, pp. 3a, 8b.

14. Polk, *Address to People of Tennessee* (1839), pp. 3–7; *Address to Republican People of Tennessee*, p. 18; also *Proceedings of Convention of Republican Delegates in Fredericksburg*, pp. 3–5; Van Ness, *Speech at Woodstock*, pp. 4–5; Thomas Jefferson Sutherland, *Three Political Letters*, p. 12; *To Democratic Electors of Second Congressional District [of Indiana]*; and Van Buren, *Inquiry into Political Parties*, pp. 421–22.

15. Rantoul, *Oration at Scituate*, p. 4; also "Address to the People of Rhode Island, from the convention assembled at Providence on the 22d day of February, and again on the 12th day of March, 1834, to promote the establishment of a State constitution," *Report of Select Committee on Rhode Island*, pp. 151ff.; and James C. Zabriskie, in *N.J. C. C.* (1844), pp. 390–91. Cushing Strout touches on many of these themes in *American Image of the Old World.*

16. See Downs, in *La. C. C.* (1845), p. 115b; Isaac T. Preston, in ibid., p. 152a–b.

17. Morris, in *N.Y. C. C.* (1846), p. 995a; also Nathan Sanford, in *N.Y. C. C.* (1821), p. 178.

18. Dorr, Speech before the Constitutional Assembly of Rhode Island (1842), as

found in Irving Mark and Eugene L. Schwaab, eds., *Faith of Our Fathers*, p. 61; *Address of Democratic Convention [of Tennessee]*, p. 3b; "The Currency," *West. Rev.* 1, no. 1 (April 1846), 208.

19. *Brief Sketch of Parties*, p. 7; "To the Political Reader," *Am. Rev.* 12, no. 35 (November 1850), 439b; and Webster, Speech at Saratoga, in Norton, ed., *Great Revolution of 1840*, pp. 231–32; also *Facts for the People* (1840), p. 14b; and D. Francis Bacon, *Progressive Democracy*, p. 17.

20. Everett, "Education in the West" (1833), in *Importance of Practical Education*, pp. 162–63; [Colton], *Junius Tracts* no. 3, p. 15; also [Emory Washburn], review of addresses by Everett and Frederick Robinson, in *No. Am. Rev.* 41, no. 89 (October 1835), 348–66; and *Facts for the People* (1840), p. 31b; and see Norman Jacobson, "The Concept of Equality in the Assumptions and the Propaganda of Massachusetts Conservatives, 1790–1840" (Ph.D. diss., University of Wisconsin, 1951), chs. 6–7 passim.

In *America and Image of Europe*, Daniel Boorstin argues that Americans defined themselves as the antithesis of Europe at least until the twentieth century—initially with pride, later with concern, but consistently with the sense that the world beyond their shores was hostile. I think his point is well taken but tends to obscure the special commitment Americans of the Middle Period felt to vindicating themselves by maintaining the difference. See also Charles L. Sanford, "The Intellectual Origins and New-Worldliness of American Industry," *Journal of Economic History* 18 (1958), 1–6.

21. Butler, *Representative Democracy in the United States*, pp. 30–31; "Extract from the remarks of D. V. Bradford, Esq.," *Columbus* (Ohio) *Statesman, Extra*, 10 October 1840, p. 2b.

22. Gouge, *Short History of Paper Money*, p. 44; Mann, Report for 1848, *Life and Works*, 4:246, 248; also David Henshaw, *Address at Faneuil Hall*, pp. 4–5; "The Boston Association of the Friends of the Rights of Man," *Boston Quarterly Review* 1, no. 2 (April 1838), 236–38; "An Address of the Workingmen of Charlestown, Mass., to their Brethren . . . ," ibid. 4, no. 13 (January 1841), 119–22; *Proceedings of Democratic Legislative Convention in Boston*, pp. 8–9; [Levi Slamm], *The Tariff, No. 1*, p. 8a; and *Manchester* (New Hampshire) *Operative*, as quoted in *Lynn* (Massachusetts) *Awl*, 28 August 1844, p. 4.

The *Harbinger* also saw the United States in an exceptional light. It argued in 1845 that "the civilization of Europe and of the United States are of one and the same stock. They differ only as the early plant of spring differs from the mature product of the autumn." But it also pointed out that "in this country, we have new and peculiar advantages for such a work [as reorganizing society according to divine laws]. We have all the vigor of full youth, not without something of the wisdom of experience. Above all, society here is not so corrupt as to lead us to despair of a remedy. It contains ample materials for a social order which shall leave the effete civilization of the age far in the back ground, and realize the hopes which the best men in their best hours have never ceased to cherish" ([George Ripley], "Tendencies of Modern Civilization," *Harbinger* 1, no. 3 [28 June 1845], 35a). By contrast, Parke Godwin insisted that the United States and Europe suffered from the same problems and required the same radical alterations of society (*Democracy*, passim).

23. Maury, *Address on Advantages of the United States*, p. 6. In view of the attention that literary historians have lavished on writings that seem to represent America as a second Paradise, it is probably worth noting that the New World Maury describes is not so much Adamic as receptive to the impress of a liberty that has reached manhood. See also George Holley's Fourth of July oration at Peru, Illinois, in 1839: "There is no other world for another Columbus to discover, and unless the wheels of time can be stayed in their tracks, . . . there can be no possible combination of circumstances, no possible series of events, that shall be so favorable to the formation of a pure representative democracy, as those circumstances which were combined, and those events which did transpire, to consummate the establishment of our Government. Freedom, driven from all the old states, sought in this virgin world her last asylum, her noblest, fairest, final home" (p. 5).

24. [Colton], *Junius Tracts* no. 7, p. 15; also George W. Blagden, *Great Principles Associated with Plymouth Rock*, p. 23; and [Thomas R. Hazard], *Facts for the Laboring Man*, p. 28.

25. Channing, "National Literature," *Christian Examiner* 7, no. 36 (January 1830), 286; Catharine Beecher, *Evils Suffered by American Women and Children*, pp. 11b–12a.

26. Norvell, in *Mich. C. C.* (1835), p. 201, and see William Welch, in ibid., p. 107; also William N. McLeod, in *Mich. C. C.* (1850), p. 200b.

27. In addition to Boorstin, *Genius of American Politics*, and Louis Hartz, *Liberal Tradition in America*, see Yehoshua Arieli, *Individualism and Nationalism in American Ideology*, which attempts to trace the origins and account for the authority of the Americans' national identification with economic individualism.

28. For partisan Whig usage, see *Facts for the People* (1832), p. 6b; [Alonzo Potter], "Trades' Unions," *N.-Y. Rev.* 2, no. 3 (January 1838), 11; "A Public Friend," *To Female Operatives of Dover Cotton Manufactories;* and Sen. John H. Clarke, 9 February 1852, *Cong. Globe*, 32d C, 1st S, p. 136c. For partisan Democratic usage, see Rep. George Cary, 21 January 1824, *Ann. Cong.*, 18th C, 1st S, cols. 1127–32; *Proceedings of Harrison County Democratic Meeting*, cols. a–b; *Address of Democratic Central State Committee of Massachusetts*, p. 3; and Sen. William Allen, 16 December 1845, *Cong. Globe*, 29th C, 1st S, p. 58c.

29. Lindsley, *Address at Nashville*, p. 34; *Boston Post*, 18 September 1847, as quoted by John D. P. Fuller in "The Movement for the Acquisition of All Mexico, 1846–1848," *Johns Hopkins University Studies in Historical and Political Science* 54, no. 4 (1936), 81; Douglas, 11 December 1851, *Cong. Globe*, 32d C, 1st S, p. 71a; and *New Orleans Bulletin*, 1852, as quoted by Riepma, "Young America," p. 248; also Benjamin F. Hallett, *Right of the People to Establish Forms of Government*, p. 47; and Robert J. Walker, *Appeal for the Union*, p. 15.

30. Clay, *Papers*, 3:688, 701; 2:856. Critics of the American System also testified to the extra authority it acquired by its association with the national image when they sought to discredit use of the term. See, for example, Sen. John Rowan, 6 May 1828, *Reg. Deb.*, 20th C, 1st S, col. 730.

31. *Address of administration standing committee of Indiana*, pp. 2–4; [Colton], *Junius Tracts* no. 3, p. 5, and see ibid. no. 2, p. 11, and no. 3, p. 2; Jackson to L. H. Coleman, April 1824, in *Correspondence*, 3:250.

32. Robert W. Binkley Jr. discusses the heroic implications of the American System in his doctoral dissertation, "The American System: An Example of Nineteenth-Century Economic Thinking" (Columbia University, 1949).

33. Jackson, in James D. Richardson, ed., *Messages and Papers of the Presidents*, 2:581, and see his Proclamation to South Carolina, 10 December 1832, ibid., p. 654; *Proceedings and Address of Democratic County Convention at Galena*, p. 5a; and *Boston Post*, 13 September 1845, as quoted by Charles Warren, *Supreme Court in United States History*, 2:143.

This is not to deny that Americans often expressed an unrelieved hostility toward foreign investors. (See Littleton D. Teackle, in *Maryland Republican* [Annapolis], *Extra*, 21 January 1832, and *Address in relation to National Policy* [Indiana], p. 11.) Nevertheless, so far as I have taken note of such expressions they do not stress "Americanism" as the basis of their antipathy.

34. "Young America" directly and explicitly adopted this version of Americanism. See also John L. O'Sullivan, "Annexation," *Dem. Rev.* 17, no. 85 (July and August 1845), 6a–b, and "The Oregon Question," *West. Rev.* 1, no. 1 (April 1846), 186. Siert F. Riepma provides the fullest discussion of Young America in his doctoral dissertation, which elaborates the judgments reached by Merle Curti in the *American Historical Review* (Curti, "Young America," *AHR* 32 [1926], 34–55). Frederick and Lois Bannister Merk note the extent to which expansionism reflected, or capitalized upon, hostility to Great Britain, in *Monroe Doctrine and American Expansionism*, esp. ch. 2.

35. Norvell, in *Mich. C. C.* (1835), p. 209; Brent, in *La. C. C.* (1845), p. 248b.

36. Ruth M. Elson, *Guardians of Tradition*, pp. 282–83; [G. C. Collins], *Fifty Reasons why Henry Clay should be President*, p. 6b; and see Joseph Taylor, *Henry Clay*, p. 36.

37. "Leggett's Writings," *N.-Y. Rev.* 8, no. 16 (April 1841), 391; Ewing, 24 April 1852, *Cong. Globe*, 32d C, 1st S, *Appendix*, p. 532b; also Mann, Report for 1848, p. 250; and Horace Bushnell, *Common Schools*.

38. Brent, in *La. C. C.* (1845), p. 113b; also J. W. Stebbins, in *United States Senatorial Question*, p. 9b; Horatio Seymour, *Speech at Tammany Hall*, p. 4a; J. Randolph Burns, *To editor of the True Issue*, p. 2b; and Carl Schurz, "True Americanism" (1859), in *Speeches, Correspondence and Political Papers*, 1:48–72.

CHAPTER III: THE MISSION OF AMERICA

1. David W. Noble develops this argument in ch. 2 of *Historians against History*. Edward McNall Burns has assembled the most comprehensive evidence of an American missionary attitude in *American Idea of Mission*.

2. Adams, in James D. Richardson, ed., *Messages and Papers of the Presidents*, 2:316; Wirt as found in John J. Harrod, *The Academical Reader*, quoted by Ruth M. Elson, *Guardians of Tradition*, p. 297; also "Civilization: American and European," *Am. Rev.* 3, no. 6 (June 1846), 624a.

3. Greenough, *The Conquering Republic*, p. 8; Everett, "Affairs of Greece," *No. Am. Rev.* 17, no. 41 (October 1823), 423; also William H. Harrison, *Speech at the Dayton Convention*, p. 8.

4. Tefft, *The Far West*, pp. 35–36; Jewett, *Oration in Vigo County*, p. 12.

5. "Mr. Forrest's Oration," *Dem. Rev.* 3, no. 9 (September 1838), 56; Wood, 21 January 1824, *Ann. Cong.*, 18th C, 1st S, col. 1133.

6. Fillmore, in Richardson, ed., *Messages and Papers of the Presidents*, 5:179–80; Clay as quoted by Arthur A. Ekirch Jr., *Ideas, Ideals, and American Diplomacy*, p. 36; also Rep. George Cary, 21 January 1824, *Ann. Cong.*, 18th C, 1st S, col. 1132; Rep. Alfred Cuthbert, 23 January 1824, ibid., cols. 1167–68; and Rep. Joseph Hemphill, 13 April 1826, *Reg. Deb.*, 19th C, 1st S, col. 2239.

7. Walker, in Myer Moses, *Full Annals of the Revolution in France*, p. 110; and see Franklin Pierce's toast as Fourth of July orator at Hillsborough, New Hampshire, in 1828: "Ancient and modern Greece. Our fathers were inspired by the chivalrous deeds of the former; we pay the debt by presenting a cheering example to the latter" (*Republican Sentiment of New-Hampshire*, p. 20a).

8. [Slamm], *Injustice of the Tariff*, p. 6; "The Oregon Question," *West. Rev.* 1, no. 1 (April 1846), 187; also Lewis Cass, 6 April 1848, *Cong. Globe*, 30th C, 1st S, *Appendix*, p. 465b.

9. Buckingham, *Oration delivered at Trenton*, p. 14; also *Address to People of Maryland*, p. 3; O. P. Jackson, *Oration at New Orleans*, p. 19; Caleb Atwater, *Essay on Education*, p. 122; and James C. Conkling, *Oration in Sprinfield*, p. 5b.

10. [Brooks], *Remarks on Europe*, p. 42.

11. Rives, 6 April 1826, *Reg. Deb.*, 19th C, 1st S, col. 2083; also Rep. Alexander Smyth, 26 January 1824, *Ann. Cong.*, 18th C, 1st S, col. 1212; Sen. John H. Clarke, 9 February 1852, *Cong. Globe*, 32d C, 1st S, p. 139c; and Article 11 of the Democratic platform for 1852.

12. Maury, *Address on Advantages of the United States*, p. 24. The clauses I have omitted from this overheated paragraph are all partisan Whig criticisms of the national Democratic administration.

13. American attitudes toward European affairs are closely examined in John G. Gazley, *American Opinion of German Unification*, and Arthur J. May, *Contemporary American Opinion of Mid-Century Revolutions*, two old-fashioned studies that have much to recommend them. Merle Curti, "The Impact of the Revolutions of 1848 on American Thought," in Edward N. Saveth, ed., *Understanding the American Past*, pp. 244–58, and Eugene N. Curtis, "American Opinion of the French Nineteenth-Century Revolutions," *AHR* 29 (1924), 249–70, are useful brief studies. Curtis examines American attitudes toward the July Revolution in "La Révolution de 1830 et l'Opinion Publique en

Amérique," *La Révolution de 1848 et les Révolutions du XIXe Siècle, 1830–1848–1870* 17 (1921), 64–73, 81–118; and see Henry Blumenthal, *Reappraisal of Franco-American Relations*, ch. 1.

14. Douglas, 11 December 1851, *Cong. Globe*, 32d C, 1st S, p. 71a; and see the further discussion of interventionist sentiment to follow.

15. Seward, 12 December 1851, ibid., p. 89c.

16. See particularly John W. Oliver, "Louis Kossuth's Appeal to the Middle West—1852," *MVHR* 14 (1928), 481–96, and Andor M. Leffler, "The Kossuth Episode in America" (Ph.D. diss., Western Reserve University, 1949), esp. chs. 3, 6, 7.

17. Cass, 4 January 1850, *Cong. Globe*, 31st C, 1st S, *Appendix*, p. 55b–c; Foote, 8 January 1850, ibid., pp. 43a–46c, esp. pp. 43c, 44a; and Buel, 20 February 1850, ibid., pp. 144a, 147c; and see Donald S. Spencer, "Lewis Cass and Symbolic Intervention: 1848–1852," *Michigan History* 53 (1969), 1–17.

18. Foote, 3 December 1851, *Cong. Globe*, 32d C, 1st S, p. 23a; Cass, 11 December 1851, ibid., pp. 66c–69a, 68a; Douglas, 11 December 1851, ibid., pp. 70b–71b.

19. Walker, 16 December 1851, ibid., p. 106a, and see the remarks of Rep. David T. Disney, 31 December 1851, ibid., pp. 172a–173a. It is true that Sen. Robert F. Stockton of New Jersey, formerly commodore of the flotilla that had seized California at the outbreak of the Mexican War, not only condemned American neutrality but insisted that the United States was engaged in a critical competition with Great Britain for "ascendency" on the high seas. But Stockton was an oddly idiosyncratic figure, laboring a distinctly military outlook and pressing geopolitical considerations that would not be fashionable for another fifty years. (See his speech of 10 December 1851, ibid., p. 51b–c.)

20. Sweetser, 3 January 1852, ibid., pp. 177b–c; Yates, ibid., p. 181b; and see Rep. Henry M. Fuller, 2 January 1852, ibid., p. 191b–c. It should be said that Yates and Fuller were Whigs.

21. Merle Curti deals very carefully with Austro-American relations in "Austria and the United States 1848–1852: A Study in Diplomatic Relations," *Smith College Studies in History* 11, no. 3 (1926), 141–206.

22. *Proceedings, Speeches, &c., at the Kossuth Dinner*, pp. 7b (Webster), 11a–12b (Douglas), 2a (Stanton), 2a–b (Shields), 16b (Graham). Graham, of course, was a Whig.

23. *Proceedings at Banquet of Jackson Democratic Association*, pp. 2a–3a and passim.

24. Ibid., pp. 10a–b (Douglas), 7b, 7b–8a (Cass), 11b (Lane).

25. Cass, 10 February 1852, *Cong. Globe*, 32d C, 1st S, *Appendix*, pp. 159a–165c, 159c, 164c; also William H. Seward, 9 March 1852 (ibid., pp. 243–47); and Pierre Soulé, 22 March 1852 (ibid., pp. 349–354). Again Senator Stockton expressed a more radical version of the American obligation, stressing that a day of reckoning between liberty and despotism must come before 1900. But even Stockton proposed only to forestall any declaration against interven-

tion, not to press for intervention in his own time, and he explicitly disa-
vowed going to war with Russia (an old friend to the United States) in behalf
of Hungarian independence (an impractical ideal). (See 2 February 1852,
ibid., pp. 438c–439c.)

26. Cass, ibid., p. 162c.

27. "Glances at Congress. By a reporter," *Dem. Rev.* 1, no. 1 (October 1837), 71;
The Crisis Met, p. 1; also Ross Wilkins, in *Mich. C. C.* (1835), p. 245; Isaac T.
Preston, in *La. C. C.* (1845), p. 23a; and David L. Gregg, Thomas G. C.
Davis, and Thompson Campbell, in *Ill. C. C.* (1847), pp. 531, 561–62, and
575.

28. Brown, 28 April 1852, *Cong. Globe*, 32d C, 1st S, *Appendix*, p. 511b; Norvell,
in *Mich. C. C.* (1835), p. 216; also George Camp, *Democracy*, p. 239.

29. Cass, 11 December 1851, *Cong. Globe*, 32d C, 1st S, p. 66c; *Weekly Gazette*,
29 January 1852, as found in Norman A. Graebner, ed., *Ideas and Diplomacy*,
pp. 289, 290; also Rep. Cary, 21 January 1824, *Ann. Cong.*, 18th C, 1st S,
col. 1132.

30. Seward, 9 March 1852, *Cong. Globe*, 32d C, 1st S, *Appendix*, p. 247c.

31. Eby, "America as 'Asylum': A Dual Image," *AQ* 14 (1962), 483–89. Significantly, Eby finds the idea of asylum most prevalent in the Middle States—
not in New England, where the idea of mission was supposedly strong.

32. Dix, *War with Mexico*, p. 15a.

33. *The Crisis Met*, p. 1.

34. Dix, *War with Mexico*, p. 15a.

35. For an outstanding example, see *Address to the People of the State of Illinois*, and
cf. Justin H. Smith, *Annexation of Texas*, esp. pp. 140ff., 261ff. Even when
allowance is made for the fact that Great Britain had no designs on Texas, as
the Merks demonstrate in *Monroe Doctrine and American Expansionism*, the idea
that it did was a significant aspect of American policy, as the Merks themselves point out.

36. Compare, for example, the views expressed by F. O. J. Smith in "Progress,"
Hunt's 18, no. 3 (March 1848), 260–69, with those expressed by Theodore
Sedgwick Jr. in *Thoughts on Annexation of Texas*, pp. 47–48. See also "Califor-
nia," *Am. Rev.* 3, no. 1 (January 1846), 82–99; Parke Godwin, *Political Essays*,
as quoted by Ekirch in *Ideas, Ideals, and Diplomacy*, pp. 57–58; and George
W. Bethune, *Claims of Our Country*, esp. p. 52.

37. "Retrospective View of the South-American States," *Dem. Rev.* 1, no. 2
(January 1838), 270; Elson, *Guardians of Tradition*, pp. 158ff. Even Lewis
Cass expressed misgivings about foreign capabilities during the middle of
debate on the Clarke Resolution (10 February 1852, *Cong. Globe*, 32d C, 1st
S, *Appendix*, p. 159b–c). Racial versions of the same theme are readily appar-
ent in "The War," *Dem. Rev.* 20, no. 104 (February 1847), 100, and in the
New York Evening Post as quoted by Norman Graebner, ed., *Manifest Destiny*,
p. lvi, as well as in Jasper Adams, *Moral Causes of Welfare of Nations*, p. 33.

38. See, for example, William W. Greenough's paean to *The Conquering Republic*,
esp. p. 27.

39. *Boston Times*, 22 October 1847, as quoted by Frederick and Lois B. Merk, *Manifest Destiny and Mission*, p. 122, and see Robert F. Stockton's address at Philadelphia, 30 December 1847, as found in Graebner, ed., *Manifest Destiny*, pp. 209–15. See also John D. P. Fuller, "The Movement for the Acquisition of All Mexico," as well as Merk and Merk, *Manifest Destiny and Mission*, ch. 5.

40. Bayard, *Address at West Point*, pp. 5a–9b.

41. *Address to the People of the State of Illinois*, p. 3a; also see Stephen Austin, "Address of the Honorable S. F. Austin, One of the Commissioners of Texas, delivered at Louisville, Kentucky, on the 7th of March 1836," as found in Avery Craven et al., eds., *Documentary History of the American People*, p. 272b.

42. The *Address to the People of the State of Illinois* was one of many publications that included Jackson's letter to Aaron V. Brown on the subject of annexation.

43. "The Oregon Question," *West. Rev.* 1, no. 1 (April 1846), 186; also Sen. Sidney Breese, 27 February 1844, *Cong. Globe*, 28th C, 1st S, *Appendix*, p. 226c; and Sen. William Allen, 10–11 February, 1846, ibid., 29th C, 1st S, *Appendix*, p. 839c.

44. London *Times*, 1 January 1846, as quoted by Merk and Merk in *Monroe Doctrine and American Expansionism*, pp. 84–85, and see the *Spectator*, 17 December 1845, quoted by Merk and Merk, p. 83. In 1848 John C. Calhoun discerned and deplored much the same pattern of thought as the stimulus to American interest in Yucatán, which disappeared at least in part because the civil war there was interrupted before the Americans could act (see ibid., p. 218 and ch. 8).

45. Weinberg, *Manifest Destiny*, chs. 1, 4, 5.

46. For the Merks' discussion of American attitudes, see esp. chs. 3 and 4 of *Monroe Doctrine and American Expansionism*. For instances of American reactions to apparently equitable European claims, see [John L. O'Sullivan], "Annexation," *Dem. Rev.* 17, no. 85 (July and August 1845), 9b–10a; Rep. Lewis C. Levin, 9 January 1846, as found in Graebner, ed., *Manifest Destiny*, p. 101; and Dix, *War with Mexico*, pp. 4a–9a, as well as chapter XII of this study, which deals with American attitudes toward exploitation of the continent.

47. Several different arguments testify to the presence of this underlying belief: (1) the idea that expanding the United States will literally expand the area of freedom, expressed by Reps. Alexander Duncan and John Belser and Sen. Stephen A. Douglas, among others; (2) the idea that the Mexicans will welcome American occupation, expressed by James Buchanan and (implicitly) by John L. O'Sullivan, again among others; (3) the idea that expanding the area of the United States will reinforce the influence of American example in the world and thus hasten the spread of free institutions in Europe, expressed by a number of expansionists; and (4) the idea that expansion will solve the problems of Negro slavery, expressed by O'Sullivan, Robert J. Walker, and others. In addition, even the opponents of expansion lent sup-

port to the basic idea when they argued that these ends would be served without actual intervention in Mexican affairs. These various themes are traced in Merk and Merk, *Manifest Destiny and Mission*, esp. ch. 5, and Weinberg, *Manifest Destiny*, ch. 4.

48. Smith, *82d Anniversary American Independence*, p. 18.

CHAPTER IV: EQUAL RIGHTS

1. Recent studies of the Jacksonian period have used the writings of foreign travelers to document the failures of American democracy during the Middle Period. In doing so, however, they have only confirmed the thrust of American egalitarian sentiment as distinguished from American practice. Indeed, they have sometimes imitated the travelers in employing a literal-minded or perfectionist rendering of American aspirations as a way of decrying American institutions, neglecting thereby the practical force of the ideal they invoke. See in particular Douglas Miller, *Jacksonian Aristocracy*, and Edward Pessen, *Jacksonian America*, ch. 3. Pessen acknowledges the power of American attitudes in "The Egalitarian Myth and the American Social Reality: Wealth, Mobility, and Equality in the 'Era of the Common Man,' " *AHR* 76 (1971), 1027–31.

2. The veto message rang the changes on this central theme of exploitation through legal privilege: stockholders exploiting the people, aliens exploiting native Americans, the East exploiting the South and West, the few exploiting the many, all conspiring to make some men "richer by Act of Congress." See James D. Richardson, ed., *Messages and Papers of the Presidents*, 2:576–81, 590.

3. *Address and Resolves of Democratic Members of the Massachusetts Legislature*, p. 4b, and see Frederick Robinson's address, ibid., p. 25b, and "The Credit System," *Dem. Rev.* 3, no. 11 (November 1838), 196; Bagg, in *Mich. C. C.* (1850), p. 29a; also George W. Brown, in *Texas C. C.* (1845), p. 461. The narrowing thrust of the Democratic position is apparent in the difference between Bagg's view and the preamble to a Kentucky statute of 1819 rescinding the charter of a manufacturing corporation to which banking privileges had been granted: "A bank charter, from its nature, extends and necessarily confines the powers and privileges granted, to a few, to the exclusion of the many. It, therefore, follows as an unavoidable conclusion, that if the powers and privileges granted in a bank charter operate against the public good, the people, by their legislature, have the primitive right to revoke such charter." According to this view, the public good might still be served by selective incorporations, although it appeared that popular presumption ran otherwise (the statute as quoted in Robert W. Binkley Jr., "The American System," p. 109).

4. *Address of Democratic Members of the Massachusetts Legislature*, p. 16; *Texas C. C.* (1845), p. 22; and see Bayrd Still, "State Constitutional Development in the United States, 1829–1851" (Ph.D. diss., University of Wisconsin, 1933), passim, as well as chapter VII, below. By contrast, Justices Story and

McLean were horrified by the *Charles River Bridge* decision because (among other things) it overlooked the Commonwealth's original wish to secure a river crossing at a hazardous location. See *Charles River Bridge* v. *Warren Bridge, U.S. Rep.*, 11 Peters 564ff., 609ff.

5. See Peter D. Vroom, in *N.J. C. C.* (1844), p. 161, and [Theodore Sedgwick Jr.], *Constitutional Reform*, p. 7b; and cf. Harold E. Wilson, *Hill Country of Northern New England*, p. 35.

6. Edwards, *Address to the People of Missouri*, p. 2a; Vroom, in *N.J. C. C.* (1844), p. 325.

7. Rowan, 6 May 1828, *Reg. Deb.*, 20th C, 1st S, col. 730; also *Address of Free Trade Convention* (1828), p. 3; Robert Rantoul Jr., *Memoirs*, p. 114; James K. Polk, *Address to the People of Tennessee* (1839), p. 6; [Sedgwick], *Constitutional Reform*, p. 45a; and [George N. Hickman, ed.], *Democratic Text Book*, p. 5.

8. See, for example, Jackson's first annual message, in which he discusses rotation of appointive office in terms equally applicable to elective office (Richardson, ed., *Messages and Papers of the Presidents*, 2:448–49), and *Address and Proceedings of Ohio State Convention*, p. 11. For theories of representation, see Alfred De Grazia, *Public and Republic*, ch. 5, as well as chapter VII of this study.

9. *Plain Facts for the People*, p. 2; Isaac Crary, in *Mich. C. C.* (1835), p. 304; Edwards, *Address to the People of Missouri*, p. 1b; also Lyman Evans, in *Iowa C. C.* (1844), pp. 120–21; Moses Jaques, in *N.J. C. C.* (1844), p. 109; Thompson Campbell, Horace Butler, and William R. Archer, in *Ill. C. C.* (1847), pp. 368, 371, 372; Isaac T. Preston, in *La. C. C.* (1845), pp. 150b–151a; Bagg, C. W. Chapel, and Elias Woodman, in *Mich. C. C.* (1850), pp. 319a, 389b, 430a; and the bitter dispute in *Ky. C. C.* (1849), pp. 446a–451a.

10. Zabriskie, in *N.J. C. C.* (1844), p. 391, and see Jaques, in ibid., pp. 454–60; Lemuel D. Evans, in *Texas C. C.* (1845), p. 355. As Perry Miller points out in part 2 of *Life of the Mind in America*, Federalists as well as Republicans criticized the common law, and Democrats as well as Whigs honored it as a liberal and progressive achievement of the human mind; obviously party allegiances were no more a *guarantee* of attitudes toward the law than of attitudes toward other social institutions. Nevertheless, Miller's data might more accurately be taken to show that lawyers who were Federalists sometimes criticized the law, and lawyers who were Democrats often praised it. It remains true that the severest critics of the law during the Middle Period tended either to be Democrats or to invoke democratic slogans against it. For additional examples of hostility toward the law or the legal profession, see Charles M. Haar, ed., *Golden Age of American Law*, and Anton-Hermann Chroust, *Rise of the Legal Profession*, 2:57–72.

11. "An Observer," *Enquiry into Medical Education*, passim; *New York Evening Star*, as reported in *Cincinnati Daily Gazette*, 26 January 1837, p. 2e; also William Leggett, 3 December 1836, in *Political Writings*, 2:118f.

12. *Mechanics' Free Press*, 24 October 1829, as found in Irving Mark and Eugene

L. Schwaab, eds., *Faith of Our Fathers*, p. 101; "Report of the Joint Committees of the City and County of Philadelphia," in John R. Commons et al., eds., *Documentary History of American Industrial Society*, 5:98–99; and also Robert Walker, in Myer Moses, *Full Annals of the Revolution in France* (second pagination), pp. 113–14.

13. See, for example, Harriet Martineau's remark, "Nothing in American civilisation struck me so forcibly and so pleasurably as the invariable respect paid to man, as man. Nothing since my return to England has given me so much pain as the contrast there. Perhaps no Englishman can become fully aware, without going to America, of the atmosphere of insolence in which he dwells; of the taint of contempt which infects all the intercourses of his world. He cannot imagine how all that he can say that is truest and best about the treatment of people of colour in America is neutralised on the spot, by its being understood how the same contempt is spread over the whole of society here, which is there concentrated upon the blacks" (Martineau, *Society in America*, 2:168). See also John W. Cooke, "Some Aspects of the Concept of the Free Individual in the United States, 1800–1860" (Ph.D. diss., Vanderbilt University, 1967), ch. 3.

14. Balch, *Popular Liberty and Equal Rights*, p. 21; Medary, as quoted by William G. Shade, "The Politics of Free Banking in the Old Northwest, 1837–1863" (Ph.D. diss., Wayne State University, 1966), p. 91; Rantoul, as found in his *Memoirs*, p. 150; also [Levi J.] Ham, *Remarks of Mr. Ham, of York*, p. 8b; *Proceedings of Democratic State Convention in Nashville*, p. 8a; and Vroom, in *N.J. C. C.* (1844), p. 537.

15. For instances of a clear "agricultural" bias among leading Jacksonians, see William Gouge, *Short History of Paper Money*, p. 132; Sen. Thomas Hart Benton, 26 May 1832, *Reg. Deb.*, 21st C, 2d S, cols. 973–74; and "Radicalism," *Dem. Rev.* 3, no. 10 (October 1838), 110–11; and see Carl N. Degler, "The Locofocos: Urban 'Agrarians,' " *Journal of Economic History* 16 (1956), 222–33, as well as Donald McConnell, *Economic Virtues in the United States*, passim. In *The Age of Jackson*, moreover, Arthur M. Schlesinger Jr. provides considerable evidence that Jacksonian Democracy was neither urban nor industrial in its attitudes, the general thesis of his book notwithstanding.

16. Jackson, in Richardson, ed., *Messages and Papers of the Presidents*, 3:305; Flood and Fisher, *The Convention and Its Men*, passim; also *Reasons why Present System of Auctions Ought to be Abolished*, p. 3; Benton, as in note 15; Gouge, *Short History of Paper Money*, pp. 83–84, 235; the *Democratic Review*'s fictional "Autobiography of Ferret Snap Newcraft, Esq. Being a Full Exposition and Exemplification of 'The Credit System,' " 2, no. 2 (May 1838), 167–86; Edwin Forrest, *Oration at Democratic Republican Celebration*, which was quoted approvingly by the *Review* in September (3, no. 9, p. 57); and Edward D. Barber, *Oration at Montpelier*, p. 14.

17. The *Jeffersonian*, as quoted by Shade, "Politics of Free Banking," p. 213; Pierce, in *Mich. C. C.* (1850), p. 560b; Gouge, *Short History of Paper Money*, p.

84; also John E. Fletcher, in *Iowa C. C.* (1844), p. 196; and Archer, in *Ill. C. C.* (1847), p. 272.

18. *The Crisis Met*, p. 14; also George Bancroft, *History of the United States*, 4:12; Forrest, as in note 16; Barber, *Oration at Montpelier*, p. 10; and [Owen], *Address of Democratic Convention*, pp. 2–3.

19. Gouge, *Short History of Paper Money*, pp. 35, 229; [Owen], *Address of Democratic Convention*, pp. 14–15; Mayo, in *La. C. C.* (1845), p. 343b; and "The Credit System," *Dem. Rev.* 3, no. 11 (November 1838), 211; also Rep. C. C. Cambreleng, 11 February 1835, *Reg. Deb.* 23d C, 1st S, col. 1310; Frederick Robinson, *Oration before Trades' Union of Boston*, pp. 18–20; and David L. Gregg, in *Ill. C. C.* (1847), pp. 259–60.

20. [Owen], *Address of Democratic Convention*, p. 8; Jaques, in *N.J. C. C.* (1844), p. 341; also Jackson, Fourth Annual Message, in Richardson, ed., *Messages and Papers of the Presidents*, 2:602; Barber, *Oration at Montpelier*, p. 10; and Edward Archbold, in *Ohio C. C.* (1850–1851), 2:333; and see chapter VII, appendix a.

21. Rives, *Speech on the Currency*, p. 6; Gouge, *Short History of Paper Money*, p. 228, and cf. pp. 52–53; also [John L. O'Sullivan], "The Course of Civilization," *Dem. Rev.* 6, no. 21 (September 1839), 213–14; George Camp, *Democracy*, pp. 105–6; and Walt Whitman, 26 July 1847, in *Gathering of the Forces*, 1:52; and see Louis Hartz, *Economic Policy and Democratic Thought*, pp. 79f., and Yehoshua Arieli, *Individualism and Nationalism in American Ideology*, ch. 8.

Among the authors who made explicit use of laissez-faire theory were Samuel Young, the Free Trade Convention of South Carolina (1828), and Levi D. Slamm. But even their usage contrasts markedly in tone with the arguments put forward by J. B. Say (whom they also cited) and J. R. McCulloch. Compare Young, *Discourse at Schenectady; Address of Free Trade Convention* (1828), p. 4; and [Slamm], *Injustice of the Tariff*, p. 7, with Say, *Treatise on Political Economy*, and McCulloch, *Principles of Political Economy*.

22. *Address of Democratic State Convention of Illinois*, p. 14; Gouge, *Short History of Paper Money*, p. 41; also Address of the Republican County Convention, September 1836, in *St. Lawrence Republican, Extra*, July 1837, pp. 2a, 4b; "The Banks and the Currency," *Dem. Rev.* 2, no. 5 (April 1838), 9–10; *The Crisis Met*, p. 12; James K. Polk, *Answers of Ex-Gov. Polk*, p. 29b; *Wisconsin Argus*, 23 March 1847, as found in Milo M. Quaife, ed., *The Struggle over Ratification*, pp. 337–38; and Martin Van Buren, *Inquiry into Political Parties*, p. 231.

23. Barber, *Oration at Montpelier*, p. 10; also ibid., p. 15; and "The Currency," *West. Rev.* 1, no. 1 (April 1846), 207–9.

24. See Barber, *Oration at Montpelier*, pp. 14–16, for an especially telling example of a doctrinaire Democrat who could predict only the evils arising from Whiggish intrusions on the natural economy. Other examples include Gouge, *Short History of Paper Money*, p. 126; Camp, *Democracy*, p. 54; and Joseph A. Wright, *Address at Livonia*, p. 13.

25. [O'Sullivan], "The Course of Civilization," p. 215; also Gouge, *Short History of Paper Money*, pp. 127, 133; "Radicalism," p. 103; and Martin Van Buren, *Opinions of Mr. Van Buren*, pp. 3a–4a.

Democratic attitudes toward charity frequently betrayed the same spirit. In general, the most principled Democrats were probably the strongest critics of charity as a demoralizing influence in society, although it should be said that they found growing support from conservative Whigs. For a general discussion of American attitudes toward poverty, see Benjamin J. Klebaner, "Poverty and its Relief in American Thought, 1815–1861," *Social Service Review* 38 (1964), 382–99, which nevertheless stresses the greater generosity the Americans demonstrated compared with the British during the same period.

Democratic attitudes toward bankruptcy legislation followed much the same pattern. In congressional debate during the early 1840s, Democratic leaders treated voluntary bankruptcy as the moral equivalent of suspension of specie payments, and they succeeded in repealing the law of 1841 as soon as they regained control of both houses. Similarly, vigorous Democrats as well as Whigs often opposed debtor relief and similar innovations in the state constitutional conventions, while they frequently held that the cure of depressions must be left to nature; it was improper for human beings to interfere with the natural processes of purgation and redemption. For the debate on bankruptcy legislation, see in particular *Cong. Globe*, 27th C, 2d S, *Appendix*, pp. 29b–31b (Benton), 88c–91a (Benton), 97a–98a (Young), and 147c–149a (Smith), as well as Charles Warren, *Bankruptcy in United States History*, pp. 60–81. Attitudes toward depressions are described systematically by Samuel Rezneck, "Social History of an American Depression, 1837–1843," *AHR* 40 (1935), 662–87.

26. Camp, *Democracy*, p. 177, and compare the many instances in which leading Democrats invoked a cyclical theory of wealth to characterize American society, e.g., Sen. Richard M. Johnson, 1 April 1828, *Reg. Deb.*, 20th C, 1st S, col. 573; Benton, 9 April 1828, ibid., col. 623; [Joseph Worrell et al.], *Letters Addressed to John Sergeant*, p. 5; Lewis Cass, *Address before Alumni of Hamilton College*, pp. 32–33; Rantoul, *Memoirs*, p. 137; and [Levi Slamm], *The Tariff, No. 1*, p. 6b.

27. See, for example, Gouge, *Short History of Paper Money*, pp. 117–18; Leggett, 30 December 1834, in *Political Writings* 1:142–43; and Cambreleng, 11 February 1835, *Reg. Deb.*, 23d C, 1st S, col. 1311.

28. Marvin Meyers comes close to recognizing this quality of their thought in his discussion of the elder Theodore Sedgwick, as also in elements of his treatments of Martin Van Buren, William Leggett, and Robert Rantoul Jr., in *The Jacksonian Persuasion*.

29. Alan Heimert points to their theological cast of mind when he holds that Democrats of the Middle Period inherited a "style" of thought from the Edwardsian Calvinists that differentiated them from the Whigs (see *Religion*

and the American Mind, passim). For examples, see Gouge, *Short History of Paper Money*, pp. 228, 235; "Carlyle's *French Revolution*," *Dem. Rev.* 2, no. 8 (July 1838), 324–25; and Frederick Grimke, *Nature and Tendency of Free Institutions*, pp. 109–18. Their attitude toward the cure of depressions had the same quality; see *Address of Democratic State Convention of Illinois*, p. 12.

30. Henry Christman provides a perceptive if overwritten account of the Anti-Rent movement in *Tin Horns and Calico*. Edward P. Cheyney, *The Anti-Rent Agitation*, and Herbert A. Donovan, *The Barnburners*, are also valuable.

31. "Radicalism," *Dem. Rev.*, p. 107; Naar, in *N.J. C. C.* (1844), p. 400; *Free Trade and the American System*, p. 8; also Forrest, *Oration at Democratic Republican Celebration*, pp. 17–19; Young, *Discourse at Schenectady*, pp. 5–6; and cf. Henry B. Fearon's comment: "Every man feels not merely independent in his political, but also in his personal condition. The individual acts and thinks as an individual; and society seems to have diminished charms for men, who imagine that they have sufficient resources within themselves" (*Sketches of America* [1818] as quoted by Cooke, "Some Aspects of the Concept of the Free Individual," p. 55).

32. *Memorial of "Free Trade Convention,"* p. 86; Smith, "Legislative Policy of Maine: with Reference to the Subject of Corporations," *Hunt's* 16, no. 3 (March 1847), 257; and see Ely Moore, *Address before General Trades' Union*, pp. 7–8.

33. For attacks on "avarice," see Cambreleng, 11 February 1835, *Reg. Deb.*, 23d C, 1st S, col. 1311f.; Seth Luther, *Address on Avarice*, passim; and *William Sheets, Federal Candidate*, p. 6.

34. Pierce, in *Mich. C. C.* (1850), pp. 658b–659a; also Thomas M. Wadsworth, in *La. C. C.* (1845), p. 834a–b.

35. Pierce, in *Mich. C. C.* (1850), p. 66a; Britain, ibid., p. 670a.

36. Arthur M. Schlesinger Jr. makes the strongest possible case for the Democratic party as the party of significant reform in *The Age of Jackson*. Although some of his argument is either tendentious or uncritical, there is no denying the general accuracy of his description of the party's role. What is questionable is his sense that the Democrats were consistently wise and consistently aware of what they were doing. For a discussion of the political allegiances of New York's Anti-Renters, see esp. Christman, *Tin Horns and Calico*, passim.

37. "The Currency," *West. Rev.* 1, no. 1 (April 1846), 208; also James Brent and Solomon Downs in *La. C. C.* (1845), pp. 110a, 115b.

38. "The Currency," p. 208.

39. Bryant, 13 June 1836, as found in Tremaine McDowell, ed., *William Cullen Bryant*, p. 307; also Gouge, *Short History of Paper Money*, p. 91; Frederick Robinson, in *Address and Resolves of Democratic Members of the Massachusetts Legislature*, pp. 23b–24a; "On the Elevation of the Laboring Portions of the Community," *Dem. Rev.* 7, no. 30 (June 1840), 59–62; Camp, *Democracy*, pp. 155–56; Michael Walsh, *Speeches and Writings*, p. 32; [Slamm], *Injustice of*

the Tariff, p. 11; and Walt Whitman, 2 January 1847, in *Gathering of the Forces*, 1:53–54.

40. Duncan, *Speech on Army Appropriation Bill*, p. 1b; [Slamm], *The Tariff, No. 1*, p. 3b, and see ibid., p. 9; also Jackson, veto message, in Richardson, ed., *Messages and Papers of the Presidents*, 2:590; Gouge, *Short History of Paper Money*, p. 133; Leggett, 31 December 1836, in *Political Writings*, 2:164; Rantoul, *Memoirs*, p. 260; and Camp, *Democracy*, p. 227.

41. Brownson, "The Laboring Classes," *Boston Quarterly Review* 3, no. 11 (July 1840), 358–95, and cf. his review of Francis Wayland's *Elements of Political Economy* in ibid., 1, no. 3 (July 1838), esp. p. 386; see also Arthur M. Schlesinger Jr., *Orestes A. Brownson*. The pamphlet version of Brownson's essay was prefaced by a note that clearly disclaimed any intention of putting his reform into effect immediately and insisted that he did not challenge the right of living men to own and use property as they saw fit (Brownson, *Rich against Poor*, p. 1).

42. Skidmore, *Rights of Man to Property!* ch. 5. Helène S. Zahler traces the train of thought that led from radical agrarianism to the Homestead Act in *Eastern Workingmen and National Land Policy*.

   By contrast with Skidmore, Parke Godwin repudiated virtually the whole of Democratic social belief in *Democracy, Constructive and Pacific*. His work argued that the only way to escape the social evils Democrats deplored was to abandon the individualism they insisted upon (ch. 4). See also [George Ripley], "Andrew Jackson," *Harbinger* 1, no. 3 (28 June 1845), 46b.

43. My estimate of English radical thought is based upon an extensive sampling of ephemeral radical publications in the British Museum, London University, and the Manchester Central Reference Library. Two accounts by contemporaries are also extremely helpful, R. G. Gammage, *History of the Chartist Movement*; and William Lovett, *Life and Struggles*; as are two modern collections of documents, Dorothy Thompson, ed., *The Early Chartists*; and G. D. H. Cole and A. W. Filson, eds., *British Working Class Movements*.

   There are many secondary studies of social attitudes and social agitation during the 1830s and 1840s. Among them I have found most useful Mark Hovell, *The Chartist Movement*; Cecil Driver, *Tory Radical: Oastler;* David C. Morris, "The History of the Labour Movement in England, 1825–1852: The Problem of Leadership and the Articulation of Demands" (Ph.D. diss., University of London, 1952); Asa Briggs, ed., *Chartist Studies;* E. P. Thompson, *Making of the English Working Class;* and Patricia Hollis, *The Pauper Press*. Thompson's work is especially interesting in that although he is predisposed to find evidences of class consciousness before and during the 1830s he is also too meticulous a historian to hold that class antagonism produced viable social theory. (Rather, he implies that its development waited upon the advent of Karl Marx.) For a sharply worded critique of Thompson's biases, see R. Currie and R. M. Hartwell, *"The Making of the English Working Class?"* *Economic History Review*, 2d ser. 18 (1965), 633–43.

44. Benbow, *Grand National Holiday*. Two recent studies help to put the agitation of the 1830s into perspective, John T. Ward's *The Factory Movement*, and Nicholas C. Edsall's *The anti–Poor Law Movement;* and see Michael E. Rose, "The Anti-Poor Law Movement in the North of England," *Northern History* 1 (1966), 70–91.

45. See, for example, the address and proceedings of the London Working Men's Association, as found in Thompson, ed., *The Early Chartists*, pp. 50–54, 57–66, and the criticisms leveled at merely political Chartism by Matthew Fletcher (ibid., pp. 17–18) and George J. Harney (Cole and Filson, eds., *British Working Class Movements*, pp. 356–58).

46. See particularly R. N. Soffer, "Attitudes and Allegiances in the Unskilled North, 1830–1850," *International Review of Social History* 10 (1965), 429–54, which Dorothy Thompson has sharply criticized in "Notes on Aspects of Chartist Leadership," *Bulletin of the Society for the Study of Labour History*, no. 15 (1967), pp. 28–33; and J. K. Edwards, "Chartism in Norwich," *Yorkshire Bulletin of Economic and Social Research* 19 (1967), 85–100. Jorwerth Prothero casts serious doubt on the traditional scholarly division of types of Chartism between London and the North, but his analysis does not alter the proposition that, wherever it occurred, radical Chartism tended to be in an odd sense less egalitarian than the more moderate demands made by William Lovett and his associates. For typical expressions of Tory Radicalism, see Cole and Filson, eds., *British Working Class Movements*, pp. 315–18, and Thompson, ed., *The Early Chartists*, pp. 46–49. For typical expressions of working-class radicalism, see Thompson, ed., *The Early Chartists*, pp. 67–70, 73–81, 95–114, 177–84.

47. E. P. Thompson describes early writings in this vein in ch. 16 of *Making of the English Working Class*, esp. pp. 728ff. Interestingly, he also depicts appeals to traditional social values and upper-class paternalism as the main elements of mob attitudes during the food riots of the late eighteenth century; see "The Moral Economy of the English Crowd in the Eighteenth Century," *Past & Present* 50 (1971), 76–136.

CHAPTER V: THE CONSERVATIVE ETHIC

1. These values were usually implied rather than expressed in conservative statements. They have been touched on in a number of modern studies, including Norman Jacobson, "Concept of Equality among Massachusetts Conservatives"; George A. Lipsky, *John Quincy Adams;* Major Wilson, "Analysis of the Ideas of Liberty and Union as used by Members of Congress and the Presidents from 1828 to 1861" (Ph.D. diss., University of Kansas, 1964); and Paul Goodman, "Ethics and Enterprise: The Values of a Boston Elite, 1800–1860," *AQ* 18 (1966), 437–51.

2. Both the theory conservatives held and the reception it received are epitomized in the efforts Democratic spokesmen made to keep prominent conservatives' statements of policy before the electorate long after they had

clearly become irrelevant. In 1837 the *History of the Federal and Democratic Parties in the United States*, published as a campaign document in Indiana, quoted a letter John Quincy Adams had written in 1824 in behalf of congressional aid for internal improvements as evidence that he was a Federalist like his father. Similarly, Thomas Hart Benton and other Democrats made a point of keeping alive Richard Rush's Report of 1827 as Secretary of the Treasury because it argued that national land policy should be geared to overall national interests including those of the eastern manufacturing states. (See the *History*, p. 34, and Benton, 18 January 1830, *Reg. Deb.*, 21st C, 1st S, pp. 23b–24a, which is quoted in chapter XII.)

Even so, conservatives continued to describe a paternal and shaping role for government. See for example the *Proceedings of Whigs of Chester County;* D. Francis Bacon, *Progressive Democracy;* and "Organization of the Party," *Am. Rev.* 10, no. 23 (November 1849) 443a–b; and see Glyndon G. Van Deusen, "Some Aspects of Whig Thought and Theory in the Jacksonian Period," *AHR* 63 (1958), 305–22; Lee Benson, *Concept of Jacksonian Democracy*, passim; Jonathan Messerli, *Horace Mann*, esp. pp. 102, 114, 204–5, 235–36; and Elliott R. Barkan, "The Emergence of a Whig Persuasion: Conservatism, Democratism, and the New York State Whigs," *New York History* 52 (1971), 367–95.

3. Timothy Dwight gave classic expression to the idea that property is salutary in his otherwise hostile account of American frontiersmen in *Travels in New-England and New-York*, 2:462–63. See also John Witherspoon, *Lectures on Moral Philosophy*, pp. 74–79, and the debates in the state constitutional conventions of the 1820s, cited below. Part 1 of Maurice Klain, "Property in a Free Society: A Study of Early American Political Thought" (Ph.D. diss., Yale University, 1949), gives a good general account of conservative theory between about 1780 and 1820.

4. Spencer in *N.Y. C. C.* (1821), p. 218, and see Warren Dutton, Leverett Saltonstall, and Joseph Story in *Mass. C. C.* (1820–1821), pp. 247, 275–76, 285–86. For clerical statements, see Leonard Woods, "Duties of the Rich," *Am. Nat. Preacher* 2, no. 1 (April 1827), 167–76; Thomas P. Hunt, *Book of Wealth;* and William B. Sprague, "The Uses and Abuses of Money," *Am. Nat. Preacher* 22, no. 7 (July 1848), 152–63; and cf. Francis Wayland, *Affairs of Rhode-Island*, pp. 23f.

5. The legal precedents Americans increasingly abandoned are touched on in such studies as John R. Commons, *Legal Foundations of Capitalism*, chs. 3, 6–7; Jarvis M. Morse, *A Neglected Period of Connecticut History*, esp. p. 248; Benjamin F. Wright Jr., *The Contract Clause*, ch. 1; Robert A. East, *Business Enterprise in American Revolutionary Era*, ch. 9; Merrill Jensen, *The New Nation*, pt. 4; Jacobson, "Concept of Equality," ch. 3; Curtis P. Nettels, *Emergence of a National Economy*, pp. 377–79; Edward S. Corwin, *Liberty Against Government*, ch. 3; Gottfried Dietze, *In Defense of Property*, ch. 3; and William B. Prendergast, "Some American Ideas on the Limits of Political

Authority, 1630 to 1914," (Ph.D. diss., University of Chicago, 1948), pp. 61–72. In "Property in Colonial Political Theory," *Temple University Law Quarterly* 16 (1942), 388–406, David Fellman describes the evolution even during the colonial period of a theory of absolute property rights, but his account is marred by an imperfect understanding of colonial economic practices.

Other studies trace a continuing or even an expanding commitment to law conceived as an instrument of social welfare, but it seems to me that they mistake the thrust of nineteenth-century opinion. Among them, James W. Hurst's *Law and Conditions of Freedom* apparently considers the very existence of law as a socially significant institution to be evidence of a deliberate social orientation in American policy, while the series of studies of state governments between the Revolution and the Civil War sponsored by the Committee on Research in Economic History, of which Oscar and Mary Handlins' *Commonwealth: Massachusetts* is perhaps best known, principally demonstrates the erosion of traditional mechanisms of social control.

The legal significance of eminent domain is discussed by Arthur Lenhoff in "Development of the Concept of Eminent Domain," *Columbia Law Review* 42 (1942), 596–638.

6. Parts 4 and 5 of Gordon Wood's *Creation of the American Republic* make earlier treatments of the Philadelphia convention obsolete. For the deepening anxiety of leading conservatives, see John T. Horton, *James Kent*, passim; Jacobson, "Concept of Equality," chs. 3–4; Perry Miller, *Life of the Mind in America*, pt. 2, ch. 6; and James McClellan, *Joseph Story*, pp. 196ff., 211ff., 232ff.

7. Webster, in *Mass. C. C.*, (1820–21), p. 312; also James Kent, in *N.Y. C. C.* (1821), p. 222, and William Gaston, in *No. Car. C. C.* (1835), pp. 33, 121; as well as Joseph Story, "The Science of Government" (1834), in *Miscellaneous Writings*, pp. 619–21, and Samuel G. Goodrich, *The Young American*, ch. 7.

8. Kent, in *N.Y. C. C.* (1821), pp. 220–21; Webster, in *Mass. C. C.* (1820–1821), pp. 312–13; also Gaston, in *No. Car. C. C.* (1835), p. 133. Benjamin W. Leigh essayed the same inflexible defense of property as the very definition of liberty in the Virginia convention of 1829–1830, but his attitudes were so clearly influenced by his fears for slavery that one cannot say what his position would have been had that form of property not seemed in jeopardy (see *Va. C. C.* [1829–1830], pp. 151–73).

9. For example, compare Josiah Quincy, in *Mass. C. C.* (1820–1821), pp. 251–52, with Rufus Choate's address in the convention of 1853, as found in Choate, *Addresses and Orations*, pp. 394–95, or with Francis Wayland, *Affairs of Rhode-Island*, pp. 7ff.

10. Kent, *Commentaries*, 2:257; Lieber, *Essays on Property and Labour*, pp. 192–93, and see Lieber, *Manual of Political Ethics*, 1:118–28; also J. M. V. C., "The New Constitution: Article VI—The Judiciary," *Am. Rev.* 4, no. 5 (November 1846), 529b.

11. Kent, *Commentaries*, 2:256, and see ibid., 1:389, 423, and Lieber, *Essays on*

Property and Labour, p. 173; ibid., p. 151; Kent, *Commentaries*, 2:1–4; also Lieber, *Manual of Political Ethics*, 1:116–18, 128–35, 221–23; and Henry C. Carey, *Principles of Political Economy*, 3:241. For a fuller discussion of Lieber's ambiguous organicism, see Bernard E. Brown, *American Conservatives*, pp. 26–100, and Prendergast, "Some American Ideas on Political Authority," pp. 137–55.

12. Kent, *Commentaries*, 2:276, 265–68; Lieber, *Essays on Property and Labour*, pp. 137ff. and essays 5 and 6; and see James McClellan's discussion of Joseph Story, who repudiated John Locke and asserted the authority of government, but who also went far beyond John Marshall in his opinion in the *Dartmouth College* case in his willingness to protect the rights of corporations against public power (McClellan, *Joseph Story*, pp. 196–210).

13. Henry D. Palmer and James M. Davis, in *Ill. C. C.* (1847), pp. 848, 850–51; *Minority Report of Select Committee on Rhode Island*, pp. 19–20. There were, of course, honorable exceptions to this position, above all those connected with the agitation against slavery; see the first section of chapter XIII.

14. Wright, *The Contract Clause*, chs. 1–2; Corwin, *Liberty Against Government*, ch. 3; and see Lynn L. Marshall, "The Early Career of Amos Kendall: The Making of a Jacksonian" (Ph.D. diss., University of California at Berkeley, 1962), pp. 327f.

15. Webster's arguments are summarized in *U.S. Rep.*, 4 Wheaton 551–99 and 6 Howard 513–21. See William H. Seward's *Speech in the [New York] Senate*, p. 15b, and also Maurice G. Baxter, *Daniel Webster & the Supreme Court*, chs. 4–6.

16. Webster, "Lecture before the Society for the Diffusion of Useful Knowledge," in *Writings and Speeches*, 13:69; Hoag, in *Iowa C. C.* (1844), p. 146.

17. Webster, *Writings and Speeches*, 13:66, 67, 73; also Carey, *Principles of Political Economy*, esp. vol. 1, ch. 21; vol. 2, ch. 16; vol. 3, pt. 4, ch. 9.

18. Webster, *Writings and Speeches*, 13:74.

19. "Results of Machinery," *American Quarterly Review* 12, no. 24 (December 1832), 306–7; also Edward Everett, *Address before Mercantile Library Association*, pp. 12–25 passim.

20. Conservative statements about public policy apart from corporate charters had the same general character, as for example when they justified a protective tariff on the grounds that it would foster the public welfare. See Henry Clay's speech at Cincinnati in 1830 (Clay, *Works*, 5:396–400) and his speech on the Compromise Tariff of 1832 (ibid., p. 482), as well as the statements by Massachusetts conservatives quoted by Jacobson in "Concept of Equality among Massachusetts Conservatives," esp. pp. 338, 356 n.48. Even the recurrent Whig complaint that the Democrats wished to "separate government from the people" probably echoed a traditional conservative belief that government should take an active role in the life of the nation. See, for example, a pamphlet issued by the Whig Congressional Executive Committee, *Tariff Doctrine*, pp. 2, 4.

21. *Pictures of the Times;* Underwood, *Speech on the Sub-Treasury Bill*, p. 32; also *To*

the Farmers! and Working Men!!; Life in a Log Cabin; and *Harrison Almanac for 1841.*

22. *Address of Whig State Convention [of Indiana],* p. 2a–b; [Colton], *Junius Tracts* no. 2, p. 16; and see ibid., no. 7, pp. 9–10.

23. Appleton, *Labor in Europe and the United States,* passim; Lowell, in Freeman Hunt, ed., *Lives of American Merchants,* 1:557–58, 568; [Colton], *Junius Tracts* no. 7, pp. 2, 8.

24. Hoag, in *Iowa C. C.* (1844), p. 147; Lyell as quoted by E. Douglas Branch, *The Sentimental Years,* p. 51, who notes that the cheapest share cost five hundred dollars; Upham, *Remarks in the House of Representatives,* p. 8a; also Clay, Speech on the American System (1832), in *Works,* 5:464; *Answer of Whig Members of the Legislature of Massachusetts,* p. 15; Underwood, *Speech on the Sub-Treasury Bill,* pp. 11–12; and [Colton], *Junius Tracts* no. 7, p. 3; and see Louis Hartz, *Economic Policy and Democratic Thought,* pp. 74ff.

25. See, for example, "Wayland's Political Economy," *N.-Y. Rev.* 1, no. 2 (October 1837), 392–93; *Proceedings of Whigs of Chester County,* p. 19; *Address to the People of Missouri,* pp. 21–22; William H. Harrison, *Speech at the Dayton Convention,* p. 5; "Insult to Mechanics," *The Pilot* (1840), as found in A. B. Norton, ed., *Great Revolution of 1840,* p. 223; and *The Essays of Camillus,* p. 70, as well as numerous quotations in William G. Shade's dissertation, "Politics of Free Banking."

26. Bacon, *Progressive Democracy,* p. 19; also The Public School Society of New York City, *Public Schools, Public Blessings,* pp. 5ff.; [Calvin Colton], *American Jacobinism,* p. 8; and Daniel Ullmann, *Address delivered in the Tabernacle,* pp. 35–37.

27. Webster, *Writings and Speeches,* 13:74; [Alonzo Potter], "Trades' Unions," *N.-Y. Rev.* 2, no. 1 (January 1838), p. 9; also Samuel G. Goodrich, Speech in the North End of Boston, as found in Norton, ed., *Great Revolution of 1840,* pp. 346–47; [Colton], *Junius Tracts* no. 7, p. 15; and *Journal of Commerce,* 6 April 1848, as quoted by Sigmund Diamond, *Reputation of the Businessman,* p. 36.

28. Kent, *Commentaries,* 2:266; [Colton], *American Jacobinism,* p. 6; also Gaston, in *No. Car. C. C.* (1835), p. 133; Lydia H. Sigourney, *The Boy's Reading-Book* (1839), as quoted by Ruth M. Elson, *Guardians of Tradition,* p. 265; and *A Few Plain Facts,* p. 5.

29. See, for example, Story in *Mass. C. C.* (1820–1821), pp. 286–89; Kent, *Commentaries,* 2:266; *Address to the People of Maryland,* p. 3; [Potter], "Trades' Unions," pp. 5–48 passim; and Underwood, *Speech on the Sub-Treasury Bill,* p. 12.

30. Austin, *Oration at Boston,* p. 30; Aiken, *Labor and Wages,* p. 22, and see p. 16; also Everett, *Address before Mercantile Library Association,* passim; [Colton], *Junius Tracts* no. 7, p. 9; "Public and Private Charities in Boston," *No. Am. Rev.* 61, no. 128 (July 1845), 154–58; and [Charles Brooks], *Remarks on Europe,* p. 34.

31. Compare John Lowell's account of Patrick Tracy Jackson (above, note 23)

with the argument in "Factory Labor," *Lowell Offering* 4, no. 9 (July 1844), 200; and see George S. White, *Memoir of Samuel Slater*, pp. 107–8; also Charles L. Sanford, "The Intellectual Origins and New-Worldliness of American Industry," *Journal of Economic History* 18 (1958), 1–6.

32. Webster, *Writings and Speeches*, 4:36; "A Whig from the Start" [John Calvin Adams], *Appeal to Whig National Convention*, p. 8; "Organization of the Party," p. 443a; also Samuel G. Goodrich, in Norton, ed., *Great Revolution of 1840*, pp. 346–47, and [Colton], *Junius Tracts* no. 7, p. 15.

33. See note 2 to this chapter.

34. See, for example, Thomas D. Arnold, *Arnold's Review*, p. 12, and "Report of the Committee on Ways and Means on the Bank of the United States, 13 April 1830," *Reg. Deb.*, 22d C, 1st S, *Appendix*, cols. 133, 137, 142.

35. Stratton, in *N.J. C. C.* (1844), p. 311; Kennedy, in ibid., p. 299; and see Louis Hartz's extended discussion of similar developments in Pennsylvania, in *Economic Policy and Democratic Thought*.

36. See in particular Clay's speech in the House of Representatives, 26 April 1820, in his *Papers*, 2:826–45, esp. p. 832, and his speech of 30 March 1824, ibid., 3:683–727.

37. For the first form of argument, see esp. Clay's speech in the House, 13 March 1818, in ibid., 2:467–89, as well as that of 26 April 1820, in ibid., pp. 837–39. For the second, see ibid., p. 837, and his speech at Cincinnati, 3 August 1830, in Clay, *Works*, 5:396.

38. *Politics for Farmers*, p. 3b; *Address of Friends of Domestic Industry*, pp. 12a, 11b; also *The Import Duties Considered*, pp. 4–7, and [Henry C. Carey], "What Constitutes Real Freedom of Trade?" *Am. Rev.* 12, no. 2 (August 1850), 127–40.

39. [Colton], *Junius Tracts* no. 1, esp. pp. 14, 15–16, and no. 2, pp. 2, 7, 13; also Henry Clay, *Speech at Raleigh*, pp. 5–6; and William C. Rives, *Speech on Repeal of the Tariff*, pp. 28–29.

40. Lieber, *Essays on Property and Labour*, p. 182; also Goodrich, *The Young American*, chs. 9–12, 15; and a number of articles in *Hunt's Merchants' Magazine* that simply ignored the editor's remonstrances against laissez faire: "Moral and Political Freedom," *Hunt's* 2, no. 5 (May 1840), 365–72; "The City of Troy, New York: Its Commerce, Manufactures, and Resources," ibid. 14, no. 6 (June 1846), 516; and C. F. Briggs, "The Island of Nantucket," ibid. 17, no. 4 (October 1847), 368.

41. Lieber, *Essays on Property and Labour*, p. 87; *Journal of Commerce*, 6 April 1848, as quoted by Diamond, *Reputation of the Businessman*, p. 36; [Colton], *Crisis of the Country*, p. 12; also Kent, *Commentaries*, 2: 268n, and Francis Wayland, *Elements of Political Economy*, passim, esp. p. 126; and see Benjamin J. Klebaner, "Poverty and its Relief in American Thought, 1815–1861," *Social Service Review* 38 (1964), 382–99.

42. [Colton], *Junius Tracts* no. 2, p. 3, and see no. 2, p. 5, and no. 7, p. 15; "Civilization: American and European," *Am. Rev.* 4, no. 1 (July 1846), 30a; also

Horace Bushnell's strictures on political economy in his Phi Beta Kappa oration of 1837, as found in Clark S. Northup, ed., *Representative Phi Beta Kappa Orations*, p. 5. For that matter, spokesmen for New England's manufacturers continued to depict a society in which wealthy men voluntarily bestowed charity on the poor, but the very enthusiasm they expressed for a social conscience so understood suggested how little they proposed to see government enforce it. See, for example, Aiken, *Labor and Wages*, p. 15, and Upham, *Remarks in the House of Representatives*, p. 8b.

CHAPTER VI: ENTERPRISE

1. For a typical example, see Frances Trollope, *Domestic Manners of Americans*, pp. 258–59. The attitudes of foreign travelers are discussed in considerable detail, although not with my concerns in mind, in ch. 2 of Edward Pessen's *Jacksonian America*. I have also benefited from the astute analysis of their views developed by John W. Cooke in "Some Aspects of the Concept of the Free Individual."

2. [Thomas G. Cary], "Love of Money in America," *Hunt's* 15, no. 2 (August 1846), 218, and see "The American Merchant," ibid. 2, no. 6 (June 1840), 503; and cf. Harriet Martineau, *Society in America*, 2:141–43, 151, 154; Michel Chevalier, *Society, Manners and Politics in the United States*, pp. 205–6; and Frederick von Raumer, *America and the American People*, p. 496.

3. Trollope, *Domestic Manners of Americans*, esp. p. 101. For friendly comments, see William Cobbett, *A Year's Residence in the United States*, chs. 11, 13; Martineau, *Society in America*, 2:60–61, 163–65; and *London Daily News*, 4 June 1853, as quoted by Sigmund Diamond, *Reputation of the Businessman*, pp. 1–2. Some modern criticisms of the travelers' happy view are cited in note 1 to chapter IV of this study.

4. Bremer, *America of the Fifties*, pp. 92–93; also Thomas Low Nichols, *Forty Years of American Life*, pp. 63–64; and see William H. Goetzman, "The Mountain Man as Jacksonian Man," *AQ* 15 (1963), 402–15.

5. Bremer, *America of the Fifties*, p. 93; Robert Rantoul Jr., *Memoirs*, p. 421; also George Camp, *Democracy*, pp. 224–38; and Frederick Grimke, *Nature and Tendency of Free Institutions*, pp. 109–18.

6. Evans, in *Texas C. C.* (1845), p. 671, and see George Brown and James S. Mayfield, in ibid., pp. 67–68, 624; Howard, in ibid., p. 645; also William Leggett, 3 January 1835, in *Political Writings*, 1:144; and "Radicalism," *Dem. Rev.* 3, no. 10 (October 1838), 108–9. Howard later opposed the Homestead Bill as an unwarranted intrusion on equal rights; see 21 April 1852, *Cong. Globe*, 32d C, 1st S, *Appendix*, pp. 582c–585b.

7. "European Views of American Democracy," *Dem. Rev.* 2, no. 8 (July 1838), 348; also Leggett, 3 January 1835, in *Political Writings*, 1:145–46; David Henshaw, *Remarks upon Rights and Powers of Corporations* (1837), as found in Joseph L. Blau, ed., *Social Theories of Jacksonian Democracy*, pp. 168–69; "The Credit System," *Dem. Rev.* 3, no. 11 (November 1838), 215; Hobart Ber-

rian, *Brief Sketch of Workingmen's Party*, p. 7; Calvin Britain, in *Mich. C. C.* (1850), p. 567b; M. H. Mitchell and R. P. Ranney, in *Ohio C. C.* (1850–1851), 2:476b, 477b; and see Lynn Marshall, "Early Career of Amos Kendall," pp. 260–61, and Charles G. Haines and Foster H. Sherwood, *Supreme Court in American Government and Politics 1835–1864*, pp. 34–35.

8. Preston, in *La. C. C.* (1845), p. 66a; also Myer Moses, *Oration at Tammany-Hall*, pp. 22–23; Thompson Campbell, in *Ill. C. C.* (1847), p. 518; and the words of a vigorous Texas Democrat rebuking nativist fears of foreign paupers: "Sir, no man is a pauper in this favoured land, who though 'steeped to the lips in poverty' has yet a willing mind, and a pair of strong arms. True, he may be a *pauper* in the opinion of a purse-proud, vicious, imbecile arstocracy [*sic*], but upon virgin American soil, and under equal American laws, he is not only a free man but a *rich* man" (J. Randolph Burns, *To editor of the True Issue*, p. 2a).

9. O'Sullivan as quoted by Frederick and Lois B. Merk, *Manifest Destiny and Mission*, p. 25n; [O'Sullivan], "Annexation," *Dem. Rev.* 17, no. 1 (July and August 1845), 9a; also Stephen Austin, "Address at Louisville, Kentucky" (1836), as found in Avery Craven et al., eds., *Documentary History of American People*, pp. 273b–274a, and William H. Wharton, Address in New York (1836), as found in Louis M. Hacker and Helène S. Zahler, eds., *Shaping of the American Tradition*, p. 447a. See also ch. 5 of Albert K. Weinberg's *Manifest Destiny* for a discussion of Americans' ideas about "the true title to the soil." Weinberg views claims based upon theories of the destined use of the soil as intolerable perversions of American ideals as well as of international law, but they seem to me to have been plausible corollaries of American belief. Certainly advocates of expansion regarded Europeans' hostility to American aggrandizement as evidence of their hostility to democratic ideals. "We take from no man," O'Sullivan observed in the *Morning News;* "the reverse rather—we give to man. This national policy, necessity or destiny, we know to be just and beneficent, and we can, therefore, afford to scorn the invective and imputations of rival nations" (quoted by Merk and Merk, *Manifest Destiny and Mission*, p. 25n). See also F. O. J. Smith, "Progress," *Hunt's* 18, no. 2 (March 1848), 260–69.

10. For Sedgwick's position, see *Thoughts on Annexation of Texas*. Rantoul's later career is sketched by Merle Curti in "Robert Rantoul, Jr., The Reformer in Politics," *New England Quarterly* 5 (1932), 264–80. For the creed of Progressive Democracy, see chapter I, the second section, and chapter II, the final section, in this volume. It is interesting to speculate what view we would have of Jacksonian Democracy if we were to make an extended study, not of the liberal Democratic mind as exemplified by the Old Republicans, but of the expansionist—internationalist—interventionist mind exemplified by Moses Y. Beach, Lewis Cass, Stephen A. Douglas, and Robert J. Walker, not to mention lesser enthusiasts of Young America.

11. The theory that Jacksonian democracy represented entrepreneurial forces is

most effectively presented by Bray Hammond in "Jackson, Biddle, and the Bank of the United States," *Journal of Economic History* 7 (1947), 1–23, and in *Banks and Politics in Early America*, esp. ch. 12. Nevertheless, even if one fully accepts Hammond's portrait of Jacksonian leaders as allies or agents of a fraternity of country bankers who resented the power of the central bank—and Frank O. Gatell calls the theory into question in "Sober Second Thoughts on Van Buren, the Albany Regency, and the Wall Street Conspiracy" (*JAH* 53 [1966], 19–40), one cannot explain the whole of Jacksonian democracy as a bankers' phenomenon. Presumably the bankers, and certainly men in the street, acted out of prejudice, half-truth, tradition, and a variety of novel aspirations and interests to create a society that none of them fully anticipated or intended. Lynn Marshall addresses himself to some of these considerations in "The Strange Stillbirth of the Whig Party," *AHR* 72 (1967), 445–68.

12. See Leggett, *Political Writings*, 1:142–44; 2:96–106, 265–66, 309–19, 324–27; also Theodore Sedgwick Jr., *What is a Monopoly?* (1835), as found in Blau, ed., *Social Theories of Jacksonian Democracy*, esp. pp. 221–23; and *"The Elements of Political Economy," Dem. Rev.* 8, no. 34 (October 1840), 303–6; and see Fritz Redlich's discussion of the Free Banking Act in New York, in *The Molding of American Banking*, 1:196–201; Richard Hofstadter, "William Leggett, Spokesman of Jacksonian Democracy," *Political Science Quarterly* 48 (1943), 581–94; and Louis Hartz, *Economic Policy and Democratic Thought*, pp. 47–50.

13. See in particular William G. Shade's "Politics of Free Banking," ch. 3–4, and note David L. Gregg's remarks in *Ill. C. C.* (1847), p. 257.

14. For typical Democratic arguments in behalf of the general incorporation of railroads, see remarks of J. M. Palmer and Walter B. Scates in *Ill. C. C.* (1847), pp. 322, 324–25. James W. Hurst traces the growth and reception of corporations in *The Legitimacy of the Business Corporation*, while the constitutional conventions of the Middle Period record the mixed feelings Democrats expressed. The attitudes of workingmen are described in Norman Ware's *The Industrial Worker* and exemplified in Seth Luther's *Address to Workingmen* and in "General Manufacturing Bill," *Voice of Industry*, 25 February 1848, p. 2. For the expressions of Democratic sympathizers, see *Proceedings of Democratic Legislative Convention in Boston*, p. 8.

15. These matters are discussed in chapter IV. The *Democratic Review* illustrated the thrust of Democratic doctrine in another fashion when it defended the British factory system against its parliamentary critics by arguing that the condition of British workers must "be ascribed to the operation of other causes, in the social system of the country, than to the introduction of labor-saving machinery, and the vast developement of industry and production of wealth consequent upon all such improvements," ("Cotton. [Second Article]," *Dem. Rev.* 2, no. 1 [April 1838], 33).

16. Edward Everett clearly exemplifies this transition in conservative thought in his *Address before Mercantile Library Association*.

17. J. M. V. C., "The New Constitution: Article VI—The Judiciary," *Am. Rev.* 4, no. 5 (November 1846), 529b.
18. "California," ibid. 3, no. 1 (January 1846), 85–86; Francis Lieber, *Essays on Property and Labour*, pp. 146, 150.
19. *Ill. C. C.* (1847), pp. 732–33, and cf. ibid., pp. 311, 315f., and 360, as well as Abner C. Harding, at p. 294; Whipple, in *Mich. C. C.* (1850), p. 589a. Whipple's views are the more striking in that he clearly understood and articulated the public origins of the rights corporations sought to exercise (ibid., p. 69a–b). Significantly, Whipple was a Democrat; by now, conservative Democrats (at least) had no reason to quarrel with protecting the legal position of corporations. On this point, see also Lucius Cass and Benjamin Stanton, in *Ohio C. C.* (1850–1851), 2:242b–247b and 867b–868a, as well as Oscar and Mary Handlin, *Commonwealth: Massachusetts*, chs. 5–6.
20. [H. W. Bellows], "Influence of the Trading Spirit upon the Social and Moral Life of America," *Am. Rev.* 1, no. 1 (January 1845), 98a; also Baynard Hall, *Righteousness the safeguard of nation*, pp. 8–9; Charles G. Finney, *Lectures on Revivals of Religion*, p. 435; and Horace Mann, *Thoughts for a Young Man*, pp. 55–60.
21. Here and in what follows, my judgments reflect the pioneering work of a number of astute historians. Chapter 1 of Fred Somkin's *Unquiet Eagle* is an especially provocative account of conservative moralism, while recent studies of the American idea of success have made important points about the early literature on the subject. In order of their appearance they are Irvin G. Wyllie, *The Self-Made Man in America*, perhaps better read in its unpublished version as a doctoral thesis at the University of Wisconsin (1949); John G. Cawelti, *Apostles of the Self-Made Man;* Richard Weiss, *American Myth of Success*, and a paper by Donald M. Scott, read at the 1971 meeting of the Organization of American Historians, "Making It in Ante-Bellum America: Young Men and their Careers, 1820–1860." In addition, I have found useful Sigmund Diamond, *Reputation of the Businessman;* Marie L. Ahearn, "The Rhetoric of Work and Vocation in Some Popular Northern Writings before 1860" (Ph.D. diss., Brown University, 1965); and Theodore P. Greene, *America's Heroes*, all of which serve to confirm the general patterns I describe, from points of departure somewhat different from mine.
22. *Hunt's* 1, no. 2 (August 1839), 135. Typical works stressing the requirements of character include John Frost, *The Young Merchant;* Frost, *The Young Mechanic;* Henry Ward Beecher, *Seven Lectures to Young Men;* John Todd, *The Young Man;* and William A. Alcott, *Young Man's Guide.* Alcott and Frost also stress the need for self-education.
23. For explicit religious exhortations that resemble those of the young men's guides, see Gardiner Spring, "Wealth a Fearful Snare to the Soul," *Am. Nat. Preacher* 4, no. 12 (May 1830), 369–80; Thomas S. Barrett, "The Foolish Rich Man," ibid. 6, no. 6 (November 1831), 283–88; Reuben Tincker, "The

Rich Fool," ibid. 20, no. 12 (December 1846), 265–73; and William B. Sprague, "The Uses and Abuses of Money," ibid. 22, no. 7 (July 1848), 152–63.

Biographical data here and elsewhere derive primarily from *The National Cyclopaedia of American Biography*.

24. Frost, *The Young Mechanic*, pp. 27ff.; also Alcott, *Young Man's Guide*, ch. 1; T. S. Arthur, *Arthur's Advice to Young Men*, p. 230f; Joseph F. Tuttle, "The Dignity of Progress," *Ladies' Repository, and Gatherings of the West* 6, no. 7 (July 1846), 198a; and William Howard Van Doren, *Mercantile Morals*, ch. 4.

25. [Goodrich], *Lives of Benefactors*, passim; also T. S. Arthur, *Rising in the World;* R. W. Cushman, *Elements of Success;* and Louisa C. Tuthill, *Success in Life. The Merchant*, ch. 21.

26. [Goodrich], *Lives of Benefactors*, p. 158; Cobb, as quoted by Ruth M. Elson, *Guardians of Traditon*, p. 264; Beman, *The Influence of Freedom*, p. 24; also Louisa Tuthill, *Success in Life. The Lawyer*, passim; and *Bosses and their Boys*, a tract published by the American Sunday School Union.

27. [Goodrich], *Lives of Benefactors*, p. iii; Todd, *The Young Man*, p. 26; and see Greene, *America's Heroes*, pt. 1.

28. Abbott, "The Agricultural Press Views the Yeoman: 1819–1859," *Agricultural History* 42 (1968), 46–47; Arthur, as quoted by Freeman Hunt in *Worth and Wealth*, p. 351; also John Laurie Blake, "Memoir of Samuel Slater, the Father of American Manufactures," *Hunt's* 20, no. 1 (January 1849), 30.

29. Arthur, *Arthur's Advice to Young Men*, pp. 27f., 241–42; Alcott, *Young Man's Guide*, p. 102; Van Doren, *Mercantile Morals*, pp. v–vi; also Beecher, *Seven Lectures to Young Men*, pp. 58–60.

30. Alcott, *Young Man's Guide*, p. 105; Wise, *The Young Man's Counsellor*, p. 41; also Arthur, *Arthur's Advice to Young Men*, passim; Beecher, *Seven Lectures to Young Men;* Frost, *The Young Merchant;* "How to Make a Fortune," *Ladies' Repository* 18, no. 2 (March 1858), 134–37; and see Elson, *Guardians of Tradition*, pp. 251–54, and Bernard Wishy, *The Child and the Republic*, pp. 61f.

31. Adams, *Laws of Success and Failure*, pp. 13–14; Frost, *Self-Made Men*, passim; Tuthill, *Success in Life. The Lawyer*, passim; Todd, *The Young Man*, pp. 17–37; and Alcott, *Young Man's Guide*, p. 25 (with emphasis in the original).

32. Wise, *The Young Man's Counsellor*, p. 76; Beman, *Influence of Freedom*, p. 15; and see Frost, *Self-Made Men*, passim, as well as Donald M. Scott's "Making It in Ante-Bellum America."

33. Alcott, *Young Man's Guide*, pp. 25–26, 87–95. Recurrent exhortations to make a "fortune" exemplify the same indifference to the purely practical meanings of the words the moralists employed. So, perhaps, does the fact that the "self-made man" came to mean, not a man who had worked his way up from the bottom of society, but a man who had significantly increased his wealth no matter where he started.

34. Tuthill, *Success in Life. The Merchant*, p. 81; also Frost, *Self-Made Men*, pp.

97–98; and Jonathan Wainwright, *Inequality of Individual Wealth the Ordinance of Providence* (1835), as quoted in Norman Jacobson, "Concept of Equality among Massachusetts Conservatives," p. 385.

35. "Prospectus," *The Girard Journal of Wealth, and Record and Depository of Benevolence* 1, no. 1 (8 February 1832), 1a; Huntington, *Individuality;* Hunt, *American Biographical Sketch Book*, esp. p. 365; also "Address to Whig Young Men of Connecticut," *Young Men's Whig State Convention*, p. 4b; Proceedings and Resolutions, ibid., p. 6a; and Oliver H. Smith, *Address delivered on the Fair Grounds*, pp. 9–10. I am indebted to Sigmund Diamond for the reference to the *Girard Journal of Wealth.*

36. For a clear expression of the new vocabulary of success, see T. S. Arthur's exhortation, in a biography of John Grigg, to the effect that "we want the histories of our self-made men spread out before us, that we may know the ways by which they came up from the ranks of the people" (as found in Freeman Hunt, *Worth and Wealth*, p. 351). For a typical disclaimer of formal education, see William Hunt's account of C. C. Cambreleng in his *American Biographical Sketch Book*, pp. 276f.

37. [Colton], *Junius Tracts* no. 7, pp. 15, 7.

38. Roy J. Honeywell has made a useful study of *The Educational Work of Thomas Jefferson.* For a more general treatment of republican elitism in education, see ch. 2 of my *Popular Education and Democratic Thought.* See also John William Ward, *Andrew Jackson*, which stresses the essentially public version of personal success that attached to Andrew Jackson as a self-made man.

39. Tallmadge, in *Voice of the People*, p. 6b; also [Joseph Worrell et al.], *Letters addressed to John Sergeant*, p. 14, and Cyrus Ratliff, in *La. C. C.* (1845), p. 87b.

40. [Slamm], *The Tariff, No. 1*, pp. 8b–9a; Rantoul, "Address to the Working-men of the United States of America" (1833), in *Memoirs*, p. 243, and see p. 119; also Ely Moore, *Address before the General Trades' Union*, pp. 31–32; and Isaac Preston, in *La. C. C.* (1845), p. 22a.

41. My judgments are based upon [Moses Y. Beach, comp.], *Wealth and Wealthy Citizens of New York City*, 2d ed. (New York, 1842); *Wealth and Pedigree of the Wealthy Citizens of New York City*, 3d ed. (New York, 1842); *Wealth and Biography of the Wealthy Citizens of New York City*, 5th ed. (New York, 1845); ibid., 11th ed. (New York, 1846); A Member of the Philadelphia Bar, *Wealth and Biography of the Wealthy Citizens of Philadelphia* (Philadelphia, 1845); [Hildreth?], *"Our First Men:" A Calendar of Wealth, Fashion and Gentility . . . in the City of Boston* (Boston, 1846); [William Armstrong], *The Aristocracy of New York: Who They Are, and What They Were* (New York, 1848); [Thomas L. V. Wilson], *The Aristocracy of Boston: Who They Are, and What They Were* (Boston, 1848); and Allen Forbes and J. W. Greene, *The Rich Men of Massachusetts . . .* (Boston, 1851). Next to *"Our First Men," Rich Men of Massachusetts* was most likely to engage in assessments of character and the pointing of moral les-

sons. Edward Pessen suggests that Abner Forbes and his son, not Richard Hildreth, compiled *"Our First Men."* See "The Egalitarian Myth and the American Social Reality," *AHR* (1971), 994 n. 12.

42. [Beach], *Wealth and Pedigree*, p. 2; [Hildreth?], *"Our First Men,"* p. 23; and cf. Forbes and Greene, *Rich Men of Massachusetts*, passim. Edward Pessen points out, in "Moses Beach Revisited: A Critical Examination of his *Wealthy Citizens* Pamphlets," *JAH* 58 (1971), 414–26, that Beach's figures were not reliable and that they were not taken seriously by the wealthy men themselves—facts that tend to confirm the "democratic" nature of these pamphlets.

43. A number of success handbooks published during the 1860s and early 1870s express the same limited aspiration and help to confirm the existence of a distinct "democratic" perspective. Among them were T. F. Wood, *The Money-Maker's Manual*, an idiosyncratic mixture of homely practical advice and exhortations to "get rich," and A. C. McCurdy, *Win Who Will*, an equally mixed volume stressing the magic of compound interest. By contrast, James D. Mills reiterated traditional orthodox injunctions about character in *The Art of Money Making*, and even Matthew Hale Smith, who was a prominent spokesman for business values during the 1850s, retained a large measure of the traditional moral code in *Successful Folks*. See also the discussion of Edwin T. Freedley in the last section of this chapter.

44. My remarks are based upon *Life of P. T. Barnum Written by Himself*. Constance Rourke summarizes his life and *Life* in her usual felicitous manner in *Trumpets of Jubilee*, pp. 367–426.

45. Barnum, *Life*, pp. 394–99, 396, and see *Struggles and Triumphs*, pp. 457–500, for the English lecture.

46. Major Wilson points up the political consequences of this development in "The Broker State Concept of the Union in the 1840's: A Synthesis of Whig and Democratic Views," *Louisiana Studies* 8 (1969), 321–47.

47. These remarks summarize the meanings assigned to "enterprise" and "enterprising" in virtually every English or American dictionary of the English language published between 1775 and 1860. Significantly, the definitions remain almost identical throughout that period, although accepted usage was obviously changing and the changes would be reflected in dictionaries published after the Civil War. Apart from its other merits, Nathan Miller's *Enterprise of a Free People* provides a capsule history of changing usage in its quotations from the period 1792–1838.

48. Virtually every success handbook devoted a chapter or section to "enterprise" understood as a peculiar ability to recognize and take advantage of opportunities that lesser men would miss. Louisa Tuthill refers to it as an alternative to speculation in *Success in Life. The Merchant*, ch. 11.

49. Leggett, 23 March 1835, in *Political Writings*, 1:246; Resolutions of the Democratic members, in Milo M. Quaife, ed., *Struggle over Ratification*, p. 205,

and see *Racine Advocate*, 24 March 1847, as found in ibid., p. 508; also Ezekiel Robbins, in *Ill. C. C.* (1847), pp. 80–81.

50. Polk, 10 January 1832, *Reg. Deb.*, 22d C, 1st S, col. 1532; *Resolutions and Addresses Adopted by Antimasonic Members of the Legislature of Massachusetts* (1836), as quoted by Jacobson, "Concept of Equality among Massachusetts Conservatives," p. 338; *Answer of Whig Members of the Legislature of Massachusetts*, p. 15; the New York convention as quoted by E. Douglas Branch, *The Sentimental Years*, p. 50; "The Herald—Onward!" *Dem. Rev.* 31, no. 5 (November and December 1852), 410b; and *New York Observer*, as quoted by Bernard A. Weisberger, *They Gathered at the River*, p. 150. Daniel Boorstin notes a comparable shift of meaning in the term "business"; see *Americans: The National Experience*, p. 115.

51. The Whig argument as in note 50. Besides Leggett, the *Democratic Review*, and the legislators of Wisconsin, Democratic spokesmen who used the term "enterprise" included (in chronological order of the appearances I have noted in passing) George Bancroft (1826), James Fenimore Cooper (1829), Andrew Jackson (1832), Lucius Lyon (1835), Enos T. Throop (1836), Martin Van Buren (1837), Roger B. Taney (1838), Robert Dale Owen (1840), Isaac T. Preston (1845), and Frederick Grimke (1848).

52. For one invocation of "business," see pp. 7–8 of *The Crisis Met:* "No true democrat is at war with the business interests of the people, but on the contrary, would do all in his power to help on the common welfare." Here "business" is apparently used to limit the author's meaning even though it seems to retain some of the public connotations attached to "enterprise." The *Democratic Review* also used the term in "The Great Nation of Futurity," speaking both of "our business men" and of "freedom of trade and business pursuits" (vol. 6, no. 23 [November 1839], 428, 430). See also a filler in *Hunt's Merchants' Magazine* (vol. 18, no. 3 [March 1838], 341) for evidence of the underlying egalitarian connotations of "business."

53. Freedley's works are *A Practical Treatise on Business . . . with an Inquiry into the Chances of Success and Causes of Failure in Business*, 5th ed. (Philadelphia, 1852); *Leading Pursuits and Leading Men. A Treatise on the Principal Trades and Manufactures of the United States* (Philadelphia, 1856); and *Opportunities for Industry and the Safe Investment of Capital; or A Thousand Chances to Make Money* (Philadelphia, 1859). I am indebted to W. Brodie Remington, a graduate student in history at the University of Pennsylvania, for establishing Freedley's political affiliation.

54. Freedley, *Practical Treatise on Business*, esp. 1, 5, 9–11, and 15; and see Hunt's criticism of the *Treatise* in *Worth and Wealth*, pp. 403ff.

55. Freedley, *Practical Treatise on Business*, esp. chs. 2, 8, 13–14; and cf. Hunt, *Worth and Wealth*, esp. pp. 393, 426, 433, 489f., 494.

56. Eric A. Foner has pointed up many of the tendencies of Democratic thought in *Free Soil, Free Labor, Free Men*. I shall return to the question of northern opinion during the 1850s in chapter XIII.

CHAPTER VII: THE POLITICS OF DEMOCRACY

1. [Richter?], *On Self-Government*, p. 27; Calhoun to Jackson, 4 June 1826, as quoted by Charles M. Wiltse, *John C. Calhoun*, 1:337–38; Freeman, *Oration at Natchez*, p. 25.

   Secondary treatments of democratic ideas of power and liberty are suggestive rather than conclusive. John William Ward has offered a brilliant brief estimate of specifically Democratic ideas in "Jacksonian Democratic Thought: 'A Natural Charter of Privilege,' " in Stanley Coben and Lorman Ratner, eds., *Development of an American Culture*, pp. 44–63. Other significant accounts include ch. 1 of Oscar and Mary Handlin, *The Dimensions of Liberty*, a very general treatment of American ideas; ch. 8 of Edwin Mims Jr., *The Majority of the People*, and the dissertation from which it was drawn, "Will of the People: Studies in the Background of the 'Constitutional Democracy' of the Jacksonian Period" (Harvard University, 1939), both focused on ways in which conservative apologists manipulated democratic fears of power to discredit democratic reforms of the economy; and Yehoshua Arieli, *Individualism and Nationalism in American Ideology*.

2. Jackson, in James D. Richardson, ed., *Messages and Papers of the Presidents*, 2:581, 581–89, and passim; also Sen. Thomas Hart Benton, 2 February 1831, *Reg. Deb.*, 21st C, 2d S, p. 60b; and "Senex" [Edmund Ravenel], *Address to the People*, pp. 4, 21.

3. Jackson, in Richardson, ed., *Messages and Papers of the Presidents*, 3:303; Address of the Republican County Convention, *St. Lawrence Republican*, *Extra*, July 1837, p. 10a; *Remarks of Mr. Ham, of York*, p. 8a; Polk, *Answers of Ex-Gov. Polk*, p. 27b; also *Proceedings of Democratic Republican Convention of Indiana*, p. 6; Benjamin C. Yancey, *Speech in relation to Bank of South Carolina*, p. 6; and Martin Van Buren, *Inquiry into Political Parties*, p. 166.

4. Gouge, *Short History of Paper Money*, pp. 1–7; Benton, *Thirty Years' View*, 2:58a; *Racine Advocate*, 17 March 1847, as found in Milo M. Quaife, ed., *Struggle over Ratification*, p. 500; also A. G. Caldwell, in *Ill. C. C.* (1847), p. 682; Joseph H. Bagg, in *Mich. C. C.* (1850), p. 696b; and [James H. Hammond], *The Railroad Mania*.

5. Leggett, 23 May 1834, in *Political Writings*, 1:290; also James Buchanan, Speech in the Senate (1842), as found in *Plain Facts and Considerations*, p. 21; Resolutions of a Democratic Meeting in Albany (1845), as quoted by Jabez D. Hammond, *Life of Silas Wright*, p. 567; Thomas G. C. Davis and William R. Archer, in *Ill. C. C.* (1847), pp. 432–33, 435. Marvin Meyers stresses the "dismantling" role of Jackson and Van Buren in *The Jacksonian Persuasion*, while George F. Brasington Jr. treats it as an essential element in the Democratic theory of representation in his "Representative Government in Jacksonian Political Thought" (Ph.D. diss., University of Illinois, 1958), ch. 5. See also ch. 8 of Mims, *Majority of the People*.

6. Hallett, *Oration at Oxford*, p. 29; Crary, in *Mich. C. C.* (1835), p. 598a; also Gouge, *Short History of Paper Money*, p. 41; *Proceedings of Democratic State Con-*

vention in Nashville, pp. 11a–12b; and Van Buren, *Inquiry into Political Parties*, p. 232; and see James W. Hurst, *Legitimacy of the Business Corporation*, pp. 36ff., 47ff.

7. Polk, *Address to the People of Tennessee* (1839), p. 5; Van Buren, *Opinions of Mr. Van Buren*, p. 4a.

8. *History of Federal and Democratic Parties*, p. 19; Baylor, in *Texas C. C.* (1845), p. 311; Ewing, in *N.J. C.C.* (1844), p. 64. Other expressions of antipathy toward the exercise of power included the Democratic argument against permitting members of Congress to vote according to their own best judgment if the presidential election were thrown into the House of Representatives (*Address of Jackson State Convention of Maryland*, p. 11), Sen. John Rowan's argument that the presiding officer of the Senate must not be granted the authority to call its members to order (Speech of 12 February 1828, in *Reg. Deb.*, 20th C, 1st S, col. 308), and the argument of Daniel Goodwin, president of the Michigan convention of 1850, that municipalities are no more to be trusted than private corporations with the power of eminent domain unless they are held to prior remuneration of property-holders whose lands are taken (*Mich. C. C.* [1850], p. 74b). See also C. P. Bush's statement in the same convention, "Power that is delegated for a long period is universally abused," a proposition he developed in behalf of annual elections (p. 117a).

9. Polk, 13 March 1826, *Reg. Deb.*, 19th C, 1st S, col. 1642; Rives, 5 February 1828, ibid., 20th C, 1st S, col. 1385; Brent, in *La. C. C.* (1845), p. 749b; *Racine Advocate*, 17 February 1847, as found in Quaife, ed., *Struggle over Ratification*, p. 457; also Solomon W. Downs, in *La. C. C.* (1845), p. 115a–b, and *Papers for the People*, esp. pp. 86, 91–92, 155f., 293–95. In 1828 Rives was a loyal Democrat and follower of Andrew Jackson.

10. [O'Sullivan], "Introduction," *Dem. Rev.* 1, no. 1 (October 1837), 6; also "The Course of Civilization," ibid. 6, no. 21 (September 1839), 213–14, and remarks of David Naar, in *N.J. C. C.* (1844), p. 61.

11. Jackson, Second Annual Message, in Richardson, ed., *Messages and Papers of the Presidents*, 2:509; [Robert Dale Owen], *Democratic Address*, p. 2b; also Leggett, 3 June 1837, in *Political Writings*, 2:326; Jackson, Farewell Address, in Richardson, ed., *Messages and Papers of the Presidents*, 3:301; and resolutions offered in the legislature of South Carolina by Christopher Memminger, as found in Yancey, *Speech in relation to Bank of South Carolina*, p. 3.

12. Cambreleng, 11 February 1835, *Reg. Deb.*, 23d C, 1st S, col. 1316; also Jackson, Farewell Address, in Richardson, ed., *Messages and Papers of the Presidents*, 3:299–301, 304–5; Leggett, 3 June 1837, in *Political Writings*, 2:326–27; Frederick Robinson, in *Address and Resolves of Democratic Members of the Massachusetts Legislature*, p. 25b; "European Views of American Democracy," *Dem. Rev.* 2, no. 8 (July 1838), 341–47; *Racine Advocate*, 24 March 1847, in Quaife, ed., *Struggle over Ratification*, p. 508; and Van Buren, *Inquiry into Political Parties*, pp. 420–21.

13. Chilton Williamson discusses the complex patterns of suffrage reform in *American Suffrage*. In *Public and Republic*, Alfred De Grazia traces the evolution of competing theories of representation, while George F. Brasington Jr. deals specifically with Democratic theories in "Representative Government in Jacksonian Political Thought."

14. Report of the Committee on the Representative Function, in *Mich. C. C.* (1835), pp. 535–36; Polk, *Answers of Ex-Gov. Polk*, pp. 3b–4a; Downs and Ledoux, in *La. C. C.* (1845), pp. 72a, 84b. See also a number of expressions in which the concern to protect rights is less explicitly stated yet clearly present, for example the statements by Reps. Jacob Fry Jr. and John Reynolds, cited in Brasington, "Representative Government in Jacksonian Political Thought," pp. 67n, 68, and those of Isaac E. Crary and J. Van Valkenburgh, in *Mich. C. C.* (1850), pp. 492a, 67b. By contrast, extremely conservative Democrats like John R. Grymes held that the members of a constitutional convention were themselves the sovereign power (*La. C. C.* [1845], pp. 68b–69a).

15. For examples of the Old Republican view that annual legislatures are necessary to safeguard popular liberties, see the remarks by Weldon N. Edwards, Henry Seawell, Joseph J. Daniel, and Nathaniel Macon, in *No. Car. C. C.* (1835), pp. 166, 167, 171, 176–77. (Traditional republican attitudes continued to flourish in North Carolina long after they had been abandoned elsewhere.) For more modern expressions of hostility to legislatures, see those of James F. Brent and Miles Taylor in *La. C. C.* (1845), pp. 110a–b and 294–295a, and of Zadoc Casey in *Ill. C. C.* (1847), p. 124. The referendum appeared in a number of state constitutions during the 1840s and was often debated in conventions that did not finally adopt it.

Even men who portrayed an effective role for government often betrayed a surprising hostility to the power of legislatures. In Illinois, Thomas G. C. Davis declared that "government should be so established as to give it the power to do everything necessary for the public good; and he thought we should not restrict the Legislature within limits too narrow to enable them in all cases to act for the good of all the people." Yet he also criticized a plan to give the legislature power to pass general incorporation laws, and he subsequently defended the executive veto (*Ill. C. C.* [1847], pp. 328, 433). In Michigan, Van Valkenburgh defined democracy as a vehicle for "the greatest good to the greatest number," but in practice he took this formula to mean a diminution of legislation (*Mich. C. C.* [1850], p. 444a).

16. Van Buren, *Opinions of Mr. Van Buren*, p. 12b; also "Executive Usurpation," *Dem. Rev.* 1, no. 3 (February 1838), 279–92; *Address of Democratic State Convention of Illinois*, p. 9; the debates in *N.Y. C. C.* (1846), pp. 327b–337b; and A. G. Herndon, *Of the Cass Democrat*.

17. Rowan, 20 February 1828, *Reg. Deb.*, 20th C, 1st S, col. 354; Brent, in *La. C. C.* (1845), p. 745b; and cf. remarks by John E. Fletcher, in *Iowa C. C.* (1844), p. 113, as well as those by August R. Knapp—a liberal Whig—in *Ill.*

C. C. (1847), p. 463. The elision in Brent's remarks represents the word "not," which I take to have been superfluous (an unintended double negative) and misleading.

18. Rowan as in note 17; Brent, in *La. C. C.* (1845), p. 748b; and see Rowan's remarks during debate on Foot's Resolution, 8 February 1830, *Reg. Deb.*, 21st C, 1st S, col. 139a; also N. G. Howard, *To the People of Rankin County;* Brent, in *La. C. C.* (1845), p. 748b; James Kingsley and Volney Hascall, in *Mich. C. C.* (1850), pp. 642b and 51b; and David Davis—another liberal Whig—in *Ill. C. C.* (1847), p. 462.

19. *Proceedings of Democratic Republican State Convention [of New Hampshire]*, p. 5b; Leggett, 21 November, 1834, in *Political Writings*, 1:164; also Andrew Jackson to Joseph Conn Guild, 24 April 1835, in *Correspondence*, 5:339; Thomas L. Hamer, 5 January 1837, *Reg. Deb.*, 24th C, 2d S, col. 1275; "Political Intolerance," *Dem. Rev.* 3, no. 9 (September 1838), 63; George Camp, *Democracy*, p. 101; and John R. Grymes, in *La. C. C.* (1845), p. 261a.

20. Hofstadter, *Idea of a Party System*, passim; Wallace, "Changing Concepts of Party in the United States: New York, 1815–1828," *AHR* 74 (1968), 471–91; also [O'Sullivan], "Introduction," pp. 1–15, and "Annexation," p. 5; and see Nahum Capen, *The History of Democracy*, a treatise begun well before the Civil War.

21. Wallace D. Farnham's " 'The Weakened Spring of Government': A Study in Nineteenth-Century American History," *AHR* 68 (1963), 662–80, has a good deal to say about the thrust of democratic belief. The later career of William Cullen Bryant exemplifies this same development in a somewhat different fashion. Together with other men of high principle, Bryant worked to purify American politics by such innovations as civil service reform, but in doing so he also helped to discredit democratic politics as an agency of public needs.

22. "Nathaniel Macon," *Dem. Rev.* 1, no. 1 (October 1837), 26; *The Working Man Defended. By the Author of the "Crisis Met,'* p. 4; also [Joseph Worrell et al.], *Letters to John Sergeant*, p. 68; Petition of the Non-freeholders of Richmond, in *Va. C. C.* (1829–1830), p. 28; Jackson, Farewell Address, in Richardson, ed., *Messages and Papers of the Presidents*, 3:293–308 passim; *Address and Resolves of Democratic Members of the Massachusetts Legislature*, p. 3a; Stephen Hempstead, in *Iowa C. C.* (1844), p. 103; Isaac T. Preston, in *La. C. C.* (1845), pp. 261b–262a; and Caldwell, in *Ill. C. C.* (1847), p. 682.

23. Ely Moore, *Address before General Trades' Union*, p. 8, and contrast the remarks by the editor of the *Poor Man's Guardian* (London), 5 April 1834, in which he insists on the need for power to control the economy: "I have long been of opinion that no partial measures can benefit the working classes. There must be a radical alteration of the system. A power over the land, and circulating medium, appears to me to be necessary to their regeneration. Without land of their own to cultivate, or at least a claim on its produce, they must be always subject to the caprices of individuals; and without some

control over the currency, their produce will be ever at the mercy of usury to detract from its value. . . . To monopolize either is to monopolize the sinews of existence. Universal Suffrage would break up the monopoly in both, and therefore (were there no other reason) the Trades' should join us openly in demanding Universal Suffrage" (p. 67a–b). The Michigan convention of 1850 debated the grounds of public intervention at some length; see particularly the remarks of Calvin Britain, John P. Cook, John D. Pierce, and De Witt C. Walker, in *Mich. C. C.* (1850), pp. 567a–b, 587a–b, 734b–735a, 515b.

24. Daniel, in *No. Car. C. C.* (1835), p. 334, and cf. Seawell, in ibid., p. 167.
25. *Niles' Weekly Register* 19, no. 8 (21 October 1820), 115; also Jesse Speight, in *No. Car. C. C.* (1835), pp. 86, 120–21, 334; and [Thomas W. Dorr], *Address to the People of Rhode Island* (1834), as found in *Report of Select Committee on Rhode Island*, pp. 167–68.
26. For the "reactionary" view, see James Kent in *N.Y. C. C.* (1821), p. 221, and Benjamin W. Leigh in *Va. C. C.* (1829–1830), pp. 155–58. For the "liberal" view, see Ross in *N.Y. C. C.* (1821), p. 180, and cf. Nathan Sanford and Peter R. Livingston in ibid., pp. 179 and 225. Maurice Klain discusses the importance a stake in society held in early "radical" thought in "Property in a Free Society"; and see Oscar and Mary Handlin, eds., *Popular Sources of Political Authority*, 34–39.
27. Sanford, in *N.Y. C. C.* (1821), p. 179; Non-freeholders of Richmond, in *Va. C. C.* (1829–1830), p. 28; also James T. Austin in *Mass. C. C.* (1820–1821), pp. 252–53; Peter R. Livingston and Martin Van Buren in *N.Y. C. C.* (1821), pp. 224–25, 255–65, 366–68; James Fenimore Cooper, *Notions of the Americans*, 1:263–71; Howard, *To the People of Rankin County;* and Jabez Hammond, *History of Political Parties in New York*, 2:49–51.
28. "The Sober Second-Thought of the People," *Dem. Rev.* 3, no. 11 (November 1838), 288; Davis, in *Texas C. C.* (1845), p. 120; also "How Stands the Case?" *Dem. Rev.* 3, no. 9 (September 1838), 13; "The Rank and File of Democracy. No. I. Pennsylvania," ibid. no. 12 (December 1838), 391–92; Wadsworth, in *La. C. C.* (1844), p. 129a; and Brent, in *La. C. C.* (1845), p. 745a. (The Louisiana convention first met at Jackson in August 1844, but soon adjourned to meet at New Orleans in February 1845.)
29. *Report of Select Committee on Rhode Island*, p. 41; Preston, in *La. C. C.* (1845), p. 191a; also Marcus Morton, "Address of His Excellency Marcus Morton, to the Two Branches of the Legislature," *Massachusetts House Documents, 1840*, no. 9, pp. 37–38; Jacob Frieze, *Concise History of Suffrage in Rhode Island;* and remarks of Thomas G. C. Davis and Horace Butler in *Ill. C. C.* (1847), pp. 563–64, 566. By contrast, Grymes denied that the vote was a natural right (*La. C. C.* [1845], p. 104b).
30. Rantoul, Speech at Salem, Massachusetts (1834), *Memoirs*, p. 560; Camp, *Democracy*, pp. 45, 53, and 65, and cf. Rantoul, *Memoirs*, p. 283; also Albert

Gallatin's address of welcome to Lafayette, as found in Edgar E. Brandon, ed., *A Pilgrimage of Liberty*, p. 370, and remarks of Charles S. Morgan in *Va. C. C.* (1829–1830), p. 377.

31. Fitzwilliam Byrdsall, *History of Loco-Foco Party*, p. 39; *Proceedings of Democratic Legislative Convention in Boston*, pp. 3, 10; Jaques, in *N.J. C. C.* (1844), p. 409; Hascall, in *Mich. C. C.* (1850), p. 642a; also *Preamble and Resolutions of the People of Abbeville District*, p. 5; Thomas Skidmore, *Rights of Man to Property!* pp. 146, 148–50; *Report of Select Committee on Rhode Island*, p. 42; and note Thomas H. Lewis's bitter condemnation of the idea that government preserves natural rights intact, in *La. C. C.* (1845), pp. 53a, 54a.

32. R. S. S. Andros et al., *Dear Sir;* Preston, in *La. C. C.* (1845), 66a–b; also *Report of Select Committee on Rhode Island*, p. 43; *Proceedings of Democratic State Convention in Nashville*, p. 8a; John McCoy, *To Freemen of 21st Senatorial District* [of Arkansas]; Remarks of Mr. Hensley, attorney for Horace Burnham, in *Texas C. C.* (1845), p. 61; and J. Randolph Burns, *To editor of the True Issue*, p. 1, col. c.

33. Gregg, in *Ill. C. C.* (1847), p. 530; Whitman, in *New York Aurora*, 18 April 1842, as quoted by Donald R. Harkness, "Crosscurrents: American Anti-Democracy, from Jackson to the Civil War" (Ph.D. diss., University of Minnesota, 1955), p. 164. For examples of conservative Democratic opposition, see Edward D. Ellis in *Mich. C. C.* (1835), pp. 239–40, and Grymes in *La. C. C.* (1845), p. 104b.

34. Luther, *Address to Workingmen*, p. 31; "Radicalism," *Dem. Rev.* 3, no. 10 (October 1838), 111. As O'Sullivan's argument demonstrated, even the defense of majority as opposed to minority rule often centered on the likelihood of infringements by one group on the other; see O'Sullivan as in note 10; also remarks of Phineas B. Kennedy, in *N.J. C. C.* (1844), pp. 66–67, and Downs, in *La. C. C.* (1845), p. 114b.

35. [Theodore Sedgwick Jr.], *Constitutional Reform*, p. 57b; Hempstead, in *Iowa C. C.* (1844), pp. 103–4; Brent and Preston, in *La. C. C.* (1845), pp. 56a, 57a, 99b; Ratliff, in *La. C. C.* (1844), p. 97a; also Rantoul, *Memoirs*, p. 91, and William S. Balch, *Popular Liberty and Equal Rights*, pp. 19–20.

36. Significantly, Robert Rantoul Jr. argued at South Reading (Massachusetts) in 1832 that the essence of the American experiment was its effort to substitute self-government for government. So, too, Frederick von Raumer remarked in 1846, "No country of the world is so little governed by authority as the United States; and nowhere is so much left to the immediate regulation and decision of the people themselves. . . . Moreover the right of self-government, thus granted, induces every individual to understand and take part in public affairs, lessens discontent and opposition, and leads to maturity and independence in the best sense of the word." (Rantoul, *Memoirs*, pp. 157–58; Raumer, *America and the American People*, p. 250.)

37. For an explicit avowal of this position, see ch. 1 of John Todd's *The Young Man*. I treat the implicit premises of Whig constitutionalism in chapter VIII

of this study. Many of the same issues are also dealt with in chapters X and XI, which examine American attitudes toward religion and education, respectively.

38. Camp, *Democracy*, pp. 45–46, 39, 44–45, and cf. pp. 62 and 85; also Hallett, *Oration at Oxford*, p. 35, and *Proceedings of Democratic State Convention in Nashville*, passim.

39. [O'Sullivan], "The Course of Civilization," pp. 215–16; "Territorial Aggrandizement," *Dem. Rev.* 17, no. 3 (October 1845), 244–45; [Richter], *On Self-Government*, pp. 2, 1, 6–7.

40. "Mr. Forrest's Oration," *Dem. Rev.* 3, no. 9 (September 1838), 52; Camp, *Democracy*, pp. 30–31; Balch, *Popular Liberty and Equal Rights*, p. 4; Doheny, *Principle, Progresss, and Destiny of Democracy*, p. 6.

41. "The Supreme Court," *Dem. Rev.* 1, no. 2 (January 1838), 148; also [O'Sullivan], "Introduction," p. 7; Camp, *Democracy*, pp. 183–84; Preston, in *La. C. C.* (1845), p. 720a–b; Thompson Campbell, in *Ill. C. C.* (1847), pp. 791–92; and John Perkins Jr., *Speech on Transfer of Public Lands*, pp. 9–12 and 17–18, as well as William Cobbett's observation that the Americans are obedient to the law, but "it is *the law only* that they will *bow* to. They will bow to nothing else" (Cobbett, *A Year's Residence in the United States* [1819], as quoted by John W. Cooke in "Some Aspects of the Concept of the Free Individual," p. 226).

42. Quitman, *Speech on Neutrality Laws*, pp. 17–18; and cf. remarks of Lemuel D. Evans in *Texas C. C.* (1845), p. 309. Frances Trollope bore witness to the same point of view in her hostile account of the traveler who attempted to force a heavy piece of luggage into the crowded stage-coach in which the Trollope family had booked passage. "No law, sir, can permit such conduct as this," she reports that she exclaimed, whereupon

"Law!" exclaimed a gentleman very particularly drunk; "we makes our own laws, and governs our own selves."

"Law!" echoed another gentleman of Vernon; "this is a free country—*we have no laws here*, and we don't want no foreign power to tyrannise over us." (Trollope, *Domestic Manners of the Americans*, pp. 348–49.) See also Alexis de Tocqueville's discussion of American attitudes toward the law as quoted by George W. Pierson, *Tocqueville and Beaumont in America*, p. 161, and David Grimsted, "Rioting in Its Jacksonian Setting," *AHR* 77 (1972), 366–74.

CHAPTER VIII: THE POLITICS OF WHIGGERY

1. There is an extensive literature on both the derivations and the doctrines of Whiggery. The works most pertinent to my purposes here include (in chronological order) Edwin S. Mims Jr., *Majority of the People* and "Will of the People"; Arthur M. Schlesinger Jr., *The Age of Jackson*, esp. chs. 22–23; Louis Hartz, *Liberal Tradition in America*, chs. 4–5; George F. Brasington Jr., "Representative Government in Jacksonian Political Thought," ch. 4; Glyndon Van Deusen, "Some Aspects of Whig Thought and Theory in the Jack-

sonian Period," *AHR* 63 (1958), 305–22; Richard P. McCormick, *Second American Party System;* Major Wilson, "Analysis of Ideas of Liberty and Union"; and Edward Pessen, *Jacksonian America.*

2. Barton, 9 February 1830, *Reg. Deb.*, 21st C, 1st S, p. 147a; also *Address of Great State Convention* [*of New Hampshire*]; *Address to the People of the United States on the Presidential Election;* and William S. Allen, *Oration delivered in Newburyport.*

3. Kennedy, *Quodlibet*, p. 170; also William Gaston, in *No. Car. C. C.* (1835), p. 127; Edward Everett, "The Importance of Education in a Republic" (1838), in *Orations and Speeches*, 2:317; William Henry Harrison, *Speech at Dayton Convention*, p. 7; R. S. Kennedy, in *N.J. C. C.* (1844), p. 374; and [Calvin Colton], *Junius Tracts* no. 6, p. 10; and see Ronald P. Formisano, "Political Character, Antipartyism and the Seond Party System," *AQ* 21 (1969), 683–709.

4. Barbour, in *Proceedings of Democratic Whig National Convention*, p. 12; and for appeals to the precedent of "revolution," see A. B. Norton, ed., *Great Revolution of 1840*, passim.

5. "Hamilton" [Watson], *The Whig Party*, p. 3; [Colton], *Crisis of the Country*, p. 15; and see his *Junius Tracts* no. 6, p. 10.

6. Kent, *Speech in support of an Amendment to the Constitution*, pp. 10–11; "What Shall the Whigs Do?" *Cincinnati Daily Gazette*, 17 January 1837, p. 2f; *Address to Democratic Whig Young Men of New-York*, p. 4; and see ch. 5 of Brasington, "Representative Government in Jacksonian Thought," for a study of the deliberate effort Whigs made to read Jackson's claim that he represented the people as a claim to be above the Constitution.

It should be noted that Democrats as well as Whigs were guilty of allegations and misrepresentations demeaning executive power. The point is not that the Whigs were unique, but that men who had once sympathized with powerful government and even with the executive veto now repudiated both as power infringing on freedom.

7. *Address to the People of Missouri*, p. 14a; Harrison, Inaugural Address, in James D. Richardson, ed., *Messages and Papers of the Presidents*, 4:5–21; also Harrison, *Speech at Dayton Convention*, p. 3; [John C. Montgomery], *Montgomery's Tippecanoe Almanac*, pp. 58b–59a; [Calvin Colton], *One Presidential Term;* and Henry Clay, Speech in Hanover County, in *Works*, 6:198ff.

8. [Colton], *Junius Tracts* no. 1, p. 3; also *Proceedings of Convention of Democratic Young Men for Ritner*, p. 14.

9. [Colton], *Junius Tracts* no. 1, p. 4; Rives, *Speech on Funds Receivable*, p. 10; and cf. [Colton], *Junius Tracts* no. 2, p. 14, and Rives, *Speech on Funds Receivable*, p. 11, where they underline the shift in conservative perspective by appealing to residual ideas of a fostering government. See also Richard Fletcher, *Speech to his Constituents;* Joseph R. Underwood, *Speech on the Sub-Treasury Bill*, p. 31; and Willis Green, *The Sub-Treasury;* as well as three

state-oriented polemics: *Proceedings of Convention of Democratic Young Men for Ritner;* William H. Seward, *Speech in the [New York] Senate,* p. 16a; and *"Address, of the General Committee of Whig Young Men, of New-York City."*

10. Clay, as found in Norton, ed., *Great Revolution of 1840,* p. 194.

11. Harrison, as found in ibid., p. 185.

12. Claiborne, in *La. C. C.* (1845), p. 169b, and cf. remarks by Thomas H. Lewis and Judah P. Benjamin, in ibid., pp. 53a, 54b, 88b–89a, and 222a.

13. *Answer of Whig Members of the Legislature of Massachusetts,* pp. 26–29; Henry R. Greene, Anthony Thornton, and James M. Davis, in *Ill. C. C.* (1847) pp. 534, 543, 571 respectively; *Minority Report of Select Committee on Rhode Island,* pp. 34ff.; James Kent, *Commentaries,* 2:6n; also *Address to the People of the United States on the Presidential Election.*

14. *Answer of Whig Members of the Legislature of Massachusetts,* p. 28; Warner, "Representative Government," *Am. Rev.* 7, no. 3 (March 1848), 280–85; "Human Rights according to Modern Philosophy," ibid. 2, no. 4 (October 1845), 327–40. It is also interesting, in view of the possibility that Democratic beliefs were ultimately grounded in religious dissent, that the reviewer concluded his treatment of Hurlbut's volume by insisting upon a "national conscience" based upon a "national religion." See also "Has the State a Religion?" ibid. 3, no. 3 (March 1846), 273–89, and my discussion of religion as a "free institution" in chapter X, section one, of this study.

15. [Colton], *Junius Tracts* no. 6, esp. p. 3, and cf. ibid. no. 4, esp. p. 13; also *Proceedings of a Convention of Democratic Young Men for Ritner,* p. 14; [Jacob B. Moore], *The Contrast,* p. 16; and *A Few Plain Facts,* p. 3.

16. *Minority Report of Select Committee on Rhode Island,* p. 19, and see the first and last sections of chapter V of this study. See also the clause of the Bill of Rights of Kentucky, drafted by Archibald Dixon in 1849: "That absolute, arbitrary power over the lives, liberty and property of freemen exist nowhere in a republic, not even in the largest majority." Dixon's role is discussed by Helm Bruce in "The Constitution and Constitutional Convention of 1849," in *Proceedings of Seventeenth Annual Meeting of the Kentucky State Bar Association . . . 1918,* p. 145.

17. Hornblower, in *N.J. C. C.* (1844), p. 169; Ten Eyck, in ibid., p. 170; and cf. remarks of James Parker, in ibid., pp. 170–71, as well as those of Thomas J. McKean in *Iowa C. C.* (1844), pp. 117–18, and of H. T. Backus in *Mich. C. C.* (1850), pp. 44b–45a. It is worth noting that, unlike most of his colleagues, Hornblower also urged easy amendment of the state's constitution (see *N.J. C. C.* [1844], p. 55, and appendix d to this chapter).

18. Benjamin, in *La. C. C.* (1845), p. 407a, and cf. Lewis, in ibid., p. 53a; also James M. Davis and Henry D. Palmer, in *Ill. C. C.* (1847), pp. 848, 850–51, and Edward V. Whiton, speech at Janesville (Wisconsin), as found in Milo M. Quaife, ed., *Struggle over Ratification,* p. 412.

19. Lieber, *Essays on Property and Labour,* p. 216; Lewis, in *La. C. C.* (1845), pp.

54a, 54b; also *Minority Report of Select Committee on Rhode Island*, pp. 19ff., and Nathan S. S. Beman, *Influence of Freedom*, p. 20, as well as Lieber's contention that "the modern citizen is considered to be a member of his political society for the purpose of finding his individual rights, indispensable to the fulfilment of his career as Man, the more firmly guarantied" (*Essays on Property and Labour*, p. 216).

20. Specific constitutional arrangements have been studied in some detail, but relatively little attention has been paid to the premises that supported them, and the literature on the state conventions is thin. The most comprehensive published account of developments in the states is Francis N. Thorpe, *Constitutional History of the American People*. In "State Constitutional Development in the United States," Bayrd Still focuses more directly on the differences between republican and democratic constitutions, tracing attempts to introduce democratic innovations and changes in the separation and balance of powers. Oscar and Mary Handlin offer a number of suggestive insights into American constitutional attitudes, stated in very brief compass, in ch. 2 of their *Dimensions of Liberty*, while Fletcher M. Green's *Constitutional Development in the South Atlantic States* is a useful regional study. See also the more general treatments of constitutionalism at the national level noted in the first appendix to chapter IX.

21. Clark, in *N.J. C. C.* (1844), p. 290; Conrad and Roman, in *La. C. C.* (1845), pp. 496b, 511a.

22. Harding, in *Ill. C. C.* (1847), p. 294, and cf. Christian Roselius, in *La. C. C.* (1845), p. 600b.

23. Gaston, McQueen, and Outlaw, in *No. Car. C. C.* (1835), pp. 132, 147, and 114, respectively, and cf. Emanuel Shober, in ibid., p. 172, as well as my discussion of conservative efforts to protect property by constitutional innovations, in the first section of chapter V of this study.

24. David M. Woodson, in *Ill. C. C.* (1847), p. 422; Harding and Minshall, in ibid., pp. 294, 413; and cf. Archibald Williams, in ibid., p. 466.

25. Benjamin, in *La. C. C.* (1845), p. 222a, and cf. Thomas H. Lewis, in ibid., pp. 53a, 55a, 121a; also William C. Woodbridge, in *Mich. C. C.* (1835), p. 256, and Francis Lieber, *On Civil Liberty*, 1:166–74, 209–16.

26. *Minority Report of Select Committee on Rhode Island*, p. 17; also Henry Clay, *Speech at Raleigh*, p. 4; [Colton], *Junius Tracts* no. 6, pp. 8–9; and *Address of the Whig Convention at Dover*, pp. 20–24.

27. Field, in *N.J. C. C.* (1844), pp. 62–63.

28. Woodbridge, in *Mich. C. C.* (1835), p. 256; Conrad, in *La. C. C.* (1844), p. 43. (The convention first met at Jackson in August 1844, but soon adjourned to meet at New Orleans in February 1845.)

29. Woodbridge and Conrad, as in note 28; J. M. V. C., "The New Constitution: Article VI—The Judiciary," *Am. Rev.* 4, no. 5 (November 1846), 520a–b; also "Responsibility of the Ballot Box; with an Illustration," ibid. 4, no. 5 (November 1846), 435–46; H. W. Warner, "The Republic. No. 1,"

ibid. 9, no. 4 (April 1849), 399–406; and Lieber, *On Civil Liberty*, vol. 1, chs. 24–26.

30. Lewis, in *La. C. C.* (1845), p. 54a; also McKean, in *Iowa C. C.* (1844), p. 114; Rufus Choate, "The Position and Functions of the American Bar, as an Element of Conservatism in the State" (1845), as found in Perry Miller, ed., *The Legal Mind in America*, pp. 262–63; *Address of Whig Convention at Dover;* Kent, *Commentaries*, 1:421; and see Perry Miller, *Life of the Mind in America*, bk. 2, ch. 5.

31. Nevin, "Human Freedom," *Am. Rev.* 7, no. 4 (April 1848), 406–18; "Civilization: American and European," pt. 2, ibid. 4, no. 1 (July 1846), 28a; also John Todd, *The Young Man*, ch. 1; Horace Mann, "The Necessity of Education in a Republican Government" (1838), in *Life and Works*, 2:149–51; and see chapter X of this study.

32. Porter, *Outlines of Oration of Judge Porter*, p. 21; also George Kent, *Characteristics and Claims of the Age*, pp. 12–13; Lieber, *On Civil Liberty*, chs. 24–26; and F. B. Sexton, *Human Progress*, pp. 17–18.

33. *Address of Friends of Domestic Industry*, p. la; *Reception of Mr. Webster at Boston*, p. 28; and cf. Chief Justice Marshall's dictum in *McCulloch* v. *Maryland:* "This provision [of necessary and proper powers] is made in a constitution, intended to endure for ages to come, and consequently, to be adapted to the various *crises* of human affairs. To have prescribed the means by which government should, in all future time, execute its powers, would have been to change, entirely, the character of the instrument, and give it the properties of a legal code. It would have been an unwise attempt to provide, by immutable rules, for exigencies which, if foreseen at all, must have been seen dimly, and which can be best provided for as they occur" (*U.S. Rep.*, 4 Wheaton 415).

34. Webster, 26 January 1830, *Reg. Deb.*, 21st C, 1st S, pp. 77b–80a, and cf. Webster, *Speech at Dinner Given Him in Philadelphia*, p. 4. His statements obviously followed in a path laid out by Marshall in *Martin* v. *Hunter's Lessee* and *McCulloch* v. *Maryland*, which are ably discussed by Charles Grove Haines in *The Supreme Court in American Government and Politics*, pp. 340f., 345f. They are the more striking when we contrast them with the essentially prudential arguments of other advocates of the power of the Supreme Court (see the remarks of Sens. Barton, Holmes, Clayton, Livingston, Johnston, and Robbins in *Reg. Deb.*, 21st C, 1st S, pp. 152a–b, 161a–b, 227a–29b, 266a–70b, 284–88b, and 435b–36b). For a discussion of the theory of nullification as a theory of liberty, see the last section of chapter IX of this study.

35. Poindexter, 17 April 1834, *Reg. Deb.*, 23d C, 1st S, col. 1337; Sprague, 29 January 1834, ibid., cols. 386–87.

36. Everett, 9 March 1826, *Reg. Deb.*, 19th C, 1st S, col. 1573; Henry, *Importance of Exalting Intellectual Spirit of Nation;* Harrison, Inaugural Address, in Richardson, ed., *Messages and Papers of the Presidents*, 4:10–11; Warner, "The Republic, Number 2," *Am. Rev.* 9, no. 5 (May 1849), 476–87, and "Number

4," ibid. 10, no. 3 (September 1849), 278–95; also Aaron O. Dayton, *Address before Whig and Cliosophic Societies*, pp. 13–16, and Henry W. Hilliard, *The Spirit of Liberty*, p. 13.

37. See, for example, *Proceedings of National Republican Convention of Young Men*, p. 9, and Daniel Webster, in *Journal of Proceedings of National Republican Convention at Worcester*, pp. 35ff., 74–75.

38. "To the Freemen of New York," in *Proceedings of Whig State Convention at Utica*, p. 8; Barbour, in *Proceedings of Democratic Whig National Convention*, p. 13; Clay, Speech at Taylorsville, Virginia, as found in Norton, ed., *Great Revolution of 1840*, pp. 187–212; and cf. Clay's speech at Nashville, ibid., pp. 270–84; [Colton], *One Presidential Term*, p. 3; and a number of other speeches in Norton's book, as well as the barbed observation in the *Democratic Review* that the Whigs had no program except the wish to "heal the wounds of the bleeding Constitution" and "to 'drive out the Philistines', and enter themselves upon the enjoyment of the milk and honey of the Promised Land" (*Dem. Rev.* 3, no. 9 [September 1838], 9).

39. [Colton], *Junius Tracts* no. 6, p. 12.

40. Clay, *Speech at Raleigh*, p. 2, and note the motto of the *American Review*, launched in 1844: "To Stand by the Constitution."

41. For the long-range tendency of federal judicial opinions on social and economic questions, see Benjamin F. Wright Jr., *The Contract Clause;* Edward S. Corwin, *Liberty Against Government;* and John R. Commons, *Legal Foundations of Capitalism*, as well as chapter V of this study.

42. See, for example, Chancellor Kent's unflinching statement of the theory of judicial review in his *Commentaries on American Law*, in which he clearly transforms issues of politics into issues of law: "The courts of justice have a right, and are in duty bound, to bring every law to the test of the constitution, and to regard the constitution, first of the United States, and then of their own state, as the paramount or supreme law, to which every inferior or derivative power and regulation must conform. . . . The judicial department is the proper power in the government to determine whether a statute be or be not constitutional. The interpretation or construction of the constitution, is as much a judicial act, and requires the exercise of the same legal discretion, as the interpretation or construction of a law" (Kent, *Commentaries*, 1:421).

43. Ibid., 1:273; also *Iowa Standard*, 14 November 1844, as found in *Iowa C. C.* (1844), pp. 208–9; and the observations of two conservative Democrats, A. Dunn and George Eustis, in *La. C. C.* (1845), pp. 270a, 167b.

44. Kent, *Commentaries*, 1:422, and compare Lieber, *On Civil Liberty*, vol. 1, ch. 18 and pp. 241–49.

45. Giles, in *No. Car. C. C.* (1835), p. 333; J. M. V. C., "The New Constitution: Article VI—The Judiciary," p. 531a.

46. Kent, *Commentaries* (4th ed.), 1:450n; McKean, in *Iowa C. C.* (1844), pp. 117–18.

47. Kent, *Commentaries* (1st ed.), 1:273–74; Giles, as in note 45; McKean, as in note 46; "Responsibility of the Ballot Box; with an Illustration," p. 440a; also John H. Tweedy, in *Wisc. C. C.* (1846), pp. 497–500.
48. J. M. V. C., "The New Constitution: Article VI—The Judiciary," p. 520.
49. See the remarks of Archibald Williams and Samuel D. Lockwood, in *Ill. C. C.* (1847), pp. 743–44, 763; and of Kirkpatrick, in *Iowa C. C.* (1844), p. 112.
50. "Responsibility of the Ballot Box; with an Illustration," p. 440a.
51. Webster, 26 January 1830, *Reg. Deb.*, 21st C, 1st S, pp. 77b–78a, and cf. the remarks of Sens. Barton, Holmes, Clayton, Livingston, Johnston, and Robbins, as cited in note 34; Webster, *Speech at Dinner Given Him in Philadelphia*, p. 4; and see his speech of 1826 defending expansion of the Supreme Court as a necessary but not a dangerous innovation (*Writings and Speeches*, 5:150–77).
52. Story, *Commentaries on the Constitution*, 3:425–26, and see the statement made in the Senate by William Harper of South Carolina in 1826: "The Constitution has laid down the fundamental and immutable laws of justice for our Government; and the majority that constitutes the Government should not violate these. The Constitution is made to control the Government; it has no other object; and though the Supreme Court cannot resist public opinion, it may resist a temporary majority and may change that majority" (quoted by Warren, in *Supreme Court in United States History*, 1:671); Kent, *Commentaries*, 1:274.
53. Romeyn, *Our Country and her Claims*, p. 21.

CHAPTER IX: THE CONSTITUTION OF DEMOCRACY

1. Root, in *N.Y. C. C.* (1821), p. 223; Tallmadge, in *From the Albany Daily Advertiser*, pp. 8–9.
2. Norvell, in *Mich. C. C.* (1835), p. 258; Preston, in *La. C. C.* (1845), p. 191a.
3. Preston, in *La. C. C.* (1845), p. 150b, and cf. p. 620a; *Proceedings and Address of Democratic County Convention at Galena*, p. 7b; and see my discussion of the right of instruction, exemplified in the same proceedings at p. 6b, in chapter VII of this study.
4. See, for example, Thomas W. Dorr's *Address to the People of Rhode Island*, as found in *Report of Select Committee on Rhode Island*, p. 165; the resolutions of a suffrage convention (1841?), ibid., p. 406; the Report of the Committee, ibid., pp. 32–41; and remarks of Shepherd Leffler, in *Iowa C. C.* (1841), p. 249.
5. Preston, in *La. C. C.* (1845), p. 415a; Naar, in *N.J. C. C.* (1844), p. 61; also *Report of Select Committee on Rhode Island*, pp. 32–41; James Brent and Solomon Downs, in *La. C. C.* (1845), pp. 845a, 410a; and Michael Doheny, *Principle, Progress, and Destiny of Democracy*, p. 5.
6. Ratliff, in *La. C. C.* (1845), p. 87b; Evans, in *Texas C. C.* (1845), p. 309.
7. Turner, in *Report of Select Committee on Rhode Island*, p. 1011; Memorial of the Democratic Members of the General Assembly of Rhode Island, ibid., p. 2;

the Report of the Committee, ibid., p. 83; *Facts involved in the Rhode Island Controversy*, p. 34; Thomas G. C. Davis, in *Ill. C. C.* (1847), p. 76; and Andrew Jackson to Francis Preston Blair, 23 May 1842, in *Correspondence*, 6:153.

8. All of these attitudes are exemplified at the same locations in the documents I have already cited in notes 1 through 7. In this connection it is worth noting that four states gave up unicameral legislatures; see Alfred De Grazia, *Public and Republic*, pp. 137–38.

9. *Report of Select Committee on Rhode Island*, p. 27; Hallett, *Right of the People to Establish Forms of Government*, p. 52.

10. See Address of the State Committee (1841), in *Report of Select Committee on Rhode Island*, p. 416; Memorial of the Democratic Members, ibid., p. 3; and Report of the Committee, ibid., pp. 32–41; as well as the discussion of attitudes and events in Arthur H. Mowry, *The Dorr War*. As Bayrd Still notes, the revised constitution adopted by the legislature in 1842 was very much a classic democratic instrument, limiting the power of the legislature to contract debts, to lend its credit, or to establish corporations. (Still, "State Constitutional Development in the United States," pp. 157ff.).

11. Brent, in *La. C. C.* (1845), p. 748a; Fletcher, in *Iowa C. C.* (1844), p. 113; also Norvell, in *Mich. C. C.* (1835), p. 355; and Resolutions of the Democratic members, in Milo M. Quaife, ed., *Struggle over Ratification*, p. 205.

12. Church, in *Mich. C. C.* (1850), p. 236a; *Racine Advocate*, 2 December 1846, as found in Quaife, ed., *Struggle over Ratification*, p. 213; also David Naar and Peter D. Vroom, in *N.J. C. C.* (1844), pp. 61, 288, and Miles Taylor in *La. C. C.* (1845), p. 490a.

13. Brent, in *La. C. C.* (1845), p. 845a; Preston, in ibid., p. 415b.

14. Tallmadge, in *From the Albany Daily Advertiser*, p. 8; Zabriskie, in *N.J. C. C.* (1844), pp. 169–70; also Isaac E. Crary, in *Mich. C. C.* (1835), p. 287.

15. Stokes, in *N.J. C. C.* (1844), p. 60; also [John L. O'Sullivan], "Introduction," *Dem. Rev.* 1, no. 1 (October 1837), 5–8; James K. Polk, Inaugural Address, in James D. Richardson, ed., *Messages and Papers of the Presidents*, 4:375; and see the revealing analogy between a constitutional prohibition on banks and a bill of rights, drawn by Walter B. Scates and A. G. Caldwell in *Ill. C. C.* (1847), pp. 264, 682.

16. For examples of liberal protest, see Preston, in *La. C. C.* (1845), p. 191a; Bush, in *Mich. C. C.* (1850), p. 608b; and Joseph H. Bagg and John D. Pierce, in ibid., pp. 265a–b, 549a. For examples of conservative protest, see William B. Ewing, in *N.J. C. C.* (1844), p. 327; James S. Mayfield, in *Texas C. C.* (1845), p. 342; George Eustis and Bernard Marigny, in *La. C. C.* (1845), pp. 655b, 693b; and the *Southport* (Wisconsin) *Telegraph*, 23 October 1846, as found in Quaife, ed., *Struggle over Ratification*, pp. 182–83. It is suggestive that when Bagg and Pierce pressed for greater freedom for the legislature, they had in mind leaving it free to deal with the vexed question of public schools, which could well be taken to be something the convention

should leave alone. By contrast, Bush and Preston sought to free it to deal with taxation and electoral districts, respectively, which few Democrats were willing to trust to the legislature.

17. Norvell, in *Mich. C. C.* (1835), p. 203; Scates, in *Ill. C. C.* (1847), p. 327; also the *Racine Advocate*, 3 February 1847, as found in Quaife, ed., *Struggle over Ratification*, pp. 445–46; and Elisha P. Hurlbut, *Essays on Human Rights*, as quoted by Alfred De Grazia, *Public and Republic*, p. 137.

18. Scates, in *Ill. C. C.* (1847), p. 263; [Sedgwick], *Constitutional Reform*, pp. 1b, 5a, and see p. 25a; also A. H. Hanscom, in *Mich. C. C.* (1850), p. 351a–b.

19. Gregg, in *Ill. C. C.* (1847), pp. 438–39; Davis, in ibid., p. 434; and see Vroom's insistence upon a distinctly constituted senate in the New Jersey convention, partly in order to make up for the convention's refusal to adopt an executive veto (*N.J. C. C.* [1844], p. 228); also the debate in *N.Y. C. C.* (1846), pp. 327b–337b. The analysis of types of state constitutions in Bayrd Still's "State Constitutional Development in the United States" remains relevant on this point: in effect, Still distinguishes between "early" constitutions (no matter what their date) geared to a powerful and active legislature, and "late" constitutions (meaning second or third instruments of government) committed to a stronger executive and more effective restrictions on the legislature.

20. *Racine Advocate*, 3 February 1847, as found in Quaife, ed., *Struggle over Ratification*, p. 447; and cf. Gregg, in *Ill. C. C.* (1847), p. 440.

21. Van Zandt, in *Texas C. C.* (1845), p. 141.

22. "Radicalism," *Dem. Rev.* 3, no. 10 (October 1838), 99; also "Congressional History. The Second Session of the Twenty-Fifth Congress," ibid. no. 10, p. 106, and "The Northeastern Boundary Question," ibid. no. 9 (September 1838), 49n. For an early example of Democratic "Calvinism," see Rep. George McDuffie's remark during debate on his proposal to elect the president by electoral districts rather than states: "No political millenium [*sic*] has opened upon us. The nature of man is unchanged. We can only hope for exemption from the corruption and depravity which history records of other countries, by avoiding the imperfection in our political organization that produced those evils in their systems" (*Reg. Deb.*, 31 March 1826, 19th C, 1st S, col. 1952). In ch. 31 of *The Age of Jackson*, Arthur M. Schlesinger Jr. discusses the logic that led not only Orestes Brownson but also other less idiosyncratic Democrats to adopt a rigidly constrictive constitutionalism on the national level as the only plausible means of controlling the mistakes men make when they have power. See also my discussion of conservative Democrats' attitudes, in appendix g to this chapter.

23. Camp, *Democracy*, p. 214.

24. [Sedgwick], *Constitutional Reform*, p. 2b; also Address of the State Committee, in *Report of Select Committee on Rhode Island*, p. 416; the Report of the Committee, ibid., p. 32; Leffler, in *Iowa C. C.* (1844), pp. 8–9; and Pierre Soulé, in *La. C. C.* (1845), p. 729 a–b.

494 · NOTES: CONSTITUTION OF DEMOCRACY ·

25. [Sedgwick], *Constitutional Reform*, p. 52b; the *Jeffersonian*, as quoted by Amasa Read, in *La. C. C.* (1845), p. 743a.
26. Norvell, in *Mich. C. C.* (1835), pp. 354–55; Crary, in ibid., p. 287; also Ross Wilkins, in ibid., p. 287; Brent, in *La. C. C.* (1845), p. 748a; and Edward G. Ryan, in *Wisc. C. C.* (1846), pp. 592–603. I have corrected an obvious typographical error in Crary's statement, which reads "Legislative and Judicial." Brent's paragraph continues with the general theory of checks and balances quoted on p. 225.
27. Robinson, *Oration before Trades' Union of Boston*, p. 17; Brent, in *La. C. C.* (1845), p. 751a; and see Fletcher, in *Iowa C. C.* (1844), pp. 192–95.
28. Camp, *Democracy*, p. 65; Polk, 13 March 1826, *Reg. Deb.*, 19th C, 1st S, col. 1652; Doheny, *Principle, Progress, and Tendency of Democracy*, p. 5.
29. See *History of Federal and Democratic Parties*, p. 30, and cf. the debate on Senator Foot's resolution in *Reg. Deb.*, 21st C, 1st S, esp. pp. 87b–88b (Hayne), 112a–b (Benton), 132b–139b (Rowan), 184a–185b (Woodbury), 204a (Smith), and 213a–b (Grundy); remarks by John D. Pierce, in *Mich. C. C.* (1850), pp. 735b–736a; and the account of public reactions to controversial decisions in Charles Warren, *Supreme Court in United States History*, 1:514–24, 715–28.
30. Rowan, 8 February 1830, *Reg. Deb.*, 21st C, 1st S, p. 139c; "The Supreme Court of the United States. Its Judges and Jurisdiction," *Dem. Rev.* 1, no. 2 (January 1838), 143, 144; Jackson, in Richardson, ed., *Messages and Papers of the Presidents*, 2:581–82; M. Hall McAllister, *Address to Democratic Republican Convention of Georgia*, p. 10; and see the remarks by Rowan on 20 February 1828, *Reg. Deb.*, 20th C, 1st S, col. 349.
31. *Dem. Rev.* 1, no. 2 (January 1838), 168–72, 171, 172; "European Views of American Democracy—No. II. M. de Tocqueville," *ibid.* 2, no. 8 (July 1838), 338; Soulé, in *La. C. C.* (1845), p. 214a; and see the remarks by A. S. Robertson in *Mich. C. C.* (1850), p. 695a. The "revolution" the *Review* hailed included the decisions of the first Taney Court, especially the *Charles River Bridge* case (which denied exclusive rights to the original grantee), *The Mayor of New York* v. *Miln* (authorizing the states to regulate immigration), and *Briscoe* v. *Bank of Kentucky* (authorizing a bank owned by a state to issue banknotes, the federal prohibition on state currencies notwithstanding).
32. Hunt, *Speech at Mass Meeting of Mechanics*, p. 1a; and see *The Crisis Met*, p. 2.
33. Walker, in Myer Moses, *Full Annals of the Revolution in France* (second pagination), p. 114; Garland, *Principles of Democracy*, pp. 19–20; Bancroft, *History of the United States*, 4:13.
34. *Proceedings of Democratic Republican Convention of Indiana*, p. 8; "Executive Usurpation," *Dem. Rev.* 1, no. 3 (February 1838), 282–83; Gardiner, ed., *The Great Issue*, p. 19.
35. "Executive Usurpation," p. 291; *Address of Democratic State Convention of Illinois*, p. 9.

36. Jackson, in Richardson, ed., *Messages and Papers of the Presidents*, 2:581–88, 3:90–93.
37. Special Message of 16 January 1833, in ibid., 2:617–25, 631–32; Nullification Proclamation, in ibid., pp. 641–43, 648–51, 652–55.
38. Arthur M. Schlesinger Sr. strongly pressed the idea that states' rights was merely a rationalization, in "The State Rights Fetish," in *New Viewpoints in American History*, pp. 220–44, but I have found Louis Hartz's "South Carolina vs. the United States," in Daniel Aaron, ed., *America in Crisis*, pp. 73–89, far more relevant to an understanding of its recurrence in American political discourse.
39. Emmet as quoted by Warren, *Supreme Court in United States History*, 1:619; Jackson, in Richardson, ed., *Messages and Papers of the Presidents*, 2:590; Joseph A. Wright, *Address at Livonia*, p. 13; also *Memorial and Resolutions adopted at Anti-Tariff Meeting at Sumter District; New York Evening Post*, 7 August 1835, as quoted by Warren, *Supreme Court in United States History*, 1:810–11; Joseph J. Daniel and John Branch, in *No. Car. C. C.* (1835), pp. 163, 165; *Address of Democratic State Convention of Illinois*, p. 2; Orestes Brownson, "Constitutional Government," *Boston Quarterly Review* 5, no. 17 (January 1842), 39–50; *Proceedings of Democratic State Convention in Nashville*, p. 9a–b; "New Territory versus No Territory," *Dem. Rev.* 21, no. 112 (October 1847), 292–94; and Cyrus Ratliff, in *La. C. C.* (1845), p. 499b. Avowed conservatives also increasingly insisted that decentralization was the key to American liberty; see not only Francis Lieber, *On Civil Liberty*, chs. 21, 23, 34, but also Daniel D. Barnard, *Political Aspects and Prospects in Europe*, pp. 27–28.
40. *Preamble and Resolutions of the People of Abbeville District*, p. 5; *Address of the Citizens of Richland Dist.*, p. 4; and see the discussion of southern views in chapter XIII, below.
41. Hamilton, in *Proceedings of State Rights Celebration at Charleston*, pp. 28–29; also Hamilton, *Speech on Operation of Tariff*, pp. 7–8, 13; and Address of the State Rights and Free Trade Party of Charleston, in *The Constitution of the State Rights and Free Association of South Carolina*, pp. 2–3.
42. *Exposition and Protest*, pp. 5–7, 26–38; and cf. Calhoun's *Discourse on the Constitution and Government of the United States*, in *Works*, 1:321–40, which challenges the legitimacy of the Judiciary Act of 1789 on the same grounds.
43. *Exposition and Protest*, pp. 22, 29, 33–34.
44. *Address to the People of South Carolina*, in *Report, Ordinance, and Addresses of Convention of South Carolina*, pp. 7–8, and cf. Hamilton, *Speech on Operation of Tariff*, pp. 15ff.
45. For conflicting views of the measures necessary to secure southern liberties, see *Proceedings of State Rights Celebration at Charleston* (1830), passim; also John Calhoun's arguments in his Fort Hill Address (1831) and his remarks on the Force Bill (1833), in his *Works*, 6:124–26 and 2:197–262.
46. *Address to the People of Mississippi*, pp. 17–18.

CHAPTER X: RELIGION AS A FREE INSTITUTION

1. Adams, *Moral Causes of Welfare of Nations*, pp. 12–13; also George W. Benedict, *Oration at Burlington*, pp. 25–26; William Wirt, *Address before Peithessophian and Philoclean Societies*, pp. 10–11; H. W. Warner, "The Republic. No. 1," *Am. Rev.* 9, no. 4 (April 1849), 399b; and Daniel D. Barnard, *Political Aspects and Prospects in Europe*, pp. 26, 48. See also Wilson Smith, *Professors and Public Ethics*.

2. Francis Wayland, *Elements of Political Economy*, p. 194; George Robertson, *Address on behalf of Deinologian Society*, p. 13; Todd, *The Young Man*, p. 22; also Jasper Adams, *Relation of Christianity to Civil Government*, p. 19; Daniel Ullmann, *Address delivered in the Tabernacle*, pp. 24–25; Christian Roselius, in *La. C. C.* (1845), p. 234b; and Horace Mann, Report for 1848, *Life and Works*, 4:286–90. For a sensitive treatment of the authority of virtue in Massachusetts, see Jane M. Johnson, " 'Through Change and Through Storm': A Study of Federalist-Unitarian Thought, 1800–1860" (Ph.D. diss., Radcliffe College, 1958).

3. Kent, *Characteristics and Claims of the Age*, pp. 41–42; Beman, *Claims of Our Country*, p. 33; also Wayland, *Elements of Political Economy*, p. 116; Charles J. Stillé, *The Social Spirit*, p. 11; Mann, Report for 1845, *Life and Works*, 4:16; George W. Eaton, *Address before Sigma Phi*, pp. 17–19; and George Putnam, *Sermon delivered before His Excellency George N. Briggs;* and see chapter XI, note 6.

4. "Reflections suggested by the Obsequies of John Adams and Thomas Jefferson," *Christian Examiner* 3, no. 4 (July and August, 1826), 325; Review of *An Inquiry into the Moral and Religious Character of the American Government*, in *N.-Y. Rev.* 3, no. 2 (October 1838), 473; and cf. D. F. Robertson, *National Destiny and Our Country*, pp. 23–26, 42–47.

5. "Human Rights according to Modern Philosophy," *Am. Rev.* 2, no. 4 (October 1845), 340b; "Has the State a Religion?" ibid. 3, no. 3 (March 1846), 273–89; and cf. Stillé, *The Social Spirit*, passim. Significantly, to substantiate his position the author of "Has the State a Religion?" cited both Daniel Webster in the Girard Will case and Chancellor Kent in *The People* v. *Ruggles*.

6. American religious history has recently begun to acquire great range and depth. Among the works I have found most useful for my purposes here have been (in order of their appearance) John R. Bodo, *Protestant Clergy and Public Issues;* Charles C. Cole Jr., *Social Ideas of Northern Evangelists;* Charles I. Foster, *An Errand of Mercy;* Clifford S. Griffin, *Their Brothers' Keepers;* James Ward Smith and A. Leland Jamison, eds., *Shaping of American Religion;* Winthrop S. Hudson, *American Protestantism;* Sidney E. Mead, *The Lively Experiment;* and Mark De Wolfe Howe, *The Garden and the Wilderness*.

7. For perspectives on the orthodox evangelical crusade see, in addition to the works cited in note 6, Clifford S. Griffin, "Religious Benevolence as Social Control, 1815–1860," *MVHR* 44 (1957), 423–44; Perry Miller, "From the Covenant to the Revival," in Smith and Jamison, eds., *Shaping of American*

Religion, 1:322–68; William Lee Miller, "American Religion and American Political Attitudes," ibid., 2:81–118; Perry Miller, *Life of the Mind in America*, bk. 1, chs. 1–2; Fred Somkin, *Unquiet Eagle*, ch. 1; Bertram Wyatt-Brown, "Prelude to Abolitionism: Sabbatarian Politics and the Rise of the Second Party System," *JAH* 58 (1971), 316–41; and W. David Lewis, "The Reformer as Conservative: Protestant Counter-Subversion in the Early Republic," in Stanley Coben and Lorman Ratner, eds., *Development of an American Culture*, pp. 64–91 (this essay is a general synthesis of existing secondary accounts). Recently Lois W. Banner has challenged the implicit bias of modern commentators who see in religious benevolence an attempt, whether conscious or not, to maintain some kind of control over the democracy. Although her observations are a necessary corrective to these unsympathetic critics of the evangelical crusade, they actually reinforce the proposition that many advocates of benevolence perceived it as an indispensable remedy for the ills of a nation given over to materialism and a dubious standard of politics. (See Banner, "Religious Benevolence as Social Control: A Critique of an Interpretation," *JAH* 60 [1973], 23–41.)

For various aspects of specifically New England developments, see Richard L. Power, "A Crusade to Extend Yankee Culture, 1820–1865," *New England Quarterly* 13 (1940), 638–53; James F. Maclear, " 'The True American Union' of Church and State: The Reconstruction of the Theocratic Tradition," *Church History* 28 (1959), 41–62; and J. Earl Thompson Jr., "A Perilous Experiment," chs. 6–7, as well as the last section of this chapter.

8. Beecher, *Autobiography*, 1:273, 274, 261; and see Vincent Harding, "Lyman Beecher and the Transformation of American Protestantism, 1776–1863" (Ph.D. diss., University of Chicago, 1965), as well as Barbara Cross's introduction to the John Harvard Library edition of the autobiography, and Sidney E. Mead's *Nathaniel William Taylor*.

9. Beecher, *Autobiography*, 1:344; Beecher, *Lectures on Political Atheism*, pp. 59–60, 75–77.

10. Beecher, *Lectures on Political Atheism*, pp. 137–38.

11. Chapin, *Spirit of the Age*, p. 8; Wylie, *Religion and State*, esp. p. 16; Southwick, *Oration before Albany County Temperance Society*, p. 28; and cf. Baynard Hall, *Righteousness the safe-guard of nation*, p. 15.

12. Chapin, *Spirit of the Age*, p. 8; Wylie, *Religion and State*, pp. 5, 11–14; Southwick, *Oration before Albany County Temperance Society*, p. 14, and see his tract of 1834, *A Layman's Apology*, passim; also Hall, *Righteousness the safe-guard of nation*, passim; and Mark Hopkins, *Sermon delivered before His Excellency Edward Everett*.

13. Southwick, *Oration before Albany County Temperance Society*, p. 28, and cf. pp. 41–42; also Hall, *Righteousness the safe-guard of nation*, pp. 7–8; Calvin Colton, *History and Character of American Revivals*, pp. 30–31; and Charles G. Finney, *Lectures on Revivals of Religion*, pp. 305–6.

14. Bent, *Oration at Raynham*; Aydelott, *Our Country's Evils*, p. 37; also William

Twining, *Address on Moral Education*, p. 9; Humphrey Moore, *Address in Pembroke*, esp. pp. 4, 9–10; Notice of the *Annual Report of the American Bible Society*, in *Ladies' Repository, and Gatherings of the West* 6, no. 6 (June 1846), 190b; and Philip S. Cleland, *The Higher Law*, pp. 10–11.

15. Hopkins, *Sermon delivered before His Excellency Edward Everett*, esp. pp. 18–19; Hopkins, "The Sabbath and Free Institutions," *Am. Nat. Preacher* 21, no. 6 (June 1847), 125–41; Chapin, *Relation of the Individual to the Republic*, p. 9.

16. Aydelott, *Our Country's Evils*, pp. 37–38; Sparrow, *The Nation's Privileges*, p. 31; *New York Recorder* as quoted in *Home Missionary* 19, no. 5 (September 1846), 117a–b; also Josiah Bent Jr., *National Jubilee*, p. 11; Lyman Beecher, "The Gospel the Only Security for Eminent and Abiding National Prosperity," *Am. Nat. Preacher* 3, no. 10 (March 1829), 145–51; Adams, *Relation of Christianity to Civil Government*, p. 27; Twining, *Address on Moral Education*, p. 10; George Putnam, *Our Political Idolatry;* John M. Austin, *Source and Perpetuity of Republicanism;* Whitefoord Smith, *Oration at South Carolina College;* and I. N. Wyckoff, *Stability of the Times.*

17. Bushnell, "American Politics," *Am. Nat. Preacher* 14, no. 12 (December 1840), 189–204; Bushnell, *The Census and Slavery*, p. 19; Bushnell, "The Fathers of New England" (1849), as quoted by Gordon Harland, in "The Crisis of American Protestantism," *Frontier* 6 (1963), 250; and cf. Bushnell, *Politics under the Law of God.*

18. Beecher, "The Scriptural Philosophy of Congregationalism and of Councils," *Bibliotheca Sacra* 22, no. 86 (April 1865), 309–10.

19. Hopkins, *The Sabbath and Free Institutions*, pp. 3–4; and see Hudson, *American Protestantism*, esp. pp. 64ff. and 99ff., and Sidney Ahlstrom, "The Puritan Ethic and the Spirit of American Democracy," in George L. Hunt, ed., *Calvinism and the Political Order*, pp. 88–107.

20. For useful general treatments of these developments, see William W. Sweet, *Religion in Development of American Culture;* Mead, *The Lively Experiment*, ch. 3; and Alan Heimert, *Religion and the American Mind.* Pertinent state and regional studies include William A. Robinson, *Jeffersonian Democracy in New England;* Richard J. Purcell, *Connecticut in Transition;* Wesley M. Gewehr, *Great Awakening in Virginia*, ch. 8; and William G. McLoughlin, *New England Dissent*, chs. 41–63.

21. The best single treatment of Republican skepticism is probably Daniel Boorstin's *Lost World of Thomas Jefferson*, which deals with the attitudes and assumptions common to Federalist as well as Republican intellectuals. Other relevant works include Yehoshua Arieli's *Individualism and Nationalism in American Ideology*, ch. 7, and Albert Post's *Popular Freethought in America.*

22. "Further Extracts from the Private Diary of a Certain Bank Director," *Dem. Rev.* 3, no. 12 (December 1838), 363–65, and cf. William Leggett, 3 December 1837, in *Political Writings*, 2:114–15. In his discourse on *The History of Liberty*, moreover, the Reverend Leander Ker clearly articulated the essen-

tial democratic theory of liberty in its relationship to Christianity, albeit in a highly conservative vein (pp. 16–21).

23. Polk, in James D. Richardson, ed., *Messages and Papers of the Presidents*, 4:629; and see chapter I of this study.
24. "Radicalism," *Dem. Rev.* 3, no. 10 (October 1838), 105; George Camp, *Democracy*, p. 244.
25. Ibid., pp. 141–42; Grimke, *Nature and Tendency of Free Institutions*, pp. 546–47; also Rep. Jacob C. Isacks, 16 March 1826, *Reg. Deb.*, 19th C, 1st S, cols. 1703–4; William Gibbes Hunt, *Address at Nashville*, pp. 8–9; and Samuel J. Bayard, *Address at West Point*, p. 8b.
26. Wood, 14 March 1826, *Reg. Deb.*, 19th C, 1st S, cols. 1680–81, 1679; also Camp, *Democracy*, pp. 148–58; [Theodore Sedgwick Jr.], *Constitutional Reform*, p. 4a–b; and Grimke, *Nature and Tendency of Free Institutions*, bk. 1, chs. 5, 8; bk. 3, ch. 5; and see bk. 4, ch. 8 (new in the 1856 edition).
27. "European Views of American Democracy. M. de Tocqueville," *Dem. Rev.* 2, no. 8 (July 1838), 350, 351; and see Isaac William Hayne, *An Oration in Columbia*, p. 5.
28. "Mr. Forrest's Oration," *Dem. Rev.* 3, no. 9 (September 1838), 51–52.
29. "Claims of the Beautiful Arts," ibid. 3, no. 11 (November 1838), 262; [O'Sullivan], "The Course of Civilization," ibid. 6, no. 21 (September 1839), 216–17; and see "The Northeastern Boundary Question," ibid. 3, no. 9 (September 1838), 47–48, as well as the citations in chapter VII, note 40.
30. Camp, *Democracy*, pp. 73–74; "The Course of Civilization," p. 214.
31. Poinsett, *Substance of a Speech at Seyle's*, p. 4n; Van Valkenburgh, in *Mich. C. C.* (1850), p. 158a; and cf. the same speaker on opening prayers, ibid., pp. 4b–5a.
32. Camp, *Democracy*, pp. 57, 124.
33. Zabriskie, in *N.J. C. C.* (1844), p. 68; also Review of Thomas Carlyle's *The French Revolution*, in *Dem. Rev.* 2, no. 4 (July 1838), 328, and Fitzwilliam Byrdsall, *History of Loco-Foco Party*, p. 189.
34. Channing, "Spiritual Freedom. Discourse Preached at the Annual Election, May 26, 1830," in *Works*, 4:67–103, 83.
35. Channing, "Remarks on Associations," in ibid., 1:281–332, 306; Channing, "Self-Culture. An address introductory to the Franklin Lectures, delivered at Boston, Sept., 1838," in ibid., 2:347–411, 411.
36. Parker, "The Laboring Classes," in *Social Classes in a Republic*, pp. 48–51; "The Mercantile Classes," in ibid., pp. 23, 18, 18–19; "The Perishing Classes," in ibid., pp. 103–4, 136.
37. Ibid., pp. 13–18, 127–36; "The Education of the Laboring Classes," in ibid., p. 87.
38. These themes run through Emerson's writings but come to a focus in "Self Reliance," in *Works*, 2:47–87. Yehoshua Arieli has a penetrating discussion of the differences between democratic atomism and Emersonian individualism

in chs. 9 and 12 of *Individualism and Nationalism in American Ideology*. For the *Democratic Review*'s estimate of Channing, see "Channing on 'Self-Culture,' " *Dem. Rev.* 5, no. 13 (January 1839), 85–91, and "On the Elevation of the Laboring Portion of Society," ibid. 7, no. 30 (June 1840), 529–39.

CHAPTER XI: THE USES OF EDUCATION

1. Orestes Brownson bore witness to the ultimate weakness of contemporary Protestantism as a bulwark for free institutions both in his conversion to Roman Catholicism and in his writings on the subject, especially "Catholicity Necessary to Sustain Popular Liberty" (1845), in *Works*, 10:1–16. For a Protestant expression of some of the same fears, see Joseph Tuckerman, *Principles and Results of Ministry at Large*, pp. 34–45.

2. The literature on educational reform is uneven. Among the most useful works are Merle Curti, *Social Ideas of American Educators*; Howard K. Beale, *History of Freedom of Teaching in American Schools*; Sidney L. Jackson, *America's Struggle for Free Schools*; Lawrence Cremin, *The American Common School*; my own *Popular Education and Democratic Thought*; Michael Katz, *Irony of Early School Reform*; Robert H. Wiebe, "The Social Functions of Public Education," *AQ* 21 (1969), 147–64; Raymond A. Mohl, "Humanitarianism in the Preindustrial City: The New York Society for the Prevention of Pauperism, 1817–1823," *JAH* 57 (1970), 576–99; and my "Popular Education and Democracy in American and English Thought," in *American Writings on Popular Education*, pp. xiii–lx.

3. Stowe, *Report on Elementary Instruction in Europe*, as found in Edgar W. Knight, ed., *Reports on European Education*, p. 256; Holley, *Oration at Peru*, p. 7; Walker, in *Mich. C. C.* (1850), p. 552a; also Thaddeus Stevens, A Plea for Free Schools (1835), in Thomas E. Finegan, ed., *Free Schools*, pp. 59–60; Daniel Webster, Remarks to the Ladies of Richmond (1840), in *Writings and Speeches*, 3:107; William H. Seward, *Elements of Empire in America*, p. 32; Horace Mann, Report for 1845, *Life and Works*, 4:15–17; and *Address in relation to Free Common Schools* (Indiana), p. 13.

4. Seward, *Discourse on Education*, p. 5; "Speech of William Cost Johnson," *N.-Y. Rev.* 10, no. 19 (January 1842), 175; Mann, Report for 1848, *Life and Works*, 4:269; and cf. Seward, "Internal Improvements and Education" (1835), in *Works*, 3:131–33.

5. Stowe, "The Education of Immigrants," in *Transactions of the Western Literary Institute*, 5:66; Mann, "The Necessity of Education in a Republican Government," *Life and Works*, 2:174–75; Benjamin, in *La. C. C.* (1845), p. 906a–b; also Seward, Message of 1841, in Charles Z. Lincoln, ed., *Messages from the Governors*, 3:882–87, and [Catharine Beecher], *Duty of American Women to their Country*.

6. Kent, *Address delivered at New Haven*, pp. 47–48; and cf. Lyman Beecher, *Address at Miami University*, pp. 3–4, 41–43; Horace Bushnell, Oration at New Haven, in Clark S. Northup, ed., *Representative Phi Beta Kappa Orations*,

pp. 19–23; William C. Handley, *Anniversary Oration at Mercer University;* and William H. Seward, *The Destiny of America*, pp. 22–25; and see chapter X, note 3.

7. [Channing], "The Abuses of Political Discourse," *No. Am. Rev.* 4, no. 11 (January 1817), 193–201; [Sparks], "Appropriation of Public Lands for Schools," ibid. 13, no. 33 (October 1821), 310–42; [Kingsley], "Connecticut School Fund," ibid. 16, no. 38 (April 1823), 379–96; [Ticknor], "Free Schools of New England," ibid. 19, no. 45 (October 1824), 448–57; [Dewey], "Popular Education," ibid. 23, no. 52 (July 1826), 49–67.

8. Picket, "Opening Address," *Transactions of the Western Literary Institute*, 6 (1837), 38–40; Campbell, "Closing Address," ibid. 6, pp. 253–56; Picket, ibid. 6, p. 42; Stowe, "Report, on the Course of Instruction in the Common Schools of Prussia and Wirtemberg," ibid. 7 (1838), 204–28; Lewis, "The Expediency of Adopting Common School Education to the Entire Wants of the Community," ibid., pp. 52–60; and see Allen O. Hansen, *Early Educational Leadership in Ohio Valley.*

9. Wilson, "Universal Instruction," *Transactions of the Western Literary Institute* 6 (1837), 64–66; Thomas S. Grimké, "American Education," ibid. 4 (1835), 103–4; T. J. Biggs, "Lecture on Domestic Education," ibid. 5 (1836), 47–59; Aydelott, "Address on the Duties of American Citizens," ibid. 9 (1840), 50–62; and the anonymous introduction to vol. 5, p.5.

10. Bushnell, *Common Schools*, p. 5. For examples of Protestant pressure for truly religious schools, see "Religious Instruction in Common Schools," *Biblical Repertory and Princeton Review* 13, no. 3 (July 1841), 315–68, and D. F. Robertson, *National Destiny and Our Country*, pp. 28–34, as well as Lewis J. Sherrill, *Presbyterian Parochial Schools*, and Raymond B. Culver, *Horace Mann and Religion in Massachusetts.*

11. Sidney Jackson is especially sensitive to the ways in which conservatives viewed the schools as an agency of social control; see *America's Struggle for Free Schools*, ch. 3–5, 9. A number of contemporaries clearly perceived them as the moral equivalent of a religious establishment; see Mann, Report for 1848, *Life and Works*, 4:312, and Bushnell, *Common Schools*, pp. 6–8. Other writers also implied as much; see particularly Baynard Hall, *Righteousness the safe-guard of nation*, pp. 15–18, and [Catharine Beecher], *Duty of American Women to their Country.* See also Mead, *The Lively Experiment*, ch. 4; David Tyack, "The Kingdom of God and the Common School," *Harvard Educational Review* 36 (1966), 447–69; and Paul H. Mattingly, "Educational Revivals in Ante-Bellum New England," *History of Education Quarterly* 11 (1971), 39–71. Mattingly stresses the evangelical attitudes with which leading advocates of educational reform approached their cause, pressing their hearers to undertake it as a duty rather than a professional career.

12. Kent, *Address delivered at New Haven*, p. 16; [Packard], *Thoughts on Popular Education*, p. 16; Field, in *N.J. C. C.* (1844), p. 402; and see "Religious Instruction in Common Schools," p. 317. The examples of New England–born fig-

ures who appealed to the precedents of the 1640s are legion; see, for example, James G. Carter, *Essays upon Popular Education*, pp. 19–20; Caleb Cushing, "Introductory Lecture," *Introductory Discourse and Lectures before the American Institute of Instruction, 1834*, pp. 25–28; and "An Appeal to the Citizens of Massachusetts, in behalf of their Public Schools," *Common School Journal* 2, no. 4 (15 February 1840), 54.

13. "American Education," *No. Am. Rev.* 48, no. 102 (January 1839), 310, and cf. Carter, *Essays upon Popular Education*, pp. 20–21; Mann, Report for 1846, *Life and Works*, 4:116–30; and Noah Porter, *Necessity of Improving the Common Schools*, p. 16. For examples of outright hostility to tax support as "agrarianism," see "Agrarian and Education Systems," *Southern Review* 6, no. 11 (August 1830), 1–32; and William Harper, *Anniversary Oration*, p. 12.

14. Webster, in *Mass. C. C.* (1820–1821), pp. 314, 315; Picket, "Opening Address," pp. 51–52; also Edward Everett, "Education Favorable to Liberty, Knowledge, and Morals" (1835), *Orations and Speeches*, 1:599–633; Mann, "The Necessity of Education in a Republican Government," pp. 183–84; and William Slocomb, "Address on Education," *Transactions of the Western Literary Institute*, 8 (1839), 242. Webster used the same phrases in "First Settlement of New England" (1820), *Writings and Speeches*, 1:217–18.

15. Eaton, as quoted by David M. Ludlum, *Social Ferment in Vermont*, p. 237; also Carter, *Essays upon Popular Education*, pp. 20–21; Stevens, Plea for Free Schools, pp. 61–62, 65; James Parker, in *N.J. C. C.* (1844), p. 403; and Bushnell, *Common Schools*, pp. 7–8; and see Ruth M. Elson, *Guardians of Tradition*, esp. p. 145.

16. Mann, Report for 1848, pp. 250–51; also Edward Everett, "On the Importance of Scientific Knowledge to Practical Men . . ." (1827), *Orations and Speeches*, 1:256–66, 269–70; Everett, "Fourth of July at Lowell" (1830), ibid. 2:54–65; William H. Seward, Address at a Sunday-School Celebration (1839), *Works*, 3:209–10; and Seward, Address of August 15, 1839, ibid., p. 213.

17. Michael Katz has demonstrated the existence of significant class divisions over educational reform in the first part of his book, *Irony of Early School Reform*, which deals with popular attitudes toward the public high school in Beverly, Massachusetts. Political histories of other states often indicate a comparable division of opinion; see, for example, Lee Benson, *The Concept of Jacksonian Democracy*, chs. 5, 14.

18. "Amos Kendall," *Dem. Rev.* 1, no. 4 (March 1838), 404; Judd, in *Wisc. C. C.* (1846), p. 569; and cf. remarks of Charles Reemelin and William Sawyer in *Ohio C. C.* (1850–1851), 2:11a, 16b–17b.

19. Morton, "Address of His Excellency Marcus Morton, to the Two Branches of the Legislature," *Massachusetts House Documents, 1840*, no. 9, pp. 29–31; Report of the Committee on Education, ibid., no. 49, p. 6; "Public Instruction in Michigan," *Dem. Rev.* 2, no. 8 (July 1838), 374.

20. Luther, *Address to Workingmen*, pp. 21–22; Report of the Joint Committees of

the City and County of Philadelphia, in John Commons et al., eds., *Documentary History of American Industrial Society*, 5:96–101, 103–5; Resolutions of a Workingmen's convention in Boston (1833), as quoted by Leonard D. White, *The Jacksonians*, p. 407; also Stephen Simpson, *The Working Man's Manual*, pp. 24–26, 200–1; Frances Wright, *Lecture on Existing Evils*, passim; Robert Walker, in Myer Moses, *Full Annals of the Revolution in France* (second pagination), pp. 113–14; and the accounts in Fitzwilliam Byrdsall, *History of Loco-Foco Party*, pp. 88–89, 172, and Hobart Berrian, *Brief Sketch of Workingmen's Party*, passim.

21. Skidmore, *Rights of Man to Property!* p. 369; Brownson, "The Laboring Classes," *Boston Quarterly Review* 3, no. 11 (July 1840), 364–66, 375; "Education," *Voice of Industry*, 14 January 1848, 2e; also [Paul Brown], *The Radical: And Advocate of Equality*, esp. pp. 7–10, 78–80, 127–28, 144–47; "The Boston Association of the Friends of the Rights of Man," *Boston Quarterly Review* 1, no. 2 (April 1838), 229; and *The Condition of Labor*, esp. pp. 10, 30.

22. Report of the Joint Committees of Philadelphia, in Commons et al., eds., *Documentary History of American Industrial Society*, 5:99; Berrian, *Brief Sketch of Workingmen's Party*, p. 2; and cf. the Declaration of Rights of the Equal Rights Party (written by Moses Jaques), in Jabez D. Hammond, *History of Political Parties in New York*, 2:497.

23. Rantoul, "An Address to the Workingmen of the United States of America," *Memoirs*, p. 240; Woodbury, "An Address on the Remedies for Certain Defects in American Education," *Writings*, 3:53; also Lewis Cass, *Address before Alumni of Hamilton College*, p. 7; Resolutions of the Democratic members of the legislature of Wisconsin (1847), as found in Milo M. Quaife, ed., *Struggle over Ratification*, p. 321; Hammond, *History of Political Parties in New York*, 2:536; and see ch. 4 of my book, *Popular Education and Democratic Thought*.

24. Preston, in *La. C. C.* (1845), p. 269a; [O'Sullivan], "The Great Nation of Futurity," *Dem. Rev.* 6, no. 23 (November 1839), 428; and cf. remarks of Horace Butler in *Ill. C. C.* (1847), p. 568, and chapter X, note 25.

25. Williams, in *Mich. C. C.* (1835), pp. 223–24; "Of the Intelligence of the People," *Dem. Rev.* 8, no. 34 (October 1840), 360–66, 365; "Mr. Forrest's Oration," ibid. 3, no. 9 (September 1838), 55; also George Bancroft, *Oration before the Democracy of Springfield*, pp. 20–21, 24; Bancroft, "The Office of the People in Art, Government, and Religion" (1835), in his *Literary and Historical Miscellanies*, pp. 428–30; William Leggett, *Political Writings*, passim; and "Report of the Committee on Education" (written by George Mayo), in *La. C. C.* (1845), pp. 316–19.

26. Van Valkenburgh, in *Mich. C. C.* (1850), p. 266a, and cf. Calvin Britain, in ibid., p. 274b; Bevans, as found in *Wisc. C. C.* (1846), 575; and note Henry L. Pinckney, *Necessity of Popular Enlightenment to the State*, passim.

27. Pierce, as found in Charles O. Hoyt and R. Clyde Ford, *John D. Pierce*, p. 94; Moore, in *Mich. C. C.* (1850), p. 543a.

28. For examples of the connections Whigs often made between internal improvements and education, see William H. Seward, "Internal Improvements and Education" (1835), pp. 128–34, and *Missouri Statesman*, 27 May 1853, as quoted by James N. Primm, *Economic Policy in Development of Missouri*, p. 108.

29. Morton, "Address of His Excellency Marcus Morton, to the Two Branches of the Legislature," p. 31; also Robert Rantoul Jr., *Oration before Gloucester Mechanic Association*, p. 4; and Levi Woodbury, "Importance of Science to the Arts" (1831), *Writings*, 3:16, a statement that parallels Edward Everett's cited in note 14. For a classic debate on free schools, demonstrating the essentially nonpartisan character of both advocacy and criticism, see *Mich. C. C.* (1850), pp. 136–40, 256–76, 535–55, 774–91.

30. For an argument from efficiency, see Mann, Report for 1843, *Life and Works*, 3:241–42. For expressions of the belief that education liberates, see ibid., pp. 378–79, and Henry Barnard, Eighth Annual Report (1853), as found in John S. Brubacher, ed., *Henry Barnard on Education*, p. 74.

31. Channing, "Remarks on Education" (1833), *Works*, 1:369–87, 381–82; and cf. the educational aspects of his *Remarks on Associations formed by the Working Classes*, passim; "Self-Culture" (1838), *Works*, 2:347–411; and "Lectures on the Elevation of the Laboring Portion of the Community" (1840), ibid., 5:151–230, in which he repeatedly demands that reformers contrive to call forth the man in the student of any age or condition.

32. Seward, *Discourse on Education*, p. 9. For other comparable statements by prominent political advocates of educational innovation, see William H. Marcy's messages to the legislature of New York in 1834, 1836, and 1837, in Lincoln, ed., *Messages from the Governors*, 3:455–56, 537–40, 611–15; Edward Everett's message of 1837, in *Massachusetts Senate Documents, 1837*, no. 1, pp. 6–7; his "Superior and Popular Education" (1837), *Orations and Speeches*, 2:224–29; and his "Normal Schools" (1839), in ibid., 335–62; and Daniel Webster, "Remarks on Common Schools" (1838), *Writings and Speeches*, 13:104–5. Typical statements by educational reformers include Carter, *Essays upon Popular Education*, pp. 10–16, 33–34, 42–50; the review by [Orville Dewey] in *No. Am. Rev.* 24, no. 54 (January 1827), 156–69; Catharine Beecher, *Suggestions respecting Improvements in Education*; the review by [Samuel Sewall] in *No. Am. Rev.* 30, no. 67 (April 1830), 323–37; [A. P. Peabody], "The District School Library," ibid. 50, no. 107 (April 1840), 505–15; [George B. Emerson] on Mann's first three Annual Reports, ibid. 52, no. 110 (January 1841), 149–91; and [George S. Hilliard], "The School and the Schoolmaster," ibid., 57, no. 120 (July 1843), 149–55.

33. Mann, Report for 1845, pp. 36–41, and compare the pedagogical discussions in his Seventh, Ninth, and Eleventh Reports, ibid. 3:278–79, 303–44, 373–79, 389–402, 435–522, and 4:163–71. For an extended critique of Mann's attitudes, see Jonathan Messerli, *Horace Mann*, passim. Paul H. Mattingly argues that improvements in pedagogy were not important to the

educational reformers of the Middle Period because they were committed only to the improvement of character, but it seems to me that he exaggerates the bias the reformers obviously felt toward the development of virtue (Mattingly, "Educational Revivals in Ante-Bellum New England," pp. 39–71). Bernard Wishy traces the liberalizing of attitudes toward children and childhood education in *The Child and the Republic.*

34. For early statements of this point of view, made against a republican rather than a democratic background, see Charles Jared Ingersoll, *Discourse Concerning Influence of America on the Mind,* pp. 36–37; Edward Everett, "The Circumstances Favorable to the Progress of Literature in America" (1824), *Orations and Speeches,* 1:9–44; John Quincy Adams, 8 February 1832, *Reg. Deb.,* 22d C, 1st S, col. 1773; and the remarks by Joseph D. McCarson and Hugh McQueen, in *No. Car. C. C.* (1835), pp. 187, 199.

35. "America for the Americans," *Putnam's Monthly* 5, no. 29 (May 1855), 540b; Stanton, *Ultraists–Conservatives–Reformers,* pp. 33–34; also Carl Schurz, "True Americanism" (1859), *Speeches, Correspondence and Political Papers,* 1:60–62.

36. "Dangers and Safeguards of the Union," *Am. Rev.* 9, no. 2 (February 1849), 119a.

37. Hornblower, in *N.J. C. C.* (1844), p. 131; Barnard, in Brubacher, ed., *Henry Barnard on Education,* p. 75; Beman, *Influence of Freedom,* p. 18; and see Daniel D. Barnard, *Political Aspects and Prospects in Europe,* p. 27.

CHAPTER XII: THE FRONTIER WEST
AS IMAGE OF AMERICAN SOCIETY

1. See Chapter X, notes 26 and 27; also John D. Pierce, in *Mich. C. C.* (1850), p. 659b, and Rep. George W. Julian's defense of the Homestead Bill, 29 January 1851, *Cong. Globe,* 31st C, 2d S, *Appendix,* p. 137a.

2. The classic studies of American land policy and polemics are (in chronological order) Raynor G. Wellington, *Political and Sectional Influence of Public Lands;* George M. Stephenson, *Political History of Public Lands;* Benjamin H. Hibbard, *History of Public Land Policies;* and Roy M. Robbins, *Our Landed Heritage.*

3. R. M. Johnson, 1 April 1828, *Reg. Deb.,* 20th C, 1st S, col. 576; Skelton, 19 March 1852, *Cong. Globe,* 32d C, 1st S, *Appendix,* p. 382c. Skelton's remark was a rebuttal to Rep. Thomas J. D. Fuller of Maine, whose argument is quoted at pages 303–4 of this chapter.

4. Hayne, 19 January 1830, *Reg. Deb.,* 21st C, 1st S, p. 34a–b; and cf. Sen. Johnson's remarks, ibid., 20th C, 1st S, cols. 574–75.

5. Benton, 18 January 1830, *Reg. Deb.,* 21st C, 1st S, p. 24a.

6. "How Stands the Case?" *Dem. Rev.* 3, no. 9 (September 1838), 10; Andrew Johnson, 29 April 1852, *Cong. Globe,* 32d C, 1st S, *Appendix,* p. 530c.

7. Bancroft, *History of the United States,* 5:165; Smith, 20 January 1841, *Cong. Globe,* 26th C, 2d S, *Appendix,* p. 196c.

8. Lewis, 7 January 1830, *Reg. Deb.*, 21st C, 1st S, p. 505b; Young, 7 January 1841, *Cong. Globe*, 26th C, 2d S, *Appendix*, p. 41a. The Representative from Vermont was Jonathan Hunt, who had sponsored a resolution recommending distribution to the states of the proceeds from the sale of public lands.

9. Gouge, *Short History of Paper Money*, pp. 43–44; "Thoughts on the Times," *Dem. Rev.* 6, no. 24 (December 1839), 447–62, esp. p. 454; also Robert Dale Owen, "One of the Problems of the Age," ibid. 14, no. 68 (February 1844), 167a–b, and "Pamphlets for the People," ibid. 33, no. 3 (September 1853), 216.

10. Fuller, 30 March 1852, *Cong. Globe*, 32d C, 1st S, *Appendix*, p. 390b; "New Territory versus No Territory," *Dem. Rev.* 21, no. 112 (October 1847), 291–92.

11. Allen as quoted by Schlesinger, *The Age of Jackson*, p. 153; Rhett, in ibid., p. 346; and cf. Orestes Brownson, "The Laboring Classes," *Boston Quarterly Review* 3, no. 11 (July 1840), 372.

12. Smith, *Virgin Land*, ch. 13, and note the editorial remark made by the *Wilmington* (North Carolina) *Daily Journal* in May 1854 to the effect that of all the measures by which the abolitionists seek to ruin the South, the Homestead Bill is "beyond comparison, the most iniquitous and most efficient for their evil purposes" (as quoted by Stephenson, *Political History of Public Lands*, p. 155). Rep. George W. Julian clearly justified their fears in his defense of the homestead principle on 29 January 1851 (*Cong. Globe*, 31st C, 2d S, *Appendix*, p. 139b–c).

13. Fuller, as in note 10; Evans, in *Young America*, 11 September 1847, as quoted by Joseph G. Rayback in "Land for the Landless" (Master's thesis, Western Reserve University, 1936), pp. 17–18; Pierce, in *Mich. C. C.* (1850), p. 659b; Dunham, 6 April 1852, *Cong. Globe*, 32d C, 1st S, *Appendix*, p. 410c; and cf. remarks of Robert Lucas, in *Iowa C. C.* (1844), pp. 159–60.

14. Kirkland, "The West, the Paradise of the Poor," *Dem. Rev.* 15, no. 74 (August 1844), 189b–190a; and cf. editorial remarks of the *Chicago Democrat*, 14 February 1848, as quoted by Rayback, "Land for the Landless," p. 21.

15. I have borrowed freely here from my own essay, "The Frontier West as Image of American Society: Conservative Attitudes before the Civil War," *MVHR* 46, no. 4 (March 1960), 593–614, which comments briefly on modern historiography as well as antebellum attitudes.

16. Morris, in Charles C. Tansill, ed., *Documents Illustrative of the Formation of the Union*, p. 357; Griswold, 25 October 1803, *Ann. Cong.*, 8th C, 1st S, col. 465; Pollock, 25 January 1845, *Cong. Globe*, 28th C, 2d S, p. 177b–c; and cf. [Daniel D. Barnard], "The Whigs and the War," *Am. Rev.* 6, no. 4 (October 1847), 333a–338a, 345b–346b.

17. Rush, as quoted by Harry G. Good, *Benjamin Rush and American Education*, p. 205; Richard Rush, as quoted by Wellington, *Political and Sectional Influence of Public Lands*, p. 28n; Greeley, in the *Log Cabin*, as quoted by Robbins, *Our Landed Heritage*, p. 83; *The Contrast: Whig and Democratic Platforms*, p. 7b;

and see the discussion of the opposition in Rayback, "Land for the Landless," esp. pp. 19, 33.

18. Dwight, *Travels in New-England and New-York*, 2:459.

19. White, "Influence of Colleges, especially on Western Education and Civilization," *Biblical Repository and Classical Review*, 3d ser., 4, no. 15 (July 1848), 383; and cf. "Western Literature," *N.-Y. Rev.* 5, no. 10 (October 1839), 384–86.

20. Neal, *Oration, Portland*, p. 25; "Responsibility of the Ballot Box," *Am. Rev.* 4, no. 5 (November 1846), 436a–b; and cf. Horace Bushnell, "Barbarism the First Danger," *Am. Nat. Preacher* 21, no. 9 (September 1847), 200.

21. "An Estimate of the Present and Future Physical, Civil, and Moral Power of the West, Including the Country Watered by the Mississippi and its Tributaries," *Quarterly Register and Journal of the American Education Society* 1, no. 4 (April 1828), 63a; "Political Power Moving Westward," *Home Missionary* 14, no. 12 (April 1842), 278.

22. [James Flint], Review of *Recollections of the Last Ten Years*, in *No. Am. Rev.* 23, no. 53 (October 1826), 355–56; "Estimate of the Present and Future Power of the West," p. 64a–b; and cf. Lyman Beecher, *Plea for the West*.

23. "Requisite qualifications of a Ministry adapted to the Wants of the West," *Biblical Repertory and Theological Review* [*Princeton Review*] 8, no. 3 (July 1836), 382.

24. Everett, "Education in the West" (1833), in *Importance of Practical Education*, pp. 164–65, 168–69.

25. Ibid., p. 169.

26. Bushnell, "Barbarism the First Danger," p. 219; and see a Baptist view of Lyman Beecher's *Plea for the West*, in "Condition and Wants of the West," *Christian Review* 1, no. 2 (June 1836), 248–63.

27. My essay "The Frontier West as Image of American Society: Conservative Attitudes before the Civil War," traces the changes in conservative thought more schematically than I do here. It also speculates rather inadequately on the causes for those changes.

28. Review of *Condensed Geography and History of the Western States, or the Mississippi Valley*, in *American Quarterly Review* 5, no. 10 (June 1829), 356; [Clarke], Review of *History of the Commonwealth of Kentucky* and *Sketches of History, Life, and Manners in the West*, in *No. Am. Rev.* 43, no. 92 (July 1836), 28; Peck, *New Guide to the West*, p. 114; and cf. Timothy Flint, *Condensed Geography and History of the Western States*, 1:207.

29. Beecher, *Plea for the West*, p. 12; Porter, *Educational Systems of Puritans and Jesuits Compared*, p. 94.

30. Bushnell, "Barbarism the First Danger," p. 211; [E. Judson], "The Evangelization of the West. How Shall It Be Effected? And by Whom?" *New Englander* 4, no. 13 (January 1846), 38.

31. [Felton], "Forest Life," *No. Am. Rev.* 55, no. 117 (October 1842), 511; "Uses and Abuses of Lynch Law," *Am. Rev.* 11, no. 28 (May 1850), 459–61.

32. [Everett], Review of *Condensed Geography and History of the Western States*, in *No. Am. Rev.* 28, no. 62 (January 1829), 82.
33. Cushing, as quoted by Fred Somkin, *Unquiet Eagle*, p. 96; Seward, *Elements of Empire in America*, p. 26; and cf. *Address of Louisiana Native American Association to Citizens of Louisiana*, p. 13.
34. Clay, *Papers*, 2:829; Burges, 13 January 1830, *Reg. Deb.*, 21st C, 1st S, p. 521b; "Western Prairies," *Am. Rev.* 11, no. 28 (May 1850), 528b.
35. Greeley, as quoted by Robbins, *Our Landed Heritage*, p. 102; Julian, 29 January 1851, *Cong. Globe*, 31st C, 2d S, *Appendix*, p. 138b; and see Ruth M. Elson, *Guardians of Tradition*, pp. 180–84.
36. Lanman, "Agricultural Commerce of the United States," *Hunt's* 5, no. 3 (September 1841), 219.
37. Seward, 11 March 1850, *Cong. Globe*, 31st C, 1st S, *Appendix*, pt. 1, 267c–268a; Sparrow, *The Nation's Privileges*, pp. 32–34.
38. Martineau, *Society in America*, 1:291–92.
39. R. M. Johnson, 1 April 1828, *Reg. Deb.*, 20th C, 1st S, col. 573.
40. Holmes, as quoted by Roger B. Stein, *John Ruskin and Aesthetic Thought*, p. 16; *Kendall's Expositor*, as quoted in *Answers of Ex-Gov. Polk*, p. 32b. It should be noted that Holmes referred to the whole of the United States, not to the West alone, but the effect was the same. See also the comment by Perry Miller in "The End of the World" to the effect that the nineteenth century saw the final transformation of the seventeenth-century New Englanders' religious effort into a limitless agricultural and industrial expansion (*Errand into the Wilderness*, p. 236, and cf. Roderick Nash, *Wilderness and the American Mind*, ch. 2, on the views of ordinary men). So far as Kendall is concerned, Lynn Marshall notes that he expressed romantic visions of the West mainly to confirm his own gentility, but that in unguarded moments he was far more likely to perceive the region as a resource inviting exploitation. On one occasion he wrote of an impressively wild scene, "With improvements, the place might be made singularly romantic" (Marshall, "Early Career of Amos Kendall," pp. 57–58, and see p. 139.
41. The best published account of the agitation is in chs. 10, 12, and 13 of Stephenson, *Political History of Public Lands*, but see also Rayback, "Land for the Landless."
42. Grund, *The Americans*, p. 208; Perkins, *Speech on Transfer of Public Lands*, p. 17; and see John D. Freeman, *Oration at Natchez*, pp. 31–32.
43. "Claims of the West," *Quarterly Christian Spectator*, 3d ser., 6, no. 4 (December 1834), 514.
44. Kent, *Address at Union College*, pp. 11–13; "Western Literature," p. 384.
45. Romeyn, *Our Country and her Claims*, p. 8; Scott, "The Great West," *De Bow's Review* 15, no. 1 (July 1853), 50; also George Holley, *Oration at Peru*, p. 10; Abram P. Maury, *Address on Advantages of the United States*, p. 22; John A. Wilstach, *Imperial Period of National Greatness*, p. 12; and James C. Conkling, *Oration in Springfield*, p. 7b; and see the comment by Harriet Martineau, in *Society in America*, 2:164.

46. Kent, *Address at Union College*, p. 4; Olney, as quoted by Elson, *Guardians of Tradition*, p. 184; and see David A. Bokee, *Oration in Brooklyn*, p. 9b.
47. Grow, 30 March 1852, *Cong. Globe*, 32d C, 1st S, *Appendix*, p. 428b; also Sen. John P. Hale, 10 January 1851, *Cong. Globe*, 31st C, 2d S, p. 213c.
48. Seymour, *Speech at Tammany Hall*, p. 4a; also Isaac T. Preston, in *La. C. C.* (1845), p. 23a.
49. Dunham, 6 April 1852, *Cong. Globe*, 32d C, 1st S, *Appendix*, p. 410a; Dawson, 3 March 1852, ibid., p. 261a; and see remarks by Sen. John A. Dix during his defense of the war with Mexico, 26 January 1848, *Cong. Globe*, 30th C, 1st S, p. 257a; also those of John Tyler in his last annual message, in James D. Richardson, ed., *Messages and Papers of the Presidents*, 4:336.
50. Crary, in *Mich. C. C.* (1835), pp. 303–4; also James Brent, in *La. C. C.* (1845), p. 744a; *Racine Advocate*, 27 January 1847, as found in Milo M. Quaife, ed., *Struggle over Ratification*, p. 444; and Van Valkenburgh, in *Mich. C. C.* (1850), p. 67b.
51. "The Poetry of the West," *Dem. Rev.* 9, no. 1 (July 1841), 25.
52. Allan, *Oration at Centre College*, p. 15; Foote, *National Characteristics*, p. 31; and cf. remarks by Rep. Orin Fowler of Massachusetts, 31 March 1852, *Cong. Globe*, 32d C, 1st S, *Appendix*, p. 396a.
53. Lanman, "The Progress of the Northwest," *Hunt's* 3, no. 1 (July 1840), 39; Peck, "Elements of Western Character," *Christian Review* 16, no. 63 (January 1851), 77–95, 93–94, 95.
54. Thayer, 7 January 1858, *Cong. Globe*, 35th C, 1st, S, pp. 228c–229a.
55. Upham, "Kanzas and Nebraska," *No. Am. Rev.* 80, no. 166 (January 1855), 93–96, 96–97. Upham may have drawn upon, but he also clearly went beyond, George P. Marsh's accolade to the uniqueness of the American experience in *The American Historical School*, p. 27.
56. "Western Prairies," p. 528a; and see Roy E. Basler, *The Lincoln Legend*, p. 133.

CHAPTER XIII: CONSEQUENCES

1. For specific examples of this general tendency, see Louis Hartz, *Economic Policy and Democratic Thought;* William G. Shade, "Politics of Free Banking"; and Harry N. Scheiber, *Ohio Canal Era.*
2. The best single work on the developments I am interested in is Eric Foner's *Free Soil, Free Labor, Free Men;* if it were not for the fact that his study begins with the ideology of the Republican party and traces its origin to a handful of rather broadly stated ideas derived from the Jacksonian era, rather than establishing the ideas of the era and tracing them to their consequences in the confrontations of the 1850s, my analysis here might be unnecessary. Even so, it is worth noting that Foner's tendency to render ideas as the expressions of practical interests or as the instruments of Republican polemics works to limit his perceptions of their importance as sources of American behavior.

Other studies having major significance for my analysis include (in alphabetical order) Avery Craven, *Coming of the Civil War;* David Brion Davis, *The Slave Power Conspiracy;* Allan Nevins, *Ordeal of the Union;* Nevins, *The Emergence of Lincoln;* and Charles Warren, *Supreme Court in United States History,* vol. 2.

3. The literature on abolition and antislavery is large without necessarily being illuminating. Putting aside the studies that have sought to explain the rise of abolition by biographical or sociological analysis, which may be accurate but which is irrelevant to my purposes here, I have made the largest use of a number of essentially intellectual and institutional accounts of the movement. Chief among them have been Gilbert H. Barnes, *The Anti-Slavery Impulse;* Timothy L. Smith, *Revivalism and Social Reform;* Stanley Elkins, *Slavery;* Louis Filler, *The Crusade against Slavery;* Dwight L. Dumond, *Antislavery*—useful in spite of its reverence for the abolitionists—and Russel B. Nye, *Fettered Freedom.*

4. Ladd, *Essay on a Congress of Nations,* p. 607; Finney, *Lectures on Revivals of Religion,* p. 150. Ladd presented a less insistent rendering of his exhortation in an earlier version of his essay, *Dissertation on a Congress of Nations;* and cf. the instructions of the American Anti-Slavery Society to its agents, as quoted by Dumond, *Antislavery,* p. 180b.

5. Finney, *Lectures on Revivals of Religion,* p. 298; Whittier, "Justice and Expediency; or, Slavery considered with a view to its rightful and effectual remedy, Abolition," *Anti-Slavery Reporter* 1, no. 4 (September 1833), 60b; and cf. William Lloyd Garrison's famous "recantation" of colonization in the *Liberator* for 1 January 1831.

6. Finney, *Lectures on Revivals of Religion,* pp. 301–2; Weld, in *History of Pennsylvania Hall,* p. 123; and cf. the Declaration of the Antislavery Convention of 1833, which appears in *Old South Leaflets* no. 81, pp. 7–9.

7. *Politics and the Pulpit,* passim, esp. pp. 49–53; Gannett, *Relation of the North to Slavery,* passim; Cleland, *The Higher Law,* p. 8; also George Putnam, *God and our Country;* William H. Marsh, *God's Law Supreme;* and Hiram C. Estes, *The Condition of our Country.*

8. Robertson, *National Destiny and Our Country,* p. 41; Brooks, *Appeal for the Right,* p. 12; also John C. Holbrook, *Our Country's Crisis,* and George B. Cheever, *The Sin of Slavery,* esp. p. 15; and see George I. Rockwood, *Cheever, Lincoln and the Civil War.*

9. Robertson, *National Destiny and Our Country,* p. 41; Whittlesey, *The Perils of Liberty,* p. 14; also Brooks, *Appeal for the Right,* p. 13; S. G. Spees, *Discourse on University Liberty,* pp. 16–21; and Joseph E. Roy, *Kansas,* pp. 28–30.

10. Rice, *Harper's Ferry,* pp. 7, 7–8, and see p. 15, as well as Whittlesey, *Perils of Liberty,* p. 10.

11. Weller, 9 April 1853, as found in *Debate in the Senate,* p. 12b; also Caleb Cushing, *Oration before Tammany Society,* passim; and Daniel W. Voorhees, "The American Citizen," in *Speeches,* pp. 45–53.

12. Shields, *Speech on the Territorial Question,* p. 15; also "European Views of

American Democracy—No. II. M. de Tocqueville," *Dem. Rev.* 2, no. 8 (July 1838), 352–53; "Annexation," ibid. 17, no. 85 (July and August 1845), 7a–8b; and John A. Dix, "Speech on the Bill to establish a territorial government in Oregon," as found in O. C. Gardiner, ed., *The Great Issue*, esp. p. 162.

13. Britain, in *Mich. C. C.* (1850), p. 403a; Brownson, "The Presidential Election," *Brownson's Quarterly Review* 13, no. 4 (October 1856), 511. For a truly venomous attack on "Puritanism" and "fanaticism" by an old-line Democratic leader, see [John] Reynolds, *Reynolds' Olive Branch*, pp. 2–3, 13–19, 24; but see also the statement of a more moderate opponent of religious "fanaticism" in Samuel S. Hayes, *The Issues in Illinois*, esp. pp. 3b–4b, as well as Stephen A. Douglas's rebuke to the clergy, 14 March 1854, *Cong. Globe*, 33d C, 1st S, p. 618a.

14. Seymour, *Speech at Tammany Hall*, p. 9b; *Proceedings and Address of Democratic State Convention at Syracuse*, pp. 9–27; and cf. "Further Extracts from the Private Diary of a Certain Bank Director," *Dem. Rev.* 3, no. 12 (December 1838), 363–65.

15. Barnes, *Inquiry into Scriptural Views of Slavery*, chs. 2, 5, 7; Weld, *American Slavery As It Is*, passim; Sumner, "The Barbarism of Slavery," in *The Campaign of 1860*, Albany Evening Journal Tracts no. 10; also Spees, *Discourse on Universal Liberty*, p. 9; and Charles Hawley, *True Social and Civil Life*, pp. 21–26. George M. Frederickson briefly discusses the "white nationalism" of many antislavery spokesmen in ch. 5 of *The Black Image in the White Mind;* and see William H. and Jane H. Pease, "Antislavery Ambivalence: Immediatism, Expediency, Race," *AQ* 17 (1965), 682–95.

16. Weld, *American Slavery As It Is*, p. 7a; Edward Beecher, *Narrative of Riots at Alton;* and see Larry Gara, "Slavery and the Slave Power: A Crucial Distinction," *Civil War History* 15 (1969), 5–18, as well as Nye, *Fettered Freedom*, chs. 2, 4.

17. For expressions of antislavery sentiment that reveal an essentially conservative hostility toward mobocracy and popular prejudices, see not only Edward Beecher's *Narrative of Riots at Alton* but also *Narrative of the Late Riotous Proceedings in Cincinnati* (1836) and Albert Barnes, "The Supremacy of the Laws," *Am. Nat. Preacher* 12, no. 8 (August 1838), 113–28; as well as ch. 5 of Nye, *Fettered Freedom*.

18. Sickles, *Remarks on Relations of North and South*, p. 14; and cf. Reynolds, *Reynolds' Olive Branch*, pp. 3, 7–8.

19. Dix, *Speech on the Three Million Bill*, p. 11; Resolutions offered by Mr. Smith, of Wayne, as found in Gardiner, ed., *The Great Issue*, p. 51; and see Chaplain W. Morrison, *Democratic Politics and Sectionalism*, and Eugene H. Berwanger, *The Frontier Against Slavery*, as well as Eric Foner, "The Wilmot Proviso Revisited," *JAH* 56 (1969), 262–79.

20. *Address of Democratic Members of the New-York Legislature*, p. 15a; Field, as found in Gardiner, ed., *The Great Issue*, pp. 55–57.

21. [Chase], *Appeal of The Independent Democrats*, p. 6; Law, letter to G. A. Scroggs, Esq., 3 July 1856, as found in *Tracts for Americans*, p. 12a; also Rep. Caleb Lyon, *The Covenant of Freedom*, pp. 1a, 2b; and Timothy C. Day, *The Humbug and the Reality*, p. 7b.

22. Hamlin, *Kansas—Lecompton Constitution*, p. 6b; Burlingame, as found in *Speeches of Joseph T. Buckingham [et al.] at Free Democratic Meeting*, p. 15a.

23. Wade, as found in *The Nebraska Question*, p. 65b; also John Hardy, *Letter to a New-Jersey Farmer*, passim; and William H. Fry, *Republican "Campaign" Textbook*, p. 15; and see Foner, *Free Soil, Free Labor, Free Men*, ch. 6. In "The Natural Limits of Slavery Expansion: Kansas–Nebraska, 1854," *Kansas Historical Quarterly* 34 (1968), 32–40, Charles D. Hart deals systematically with the opinions that members of Congress expressed about the feasibility of slavery in the new territory. As he points out, their views varied widely; he fails, however, to stress the significance of the fact that northern Whigs were almost unanimous in insisting that slavery could or would be extended. Their agreement on this point, which contrasted with the mixed opinions expressed by southern Whigs and northern Democrats, suggests that the northerners thought they had found a sure charge with which to belabor their opponents.

24. Dixon, *Speech on the Thirty Million Bill*, p. 29; and cf. Rep. James Wilson, *Speech on Political Influence of Slavery*, esp. pp. 4, 16; and Hawley, *True Social and Civil Life*, p. 21. The Senator from South Carolina was James H. Hammond, who had delivered his famous "mudsill" speech on 4 March 1858.

25. "One of the People" [Moody], *Plain Statement to Honest Democrats*, p. 25; also Rep. James Dixon, *Speech against Extension of Slave Territory*, p. 13; and Benjamin F. Wade, in *The Nebraska Question*, pp. 66b–67a; and see Andrew W. Crandall, *Early History of Republican Party*, pp. 68–74.

26. Hammond, "Freedom National—Slavery Sectional," *The Campaign of 1860, Albany Evening Journal Tracts* no. 4, p. 8a; also Horace Bushnell, "Barbarism the First Danger," *Am. Nat. Preacher* 21, no. 9 (September 1847), 210; and George W. Julian, 29 January 1851, *Cong. Globe*, 31st C, 2d S, *Appendix*, pp. 135c–136b; and see Foner, *Free Soil, Free Labor, Free Men*, ch. 2.

27. Lincoln, Special Message to Congress, 4 July 1861, in *Collected Works*, 4:438, and cf. his message of 3 December, in ibid., 5:52–53; and also his speeches at Springfield (26 June 1858 and 17 July 1858), in ibid., 2:403–6, 519–20, and his speeches at Galesburg (7 October 1858) and Alton (15 October 1858) in ibid., 3:220–22, 299–304.

28. [Colton], *Junius Tracts* no. 9, p. 12; also Rep. Andrew Stewart, 22 January 1845, *Cong. Globe*, 28th C, 2d S, p. 174c; Rep. Edward S. Hamlin, *Speech on Annexation of Texas*, pp. 14–15; and see Justin H. Smith, *Annexation of Texas*, and Norman L. Trusty, "Massachusetts Public Opinion and the Annexation of Texas, 1835–1845" (Ph.D. diss., Boston University, 1964).

29. Weed, as quoted by Glyndon Van Deusen, *Thurlow Weed*, pp. 148–49; Wilson, *Speech on Political Influence of Slavery*, p. 10; also *To Voters of Second Con-*

gressional District of Ind., pp. 25–26, and *Address adopted by Whig State Convention at Worcester*, p. 11.

30. Webster, 7 March 1850, *Cong. Globe*, 31st C, 1st S, pp. 269c–276c, esp. pp. 274a–275a; and see Holman Hamilton, *Prologue to Conflict*.

31. Charles W. Upham clearly expressed the Whig sense that the South must either keep the sectional bargain or jeopardize the nation's peace and unity in his *Eulogy of Zachary Taylor*, esp. pp. 38–39, as well as in subsequent speeches.

32. Seward, 17 February 1854, as found in *The Nebraska Question*, p. 98a; and see the speech by M. L. Rickerson in the New York legislature in behalf of Seward's candidacy for reelection, in *United States Senatorial Question*, p. 24a. At the same time, Seward's speech also illustrated the Whigs' continued appeal to constitutional stasis. Far from invoking the "higher law" that he had employed against the Compromise of 1850, Seward pleaded with the Senate to uphold that resolution of sectional issues.

33. See *Kansas Affairs*, p. 4; also "One of the People," *The Coming Struggle*, passim; the petition circulated in Illinois in 1856 asking for a special session of the state legislature to help protect the lives and property of prospective settlers in the Territory (*To his Excellency, JOEL A. MATTESON*); and the remark made by Charles Ballance, an Old Line Whig in Illinois, to Lyman Trumbull: "With regard to general politics," he wrote in 1860, "our people are generally moderate men—opposed to extremes . . . and are willing to be foiled in our projects, provided the union is safe—provided the country is quiet and prosperous. The majority of us are opposed to the fugitive slave law, but for the sake of peace we say let it be enforced; but when an attempt is made to open up the slave trade, or force slavery into the territories . . . there is no difference of opinion here" (as quoted by Foner, *Free Soil, Free Labor, Free Men*, p. 209).

34. "Address to the People of the United States," *Republican Documents*, p. 15.

35. Wright, *Two Letters to Gov. Hunt*, p. 16; "A Democrat," *Address to Voters of Indiana*, p. 16. For an early expression of this same view, see Rep. Harmon S. Conger, *Speech on the bill Organizing Government in Oregon*, pp. 5–6; and cf. "A Whig of the Free States" [John Calvin Adams], *A Northern No!* passim.

36. For the Lincoln-Douglas debates, see Paul M. Angle, ed., *Created Equal?* esp. pp. 77–80, 218–20, 308–11, 355–57, 394–96; Evarts, "The Issues of the Day," in *The Campaign of 1860, Albany Evening Journal Tracts* no. 18, p. 11; and see the account of contemporary attitudes toward the Court both before and after the decision, in Warren, *Supreme Court in United States History*, 2:207–309 passim.

37. Leach, *Bogus Democracy Exposed*, p. 7b; also Rep. Israel Washburn Jr., 10 January 1859, *Cong. Globe*, 35th C, 2d S, pp. 299a–302c.

38. Dix, *Speech on the Three Million Bill*, p. 13; Shields, *Speech on the Territorial Question*, p. 11.

39. David Wilmot, Address at the Herkimer Convention (1847), in Gardiner,

ed., *The Great Issue*, p. 62, and cf. the Address of the Utica Convention (1848), ibid., esp. pp. 85–92; Chase, 9 April 1853, as found in *Debate in the Senate*, p. 10a; and see Foner, *Free Soil, Free Labor, Free Men*, ch. 3, which stresses the Democratic origins of the campaign against the Slave Power.

40. *Free Soil, Free Speech, Free Men* (1856), p. 6; McCarty, as found in *Popular Sovereignty*, p. 4a.
41. McCarty, in ibid., p. 4b; Montgomery, *Speech on Admission of Kansas*, p. 1b; and cf. *Proceedings of State Rights Democracy Of Pennsylvania*, passim, as well as Foner, *Free Soil, Free Labor, Free Men*, ch. 5.
42. Hamlin, *Kansas—Lecompton Constitution*, p. 5a; and see Warren, *Supreme Court in United States History*, 2:279–309 passim.
43. Wilson, *Speech on Political Influence of Slavery*, p. 14; Wilstach, *Imperial Period of National Greatness*, p. 11; also Wade, 6 February 1854, as found in *The Nebraska Question*, p. 65a; and Sen. James Dixon, *Speech on the Thirty Million Bill*, pp. 29–30.
44. Dixon, ibid., p. 30; also [Moody], *Plain Statement to Honest Democrats*, pp. 23–26; Hammond, "Freedom National—Slavery Sectional," p. 8a; and see Ruth M. Elson, *Guardians of Tradition*, pp. 172–76, 314.
45. Seward, 11 March 1850, *Cong. Globe*, 31st C, 1st S, *Appendix*, p. 265a; also Sumner, 21 February 1854, as found in *The Nebraska Question*, p. 119b; and "One of the People," *The Coming Struggle*, pp. 4–5.
46. Seward, "The Irrepressible Conflict," in *The Campaign of 1860, Albany Evening Journal Tracts* no. 1; "Organization of the Party," *Am. Rev.* 10, no. 23 (November 1849), 444b; also [Moody], *Plain Statement to Honest Democrats*, p. 30; and R. V. Marsh, *Speech in the Vermont House*, pp. 10–11. Robert T. Oliver points out, in "William H. Seward on the 'Irrepressible Conflict,'" in J. Jeffery Auer, ed., *Antislavery and Disunion*, pp. 29–50, that Seward did not intend to exacerbate sectional tensions and that only his prominence as a prospective Republican presidential candidate lent significance to his unpremeditated expression of intransigence. The point is well taken, but it reinforces the proposition that conservative critics of slavery were led to embrace an ever broader definition of the differences between the North and the South without fully realizing what they were doing.
47. Hammond, "Freedom National—Slavery Sectional," p. 13b; Evarts, "The Issues of the Day," p. 13a.
48. Lincoln, as found in Angle, ed., *Created Equal?* pp. 1–2; and see the form letter the Republican party sent to its workers in Illinois, which held that "Illinois may be regarded as the center battle ground, or turning point, between the hosts of Freedom and the powers of Slavery. Let every true man act well his part!" (*Dear Sir: Confiding in your zeal and activity in behalf of Jeffersonian principles. . . .*) See also Don E. Fehrenbacher, "The Origins and Purpose of Lincoln's 'House-Divided' Speech," *MVHR* 46 (1960), 615–43, and "A New Look at the Great Debates," in *Prelude to Greatness*, pp. 96–120, both of which stress the political as well as the moral necessity Lincoln felt to distinguish his views from those of Stephen A. Douglas.

49. Hammond, *Address at Mashapaug Lake*, p. 28. Carl Schurz developed the historic imperatives of American freedom even more clearly in "True Americanism" (1859), *Speeches, Correspondence and Political Papers*, 1:48–72, and in his campaign speeches for Abraham Lincoln, several of which appear in *The Campaign of 1860*.

50. Mann, *Speech on Institution of Slavery*, pp. 10b, 11b. For more clearly religious expressions of the belief, see Brooks, *Appeal for the Right*, pp. 16–17, and Cleland, *The Higher Law*, p. 11. As Eric Foner notes, many Republicans clearly believed that putting an end to the expansion of slavery would also doom it in the South; hence they felt no need to consider the practical effects of their proposals (Foner, *Free Soil, Free Labor, Free Men*, pp. 115–23).

51. "One of the People," *The Coming Struggle*, p. 8; Fry, *Republican "Campaign" Text-book*, p. 108; and cf. Seward, 11 March 1850, *Cong. Globe*, 31st C, 1st S, *Appendix*, p. 264b.

52. See, for example, Leach, *Bogus Democracy Exposed*, pp. 7a–8b, and J. W. Gordon, *Indiana Democracy since 1854*, pp. 2–3.

53. Lincoln, Speech at Springfield, 26 June 1857, in *Collected Works*, 2:406; and cf. Angle, ed., *Created Equal?* pp. 33–34, 76–77, 81–82, 205–6, 298, 378–80, 384–86.

54. *Address of Democratic Members of the New-York Legislature*, p. 14a; and cf. Lyon, *Covenant of Freedom*, p. 2b.

55. Grover, as found in Gardiner, ed., *The Great Issue*, p. 108; *Free Soil, Free Speech, Free Men* (1856), p. 8; and cf. *Address of Democratic Members of the New-York Legislature*, p. 4a–b, and [Chase], *Appeal of The Independent Democrats*, pp. 1, 6–7, as well as Major Wilson's argument to the effect that westward expansion really defined the Union in all of its complexity and all of its promise for many liberal Democrats (Wilson, "Analysis of Ideas of Liberty and Union," ch. 4, and "The Free Soil Concept of Progress and the Irrepressible Conflict," *AQ* 22 [1970], 769–90).

56. Gardiner, ed., *The Great Issue*, pp. 19–20, and cf. pp. 7, 17.

57. Major Wilson discusses the attitudes of the Free Soil Democrats in "The Free Soil Concept of Progress and the Irrepressible Conflict." For Democratic charges of apostasy, see [John Van Buren], "Address to the Democratic Electors of the State of New-York" (1847), in Gardiner, ed., *The Great Issue*, pp. 51–54; [Van Buren], "Address of the Utica Convention" (1848), in ibid., pp. 88–89; *Address of Democratic Members of the New-York Legislature* (1848), p. 2a–b; Resolutions of the Democratic meeting at Indianapolis, as found in *Popular Sovereignty* (1858), p. 7b; the Address by Judge S. D. Johnston of Kansas, in ibid., p. 22b; and *Proceedings of State Rights Democracy of Pennsylvania* (1859), passim.

58. Hamlin, *Kansas—Lecompton Constitution*, p. 1a–b; also Rep. John Hickman, *Southern Sectionalism*, p. 8b.

59. Hammond, "Freedom National—Slavery Sectional," p. 10b, and cf. p. 6a; also Leach, *Bogus Democracy Exposed*, p. 6b.

60. Seward, 11 March 1850, *Cong. Globe*, 31st C, 1st S, *Appendix*, p. 264b;

Upham, "Kanzas and Nebraska," *No. Am. Rev.* 80, no. 166 (January 1855), 96.

61. Benton, as quoted by Benjamin Perley Poore, *Perley's Reminiscences*, 1:409–10.

62. Voorhees, "The American Citizen," *Speeches*, pp. 55, 54, and cf. the views expressed by Caleb Cushing, as quoted by Claude M. Fuess, *Life of Caleb Cushing*, 2:224–25.

63. Cox, 14 January 1861, *Cong. Globe*, 36th C, 2d S, p. 377c; also Reynolds, *Reynolds' Olive Branch*, pp. 3–4; and S. E. Perkins, *Speech at a Mass Meeting at Richmond, Ind.*, passim.

64. Tibbatts, *Speech on Reannexation of Texas*, p. 13a; Sickles, *Remarks on Relations of North and South*, p. 7. Tibbatts made the remark quoted here in 1844; it is appended to his speech of 1845.

65. Cushing, *Oration before Tammany Society*, p. 15, and cf. Reynolds, *Reynolds' Olive Branch*, pp. 4–5.

66. Cushing, *Oration before Tammany Society*, p. 14; also Benjamin Bailey, *Speech at Democratic County Convention*, esp. p. 2a, and Seymour, *Speech at Tammany Hall*, passim.

67. *Nashville Union American*, 5 April 1860, as quoted by George M. Stephenson, *Political History of Public Lands*, pp. 233–34; and see Stephenson's discussion of the homestead agitation, ibid., chs. 10–13. For a useful brief account of economic issues, see Henry H. Simms, *Decade of Sectional Controversy*, ch. 8.

68. Seymour, *Speech at Tammany Hall*, p. 1b, and cf. Frederick Grimke, *Nature and Tendency of Free Institutions*, bk. 2, ch. 1.

69. Sutherland as found in Mann, *Speech on Institution of Slavery*, p. 11a; Medary, in *Official Proceedings of National Democratic Convention [of] 1856*, p. 11; and see Hayes, *Issues in Illinois*, pp. 4b–5a, a moderate but no less significant criticism of Abraham Lincoln's high-handed attitudes toward the Supreme Court and the *Dred Scott* decision, which undertakes an explicit defense of the role and authority of the Court.

70. Buel, *Speech in Defence of the Constitution and the Union*, pp. 17–19; Buchanan, as quoted by James G. Randall and David Donald, *Civil War and Reconstruction*, p. 116; Sickles, *Remarks on Relations of North and South*, p. 16; and see Arthur Bestor, "The American Civil War as a Constitutional Crisis," *AHR* 69 (1964), 327–52, which exemplifies as well as examines the juridical perspectives that Americans brought to bear on the sectional crisis.

71. Northern reactions to the *Dred Scott* decision are usefully summarized in Warren, *Supreme Court in United States History*, vol. 2, ch. 26. One contemporary comment points up the difficulties it was virtually bound to cause: at some time during the 1850s Martin Van Buren wrote that the United States had been spared constitutional convulsions for many years because "the Supreme Court has occupied itself with its legitimate duties—the administration of justice between man and man—without being, as formerly, constantly assailed by applications for latitudinarian construction of the consti-

tution in support of enormous corporate pretensions. We might, perhaps, have expected that in such a calm even Mr. Jefferson's alarm, if he had lived to see it, would at least in some degree have subsided; but this state of things can only be expected to last until a similar or equally strong interest is brought under discussion of a character to excite the whole country and to enlist the sympathies of a majority of the Court and requiring the intervention of that high tribunal to sustain its unconstitutional assumptions, by unauthorized and unrestrained construction. Whether the institution of domestic slavery is destined to be such an interest remains to be seen" (Van Buren, *Autobiography*, p. 184).

72. For the origins of popular sovereignty, see Joseph G. Rayback, *Free Soil: The Election of 1848*, pp. 115–19.

73. The clearest assessment of Douglas's doctrine is to be found in ch. 3 of Damon Wells' *Stephen Douglas*, which I find more telling than pt. 2 of Harry V. Jaffa's *Crisis of the House Divided*, a study in conservative casuistry. See also James C. Malin, *The Nebraska Question*, ch. 1, and Wilson, "Analysis of Ideas of Liberty and Union," ch. 10; and Douglas's remarks in Angle, ed., *Created Equal?*, pp. 18–20. Robert W. Johannsen's *Stephen A. Douglas* appeared after I had written these lines.

74. For examples of an obvious and obviously unsuccessful effort to maintain popular sovereignty as a "democratic" principle in the face of growing northern hostility, see the remarks of Henry B. Payne in *Popular Sovereignty*, p. 30a; those of John A. Dix in *Grand Mass Meeting of the Democracy of New York!* pp. 2–3; and Hayes, *Issues in Illinois*, pp. 4b–5a.

75. Lincoln, as found in Angle, ed., *Created Equal?* pp. 143–44. As Don M. Fehrenbacher points out, Douglas had jeopardized his standing with southern Democrats by opposing the Lecompton Constitution well before he articulated the so-called Freeport Doctrine; hence it is impossible to attach great significance to that doctrine as an obstacle to his candidacy for President. Nevertheless this consideration applies only to his influence on southern opinion, whereas it seems quite clear that Lincoln intended to embarrass Douglas in the North, not the South (see Fehrenbacher, "Lincoln, Douglas, and the 'Freeport Question,' " *AHR* 66 [1961], 599–617).

76. *Exposition and Protest*, esp. pp. 6–7; *Address to the People of the United States*, in *Report, Ordinance, and Addresses of Convention of South Carolina*, pp. 31–34; *Proceedings of Jackson and Barbour Convention*, p. 7b; also *Address of Citizens of Richland Dist.*, p. 8; George McDuffie, *Speech at a Public Dinner*, esp. pp. 23–24; and the monthly *Political Tracts* published by the State Rights and Free Trade Association in Charleston in 1831–1832, esp. no. 3, *Catechism on the Tariff*; no. 4, *Taxes! Taxes! Taxes!*; no. 6, *The Prospect before Us*; and no. 8, *Free Trade and the American System*.

77. *Address to the People of the United States*, p. 15; *Address of Citizens of Richland Dist.*, p. 10; also *Memorial of Chamber of Commerce of Charleston*; Rep. McDuffie, 18 April 1828, *Reg. Deb.*, 20th C, 1st S, col. 2397; Sen. Robert Y. Hayne,

16 January 1832, ibid., 22d C, 1st S, col. 94; and *Catechism on the Tariff*, p. 7. For later charges of northern injustice, see *Proceedings of Democratic State Convention [of South Carolina]*, p. 10, and Thomas P. Kettell, *Southern Wealth and Northern Profits*, ch. 10. Weymouth T. Jordan documents the lasting sense of deprivation and "unnatural" intrusions on the southern economy in *Rebels in the Making*, ch. 1.

78. For examples of the charge of corruption, see the *Report of Committee of Twenty-One to Convention of South Carolina* in *Report, Ordinance, and Addresses of Convention of South Carolina*, pp. 5–6, and *Free Trade and the American System*, p. 11. For examples of unconquerable doubts that the federal constitution as it existed could maintain southern rights, see not only John C. Calhoun's writings, but also William Harper, *Remedy by State Interposition (Political Tracts* no. 5), passim.

79. Cheves, "Letter on Southern Wrongs, September 1844," in *Southern State Rights Tract No. 1*, pp. 1–14; and see "One of the People," *To Hon. W. J. Grayson*, pp. 7–8, as well as Jesse T. Carpenter, *The South as Conscious Minority*, chs. 4–5, and Wilson, "Analysis of Ideas of Liberty and Union," ch. 9.

80. Holmes, 14 January 1845, *Cong. Globe*, 28th C, 2d S, *Appendix*, p. 108b. Whigs clearly joined Democrats in reacting to northern prescriptions; see, for example, Rep. Abraham Venable, 1 June 1848, *Cong. Globe*, 30th C, 1st S, *Appendix*, p. 652b; *Political Acts and Opinions of Lewis Cass*, passim; Rep. Humphrey Marshall, *California and New Mexico*, p. 3a–b; and Sen. Archibald Dixon, 4 February 1854, *Cong. Globe*, 33d C, 1st S, pp. 142c–144a. For comparable statements by Democratic spokesmen during the 1850s, see Aaron V. Brown, *Address on Parties and Issues*, passim; *Official Proceedings of Democratic and Anti-Know-Nothing State Convention of Alabama*, p. 8; Robert J. Walker, *Appeal for the Union*, pp. 1–3; and "Vivo in Silvis," *Pamphlet on Equal Rights*, passim.

81. Calhoun, 6 February 1837, in *Works*, 2:628–29; "One of the People," *To Hon. W. J. Grayson*, pp. 8–10.

82. For an explicit example of southern attitudes toward the Court as a means of protection, see the *Southern Quarterly Review* for 1855 as quoted by Charles Warren: "The issue between the North and South on the subject of slavery affords an illustration of the necessity for a perfectly independent Judiciary, and shows how difficult it is for a Judge, responsible to the people of a particular section, to decide with impartiality, where the conflicting claims of two sections are involved. The Federal Judiciary, in its freedom from bias, has been the great trust of the South for the preservation of those rights which only need for their support a just interpretation of the Constitution and an unprejudiced judgment on the principles of law" (Warren, *Supreme Court in United States History*, 2:277).

83. Marshall, *Speech in the House of Representatives* (1859), passim; and see Steven A. Channing, *Crisis of Fear*. Washburn's speech is cited in note 37.

84. Campbell, 15 April 1842, *Cong. Globe*, 27th C, 2d S, *Appendix*, p. 337c;

Wise, 26 January 1842, *Cong. Globe*, p. 173c. Significantly, both Campbell and Wise began political life as Whigs but moved into the Democratic party in response to sectional controversy.

85. Fitzhugh, *Sociology for the South* and *Cannibals All; Virginia South Side Democrat*, as quoted by Crandall, *Early History of Republican Party*, pp. 77–78. The standard treatments of proslavery thought include William S. Jenkins, *Pro-Slavery Thought in the Old South;* Arthur Y. Lloyd, *The Slavery Controversy;* and Louis Hartz, *Liberal Tradition in America*, chs. 6–7.

86. For a useful brief discussion of northern responses to the proslavery argument, see Yehoshua Arieli, *Individualism and Nationalism in American Ideology*, pp. 298–309.

87. Henry Nash Smith discusses the southern argument and its consequences in chapters 12 and 13 of *Virgin Land*.

88. The invasion of Kansas, the agitation of imperial hopes, and the clamor to reopen the slave trade are discussed in Nevins, *Ordeal of the Union*, vol. 1, ch. 16, and vol. 2, ch. 10–12, and *Emergence of Lincoln*, vol. 1, ch. 16, and vol. 2, ch. 1 and app. 3.

89. Obviously these generalizations cannot be documented in detail here. For a revealing picture of a hesitant northern moralist who became increasingly inflexible (not to mention increasingly committed to democracy) as the war progressed, see Henry Ward Beecher's collected addresses of the period, *Freedom and War*.

90. Julia Ward Howe, "The Battle Hymn of the Republic," in Daniel J. Boorstin, ed., *An American Primer*, 1:382; and see not only William G. McLoughlin's discussion, in ibid., pp. 380–85, but also Ernest L. Tuveson, *Redeemer Nation*, pp. 199–202, which does far better the kind of literary analysis attempted by Edmund Wilson in *Patriotic Gore*, pp. 92–95.

91. Stephens to Lincoln, 30 December 1860, as found in Stephens, *Constitutional View of the War between the States*, 2:270.

92. For Douglas's role in 1860–1861, see Lionel Crocker, "The Campaign of Stephen A. Douglas in the South, 1860," in Auer, ed., *Antislavery and Disunion*, pp. 262–78, and Wells, *Stephen Douglas*, ch. 7, which stresses the long period during which Douglas sought to achieve a compromise between the North and the South as an alternative to war. Johnson's convictions were expressed in the Senate on 19 December 1860, *Cong. Globe*, 36th C, 2d S, pp. 134–43, esp. p. 142c.

93. For Lincoln's Second Inaugural I have used the version in his *Collected Works*, 8:333. Lincoln's religious beliefs are persuasively discussed by George Fox in *Abraham Lincoln's Religion;* with less insight by William J. Wolf in *The Almost Chosen People* and Edmund Wilson in *Patriotic Gore*, ch. 3.

94. Here I follow the version prepared by reporters who were at the scene, as found in Lincoln's *Collected Works*, 7:19–21.

BIBLIOGRAPHY

BIBLIOGRAPHICAL NOTE

This study is based upon a wide sampling of surviving publications (books, pamphlets, magazines, legislative proceedings, and official documents) of the years 1820–1850. I have made extensive use of the holdings of the American Antiquarian Society, which lend themselves to a fairly systematic sampling of publications of the period, and of the collections of other major research libraries such as the New York Public Library and the State Library of New York, where sampling of the literature is less convenient because of the manner in which it is stored or catalogued. I have also made a deliberate effort to counteract the regional bias that develops when one relies upon such collections to document the attitudes of Americans who lived in the South and West, whose thoughts were either less often committed to print or less likely to survive than those of their contemporaries in the Northeast. For this purpose I have examined perhaps half of the seemingly relevant titles named in the check lists of southern and western imprints originally compiled under the auspices of the W.P.A. and in some cases updated since then.

In approaching all of these materials I have tended, for reasons explained in my preface, to scant formal disquisitions on important philosophical topics (e.g., the idea of progress, the principles of liberty) and to pay relatively little attention to the statements of major literary commentators on American life. On the other hand, I have paid close attention to the deliberations of state constitutional conventions, the writings of journalists and polemicists, and the rhetorical effusions of politicians and other public men. Among the public and semi-popular sources I might have consulted, however, I have made very little use of contemporary newspapers, for two main reasons. First, such sampling as I attempted suggested that they commonly printed polemical materials that were in most respects the same as the materials that found their way into other kinds of publication; hence there was no pressing need to read them systematically. Second—and quite apart from such duplication—the labor of reading them *well* seemed disproportionate to the results that could be obtained. In order to make a truly effective use of newspapers it would probably be necessary to become a well-informed historian of the area in which each of them circulated, a task that could not be completed by one person in a lifetime.

For reasons of economy, titles listed under "Abbreviations Used in Appendices and Notes" are not repeated in this bibliography. For the reader's convenience, I have indicated in parentheses the location of every primary source that is not recorded for that location in the *National Union Catalog* of pre-1956 imprints or in the *Union List of Serials*. (Because the former is still in process of publication, I have chosen to record locations for all but the most common titles that are to be catalogued in its prospective volumes.) The multiplicity of these entries is eloquent testimony to the assistance a great many libraries have given me.

PRIMARY SOURCES

An Account of the Great Whig Festival, held in the City of Baltimore, on Thursday, Nov. 12th, 1835. Baltimore, 1835.

Adams, Jasper. Laws of Success and Failure in Life: An Address delivered 30th October, 1833, In the Chapel of the College of Charleston before the Euphradian Society. Charleston, S.C., 1833.

——. The Moral Causes of the Welfare of Nations: An Oration, delivered 1st November, 1834, in the Chapel, before the Society of the Graduates of the College of Charleston. Charleston, S.C., 1834. (MWA)

——. The Relation of Christianity to Civil Government in the United States: A Sermon, Preached . . . before the Convention of the Protestant Episcopal Church of the Diocese of South-Carolina. Charleston, S.C., 1833. (MWA)

Adams, John Calvin [A Whig from the Start]. An Appeal to the Whig National Convention, in favor of the nomination of Daniel Webster to the Presidency. New York, 1848. (N)

—— [A Whig of the Free States]. A Northern No! addressed to the Delegates from the Free States to the Whig National Convention at Philadelphia. N.p., n.d. (NN)

Address adopted by the Whig State Convention, at Worcester, September 18, 1848. Together with the Resolutions and Proceedings. N.p. [Massachusetts], n.d. (NN)

Address and Proceedings of the Ohio State Convention which met at Columbus, O. January 9, 1832, to Nominate a Governor. . . . Columbus, Ohio, 1832. (NN)

Address and Resolves of the Democratic Members of the Massachusetts Legislature of 1838, with a Sketch of Some Debates. N.p., n.d. (MWA)

An Address in relation to Free Common Schools. By a committee of the state education convention, held May 26, 1847. Indianapolis, Ind., 1847. (InHi)

An Address in relation to National Policy, Adopted by the Democratic State Convention, Held at Indianapolis, on the Eighth of January, 1844. Indianapolis, Ind., n.d.

Address of the administration standing committee to their fellow-citizens of Indiana. N.p., 1828. (InHi)

Address of the Citizens of Richland Dist. to the Citizens of South Carolina. Columbia, S.C., 1828. (ScU)

Address of the Democratic Central State Committee of Massachusetts. 1845. Boston Post. Extra. N.p., n.d. (NN)

Address of the Democratic Convention. N.p. [Tennessee, 1843]. (NN)

Address of the Democratic Members of the Legislature of the State of New-York. Albany Atlas, Extra, April 1848. (N)

Address of the Democratic Members of the Massachusetts Legislature to their Constituents and the People, at the close of the session for 1841. Boston Post. Extra. N.p., n.d. (MWA)

Address of the Democratic-Republican Central Committee to the Freemen of New-Hampshire. Concord, N.H., [1838]. (MWA)

Address of the Democratic State Convention, To the People of the State of Illinois. Springfield, Ill., 1841. (MoSMerc)

Address of the Free Trade Convention to the People of the United States. N.p. [South Carolina, 1828]. (ScU)

Address of the Friends of Domestic Industry, Assembled in Convention at New York, October 26, 1831. N.p., n.d. (MWA)

"Address, of the General Committee of Whig Young Men, of New-York City, to the Young Men of the State." With Notes, by a Democratic Republican. New York, 1834. (NN)

Address of the Great State Convention in favor of the Friends of the Administration, assembled at the Capitol in Concord, June 12, 1828 . . . . Concord, N.H., 1828. (NN)

Address of the Jackson Convention To the People of Missouri. N.p., [1828]. (MoHi)

Address of the Jackson State Convention to the People of Maryland, on the Late and Approaching Election of President. Baltimore, 1827. (NN)

Address of the Louisiana Native American Association to the Citizens of Louisiana and the Inhabitants of the United States. New Orleans, 1839. (NN)

Address of the Republican General Committee of Young Men of the City and County of New York, Friendly to the Election of Gen. Andrew Jackson to the Presidency, to the Republican Electors of the State of New-York. New York, 1828.

Address of the Whig Convention of Three Hundred Delegates, assembled at Dover, on the eighth day of June, 1852, To the People of the State of Delaware. Philadelphia, 1852. (N)

Address of the Whig State Convention. Indianapolis, 1844. (In)

Address of the Democratic Whig Young Men of the City and County of New-York: In Primary Meetings Assembled. N.p., [1841]. (NN)

Address to the People of Connecticut, Adopted at the State Convention, Held at Middletown August 7, 1828. with the Proceedings of the Convention. Hartford, Conn., 1828. (NN)

An Address, to the People of Maryland, from their Delegates to the Late National Republican Convention: Made in Obedience to a Resolution of That Body. Baltimore, 1832.

Address to the People of Mississippi, by the Committee appointed by the State Rights' Convention, assembled at Jackson, May 21, 1834. Jackson, Miss., 1834. (NN)

An Address to the People of the State of Illinois, on the Annexation of Texas to the United States, Reported, by a committee appointed for the purpose, to a meeting of the friends of Annexation, held in the State House, in Springfield, on the 8th of June, 1844. N.p., n.d. (MoSMerc)

Address to the People of the State of Missouri. N.p., [1840]. (MoHi)

An Address to the People of the United States, on the Subject of the Presidential Election: with a Special Reference to the Nomination of Andrew Jackson, Containing Sketches of his Public and Private Character. By a Citizen of the United States. N.p., 1828.

Address to the Republican People of Tennessee, by the Central Corresponding Committee of the State [No. 1.]. Nashville, Tenn., [1840].

"Address to the Whig Young Men of Connecticut," in *Young Men's Whig State Convention*. N.p., [1840]. (NN)

"Agrarian and Education Systems." *Southern Review* 6, no. 11 (August 1830), 1–32.

Aiken, John. *Labor and Wages, At Home and Abroad: in a Series of Newspaper Articles*. Lowell, Mass., 1849. (N)

Alcott, Amos Bronson. *Essays on Education (1830–1862)*. Edited by Walter Harding. Gainesville, Fla.; Scholars' Facsimiles & Reprints, 1960.

Alcott, William A. *The Young Man's Guide*. 2d ed. Boston, 1834. (NN)

Allan, James S. *Oration delivered before the Chamberlain Philosophical and Literary Society of Centre College, on the Fourth of July, 1835*. Cincinnati, Ohio, 1835.

Allen, William S. *An Oration, delivered in Newburyport, on the Fifty-fourth Anniversary of the Declaration of American Independence*. Newburyport, Mass., 1830.

"America for the Americans." *Putnam's Monthly* 5, no. 29 (May 1855), 533–41.

American Institute of Instruction. *The Introductory Discourse and the Lectures delivered before the American Institute of Instruction in Boston, August, 1834–1850*. Boston, 1835–1851.

American Lyceum of Science and the Arts, Composed of Associations for Mutual Instruction, and Designed for the General Diffusion of Useful and Practical Knowledge. Worcester, Mass., 1827. (MWA)

American Quarterly Review, vols. 1–22. Philadelphia, 1827–1837.

Andrews, Stephen Pearl. *True Constitution of Government in the Sovereignty of the Individual, as the Final Development of Protestantism, Democracy, and Socialism*. The Science of Society, no. 1. New York, 1851.

Andros, R. S. S., et al., County Committee. *Dear Sir: The approaching election.* . . . Broadside, dated Taunton, [Mass.], November 10, 1842. (MWA)

Angle, Paul M., ed. *Created Equal? The Complete Lincoln-Douglas Debates of 1858*. Chicago, Univ. of Chicago Press, 1958.

Answer of the Whig Members of the Legislature of Massachusetts . . . to the Address of His Excellency Marcus Morton, delivered in the Convention of the Two Houses, January 22, 1840. Boston, 1840. (NN)

Anti-Masonic Party. *The Proceedings of the Second United States Anti-Masonic Convention, Held at Baltimore, September, 1831*. . . . Boston, 1832. (N)

Appeal of The Independent Democrats in Congress, to the People of the United States. Shall Slavery Be Permitted in Nebraska? N.p., [1854]. (MWA)

"An Appeal to the Citizens of Massachusetts, in behalf of their Public Schools." *Common School Journal* 2, no. 4 (15 February 1840), 54–56.

Appleton, Nathan. *Labor, its Relations in Europe and the United States Compared*. Boston, 1844. (MH)

Argus Extra. Democratic State Convention. [Albany, N.Y., 1838]. (N)

Armstrong, William [An Old Resident]. *The Aristocracy of New York: Who They Are, and What They Were*. . . . New York, 1848.

Arnold, Thomas D. *Arnold's Review. To the Freemen of the Counties of Cocke, Sevier,*

Blount, Jefferson, Grainger, Claiborne, and Knox. Dated Knoxville, [Tenn.], May 24, 1827. N.p., n.d. (T)

Arthur, T. S. *Arthur's Advice to Young Men on their Duties and Conduct in Life.* Philadelphia, [1848].

——. *Rising in the World; or, A Tale for the Rich and the Poor.* New York, 1848. (NN)

"The Attitude of the South." *Commercial Review of the South and West: Agricultural, Commerical, Industrial Progress & Resources (De Bow's Review)* 29, no. 1 (July 1860), 25–31.

Atwater, Caleb. *An Essay on Education.* Cincinnati, Ohio, 1841.

Austin, Ivers J. *An Oration delivered by Request of the City Authorities before the Citizens of Boston.* Boston, 1839.

Austin, John M. *The Source and Perpetuity of Republicanism, A Discourse delivered in Auburn, N.Y., on Sunday Evening, October 27, 1844.* Auburn, N.Y., 1844. (N)

Austin, Samuel. *An Oration, pronounced at Newport, Rhode-Island, July 4, 1822.* Newport, 1822.

Aydelott, B. P. *Our Country's Evils and Their Remedy.* Concinnati, Ohio, 1843.

Bacon, D. Francis. *Progressive Democracy. A Discourse, on the History, Philosophy and Tendency of American Politics, delivered in National Hall, New-York City, before a Large Mass-Meeting of Whigs and Young Men.* New York, 1844.

Bailey, Benjamin. *Speech of the Hon. Benjamin Bailey, Delivered at the Democratic County Convention, held at Carmel, on Saturday Afternoon, October 8, 1853.* N.p. [New York State], n.d.

Baird, Robert. *View of the Valley of the Mississippi; or the Emigrant's and Traveller's Guide to the West. . . .* Philadelphia, 1832.

Balch, William S. *Popular Liberty and Equal Rights. An Oration, delivered before the Mass Convention, of the R. I. Suffrage Association . . . July Fifth, 1841.* Providence, R. I., 1841.

Baltimore Republican, 8 November 1828. (MWA)

Bancroft, George. *History of the United States from the Discovery of the American Continent. . . .* 10 vols. Boston, 1834–1874.

——. *Literary and Historical Miscellanies.* New York, 1855.

——. *An Oration delivered before the Democracy of Springfield and neighboring towns, July 4, 1836.* Springfield, Mass., 1836. (MWiW)

Barber, Edward D. *An Oration, Delivered before the Democrats of Washington County, at Montpelier, on the 4th of July, 1839.* N.p. [Vermont], 1839. (NN)

Barbour, B[enjamin] J. *An Address delivered before the Literary Societies of the Virginia Military Institute, at Lexington, On the 4th of July, 1854.* Richmond, Va. 1854. (N)

Barnard, Daniel D. *An Address Delivered at Amherst, before the Literary Societies of Amherst College, August 27, 1839.* Albany, N.Y., 1839.

——. *Political Aspects and Prospects in Europe: A Lecture delivered before the Young Men's Association in the City of Albany, January 31, 1854.* Albany, N.Y., 1854. (N)

Barnes, Albert. *The Church and Slavery*. 2d ed. Philadelphia, 1857. (MWiW)
——. *An Inquiry into the Scriptural Views of Slavery*. Philadelphia, 1857; reprint ed., New York, Negro Univs. Press, 1969. [First published in 1846.]
Barnum, P[hineas] T. *Life of P. T. Barnum Written by Himself*. New York, 1855.
——. *Struggles and Triumphs: or Forty Year's Recollections of P. T. Barnum*. Hartford, Conn., 1870.
Barton, Ira. *An Oration, delivered at Oxford, on the Forty-sixth Anniversary of American Independence*. Cambridge, Mass., 1822.
Bayard, Samuel J. *Address . . . at West Point, before the Graduating Class of Cadets, June 16, 1854. . . .* Camden, N.J., 1854. (N)
[Baylies, Francis.] *The Contrast; or, Military Chieftains and Political Chieftains*. Albany, N.Y., 1828.
[Beach, Moses Yale, comp.] *Wealth and Biography of the Wealthy Citizens of New York City*. For these and similar titles, see chapter VI, note 41 of this study.
[Beecher, Catharine.] *The Duty of American Women to their Country*. New York, 1845. (NN)
——. *The Evils Suffered by American Women and American Children: The Causes and the Remedy. Presented in an Address to Meetings of Ladies in Cincinnati, Washington, [etc.]. . . . Also, An Address to the Protestant Clergy of the United States*. New York, 1846.
——. *Suggestions respecting Improvements in Education, presented to the trustees of the Hartford Female Seminary. . . .* Hartford, Conn., 1829.
Beecher, Edward. *Narrative of Riots at Alton: in connection with the Death of Rev. Elijah P. Lovejoy*. Alton, Ill., 1838. (MWA)
——. "The Scriptural Philosophy of Congregationalism and of Councils." *Bibliotheca Sacra* 22, no. 86 (April 1865), 284–315.
Beecher, Henry Ward. *Freedom and War. Discourses on Topics Suggested by the Times*. Boston, 1863. (MWiW)
——. *Seven Lectures to Young Men on Various Important Subjects. . . .* Indianapolis, Ind., and Cincinnati, Ohio, 1844. (NN)
Beecher, Lyman. *An Address delivered at the Tenth Anniversary Celebration of the Union Literary Society of Miami University, September 29, 1835*. Cincinnati, Ohio, 1835.
——. *Autobiography, Correspondence, etc. of Lyman Beecher, D.D*. Edited by Charles Beecher. 2 vols. New York, 1864–1865.
——. *Lectures on Political Atheism and Kindred Subjects. . . .* (Beecher's *Works*, vol. 1). 3 vols. Boston, 1852.
——. *A Plea for the West*. 2d ed. Cincinnati, Ohio, and New York, 1835.
Beman, Nathan S. S. *The Claims of Our Country on Young Men: An Address before the Literary Societies in Hamilton College, . . . July 25, 1843*. Troy, N.Y., 1843. (N)
——. *The Influence of Freedom on Popular and National Education: A Lecture, delivered at the Opening of the Association Lecture Room, in the Athenaeum, Troy, February 24, 1846*. Troy, N.Y., 1846. (N)

——. *The Western Continent: A Discourse, delivered in the First Presbyterian Church, Troy, July Fourth, 1841.* Troy, N.Y., 1841. (N)

Benbow, William. *Grand National Holiday, and Congress of the Productive Classes, &c.* London, [1831].

Benedict, George W. *An Oration, delivered at Burlington, Vt. on the Fourth of July 1826.* Burlington, 1826. (N)

Bent, Josiah Jr. *National Jubilee. An Oration delivered at Braintree, July 4, 1826 . . . on the Fiftieth Anniversary of American Independence.* Boston, 1826.

Bent, N.T. *An Oration delivered at a Temperance Celebration of American Independence, at Raynham, July 4, 1842.* Taunton, Mass., 1842.

Benton, Thomas Hart. *Thirty Years' View; or, A History of the Working of the American Government for Thirty Years, from 1820 to 1850.* 2 vols. New York, 1854–1856.

Bergen, John G. *A Discourse on the Providence of God, over the Revolutions of Europe, in the Year 1848.* Springfield, Ill., 1849.

Berrian, Hobart. *A Brief Sketch of the Origin and Rise of the Workingmen's Party in the City of New York.* Washington, D.C., [1840].

Bethune, George W. *The Claims of Our Country on its Literary Men. An Oration before the Phi Beta Kappa Society of Harvard University, July 19, 1849.* Cambridge, Mass., 1849.

Blagden, George W. *Great Principles Associated with Plymouth Rock. An Address delivered before the Pilgrim Society of Plymouth, December 22, 1834.* Boston, 1835. (NN)

Blau, Joseph, ed. *Social Theories of Jacksonian Democracy: Representative Writings of the Period 1825–1850.* New York, Liberal Arts Press, 1954.

Bokee, David A. *Oration delivered . . . in the First Baptist Church, Brooklyn, July 4th, 1851.* [Brooklyn, N.Y., 1851.]

Boorstin, Daniel J., ed. *An American Primer.* 2 vols. Chicago, Univ. of Chicago Press, 1953.

Bosses and their Boys. Philadelphia, [1853].

Boston Quarterly Review, vols. 1–5. Boston, 1838–1842.

Brace, Charles Loring. *The Life of Charles Loring Brace, Chiefly Told in his Own Letters.* Edited by his Daughter. New York, 1894.

Brandon, Edgar E., ed. *A Pilgrimage of Liberty: A Contemporary Account of the Triumphal Tour of General Lafayette Through the Southern and Western States in 1825. . . . .* Athens, Ohio, Lawhead Press, 1944.

Bremer, Fredrika. *America of the Fifties.* Edited by Adolph A. Benson. New York, American-Scandinavian Foundation, 1924.

A Brief Report of the Debates in the Anti-Masonic State Convention of the Commonwealth of Massachusetts, Held in Faneuil Hall, Boston, December 30, 31, 1829, and January 1, 1830. Boston, 1830.

A Brief Sketch of Parties, the British and American, as connected with the American System: together with an account of the Extraordinary Doings of the Maine Legislature for 1831. Portland, Me., 1831. (MWA)

Brooks, A. L. *An Appeal for the Right. A sermon preached by Rev. A. L. Brooks, Pastor of the Third Presbyterian Church, Chicago.* Chicago, 1856.

[Brooks, Charles.] *Remarks on Europe, Relating to Education, Peace and Labor; and their Reference to the United States.* New York, 1846. (MWA)

Brown, Aaron V. *An Address on the Parties and Issues of the Presidential Election . . . delivered at Philadelphia, before the Key-Stone Club of that City, August 15, 1856.* Nashville, Tenn., 1856.

[Brown, Paul.] *The Radical: and Advocate of Equality: Presenting a Series of Expostulatory Animadversions on the Present State of Practical Politics and Morals; with a View to an Access of Improvement. Addressed to the People of the United States.* Albany, N.Y., 1834. (MH)

Brown, Samuel R. *The Western Gazetteer; or Emigrant's Directory, containing a geographical description of the western states and territories. . . .* Auburn, N.Y., 1817.

Brownlow, William G. *A Political Register, Setting Forth the Principles of the Whig and Locofoco Parties in the United States, with the Life and Public Services of Henry Clay. . . .* Jonesborough, Tenn., 1844. (NN)

Brownson, Orestes A. "The Presidential Election." *Brownson's Quarterly Review* (N.Y. ser.) 13, no. 4 (October 1856), 504–13.

——. *The Rich Against the Poor. The Laboring Classes. From the Boston Quarterly Review of July, 1840.* N.p., n.d. (N)

——. *The Works of Orestes A. Brownson.* Collected and arranged by Henry F. Brownson. 20 vols. Detroit, Mich., T. Nourse, 1882–1907.

Brubacher, John S., ed. *Henry Barnard on Education.* New York, McGraw-Hill, 1931.

Bryant, William Cullen. *See* Tremaine McDowell.

Buckingham, Edgar. *An Oration delivered at Trenton, Oneida County, New-York, July 4, 1842.* Utica, N.Y., 1842.

Buel, Alexander W. *Speech of Hon. Alex. W. Buel, in Defence of the Constitution and the Union. Delivered at a Public Dinner Given to him by his Fellow-Citizens, at Detroit, November 19, 1850.* Washington, D.C., 1851. (MWA)

——. *Speech of Hon. Alex. W. Buel, of Michigan, on Hungarian Independence, delivered in the House of Representatives, February 20, 1850.* Washington, D.C., 1850. (MWA)

Buffinton, James. *Kansas—the Lecompton Constitution. Speech of Hon. James Buffinton, of Mass., Delivered in the House of Representatives, March 24th, 1858.* Washington, D.C., 1858. (MWA)

Burges, Tristam. *Remarks Sent to the People Who Celebrated the 4th of July, 1835, at Woonsocket Falls.* Woonsocket Falls, R.I., 1835.

Burns, J. Randolph. *To the editor of the True Issue.* Texas broadside, n.p., [1856]. (TxU)

Bushnell, Horace. *The Census and Slavery: A Thanksgiving Discourse, delivered in the Chapel at Clifton Springs, N.Y., November 29, 1860.* Hartford, Conn., 1860. (MWA)

———. *Common Schools: A Discourse on the Modifications Demanded by the Roman Catholics, Delivered in the North Church, Hartford, March 25, 1853.* Hartford, Conn., 1853.

———. *A Discourse on the Moral Uses of the Sea. Delivered on board the packet-ship Victoria, at sea, July 1845.* New York, 1845. (N)

———. *Politics under the Law of God. A Discourse, delivered in the North Congregational Church, Hartford; on the Annual Fast of 1844.* Hartford, Conn., 1844. (NN)

———. "The True Wealth or Weal of Nations," in Clark S. Northup, ed., *Representative Phi Beta Kappa Orations.* 2d ed. New York, Elisha Parmele Press, 1930. Pp. 1–23.

Butler, Benjamin F. *Representative Democracy in the United States: An Address delivered before the Senate of Union College, on the 26th July, 1841.* Albany, N.Y., 1841.

Byrdsall, Fitzwilliam. *The History of the Loco-Foco, or Equal Rights Party: Its Movements, Conventions and Proceedings.* New York, 1842. (MH)

Calhoun, John C. *The Works of John C. Calhoun.* Edited by Richard K. Crallé. 6 vols. New York, 1851–1856.

Camillus [pseud.]. *The Essays of Camillus, addressed to the Hon. Joel Holleman. . . .* Norfolk, Va., 1841. (NN)

Camp, George S. *Democracy.* New York, 1841. (MWiW)

The Campaign of 1860, comprising the Speeches of Abraham Lincoln . . . [et al.]. Albany Evening Journal Tracts, nos. 1–18. Albany, N.Y., 1860 (N)

Capen, Nahum. *The History of Democracy: or, Political Progress, Historically Illustrated, from the Earliest to the Latest Periods.* Hartford, Conn., 1874. (NN)

Carey, Henry C. *Principles of Political Economy.* 3 vols. Philadelphia, 1837–1840.

[Carey, Mathew.] *The Crisis. An Appeal to the Good Sense of the Nation, Against the Spirit of Resistance and Dissolution of the Union.* 3d ed., corr. Philadelphia, 1832.

Carter, James G. *Essays upon Popular Education, Containing a Particular Examination of the Schools of Massachusetts, and an Outline of an Institution for the Education of Teachers.* Boston, 1826. (N)

Cass, Lewis. *Address . . . delivered, by appointment, before the association of the alumni of Hamilton College, at their anniversary meeting, August 25, 1830.* Utica, N.Y., 1830. (N)

The Cass Platform. [Washington, D.C., 1848.] (NN)

Channing, William Ellery. "National Literature." *Christian Examiner* 7, no. 36 (January 1830), 268–95.

———. *Remarks on the Associations Formed by the Working Classes of America. . . .* London, 1833.

———. *The Works of William Ellery Channing.* 1st complete American ed. 6 vols. Boston, 1841.

Chapin, Edwin H. *The Relation of the Individual to the Republic. A Sermon delivered before His Excellency Marcus Morton . . . at the Annual Election, on Wednesday, January 3, 1844.* Boston, 1844.

Chapin, Edwin H. *The Responsibilities of a Republican Government. A Discourse, preached Fast Day, April 8, 1846*. Boston, 1841. (NN)

Chapin, Stephen. *The Spirit of the Age. An Address, delivered before the Evangelical Society of the Columbian College, D.C. April 6, 1835*. Washington, D.C., 1835. (MH)

Chase, Salmon P., and Charles D. Cleland. *Anti-Slavery Addresses of 1844 and 1845*. London and Philadelphia, 1867. (MWA)

[Chase, Salmon P., et al.] *Appeal of The Independent Democrats in Congress, to the People of the United States. Shall Slavery Be Permitted in Nebraska?* N.p., [1854]. (MWA)

Cheever, George B. *The Century of Preparation, and the Means and Time of Fulfillment. A Sermon delivered before the Foreign Missionary Society of New York and Brooklyn, April 9th, 1854*. . . . New York, 1854. (MWA)

——. *The Sin of Slavery the Guilt of the Church, and the Duty of the Ministry. An Address delivered before the Abolition Society at New York, on Anniversary Week, 1858*. Boston and Cleveland, 1858.

Chevalier, Michel. *Society, Manners and Politics in the United States: Letters on North America*. Trans. from the 3d Paris ed. Boston, 1839.

Cheves, Langdon. "Letter on Southern Wrongs, September 1844." In *Southern State Rights, Anti-Tariff & Anti-Abolition Tract No. 1*. Charleston, S.C., 1844. Pp. 1–14. (NN)

Choate, Rufus. *Addresses and Orations*. 2d ed. Boston, 1878.

Cincinnati Daily Gazette, 26 January 1837.

"Claims of the West." *Quarterly Christian Spectator* (3d ser.) 6, no. 4 (December 1834), 513–24.

Clay, Henry. *Mr. Clay's Speech, Delivered in the City of Raleigh, N.C. April 13, 1844*. 4th ed. [New York], n.d.

——. *The Papers of Henry Clay*. Edited by James F. Hopkins. Lexington, Ky., Univ. Press of Ky., 1959–.

——. *The Works of Henry Clay*. . . . Edited by Calvin Colton. 7 vols. New York, [1890].

Cleland, Philip S. *The Higher Law. A Sermon, delivered in Greenwood, Ind., on Thanksgiving Day, November 20, 1856*. Indianapolis, 1856. (In)

Clowes, Timothy. *An Oration delivered at the Request of the citizens of Hempstead, L. I. The 57th Anniversary of American Independence*. Hempstead, N.Y., [1833]. (NNHi)

Cobbett, William. *A Year's Residence in the United States of America*. . . . 3 vols. London, 1818–1819.

Cole, G. D. H., and A. W. Filson, eds. *British Working Class Movements: Selected Documents 1789–1875*. London and New York, 1965.

Collins, George C. [An Irish Adopted Citizen]. *Fifty Reasons why Hon. Henry Clay should be Elected President of the United States*. Baltimore, 1844.

Colton, Calvin [Junius]. *American Jacobinism. Being a Sequel to the "Crisis of the Country."* N.p., [1840].

——. [Junius]. *The Crisis of the Country.* N.p., [1840].

——. *History and Character of American Revivals of Religion.* London, 1832. (NN)

——. *The Junius Tracts.* New York, 1843–1844.

——. [Junius]. *One Presidential Term.* N.p., [1840]. (NN)

——. *Thoughts on the Religious State of the Country; with Reasons for Preferring Episcopacy.* 2d ed. New York, 1836.

Commons, John R., et al., eds. *A Documentary History of American Industrial Society.* Prepared under the auspices of the American Bureau of Industrial Research, with the cooperation of the Carnegie Institution of Washington. 10 vols. Cleveland, Ohio, A. H. Clark, 1910–1911.

A Compilation of Political Historic Sketches, or, The Democratic and Federal Parties in the United States. From their Origin to A. D. 1838. . . . Carrollton, Ohio, 1838.

"Condition and Wants of the West." *Christian Review* 1, no. 2 (June 1836), 248–63.

The Condition of Labor. An Address to Members of the Labor Reform League of New England. Boston, 1847. (NN)

Conger, Harmon S. *Speech of Mr. Conger, of New-York, on the bill Organizing a Government in the Territory of Oregon. Delivered in the House of Representatives of the U. S., July 25, 1848.* Washington, D.C., 1848. (N)

Conkling, James C. *Oration . . . delivered in Springfield, Ill., July 4th, 1857.* N.p., n.d. (IHi)

The Constitution of the State Rights and Free Trade Association of South Carolina, with the Address Prefixed as adopted by the State Rights and Free Trade Party of Charleston . . . 25th July, 1831. Charleston, S.C., 1831. (NN)

The Contrast; The Whig and Democratic Platforms—the Whig and Democratic Candidates for the Presidency. N.p., [1852].

Cooley, James E. *Speech of the Hon. James E. Cooley, before the Democracy of Syracuse, in Mass Meeting Assembled, on Tuesday Evening, Nov. 1, 1853.* Syracuse, N.Y., 1853. (N)

Cooper, James Fenimore. *Notions of the Americans Picked Up by a Traveling Bachelor.* 2 vols. Philadelphia, 1828.

Cooper, Thomas. *The Life of Thomas Cooper.* London, 1872.

Cox, Samuel H. *The Bright and Blessed Destination of the World: A Discourse delivered at Pittsfield, Mass., on . . . Tuesday, Sept. 11, 1849, before the American Board of Commissioners for Foreign Missions.* New York, 1849. (MWA)

Craven, Avery, et al., eds. *A Documentary History of the American People.* Boston, Ginn, 1951.

The Crisis Met. A Reply to Junius. New York, 1846. (NN)

Cushing, Caleb. *Oration . . . before the Tammany Society, or Columbian Order at Tammany Hall, On Monday, July 5th, 1858.* New York, 1858. (N)

Cushman, R. W. *Elements of Success. An Address delivered before the First Annual Meeting of the Alumni Association of Columbian College, Washington, D.C.* Washington, 1848. (MH)

Day, Timothy C. *The Humbug and the Reality. An Address to the People of the First Congressional District of Ohio.* Washington, D.C., 1856. (NN)

Dayton, Aaron Ogden. *Address delivered before the American Whig and Cliosophic Societies of the College of New Jersey. September 24, 1839.* Princeton, N.J., 1839. (NN)

Dear Sir: Confiding in your zeal and activity in behalf of Jeffersonian principles. . . . Form letter, dated State Central Committee Rooms, Chicago, April 23, 1858. (IHi transcript)

Debate in the Senate of the United States. Public Printing—Ohio Politics—The Old Line and Independent Democracy. In Senate, Saturday, April 9th, 1853. N.p., n.d. (NN)

A Democrat [pseud.]. *An Address to the Voters of Indiana.* Indianapolis, Ind., 1856.

Democratic State Convention. Argus Extra. [Albany, N. Y., 1838.] (N)

Dewey, Chester. "Permanence of Free Institutions." *Biblical Repository and Classical Review* 8, no. 24 (October 1836), 257–85.

Dix, John A. *Address delivered before the Alpha Phi Delta and Englossian Societies of Geneva College on the 7th of August, 1839.* Albany, N.Y., 1839. (MWA)

——. *An Address delivered by John A. Dix, Before the Democracy of Herkimer County, at the Village of Herkimer, on the 4th of July, 1840.* N.p., n.d. (N)

——. *Speech of Hon. John A. Dix, on the Three Million Bill. Delivered in the Senate of the United States, March 1, 1847.* Washington, D.C., 1847. (MWA)

——. *The War with Mexico. Speech of Hon. John A. Dix, of New York, in the Senate of the United States, January 26, 1848, on the Bill reported from the Committee on Military Affairs to raise, for a limited time, an additional Military Force.* Washington, D.C., n.d. (MWA)

Dixon, James. *Speech of Hon. James Dixon, on the Thirty Million Bill, for the Acquisition of Cuba. Delivered in the Senate of the United States, February 25, 1859.* Washington, D.C., 1859. (MWA)

——. *Speech of James Dixon, of Connecticut. Delivered in the Senate of the United States, February 9, 1858.* Washington, D.C., 1858. (MWA)

——. *Speech of Mr. Dixon, of Connecticut, against the Extension of Slave Territory. Delivered in the House of Representatives of the U. S. Feb. 9, 1847.* Washington, D.C., 1847. (MWA)

Doheny, Michael. *The Principle, Progress, Tendency, Obligations and Destiny of Democracy.* New York, 1853. (N)

Drake, Charles D. *The Duties of American Citizens: An Address delivered before the Franklin Society of St. Louis, on the occasion of its Second Anniversary, January 7th, 1837.* St. Louis, 1837.

Duncan, [Alexander]. *Speech of Mr. Duncan, of Ohio, In the House of Representatives, Feb. 19, in Committee on the Army Appropriation Bills.* N.p., [1845]. (NN)

Dwight, Timothy. *Travels in New-England and New-York.* 4 vols. New Haven, Conn., 1821–1822.

[Dyer, Oliver.] *Oliver Dyer's Phonographic Report of the Proceedings of the National Free Soil Convention at Buffalo, N.Y. August 9th and 10th, 1848.* Buffalo, N.Y., n.d. (N)

Eaton, George Washington. *Address, and Poem, delivered before the Beta of the Sigma Phi, at its Anniversary Meeting, Clinton, July 26th, 1842*. Utica, N.Y., 1842. (N)

"Education." *Voice of Industry* 3, no. 27 (14 January 1848), 2. (MB)

Edwards, John C. *Address of John C. Edwards, to the People of Missouri*. N.p., [1844]. (MoHi)

———. *Inaugural Address of Governor Edwards. Delivered in the Hall of Representatives, November 20, 1844*. N.p., n.d. (NN)

Ellsworth, Henry L. *The Crisis. Free Soil vs. Slavery Extension. An Address, Delivered at a Public Meeting in the City of Lafayette, Indiana, on the evening of August 11th, 1848*. Lafayette, Ind., 1848.

Emerson, Ralph Waldo. *The Complete Works of Ralph Waldo Emerson*. Edited by Edward W. Emerson. 11 vols. Boston, 1894–1895.

———. *The Works of Ralph Waldo Emerson*. Riverside ed. 12 vols. Boston, 1883–1893.

Estes, Hiram C. *The Condition of our Country—Its Perils and its Help. A Sermon preached in East Trenton, Maine, August 24 and September 1, 1856*. Ellsworth, Me., 1856. (NNHi)

"An Estimate of the Present and Future Physical, Civil, and Moral Power of the West, Including the Country Watered by the Mississippi and its Tributaries." *Quarterly Register and Journal of the American Education Society* 1, no. 4 (April 1828), 61–65.

Everett, Alexander H. *A Discourse on The Progress and Limits of Social Improvement; including a General Survey of the History of Civilization. Addressed to the Literary Societies of Amherst College, at their Public Anniversary Meeting, August 27, 1833*. Boston, 1834 (MWA)

———. *An Oration delivered at Holliston, Mass. on the Fourth of July, 1839, at the Request of the Democratic Citizens of the Ninth Congressional District*. Boston, 1839. (MWA)

———. *An Oration: delivered at the Request of the City Government, before the Citizens of Boston, on the 5th of July, 1830*. Boston, 1830.

Everett, Edward. *An Address, delivered before the Mercantile Library Association, at the Odeon in Boston, September 13, 1838*. Boston, 1838.

———. "Address of His Excellency Edward Everett, to the Two Branches of the Legislature, on the Organization of the Government, for the Political Year . . . 1837." *Documents Printed by Order of the Senate of . . . Massachusetts, 1837*, no. 1. Boston, 1837.

———. *Importance of Practical Education and Useful Knowledge*. . . . New York, 1847.

———. *Orations and Speeches on Various Occasions*. 2d ed. 4 vols. Boston, 1850–1868.

———. *Speech of Mr. Everett, on the Proposition to Amend the Constitution of the United States, respecting the Election of President and Vice President. Delivered in the House of Representatives March 9, 1826*. Washington, D.C., 1826.

Ewing, John. *Circular. To the citizens of the Senatorial District embracing Knox, Daviess and Martin Counties*. Dated Indianapolis, January 26, 1826. N.p., n.d. (In)

Exposition and Protest, reported by the Special Committee of the House of Representatives, on the Tariff; Read and Ordered to be Printed, Dec. 19th, 1828. Columbia, S.C., 1829. (MWA)

"Extract from the remarks of D. V. Bradford, Esq." *Columbus* (Ohio) *Statesman, Extra,* 10 October 1840. P. 2.

"Factory Labor." *Lowell Offering* 4, no. 9 (July 1844), 100.

Facts for the People. First published at Philadelphia, Pennsylvania, and Re-published at Frankfort, Kentucky, October, 1832. (MWA)

Facts for the People. The Various Charges against General W. H. Harrison Briefly Stated and Refuted, and Some of the Objections to the Present Administration Enumerated. Jonesborough, Tenn., 1840. (T)

Facts involved in the Rhode Island Controversy with Some Views upon the Rights of Both Parties. Boston, 1842. (MWA)

A Few Plain Facts, Addressed to the People of Pennsylvania. By a Citizen of Pennsylvania. Philadelphia, 1844.

[Fillmore, Millard.] *Mr. Fillmore at Home. His Reception at New York and Brooklyn, and Progress through the State to his Residence in Buffalo.* Buffalo, N.Y., n.d. (N)

Finegan, Thomas E., ed. *Free Schools: A Documentary History of the Free School Movement in New York State.* Fifteenth Annual Report of the New York State Education Department, 1917–18. Vol. 1. Albany, N.Y., Univ. of State of N.Y., 1921.

Finney, Charles G. *Lectures on Revivals of Religion.* Edited by William G. McLoughlin. Cambridge, Mass., Harvard Univ. Press, 1960.

Fitzhugh, George. *Cannibals All! or, Slaves without Masters.* Richmond, Va., 1857. (MH)

——. *Sociology for the South, or the Failure of Free Society.* Richmond, Va., 1854. (MH)

Fletcher, Richard. *Speech of Richard Fletcher to his Constituents, delivered in Faneuil Hall, Monday, Nov. 6, 1837.* N.p., n.d. (MWA)

Flint, Timothy. *A Condensed Geography and History of the Western States, or the Mississippi Valley.* 2 vols. Cincinnati, Ohio, 1828.

Flood, Charles B., and E. Burke Fisher. *The Convention and Its Men.* Columbus, Ohio, 1850. (MH-L)

Foote, Thomas M. *National Characteristics. An Address delivered before the Literary Societies of Hamilton College, July 24, 1848.* Buffalo, N.Y., 1848.

Forbes, Abner, and J. W. Green. *The Rich Men of Massachusetts.* . . . Boston, 1851.

——. *The Rich Men of Massachusetts.* . . . 2d ed., enl. and improved. Boston, 1852.

Forrest, Edwin. *Oration delivered at the Democratic Republican Celebration of the Sixty-Second Anniversary of the Independence of the United States, in the City of New York, Fourth July, 1838.* New York, 1838.

Fowler, John W. *Society: Its Progress and Prospects, and the Influence of American Example and Agency on its Ultimate Destiny. A Lecture delivered before the Young Men's Association of the City of Utica, April 14th, 1843.* Utica, N.Y., 1843. (NN)

Freedley, Edwin T. *Opportunities for Industry and the Safe Investment of Capital; or, A Thousand Chances to Make Money.* Philadelphia, 1859. (NN)

———. *A Practical Treatise on Business: or How to Get, Save, Spend, Give, Lend, and Bequeath Money: with an Inquiry into the Chances of Success and Causes of Failure in Business.* 5th ed. Philadelphia, 1852. (MWA)

———, ed. *Leading Pursuits and Leading Men. A Treatise on the Principal Trades and Manufactures of the United States.* . . . Philadelphia, 1856. (NN)

Freeman, John D. *An Oration, delivered on the Fourth of July, A.D. 1839, before the Fencibles, Guards, Hussars, Light Guards, Light Artillery, Mechanics Association, and Citizens of Natchez.* Natchez, Miss., 1839.

Free-Masonry, in reply to Anti-Masonry, in the American *Quarterly Review, for March, 1830.* Boston, 1830. (MWA)

Free Soil, Free Speech, Free Men. Proceedings of the Democratic Republican State Convention, At Syracuse, July 24, 1856. The Address and Resolutions, with the List of Delegates. Albany, N.Y., 1856. (N)

Free Trade and the American System: A Dialogue between a Merchant and a Planter. Political Tract, No. 8 (April 1, 1832). Charleston, S.C., 1832. (NN)

Frieze, Jacob. *A Concise History, of the Efforts to Obtain an Extension of the Suffrage in Rhode Island; from the Year 1811 to 1842.* Providence, R.I., 1842.

From the Albany Daily Advertiser. General Tallmadge's Speech. N.p. [1824]. (NN)

Frost, John. *Self-Made Men of America.* New York, 1848.

———. *The Young Mechanic.* New York and Boston, 1843.

———. *The Young Merchant.* 2d ed. Boston, 1840.

Fry, William H. *Republican "Campaign" Text-book, for the Year 1860.* New York, 1860. (NN)

Gannett, Ezra S. *Relation of the North to Slavery. A Discourse preached in the Federal Street Meetinghouse, in Boston, on Sunday, June 11, 1854.* Boston, 1854.

———. *Religion Conducive to Prosperity in this Life. A Sermon Preached July 21, 1861, the Sunday after the Funeral of the Late Hon. Nathan Appleton, of Boston.* Boston, 1861. (MWA)

———. *The State of the Country: A Discourse Preached in the Federal Street Meetinghouse, in Boston, on Sunday, June 8, 1856.* Boston, 1856. (MWA)

———. *Thanksgiving for the Union: A Discourse delivered in the Federal-Street Meetinghouse in Boston, on Thanksgiving-Day, November 28, 1850.* Boston, 1850. (MWA)

Gardiner, O[liver] C., ed. *The Great Issue: or, The Three Presidential Candidates; Being a Brief Historical Sketch of the Free Soil Question in the United States.* . . . New York, 1848. (MWA)

Garland, Hugh A. *The Principles of Democracy Identical with the Moral Improvement of Mankind. An Oration, Pronounced in Castle Garden, July 27, 1840* . . . *in Celebration of the Second Declaration of Independence, or the Passage of the Independent Treasury Bill.* New York, [1840].

"General Manufacturing Bill." *Voice of Industry,* 25 February 1848, p. 2.

Gilpin, Henry D. *A Speech Delivered at the Democratic Celebration by the Citizens of The Second Congressional District of Pennsylvania* . . . *July 4th 1834.* N.p., n.d.

The Girard Journal of Wealth, and Record and Depository of Benevolence 1, no. 1 (8 February 1832). (MH-BA photostat)

Godwin, Parke. *Democracy, Constructive and Pacific.* New York, 1844. (NN, film)

Goodrich, Samuel G. *Lives of Benefactors.* New York, 1844.

——. *The Young American: or Book of Government and Law.* . . . 8th ed. New York, 1847. (MWiW)

Gordon, J. W. *Indiana Democracy since 1854. Judged by its Record! Speech by J. W. Gordon. Delivered at Cumberland, July 7th, 1860.* Indianapolis, n.d. (In)

Gouge, William M. *A Short History of Paper Money and Banking in the United States . . . to which is prefixed An Inquiry into the Principles of the System.* . . . Philadelphia, 1833.

Graebner, Norman, ed. *Ideas and Diplomacy: Readings in the Intellectual Tradition of American Foreign Policy.* New York, Oxford Univ. Press, 1964.

——. *Manifest Destiny.* New York, Bobbs, 1968.

Grand Mass Meeting of the Democracy of New York! The Administration Fully Sustained. Speeches of Hon. John A. Dix, Hon. R. M. McLane, John Van Buren, and Hon. John Cochrane. N.p., [1858]. (MWA)

Greeley, Horace. *Hints Toward Reforms, in Lectures, Addresses, and Other Writings.* New York, 1850.

——. *An Overland Journey, from New York to San Francisco, in the Summer of 1859.* New York, 1860.

——, and John F. Cleveland, comps. *A Political Text-Book for 1860.* . . . New York, 1860. (N)

Green, Willis. *Address of the Hon. Willis Green, of Kentucky, before the Alexandria (D.C.) Clay Club.* N.p., [1844].

——. *The Sub-Treasury: A Tract for the Times.* Washington, D.C., 1844. (NN)

[Greene, Charles G.] *The Identity of the Old Hartford Convention Federalists with the Modern Whig, Harrison Party. Carefully Illustrated by Living Specimens, and Dedicated to the Young Men of the Union. Boston Morning Post. Extra.* August 1840. (NN)

Greenough, William W. *The Conquering Republic. An Oration delivered before the Municipal Authorities of the City of Boston, July 4, 1849.* Boston, 1849.

Grimke, Frederick. *The Nature and Tendency of Free Institutions.* Edited by John W. Ward. Cambridge, Mass., Harvard Univ. Press, 1968.

Grund, Francis. *The Americans, in their Moral, Social, and Political Relations.* Boston, 1837.

Haar, Charles M., ed. *The Golden Age of American Law.* New York, Braziller, 1965.

Hacker, Louis M., and Helène S. Zahler, eds. *The Shaping of the American Tradition.* New York, Columbia Univ. Press, 1947.

Hall, Baynard R. *Righteousness the safe-guard and glory of a nation. A Sermon Preached in the Representative Hall, at Indianapolis, Indiana; December 31st, 1826.* N.p., 1827.

Hallett, Benjamin F. *Facts for Candid Men and True Democrats. Speech . . . at the*

Democratic Mass Meeting in Syracuse, July 22, 1848. Albany, N.Y., 1848. (NN)

——. *Oration before the Democratic Citizens of Oxford, and the Adjoining Towns, in Worcester County, Massachusetts, July 5, 1841.* Boston, 1841. (NN)

——. *The Right of the People to Establish Forms of Government. Mr. Hallett's Argument in the Rhode Island Cases, before the Supreme Court of the United States, January 1848.* . . . Boston, 1848. (MWA)

Ham [Levi A.]. *Remarks of Mr. Ham, of York, in the Senate of Maine, February 13, 1838.* . . . N.p., n.d. (MWA)

Hamilton, James Jr. *A Speech on the Operation of the Tariff on the Interests of the South* . . . *delivered at Walterborough, on the 21st Oct. 1828.* . . . Charleston, S.C., 1828.

Hamlin, E[dward] S. *Speech of E. S. Hamlin, of Ohio, on the Annexation of Texas. Delivered in the House of Representatives, U. S., Jan. 9, 1845.* Washington, D.C., n.d. (MWA)

Hamlin, Hannibal. *Kansas—Lecompton Constitution. Speech of Hon. Hannibal Hamlin, of Maine, in the Senate of the United States, March 9 and 10, 1858.* [Washington, D.C., 1858.] (MWA)

Hammond, Charles. *An Address delivered at Mashapaug Lake, Before the Citizens of Union, Conn., and the Neighboring Towns, at their Temperance Celebration of the National Anniversary, July 4th, 1853.* Worcester, Mass., 1853.

Hammond, Jabez D. *The History of Political Parties in the State of New-York.* 3d. ed., rev. 2 vols. Cooperstown, N.Y., 1845.

——. *Life and Times of Silas Wright, Late Governor of the State of New York.* Syracuse, N.Y., 1848.

[Hammond, James H.] *The Railroad Mania: and Review of the Bank of the State of South-Carolina, A Series of Essays by Anti-Debt.* Charleston, S.C., 1848. (MH)

Hanckel, Thomas M. *Oration delivered on the Fifth Anniversary of the South Carolina Historical Society,* . . . *May 23, 1860.* Charleston, S.C., 1860. (NNHi)

Handerson, [Phineas]. *Mr. Handerson's Address, Delivered at Keene, February 22, 1838, Being the Anniversary of Washington's Birth Day.* N.p., n.d. (MWA)

Handley, William C. *An Anniversary Oration, delivered before the Phi-Delta Society, of Mercer University, on the 22d February, 1847.* Penfield, Ga., 1847. (MWA)

Handlin, Oscar, and Mary Handlin, eds. *The Popular Sources of Political Authority: Documents on the Massachusetts Constitution of 1780.* Cambridge, Mass., Harvard Univ. Press, 1966.

The Harbinger, devoted to social and political progress, vol. 1. New York, 1845.

Hardy, John. *Letter to a New-Jersey Farmer.* New York, [1856]. (MWA)

Harper, William. *Anniversary Oration; Delivered* . . . *in the Representative Hall, on the 9th of December, 1835.* South Carolina Society for the Advancement of Learning, publication no. 2. Columbia, S.C., 1836.

——. *The Remedy by State Interposition, or Nullification; Explained and Advocated by Chancellor Harper, in his Speech at Columbia, (S.C.) on the Twentieth September, 1830. Political Tract No. 5* (January 1832). Charleston, S.C., 1832. (MWA)

The Harrison Almanac for 1841. New York, 1840. (NN)

Harrison, William Henry. *Gen. Harrison's Speech at the Dayton Convention, September 10, 1840.* [Boston, 1840.] (NNHi)

Hawley, Charles. *A True Social and Civil Life: A Discourse delivered Thanksgiving Day, November 24, 1859, in the Second Presbyterian Church. . . .* Auburn, N.Y., 1860.

Hayes, Samuel S. *The Issues in Illinois. Speech of Hon. Samuel S. Hayes. At the Democratic Meeting at Metropolitan Hall, October 18th, 1858.* N.p., n.d.

Hayne, Isaac W. *An Oration, delivered in the Third Presbyterian Church in Columbia, on the Fourth of July, 1831.* Columbia, S.C., 1831. (NNHi)

[Hazard, Thomas R.] *Facts for the Laboring Man: By a Laboring Man.* Newport, R.I., 1840. (MWA)

Headley, J[oel] T. *The One Progressive Principle. delivered before the Literary Societies of the University of Vermont, August, 1846.* New York, 1846.

Henry, Caleb S. *The Importance of Exalting the Intellectual Spirit of the Nation; and Need of a Learned Class. A Discourse Pronounced before the Sigma Nu Society of the University of Vermont. August 3, 1836.* Burlington, N.J., 1836.

Henshaw, David. *An Address, delivered before an Assembly of Citizens . . . at Faneuil Hall, Boston, July 4, 1836.* Boston, 1836. (MH)

Herndon, A. G. *Of the Cass Democrat. To My Democratic Friends in Illinois.* Illinois broadside, n.p., n.d. (ICHi)

Hibbard, Harry. *Letter from Hon. Harry Hibbard, to Stephen Pingry and other Citizens of New Hampshire.* Dated Washington, D.C., February 14, 1852. Np., n.d.

[Hickman, George H., ed.] *The Democratic Text Book, being A Compendium of the Principles of the Democratic Party.* New York and Philadelphia, 1848. (NN)

Hickman, John. *Southern Sectionalism. Speech of Hon. John Hickman, of Penn. Delivered in the U. S. House of Representatives, May 1, 1860.* N.p., n.d. (N)

[Hildreth, Richard.] *"Our First Men:" A Calendar of Wealth, Fashion and Gentility; Containing a List of Those Persons Taxed in the City of Boston, Credibly Reported To Be Worth One Hundred Thousand Dollars, with Biographical Notices of the Principal Persons.* Boston, 1846. (MWA)

——. *A Review of "An Oration delivered before the Young Men of Boston, on the Fourth of July, M DCCC XXXI."* N.p., n.d. (NN)

Hilliard, Henry W. *The Spirit of Liberty. An Oration, delivered before the Literary Societies of the University of Virginia. On the 27th July, 1859.* Montgomery, Ala., 1860. (A-Ar)

History of Pennsylvania Hall, which was Destroyed by a Mob, on the 17th of May 1838. Philadelphia, 1838. (MWA)

A History of the Federal and Democratic Parties in the United States, from their Origin to the Present Time. By a Citizen of Wayne County, Ind. Richmond, Ind., 1837.

Holbrook, John C. *Our Country's Crisis, A Discourse delivered in Dubuque, Iowa, on Sabbath evening, July 6, 1856.* N.p., n.d. (N)

Holley, George W. *An Oration, Delivered on the Fourth of July, 1839. At Peru, La Salle County, Ill.* Chicago, 1839.

Hopkins, Mark. *The Sabbath and Free Institutions. A Paper Read Before the National Sabbath Convention, Saratoga, Aug. 13, 1863 . . . on Invitation of the New York Sabbath Committee.* New York, 1863. (MWA)

———. *A Sermon delivered before His Excellency Edward Everett, Governor . . . on the Anniversary Election, January 2, 1839.* Boston, 1839. (MWA)

The House that Jonathan Built, Or Political Primer for 1832. Philadelphia, 1832.

Howard, N. G. *To the People of Rankin County.* Mississippi broadside, dated July 2, 1832.

"How to Make a Fortune." *Ladies' Repository* (Cincinnati) 18, no. 3 (March 1858), 134–37.

Hunt, Benjamin F. *Speech of Col. Benj. Faneuil Hunt, of Charleston, South Carolina, delivered at the request of the Democratic Republican General Committee, at the Mass Meeting of the Mechanics and Working Men of New-York, in Reply to the Doctrines of Daniel Webster, on the Currency and a National Bank.* [New York, 1840.]

Hunt, Freeman, ed. *Lives of American Merchants.* 2 vols. New York, 1856–1858.

———. *Worth and Wealth: A Collection of Maxims, Morals and Miscellanies for Merchants and Men of Business.* New York, 1856. (NN)

Hunt, Thomas P. *The Book of Wealth; in which it is Proved from the Bible, that it is the Duty of Every Man, to Become Rich.* New York, 1836.

Hunt, William. *The American Biographical Sketch Book.* New York, 1849. (LN)

Hunt, William Gibbes. *An Address, Delivered at Nashville, Tenn. April 6, 1831, At the Request of the Literary Societies of the University of Nashville.* Nashville, Tenn., 1831.

Huntington, B. W. *Individuality. An Address, delivered before The Philomathic Society of the University of Alabama, at its twelfth anniversary.* Tuscaloosa, Ala., 1845. (AU)

The Import Duties Considered in relation to the Happiness of the People and Prosperity of the Union. By a Friend of the Administration. Philadelphia, 1832. (MWA)

Ingersoll, Charles J. *A Discourse Concerning the Influence of America on the Mind.* Philadelphia, 1823. (MH)

Jackson, Andrew. *Correspondence.* Edited by J. S. Bassett. 7 vols. Washington, D.C., Carnegie Institution, 1926–1935.

Jackson, O. P. *An Oration, delivered by O. P. Jackson, Esq. on the Fourth of July, 1835. . . .* New Orleans, 1835.

James Buchanan, His Doctrines and Policy as Exhibited by Himself and Friends. [New York, 1856.] (MWA)

Jewett, M. Augustus. *An Oration, delivered before the Citizens of Vigo County, Indiana, in the Court-House in Terre-Haute, July 4, 1840.* Terre Haute, Ind., 1840.

Journal of Proceedings of the National Republican Convention, Held at Worcester, October 11, 1832. Boston, 1832. (NN)

[Judson, E.] "The Evangelization of the West. How Shall It Be Effected? And by Whom?" *New Englander* 4, no. 13 (January 1846), 29–39.

Kansas Affairs. Report of the Select Committee to Whom was Referred So Much of the Governor's Message as Relates to Slavery and the Affairs in Kansas. . . . N.p. [Vermont, ca. 1856]. (MWA)

Kendrick, Asahel. *The Ancient and Modern Civilizations Contrasted. An Address delivered before the Aeonian Society of the Hamilton Literary and Theological Institution, on Wednesday, July 30, 1845.* Hamilton, N.Y., 1845. (MWA)

[Kennedy, John P.] *Quodlibet.* . . . Philadelphia, 1840.

Kent, George. *The Characteristics and Claims of the Age in Which We Live. An Oration, Pronounced at Dartmouth College, August 23, 1832, before the New-Hampshire Alpha of the Phi Beta Kappa Society.* Concord, N.H., 1832. (MWA)

Kent, James. *An Address Delivered at New Haven before the Phi Beta Kappa Society, September 13, 1831.* New Haven, Conn., 1831.

———. *Commentaries on American Law.* 4 vols. New York, 1826–1830.

Kent, Joseph. *Speech of Joseph Kent, of Maryland, in support of An Amendment to the Constitution to Restrain the Veto Power of the President of the United States. Delivered in the Senate of the United States, on the 20th of February, 1835.* Washington, D.C., 1835. (MWA)

Kent, William. *An Address, Pronounced before the Phi Beta Kappa Society of Union College, At Schenectady, on Tuesday, July 27th, 1841.* New York, 1841. (N)

Kenyon, Cecelia S., ed. *The Antifederalists.* Indianapolis, Ind., Bobbs, 1966.

Ker, Leander. *The History of Liberty, Its Origin, Character and Progress. An Address delivered before the Athenaean Society, of the University of Missouri . . . 30th of July, 1845.* Columbia, Mo., 1845. (MoHi)

Kettell, Thomas P. *Southern Wealth and Northern Profits, as Exhibited in Statistical Facts and Official Figures.* . . . New York, 1860.

Knight, Edgar W., ed. *Reports on European Education.* New York, McGraw-Hill, 1930.

Ladd, William. *A Dissertation on a Congress of Nations.* 2d ed. Boston, 1832. (MWA)

———. *An Essay on a Congress of Nations, for the Adjustment of International Disputes without Resort to Arms.* . . . Boston, 1840. (MH-A)

Lanman, James H. *History of Michigan.* . . . New York, 1841. (MWiW)

Leach, D. C. *Bogus Democracy Examined and Exposed. Speech of Hon. D. C. Leach, of Michigan. Delivered in the House of Representatives, March 14, 1860.* Washington, D.C., n.d. (MWA)

Lecompte, Joseph. *To the People of the Sixth Congressional District of Kentucky.* Letter dated February 28, 1829. N.p., n.d. (MWA)

Leggett, William. *A Collection of the Political Writings of William Leggett.* Edited by Theodore Sedgwick Jr. 2 vols. New York, 1840.

Lieber, Francis. *Essays on Property and Labour.* . . . New York, 1841. (MWiW)

———. *Manual of Political Ethics designed chiefly for the Use of Colleges and Schools at Law.* 2 vols. Boston, 1838–1839.

——. *On Civil Liberty and Self-Government.* 2 vols. Philadelphia, 1853.

Life in a Log Cabin, with Hard Cider. Philadelphia, 1840. (NN)

Lincoln, Abraham. *The Collected Works of Abraham Lincoln.* Edited by Roy P. Basler. 9 vols. New Brunswick, N.J., Rutgers Univ. Press, 1953.

Lincoln, Charles Z., ed. *State of New York. Messages from the Governors, Comprising Executive Communications to the Legislature and Other Papers Relating to Legislation from the Organization of the First Colonial Assembly in 1683 to and Including the Year 1906, with Notes.* 11 vols. Albany, N.Y., published by authority of the state, 1909.

Lindsley, Philip. *An Address, delivered at Nashville, Ten. Feb. 22, 1832 . . . on the Occasion of the Centennial Birth Day of George Washington.* Nashville, Tenn., 1832. (T)

Locke, John. *Two Treatises of Government.* Edited by Peter Laslett. Rev. ed. Cambridge, Cambridge Univ. Press, 1963.

Lovett, William. *Life and Struggles of William Lovett in his Pursuit of Bread, Knowledge, and Freedom.* 2 vols. London, Dutton, 1920.

Luther, Seth. *An Address on the Origin and Progress of Avarice.* Boston, 1834. (NN)

——. *An Address on the Right of Free Suffrage. . . .* Providence, R.I., 1833. (MWA)

——. *An Address to the Workingmen of New England, on the State of Education, and on the Condition of the Producing Classes in Europe and America. . . .* 2d. ed. New York, 1833. (MH)

Lynn (Massachusetts) *Awl,* 28 August 1844.

Lyon, Caleb. *The Covenant of Freedom. Speech of Hon. Caleb Lyon, of Lyonsdale, New York, in the House of Representatives, May 8, 1854.* Washington, D.C., n.d. (MWA)

McAllister, M. Hall. *Address to the Democratic Republican Convention of Georgia. Delivered by M. Hall McAllister At Milledgeville, on 4th July, 1840.* Milledgeville, Ga., 1840. (NN)

McCoy, John. *To the Freemen of the Counties of Ozark, Taney, and Greene which compose the 21st Senatorial District. June 30, 1845.* Missouri broadside, n.p., dated June 30, 1845. (MoHi typescript)

McCulloch, J. R. *The Principles of Political Economy.* New ed. Edinburgh, 1843.

McCurdy, A. C. *Win Who Will; or, the Young Man's Key to Fortune. Being a Practical Treatise on Money-Getting, The Mystery of Accumulation, and Causes of Failure. . . .* Philadelphia, 1872. (MH-BA)

McDowell, Tremaine, ed. *William Cullen Bryant: Representative Selections.* New York, Am. Book, 1935.

McDuffie, George. *Speech . . . at a Public Dinner Given to Him by the Citizens of Charleston, (S.C.) May 19, 1831. . . .* Charleston, 1831. (NNHi)

McKenney, Thomas L. [Aristides]. *Essays on the Spirit of Jacksonism, as Exemplified in its Deadly Hostility to the Bank of the United States, and in the Odious Calumnies Employed for its Destruction.* Philadelphia, 1835. (NN)

Mann, Horace. *A Few Thoughts for a Young Man: A Lecture, delivered before the Bos-*

ton Mercantile Library Association, on its 29th Anniversary. Boston, 1850. (NN)

Mann, Horace. *Life and Works of Horace Mann.* Edited by Mary S. Mann. 5 vols. Boston and New York, 1891.

———. *Speech of Hon. Horace Mann, of Massachusetts, on the Institution of Slavery. Delivered in the House of Representatives, August 17, 1852.* Washington, D.C., n.d. (NN)

Manning, William. Samuel Eliot Morison, ed., "William Manning's *The Key of Libberty.*" *William and Mary Quarterly,* 3d ser., 13 (1956), 202–54.

Mark, Irving, and Eugene L. Schwaab, eds. *The Faith of Our Fathers: An Anthology Expressing the Aspirations of the American Common Man 1790–1860.* New York, Knopf, 1952.

Marsh, George P. *The American Historical School: A Discourse delivered before the Literary Societies of Union College.* Troy, N.Y., 1847. (N)

Marsh, R. V. *Speech of R. V. Marsh, of Brandon. Delivered in the House of Representatives of the State of Vermont, on the 7th day of November, 1856.* N.p., n.d. (MWA)

Marsh, William H. *God's Law Supreme. A Sermon, Aiming to Point out the Duty of a Christian People in Relation to the Fugitive Slave Law: Delivered at Village Corners, Woodstock, Conn., on the Day of the Annual Thanksgiving, Nov. 28, 1850, and Subsequently Repeated, By Request, in Southbridge, Mass.* Worcester, Mass., n.d. (MWA)

Marshall, [Edward C.] *American Progress—Judge Douglas—The Presidency. Speech of Mr. Marshall, of California, in the House of Representatives, March 11, 1852, in Reply to the Speech of Mr. Breckinridge, of Kentucky.* Washington, D.C., n.d. (MWA)

Marshall, H[umphrey]. *California and New Mexico. Speech of Hon. H. Marshall, of Kentucky, in the House of Representatives, April 3, 1850, In Committee of the Whole on the state of the Union, on the President's message transmitting the Constitution of California.* Washington, D.C., n.d. (MWA)

———. *Speech of Hon. Humphrey Marshall, of Kentucky, in the House of Representatives, January 19, 1859.* Washington, D.C., n.d. (MWA)

Martineau, Harriet. *Society in America.* 2 vols. New York, 1837.

Maryland Republican. Extra. Annapolis, Md., January 21, 1832. (N)

Maury, A. P. *Address on the Peculiar Advantages of the United States in Comparison with Other Nations. . . .* Nashville, Tenn., 1847. (T)

Meek, Alexander B. *Americanism in Literature: An Oration before the Phi Kappa and Demosthenian Societies of the University of Georgia, at Athens, August 4, 1844.* Tuscaloosa, Ala., 1844. (AAr)

A Member of the Philadelphia Bar [pseud.]. *Wealth and Biography of the Wealthy Citizens of Philadelphia. . . .* Philadelphia, 1845. (NN)

The Memorial and Resolutions adopted at the Anti-Tariff Meeting, held at Sumter District, South Carolina, on Monday the 3d of September, 1827. Charleston, S.C., 1827. (NNHi)

The Memorial of the Chamber of Commerce, and of the Citizens of Charleston, against the

Tariff on Woollen Goods, Proposed at the 2d Session of the 19th Congress. Charleston, S.C., 1827. (MWA)

Memorial of the Committee Appointed by the "Free Trade Convention," Held at Philadelphia, in September and October, 1831, To Prepare and Present a Memorial to Congress, Remonstrating Against the Existing Tariff of Duties. New York, 1832. (MWA)

Miller, Perry, ed. *The Legal Mind in America.* New York, Doubleday, 1962.

Mills, James D. *The Art of Money Making; or The Road to Fortune: A Universal Guide for Honest Success.* New York, 1872. (NN)

Milroy, Samuel. *An Address, delivered by Gen. Samuel Milroy, before the Delphi "Hickory Club," at its first organized meeting for 1844.* N.p. [Indiana], n.d. (In)

Miner, Charles. *An Address, delivered at the Democratic Whig Festival, at Wilkes-Barre, Penn., December 4, 1840, in honor of the election of Gen. Wm. Henry Harrison.* Wilkes-Barre, 1841. (NN)

Minority Report of the Select Committee, to whom were referred the memorial of the democratic members of the Legislature of Rhode Island. . . . 28th Congress, 1st Session, *House Report* No. 581.

[Montgomery, John C.] *Montgomery's Tippecanoe Almanac, for the Year 1841. . . .* 4th ed., enl. and improved. Philadelphia, n.d. (NN)

Montgomery, William. *Speech of Hon. William Montgomery, of Pennsylvania, on the Admission of Kansas, and in Defence of His Compromise Bill. Delivered in the House of Representatives, March 19, 1858.* N.p., n.d. (NN)

Moody, Loring [One of the People]. *A Plain Statement addressed to all Honest Democrats.* Boston, 1856. (NNHi)

Moore, Ely. *Address delivered before the General Trades' Union of the City of New York . . . December 2, 1833.* New York, 1833.

Moore, Humphrey. *An Address delivered before the Temperance Society in Pembroke, July 4, 1836.* Concord, N.H., 1836. (MWA)

[Moore, Jacob B.] *The Contrast; or, Plain Reasons why William Henry Harrison Should be Elected President of the United States, and Why Martin Van Buren Should Not be Re-elected.* New York, 1840. (NN)

Moore, Samuel H. *Remarks of the Hon. Samuel H. Moore, of Virginia, in the House of Representatives, on Monday, March 10, 1834. On the Resolutions of Virginia, Relative to the Removal of the Public Deposites.* N.p., n.d. (MWA)

"The Moralist." *Universalist, and Ladies' Repository* 4, no. 6 (December 1835), 247–50.

Morton, Marcus. "Address of His Excellency Marcus Morton, to the Two Branches of the Legislature, on the Organization of the Government, for the Political Year . . . 1840." *Documents Printed by Order of the House of Representatives of . . . Massachusetts, 1840,* no. 9. Boston, 1840.

Moses, Myer. *Full Annals of the Revolution in France, 1830, to Which is Added, A Full Account of the Celebration of Said Revolution in the City of New-York.* New York, 1830. (NN)

——. *Oration, delivered at Tammany-Hall, on the Twelfth May, 1831, being the Forty-*

Second Anniversary of the Tammany Society, Or, Columbian Order. New York, 1831. (NN)

"Mr. Pepperage's Fourth of July Oration." *Putnam's Monthly Magazine* 6, no. 1 (July 1855), 91–98.

Narrative of the Late Riotous Proceedings against the Liberty of the Press, in Cincinnati. . . . Addressed to the People of Ohio, by the Executive Committee of the Ohio Anti-Slavery Society. Cincinnati, Ohio, 1836. (NN)

Neal, John. *Oration, Portland, July 4, 1838.* Portland, Me., 1838. (NN)

The Nebraska Question comprising Speeches in the United States Senate by Mr. Douglas [et al.] *. . . together with The History of the Missouri Compromise. . . .* New York, 1854. (N)

Nichols, Thomas Low. *Forty Years of American Life, 1821–1861.* New York, Stackpole, 1937.

Northup, Clark S., ed. *Representative Phi Beta Kappa Orations.* 2d ed. New York, Elisha Parmele, 1930.

Norton, A. B., ed. *The Great Revolution of 1840. Reminiscences of the Log Cabin and Hard Cider Campaign.* Mount Vernon, Ohio, and Dallas, Texas, 1888. (NN)

An Observer [pseud.]. *An Enquiry into the Present System of Medical Education, in the State of New-York. Respectfully Submitted to the Consideration of the Members of the Legislature.* Albany, N.Y., 1830. (MWA)

Official Proceedings of the Democratic and Anti-Know-Nothing State Convention of Alabama, held in . . . Montgomery. . . . Montgomery, Ala., 1856.

Official Proceedings of the National Democratic Convention, Held in Cincinnati, June 2–6, 1856. Cincinnati, Ohio, 1856. (N)

Old South Leaflets, General Series. Published by The Directors of the Old South Work. Boston, n.d.

One of the People [pseud.]. *The Coming Struggle: or, Shall Kansas be a Free or a Slave State?* Philadelphia, 1856. (NNHi)

——. *To the Hon. W. J. Grayson.* N.p., n.d. (NNHi)

—— *See* Loring Moody.

"Our First Men." See Richard Hildreth.

[Owen, Robert Dale.] *Address of the Democratic Convention of 1840. (Together with an Abstract of the Proceedings.)* N.p. [Indiana], n.d.

——. *Democratic Address. At an adjourned meeting of the Democratic Party of the State of Indiana, held in the Hall of Representatives at Indianapolis, on Saturday the 10th of February, 1838. . . .* N.p., n.d. (In)

Packard, Frederick A. [A Citizen of Pennsylvania]. *Thoughts on the Condition and Prospects of Popular Education in the United States. . . .* Philadelphia, 1836. (MH)

Papers for the People. To Be Issued Weekly during the Campaign, under the Patronage of the Entire Democratic Delegation in Congress. New York, 1852. (NN)

Parker, Joel. *Progress. An Address before the Phi Beta Kappa Society of Dartmouth College, July 29, 1846.* Hanover, N.H., 1846. (MWA)

Parker, Theodore. *Lessons from the World of Matter and the World of Man.* Edited by Rufus Leighton. *Works of Theodore Parker,* Centenary ed., vol. 5. Boston, American Unitarian Association, 1908.

——. *Sins and Safeguards of Society.* Edited by Samuel B. Stewart. *Works of Theodore Parker,* Centenary ed. Boston, American Unitarian Association, n.d.

——. *Social Classes in a Republic.* Edited by Samuel A. Eliot. *Works of Theodore Parker,* Centenary ed., vol. 19. Boston, American Unitarian Association, n.d.

Parsons, Theophilus Jr. *Memoir of Theophilus Parsons.* . . . Boston, 1859. (MWiW)

Peabody, Elizabeth P. *Record of a School: Exemplifying the General Principles of Spiritual Culture.* 2d ed. Boston and New York, 1835. (NN)

Peck, J. M. "Elements of Western Character." *Christian Review* 16, no. 63 (January 1851), 77–95.

——. *A Guide for Emigrants, containing Sketches of Illinois, Missouri and the Adjacent Parts.* Boston, 1831. (N)

——. *A New Guide for Emigrants to the West.* . . . Boston, 1836. (N)

Perkins, John Jr. *Speech . . . on the Transfer to the States, by the General Government, of the Administration of the Public Lands within their Limits.* Washington, D.C., 1854. (NN)

Perkins, Samuel Elliott. *Speech of Judge Perkins at a Mass Meeting held at Richmond, Indiana, September 25, 1860.* N.p., n.d. (InU)

Pictures of the Times; or, A Contrast between the Effects of the True Democratic System, as displayed under Jefferson, Madison and Jackson in former times, and the Effects of the Aristocratic Sub-Treasury System, as displayed in Martin Van Buren's Time. Philadelphia, 1840. (NN)

Pinckney, Henry L. *The Necessity of Popular Enlightenment to the Honor and Welfare of the State. An Oration delivered before The Literary Societies of the South Carolina College. On the 3d of December, 1844.* Columbia, S.C., 1845. (NNHi)

Plain Facts and Considerations: Addressed to the People of the United States, without Distinction of Party. Boston, 1856. (NN)

Plain Facts for the People. From the Morning Courier & New-York Enquirer, June 23, 1831. N.p., [1832]. (N)

Poinsett, Joel R. *Substance of a Speech, delivered . . . at a Public Meeting held at Seyle's, 5th October, 1832.* Charleston, S.C., 1832. (NN)

Political Acts and Opinions of Lewis Cass, the Democratic Candidate for the Presidency. Richmond, Va., [1848]. (NN)

The Political Mirror: or Review of Jacksonism. New York, 1835. (NN)

"Political Power Moving Westward." *Home Missionary* 14, no. 12 (April 1842), 277–78.

Political Tracts. See State Rights and Free Trade Association.

Politics and the Pulpit: A Series of Articles Which Appeared in the Journal of Commerce and in The Independent, during the Year 1850. . . . New York, 1851. (NN)

546 · BIBLIOGRAPHY ·

Politics for Farmers. From Niles's Register. N.p., [1830]. (MWA)

Polk, James K. *Address of James K. Polk to the People of Tennessee, April 3, 1839.* Columbia, Tenn., 1839. (T)

———. *Address of James K. Polk, to the People of Tennessee.* Nashville, Tenn., 1841. (NN)

———. *Answers of Ex-Gov. Polk, to Two Series of Interrogatories Propounded to him and Gov. Jones, through the Presses of Memphis; together with a Letter, to the People of Tennessee. . . .* Memphis, Tenn., 1843. (NN)

Popular Sovereignty. Proceedings of the Democratic State Convention, held at Indianapolis, Indiana, February 23d, 1858. . . . Indianapolis, Ind., 1858. (ICN)

Porter, Benjamin F. *Outlines of the Oration of Judge Porter, before the Republican Society, and other Citizens of Tuskaloosa [sic] County; at Hopewell, July 4, 1845.* Tuskaloosa, Ala., 1845. (AU)

Porter, James M. *An Address to the Mechanics of Easton, Pennsylvania, delivered at their request . . . on the Fourth of July, 1835.* Easton, 1835. (NN)

Porter, John K. *An Address delivered before the Young Men's Association, of the City of Albany, on the Twenty-second Day of February, 1850.* Albany, N.Y., 1850. (N)

Porter, Noah. *The Educational Systems of the Puritans and Jesuits Compared. A Premium Essay, Written for "The Society for the Promotion of Collegiate and Theological Education at the West."* New York, 1851. (MH)

———. *The Necessity and Means of Improving the Common Schools of Connecticut.* Hartford, Conn., 1846. (MH)

Preamble and Resolutions, Adopted at the Great Anti-Tariff Meeting, of the People of Abbeville District, On Thursday, 25th Sept., 1828. Columbia, S.C., 1830. (ScU)

Proceedings and Address of the Democratic County Convention, Held at Galena, in the County of Jo Daviess, in the State of Illinois, on the 22d February, 1839. Galena Democrat & Advertiser, Extra. N.p., n.d.

Proceedings and Address, of the Democratic State Convention, held at Syracuse, January Tenth and Eleventh, 1856. Albany, N.Y., 1856. (NN)

Proceedings and Address of the Republican County Convention, Held at Ballston Spa, October 20, 1831. N.p., n.d. (N)

Proceedings at the Banquet of the Jackson Democratic Association, Washington, Eighth of January, 1852. Washington, D.C., n.d. (NN)

Proceedings at the Dinner to the Honorable Isaac Hill, at the Eagle Coffee House, Concord, N.H. August 8, 1832. N.p., n.d. (N)

Proceedings of a Convention of Democratic Young Men, Delegates from the Citizens of Pennsylvania, In Favour of the Re-election of Joseph Ritner . . . at Reading, June 4th, 1838. Reading, Pa., 1838. (N)

Proceedings of a Convention of Republican Delegates, from the Adjacent counties, held in Fredericksburg, on the 4th July, 1836, including An Address to the Republicans of Virginia. Fredericksburg, Va., 1836. (NN)

Proceedings of the Celebration of the 4th of July, 1831, at Charleston, S.C., by the State Rights and Free Trade Party. . . . Charleston, 1831. (NNHi)

Proceedings of the Democratic Legislative Convention, held in Boston, March 1840. Boston, n.d. (NN)

Proceedings of the Democratic Republican Convention of the State of Indiana, Friendly to the nomination of MARTIN VAN BUREN and RICHARD M. JOHNSON. . . . N.p., n.d.

Proceedings of the Democratic Republican State Convention, Holden at Concord, June 20, 1832. Concord, N.H., 1832. (NN)

Proceedings of the Democratic State Convention, Held in Nashville on the 23d of November, 1843, for the Purpose of Electing Delegates to Represent The State of Tennessee in the National Convention, for the Nomination of Candidates for President and Vice President. Nashville, 1843. (NN)

Proceedings of the Democratic State Convention . . . 1843. Columbia, S.C., 1843. (NN)

Proceedings of the Democratic Whig National Convention, which assembled at Harrisburg, Pennsylvania, on the Fourth of December, 1839. . . . Harrisburg, Pa., 1839. (N)

Proceedings of the Harrison County Democratic Meeting. Indiana broadside, n.p., dated April 15, 1840. (In)

Proceedings of the Jackson and Barbour Convention of North Carolina. Raleigh, N.C., [1832]. (NN)

Proceedings of the Merchants' Great Democratic Meeting at the New York Exchange, On Thursday, 20 October, 1856; Correspondence of the Committees, and Speech of Governor Floyd, of Virginia. New York, n.d. (NN)

Proceedings of the National Republican Convention of Young Men, which assembled in the city of Washington, May 7, 1832. Washington, D.C., 1832. (N)

Proceedings of the Opponents of the Present Administration. Held in the City of Washington, February 15 and 18, 1840. . . . N.p., n.d. (N)

The Proceedings of the Second United States Anti-Masonic Convention, Held at Baltimore, September, 1831. . . . Boston, 1832. (N)

Proceedings of the State Convention of the State Rights Democracy Of Pennsylvania, Held at Harrisburg, on Wednesday, April 13, 1859. Harrisburg, Pa., 1859. (N)

Proceedings of the State Rights Celebration, at Charleston, S.C. July 1st, 1830. . . . Charleston, 1830. (NNHi)

Proceedings of the Whigs of Chester County, Favorable to a Distinct Organization of the Whig Party. West Chester, Pa., [1838]. (MWA)

Proceedings of the Whig State Convention, held at Utica, on Wednesday and Thursday, The 12th and 13th of August, 1840. . . . Albany, N.Y., 1840. (NN)

Proceedings, Speeches, &c., at the Dinner Given to Louis Kossuth, at the National Hotel, Washington, Jan. 7, 1852. N.p., n.d. (NN)

"Proposed City Loan." *Cincinnati Daily Gazette,* 2 January 1837, p. 2a.

A Protestant Episcopalian [pseud.]. *A Letter to the Right Rev. L. Silliman Ives, Bishop of the Protestant Episcopal Church in the State of North Carolina, Occasioned by his Late Address to the Convention of his Diocese.* Washington, D.C., dated December 1846. (MWA)

A Public Friend [pseud.]. *To the Female Operatives of the Dover Cotton Manufactories.* New Hampshire broadside, n.p., dated July 26th, 1842. (MWA)

The Public Schools, Public Blessings. By a Father. Published for Gratuitous Distribution by the Executive Committee of the Public School Society. New York, 1837. (N)

Putnam, George. *God and our Country. A Discourse delivered in the First Congregational Church in Roxbury, on Fast Day, April 8, 1847.* Boston, 1847. (MWA)

——. *Our Political Idolatry. A Discourse delivered in the First Church in Roxbury, on Fast Day, April 6, 1843.* Boston, 1843. (MWA)

——. *A Sermon delivered before His Excellency George N. Briggs . . . at the Annual Election, Wednesday, Jan. 7, 1846.* Boston, 1846. (MWA)

Quaife, Milo M., ed. *The Struggle over Ratification, 1846–1847.* Publications of the State Historical Society of Wisconsin. Collections, vol. 28. Madison, Wis., The Society, 1920.

Quandary, Christopher [pseud.]. *Some Serious Considerations on the Present State of Parties, with regard to the Presidential Election.* Richmond, Va., 1827. (NN)

Quitman, John A. *Speech of John A. Quitman, of Mississippi, on the Subject of the Neutrality Laws; delivered in Committee of the Whole House on the State of the Union, April 29, 1856.* Washington, D.C., 1856. (NN)

Rantoul, Robert Jr. *Memoirs, Speeches and Writings of Robert Rantoul, Jr.* Edited by Luther Hamilton. Boston, 1854.

——. *An Oration delivered before the Democrats and Antimasons, of the County of Plymouth, at Scituate, on the Fourth of July, 1836.* Boston, 1836. (NN)

——. *An Oration, delivered before the Gloucester Mechanic Association, on the Fourth of July, 1833.* Salem, Mass., 1833. (MH)

——. *An Oration, delivered before the Inhabitants of the Town of South Reading and its Vicinity, on the Fourth of July, 1832.* Salem, Mass., 1832. (MH)

Raumer, Frederick von. *America and the American People.* Transl. from German by William W. Turner. New York, 1846.

Ravenel, Edmund [Senex]. *An Address to the People, on the Subject of Renewing the Charter of the United States Bank, with a List of Foreign Stockholders, and Notes.* Charleston, S.C., 1832. (ScU)

Read, Daniel. *An Address delivered before the Mechanics Institute of Bloomington, At the Celebration of their Anniversary, February 22d, 1844.* Bloomington, Ind., 1844. (In)

Reasons why The Present System of Auctions Ought to be Abolished. New York, 1828. (N)

Reception of Mr. Webster at Boston, September 30, 1842. With his Speech, delivered in Faneuil Hall on that Occasion. Boston, 1842. (NN)

"Reflections suggested by the Obsequies of John Adams and Thomas Jefferson." *Christian Examiner* 3, no. 4 (July and August 1826), 315–30.

"Reformers and Reforms." *Ladies' Repository* 11, no. 8 (August 1851), 287–88.

"Religious Instruction in Common Schools." *Biblical Repertory and Princeton Review* 13, no. 3 (July 1841), 315–68.

Report of the Select Committee, to whom were referred the memorial of the democratic members of the Legislature of Rhode Island. . . . 28th Congress, 1st Session, House Report no. 546. Also titled *Report of the Select Committee on the Interference of the Executive in the Affairs of Rhode Island.*

The Report, Ordinance, and Address of the Convention of The People of South Carolina. Adopted, November 24th, 1832. Columbia, S.C., 1832. (MWA)

Republican Documents. Official Proceedings of the Republican Convention convened in the City of Pittsburgh, Pennsylvania, on the Twenty-Second of February, 1856. New York, 1856. (NN)

The Republican Sentiment of New-Hamshire, July 4, 1828; Exhibited in her Anniversary Celebrations. N.p., n.d. (MWA)

"Requisite qualifications of a Ministry adapted to the Wants of the West." *Biblical Repertory and Theological Review* 8, no. 3 (July 1836), 380–90.

Reynolds, [John]. *Reynolds' Olive Branch. A Democratic Address delivered by Ex-Gov. Reynolds, in the State House, Springfield, Ill., to a Large and Intelligent Assembly, on the 14th January, 1857.* Belleville, Ill., 1857. (ICHi)

Rice, Daniel. *Harper's Ferry—Its Lessons. A Sermon, Preached in the Second Presbyterian Church. Lafayette, Indiana, Dec. 11, 1859.* Lafayette, 1860. (In)

Richardson, James D., ed. *A Compilation of the Messages and Papers of the Presidents.* 10 vols. N.p., published by authority of Congress, 1899.

[Richter, M. A.?] *On Self-Government; Together with General Plans of a State Constitution, and a constitution for a Confederation of States.* . . . Boston, 1847. (MWA)

Riell, Henry E. *An Appeal to the Voluntary Citizens of the United States, from all Nations, on The Exercise of their Elective Franchise, at the Approaching Presidential Election.* New York, 1844. (NN)

Ritner, Joseph. *Vindication of General Washington from the Stigma of Adherence to Secret Societies, by Joseph Ritner, Governor of the Commonwealth of Pennsylvania, Communicated by Request of the House of Representatives, to that Body, on the 8th of March, 1837.* . . . Harrisburg, Pa., 1837. (MWA)

Rives, William C. *Letter from the Hon. William C. Rives, of Virginia.* N.p., [1840]. (MWA)

———. *Speech of Mr. Rives, of Virginia, in Support of the Bill Introduced by Him Designating the Funds Receivable in Payment of the Public Revenue, and in Opposition to the Sub-Treasury Scheme.* Washington, D.C., 1837. (MWA)

———. *Speech of Mr. Rives, of Virginia, on the Currency of the United States, and the Collection of the Public Revenue. Delivered in the Senate U. S. January 10, 1837.* Washington, D.C. 1837. (MWA)

———. *Speech of Mr. Wm. C. Rives, of Virginia, on Mr. McDuffie's Proposition to Repeal the Tariff Act of 1842. Delivered in the Senate of the United States, Monday, May 27, 1844.* N.p., n.d. (NN)

Robertson, D. F. *National Destiny and Our Country.* New York, 1851. (N)

Robertson, George. *Address on behalf of the Deinologian Society of Centre College, on the 4th of July, 1834.* Lexington, Ky., 1834. (NN)

Robinson, Frederick. *An Oration delivered before the Trades' Union of Boston and Vicinity, July 4, 1834*. Boston, 1834. (NN)

Romeyn, Theodore. *Our Country and her Claims. An Address, delivered before the Philoclean and Peithessophian Societies of Rutgers College . . . July 27, 1847*. New Brunswick, N.J., 1847. (NNHi)

Roy, Joseph E. *Kansas—her Struggle and her Defense. A Discourse preached in the Plymouth Congregational Church of Chicago, Sabbath afternoon, June 1, 1856*. [Chicago], 1856. (MH)

St. Lawrence Republican, Extra. Ogdensburgh, N.Y., July 1837. (NN)

Say, J. B. *A Treatise on Political Economy*. Transl. from 4th French ed. by C. R. Prinsep. 3d Amer. ed. Philadelphia, 1827.

Schurz, Carl. *Speeches, Correspondence and Political Papers*. Edited by Frederick Bancroft. 6 vols. New York, Putnam, 1913.

Scott, Jessup W. "The Great West." *Commercial Review of the South and West* [*De Bow's Review*] 15, no. 1 (July 1853), 50–53.

[Sedgwick, Theodore Jr.] *Constitutional Reform, in a Series of Articles Contributed to the Democratic Review, upon Constitutional Guaranties in Political Government . . . to which are Added Two Letters of the Hon. Michael Hoffman. . . .* Edited by Thomas P. Kettell. New York, 1846. (N)

——. *Thoughts on the Proposed Annexation of Texas to the United States . . . together with the Address of Albert Gallatin, LL.D. . . .* 2d ed. New York, 1844. (NN)

Seward, William H. *The Destiny of America: Speech of William H. Seward at the Dedication of Capital University, at Columbus, Ohio, September 14, 1853*. Albany, N.Y., 1853. (NN)

——. *Discourse on Education, Delivered at Westfield, July 26, 1837*. Albany, N.Y., 1837. (NN)

——. *The Elements of Empire in America*. New York, 1844. (NN)

——. *Speech . . . in the Senate, Against Gov. Marcy's Six Million Mortgage. Delivered April 10, 1834*. N.p., 1834. (N)

——. *The Works of William H. Seward*. Edited by George E. Baker. 3 vols. New York, 1853.

Sexton, F. B. *Human Progress: An Address before the Literary Societies of Austin College June 22nd, 1858*. Houston, Texas, 1858. (TxU)

Seymour, Charles C. C. *Self-Made Men*. New York, 1858. (NN)

Seymour, Horatio. *Speech of Hon. Horatio Seymour, delivered at Tammany Hall, Friday Evening, Sept. 28, 1855*. N.p., n.d. (NN)

Shand, Peter J. *An Oration delivered before the Revolution and Cincinnati Societies of Charleston, South-Carolina, on The Fifth of July, 1830. . . .* Charleston, 1830. (MWA)

Shields, [James]. *Speech of Mr. Shields, of Illinois, on the Territorial Question. Delivered in the Senate of the United States, April 5, 1850*. Washington, D.C., 1850. (MWA)

Short Answers to Reckless Fabrications, against the Democratic Candidate for President, James Buchanan. Philadelphia, 1856. (NN)

Sickles, D[aniel] E. *Remarks of Hon. D. E. Sickles, of N. Y., on the Relations of the North and the South, and the Duty of the North in the Present Crisis. Delivered in the House of Representatives, December 13, 1859.* N.p., n.d. (MWA)

Simpson, Stephen. *The Working Man's Manual; A New Theory of Political Economy, on the Principle of Production the Source of Wealth.* Philadelphia, 1831. (MH)

Skidmore, Thomas. *The Rights of Man to Property! Being a Proposition to Make It Equal among the Adults of the Present Generation: And to Provide for its Equal Transmission to Every Individual of Each Succeeding Generation, on Arriving at the Age of Maturity.* . . . New York, 1829. (NNHi)

Slade, W[illiam]. *To the Public.* Pamphlet dated Washington, [D.C.], December 4, 1835. (NN)

[Slamm, Levi D.] *The Injustice of the Tariff on Protective Principles. The Plebeian Tracts, No. 2.* New York, 1844. (NN)

———. *The Tariff, No. 1: Its Injustice on Principles of Revenue. Remarks on the Injustice of our System of Indirect Taxation, by a Tariff of Duties on Imported Goods.* . . . New York, 1843. (NN)

Smith, Henry. *82d Anniversary American Independence. Oration by Henry Smith, Esq., delivered at the Capitol, in the City of Albany, July 5, 1858.* Albany, N.Y., 1858. (N)

Smith, Matthew Hale. *Successful Folks. How They Win.* . . . New York, 1878. (MH)

Smith, Oliver H. *Address of the Hon. Oliver H. Smith, delivered on the Fair Grounds, at Indianapolis, before the Marion County Agricultural Society. At the Annual Fair, in the Year 1856.* Indianapolis, 1856. (In)

Smith, S. Lisle. *Eulogy upon the Life, Character and Services of Henry Clay. Pronounced before the Common Council and Citizens of Chicago, July 20, 1852.* Chicago, 1852. (ICHi)

Smith, Thomas L., et al. *To the Democratic Citizens of Floyd County, and of the State of Indiana.* Indiana broadside, n.p., [1844]. (In)

Smith, Whitefoord. *An Oration delivered before the Euphradian and Clariosophic Societies of the South Carolina College, on the 6th December, 1848.* Columbia, S.C., 1849. (NNHi)

Southwick, Solomon [Sherlock]. *A Layman's Apology, for the Appointment of Clerical Chaplains by the Legislature of the State of New-York: in a Series of Letters, Addressed to Thomas Herttell, Member of the Assembly for the City of New-York, 1833.* Albany, N.Y., 1834. (N)

———. *An Oration: delivered by invitation, before the Albany County Temperance Society, at the Reformed Dutch Church in Bethlehem, July 4th, 1838.* Albany, N.Y., 1838. (N)

Sparrow, William. *The Nation's Privileges, and their Preservation. A Sermon Preached on the Day of our National Anniversary, 1852, in Christ Church, Alexandria, Va.* Philadelphia, 1852. (MWA)

Speeches of Joseph T. Buckingham, Charles M. Ellis, Esq., and Hon. Anson Burlingame, at the Free Democratic Meeting in Faneuil Hall, October 13, 1852. Boston, 1852. (MWA)

Spees, S. G. *A Discourse on the Great American Idea—Universal Liberty. Delivered in the Second Presbyterian Church, Indianapolis, Indiana, upon Thanksgiving Day, November 25th, 1847.* Indianapolis, Ind., 1848. (In)

Stanton, Henry B. *Ultraists—Conservatives—Reformers: An Address delivered before the Adelphic Union Society of Williams College, August 20, 1850.* New York, 1850. (NN)

State Rights and Free Trade Association, South Carolina. Political Tracts. *A Catechism on the Tariff, for the use of Plain People of Common Sense. Political Tract No. 3* (September 1831). Charleston, S.C., 1831. (NNHi)

——. *Free Trade and the American System; A Dialogue between a Merchant and a Planter. Political Tract, No. 8* (April 1, 1832). Charleston, S.C., 1832. (NN)

——. *The Prospect before Us; or, Strictures on the Late Message of the President of the United States: and the Report of the Secretary of the Treasury . . . By Aristides. . . . Political Tract No. 6* (February 1832). Charleston, S.C., 1832. (NN)

——. *The Remedy by State Interposition, or Nullification; Explained and Advocated by Chancellor Harper, in his Speech at Columbia, (S.C.) on the Twentieth September, 1830. Political Tract No. 5* (January 1832). Charleston, S.C., 1832. (MWA)

——. *Taxes! Taxes! Taxes! or Tables, Shewing the Form and the Amount of the Tribute Money, Levied by the Federal Government; on Agriculture and Commerce, to be Transferred into the Pockets of Manufacturers and Sugar Planters. Political Tract No. 4* (November 1831). Charleston, S.C., 1831. (MWA)

——. *Proceedings of the Celebration of the 4th of July, 1831, at Charleston, S.C., by the State Rights and Free Trade Party. . . .* Charleston, S.C., 1831. (NNHi)

——. *Proceedings of the State Rights Celebration, at Charleston, S.C. July 1st, 1830. . . .* Charleston, 1830. (NNHi)

Stephens, Alexander H. *A Constitutional View of the Late War between the States. . . .* 2 vols. Philadelphia, 1868–1870.

Stiles, William H. *Connection Between Liberty and Eloquence. An Address delivered before the Phi Kappa and Demosthenian Societies of Franklin College, (University of Georgia,) at the Annual Commencement, August 4th, 1852.* Augusta, Ga., 1852. (MWA)

Stillé, Charles J. *The Social Spirit. A Valedictory Oration, pronounced at the departure of the senior class from the society of Brothers in Unity, Yale College, June 28, 1839.* New Haven, Conn., 1839. (MWA)

Story, Joseph. *Commentaries on the Constitution of the United States. . . .* 3 vols. Boston and Cambridge, Mass., 1833.

——. *The Miscellaneous Writings of Joseph Story.* Edited by William Wetmore Story. Boston, 1852.

Summary of the Proceedings of a Convention of Republican Delegates, from the Several States in the Union, for the Purpose of Nominating a Candidate for the Office of Vice-

President of the United States; Held at Baltimore . . . May, 1832: with an Address, to the Republicans of the State of New-York, Prepared by their Delegates. . . . Albany, N.Y., 1832.

Sumner, Charles. *The Law of Human Progress: An Oration before the Phi Beta Kappa Society of Union College, Schenectady. July 25th, 1848.* Boston, 1849. (N)

Sutherland, Thomas Jefferson. *Three Political Letters, addressed to Dr. Wolfred Nelson, Late of Lower Canada, Now of Plattsburgh, N.Y.* New York, 1840. (NN)

Tansill, Charles C., ed. *Documents Illustrative of the Formation of the Union of the American States.* Washington, D.C., Government Printing Office, 1927.

Taylor, Joseph W. *Henry Clay: his Life, Character, and Services.* Eutaw, Ala., 1852. (AU)

Taylor, Nathaniel W. *Concio ad Clerum. A Sermon delivered in the chapel of Yale College, September 18, 1828.* New Haven, Conn., 1828. (N)

Tefft, Benjamin F. *The Far West, its Present, Past and Future: An Inaugural Address delivered to the Trustees of the Indiana Asbury University, at the Annual Commencement, August 20, 1845.* Indianapolis, 1845. (In)

Thompson, Dorothy, ed. *The Early Chartists.* London, Macmillan, 1971.

Thoreau, Henry D. *The Writings of Henry David Thoreau.* New Riverside ed. 11 vols. Boston, 1894–1895.

Tibbatts, John W. *Speech of Hon. John W. Tibbatts, of Kentucky, on the Reannexation of Texas; delivered in the House of Representatives, January 13, 1845.* Washington, D.C., 1845. (NN)

——. *Speech of Mr. Tibbatts, of Kentucky, on the Question of the Reannexation of Texas, together with His Remarks on the Tariff, delivered in the House of Representatives, May 7, 1844.* Washington, D.C., 1844. (NN)

Todd, John. *The Young Man. Hints addressed to the Young Men of the United States.* Northampton, Mass., 1844. (MWA)

To his Excellency, JOEL E. MATTESON, Governor of the State of Illinois. Illinois broadside, n.p., n.d. (KHi)

To the Democratic Electors of the Second Congressional District. Broadside authorized by Corresponding Democratic Committee, Second Congressional District of Indiana. Dated July 26, 1849. N.p., n.d. (In)

To the Farmers! and Working Men!! The Democracy of the Country! (Democratic Tract, No. 12). N.p. [Pennsylvania], 1840. (NN)

To the Voters of the Second Congressional District of Ind. [Whig tract.] N.p., [1847]. (In)

Tracts for Americans. Fillmore's Political History and Position. George Law and Chauncey Shaffer's Reasons for Repudiating Fillmore and Donelson. . . . Speech of Hon. E. B. Morgan, of N.Y., in U. S. House of Representatives, Aug. 4, 1856. N.p., n.d. (NN)

Transactions of the . . . Annual Meeting[s] of the Western Literary Institute and College of Professional Teachers Held in Cincinnati, 1834–1840. Cincinnati, Ohio, 1835–1841.

Trollope, Frances. *Domestic Manners of the Americans*. The English Library, edited by J. Isaacs. London, Routledge, 1927.

"The True Progress of Society." *Biblical Repertory and Princeton Review* 24, no. 1 (January 1852), 16–38.

Tuckerman, Joseph. *The Principles and Results of the Ministry at Large, in Boston*. Boston, 1838. (MWA)

Tuthill, L[ouisa] C. *Success in Life. The Lawyer*. New York, 1850. (MWiW)

——. *Success in Life. The Merchant*. New York, 1850. (NN)

Tuttle, Joseph F. "The Dignity of Progress." *Ladies' Repository, and Gatherings of the West* 6, no. 7 (July 1846), 198.

——. "The West and Western Eloquence." *Biblical Repository and Classical Review*, 3d ser., 1, no. 4 (October 1845), 638–69.

Twining, William. *Address on Moral Education, Based on the Study of the Bible as a School Book*. . . . Rising Sun, Ind., 1836. (In)

Ullmann, Daniel. *An Address delivered in the Tabernacle, before the Tippecanoe and other Harrison Associations, of the City of New York, at the celebration of the Anniversary of the Birth Day of Washington, and the Recent Triumph of Sound Principles, in the Election of William Henry Harrison, to the Presidency of the U.S. Feb'y. 22, 1841*. New York, 1841. (NN)

Underwood, [Joseph R.] *Speech of Mr. Underwood, of Kentucky, on the Sub-Treasury Bill. Delivered in the House of Representatives, June 8, 1840*. Washington, D. C. 1840. (MWA)

United States Senatorial Question. Speeches Delivered in the Assembly of the State of New-York. . . . Albany, N.Y., 1855. (N)

Upfold, George. *The Distinguishing goodness of God to the American People: A Discourse, delivered in Trinity Church, On Thursday, November 23d, 1848, the day of Annual Thanksgiving appointed by the Governor of the Commonwelth*. Pittsburgh, Pa., 1848. (MWA)

Upham, Charles W. *Eulogy on the Life and Character of Zachary Taylor, President of the United States, July 18, 1850*. . . . Salem, Mass., 1850. (MWA)

——. *Remarks of Hon. Charles W. Upham, of Mass., delivered in the House of Representatives, February 27, 1855, on Mediation in the Eastern War—The Institutions of Massachusetts—The Ordinance of 1787*. Washington, D.C., 1855. (MWA)

Upham, W[illiam]. *The Compromise Bill. Speech of Hon. W. Upham, of Vermont, in the Senate of the United States, July 26, 1848*. Washington, D.C., n.d. (MWA)

Van Buren, Martin. *The Autobiography of Martin Van Buren*. Edited by J. C. Fitzpatrick. Annual Report of the American Historical Association for the Year 1918. 2 vols. Washington, D.C., Government Printing Office, 1920. Vol. 2.

——. *Inquiry into the Origin and Course of Political Parties in the United States*. Edited by his Sons. New York, 1867. Reprint ed., New York, Kelley, 1967.

——. *Opinions of Mr. Van Buren, on the Subject of a National Bank, Distribution of the Proceeds of the Public Lands, an Exchequer or Government Fiscal Agent, a Tariff, the Veto Power, and a National Convention*. N.p., [1843]. (NN)

Van Doren, William H. *Mercantile Morals; or, Thoughts for Young Men Entering Mercantile Life.* New York, 1852. (MH-BA)

Van Ness, C[ornelius] P. *Speech of the Hon. C. P. Van Ness, delivered at the Late Democratic Convention at Woodstock, Vermont, And published by the request of the State Committee.* Burlington, Vt., 1840. (NN)

Vivo in Silvis [pseud.]. *A Pamphlet on Equal Rights and Privileges, to the People of the United States. Andrew County, Missouri.* St. Joseph, Mo., 1856. (NN)

A Voice from the Interior. Who Shall Be President? the Hero of New-Orleans, or John the Second, of the House of Braintree. Boston, 1828. (NN)

The Voice of the People, and the Facts, in Relation to the Rejection of Martin Van Buren by the U.S. Senate. New York Standard—Extra. New York, 1832. (NN)

Voice of the Southwest. Proceedings of the Democratic State Convention of Tennessee at Nashville February 11, 1840. Nashville, Tenn., 1840.

Voorhees, Daniel W. *Speeches of Daniel W. Voorhees of Indiana. . . .* Compiled by Charles S. Voorhees. Cincinnati, Ohio, 1875. (NN)

Walker, Amasa. *An Address delivered before the Young Men of Boston, associated for Moral and Intellectual Improvement, on the Fiftyseventh Anniversary of American Independence.* Boston, 1833. (NN)

——. *An Oration delivered at Stoughton, Mass., July 5, 1830. . . .* Boston, 1830. (NN)

Walker, Robert. *Oration delivered at Clinton Hall, to the Journeymen Stone Cutters' Association, on the Fifty-Seventh Anniversary of American Independence, July 4, 1833.* New York, 1833. (NNHi)

Walker, Robert J. *An Appeal for the Union. Letter from the Hon. Robert J. Walker. New York, Tuesday, Sept. 30, 1856. . . .* New York, 1856. (N)

Walsh, Michael. *Sketches of the Speeches and Writings of Michael Walsh.* New York, 1843. (NN)

Ware, John. "Address delivered on the First Anniversary, Nov. 1823." In *Addresses delivered before the Association for Religious Improvement, at their First, Second, and Third Anniversaries.* Boston, 1826. (MWA)

Warren, Charles. *An Address, in Commemoration of American Independence, delivered at Palmyra, July 4, 1823.* Hallowell, Me., 1823. (MWA)

Watson, William R. [Hamilton]. *The Whig Party; its objects—its principles—its candidates—its duties—and its prospects. An Address to the People of Rhode-Island, published in the Providence Journal . . . 1844.* Providence, R.I., 1844. (NN)

Wayland, Francis. *The Affairs of Rhode-Island. A Discourse delivered in the Meeting-House of the First Baptist Church, Providence, May 22, 1842.* Providence, R.I., 1842. (NN)

——. *The Elements of Political Economy.* New York, 1837.

Webster, Daniel. *Reception of Mr. Webster at Boston, September 30, 1842. With his Speech, delivered in Faneuil Hall on that Occasion.* Boston, 1842. (NN)

——. *Speech of the Hon. Daniel Webster, of Massachusetts, at the Dinner Given to Him by the Merchants and Other Citizens of Philadelphia, December 9, 1846.* Washington, D.C., 1847. (NN)

Webster, Daniel. *The Writings and Speeches of Daniel Webster.* National ed. 18 vols. Boston: Little, 1903.

Webster, Noah, comp. *An American Dictionary of the English Language.* 2 vols. New York, 1828. (NN)

Weld, Theodore D. *American Slavery As It Is.* New York, 1839.

Welter, Rush, ed. *American Writings on Popular Education: The Nineteenth Century.* Indianapolis, Ind., Bobbs, 1971.

Western Literary Institute and College of Professional Teachers, *see Transactions.*

"What Shall the Whigs Do?" *Cincinnati Daily Gazette,* 17 January 1837, p. 3. (MWA)

Whig Congressional Executive Committee. *The Prospect Before Us, or Locofoco Impositions Exposed.* Washington, D.C., [1844]. (NN)

——. *Tariff Doctrine.* Washington, D.C., [1844]. (NN)

Whig Songs for 1844. New York, n.d. (NN)

Whipple, Edwin P. *Washington and the Principles of the Revolution: An Oration delivered before the Municipal Authorities of the City of Boston, at the Celebration of the Declaration of Independence, July 4, 1850.* 2d ed. Boston, 1850. (NN)

White, [Charles]. "Influence of Colleges, especially on Western Education and Civilization." *Biblical Repository and Classical Review,* 3d ser., 4, no. 15 (July 1848), 383–412.

White, George S. *Memoir of Samuel Slater.* 2d ed. Philadelphia, 1836. Reprint ed., New York, Kelley, 1967.

Whitman, Walt. *The Gathering of the Forces: Editorials, Literary and Dramatic Reviews and Other Material Written by Walt Whitman as Editor of the Brooklyn Daily Eagle in 1846 and 1847.* Edited by Cleveland Rodgers and John Black. 2 vols. New York, Putnam, 1920.

Whittier, John G. "Justice and Expediency; or, Slavery considered with a view to its rightful and effectual remedy, Abolition." *Anti-Slavery Reporter* 1, no. 4 (September 1833), 51–63.

Whittlesey, M. K. *The Perils of Liberty. A Sermon preached in . . . First Congregational Church in Ottawa, by the Pastor, M. K. Whittlesey.* Peoria, Ill., 1856. (ICHi)

William Sheets, Federal Candidate for the State Senate, in account with the Secretary of State. Indianapolis, September, 1852. N.p., n.d. (In)

Wilson, James. *Speech of Mr. Jas. Wilson, of N. Hampshire, on the Political Influence of Slavery . . . delivered in the House of Representatives of the United States, February 16, 1849.* Washington, D.C., 1849.

[Wilson, Thomas L. V.] *The Aristocracy of Boston: Who They Are, and What They Were. . . .* Boston, 1848. (NN)

Wilstach, John A. *The Imperial Period of National Greatness. A Lecture on the Destiny of the West, . . . before the Western Literary Union, . . . 12th of First Month, 1855.* Lafayette, Ind., 1855. (In)

Wirt, William. *An Address, delivered before the Peithessophian and Philoclean Societies of Rutgers College.* 2d ed. New Brunswick, N.J., 1830. (NN)

Wise, Daniel. *The Young Man's Counsellor: or, Sketches and Illustrations of the Duties and Dangers of Young Men.* . . . New York, 1850. (NN)

Witherspoon, John. *Lectures on Moral Philosophy.* Edited by Varnum L. Collins. Princeton, N.J., Princeton Univ. Press, 1912.

Wood, T. F. *The Money-Maker's Manual; and Secrets of Success.* . . . Vernon, N.J., 1868. (MWA)

Woodbury, Levi. *Writings of Levi Woodbury LL.D. Political, Judicial and Literary: Now First Selected and Arranged.* 3 vols. Boston, 1852.

The Working Man Defended. By the Author of the "Crisis Met." New York, 1840. (NN)

[Worrell, Joseph, et al.] *Letters addressed to John Sergeant, Manuel Eyre, Lawrence Lewis, Clement C. Biddle, and Joseph P. Norris, Esqs. Authors of An Address to the People of Pennsylvania, Adopted at a Meeting of the Friends to the Election of John Quincy Adams, held in Philadelphia, July 7, 1828: Containing Strictures on their Address. by the Committee of Correspondence, of Philadelphia, Appointed by a Republican Convention, held at Harrisburg, January 8, 1828.* Philadelphia, 1828. (NN)

Wright, D[eodatus]. *Two Letters to Gov. Hunt, In Reply to his Letter of August 8th, 1856.* N.p., n.d. (N)

Wright, Frances. *A Lecture on Existing Evils and Their Remedy.* . . . New York, 1829. (NN)

Wright, Joseph A. *An Address delivered by Gov. Joseph A. Wright, on the 6th day of October, 1853, at Livonia, Washington County, Indiana, to the District Agricultural Society.* . . . Indianapolis, Ind., 1854. (MWA)

Wright, Silas Jr. *Address delivered at the Celebration of the 63rd Anniversary of the Independence of the United States, at Canton, N.Y., Fourth of July, 1839.* Ogdensburgh, N.Y., 1839. (MWA)

Wyckoff, I. N. *The Stability of the Times: A Sermon delivered on the Fourth of July, 1852, in the Second Ref. Prot. Dutch Church, in the City of Albany.* Albany, N.Y., 1852. (MWA)

Wylie, Andrew. *Religion and State; Not Church and State. A Sermon, on Psalm 11, 10–12, Delivered, July Fourth 1830. In the Hall of the Indiana College, Bloomington.* . . . Bloomington, Ind., 1830. (In)

——. *Sermon on the Subject of the Union of Christians for the Conversion of the World, delivered in Madison, Ia., April 20, 1834.* Madison, Iowa, 1834. (In)

Yancey, Benjamin C. *Speech . . . in relation to the Bank of the State of South Carolina delivered in Committee of the Whole House, December Session of the Legislature, 1848.* Hamburg, S.C. [1849]. (ScU)

Young, Samuel. *A Discourse delivered at Schenectady, July 25, A.D. 1826. Before the New-York Alpha of the Phi Beta Kappa.* Ballston Spa, N.Y., 1826. (N)

Young Men's Whig State Convention. N.p. [Connecticut, 1840]. (NN)

SECONDARY SOURCES

Abbott, Richard. "The Agricultural Press Views the Yeoman: 1819–1859." *Agricultural History* 42 (1968), 35–48.

Adams, Ephraim. *The Power of Ideals in American History.* New Haven, Conn., Yale Univ. Press, 1913.

Ahearn, Marie L. "The Rhetoric of Work and Vocation in Some Popular Northern Writings before 1860." Ph.D. diss., Brown University, 1965.

Ahlstrom, Sidney. "The Puritan Ethic and the Spirit of American Democracy." In George L. Hunt, ed., *Calvinism and the Political Order.* Philadelphia, Westminster Press, 1965.

——. *A Religious History of the American People.* New Haven, Conn., Yale Univ. Press, 1972.

Alexander, Thomas B. *Sectional Stress and Party Strength.* Nashville, Tenn., Vanderbilt Univ. Press, 1967.

Arieli, Yehoshua. *Individualism and Nationalism in American Ideology.* Cambridge, Mass., Harvard Univ. Press, 1964.

Auer, J. Jeffery, ed. *Antislavery and Disunion, 1858–1861: Studies in the Rhetoric of Compromise and Conflict.* New York, Harper, 1963.

Bailyn, Bernard. *The Ideological Origins of the American Revolution.* Cambridge, Mass., Harvard Univ. Press, 1967.

Banner, Lois W. "Religious Benevolence as Social Control: A Critique of an Interpretation." *Journal of American History* 60 (1973), 23–41.

Barkan, Elliott. "The Emergence of a Whig Persuasion: Conservatism, Democratism, and the New York State Whigs." *New York History* 52 (1971), 367–95.

Barnes, Gilbert H. *The Anti-Slavery Impulse 1830–1844.* New York and London, Appleton, 1933. Reprint ed., Gloucester, Mass., Peter Smith, 1957.

Baskerville, Barnet. "19th Century Burlesque of Oratory." *American Quarterly* 20 (1968), 726–43.

Basler, Roy E. *The Lincoln Legend: A Study in Changing Conceptions.* Boston, Houghton, 1935.

Baxter, Maurice G. *Daniel Webster & the Supreme Court.* N.p., Univ. of Mass. Press, 1966.

Beale, Howard K. *A History of Freedom of Teaching in American Schools.* Report of the Commission on the Social Studies, American Historical Association. Part 16. New York: Scribner, 1941.

Benson, Lee. *The Concept of Jacksonian Democracy: New York as a Test Case.* Princeton, N.J., Princeton Univ. Press, 1961.

Berwanger, Eugene H. *The Frontier Against Slavery: Western Anti-Negro Prejudice and the Slavery Extension Controversy.* Urbana, Ill.: Univ. of Ill. Press, 1967.

Bestor, Arthur. "The American Civil War as a Constitutional Crisis." *American Historical Review* 69 (1964), 327–52.

——. "State Sovereignty and Slavery: A Reinterpretation of Proslavery Constitutional Doctrine, 1846–1860." *Journal of the Illinois State Historical Society* 54 (1961), 117–80.

Billington, Ray A. *The Protestant Crusade 1800–1860: A Study of the Origins of American Nativism.* New York: Macmillan, 1938.

Binkley, Robert W. Jr. "The American System: An Example of Nineteenth-Century Economic Thinking. Its Definition by its Author Henry Clay." Ph.D. diss., Columbia University, 1949.

Blumenthal, Henry. *A Reappraisal of Franco-American Relations 1830–1871.* Chapel Hill, N.C.: Univ. of N.C. Press, 1959.

Bodo, John R. *The Protestant Clergy and Public Issues 1812–1848.* Princeton, N.J., Princeton Univ. Press, 1954.

Boorstin, Daniel J. *America and the Image of Europe.* New York, Meridian Books, 1960.

——. *The Americans: The National Experience.* New York, Random House, 1965.

——. *The Genius of American Politics.* Chicago, Univ. of Chicago Press, 1953.

——. *The Lost World of Thomas Jefferson.* New York, Holt, 1948.

Boudin, Louis. *Government by Judiciary.* 2 vols. New York, Godwin, 1932.

Boyd, William K. "The Antecedents of the North Carolina Convention of 1835." *South Atlantic Quarterly* 9 (1910), 83–93, 161–76.

Branch, E. Douglas. *The Sentimental Years.* New York, Appleton, 1934.

Brasington, George F. Jr. "Representative Government in Jacksonian Political Thought." Ph.D. diss., University of Illinois, 1958.

Brauer, Kinley J. *Cotton versus Conscience: Massachusetts Whig Politics and Southwestern Expansion, 1843–1848.* Lexington, Ky., Univ. of Ky. Press, 1967.

Briggs, Asa. "The Language of 'Class' in Early Nineteenth-Century England." In Asa Briggs and John Saville, eds., *Essays in Labour History.* London, Macmillan, 1960. Pp. 43–73.

Briggs, Asa, ed. *Chartist Studies.* London, Macmillan, 1959.

Brown, Bernard E. *American Conservatives: The Political Thought of Francis Lieber and John W. Burgess.* New York, Columbia Univ. Press, 1954.

Brown, Ira V. "Watchers for the Second Coming: The Millenarian Tradition in America." *Mississippi Valley Historical Review* 39 (1952), 441–58.

Brown, Roger A. *The Republic in Peril: 1812.* New York, Columbia Univ. Press, 1964.

Bruce, Helm. "The Constitution and Constitutional Convention of 1849." *Proceedings of Seventeenth Annual Meeting of the Kentucky State Bar Association . . . 1918.* Louisville, Ky., the Association, n.d. Pp. 131–60.

Burns, Edward M. *The American Idea of Mission: Concepts of National Purpose and Destiny.* New Brunswick, N.J., Rutgers Univ. Press, 1957.

Burns, Rex S. "The Yeoman Mechanic: 'Venturous Conservative?' " *Rocky Mountain Social Science Journal* 4, no. 2 (1967), 9–21.

Cadman, John W. Jr. *The Corporation in New Jersey: Business and Politics 1791–1875.* Cambridge, Mass., Harvard Univ. Press, 1949.

Callcott, George H. *History in the United States 1800–1860: Its Practice and Purpose.* Baltimore, Johns Hopkins Univ. Press, 1970.

Carpenter, Jesse T. *The South as a Conscious Minority 1789–1861: A Study in Political Thought.* New York, N.Y. Univ. Press, 1930.

Carroll, E. Malcolm. *Origins of the Whig Party.* Durham, N.C., Duke Univ. Press, 1925.

Case, Shirley J. *The Millennial Hope: A Phase of War-Time Thinking.* Chicago, Univ. of Chicago Press, 1918.

Cawelti, John G. *Apostles of the Self-Made Man.* Chicago, Univ. of Chicago Press, 1965.

Channing, Steven A. *Crisis of Fear: Secession in South Carolina.* New York, Simon & Schuster, 1970.

Cheyney, Edward P. *The Anti-Rent Agitation in the State of New York, 1839–1846.* Publications of the University of Pennsylvania, Political Economy and Public Law Series, no. 2. Philadelphia, 1887.

Christman, Henry. *Tin Horns and Calico: A Decisive Episode in the Emergence of Democracy.* New York, Holt, 1945.

Chroust, Anton-Hermann. *The Rise of the Legal Profession in America.* 2 vols. Norman, Okla., Univ. of Okla. Press, 1965.

Cline, Myrtle. *American Attitude toward the Greek War of Independence 1821–1828.* Atlanta, Ga., privately printed, 1930.

Coben, Stanley and Lorman Ratner, eds. *The Development of an American Culture.* Englewood Cliffs, N.J., Prentice-Hall, 1970.

Cohen, Morris R. *American Thought: A Critical Sketch.* Edited by Felix S. Cohen. Glencoe, Ill., Free Press, 1954.

Coker, Francis W. "American Traditions concerning Property and Liberty," *American Political Science Review* 30 (1936), 1–23.

Cole, Arthur C. *The Whig Party in the South.* Washington, D.C., American Historical Association, 1913.

Cole, Charles C. Jr. *The Social Ideas of the Northern Evangelists 1826–1860.* New York, Columbia Univ. Press, 1954.

Commager, Henry Steele. *Majority Rule and Minority Rights.* New York, Oxford Univ. Press, 1943.

———. "The Search for a Usable Past." *American Heritage* 16, no. 2 (1965), 4–9, 90–96.

Commons, John R. *Legal Foundations of Capitalism.* New York, Macmillan, 1924.

Cooke, John W. "Some Aspects of the Concept of the Free Individual in the United States, 1800–1860." Ph.D. diss., Vanderbilt University, 1967.

Corwin, Edward S. *Liberty Against Government: The Rise, Flowering and Decline of a Famous Juridical Concept.* Baton Rouge, La., La. State Univ. Press, 1948.

Crandall, Andrew W. *The Early History of the Republican Party 1854–1856.* Boston, Badger, 1930.

Crandall, John C. "Patriotism and Humanitarian Reform in Children's Literature, 1825–1860." *American Quarterly* 21 (1969), 1–22.

Craven, Avery. *The Coming of the Civil War*. 2d ed. Chicago, Univ. of Chicago Press, 1957.
———. *The Growth of Southern Nationalism, 1848–1861. A History of The South*, Vol. 6. Baton Rouge, La., La. State Univ. Press, 1953.
Craven, Wesley F. *The Legend of the Founding Fathers*. New York, N.Y. Univ. Press, 1956.
Cremin, Lawrence A. *The American Common School: An Historic Conception*. Teachers College Studies in Education. New York, Teachers College Press, 1951.
Croly, Herbert. *Progressive Democracy*. New York, Macmillan, 1914.
Cross, Whitney R. *The Burned-over District: The Social and Intellectual History of Enthusiastic Religion in Western New York, 1800–1850*. Ithaca, N.Y., Cornell Univ. Press, 1950.
Culver, Raymond B. *Horace Mann and Religion in the Massachusetts Public Schools*. Yale Studies in the History and Theory of Religious Education, vol. 3. New Haven, Conn., Yale Univ. Press, 1929.
Currie, R., and R. M. Hartwell. "*The Making of the English Working Class?*" *Economic History Review*, 2d ser., 18 (1965), 633–43.
Curti, Merle. "Austria and the United States 1848–1852, A Study in Diplomatic Relations." *Smith College Studies in History* 11, no. 3 (1926), 141–206.
———. "The Impact of the Revolutions of 1848 on American Thought." In Edward N. Saveth, ed., *Understanding the American Past*. Boston, Little, 1954. Pp. 244–58.
———. "Robert Rantoul, Jr., The Reformer in Politics." *New England Quarterly* 5 (1932), 264–80.
———. *The Roots of American Loyalty*. New York, Columbia Univ. Press, 1946.
———. *The Social Ideas of American Educators*. Report of the Commission on the Social Studies, American Historical Association, part 10. New York, Scribner, 1935.
———. "Young America." *American Historical Review* 32 (1926), 34–55.
Curtis, Eugene N. "American Opinion of the French Nineteenth-Century Revolutions." *American Historical Review* 29 (1924), 249–70.
———. "La Révolution de 1830 et l'Opinion Publique en Amérique." *La Révolution de 1848 et Les Révolutions du XIXe Siècle, 1830–1848–1870* 17 (1921), 64–73, 81–118.
Davis, David Brion. *The Slave Power Conspiracy and the Paranoid Style*. Baton Rouge, La., La. State Univ. Press, 1969.
———. "Some Ideological Functions of Prejudice in Ante-Bellum America." *American Quarterly* 15 (1963), 115–25.
———. "Some Themes of Counter-Subversion: An Analysis of Anti-Masonic, Anti-Catholic, and Anti-Mormon Literature." *Mississippi Valley Historical Review* 47 (1960), 205–24.
Degler, Carl N. "The Locofocos: Urban 'Agrarians.'" *Journal of Economic History* 16 (1956), 322–33.

De Grazia, Alfred. *Public and Republic: Political Representation in America.* New York, Knopf, 1951.

Detweiler, Philip F. "The Changing Reputation of the Declaration of Independence: The First Fifty Years." *William and Mary Quarterly,* 3d ser., 19 (1962), 557–74.

Diamond, Sigmund. *The Reputation of the American Businessman.* Cambridge, Mass., Harvard Univ. Press, 1955.

Dietze, Gottfried. *In Defense of Property.* Chicago, Regnery, 1963.

Donald, David. *An Excess of Democracy: The American Civil War and the Social Process.* Oxford, Clarendon Press, 1960.

Donovan, Herbert A. *The Barnburners: A Study of the Internal Movements in the Political History of New York State . . . 1830–1852.* New York, N.Y. Univ. Press, 1925.

Dorfman, Joseph. *The Economic Mind in American Civilization, 1606–1918.* 3 vols. New York, Viking, 1946–1949. Vol. 2.

Driver, Cecil. *Tory Radical: The Life of Richard Oastler.* New York, Oxford Univ. Press, 1946.

Dubofsky, Melvyn. "Daniel Webster and the Whig Theory of Economic Growth: 1828–1848." *New England Quarterly* 42 (1969), 551–72.

Dumond, Dwight L. *Antislavery: The Crusade for Freedom in America.* Ann Arbor, Mich., Univ. of Mich. Press, 1961.

Earle, Edward M. "American Interest in the Greek Cause, 1821–1827." *American Historical Review* 33 (1927), 44–63.

——. "Early American Policy concerning Ottoman Minorities." *Political Science Quarterly* 42 (1927), 337–67.

East, Robert A. *Business Enterprise in the American Revolutionary Era.* New York, Columbia Univ. Press, 1938.

Eaton, Clement. *Freedom of Thought in the Old South.* Durham, N.C., Duke Univ. Press, 1940.

Eby, Cecil. "America as 'Asylum': A Dual Image." *American Quarterly* 14 (1962), 483–89.

Edsall, Nicholas C. *The anti-Poor Law Movement 1834–44.* Manchester, England, Manchester Univ. Press, 1971.

Edwards, J. K. "Chartism in Norwich." *Yorkshire Bulletin of Economic and Social Research* 19 (1967), 85–100.

Ekirch, Arthur A. Jr. *The Idea of Progress in America, 1815–1860.* Columbia University Studies in History, Economics, and Public Law, no. 511. New York, Columbia Univ. Press, 1944.

——. *Ideas, Ideals, and American Diplomacy.* New York, Appleton, 1966.

Elkins, Stanley. *Slavery: A Problem in American Institutional and Intellectual Life.* Chicago, Univ. of Chicago Press, 1959.

Ellis, Richard E. *The Jeffersonian Crisis: Courts and Politics in the Young Republic.* New York, Oxford Univ. Press, 1971.

Elson, Ruth M. *Guardians of Tradition: American Schoolbooks of the Nineteenth Century.* Lincoln, Neb., Univ. of Neb. Press, 1964.

England, J. Merton. "The Democratic Faith in American Schoolbooks, 1783–1860." *American Quarterly* 15 (1963), 191–99.

Ershkowitz, Herbert, and William G. Shade. "Consensus or Conflict? Political Behavior in the State Legislatures during the Jacksonian Era." *Journal of American History* 58 (1971), 591–621.

Farnham, Wallace D. " 'The Weakened Spring of Government': A Study in Nineteenth-Century American History." *American Historical Review* 68 (1963), 662–80.

Fehrenbacher, Don E. "Lincoln and Judicial Supremacy: A Note on the Galena Speech of July 23, 1856." *Civil War History* 16 (1970), 197–204.

——. "Lincoln, Douglas, and the 'Freeport Question.' " *American Historical Review* 66 (1961), 599–617.

——. "The Origins and Purpose of Lincoln's 'House-Divided' Speech." *Mississippi Valley Historical Review* 46 (1960), 615–43.

——. *Prelude to Greatness: Lincoln in the 1850's*. Stanford, Calif., Stanford Univ. Press, 1962.

Fellman, David. "Property in Colonial Political Theory." *Temple University Law Quarterly* 16 (1942), 388–406.

Filler, Louis. *The Crusade against Slavery, 1830–1860*. New York, Harper, 1960.

Fischer, David H. *The Revolution of American Conservatism: The Federalist Party in the Era of Jeffersonian Democracy*. New York, Harper, 1965.

Foner, Eric. *Free Soil, Free Labor, Free Men: The Ideology of the Republican Party before the Civil War*. New York, Oxford Univ. Press, 1970.

——. "The Wilmot Proviso Revisited." *Journal of American History* 56 (1969), 262–79.

Formisano, Ronald P. *The Birth of Mass Political Parties: Michigan, 1827–1861*. Princeton, N.J., Princeton Univ. Press, 1971.

——. "Political Character, Antipartyism and the Second Party System." *American Quarterly* 21 (1969), 683–709.

Foster, Charles I. *An Errand of Mercy: The Evangelical United Front, 1790–1837*. Chapel Hill, N.C., Univ. of N.C., 1960.

Fox, G. George. *Abraham Lincoln's Religion: Sources of the Great Emancipator's Religious Inspiration*. New York, Exposition, 1959.

Fredrickson, George M. *The Black Image in the White Mind: The Debate on Afro-American Character and Destiny, 1817–1914*. New York, Harper, 1971.

Freehling, William W. *Prelude to Civil War: The Nullification Controversy in South Carolina, 1816–1836*. New York, Harper, 1966.

Fritz, Henry E. "Nationalistic Response to Frontier Expansion." *Mid-America* 50 (1969), 227–43.

Fuess, Claude M. *The Life of Caleb Cushing*. 2 vols. New York, Harcourt, 1923.

Fuller, John D. P. "The Movement for the Acquisition of All Mexico, 1846–1848." *Johns Hopkins University Studies in Historical and Political Science* 54, no. 4 (1936), 1–176.

——. "The Slavery Question and the Movement to Acquire Mexico, 1846–1848." *Mississippi Valley Historical Review* 21 (1934), 31–48.

Fussell, Edwin. *Frontier: American Literature and the American West.* Princeton, N.J., Princeton Univ. Press, 1965.

Gammage, R. E. *History of the Chartist Movement 1837–1854.* Rev. ed. Newcastle and London, 1894.

Gara, Larry. "Slavery and the Slave Power: A Crucial Distinction." *Civil War History* 15 (1969), 5–18.

Gatell, Frank O. "Sober Second Thoughts on Van Buren, the Albany Regency, and the Wall Street Conspiracy." *Journal of American History* 53 (1966), 19–40.

Gazley, John G. *American Opinion of German Unification, 1848–1871.* Columbia University Studies in History, Economics, and Public Law no. 267. New York, Columbia Univ. Press, 1926.

Gewehr, Wesley M. *The Great Awakening in Virginia, 1740–1790.* Durham, N.C., Duke Univ. Press, 1930.

Goetzmann, William H. "The Mountain Man as Jacksonian Man." *American Quarterly* 15 (1963), 402–15.

Good, Harry G. *Benjamin Rush and His Services to American Education.* Berne, Ind., Witness Press, 1918.

Goodman, Paul. "Ethics and Enterprise: The Values of a Boston Elite, 1800–1860." *American Quarterly* 18 (1966), 437–51.

Goodrich, Carter. *Government Promotion of American Canals and Railroads, 1800–1890.* New York, Columbia Univ. Press, 1960.

Grampp, William D. *Economic Liberalism.* 2 vols. New York: Random House, 1965.

Green, Fletcher M. *Constitutional Development in the South Atlantic States: A Study in the Evolution of Democracy.* Chapel Hill, N.C., Univ. of N.C. Press, 1930.

Greene, Evarts B. *American Interest in Popular Government Abroad.* United States Committee on Public Information, War Information Series, no. 8 (September 1917). Washington, D.C., Government Printing Office, 1917.

Greene, Theodore P. *America's Heroes: The Changing Models of Success in American Magazines.* New York, Oxford Univ. Press, 1970.

Griffin, Clifford S. "Religious Benevolence as Social Control, 1815–1860." *Mississippi Valley Historical Review* 44 (1957), 423–44.

——. *Their Brothers' Keepers: Moral Stewardship in the United States, 1800–1865.* New Brunswick, N.J., Rutgers Univ. Press, 1960.

Grimsted, David. "Rioting in Its Jacksonian Setting." *American Historical Review* 77 (1972), 361–97.

Gunderson, Robert Gray. *The Log-Cabin Campaign.* Lexington, Ky., Univ. of Ky. Press, 1957.

Haines, Charles G. *The American Doctrine of Judicial Supremacy.* 2d ed. Berkeley, Calif., Univ. of Calif. Press, 1932.

——. *The Role of the Supreme Court in American Government and Politics 1789–1835.* Berkeley and Los Angeles, Calif., Univ. of Calif. Press, 1944.

——, and Foster H. Sherwood. *The Role of the Supreme Court in American Govern-*

ment and Politics 1835–1864. Berkeley and Los Angeles, Calif., Univ. of Calif. Press, 1956.

Hall, James W. "Concepts of Liberty in American Broadside Ballads 1850–1870." *Journal of Popular Culture* 2 (1968), 252–77.

Hamilton, Holman. *Prologue to Conflict: The Crisis and Compromise of 1850*. Lexington, Ky., Univ. of Ky. Press, 1964.

Hamilton, J. G. deRoulhac. *Party Politics in North Carolina, 1836–1860*. University of North Carolina, The James Sprunt Historical Publications, vol. 15, nos. 1–2. Durham, N.C., 1916.

Hammond, Bray. *Banks and Politics in America: From the Revolution to the Civil War*. Princeton, N.J., Princeton Univ. Press, 1957.

——. "Jackson, Biddle, and the Bank of the United States." *Journal of Economic History* 7 (1947), 1–23.

Handlin, Oscar, and Mary Handlin. *Commonwealth; A Study of the Role of Government in the American Economy: Massachusetts, 1774–1861*. New York, N. Y. Univ. Press, 1947. Rev. ed., Cambridge, Mass., Harvard Univ. Press, 1969.

——. *The Dimensions of Liberty*. Cambridge, Mass., Harvard Univ. Press, 1961.

Hansen, Allen O. *Early Educational Leadership in the Ohio Valley: A Study of Educational Reconstruction through the Western Literary Institute and College of Professional Teachers*. Journal of Educational Research Monographs, no. 5. Bloomington, Ill., Public School Publishing Co., 1923.

Harding, Vincent. "Lyman Beecher and the Transformation of American Protestantism." Ph.D. diss., University of Chicago, 1965.

Harkness, Donald R. "Crosscurrents: American Anti-Democracy, from Jackson to the Civil War (1829–1860)." Ph.D. diss., University of Minnesota, 1955.

Harland, Gordon. "The Crisis of American Protestantism." *Frontier* 6 (1963), 247–55.

Harrison, J. F. C. *Learning and Living 1790–1960: A Study in the History of the English Adult Education Movement*. London, Routledge, 1961.

Hart, Charles D. "The Natural Limits of Slavery Expansion: Kansas-Nebraska, 1854." *Kansas Historical Quarterly* 34 (1968), 32–40.

Hartz, Louis. *Economic Policy and Democratic Thought: Pennsylvania, 1776–1860*. Cambridge, Mass., Harvard Univ. Press, 1948.

——. *The Liberal Tradition in America: An Interpretation of American Political Thought since the Revolution*. New York, Harcourt, 1955.

——. "South Carolina vs. the United States." In Daniel Aaron, ed., *America in Crisis: Fourteen Crucial Episodes in American History*. New York, Knopf, 1952. Pp. 73–89.

Hay, Robert P. "The Glorious Departure of the American Patriarchs: Contemporary Reactions to the Deaths of Jefferson and Adams." *Journal of Southern History* 35 (1969), 543–55.

——. "Providence and the American Past." *Indiana Magazine of History* 65 (1969), 79–102.

Heilbroner, Robert L. *The Future as History: The Historic Currents of Our Time and the Direction in Which They Are Taking America.* New York, Harper, 1960.

Heimert, Alan. *Religion and the American Mind from the Great Awakening to the Revolution.* Cambridge, Mass., Harvard Univ. Press, 1966.

Hibbard, Benjamin H. *A History of the Public Land Policies.* New York, Macmillan, 1924.

Higham, John. *From Boundlessness to Consolidation: The Transformation of American Culture 1848–1860.* Ann Arbor, Mich.; William L. Clements Library, 1969.

Hodges, Wiley E. "The Theoretical Basis for Anti-governmentalism in Virginia, 1789–1836." *Journal of Politics* 9 (1947), 325–54.

Hoffmann, William S. *Andrew Jackson and North Carolina Politics.* The James Sprunt Studies in History and Political Science, vol. 40. Chapel Hill, N.C., Univ. of N.C. Press, 1958.

Hofstadter, Richard. *America at 1750: A Social Portrait.* New York, Knopf, 1971.

——. *Anti-intellectualism in American Life.* New York, Knopf, 1963.

——. *The Idea of a Party System: The Rise of Legitimate Opposition in the United States, 1780–1840.* Berkeley and Los Angeles, Calif., Univ. of Calif. Press, 1969.

——. "William Leggett, Spokesman of Jacksonian Democracy." *Political Science Quarterly* 48 (1943), 581–94.

Hollis, Patricia. *The Pauper Press: A Study in Working-Class Radicalism of the 1830s.* London, Oxford Univ. Press, 1970.

Honeywell, Roy J. *The Educational Work of Thomas Jefferson.* Cambridge, Mass., Harvard Univ. Press, 1931.

Horton, John T. *James Kent: A Study in Conservatism.* New York, Appleton, 1939.

Hovell, Mark. *The Chartist Movement.* 2d ed. Manchester, England, Manchester Univ. Press, 1925.

Howard, Victor B. "The 1856 Election in Ohio: Moral Issues in Politics." *Ohio History* 80 (1971), 24–44.

Howe, Mark De Wolfe. *The Garden and the Wilderness: Religion and Government in American Constitutional History.* Chicago, Univ. of Chicago Press, 1965.

Hoyt, Charles O., and R. Clyde Ford. *John D. Pierce. . . .* Ypsilanti, Mich., Scharf Tag, Label & Box Co., 1905.

Hudson, Winthrop S. *American Protestantism.* Chicago, Univ. of Chicago Press, 1961.

Hugins, Walter. *Jacksonian Democracy and the Working Class: A Study of the New York Workingmen's Movement 1829–1837.* Stanford, Calif., Stanford Univ. Press, 1960.

Hurst, James W. *The Growth of American Law: The Law Makers.* Boston, Little, 1950.

——. *Law and the Conditions of Freedom in the Nineteenth-Century United States.* Madison, Wis., Univ. of Wis. Press, 1956.

——. *The Legitimacy of the Business Corporation in the Law of the United States 1780–1870.* Charlottesville, Va., Univ. Press of Va., 1970.

Jackson, Sidney L. *America's Struggle for Free Schools: Social Tension and Education in New England and New York, 1827–1842*. Washington, D.C., American Council on Public Affairs, 1941.

Jacobson, Norman. "The Concept of Equality in the Assumptions and Propaganda of Massachusetts Conservatives 1790–1840." Ph.D. diss., University of Wisconsin, 1951.

Jaffa, Harry V. *Crisis of the House Divided: An Interpretation of the Issues in the Lincoln-Douglas Debates*. Garden City, N.Y., Doubleday, 1959.

Jenkins, William S. *Pro-Slavery Thought in the Old South*. Chapel Hill, N.C., Univ. of N.C. Press, 1935.

Jensen, Merrill. *The New Nation: A History of the United States During the Confederation 1781–1789*. New York, Knopf, 1950.

Johannsen, Robert W. *Stephen A. Douglas*. New York, Oxford Univ. Press, 1973.

Johnson, Jane M. " 'Through Change and Through Storm': A Study of Federalist-Unitarian Thought, 1800–1860." Ph.D. diss., Radcliffe College, 1958.

Jordan, Weymouth T. *Rebels in the Making: Planters' Conventions and Southern Propaganda*. Tuscaloosa, Ala., Confederate Pub., 1958.

Katz, Michael. *The Irony of Early School Reform: Educational Innovation in Mid-Nineteenth Century Massachusetts*. Cambridge, Mass., Harvard Univ. Press, 1968.

Kelley, Robert. *The Transatlantic Persuasion: The Liberal-Democratic Mind in the Age of Gladstone*. New York, Knopf, 1969.

Klain, Maurice. "Property in a Free Society: A Study of Early American Political Thought." Ph.D. diss., Yale University, 1949.

Klebaner, Benjamin J. "Poverty and its Relief in American Thought, 1815–1861." *Social Service Review* 38 (1964), 382–99.

Knoles, George H., ed. *The Crisis of the Union 1860–1861*. Baton Rouge, La., La. State Univ. Press, 1965.

Kohn, Hans. *American Nationalism: An Interpretative Essay*. New York, Macmillan, 1957.

Kraditor, Aileen. *The Ideas of the Woman Suffrage Movement, 1890–1920*. New York, Columbia Univ. Press, 1970.

Lacey, Edmund E. "Protestant Newspaper Reaction to the Kansas-Nebraska Bill of 1854." *Rocky Mountain Social Science Journal* 7 (1970), 61–72.

Lannie, Vincent P. *Public Money and Parochial Education: Bishop Hughes, Governor Seward, and the New York School Controversy*. Cleveland, Ohio, Press of Case Western Reserve Univ., 1968.

Larrabee, Stephen A. *Hellas Observed: The American Experience of Greece, 1775–1865*. New York, N.Y. Univ. Press, 1957.

Leffler, Andor M. "The Kossuth Episode in America." Ph.D. diss., Western Reserve University, 1949.

Lenhoff, Arthur. "Development of the Concept of Eminent Domain." *Columbia Law Review* 42 (1942), 596–638.

Levy, Leonard W. *The Law of the Commonwealth and Chief Justice Shaw: The Evolution of American Law, 1830–1860.* Cambridge, Mass., Harvard Univ. Press, 1957.

Lewis, Richard W. B. *The American Adam: Innocence, Tragedy and Tradition in the Nineteenth Century.* Chicago, Univ. of Chicago Press, 1955.

Lillibridge, G. D. *Beacon of Freedom: The Impact of American Democracy upon Great Britain 1830–1870.* Philadelphia, Univ. of Pa. Press, 1955.

Lipsky, George A. *John Quincy Adams: His Theory and Ideas.* New York, Crowell, 1950.

Lloyd, Arthur Y. *The Slavery Controversy, 1831–1860.* Chapel Hill, N.C., Univ. of N.C. Press, 1939.

Ludlum, David M. *Social Ferment in Vermont, 1791–1850.* New York, Columbia Univ. Press, 1939.

McCarthy, Charles. *The Antimasonic Party: A Study in Political Anti-Masonry in the United States, 1827–1840.* Annual Report of the American Historical Association for the Year 1902. 2 vols. Washington, D.C., Government Printing Office, 1903. Vol. 1, pp. 365–574.

McClellan, James. *Joseph Story and the American Constitution: A Study in Political and Legal Thought.* Norman, Okla., Univ. of Okla. Press.

McConnell, Donald. *Economic Virtues in the United States: A History and an Interpretation.* New York, privately printed, 1930.

McCormick, Richard P. "Party Formation in New Jersey in the Jackson Era." *Proceedings of the New Jersey Historical Society* 83 (1965), 161–73.

——. *The Second American Party System: Party Formation in the Jacksonian Era.* Chapel Hill, N.C., Univ. of N.C. Press, 1969.

McCurdy, Frances L. "The Genius of Liberty." *Missouri Historical Review* 57 (1963), 331–43.

Maclear, J. F. "The Republic and the Millennium." In Elwyn A. Smith, ed., *The Religion of the Republic.* Philadelphia, Fortress Press, 1971. Pp. 183–216.

——. " 'The True American Union' of Church and State: The Reconstruction of the Theocratic Tradition." *Church History* 28 (1959), 41–62.

McLoughlin, William G. *The Meaning of Henry Ward Beecher: An Essay on the Shifting Values of Mid-Victorian America, 1840–1870.* New York, Knopf, 1970.

——. *New England Dissent, 1630–1833.* 2 vols. Cambridge, Mass., Harvard Univ. Press, 1971.

Malin, James C. *The Nebraska Question, 1852–1854.* Lawrence, Kans., privately printed, 1953.

Marshall, Lynn L. "The Early Career of Amos Kendall: The Making of a Jacksonian." Ph.D. diss., University of California at Berkeley, 1962.

——. "The Strange Stillbirth of the Whig Party." *American Historical Review* 72 (1967), 445–68.

Martin, Howard H. "Orations on the Anniversary of American Independence, 1776–1876." Ph.D. diss., Northwestern University, 1955.

——. " 'Style' in the Golden Age." *Quarterly Journal of Speech* 43 (1957), 374–82.

Marx, Leo. *The Machine in the Garden: Technology and the Pastoral Ideal in America.* New York, Oxford Univ. Press, 1964.

Mattingly, Paul H. "Educational Revivals in Ante-Bellum New England." *History of Education Quarterly* 11 (1971), 39–71.

May, Arthur J. *Contemporary American Opinion of the Mid-Century Revolutions in Central Europe.* Philadelphia, privately printed, 1927.

Mead, Sidney E. *The Lively Experiment: The Shaping of Christianity in America.* New York, Harper, 1963.

——. *Nathaniel William Taylor.* Chicago, Univ. of Chicago Press, 1942.

Merideth, Robert. *The Politics of the Universe: Edward Beecher, Abolition, and Orthodoxy.* Nashville, Tenn., Vanderbilt Univ. Press, 1968.

Merk, Frederick, and Lois Bannister Merk. *Manifest Destiny and Mission in American History: A Reinterpretation.* New York, Knopf, 1963.

—— and ——. *The Monroe Doctrine and American Expansionism 1843–1849.* New York, Knopf, 1967.

Messerli, Jonathan. *Horace Mann: A Biography.* New York, Knopf, 1972.

Meyers, Marvin. *The Jacksonian Persuasion.* Stanford, Calif., Stanford Univ. Press, 1957.

Michaelsen, Robert S. "The American Gospel of Work and the Protestant Doctrine of Vocation." Ph. D. diss., Yale University, 1951.

Miller, Douglas T. *Jacksonian Aristocracy: Class and Democracy in New York, 1830–1860.* New York, Oxford Univ. Press, 1967.

Miller, Nathan. *The Enterprise of a Free People: Aspects of Economic Development in New York State during the Canal Period, 1792–1838.* Ithaca, N.Y., Cornell Univ. Press, 1962.

Miller, Perry. *Errand into the Wilderness.* Cambridge, Mass., Harvard Univ. Press, 1956.

——. *The Life of the Mind in America; from the Revolution to the Civil War.* New York, Harcourt, 1965.

——. *Nature's Nation.* Cambridge, Mass., Harvard Univ. Press, 1967.

Mims, Edwin Jr. *The Majority of the People.* New York, Modern Age, 1941.

——. "The Will of the People: Studies in the Background of the 'Constitutional Democracy' of the Jacksonian Period." Ph.D. diss., Harvard University, 1939.

Mohl, Raymond A. "Humanitarianism in the Preindustrial City: The New York Society for the Prevention of Pauperism, 1817–1823." *Journal of American History* 57 (1970), 576–99.

Morris, David C. "The History of the Labour Movement in England, 1825–1852: The Problem of Leadership and the Articulation of Demands." Ph.D. diss., University of London, 1952.

Morrison, Chaplain W. *Democratic Politics and Sectionalism: The Wilmot Proviso Controversy.* Chapel Hill, N.C., Univ. of N.C. Press, 1967.

Morse, Jarvis M. *A Neglected Period of Connecticut's History, 1818–1850.* New Haven, Conn., Yale Univ. Press, 1933.

Mowry, Arthur M. *The Dorr War or The Constitutional Struggle in Rhode Island.* Providence, R.I., Preston & Rounds, 1901.

Nagel, Paul C. *One Nation Indivisible: The Union in American Thought 1776–1861.* New York, Oxford Univ. Press, 1964.

———. *This Sacred Trust: American Nationality 1798–1898.* New York, Oxford Univ. Press, 1971.

Nash, Roderick. *Wilderness and the American Mind.* New Haven, Conn., Yale Univ. Press, 1967.

The National Cyclopaedia of American Biography. 51 vols. New York, White, 1898–1969.

Nettels, Curtis P. *The Emergence of a National Economy, 1775–1815. The Economic History of the United States,* edited by Henry David et al., vol. 2. New York, Holt, 1962.

Neufeld, Maurice F. "Realms of Thought and Organized Labor in the Age of Jackson." *Labor History* 10 (1969), 5–43.

Nevins, Allan. *The Emergence of Lincoln.* 2 vols. New York, Scribner, 1951.

———. *Ordeal of the Union.* 2 vols. New York, Scribner, 1947.

Newmyer, R. Kent. "Daniel Webster as Tocqueville's Lawyer: The *Dartmouth College* Case Again." *American Journal of Legal History* 11 (1967), 127–47.

Nichols, Roy F. *The Disruption of American Democracy.* New York, Macmillan, 1948.

Noble, David W. *Historians against History: The Frontier Thesis and the National Covenant in American Historical Writing since 1830.* Minneapolis, Minn., Univ. of Minn. Press, 1965.

Nye, Russel B. *Fettered Freedom: Civil Liberties and the Slavery Controversy 1830–1860.* Lansing, Mich., Mich. State Univ. Press, 1963. [Second edition of a work first published in 1948.]

———. *This Almost Chosen People: Essays in The History of American Ideas.* N.p., Mich. State Univ. Press, 1966.

Oliver, John W. "Louis Kossuth's Appeal to the Middle West—1852." *Mississippi Valley Historical Review* 14 (1928), 481–96.

Ostrander, Gilman. *The Rights of Man in America 1606–1861.* Columbia, Mo., Univ. of Mo. Press, 1960.

Parish, Peter J. "Daniel Webster, New England, and the West." *Journal of American History* 54 (1967), 524–49.

Pearce, Roy H. *The Savages of America: A Study of the Indian and the Idea of Civilization.* Rev. ed. Baltimore, Johns Hopkins Univ. Press, 1965.

Pease, William H. and Jane H. Pease. "Antislavery Ambivalence: Immediatism, Expediency, Race." *American Quarterly* 17 (1965), 682–95.

Pessen, Edward. "The Egalitarian Myth and the American Social Reality: Wealth, Mobility, and Equality in the 'Era of the Common Man.'" *American Historical Review* 76 (1971), 989–1034.

——. *Jacksonian America: Society, Personality, and Politics.* Homewood, Ill., Dorsey Press, 1969.

——. "Moses Beach Revisited: A Critical Examination of His *Wealthy Citizens* Pamphlets." *Journal of American History* 58 (1971), 414–26.

——. *Most Uncommon Jacksonians: The Radical Leaders of the Early Labor Movement.* Albany, N.Y., State Univ. of N.Y. Press, 1967.

——. "The Workingmen's Movement of the Jacksonian Era." *Mississippi Valley Historical Review* 43 (1956), 428–47.

Pierson, George W. *Tocqueville and Beaumont in America.* New York, Oxford Univ. Press., 1938.

Poage, George R. *Henry Clay and the Whig Party.* Chapel Hill, N.C., Univ. of N.C. Press, 1936.

Poore, Benjamin Perley. *Perley's Reminiscences of Sixty Years in the National Metropolis.* . . . 2 vols. Philadelphia, 1886.

Post, Albert. *Popular Freethought in America, 1825–1850.* New York, Columbia Univ. Press, 1943.

Potter, David M. *The South and the Sectional Conflict.* Baton Rouge, La., La. State Univ. Press, 1968.

Power, Richard L. "A Crusade to Extend Yankee Culture, 1820–1865." *New England Quarterly* 13 (1940), 638–53.

Prendergast, William B. "Some American Ideas on the Limits of Political Authority, 1630 to 1914." Ph.D. diss., University of Chicago, 1948.

Primm, James Neal. *Economic Policy in the Development of a Western State: Missouri 1820–1860.* Cambridge, Mass., Harvard Univ. Press, 1954.

Prothero, Jorwerth. "Chartism in London." *Past & Present* 44 (1969), 76–105.

Purcell, Richard J. *Connecticut in Transition, 1775–1818.* Washington, D.C., American Historical Association, 1918.

Randall, James G., and David Donald. *The Civil War and Reconstruction.* 2d ed. Boston, Heath, 1961.

Rayback, Joseph G. *Free Soil: The Election of 1848.* Lexington, Ky., Univ. Press of Ky., 1971.

——. "Land for the Landless." Master's thesis, Western Reserve University, 1936.

Redlich, Fritz. *The Molding of American Banking.* 2 vols. New York, Hafner Pub. Co., 1947–1951.

Remini, Robert V. *Andrew Jackson.* New York, Twayne, 1966.

——. *The Election of Andrew Jackson.* Philadelphia, Lippincott, 1963.

Rezneck, Samuel, "Social History of an American Depression, 1837–1843." *American Historical Review* 40 (1935), 662–87.

Riepma, Siert F. " 'Young America': A Study in American Nationalism before the Civil War." Ph.D. diss., Western Reserve University, 1939.

Robbins, Roy M. "Horace Greeley: Land Reform and Unemployment, 1837–1862." *Agricultural History* 7 (1933), 18–41.

Robbins, Roy M. *Our Landed Heritage: The Public Domain, 1776–1936*. Princeton, N.J., Princeton Univ. Press, 1942.

Robinson, William A. *Jeffersonian Democracy in New England*. New Haven, Conn., Yale Univ. Press, 1916.

Rockwood, George I. *Cheever, Lincoln and the Causes of the Civil War*. Worcester, Mass., privately printed, 1936.

Rose, Michael E. "The Anti–Poor Law Movement in the North of England." *Northern History* 1 (1966), 70–91.

Rourke, Constance. *Trumpets of Jubilee*. New York, Harcourt, 1927.

Russel, Robert R. "Constitutional Doctrines with Regard to Slavery in the Territories." *Journal of Southern History* 32 (1966), 466–86.

———. "The Issues in the Congressional Struggle Over the Kansas-Nebraska Bill, 1854." *Journal of Southern History* 29 (1963), 187–210.

Russo, David J. "The Major Political Issues of the Jacksonian Period and the Development of Party Loyalty in Congress, 1830–1840." *Transactions of the American Philosophical Society*, new ser., 62, pt. 5 (1972).

Sanford, Charles L. "The Intellectual Origins and New-Worldliness of American Industry." *Journal of Economic History* 18 (1958), 1–6.

Scheiber, Harry N. *Ohio Canal Era: A Case Study of Government and the American Economy, 1820–1861*. Athens, Ohio, Ohio Univ. Press, 1969.

———. "The Road to *Munn*: Eminent Domain and the Concept of Public Purpose in the State Courts." *Perspectives in American History* 5 (1971), 327–402.

Schlatter, Richard. *Private Property: The History of an Idea*. London, G. Allen, 1951.

Schlesinger, Arthur M. *New Viewpoints in American History*. New York, Macmillan, 1932.

Schlesinger, Arthur M. Jr. *The Age of Jackson*. Boston, Little, 1945.

———. *Orestes A. Brownson*. Boston, Little, 1939.

Schneider, Herbert W. *A History of American Philosophy*. New York, Columbia Univ. Press, 1946.

Schultz, Harold S. *Nationalism and Sectionalism in South Carolina 1852–1860: A Study of the Movement for Southern Independence*. Durham, N.C., Duke Univ. Press, 1950.

Scott, Donald M. "Making It in Ante-Bellum America: Young Men and their Careers, 1820–1860." Paper read at the annual meeting of the Organization of American Historians, April 1971.

See, Ruth Douglas. "The Protestant Doctrine of Vocation in the Presbyterian Thought of Nineteenth-Century America." Ph.D. diss., New York University, 1952.

Shade, William G. "The Politics of Free Banking in the Old Northwest, 1837–1863." Ph.D. diss., Wayne State University, 1966.

Sharp, James R. *The Jacksonians versus the Banks: Politics in the States after the Panic of 1837*. New York, Columbia Univ. Press, 1970.

Shepard, Odell. *Pilgrim's Progress: The Life of Bronson Alcott*. Boston, Little, 1937.

Sherrill, Lewis J. *Presbyterian Parochial Schools 1846–1870.* New Haven, Conn., Yale Univ. Press, 1932.

Shine, Mary Lambert. "Ideas of the Founders of the American Nation on Landed Property." Ph.D. diss., University of Wisconsin, 1922.

Silbey, Joel H. *The Shrine of Party: Congressional Voting Behavior 1841–1852.* Pittsburgh, Pa., Univ. of Pittsburgh Press, 1967.

Simms, Henry H. *A Decade of Sectional Controversy 1851–1861.* Chapel Hill, N.C., Univ of N.C. Press, 1942.

Smith, Henry Nash. *Virgin Land: The American West as Symbol and Myth.* Cambridge, Mass., Harvard Univ. Press, 1950.

Smith, James Ward, and A. Leland Jamison, eds. *The Shaping of American Religion.* 5 vols. Princeton, N.J., Princeton Univ. Press, 1961.

Smith, Justin H. *The Annexation of Texas.* New York, Baker & Taylor, 1911.

Smith, Timothy L. "Congregation, State, and Denomination: The Forming of the American Religious Structure." *William and Mary Quarterly,* 3d ser., 25 (1968), 155–76.

——. "Protestant Schooling and American Nationality, 1800–1850." *Journal of American History* 53 (1967), 679–95.

——. *Revivalism and Social Reform in Mid-Nineteenth-Century America.* New York and Nashville, Abingdon, 1957.

Smith, Wilson, *Professors & Public Ethics: Studies of Northern Moral Philosophers before the Civil War.* Ithaca, N.Y., Cornell Univ. Press, 1956.

Soffer, R. N. "Attitudes and Allegiances in the Unskilled North, 1830–1850." *International Review of Social History* 10 (1965), 429–54.

Somkin, Fred. *Unquiet Eagle: Memory and Desire in the Idea of American Freedom, 1815–1860.* Ithaca, N.Y., Cornell Univ. Press, 1967.

Spencer, Donald S. "Lewis Cass and Symbolic Intervention: 1848–1852." *Michigan History* 53 (1969), 1–17.

Stampp, Kenneth M. *And the War Came: The North and the Secession Crisis, 1860–1861.* Baton Rouge, La., La. State Univ. Press, 1950.

Stanley, John L. "Majority Tyranny in Tocqueville's America: The Failure of Negro Suffrage in 1846." *Political Science Quarterly* 84 (1969), 412–35.

Stearns, Bertha M. "Early Factory Magazines in New England: The Lowell Offering and Its Contemporaries." *Journal of Economic and Business History* 2 (1930), 685–705.

Stein, Roger B. *John Ruskin and Aesthetic Thought in America, 1840–1900.* Cambridge, Mass., Harvard Univ. Press, 1967.

Stephenson, George M. *The Political History of the Public Lands, from 1840–1862. . . .* Boston, Badger, 1917.

Still, Bayrd. "State Constitutional Development in the United States, 1829–1851." Ph.D. diss., University of Wisconsin, 1933.

Strout, Cushing. *The American Image of the Old World.* New York, Harper, 1963.

Sweet, William W. *Religion in the Development of American Culture 1765–1840.* New York, Scribner, 1952.

Taylor, George R. *The Transportation Revolution, 1815–1860. The Economic History of the United States*, edited by Henry David et al., vol. 5. New York, Rinehart, 1951.

Taylor, William R. "Toward a Definition of Orthodoxy: The Patrician South and the Common Schools." *Harvard Educational Review* 36 (1966), 412–26.

Temple, Henry W. "William H. Seward." In Samuel Flagg Bemis, ed., *The American Secretaries of State and their Diplomacy*. 10 vols. New York, Knopf, 1927–1929, 7:29–36.

Thistlethwaite, Frank. *The Anglo-American Connection in the Early Nineteenth Century*. Philadelphia, Univ. of Pa. Press, 1959.

Thomas, John L. "Romantic Reform in America, 1815–1865." *American Quarterly* 22 (1965), 656–81.

Thomases, Jerome. "Freeman Hunt's America." *Mississippi Valley Historical Review* 30 (1943), 395–407.

Thompson, Dorothy. "Notes on Aspects of Chartist Leadership." *Bulletin of the Society for the Study of Labour History* no. 15 (1967), 28–33.

Thompson, E. P. *The Making of the English Working Class*. London, Gollancz, 1964.

———. "The Moral Economy of the English Crowd in the Eighteenth Century." *Past & Present* 50 (1971), 76–136.

Thompson, J. Earl Jr. "A Perilous Experiment: New England Clergymen and American Destiny 1796–1826." Ph.D. diss., Princeton University, 1966.

Thorpe, Francis N. *A Constitutional History of the American People 1776–1850*. 2 vols. New York, 1898.

Trusty, Norman L. "Massachusetts Public Opinion and the Annexation of Texas, 1835–1845." Ph.D. diss., Boston University, 1964.

Turner, Frederick J. *The Frontier in American History*. New York, Holt, 1920.

Tutorow, Norman E. "Whigs of the Old Northwest and Texas Annexation, 1836–April 1844." *Indiana Magazine of History* 66 (1970), 56–69.

Tuveson, Ernest L. *Redeemer Nation: The Idea of America's Millennial Role*, Chicago, Univ. of Chicago Press, 1968.

Tyack, David. "The Kingdom of God and the Common School: Protestant Ministers and the Educational Awakening in the West." *Harvard Educational Review* 36 (1966), 447–69.

Van Deusen, Glyndon. *The Jacksonian Era, 1828–1848*. New York, Harper, 1959.

———. "Some Aspects of Whig Thought and Theory in the Jacksonian Period." *American Historical Review* 43 (1958), 305–22.

———. *Thurlow Weed, Wizard of the Lobby*. Boston, Little, 1947.

———. *William Henry Seward*. New York, Oxford Univ. Press, 1967.

Wallace, Michael. "Changing Concepts of Party in the United States: New York, 1818–1828." *American Historical Review* 74 (1968), 453–91.

Ward, John T. *The Factory Movement 1830–1855*. London, Macmillan, 1962.

Ward, John William. *Andrew Jackson: Symbol for an Age.* New York, Oxford Univ. Press, 1955.

Ware, Edith E. *Political Opinion in Massachusetts during Civil War and Reconstruction.* Columbia University Studies in History, Economics and Public Law, no. 175. New York, Columbia Univ. Press, 1916.

Ware, Norman. *The Industrial Worker, 1840–1860: The Reaction of American Industrial Society to the Advance of the Industrial Revolution.* Boston, Houghton, 1924.

Warren, Charles. *Bankruptcy in United States History.* Cambridge, Mass., Harvard Univ. Press, 1935.

——. *The Supreme Court in United States History.* Rev. ed. 2 vols. Boston, Little, 1926.

Weaver, Richard M. *The Ethics of Rhetoric.* Chicago, Univ. of Chicago Press, 1953.

Weber, Max. *The Protestant Ethic and the Spirit of Capitalism.* Transl. by Talcott Parsons. New York, Scribner, 1958.

Weinberg, Albert K. *Manifest Destiny: A Study of Nationalist Expansionism in American History.* Baltimore, Johns Hopkins Univ. Press, 1935.

Weisberger, Bernard A. *They Gathered at the River: The Story of the Great Revivalists and Their Impact upon Religion in America.* Boston, Little, 1958.

Weiss, Richard. *The American Myth of Success, From Horatio Alger to Norman Vincent Peale.* New York, Basic Books, 1969.

Wellington, Raynor G. *The Political and Sectional Influence of the Public Lands, 1828–1842.* Cambridge, Mass., Riverside, 1914.

Wells, Damon. *Stephen Douglas: The Last Years, 1857–1861.* Austin, Tex., Univ. of Tex. Press, 1971.

Welter, Rush. "The Frontier West as Image of American Society: Conservative Attitudes before the Civil War." *Mississippi Valley Historical Review* 46 (1960), 593–614.

——. "The Frontier West as Image of American Society, 1776–1860." *Pacific Northwest Quarterly* 52 (1961), 1–6.

——. "The Idea of Progress in America: An Essay in Ideas and Method." *Journal of the History of Ideas* 16 (1955), 401–15.

——. *Popular Education and Democratic Thought in America.* New York, Columbia Univ. Press, 1962.

White, Leonard D. *The Jacksonians: A Study in Administrative History, 1829–1861.* New York, Macmillan, 1954.

Wickwar, W. Hardy. "Foundations of American Conservatism." *American Political Science Review* 41 (1947), 1105–17.

Wiebe, Robert H. "The Social Functions of Public Education." *American Quarterly* 21 (1969), 147–64.

Williams, William A. *The Contours of American History.* London, J. Cape, 1961.

Williamson, Chilton. *American Suffrage: From Property to Democracy.* Princeton, N.J., Princeton Univ. Press, 1960.

Wilson, Edmund. *Patriotic Gore: Studies in the Literature of the Civil War*. New York, Oxford Univ. Press, 1962.

Wilson, Harold E. *The Hill Country of Northern New England*. New York, Columbia Univ. Press, 1936.

Wilson, Major L. "An Analysis of the Ideas of Liberty and Union as used by Members of Congress and the Presidents from 1828 to 1861." Ph.D. diss., University of Kansas, 1964.

——. "The Broker State Concept of the Union in the 1840's: A Synthesis of Whig and Democratic Views." *Louisiana Studies* 8 (1969), 321–47.

——. "The Concept of Time and the Political Dialogue in the United States, 1828–48." *American Quarterly* 19 (1967), 619–44.

——. "The Free Soil Concept of Progress and the Irrepressible Conflict." *American Quarterly* 22 (1970), 769–90.

——. "Of Time and the Union: Kansas-Nebraska and the Appeal from Prescription to Principle." *Midwest Quarterly* 10 (1968), 73–87.

——. "Of Time and the Union: Webster and his Critics in the Crisis of 1850." *Civil War History* 14 (1968), 293–306.

Wiltse, Charles M. *John C. Calhoun*. 3 vols. Indianapolis, Ind., Bobbs, 1944–1951.

Wishy, Bernard. *The Child and The Republic: The Dawn of Modern American Child Nurture*. Philadelphia, Univ. of Pa. Press, 1968.

Wolf, William J. *The Almost Chosen People: A Study of the Religion of Abraham Lincoln*. Garden City, N.Y., Doubleday, 1959.

Wood, Gordon S. *The Creation of the American Republic 1776–1787*. Chapel Hill, N.C., Univ. of N.C. Press, 1969.

Wright, Benjamin F. Jr. *The Contract Clause of the Constitution*. Cambridge, Mass., Harvard Univ. Press, 1938.

Wyatt-Brown, Bertram. "Prelude to Abolitionism: Sabbatarian Politics and the Rise of the Second Party System." *Journal of American History* 58 (1971), 316–41.

Wyllie, Irvin G. *The Self-Made Man in America*. New Brunswick, N.J., Rutgers Univ. Press, 1954.

——. "The Cult of the Self-Made Man in America 1830–1910." Ph.D. diss., University of Wisconsin, 1949.

Zahler, Helène S. *Eastern Workingmen and National Land Policy, 1829–1862*. New York, Columbia Univ. Press, 1941.

INDEX

Abbeville District (South Carolina), 245
Abbott, Richard, 144
Abolition, 440 k
Abolitionists, 333, 351; criticized by southerners, 383–84; Democratic target, 339; influence of, 351, 352, 361–62
Abrahams, John, 153
Accommodation between parties, 129, 137–41, 152, 162, 411 a, 415 m
Accumulation of wealth: conservative idea, 128, 138–39; democratic idea, 132, 152; Freedley's view, 153, 159; in U.S., 130, 131; see also Exploitation of resources; Wealth
Adamic man, 45–46; see also Eden, Garden of
Adams, Jasper, 146–47, 254
Adams, John, 23, 28, 46, 151
Adams, John Calvin, 123
Adams, John Quincy, 123; criticized, 28, 170; defended, 191; quoted, 46
Addresses: commencement, 16; in New England, 9, 16–17, 17, 209; in New Jersey, 218, 322–23; in New York, 24, 35, 255, 322, 323, 326; in the South, 22, 149, 254, 259–60, 260, 372; in the West, 4, 5, 21, 255, 260, 325
  Phi Beta Kappa, 6, 17, 133, 255, 279, 316, 400 k
  Washington's birthday, 4, 6–7
Address to the People (Missouri), 193
Address to the People (South Carolina), 247
Address to the People of Mississippi (Quitman et al.), 248–49
Address to the People of the State of Illinois, 70–71
Address to the Voters of Indiana, 354
"Agrarianism": conservative fears of, 107, 108–9, 278–79, 410 b; conservative fears mocked, 133; equated with public schooling, 283–84; see also Radicalism
Agrarian utopia, 435 a
Agricultural premises of Democrats, 134–35
Agriculture, safeguard of republicanism, 318–19
Aiken, John, 121
Albany Argus, 3
Albany Evening Journal, 351

Albany Regency, 405 a, 420 a
Alcott, Bronson, 435 g
Alcott, William A., 142, 145, 147, 148
Alexander the Great, 148
Alien and Sedition Acts, 28, 400 b
Allan, James S., 5, 325
Allen, Samuel C., 304
"Alliances" with Europe, 55
Allston, Washington, 320
Amendment, constitutional: Democratic views, in the states, 12–13, 221–22, 226, 227–28, 229, 240, 426 g; in the U.S., 238, 240; Whig views, 112, 203–4, 205, 421 d, 424 d
"American" (catchword), 39–40, 40–41, 42
American Institute of Instruction, 295
Americanism, 38–44, 45; defined, 38; invoked, 39, 40, 41, 42, 43, 324; its larger significance, 42–44, 390; party tactic, 39, 40; relation to foreign policy, 41, 46, 51, 52
American party, 39
American Peace Society, 334
American Quarterly Review, 115, 312–13
American Review: on constitutional questions, 205, 209–10, 213–14, 215, 216; on Democratic party, 15; on economic questions, 34, 138–39, 142; on expansion, 139; on freedom, 206; on history, 15–16, 16; on Lincoln, 328; on politics and government, 197, 206, 296–97; on religion, 256; on society, 127–28; on the West and western lands, 139, 309, 315, 317, 361–62; on Whig party, 123
American Slavery As It Is (Weld), 342
American System, the, 32, 39–41, 90, 124–25
American Whig Review, see *American Review*
Anglo-Saxon race, 14
Anti-Catholicism, see Nativism
Antifederalists, 226, 236, 417 a
Anti-intellectualism, 279–80, 407 c, 410 i
Antimasonic movement, 405 a, 420 a
Antimasonic party (Massachusetts), 157
Anti-Rent agitation, 93, 97
Antislavery agitation, 336; Democratic target, 339–41, 343–44, 356, 373–74,

580 · INDEX ·

Checks and balances (*Continued*)
Whigs, 209, 210, 214; party views compared, 226, 424 e, 426 g
Cheves, Langdon, 382
Chosen people (concept), 6, 21, 63, 404 i
Christian commonwealth, 312
Christian Examiner, 255–56
Christianity: hailed by conservatives, 256, 258–59, 263; identified with democracy, 261, 270; invoked, 22, 355
Christian Review, 326
Church, role of, 335–36, 336–37; *see also* Christianity; Religion
Cincinnati Weekly Gazette, 64, 192–93
Cities, 318
Civilization: invoked by conservatives, 127–28, 218, 355; O'Sullivan on, 271; tied to property, 107, 110–11, 138–39
"Civilization: American and European" (*American Review*), 127–28
Civil service reform, 438 b
Civil War: attitudes toward, 388–89, 389–90, 390–91; causes, 333, 333–79, 379–87, 387–88; interpretations, 438 d
Claiborne, W. C. C., 196
Clark, John, 427 g
Clark, Peter I., 200
Clarke, James Freeman, 313
Clarke, John H., 60
Clarke Resolution, 60–61, 64
Class, social: conservative views, 106, 115–16, 117–18, 119, 120–22; Democratic views, 84, 85, 91–92, 97–99, 103–4, 131, 136, 137, 152, 406 b; in English radical thought, 100–101, 102–3, 410 i; European views, 85, 146; Mann on, 35–36, 285; moralists' views, 143–44, 147, 150; previous views, 84, 151, 156; radical views, 95–96, 97–98; southern view, 385; *see also* Corporations; Equality
Class struggle, 85–86, 95–98, 100–103, 346
Clay, Henry, 42–43, 414 i; American System of, 39–40, 124–25; campaign statements, 31, 195, 210; defended by Whigs, 30, 211; economic views, 90, 124–25, 414 h; other views, 24, 49, 316; *see also* American System
Cleland, Philip S., 336–37
Cobb, Lyman, 144
Cobbett, William, 131
Coercion in government, *see* Authority; Opinion versus force; Power

Colleges, *see* Education, higher
Cole, Thomas, 399 g
College graduates, *see* Scholars in politics
College of Physicians and Surgeons (New York), 82
Colleges, 16, 83; in the West, 433 a
Collins, G. C., 42–43
Colton, Calvin: on Clay, 210–11; on domestic economic questions, 34–35, 116–17, 118, 120, 150, 194; on foreign economic questions, 40, 125–26, 126; on political questions, 30, 127, 192, 197; on slavery, 350–51; on Whigs, 210–11
Commerford, John, 409 h
Common law, 82, 421 e; *see also* Law
Common schools: conservative views, 277, 280–81, 283–84, 291, 433 c; Democratic views, 286, 291, 292; equated to churches, 282, 283; in New England, 282–83; religious views of, 281–82, 434 f; seen as national heritage, 282–83, 433 d; *see also* Education
Communist Manifesto, 8
Competence, professional, 82–83
Complacency, national, 10–11, 27, 44; criticized, 18–19; reinforced, 19, 20–21, 22
Compromise of 1850, 340, 347, 351, 352, 361, 370, 383–84; *see also* California
Concurrent majority (concept), 429 i
Condition of labor, the, 34, 136, 473 n15
Conduct of life (Protestant concern), 143
Confrontation (concept): between good and evil, 336, 337–39, 359, 389; history viewed as, 72
between liberty and despotism: domestic, 27, 31; international, 22, 34–35, 56–57, 58, 69–73; over slavery, 360–61
between liberty and slavery: invoked by conservatives, 338–39, 370, 371; invoked by Democrats, 367–68, 371; invoked by Lincoln Republicans, 363, 364, 365
Confrontations, sectional, 333, 336–39, 440 i
Congregational polity, 264
Connecticut, disestablishment in, 154, 155, 257–58, 259
"Conquest" of Mexico, 69, 73
Conrad, Charles M., 200, 204–5
Conscience, appeals to, 334–36, 364
Consensus: on common schools, 292–93; of parties, 411 a; *see also* Accommodation
Conservatism: defined, 395 b, 410 a; de-

582   · INDEX ·

Corporations (*Continued*)
position of, 97, 140, 409 f; origins of, 78, 105–6, 169, 406 b, 458 *n*3; radical criticisms of, 136, 179; *see also* Banks of issue; Charters of incorporation; Class social; Free Banking; Incorporation, general
Corruption, fear of: among Democrats, 172–73, 178; in England, 417 a; among southerners, 245, 381
Corwin, Edward S., 112–13
Courts, 112–13, 140, 169; *see also* Law
Covenant theology, 413 f
Cox, Samuel S., 372–73
Crary, Isaac, 169, 234, 324–25
Craven, Avery, 440 j
Credit, private, 148
Credit system, 88; *see also* Banks of issue; Second Bank of the United States
Crisis Met, The, 9, 63, 65–66, 87, 478 *n*52
Cuba, 348–49, 387
Curtis, George William, 435 h
Cushing, Caleb, 316, 373–74, 374
Cycle of fortune (concept), 91–92, 120, 143

Dallas, George M., 378
Daniel, Joseph J., 180, 409 f
Dartmouth College v. *Woodward*, 113
Davis, David Brion, 438 d
Davis, James, 182
Davis, Thomas G. C., 230, 481 *n*15
Dearborn, H. A. S., 415 l
Debtor relief, 96, 462 *n*25
Declaration of Independence: influence of, 419 e, 439 f; invoked, 21, 176, 355, 365–66; Jacksonian sense of, 11–12
Deference, 279–80, 405 a
Delaware, 352
Democracy: conservative views, 14–15, 16–17, 115–16, 120–22, 127, 195–200, 295–97, 410 a; criticized, 14, 15, 18, 19, 386
democratic views: common opinions, 77–100, 103–4, 165–73, 173–79, 221, 226–28; implications of, 174–76, 185; influence on Christianity, 271; material basis of, 268–69; origins of, 405 a, 406 b; theoretical formulations of, 178–79, 185, 233
early Republican view, 424 e; English view, 7; equated with Christianity, 261, 270; equated with constitutionalism,

211, 218, 231–33, 242–43; equated with education, 267–68, 290, 295–97; invoked by antislavery conservatives, 345, 350, 352–55; moralists' ideas of, 150, 341–42; seen at stake in Civil War, 390, 391; Taylor's view, 407 b; Whig views, 190, 191, 195–96, 197, 208–9, 211, 427 g; *see also* Class, social; Majority rule; Republicanism; Sovereignty of the people
Democracy, Progressive, 13, 61, 74, 135, 404 j
Democrat (name claimed by Whigs), 29–31
Democrat, defined, 395 b
Democratic creed, 184–85, 242, 243; its influence, 332, 373–79, 379–81, 383–84
Democratic National Convention (1856), 375
Democratic party, 405 a; criticized by Whigs, 14–15, 30–31, 34, 191; hailed by its partisans, 167, 177–78; influence on sectional crisis, 371–79; invoked by Free Soil Democrats, 357; name adopted by Whigs, 29, 30, 31; name challenged by Whigs, 29–30, 30–31, 197; partisan allegiances, 235–36, 420 a, 425 g; target of Lincoln Republicans, 347, 352, 355; vehicle of democratic principles, 97, 395 b, 405 a
Democratic party in the states: Georgia, 238; Illinois, 89, 221, 223, 242; Indiana, 28, 88, 170, 172, 241, 357, 358; Louisiana, 412 d; Massachusetts, 78–79, 79, 183; New Hampshire, 177; New York, 27, 166–67, 417 a; New York, views on sectional issues, 341, 345–46, 366, 367, 368; Ohio, 35; Rhode Island, 222; Tennessee, 32, 33
Democratic principle, 71
Democratic Review: on constitutional questions, 229–30, 233, 237–38, 239, 241; on economic questions, 88, 91, 133, 158, 473 *n*15; on educational questions, 286, 287, 290; on expansion, 134, 404 j; on immigration, 62–63; on Macon, 178; on morality and religion, 187, 266, 269–70, 341; on national mission, 47–48; on politics and government, 171–72, 177–78, 181–82, 184–85, 185, 188, 232, 241, 266–67, 268–69; on progress, 9, 10; on South America, 68; on the West and western lands, 301, 303, 304, 306, 325; Whig target, 206
Democratic Whig National Convention (1839), 191

586   · INDEX ·

Free institutions (*Continued*)
274, 313; invoked by conservatives, 47, 53, 127, 284, 295–97, 297, 320; invoked by Democrats, 42, 189, 266, 268, 289, 291; invoked against slavery, 353, 359–64, 366–68, 369; themselves educate, 289–90, 295–97
education as free institution, 276–97; conservative views, 277–85; democratic views, 286–93; liberal views, 293–97
religion as free institution, 253–75; clerical views, 256–64; conservative views, 253–56; Democratic views, 264–72; liberal views, 273–75
the West as free institution: common views, 319–28; conservative views, 306–19; Democratic views, 299–306
Free labor: invoked by conservatives, 348, 360, 369; invoked by Democrats, 346, 367, 440 h; southern target, 386
Free land, *see* Homestead legislation
Freeman, John D., 166
Freeport Doctrine, 517 *n*75
Free religion, 305
Free schools, 305, 386; *see also* Common schools
Free society (concept), 407 d, 411 a, 419 g; derided, 386
"Free soil," 440 h
Free Soil Democrats (New York), 357
Free Soil party, 367
Free speech, 342–43, 343–44, 374, 439 h, 440 h
Free Suffrage movement (Rhode Island), 5, 203, 225
Free trade, 124–26, 162, 305
Free Trade and the American System (South Carolina), 94
Free Trade Convention (Philadelphia), 94–95
Free will, 186, 187, 386
Frémont, John Charles, 347, 364
Friends of Domestic Industry, 126, 207
Frontier, *see* West
Frontiersmen, *see* Pioneers
Frost, John, 142, 143, 147
Fry, William H., 365
Fugitive Slave Law, 372, 376, 513 *n*33
Fuller, Thomas J. D., 303–4, 305
Fundamental law, 204–5, 421 e
Funding system, 32
Future, the, 7–9, 20–22, 25; clerical views, 20–21; conservative views, 7, 16–17, 24;

liberal views, 8–9; secular views, 21–22; views challenged, 9–11, 18–19; *see also* Change, social; Progress (concept)

"Gag rule," 343
Galena Jeffersonian, 86
Gannett, Ezra S., 336
Gardiner, Oliver C., 241, 367–68
Garland, Hugh A., 240
Gaston, William, 201
General Will, the, 233
George, Henry, 85
Georgia, Democratic party, 238
Giddings, Joshua R., 403 f
Giles, John, 213
Gilpin, Henry D., 9
Girard, Stephen, 149
Girard Journal of Wealth, 149
Gloucester Democrat, 84
"Go ahead" (slogan), 37, 74, 131
God: his role in history, 6, 19–20; invoked by clergy, 6, 8, 19, 148, 313; invoked by conservatives, 9–10, 46, 46–47, 47, 111; invoked by Democrats, 63, 87, 186; invoked against slavery, 370, 390 (*see also* Higher law)
Godwin, Parke, 19, 399 h
Goodrich, Samuel G., 143–44 passim
Gouge, William, 35, 87, 88, 89, 167, 303
Government: antithesis of liberty, 166 (*see also* Power, antithesis of liberty); conservative views, 196, 197, 254, 273; Democratic views, 183, 189, 226–28, 229–30, 231, 233; early republicans' views, 417 a; English views, 100–102, 417 a; Whig views, 198–99, 210; *see also* Government, role of; Rights, natural
Government, of U.S., 324
Government, role of, 331, 416 a; conservative views, 105, 106–7, 112–13, 122–23, 124, 127–28, 208, 217, 254, 410 a; conservative views redefined, 116–17, 122–24, 126–27, 127–28, 193–95; Democratic views, 78, 87, 88, 92–94, 95–98, 161–62, 165–73, 184–85, 226–27, 228, 231–32, 242–43, 306, 374–75, 409 g, 417 a, 420 h, 424 e, 427 g, 481 *n*15; judicial views, 112–13; Lincoln Republican views, 438 e; in moral reform, 258–61, 262–63, 264; National Republican views, 210; postbellum views, 409 f; with respect to property, 107, 107–8, 111–12, 410 b; in republican era, 78, 406 b, 410 b; southern